KIERKEGAARD AND THE GREEK WORLD

TOME I: SOCRATES AND PLATO

Kierkegaard Research: Sources, Reception and Resources
Volume 2, Tome I

Kierkegaard Research: Sources, Reception and Resources
is a publication of the Søren Kierkegaard Research Centre

This volume was published with the generous financial support
of the Danish Agency for Science, Technology and Innovation

Kierkegaard and the Greek World

Tome I: Socrates and Plato

Edited by
JON STEWART AND KATALIN NUN

ASHGATE

Published by
Ashgate Publishing Limited
Wey Court East
Union Road
Farnham
Surrey, GU9 7PT
England

Ashgate Publishing Company
Suite 420
101 Cherry Street
Burlington
VT 05401-4405
USA

www.ashgate.com

British Library Cataloguing in Publication Data
Kierkegaard and the Greek world.
Tome 1, Socrates and Plato. – (Kierkegaard research : sources, reception and resources ; v. 2)
1. Kierkegaard, Søren, 1813–1855–Knowledge–Greek philosophy. 2. Socrates–Influence. 3. Plato–Influence.
I. Series II. Stewart, Jon (Jon Bartley) III. Nun, Katalin
198.9–dc22

Library of Congress Cataloging-in-Publication Data
Kierkegaard and the Greek world / edited by Jon Stewart and Katalin Nun
p. cm. — (Kierkegaard research : sources, reception and resources)
Includes bibliographical references and index.
ISBN 978-0-7546-6981-4 (v. 2, t. 1 : hardcover : alk. paper)
1. Kierkegaard, Søren, 1813–1855—Sources. 2. Philosophy, Ancient.
3. Philosophers, Ancient.
I. Stewart, Jon (Jon Bartley) II. Nun, Katalin

B4377.K45526 2009
198'.9—dc22

2009022905

ISBN 9780754669814 (hbk)

Cover design by Katalin Nun

Mixed Sources
Product group from well-managed forests and other controlled sources
www.fsc.org Cert no. SGS-COC-2482
© 1996 Forest Stewardship Council
FSC

Printed and bound in Great Britain by
TJ International Ltd, Padstow, Cornwall

Contents

List of Contributors

Rick Anthony Furtak, Department of Philosophy, Colorado College, 14 E. Cache La Poudre, Colorado Springs, CO 80903, USA.

Janne Kylliäinen, University of Helsinki, Department of Philosophy, P.O. Box 9 (Siltavuorenpenger 20 A), 00014, Finland.

William McDonald, School of Social Science, University of New England, Armidale, NSW, 2351 Australia.

Marius Timmann Mjaaland, Faculty of Theology, University of Oslo, Box 1023 Blindern, 0315 Oslo, Norway.

Paul Muench, Department of Philosophy, University of Montana, Missoula, MT 59812, USA.

Katalin Nun, Søren Kierkegaard Research Centre, Farvergade 27 D, 1463 Copenhagen K, Denmark.

Tonny Aagaard Olesen, Søren Kierkegaard Research Centre, Farvergade 27 D, 1463 Copenhagen K, Denmark.

David D. Possen, Whitney Humanities Center 325, Yale University, 53 Wall St., P.O. Box 208298, New Haven, CT 06520-8298, USA.

Harald Steffes, Evangelische Kirchengemeinde Wachtberg, Am Langenacker 12, 53343 Wachtberg, Germany.

Eric Ziolkowski, Religious Studies Department, Lafayette College, Easton, PA 18042–1780, USA.

Preface

The present volume features articles that employ source-work research to trace Kierkegaard's understanding and use of authors from the Greek tradition. The articles treat a series of figures of varying importance in Kierkegaard's authorship, ranging from early Greek poets to late classical philosophical schools. This volume is also interdisciplinary, featuring articles on Kierkegaard's use of Greek philosophers, historians, dramatists, and literary writers.

In general it can be said that the Greeks collectively constitute one of the single most important body of sources for Kierkegaard's thought, not far behind the Danish and German sources. He studied Greek from an early age and was profoundly inspired by what might be called the Greek spirit. Although he is generally regarded as a Christian thinker, he was nonetheless consistently drawn back to the Greeks for ideas and impulses on any number of topics. He frequently contrasts ancient Greek philosophy, characterized by its emphasis on the lived experience of the individual in daily life, with the abstract German philosophy that was in vogue during his own time. It has been argued that he modeled his work on that of the ancient Greek thinkers specifically in order to contrast his own activity with that of his contemporaries.[1]

Surely the most profound single Greek influence on Kierkegaard was the figure of Socrates, who appears repeatedly throughout the authorship.[2] This is evident from his earliest scholarly work, most notably his dissertation, *The Concept of Irony*, where he offers a detailed interpretation of the Socrates character as portrayed in the works of Plato, Xenophon and Aristophanes. The Socrates figure that emerges from this study—a genuinely ignorant ironist whose "mission" is to destroy claims to knowledge even though he is unable to offer any positive alternative—returns throughout Kierkegaard's authorship, both in the pseudonymous works as well as those signed in his own name. Socrates plays a major role in books such as *Philosophical Fragments* and the *Concluding Unscientific Postscript*, but he is also present in more religiously-oriented writings, where he is referred to indirectly, often as a "simple wise man of old."[3] The figure of Socrates is also significant for

---

1 See Jon Stewart, *Kierkegaard's Relations to Hegel Reconsidered*, Cambridge and New York: Cambridge University Press 2003, pp. 644ff.; Rick A. Furtak, *Wisdom in Love: Kierkegaard and the Ancient Quest for Emotional Integrity*, Notre Dame, Indiana: University of Notre Dame Press 2005, pp. 42ff.

2 See Jens Himmelstrup, *Søren Kierkegaards Opfattelse af Sokrates*, Copenhagen: Arnold Busck 1924; Paul Muench, "Kierkegaard's Socratic Point of View," *Kierkegaardiana*, vol. 24, 2007, pp. 132–63.

3 For passages where the "simple wise man" is explicitly identified as Socrates, see *SKS* 4, 310 / *CA*, 3; *SKS* 4, 228 / *PF*, 19.

Kierkegaard in less public ways. In a journal entry from near the end of his life, for example, Socrates is described as a "man with whom I have had an inexplicable rapport from my earliest days, even before I began a serious study of Plato."[4] In what proved to be virtually a death-bed reflection on his own life, Kierkegaard refers to Socrates as follows in an oft-cited slogan from the final edition of *The Moment*: "The only analogy I have before me is Socrates; my mission is a Socratic mission."[5]

But Socrates was by no means the sole Greek thinker to have captured Kierkegaard's imagination. Although there is no indication that Kierkegaard made a systematic study of Aristotle, there are clear signs that he was aware of specific concepts and analyses from the major Aristotelian works, which he refers to periodically throughout his authorship. Moreover, in addition to individual philosophers, he also refers to the various schools of Greek thought, such as the Eleatics, the Skeptics, and the Stoics. Perhaps as a result of his early studies, he was also an avid reader of the Greek poets, both epic and dramatic. He frequently refers to them to provide examples to illustrate ideas that he wishes to develop.

The present volume has been organized so as to reflective the full spectrum of Kierkegaard's Greek sources. Tome I is dedicated to the different pictures of Socrates. It contains, as noted, a series of articles on Plato, who is clearly his main Greek source in general. In addition, a second section features articles on Xenophon and Aristophanes, the other ancient sources of Socrates discussed by Kierkegaard. A third section contains articles that treat the reception of the figure of Socrates in the Germanophone world and in Denmark respectively.

Tome II features articles dedicated to the rest of Kierkegaard's Greek sources, beginning with a section containing several articles on different aspects of Aristotle's writings that influenced his thought. This is followed by another section featuring analyses of other Greek philosophers and philosophical schools who were important for him. Finally, a third section explores Kierkegaard's uses of a handful of Greek poets, dramatists and historians.

The present volume presented specific challenges that required specific solutions. For this reason, the organization of the material in this volume deviates slightly from the norm in this series on a couple of points. Unlike most of the other volumes where Kierkegaard's relation to a given author is treated in a single comprehensive article, this volume includes several articles on Plato and Aristotle—the Greek thinkers to whom Kierkegaard was most indebted. Especially in the case of Plato, it was deemed implausible to expect that a single article could exhaustively cover Kierkegaard's multi-faceted interpretation of the primary texts. To remedy this problem, different aspects of Plato's influence were identified and assigned individual articles in such a way that there would be the broadest possible coverage with a minimum of overlap. Thus, each of the articles on Plato begins with a focus on a single theme grounded in a question arising from one Platonic work (and in selected cases, from two works).

In this context a methodological deviation from other volumes arose from the fact that Kierkegaard's use of Plato tends to be thematic rather than book-based. It is the general principle of the "Sources" part of this series to present Kierkegaard's

4 *SKS* 25, 225, NB28:15 / *JP* 6, 472. (Translation modified.)

5 *SKS* 13, 405 / *M*, 341.

sources in terms of specific works by specific authors. This strategy, however, proved impossible in this case due to the fact that Plato's treatment of any number of issues of interest to Kierkegaard is often scattered through a handful of different dialogues. With this in mind, it was decided to allow a departure from the usual focus on the *work* as source and to shift over to a focus on *theme*. This said, however, an attempt has nonetheless been made to identify the key texts where the given themes appear, even though the authors have not been obliged to confine themselves to these texts. The appearance of the titles of the Platonic dialogues in the titles of the articles featured here should thus be understood with these caveats. They are intended to provide the reader with a quick general overview, but in no way are they necessarily absolutely representative of the content of every article.

Another deviation from the general principles of this series concerns the bibliographies. In the other volumes each article contains its own individual bibliography concerning Kierkegaard's relation to the figure in question. This principle, however, could not be followed in the case of the multiple articles on Plato and Aristotle featured here. First, with regard to the primary texts of these thinkers that Kierkegaard owned, that is, the first rubric in the bibliographies, it would have been absurd to repeat these each time in the bibliography of each individual article. With regard to the second rubric of the bibliography, that is, contemporary accounts of Plato and Aristotle found in works in Kierkegaard's private library, there is so much thematic overlap that it would have been impossible to create discrete bibliographies tailored to each specific article. To do so would only have resulted in a number of forced attempts to categorize individual works and accounts into specific rubrics, where they do not always fit so cleanly. The third section of the bibliography, that is, current secondary literature on Kierkegaard's use of Plato and Aristotle, falls victim to this same problem. For these reasons it was deemed counterproductive to provide individual bibliographies for each individual article on these thinkers. As a result, the bibliographies for the articles on Plato and Aristotle have been collected and included as independent units following each set of articles.

One final discrepancy between this volume and the rest of the series is worthy of mention. Kierkegaard's study of Plato was not confined to an investigation of Plato's primary texts. In the seventeenth, eighteenth and nineteenth centuries, there were thriving fields of Plato studies in both Germany and Denmark. Figures such as Tennemann, Hamann, Ast, Hegel, and Schleiermacher were profoundly influential for Kierkegaard's understanding and interpretation of the primary texts. Similarly, in Denmark figures such as Poul Martin Møller and Adam Oehlenschläger gave important treatments of Plato in their lectures and writings. Given this, it was deemed important to convey this dimension of Kierkegaard's understanding of Plato with individual articles on the later Plato reception in these countries. While individual articles appear elsewhere in this series on figures such as Hamann, Hegel, and Schleiermacher, their specific importance for Kierkegaard's understanding of Plato is not treated extensively there; in these articles the authors have been obliged to focus on the many other aspects of the thought of these figures that were significant for Kierkegaard. Thus, the material that is relevant for Plato is treated specifically in the overview articles featured in this volume.

In recent years more and more attention has been dedicated to Kierkegaard's use of Socrates and other Greek thinkers as Kierkegaard scholars have become increasingly aware of the significance of these sources for understanding his works. The present volume will, it is hoped, foster and expand on this productive trend. Despite this trend, Kierkegaard's study and use of other Greek figures, such as the historians and the poets, remains sadly unexplored, even though references to them appear throughout his *corpus*. Some of the articles on these early Greek figures featured here are thus virtually the first of their kind. It is the hope of this series that all of these articles, together with the accompanying bibliographies, will provide a solid starting point for future research.

Acknowledgements

This volume owes its existence to a generous grant from the Danish Agency for Science, Technology and Innovation from 2005 to 2007. The host institute of this series, the Søren Kierkegaard Research Centre at the University of Copenhagen, has repeatedly been of great assistance in the realization of this ambitious project. Cynthia Lund and Gordon Marino of the Hong-Kierkegaard Library at St. Olaf College were kind enough to facilitate a research stay in the fall of 2006, which allowed the editors of the present volume to do the necessary bibliographical work for the articles featured here. We gratefully acknowledge their boundless help and generosity. This volume was also made possible by the capable assistance of Nicholas Wain, Rachel Lynch, Sarah Charters, Philip Hillyer, and the kind staff at Ashgate.

We would also like to thank Finn Gredal Jensen for his enormous help as advisor to this volume in general and specifically for his assistance with the numerous Greek quotations in the featured articles. A word of gratitude is also due to the rest of the editorial and advisory board of the present series: Peter Šajda, István Czakó, David D. Possen, and Heiko Schulz. We are also thankful to Brian Soderquist for his help at the initial stages of this project. This volume and its important contribution to Kierkegaard studies would not have been possible without their help.

List of Abbreviations

Danish Abbreviations

B&A *Breve og Aktstykker vedrørende Søren Kierkegaard*, ed. by Niels Thulstrup, vols. 1–2, Copenhagen: Munksgaard 1953–54.

Bl.art. *S. Kierkegaard's Bladartikler, med Bilag samlede efter Forfatterens Død, udgivne som Supplement til hans øvrige Skrifter*, ed. by Rasmus Nielsen, Copenhagen: C.A. Reitzel 1857.

EP *Af Søren Kierkegaards Efterladte Papirer*, vols. 1–9, ed. by H.P. Barfod and Hermann Gottsched, Copenhagen: C.A. Reitzel 1869–81.

Pap. *Søren Kierkegaards Papirer*, vols. I to XI–3, ed. by Peter Andreas Heiberg, Victor Kuhr and Einer Torsting, Copenhagen: Gyldendalske Boghandel, Nordisk Forlag, 1909–48; second, expanded ed., vols. I to XI–3, by Niels Thulstrup, vols. XII to XIII supplementary volumes, ed. by Niels Thulstrup, vols. XIV to XVI index by Niels Jørgen Cappelørn, Copenhagen: Gyldendal 1968–78.

SKS *Søren Kierkegaards Skrifter*, ed. by Niels Jørgen Cappelørn, Joakim Garff, Jette Knudsen, Johnny Kondrup, Alastair McKinnon, and Finn Hauberg Mortensen, Copenhagen: Gads Forlag 1997ff.

SV1 *Samlede Værker*, ed. by A.B. Drachmann, Johan Ludvig Heiberg and H.O. Lange, vols. I–XIV, Copenhagen: Gyldendalske Boghandels Forlag 1901–06.

English Abbreviations

AN *Armed Neutrality*, trans. by Howard V. Hong and Edna H. Hong, Princeton: Princeton University Press 1998.

AR *On Authority and Revelation, The Book on Adler,* trans. by Walter Lowrie, Princeton: Princeton University Press 1955.

ASKB *The Auctioneer's Sales Record of the Library of Søren Kierkegaard*, ed. by H.P. Rohde, Copenhagen: The Royal Library 1967.

BA *The Book on Adler*, trans. by Howard V. Hong and Edna H. Hong, Princeton: Princeton University Press 1998.

C *The Crisis and a Crisis in the Life of an Actress*, trans. by Howard V. Hong and Edna H. Hong, Princeton: Princeton University Press 1997.

CA *The Concept of Anxiety*, trans. by Reidar Thomte in collaboration with Albert B. Anderson, Princeton: Princeton University Press 1980.

CD *Christian Discourses*, trans. by Howard V. Hong and Edna H. Hong, Princeton: Princeton University Press 1997.

CI *The Concept of Irony*, trans. by Howard V. Hong and Edna H. Hong, Princeton: Princeton University Press 1989.

CIC *The Concept of Irony*, trans. with an Introduction and Notes by Lee M. Capel, London: Collins 1966.

COR *The Corsair Affair*; *Articles Related to the Writings*, trans. by Howard V. Hong and Edna H. Hong, Princeton: Princeton University Press 1982.

CUP1 *Concluding Unscientific Postscript*, vol. 1, trans. by Howard V. Hong and Edna H. Hong, Princeton: Princeton University Press 1992.

CUP2 *Concluding Unscientific Postscript*, vol. 2, trans. by Howard V. Hong and Edna H. Hong, Princeton: Princeton University Press 1992.

EO1 *Either/Or*, Part I, trans. by Howard V. Hong and Edna H. Hong, Princeton: Princeton University Press 1987.

EO2 *Either/Or*, Part II, trans. by Howard V. Hong and Edna H. Hong, Princeton: Princeton University Press 1987.

EOP *Either/Or*, trans. by Alastair Hannay, Harmondsworth: Penguin Books 1992.

EPW *Early Polemical Writings*, among others: *From the Papers of One Still Living*; *Articles from Student Days*; *The Battle Between the Old and the New Soap-Cellars*, trans. by Julia Watkin, Princeton: Princeton University Press 1990.

EUD *Eighteen Upbuilding Discourses*, trans. by Howard V. Hong and Edna H. Hong, Princeton: Princeton University Press 1990.

FSE *For Self-Examination*, trans. by Howard V. Hong and Edna H. Hong, Princeton: Princeton University Press 1990.

FT *Fear and Trembling*, trans. by Howard V. Hong and Edna H. Hong, Princeton: Princeton University Press 1983.

FTP *Fear and Trembling*, trans. by Alastair Hannay, Harmondsworth: Penguin Books 1985.

JC *Johannes Climacus, or De omnibus dubitandum est*, trans. by Howard V. Hong and Edna H. Hong, Princeton: Princeton University Press 1985.

JFY *Judge for Yourself!*, trans. by Howard V. Hong and Edna H. Hong, Princeton: Princeton University Press 1990.

JP *Søren Kierkegaard's Journals and Papers*, vols. 1–6, ed. and trans. by Howard V. Hong and Edna H. Hong, assisted by Gregor Malantschuk (vol. 7, Index and Composite Collation), Bloomington and London: Indiana University Press 1967–78.

KAC *Kierkegaard's Attack upon "Christendom," 1854–1855*, trans. by Walter Lowrie, Princeton: Princeton University Press 1944.

KJN *Kierkegaard's Journals and Notebooks*, vols. 1–11, ed. by Niels Jørgen Cappelørn, Alastair Hannay, David Kangas, Bruce H. Kirmmse, George Pattison, Vanessa Rumble, and K. Brian Söderquist, Princeton and Oxford: Princeton University Press 2007ff.

LD *Letters and Documents*, trans. by Henrik Rosenmeier, Princeton: Princeton University Press 1978.

LR *A Literary Review*, trans. by Alastair Hannay, Harmondsworth: Penguin Books 2001.

M *The Moment and Late Writings*, trans. by Howard V. Hong and Edna H. Hong, Princeton: Princeton University Press 1998.

P *Prefaces*, trans. by Todd W. Nichol, Princeton: Princeton University Press 1997.

PC *Practice in Christianity*, trans. by Howard V. Hong and Edna H. Hong, Princeton: Princeton University Press 1991.

PF *Philosophical Fragments*, trans. by Howard V. Hong and Edna H. Hong, Princeton: Princeton University Press 1985.

PJ *Papers and Journals: A Selection*, trans. by Alastair Hannay, Harmondsworth: Penguin Books 1996.

PLR *Prefaces: Light Reading for Certain Classes as the Occasion May Require*, trans. by William McDonald, Tallahassee: Florida State University Press 1989.

PLS *Concluding Unscientific Postscript*, trans. by David F. Swenson and Walter Lowrie, Princeton: Princeton University Press 1941.

PV *The Point of View* including *On My Work as an Author*, *The Point of View for My Work as an Author*, and *Armed Neutrality*, trans. by Howard V. Hong and Edna H. Hong, Princeton: Princeton University Press 1998.

PVL *The Point of View for My Work as an Author* including *On My Work as an Author*, trans. by Walter Lowrie, New York and London: Oxford University Press 1939.

R *Repetition*, trans. by Howard V. Hong and Edna H. Hong, Princeton: Princeton University Press 1983.

SBL *Notes of Schelling's Berlin Lectures*, trans. by Howard V. Hong and Edna H. Hong, Princeton: Princeton University Press 1989.

SLW *Stages on Life's Way*, trans. by Howard V. Hong and Edna H. Hong, Princeton: Princeton University Press 1988.

SUD *The Sickness unto Death*, trans. by Howard V. Hong and Edna H. Hong, Princeton: Princeton University Press 1980.

SUDP *The Sickness unto Death*, trans. by Alastair Hannay, London and New York: Penguin Books 1989.

TA *Two Ages: The Age of Revolution and the Present Age. A Literary Review*, trans. by Howard V. Hong and Edna H. Hong, Princeton: Princeton University Press 1978.

TD *Three Discourses on Imagined Occasions*, trans. by Howard V. Hong and Edna H. Hong, Princeton: Princeton University Press 1993.

UD *Upbuilding Discourses in Various Spirits*, trans. by Howard V. Hong and Edna H. Hong, Princeton: Princeton University Press 1993.

WA *Without Authority* including *The Lily in the Field and the Bird of the Air, Two Ethical-Religious Essays, Three Discourses at the Communion on Fridays, An Upbuilding Discourse, Two Discourses at the Communion on Fridays*, trans. by Howard V. Hong and Edna H. Hong, Princeton: Princeton University Press 1997.

WL *Works of Love*, trans. by Howard V. Hong and Edna H. Hong, Princeton: Princeton University Press 1995.

WS *Writing Sampler*, trans. by Todd W. Nichol, Princeton: Princeton University Press 1997.

PART I

Plato's Socrates

Apology:
Kierkegaard's Socratic Point of View

Paul Muench

Not long before he died in 1855, Søren Kierkegaard composed a brief essay entitled "My Task."[1] In this relatively neglected work he argues that if we want to understand him and the philosophical activities he has been engaged in, then there is only one instructive object of comparison: Socrates and the role he played as philosophical gadfly in ancient Athens. In this article I critically discuss this text and consider in particular Kierkegaard's claim that his refusal to call himself a Christian—in a context where it was the social norm to do so—is methodologically analogous to Socrates' stance of ignorance.

I. The Moment, *10: "My Task"*

When Kierkegaard died on November 11, 1855, age 42, he left behind among his papers the finished manuscript for the tenth issue of his serial *The Moment*. This final issue includes a section, dated September 1, 1855, that is entitled "My Task" and that turns out to be in effect Kierkegaard's last pronouncement upon the various activities he has been engaged in as a writer and thinker since the completion and defense of his dissertation.[2] It is thus also the last in a series of works within

This article is an abridged version of one that originally appeared in *Kierkegaardiana*, vol. 24, 2007, pp. 132–63 and is reprinted by permission of *Kierkegaardiana*. Thanks to Bridget Clarke, Ben Eggleston, Róbert Haraldsson, Brian Söderquist, and Jon Stewart for helpful comments on an earlier draft.

1 *SKS* 13, 404–11 / *M*, 340–7.

2 Kierkegaard defended his *magister* dissertation on September 29, 1841. In general, when Kierkegaard discusses his activities as a writer and thinker he excludes from consideration his dissertation and the juvenilia that preceded it (including his first published book, *From the Papers of One Still Living*, a critique of Hans Christian Anderson's *Only a Fiddler*). While scholars generally mark the beginning of his authorship proper with the publication of *Either/Or* (February 15, 1843), Kierkegaard makes clear in the text we are considering here that he conceives of what he is calling his task as something upon which he "has spent not only fourteen years but essentially his entire life" (*SKS* 13, 408 / *M*, 343–4). If we focus on the first half of this quotation, it appears that Kierkegaard thinks that what he is describing in the fall of 1855 has been going on for 14 years (which would take us back to the fall of 1841 and to the time when he defended his dissertation). For Kierkegaard, as with many graduate students,

Kierkegaard's *corpus* that (either entirely or in part) are explicit reflections about his methodology and that often include remarks about how to understand some of his other individual works or how to conceive of them as a part of a larger philosophical and religious undertaking. To take an analogy from literary studies, just as there are works of literature and works of criticism, so can we find within Kierkegaard's *corpus* a number of works that primarily seek to illuminate a certain subject matter or existential stance while also seeking to have an existential impact on the reader; at the same time, there exists a second, smaller class of writings that serves a more critical, methodological function, offering us ways in which Kierkegaard thinks we ought to approach the first class of writings together with general remarks about the overall point of view that he claims informs his authorship and about the basic method that he employs.[3] While most of these methodological texts have received a significant amount of attention from scholars (especially *The Point of View*), the text we are considering, "My Task," remains relatively neglected.[4] Having spent several years reflecting about his authorship (and composing a number of texts in the process), Kierkegaard makes one last effort in "My Task" to draw everything together for his reader and to present in as compressed and distilled a manner as possible the essence of what he takes his task to have been. As a result, despite its neglect, this text is perhaps the best single document we have for obtaining a basic picture of how Kierkegaard conceives of his own activities as a writer and thinker.

---

the completion and defense of his dissertation marks both the end of his apprenticeship and the beginning of his mature work.

3 Excluding the many reflections of a critical nature that can be found in Kierkegaard's journals, the chief examples in Kierkegaard's *corpus* of this sort of critical, methodological text include (1) An appendix (entitled "A Glance at a Contemporary Effort in Danish Literature") found in the middle of the 1846 pseudonymous work *Concluding Unscientific Postscript* (*SKS* 7, 228–73 / *CUP1*, 251–300), in which the pseudonymous author Johannes Climacus discusses all of the previous works that have been published (those by the other pseudonymous authors, his own earlier book *Philosophical Fragments*, and works that appeared under Kierkegaard's own name) and that Kierkegaard calls "a section with which [he] would ask the reader to become familiar" (*SV1* XIII, 523 / *PV*, 31); (2) a short document entitled "A First and Last Explanation" that Kierkegaard attached without page numbers to the end of the *Postscript*, where he acknowledged for the first time that he was the creator of the various pseudonymous authors and their respective books (*SKS* 7, 569–73 / *CUP1*, 625–30); (3) *The Point of View*, written in 1848 but not published until after Kierkegaard's death, and the most substantial of this group of texts; (4) *On My Work as an Author* (*SKS* 13, 7–27 / *PV*, 1–20), a short work published in 1851 (partly an extract of *The Point of View*); (5) "Armed Neutrality" (*Pap.* X–5 B 107, pp. 288–301 / *PV*, 127–41), another short work that remained unpublished during Kierkegaard's lifetime; and (6) the text we are examining here, "My Task." For a discussion of the dangers of attaching too much significance to any one of these texts, see Joakim Garff, "Argus' Øjne: 'Synspunktet' og synspunkterne for Kierekgaards 'Forfatter-Virksomhed,' " *Dansk Teologisk Tidsskrift*, no. 52, 1989, pp. 161–89; reprinted in *Kierkegaardiana*, vol. 15, 1991, pp. 29–54.

4 For one discussion see Bruce Kirmmse, " 'I am not a Christian'—A 'Sublime Lie'? Or: 'Without Authority,' Playing Desdemona to Christendom's Othello," in *Anthropology and Authority: Essays on Søren Kierkegaard*, ed. by Poul Houe, Gordon D. Marino, and Sven Hakon Rossel, Amsterdam: Rodopi 2000, pp. 129–36.

Over the space of just a few pages Kierkegaard eloquently sketches for us what he takes to be his contemporary situation, a situation where the authentic practice of Christianity has almost ceased to exist while it nevertheless remains the cultural norm for people (notably his fellow citizens of Copenhagen) to continue to conceive of themselves as Christians. In Kierkegaard's view, there is a striking lack of fit between how his contemporaries picture their lives and how they actually live those lives: he contends that they self-deceptively think they are Christians while failing to put into practice the Christian ideal. In response to this situation Kierkegaard openly refuses to call himself a Christian and at times even denies that he is a Christian: "I do not call myself a Christian, do not say of myself that I am a Christian"; "It is altogether true: I am not a Christian."[5] He realizes that a person who openly declares that they do not call themselves a Christian is in danger of sounding a bit odd in a society where it goes without saying that everyone is a Christian, especially someone like him who has principally devoted himself to writing about what it is to be a Christian:

> Yes, I well know that it almost sounds like a kind of *lunacy* in this Christian world—where each and every one is Christian, where being a Christian is something that everyone naturally is—that there is someone who says of himself, "I do not call myself a Christian," and someone whom Christianity occupies to the degree to which it occupies me.[6]

In response to such a claim, those who have a general familiarity with Kierkegaard's writings may feel the strong desire to object: Isn't this a strange thing for Kierkegaard of all people to say? Don't we know he is a Christian, an exemplary Christian who has had a significant impact on theology, on philosophy and on countless other fields and whose writings remain personally moving to some, personally repugnant to others, precisely for their very Christian orientation and emphasis? One might even feel like exclaiming, "If he isn't a Christian who is?!" Yet, at least in this text, Kierkegaard declares "I am not a Christian" and insists that "anyone who wants to understand [his] totally distinct task must train himself to be able to fix his attention on this" very phrase and the fact that he, Kierkegaard, "continually" repeats it.[7]

In fact, Kierkegaard might not be all that surprised by expressions of puzzlement of this sort from those who take themselves to be familiar with his texts. Though he claims in "My Task" that his authorship was "at the outset stamped 'the single individual—I am not a Christian,' " this is the first time he has openly avowed that this is his position.[8] Kierkegaard suggests that those who think they know he is a Christian (and what is supposed to follow from this) are almost certain to

5 *SKS* 13, 404 / *M*, 340. (Translation modified.) *SKS* 13, 407 / *M*, 342–3.

6 *SKS* 13, 404 / *M*, 340. (My emphasis.)

7 *SKS* 13, 404 / *M*, 340. (My emphasis; translation modified.)

8 *SKS* 13, 408 / *M*, 344. There are, however, other places within Kierkegaard's *corpus* where the significance of denying that one is a Christian is discussed further. This position is most notably associated with the pseudonymous author Johannes Climacus as he presents himself in his second book *Concluding Unscientific Postscript* (cf. *SV1* XIII, 532 / *PV*, 43. *SKS* 13, 14–5 / *PV*, 8). Among Kierkegaard's methodological texts, the other main place where he

misunderstand him, for he openly rejects the idea that there is anything analogous in the entire history of Christianity to the stance he adopts and the task he pursues. He contends that this is "the first time in 'Christendom' " that *anyone* has approached things in this particular manner:

> The point of view I have exhibited and am exhibiting is of such a distinctive nature that in eighteen hundred years of Christendom there is quite literally nothing analogous, nothing comparable that I have to appeal to. Thus, in the face of eighteen hundred years, I stand quite literally alone.[9]

Since Kierkegaard clearly cannot mean by this claim that he is the first person ever to declare that he is not a Christian (since this is something atheists and people who practice other religions do as a matter of course), he must attach a special significance to the fact that he utters this phrase in a context where it has become the norm for people to declare themselves to be Christians and even to conceive of themselves as Christians while living lives that in no way reflect these supposed commitments.

Kierkegaard's claim that there is no one analogous to him in 1,800 years of Christianity is not the only thing, however, that is extraordinary about this passage. Immediately after he claims that he stands alone in Christendom, Kierkegaard makes the perhaps even more remarkable claim that there does exist one person prior to him whose activity is analogous: "The only analogy I have before me is Socrates; my task is a Socratic task, to audit the definition of what it is to be a Christian."[10] That is, Kierkegaard claims that Socrates, a non-Christian pagan philosopher, is his one true predecessor, that Socrates' philosophical activity is the only thing analogous to his activity as a writer and thinker, such that we should conceive of his task—supposedly unique within Christianity—as a *Socratic* task. I think this is a remarkable claim. If Socrates really provides the only analogy to Kierkegaard and if Kierkegaard's task truly is as thoroughly Socratic as he seems to be suggesting, then we may be in the presence here of a thought that ultimately has the potential to revolutionize the very way we think about Kierkegaard and how we approach his texts.

II. Kierkegaard's Socratic Stance: "I am Not a Christian"

The idea that Kierkegaard is in some sense a Socratic figure is bound to strike most scholars of Kierkegaard as obvious. Any random selection of secondary literature is certain to include the occasional appeal to Kierkegaard's lifelong interest in Socrates, and interpretations abound that seek to shore up whatever is being argued for with the thought that, after all, Kierkegaard modeled himself on Socrates, had a penchant for irony and indirection, and so on and so forth. But while it would be surprising to discover someone who claimed to be familiar with Kierkegaard's writings and

---

ties the denial of being a Christian to his own stance is in the text "Armed Neutrality" (see, for example, *Pap*. X–5 B 107, p. 298 / *PV*, 138–9).

9 *SKS* 13, 404–5 / *M*, 340–1. (Translation modified.) Cf. *SKS* 25, 347, NB29:87 / *JP* 6, 6872.

10 *SKS* 13, 405 / *M*, 341.

yet who had no idea that Socrates was an important figure for him, we still lack a detailed, in-depth treatment of the matter. This is not to say that there do not exist any studies of Kierkegaard's conception of Socrates or any helpful accounts of what might be called Kierkegaard's Socratic method. But these are surprisingly few in number.[11] One reason I think "My Task" is a useful place to start is that this text is fairly compressed and schematic in nature. Kierkegaard is here not so much trying to put a Socratic method into practice as to invite us to take up a point of view that he thinks makes *intelligible* many of the activities he has been engaged in as a writer and thinker since the publication of his dissertation. This means that once the point of view at issue becomes clear we will have to turn to other parts of Kierkegaard's *corpus* if we want to obtain a more detailed grasp of how his task actually gets implemented in practice and what it is more specifically about this task that he thinks makes it quintessentially Socratic.[12]

Let's consider further Kierkegaard's comparison of himself to Socrates in "My Task." I want to make clear up front that in my view the single most important text for Kierkegaard's thinking about Socrates is Plato's *Apology*.[13] This is a text to

---

11 On Kierkegaard's conception of Socrates see, for example, Jens Himmelstrup, *Søren Kierkegaards Opfattelse af Sokrates*, Copenhagen: Arnold Busck 1924; Winfield Nagley, "Kierkegaard's Early and Later View of Socratic Irony" (abbreviated "Kierkegaard's Views of Socratic Irony"), *Thought*, no. 55, 1980, pp. 271–82; Harold Sarf, "Reflections on Kierkegaard's Socrates," *Journal of the History of Ideas*, no. 44, 1983, pp. 255–76; Mary-Jane Rubenstein, "Kierkegaard's Socrates: A Venture in Evolutionary Theory," *Modern Theology*, no. 17, 2001, pp. 442–73. On Kierkegaard's Socratic method see, for example, Mark C. Taylor, "Socratic Midwifery: Method and Intention of the Authorship," in *Kierkegaard's Pseudonymous Authorship: A Study of Time and the Self*, Princeton, New Jersey: Princeton University Press 1975, pp. 51–62; Pierre Hadot, "The Figure of Socrates," in *Philosophy as a Way of Life*, ed. by Arnold I. Davidson, trans. by Michael Chase, Oxford: Blackwell 995, pp. 147–78; Paul Muench, "The Socratic Method of Kierkegaard's Pseudonym Johannes Climacus: Indirect Communication and the Art of 'Taking Away,' " in *Søren Kierkegaard and the Word(s)*, ed. by Poul Houe and Gordon D. Marino, Copenhagen: C.A. Reitzel 2003, pp. 139–50.

12 That, however, is a much larger project which lies beyond the scope of this article. I have made a start on this project in "Climacus' Socratic Method" where I argue that Kierkegaard's pseudonymous author Johannes Climacus represents Kierkegaard's "idealization of the Socratic within the context of nineteenth century Danish Christendom" (p. 139).

13 This claim may come as a surprise to those readers who are familiar with Kierkegaard's dissertation and the special role he assigns to Aristophanes' depiction of Socrates. Thus the third and seventh theses that Kierkegaard attached to his dissertation read: "III. If a comparison is made between Xenophon and Plato, one will find that the first takes too much from Socrates, the second raised him too high; neither of them finds the truth"; "VII. Aristophanes has come very close to the truth in his depiction of Socrates" (*SKS* 1, 65 / *CI*, 6). Without wanting to detract from Kierkegaard's very provocative discussion of Aristophanes' *Clouds* (*SKS* 1, 179–203 / *CI*, 128–53), where he convincingly makes the case that this text has things to teach us about Socrates, it is worth keeping in mind that the scope of these two theses about the relative merits of Xenophon vs. Plato vs. Aristophanes does not arguably extend to the whole of Kierkegaard's discussion of Socrates within the dissertation. Rather, these theses only concern the first chapter ("The Conception Made Possible"), in which Kierkegaard seeks to show that

which he returns again and again in his writings about Socrates and which exhibits for him the Socratic ideal: a life that simultaneously is directed at the cultivation of the self together with the aim of engaging one's fellow citizens and getting them to examine themselves more closely. In the case of "My Task," we are invited to compare Kierkegaard's situation and the events that have unfolded in his life to the drama of Socrates' life as it is recounted by him in the *Apology.*[14] Recall that a significant portion of Socrates' defense speech consists of a more general account of how he came to practice philosophy and why he thinks such a life is worth pursuing, together with his explanation of why so many people have been slandering him over the years. Let me briefly recall the main cast of characters who make an appearance in Socrates' account of his life: (1) *the Sophists*, professional teachers and sometimes rivals of Socrates with whom he is often confused by the general public;[15] (2) *the*

---

his own conception of Socrates is capable of accounting for the differences found in the three principal contemporary depictions of him, each of which Kierkegaard believes is ultimately a *distortion* of the truth (whether this distortion results from Xenophon's shallowness, Plato's desire to idealize his teacher, or Aristophanes' aims as a comic playwright). He writes, "even though we lack an altogether reliable conception of [Socrates], we do have in recompense all the various nuances of misunderstanding" (*SKS* 1, 180 / *CI*, 128). Kierkegaard argues that by tracing these various distortions and their interrelationships we place ourselves in a position where we can in effect triangulate back to their common Socratic source, arriving at what he takes to be the truth about Socrates, namely that his standpoint is best understood to embody a radical kind of irony (see *SKS* 1, 204–5 / *CI*, 154; for some significant respects in which Kierkegaard later modifies this view, see Nagley, "Kierkegaard's Views of Socratic Irony"; Rubenstein, "Kierkegaard's Socrates"). Thus while Aristophanes may be held to be *closer* to the truth than either Xenophon or Plato, Kierkegaard nevertheless does not think that *any* contemporary of Socrates has accurately depicted him; nor, for that matter, that anyone else has an accurate conception of him: the ultimate aim of his dissertation is to argue that it is only Søren Kierkegaard who has actually arrived at the truth about Socrates. —But where does this leave my original claim about Plato's *Apology*? Interestingly, Kierkegaard places the *Apology,* in a special class of its own, apart from Plato's other writings (and so, I would argue, apart from the criticism raised against Plato in the third thesis). Calling the *Apology*, "a historical document" (*SKS* 1, 134 / *CI*, 76) that "must be assigned a preeminent place when the purely Socratic is sought" (*SKS* 1, 138 / *CI*, 80). Kierkegaard holds both that "a reliable picture of the *actual* Socrates is seen in the *Apology*" and that "in this work we do have, according to the view of the great majority, a historical representation of Socrates' *actuality*" (*SKS* 1, 177 / *CI*, 126; my emphasis). As the argument of *The Concept of Irony* unfolds (proceeding from Kierkegaard's treatment of the ancient sources, to his discussion of Socrates' trial, to his consideration of Socrates' significance as a world-historical figure), Kierkegaard repeatedly appeals to the *Apology,* and not unreasonably treats it as the final authority upon which any conception of Socrates ultimately must rest. This means in effect that whether we are ultimately convinced by Kierkegaard's overall argument in his dissertation will in large part depend on whether we are convinced by his reading of Plato's *Apology,* itself, which he provocatively claims "is in its entirety an ironic work" (*SKS* 1, 99 / *CI*, 37).

14 All references to Plato's writings are to *Complete Works of Plato*, ed. by John M. Cooper, Indianapolis: Hackett Publishing Company 1997.

15 In the *Apology*, Socrates singles out by name Gorgias, Prodicus, and Hippias (Protagoras is notably absent from this list) as examples of those who "can go to any city and persuade the young, who can keep company with anyone of their own fellow-citizens they want without

god, who manifests himself through the oracle at Delphi and perhaps through the related phenomenon of Socrates' daimonion or divine sign;[16] (3) the broader group of *those reputed to be wise* (represented by the politicians, the poets, and the craftsmen) with whom Socrates converses, along with the public at large which often listens to their discussions;[17] (4) *the young Athenian men* who follow Socrates around and who enjoy listening to him question those reputed to be wise;[18] and (5) *Socrates* himself, who claims that the only sense in which he is wise is that he "do[es] not think [he] know[s] what [he] do[es] not know," and who believes that the god ordered him to "live the life of a philosopher, to examine [himself] and others," thereby serving as a kind of gadfly who awakens people from their ethical slumbers.[19] Socrates offers this account of his life as a part of the defense speech he delivers before the jury. If we leave aside the character of Meletus and Socrates' other immediate accusers, there exist within the larger dramatic context of Socrates' defense two other significant characters worth mentioning: (6) *Socrates' jury*, a selection of his Athenian peers which also serves as a kind of literary analogue for the readers of Plato's text, who themselves are invited to arrive at their own judgment about Socrates' guilt or innocence;[20] and (7) *Plato*, who is represented as one of the young men in attendance

---

paying, to leave the company of these, to join themselves, pay them a fee, and be grateful besides" (*Apology*, 19e–20a). Socrates contrasts any wisdom he might be said to possess (what he terms "human wisdom") with that which might be possessed by the Sophists in question: "those whom I mentioned just now may be wise with a wisdom more than human, or else I don't know what to say about it" (*Apology*, 20d–e; translation modified following *Plato: Apology*, ed. by James J. Helm, Wauconda, Illinois: Bolchazy-Carducci Publishers 1997, p. 20).

16 On the oracle at Delphi: "You know Chaerephon….Surely you know the kind of man he was, how impulsive in any course of action. He went to Delphi at one time and ventured to ask the oracle…if any man was wiser than I, and the Pythian [priestess] replied that no one was wiser" (*Apology*, 21a; cf. 33c). On Socrates' *daimonion*: "I have a divine or spiritual sign which Meletus has ridiculed in his deposition. This began when I was a child. It is a voice, and whenever it speaks it turns me away from something I am about to do, but it never encourages me to do anything" (*Apology*, 31d; cf. 40a–c).

17 See *Apology*, 21b–23b.

18 On the young men: "The young men who follow me around of their own free will, those who have most leisure, the sons of the very rich, take pleasure in hearing people questioned….They enjoy hearing those being questioned who think they are wise, but are not. And this is not unpleasant" (*Apology*, 23c; 33c).

19 *Apology*, 21d; 28e–29a. Socrates claims that it is because he has pursued this god-given task that he has not been a conventionally model public servant and that his own personal affairs have been neglected: "Because of this occupation, I do not have the leisure to engage in public affairs to any extent, nor indeed to look after my own, but I live in great poverty because of my service to the god" (*Apology*, 23b; cf. 31b–c). On being a gadfly: "I was attached to the city by the god—though this seems a ridiculous thing to say—as upon a great and noble horse which was somewhat sluggish because of its size and needed to be stirred up by a kind of gadfly. It is to fulfill some such function that I believe the god has placed me in the city" (*Apology*, 30e).

20 Myles Burnyeat, for example, argues that "readers are invited…to reach a verdict on the case before [them]" ("The Impiety of Socrates," *Ancient Philosophy*, no. 17, 1997, pp. 1–12, see p. 2).

at Socrates' trial and who, in turn, is also the writer and thinker who has composed the text in question.[21]

I want to suggest that Kierkegaard models what he is doing in "My Task"—speaking more generally about his method and overall approach—on the account that Socrates develops in the *Apology* and that he invites us to treat his contemporary situation as a modern analogue to the one faced by Socrates in Athens. As the text unfolds and he develops his claim that Socrates provides his only analogy, Kierkegaard proceeds to single out a variety of characters each of whom corresponds to one of the major characters in the Socratic drama (the Sophists, the god, those reputed to be wise along with the wider public, the young Athenian men who follow Socrates, Socrates himself, Socrates' jury, Plato's readers, and Plato).[22] Simplifying a bit, the main characters discussed by Kierkegaard are the following: (1) *the pastors and theologians*, who make a profession of proclaiming what it is to be a Christian and whom Kierkegaard calls "sophists"; (2) *the public*, who conceive of themselves as Christians but who do not actually live in accord with the Christian ideal; (3) *Kierkegaard qua Socratic figure*, who denies he is a Christian and who helps to make his fellow citizens aware of a deeper sense in which they are not Christians (since they think they are Christians when they are not); (4) *the Christian God of Love*, who Kierkegaard believes has singled him out to be the gadfly of Copenhagen; (5) *Kierkegaard's readers*, individual members of the public who are isolated as individuals by Kierkegaard's texts and whom he seeks to engage as interlocutors; and (6) *Kierkegaard qua writer and critic*, who decides how to dramatize the Socratic engagement of his audience and who offers interpretive tools for understanding his texts.

Let us start with the pastors and theologians and the larger public. Kierkegaard argues that the cultural phenomenon presenting itself as Christianity—what he calls "Christendom" (*Christenhed*)—is permeated by a kind of sophistry. In particular, he compares the pastors and theologians of his day to the Sophists[23] battled by Socrates:

---

21 In general Plato does not cast himself as a character in his writings. The *Apology*, is one of two places within his *corpus* where he is mentioned by name, and the one place where Plato stresses that he—the author of the text in question—was present at the set of events his text purports to represent (see *Apology*, 38b, 34a; Plato, *Phaedo*, 59b). While this device in no way ensures that what is represented is somehow more veridical (for there are plenty of uses of this device by ancient authors where we have independent reasons for thinking that the author in question could not have been present), the fact that Plato only avails himself of this device once in his entire *corpus* surely suggests that he attaches a special significance to asserting that he was in fact a first-hand witness of Socrates' defense.

22 The one exception being perhaps the young men who follow Socrates around and who enjoy listening to him examine those reputed to be wise. Kierkegaard does not present himself as someone who has had such followers, but he remains deeply interested in the youth and the problems a Socrates faces when seeking to interact with them. See, for example, his discussion of Alcibiades at *SKS* 1, 108–13 / *CI*, 47–52. *SKS* 1, 234–9 / *CI*, 187–92. *SKS* 4, 231–2 / *PF*, 24. *SKS* 26, 66–7, NB31:92 / *JP* 4, 4300.

23 In general, when Kierkegaard speaks of the Sophists he primarily has in mind, above all, Protagoras as he is portrayed in Plato's *Protagoras* (see, for example, *SKS* 1, 94–5 / *CI*, 33. *SKS* 1, 113–22 / *CI*, 52–62), together with Hippias and Prodicus (as also portrayed there:

" 'Christendom' lies in an abyss of sophistry that is much, much worse than when the Sophists flourished in Greece. Those legions of pastors and Christian assistant professors are all Sophists....who by falsifying the definition of Christian have, for the sake of the business, gained millions and millions of Christians."[24]

If the pastors and theologians correspond to the professional teachers of virtue in Socrates' day, then the larger Christian public corresponds more broadly to those in Athens who think they know what virtue is when they do not. One of Kierkegaard's main polemics is against the official Danish church and its representatives, the pastors and theologians. He contends that the church has become a business (whose main goal, then, is to make money and to perpetuate itself as an institution), and thus a body that out of self-interest obscures the true Christian message, employing a watered-down version in order for the sake of profits to maximize the total number of Christians.[25] At the same time Kierkegaard also conceives of the public itself as

---

see *SKS* 1, 248 / *CI*, 203), Gorgias, Polus, and Callicles as portrayed in Plato's *Gorgias* (see, for example, *SKS* 1, 94 / *CI*, 33. *SKS* 1, 95–6 / *CI*, 33–4. *SKS* 1, 98 / *CI*, 36), and Polemarchus and Thrasymachus as portrayed in the first book of Plato's *Republic* (see *SKS* 1, 163–71 / *CI*, 109–19). His more general discussion of Socrates' relationship to the Sophists can be found at *SKS* 1, 246–59 / *CI*, 201–14. That being said, a word of caution may be in order concerning the term "sophist." Henry Sidgwick famously argued that this term does not have a univocal application ("The Sophists," in *Lectures on the Philosophy of Kant and Other Philosophical Lectures and Essays*, London: Macmillan 1905, pp. 323–71). He claims that even within Plato's *corpus* we ought to distinguish between (1) Sophists like Protagoras who claim to teach the art of virtue and who prefer delivering speeches to the give and take of Socrates' question-and-answer approach and (2) those Sophists who more closely "ape" Socrates' own methods and so represent a "post-Socratic Sophistry" (caricatured in Plato's *Euthydemus*) where "instead of pretentious and hollow rhetoric we have perverse and fallacious dialectic" (p. 343; p. 334). Sidgwick further calls into question the legitimacy of assimilating Callicles and Thrasymachus (open defenders of an egoistic moral skepticism) to the first group of Sophists. It may be worth noting, however, that this latter claim seems partly to rest on Sidgwick's being under the impression that Plato does not portray Protagoras as someone Socrates attacks because his doctrines are "novel or dangerous" but only because they are "superficial and commonplace," a view Kierkegaard surely would not be alone in rejecting (p. 360; cf. Plato, *Meno*, 91e).

24 *SKS* 13, 405 / *M*, 341. (Translation modified.) *SKS* 13, 404 / *M*, 340. It should be noted, however, that one dissimilarity between the pastors and theologians under criticism by Kierkegaard and the Sophists of Socrates' day is that while the former are part of the official establishment and as such were generally recognized as legitimate authorities, the latter were usually outsiders who traveled to Athens and who were often viewed with considerable suspicion by those in power. Compare Anytus' discussion of the Sophists in Plato's *Meno* (91b–92c).

25 At the close of "My Task," Kierkegaard addresses the common man (*menige Mand*) and warns him to "avoid the pastors, avoid them, those abominations whose job is to hinder you in even becoming aware of what true Christianity is and thereby to turn you, muddled by gibberish and illusion, into what they understand by a true Christian, a contributing member of the state Church, the national Church, and the like. Avoid them; only see to it that you willingly and promptly pay them the money they are to have. One must at no price have money differences with someone one scorns, lest it be said that one was avoiding them in order to get out of paying. No, pay them double so that your disagreement with them can

a distinct force to be reckoned with, as an abstract crowd or mob whose existence is predicated on the failure of people to cultivate and maintain themselves *qua* individuals. He invites us to imagine the contemporary situation of Christendom to consist of hordes of people, all running around calling themselves Christians and conceiving of themselves as Christians, often under the direct influence and guidance of the pastors and theologians, while next to no one is actually living a true, authentic Christian life. In this way he upholds a distinction between the pastors and theologians (sophists proper), who make a living advocating what it is to be a Christian, and the larger population, who more generally think they are Christians when they are not and whom Kierkegaard generically calls "the others" (*de Andre*).[26]

Kierkegaard casts himself in the role of Socrates and, accordingly, depicts himself as someone who both seeks to reform the larger public and combats the corrupting influence of the pastors and theologians. By making such pronouncements about his contemporary situation and by presenting himself as someone who is capable of observing such patterns of behavior and even of diagnosing what can lead to such a state of things, Kierkegaard is aware that he might appear to be setting himself up as an extraordinary Christian. But he denies that he is any such thing and suggests that his refusal to call himself a Christian at all partly helps to block such attributions: "I do not call myself a Christian. That this is very awkward for the sophists I understand very well, and I understand very well that they would much prefer that with kettledrums and trumpets I proclaimed myself to be the only true Christian."[27] Recall that Kierkegaard is well aware that his refusal to call himself a Christian is bound to strike his contemporaries as a bit odd against the backdrop of a society where everyone as a matter of course calls themselves a Christian. Despite this appearance of bizarreness, Kierkegaard contends that there are two significant reasons why he continues to assert this about himself. First, he ties his refusal to call himself a Christian, or in any way to modify this statement, to his desire to maintain a proper relationship with an omnipotent being, a being he later characterizes as the Christian "God of Love": "I neither can, nor will, nor dare change my statement: otherwise perhaps another change would take place—that the power, an omnipotence [*Almagt*] that especially uses my powerlessness [*Afmagt*], would wash his hands of me and let me go my own way."[28] At the same time, Kierkegaard ties his stance of

---

become obvious: that what concerns them does not concern you at all, money, and that, on the contrary, what does not concern them concerns you infinitely, Christianity" (*SKS* 13, 410–1 / *M*, 347).

26 In the *Apology*, Socrates makes clear that independent of any danger the Sophists may represent, he takes it to be the case that the Athenian populace as a whole (which after all, in the form of the jury, will put him to death) is itself a significant force: "Do not be angry with me for speaking the truth; no man will survive who genuinely opposes you or any other crowd and prevents the occurrence of many unjust and illegal happenings in the city. A man who really fights for justice must lead a private, not a public, life if he is to survive for even a short time" (*Apology*, 31e–32a; cf. Plato, *Republic*, 492a–493c).

27 *SKS* 13, 406 / *M*, 341–2. (Translation modified.)

28 *SKS* 13, 404 / *M*, 340. (Translation modified.) Thus refusing to call himself a Christian is, in part, an expression of Kierkegaard's religious convictions and may be tied to his idea

one who does not call himself a Christian to an ability to make his contemporaries ("the others") aware of an even deeper sense in which he claims that they are not Christians:

> I am not a Christian—and unfortunately I can make it manifest that the others are not either—indeed, even less than I, since they imagine themselves to be that, or they falsely ascribe to themselves that they are that. I do not call myself a Christian (keeping the ideal free), but I can make it manifest that the others are that even less.[29]

He seems to think that adopting a position of one who refuses to call himself a Christian makes him an especially tenacious interlocutor, someone whom his contemporaries will not be able to shake off very easily: "Just because I do not call myself a Christian it is impossible to get rid of me, having as I do the confounded characteristic that I can make it manifest—also *by means of* not calling myself a Christian—that the others are that even less."[30] Kierkegaard, then, conceives his task to have a twofold structure. By denying that he is a Christian in the face of his contemporaries' wont to assert the opposite, he claims to be developing and upholding some kind of religious relationship to a divine being while also acquiring a powerful means of awakening his contemporaries and making them aware of the lack of fit between how they conceive of their lives and how they actually live them.[31]

---

that one never *is* a Christian in this life, though each person certainly can embark on the lifelong task of *becoming* a Christian.

29 *SKS* 13, 404 / *M*, 340. (Translation modified.) *SKS* 13, 405 / *M*, 341. The Danish verb phrase "*indbilde sig*" can also mean to be under an illusion or under a delusion. Those who are under the illusion that they already *are* something will not be in the practice of examining whether they *really* are that, nor will they set about trying to *become* something that they think they already are.

30 *SKS* 13, 406 / *M*, 342. (My emphasis; translation modified.)

31 Kierkegaard frequently characterizes his task in terms of these two dimensions, so that one and the same activity is partly constitutive of what in his own case he takes to be an authentic life while also being directed at helping others to gain a greater awareness of the lack of fit between their avowed commitments and how they actually live. As a result, he argues that his method of approach has an intrinsic worth to it independent of how successful it is with his interlocutors, since it helps constitute his own life whether or not, in the end, it manages to make the others more aware: "That is why this approach has intrinsic worth. Ordinarily it holds true that an approach has worth only in proportion to what is achieved by it. One judges and condemns, makes a big noise—this has no intrinsic worth, but one reckons on achieving a great deal thereby. It is different with the approach described here. Assume that a person had devoted his whole life to using it, assume that he had practiced it all his life, and assume that he had achieved nothing—he nevertheless has by no means lived in vain, because his life was true self-denial" (*SV1* XIII, 532–3 / *PV*, 44; cf. *SKS* 7, 251–4 / *CUP1*, 277–8). On the significance of self-denial for Kierkegaard, see, for example, *SKS* 9, 356, 3–4 / *WL*, 361. *SKS* 9, 194, 2–10 / *WL*, 194.

III. Socratic Ignorance

In the process of sketching his contemporary situation and characterizing both the sophist-like attributes of the pastors and theologians and the more general condition of his contemporaries (whom, he claims, think they are Christians when they are not), Kierkegaard repeatedly invokes Socrates, especially in order to throw further light on his characterization of himself as a Socratic figure. He suggests that Socrates' task in Athens has the same twofold structure as his task: Socrates is both a gadfly to his contemporaries and someone who holds that his life as a philosopher is an expression of his devotion to the god. Let's consider the image of the gadfly first. Socrates' use of this image in the *Apology* is tied to the idea of his fellow citizens' being in some sense asleep and therefore in need of being awakened. He compares their condition to that of a sluggish but noble horse which can only be stirred into life by the sting of a fly. But just as it is not uncommon for horses to kill the flies that sting them (with the quick snap of their tails), Socrates also notes that there is a certain danger involved in his being a gadfly: "You might easily be annoyed with me as people are when they are aroused from a doze, and strike out at me; if convinced by Anytus you could easily kill me, and then you could sleep on for the rest of your days, unless the god, in his care for you, sent you someone else."[32] Kierkegaard ties Socrates' ability to awaken his fellow citizens to his stance of ignorance,[33] and invites us to compare

---

32 *Apology*, 31a. The idea that a philosopher's primary role is to serve as a gadfly for her fellow citizens is rather removed from how philosophy tends to be thought of these days. Reminding ourselves that Socrates thought of his philosophical activity in these terms will better position us to appreciate the sense in which Kierkegaard might readily call himself a philosopher in spite of his general tendency to ridicule and set himself against most modern forms of philosophy.

33 Socrates' ignorance has remained an enduring source of puzzlement; this is especially so for philosophers since ignorance is normally thought to be a condition that philosophy helps one to overcome. It might seem that in so far as Socrates remains ignorant he lies outside the proper province of philosophy. One might even feel like asserting, "If Socrates is still ignorant after 70 years isn't this reason enough to admit that his method is inadequate at best and ultimately a failure?" In his essay, "Socrates' Disavowal of Knowledge," Gregory Vlastos nicely captures this sentiment and brings into view the seemingly inherent tension between Socrates' unvarying stance of ignorance and his presentation of himself as a virtuous person: "If after decades of searching Socrates remained convinced that he still knew nothing, would not further searching have become a charade—or rather worse? For he holds that virtue 'is' knowledge: if he has no knowledge, his life is a disaster, he has missed out on virtue and, therewith, on happiness. How is it then that he is serenely confident he has achieved both? [In a footnote to this passage:] His avowals of epistemic inadequacy, frequent in the dialogues, are never paralleled by admission of moral failure; the asymmetry is striking" (in *Socratic Studies*, ed. by Myles Burnyeat, Cambridge: Cambridge University Press 1994, pp. 39–66, p. 43). Socrates' stance of ignorance is sometimes treated as a rhetorical device that he uses to draw out his interlocutor. Norman Gulley, for example, claims that Socrates' profession of ignorance is "an expedient to encourage his interlocutor to seek out the truth, to make him think he is joining with Socrates in a voyage of discovery" (quoted by Vlastos, p. 39). Hence his stance of ignorance is sometimes called a mere ironic pose; consider this common dictionary definition of Socratic irony: "pretense of ignorance in a discussion to expose the

this stance with his own stance of refusing to call himself a Christian. He contends that Socrates' ignorance both effectively distinguishes him from the Sophists (who profess to be knowledgeable about virtue and the like and who are willing to teach this to others for a fee) while also serving as a means for making his fellow citizens aware of a different kind of ignorance that they themselves possess:

> O Socrates! If with kettledrums and trumpets you had proclaimed yourself to be the one who knew the most, the Sophists would soon have been finished with you. No, you were *the ignorant one*; but in addition you had the confounded characteristic that you could make it manifest (also by means of being yourself the ignorant one) that the others knew even less than you—they did not even know that they were ignorant.[34]

By likening his stance of someone who refuses to call himself a Christian to Socrates' position, Kierkegaard suggests that he shares with Socrates the ability to make people aware of a more shameful or disgraceful form of ignorance (cf. *Apology*, 29b), an ignorance that can only be counteracted through a greater attention to and cultivation of the self. The chief result of interacting with either a Socrates or a Kierkegaard is that an interlocutor comes to see that they have been self-complacent, thinking they know things they are not able to defend under examination or thinking they live a certain way that does not in fact square with their actual life. To be in such a condition is characterized by self-neglect and a lack of true intellectual curiosity, for if one thinks one is living as one imagines then no deeper self-examination is deemed necessary, and if one thinks one knows all about a subject then one feels no need to

---

fallacies in the opponent's logic" (*Webster's New World College Dictionary*, ed. by Michael Agnes, 4th ed., Cleveland: Wiley Publishing 2002, p. 755). In the *Republic*, Thrasymachus is just as suspicious of Socrates' claim to be ignorant, only he treats it as a tactic adopted by Socrates to avoid having to be questioned by others: "By Heracles, [Thrasymachus] said, that's just Socrates' usual irony. I knew, and I said so to these people earlier, that you'd be unwilling to answer and that, if someone questioned *you*, you'd be ironical and do anything rather than give an answer" (337a). In contrast to these positions Kierkegaard, who is best known for having argued in his dissertation that Socrates is an ironist through and through, never conceives of Socrates' ignorance as feigned or merely tactical, as though it did not go all the way down. See, for example, *SKS* 1, 217–24 / *CI*, 169–77. *SKS* 1, 306–8 / *CI*, 269–71. Among modern commentators who discuss Socrates' irony, Alexander Nehamas seems to come closest to Kierkegaard's position. Commenting on Vlastos' discussion, he calls the relationship between Socrates' disavowal of knowledge and his conviction that he has lived a virtuous life "Socrates' final and most complex irony. He disavows the knowledge he himself considers necessary for a life of *aretê*. But he is also 'serenely' confident in thinking that he has actually lived such a life....[If we suppose] he did live a good life, does he or does he not think that he really has that knowledge? Does he or does he not mean his disavowal seriously?... Plato's early works do not answer [these questions], and they thus endow Socrates with a further ironical dimension. Not just ironical with his interlocutors, he is ironical toward Plato himself (and so towards Plato's readers) as well, for even Plato cannot answer the question Socrates poses for him. Though Socrates is Plato's creature, his own literary character, he remains opaque to him: he is a character his own creator admits he cannot understand" (*The Art of Living: Socratic Reflections from Plato to Foucault*, Berkeley: University of California Press 1998, pp. 86–7).

34 *SKS* 13, 406 / *M*, 342. (My emphasis; translation modified.)

look into it in a more searching way. While Socrates' concern with what a person knows might on the face of it seem to be of a different order than Kierkegaard's concern with whether a person lives as a Christian, the principal focus of both of them is what we might call the practical sphere of human life, the sphere of ethics and religion, where an individual's grasp of a given ethical or religious concept is inherently tied to whether or not it plays an appropriate role in the life they lead.[35] Like Socrates, Kierkegaard focuses in particular on the tendency people have to lose track of the fundamental connection between knowing what virtue is or what it is to be a Christian and actually living a virtuous life or living an authentic Christian life.[36]

The dangers associated with Socrates' being a gadfly include the tendency of other people to grow angry with him as well as an unwillingness to take him at his word when he claims that he himself is ignorant about what he can show that the others only think they know. In the *Apology* he says that it is not uncommon for his interlocutors to grow angry in response to having been refuted by him and for them and the larger audience to assume that he must know, despite his claims of ignorance, what he has shown that they do not know:

> As a result of this investigation, gentlemen of the jury, I acquired much unpopularity, of a kind that is hard to deal with and is a heavy burden; many slanders came from these people and a reputation for wisdom, for in each case the bystanders thought that I myself possessed the wisdom that I proved that my interlocutor did not have.[37]

---

35 A passage in Plato's *Laches* nicely brings out the connection between Socrates' interest in what an individual knows and his deeper interest in examining how that person lives: "You don't appear to me to know that whoever comes into close contact with Socrates and associates with him in conversation must necessarily, even if he began by conversing about something quite different in the first place, keep on being led about by the man's arguments until he submits to answering questions about himself concerning both his present manner of life and the life he has lived hitherto. And when he does submit to this questioning, you don't realize that Socrates will not let him go before he has well and truly tested every last detail" (187e–188a; cf. *Apology*, 29e–30a).

36 One definition of sophistry might be any approach to ethical and religious matters that fosters the illusion that a theoretical knowledge of such matters is possible independent of the practical understanding that one only acquires by living a certain kind of life. Kierkegaard believes that with the rise in his day of Hegelian philosophy a new species of sophistry is born, a sophistry that holds out the promise of a systematic, theoretical comprehension of ethical and religious matters while at the same time leading individuals to neglect the proper realm of ethics and religion: namely the individual herself *qua* ethical and religious agent. Within Kierkegaard's *corpus*, the main attack against this Hegelian species of sophistry is launched by the pseudonymous author Johannes Climacus in his two books *Philosophical Fragments* and *Concluding Unscientific Postscript*.

37 *Apology*, 22e–23a; cf. 23c–24b and *Theaetetus*, 151c, where Socrates claims that "people have often before now got into such a state with me as to be literally ready to bite when I take away some nonsense or other from them." It is the condition of being "unpopular with many people" that Socrates says will lead to his "undoing, if [he] is undone, not Meletus or Anytus but the slanders and envy of many people" (*Apology*, 28a).

The characteristic ways people have of responding to Socrates' profession of ignorance have also, according to Kierkegaard, applied with respect to his denial that he is a Christian. He claims that he often faces the same kind of anger, together with a corresponding presumption about his own Christian status. But he is quick to deny that it in any way follows from his having an ability to make others aware that they are not Christians that he himself is a Christian:

> But as it went with you [Socrates] (according to what you say in your "defense," as you ironically enough have called the cruelest satire on a contemporary age)—namely that you made many enemies for yourself by making it manifest that the others were ignorant and that the others held a grudge against you out of envy since they assumed that you yourself must be what you could show that they were not—so has it also gone with me. That I can make it manifest that the others are even less Christian than I has given rise to indignation against me; I who nevertheless am so engaged with Christianity that I truly perceive and acknowledge that I am not a Christian. Some want to foist on me that my saying that I am not a Christian is only a hidden form of pride, that I presumably must be what I can show that the others are not. But this is a misunderstanding; it is altogether true: I am not a Christian. And it is rash to conclude from the fact that I can show that the others are not Christians that therefore I myself must be one, just as rash as to conclude, for example, that someone who is one-fourth of a foot taller than other people is, ergo, twelve feet tall.[38]

Part of the difficulty in taking seriously Socrates' ignorance or Kierkegaard's denial that he is a Christian is an unwillingness to accept the idea that someone in that condition could nevertheless be a skilled diagnostician and able conversation partner. We find it hard to believe that Socrates could understand his interlocutors as well as he seems to be able to (seemingly being acquainted with all the different forms that their ignorance can take) while remaining himself ignorant about the subject in question. Similarly, could Kierkegaard really be as good at depicting the various ways that a person can fall short of being a Christian whilc continuing to think they are a Christian if he were not himself that very thing? But this is to underestimate the power of self-knowledge. For Socrates and Kierkegaard to be good at diagnosing and treating different species of that more disgraceful kind of ignorance what is required first and foremost is that they have become acquainted in their own case with the phenomenon at issue, the tendency of a person to a kind of self-satisfaction where they imagine they know more than they do. This tendency is a condition they are prone to, that they need to discover and—through self-examination and self-scrutiny—learn to regulate and control. While it is clearly true that a Socrates or a Kierkegaard will not make an effective conversation partner if he cannot discuss with some precision whatever it is he suspects that his interlocutor only thinks they know, the chief qualification is that he be personally acquainted with the activity of forever being on the lookout for any such tendency in his own case. In fact, he must himself be an accomplished master of this activity (he must uphold the Delphic injunction to know thyself) if he is to be able to help others to make similar discoveries about

38 *SKS* 13, 406–7 / *M*, 342–3. (Translation modified.)

themselves and to introduce them into the rigors of a life that seeks to avoid that more disgraceful kind of ignorance in all its various manifestations.

I suspect that a further reason that we may find it difficult to take seriously Socrates' ignorance is that it does not seem to sit well with our idea of him as a philosopher. While we may certainly applaud the manner in which he helps others to overcome their more disgraceful condition of ignorance, the fact remains that Socrates still seems to fall short of a certain philosophical ideal. The image we get of him in many of Plato's dialogues is of someone who is always approaching knowledge, perhaps gaining greater and greater conviction about what he holds to be the case but never actually arriving at knowledge itself.[39] This picture of Socrates (upheld both by Plato and Aristotle and most of the philosophical tradition since them, including Hegel and the early Kierkegaard of *The Concept of Irony*) tends to conceptualize his philosophical activity as being only a part of a larger enterprise, as itself incomplete or preliminary in nature.[40] While Socrates' method of engaging his interlocutors may help cleanse them of misconceptions or remove a certain kind of self-satisfaction that stands in the way of a proper philosophical engagement of a given topic, once Socrates has done what he does well (so the story goes) then other methods are required if we are actually to gain what he has shown his interlocutors to lack. Though Kierkegaard seems to endorse a version of this picture in his dissertation, as his conception of Socrates develops in his later writings he more and more vehemently comes to reject this picture and instead maintains that Socrates'

---

39 Given the inductive nature of Socrates' enterprise, the strength of his convictions will partly rest on the quality of the interlocutor he encounters, providing him perhaps with further reason for trying to foster a philosophical culture in Athens in which someone might arise who could truly test him, a Socrates who could test Socrates (Plato arguably tries to fulfill that very role over the course of his writings): "These conclusions, at which we arrived earlier in our previous discussions are, I'd say, held down by arguments of iron and adamant, even if it's rather rude to say so. So it would seem, anyhow. And if you [Callicles] or someone more forceful than you won't undo them, then anyone who says anything other than what I'm now saying cannot be speaking well. And yet for my part, my account is ever the same: I don't know how these things are, but no one I've ever met, as in this case, can say anything else without being ridiculous" (Plato, *Gorgias*, 508e–509a). This picture of Socrates being tested by others, however, remains somewhat of an anomaly within Plato's *corpus*; his fundamental role is to be the one who asks questions. In the *Theaetetus* Socrates notes that this is how he is commonly thought of and readily ties this view of himself to his stance of ignorance: "The common reproach against me is that I am always asking questions of other people but never express my own views about anything, because there is no wisdom in me; and that is true enough. And the reason of it is this, that God compels me to attend to the travail of others, but has forbidden me to procreate. So that I am not in any sense a wise man; I cannot claim as the child of my own soul any discovery worth the name of wisdom" (150c–d).

40 In his dissertation Kierkegaard assigns Socrates an essential role in the development of a proper speculative philosophy, but contends that he should only be conceived of as someone who prepares the way for speculative philosophy without himself becoming a speculative philosopher: "In the world-historical sense [Socrates'] significance was that he set the boat of speculation afloat….He himself, however, does not go on board but merely launches the ship. He belongs to an older formation, and yet a new one begins with him" (*SKS* 1, 261 / *CI*, 217; translation modified).

philosophical activity is not a mere precursor to something else but itself the human ideal (the best ethical and religious life available outside of Christianity). Socrates' life as a philosopher is thus held by Kierkegaard to be humanly complete, and ought in his view to make a claim on us and to serve as a model that we can emulate in our own lives. Socrates' activity of examining and refuting, forever on the lookout for further instances of a person's thinking they know what they do not, becomes a life-long, ever vigilant task that he invites each of us to take part in; a task that a person will never finish, for the moment they begin to imagine that they have finished with such self-examination and self-scrutiny is the very moment when they may begin to think they know something they do not.[41]

To motivate this picture of Socrates, Kierkegaard appeals to the religious significance that Socrates attaches to his activity as a gadfly in Athens. In the face of the reputation for wisdom that he has acquired over the years, Socrates upholds his stance of ignorance and insists that it really is the case that he lacks knowledge of the very things he tests others about. But this would then seem to leave us exactly where Socrates found himself upon first hearing of the oracle's claim that no one was wiser.[42] How can it truly be the case that Socrates is both ignorant (as he insists) and the wisest among human beings? Recall that in the *Apology* Socrates offers us a way out of this apparent bind and, in the process, exhibits the very modesty that is often associated with his stance of ignorance:

> What is probable, gentlemen, is that in fact the god is wise and that his oracular response meant that human wisdom is worth little or nothing, and that when he says this man, Socrates, he is using my name as an example, as if he said: "This man among you, mortals, is wisest who, like Socrates, understands that his wisdom is worthless."[43]

---

41 On the idea of Socrates' activity being a kind of preliminary cleansing of the soul, consider this passage from Plato's *Sophist*: "They set out to get rid of the belief in one's own wisdom in another way….They cross-examine someone when he thinks he's saying something though he's saying nothing. Then, since his opinions will vary inconsistently, these people will easily scrutinize him. They collect his opinions together during the discussion, put them side by side, and show that they conflict with each other at the same time on the same subjects in relation to the same things and in the same respects. The people who are being examined see this, get angry at themselves, and become calmer toward others [ideally speaking: cf. *Apology*, 23d]. They lose their inflated and rigid beliefs about themselves that way, and no loss is pleasanter to hear or has a more lasting effect on them. Doctors who work on the body think it can't benefit from any food that's offered to it until what's interfering with it from inside is removed. The people who *cleanse the soul*, my young friend, likewise think the soul, too, won't get any advantage from any learning that's offered to it until someone shames it by refuting it, removes the opinions that interfere with learning, and exhibits it cleansed, believing that it knows only those things that it does, and nothing more" (230b–d; my emphasis). By denying that Socrates' life should be understood as incomplete, Kierkegaard radicalizes this activity of cleansing the soul, insisting that this activity is never finished, never perfected but instead is of such a nature that an individual must conceive of it as a task to which she must devote her entire life.

42 *Apology*, 20e–21b.

43 *Apology*, 23a–b.

The claim that human wisdom is worth "little or nothing" can strike people in quite different ways. In the traditional picture of Socrates (in which he battles the Sophists, destroying sophistry to make room for philosophy, though himself remaining only a preliminary step in its development), one might be inclined to restrict this claim about human wisdom to pre-philosophical forms of wisdom. As philosophy develops and becomes ever more sophisticated, a wisdom becomes possible that no longer is "little or nothing" but rather approaches the wisdom Socrates reserves for the god. In his later writings on Socrates, Kierkegaard rejects this reading and instead takes it to be the case that Socrates means to draw a strict line between the human and the divine, and to ground claims of human wisdom in an individual's ability to remain aware of that distinction.[44] On this picture the difference between a wise human being and an ignorant one is that the wise person remains aware of their ignorance in relation to the wisdom of the god; the task is to develop oneself while maintaining this awareness, thereby at the same time developing a proper relationship to the god. For Kierkegaard, then, Socrates is to be taken at his word when he says that human wisdom is worth little or nothing. He does not think that Socrates' practice of philosophy is meant to begin with this little or nothing and incrementally try to bring it as close as possible to what only the god truly possesses. Rather, it is to engage in a task of self-examination and self-scrutiny of the sort that helps a person to *fortify* themselves against the ever prevalent tendency to think they know things they do not; that is, against the tendency to lose track of the difference between the human and the divine. For Kierkegaard, Socrates' life as a philosopher embodies a rigorous task of ethical self-examination that expresses in its human modesty a deeply religious commitment. Socrates' ignorance is the point from which a person shall not be moved, not the point from which a better, more developed philosophy can begin to emerge.[45]

---

44 Kierkegaard's pseudonymous author Anti–Climacus puts it this way: "Let us never forget—but how many ever really knew it or thought it?—let us never forget that Socrates' ignorance was a kind of fear and worship of God, that his ignorance was the Greek version of the Jewish saying: The fear of the Lord is the beginning of wisdom. Let us never forget that it was out of veneration for God that he was ignorant, that as far as it was possible for a pagan he was on guard duty as a *judge* on the frontier between God and man, keeping watch so that *the deep gulf of qualitative difference* between them was maintained, *between God and man* [my emphasis], that God and man did not merge in some way, *philosophice*, *poetice* [philosophically, poetically], etc., into one. That was why Socrates was the ignorant one, and that was why the deity found him to be the wisest of men" (*SKS* 11, 211 / *SUD*, 99).

45 Compare two passages from Kierkegaard's journals: "During the most developed period of the most intellectual nation Socrates attained ignorance (ignorance, with which one [normally] begins in order to know more and more) and how? Because in radical ethicality he took his task to be that of preserving himself in ignorance, so that no temptation without and no temptation within would ever trick him into admitting that he knew something, he who nevertheless in another sense did know something….The significance of Socratic ignorance was precisely to keep ethics from becoming scholarly knowledge—instead of practice. There is nothing more dangerous than to transform into scholarly knowledge something which should be practiced" (*SKS* 22, 40, NB11:62 / *JP* 1, 972. *Pap.* XI–2 A 362 / *JP* 4, 3871).

As Kierkegaard develops the parallel between himself and Socrates, it becomes clear just how significant Socrates is for him personally. One of the ways this manifests itself stems from his claim that he stands *alone* within the Christian tradition. While underlining yet again that he thinks that "in Christendom's eighteen hundred years there is absolutely nothing comparable, nothing analogous to [his] task," he notes that there are certain burdens associated with occupying such a unique position:

> I know what it has cost, what I have suffered, which can be expressed by a single line: I was never like the others. Ah, of all the torments in youthful days, the most dreadful, the most intense: not to be like the others, never to live any day without painfully being reminded that one is not like the others, never to be able to run with the crowd, the desire and the joy of youth, never free to be able to abandon oneself, always, as soon as one would risk it, to be painfully reminded of the chain, the segregation of singularity that, to the point of despair, painfully separates a person from everything that is called human life and cheerfulness and gladness....With the years, this pain does decrease more and more; for as one becomes more and more spiritually developed, it is no longer painful that one is not like the others. To be spiritually developed is precisely: not to be like the others.[46]

With such real isolation and heartfelt loneliness in view, Kierkegaard's claim that Socrates occupied an analogous position becomes all the more poignant since this in effect ensures that there is at least one person who would be in a position to understand the difficulties of his task. Early on in "My Task," just after he claims that Socrates provides his only analogy, Kierkegaard turns and openly addresses him:

> You, antiquity's noble simple soul, you the only *human being* I admiringly acknowledge as a thinker: there is only a little preserved about you, of all people the only true martyr of intellectuality, just as great *qua* character as *qua* thinker; but how exceedingly much this little is! How I long, far from those battalions of thinkers that "Christendom" places in the field under the name of Christian thinkers...how I long to be able to speak—if only for half an hour—with you![47]

In this way Socrates becomes a kind of inner companion for Kierkegaard, someone to whom he can confide and whose example he can draw upon in his darker, lonelier moments, or in those moments perhaps when he feels least understood by his contemporaries.[48]

---

46 *SKS* 13, 408 / *M*, 344. (Translation modified.)

47 *SKS* 13, 405 / *M*, 341. (Translation modified.)

48 This also arguably marks a difference between Kierkegaard and Socrates, for however isolated Kierkegaard is, he still has the image and example of Socrates to help him maintain his bearings. Personal outpourings of this sort also mark his writings as much more a product of modernity and the Christian tradition of confession than anything we find written about Socrates. The ancient accounts of Socrates don't really concern themselves with what we might call Socrates' inner life. In the *Apology*, Socrates claims that he is the "same man" whether in public life or in private discussion: "Throughout my life, in any public activity I may have engaged in, I am the same man as I am in private life....If anyone says that...he heard anything privately that the others did not hear, be assured that he is not telling the truth" (32e–33b). Yet we often have the feeling when reading about him that there is more there,

IV. Kierkegaard as Writer and Thinker

In addition to characterizing his contemporary situation and his response to that situation in terms of the four main figures we have been discussing thus far (the pastors and theologians, the public, the Christian God of Love, and himself *qua* Socratic figure), Kierkegaard makes clear in "My Task" that he also conceives of himself as playing a role analogous to that of Plato the writer and thinker. Just as Kierkegaard often depicts (and takes part in) Socratic exchanges within his texts, so also in his capacity as a writer does he frequently engage in a conversation with the individual readers of these texts, usually addressing them in the singular as "my dear reader."[49] Though the individual reader is frequently invited by Kierkegaard to apply what has been enacted in a given work to their own life (as a reader of one of Plato's dialogues might come to examine themselves more closely in the light of certain exchanges that Plato has portrayed between Socrates and a given interlocutor), there are also cases within Kierkegaard's *corpus* where he engages the reader *qua* reader, seeking to instruct them on how to read his texts. Kierkegaard's activity in this case is akin to Socrates' attempt to inform his jury about his practice as a philosopher, and seeks to provide his reader with a more general understanding of his overall point of view and how he, the writer and thinker, thinks that his books should be read. Obviously the mere fact that Kierkegaard claims that his books mean thus and so, or that they ought to be read in the light of such and such, does not guarantee that he is right.[50] The proof lies in how illuminating we find such orienting remarks to be. Do they reveal to us ways of approaching his texts that make those texts interesting to read, and do they help us to discern patterns of argument and literary nuance that we otherwise might not properly appreciate?

The main aim of "My Task" is to provide us with a point of view from which, according to Kierkegaard, his activities as a writer and thinker become intelligible. As should have become clear by now, that point of view might be called a Socratic point of view, and it remains Kierkegaard's chief contention that Socrates is the one individual prior to him whose activity sheds any light on his task. By making such pronouncements Kierkegaard in effect presents himself as the best qualified person

---

more to him than what lies open to us. This may partly be why we continue to be fascinated by Plato's version of Socrates in particular, who seems to have a hidden depth which is never brought fully out into the open. Alexander Nehamas nicely puts it this way: "Incomprehensible and opaque, to his author as well as to us, Plato's early Socrates has acquired a solidity and robustness few literary characters can match" (Nehamas, *The Art of Living*, p. 91).

49 *SKS* 13, 409 / *M*, 345.

50 Kierkegaard would not dispute this. In *The Point of View* he says that he does not place a lot of stock in the mere fact that an author claims that their book has such and such significance: "I do not…think much of assurances in connection with literary productions and am accustomed to take a completely objective attitude to my own. If in the capacity of a third party, as a reader, I cannot substantiate from the writings that what I am saying [*qua* author] is the case,…it could never occur to me to want to win [by assurances] what I thus consider lost [with respect to the texts themselves]….*qua* author it does not help very much that I *qua* human being make assurances that I have intended this and that" (*SV1* XIII, 524 / *PV*, 33; translation modified). Cf. *SKS* 7, 229, 5–9 / *CUP1*, 252.

to offer a critical account of his authorship, and suggests that if one wants to become a good reader of his texts then one should look to him and remarks of this sort for help.[51] His claim to be the "one single person who is qualified to give a true critique of [his] work" partly rests on his belief that none of his contemporaries has properly appreciated his endeavor.[52] He contends that "there is not one single contemporary who is qualified to review [his] work" and argues that even those who sit down and try to offer a more detailed analysis only arrive at the most superficial of readings:

> Even if someone considerably better informed takes it upon himself to want to say something about me and my task, it actually does not amount to anything more than that he, after a superficial glance at my work, quickly finds some earlier something or other that he declares to be comparable.
>
> In this way it still does not amount to anything. Something on which a person with my leisure, my diligence, my talents, my education...has spent not only fourteen years but essentially his entire life, the only thing for which he has lived and breathed—then that some pastor, at most a professor, would not need more than a superficial glance at it in order to evaluate it, that is surely absurd.[53]

In the face of all the pastors and theologians who claim to find all sorts of things that are analogous to his task, Kierkegaard declares that "a more careful inspection" by them would reveal that there is nothing analogous within Christianity—and then adds, "but this is what [they do] not find worth the trouble."[54]

Kierkegaard wants us to be better readers than he thinks his contemporaries have been, to take the trouble to give his work that "more careful inspection" he claims it requires; and he encourages us to carry out this activity in the light of his suggestion that his task is a Socratic task. But this is not to say that we should expect such an inspection to be an easy one. If Kierkegaard is right and none of his contemporaries has understood him and his task, why should we think that it will necessarily fare any better in our own case? Kierkegaard is a strange, somewhat hybrid figure. He presents himself as a Socrates, someone skilled in the art of indirection and so seemingly forever elusive; and yet he demands that we try to understand him and offers us tools to assist us in our attempt. Anyone who embarks on such an enterprise should be warned up front that they are repeatedly likely to encounter moments of seeming clarity and a kind of shared intimacy with Kierkegaard (this most personal of philosophers), followed by moments of utter incomprehension and the anxiety that he is far too profound a character for our more limited sensibilities. Trying to bring Kierkegaard into focus can often seem akin to what it is like when one encounters irony in a text or meets face-to-face with an ironist:

---

51 But in doing so Kierkegaard clearly is not an easy act to follow; he seems to do everything so well himself. He composes intricate, existentially challenging texts and then proceeds to develop powerful tools for reading and interpreting those texts. Anyone who wants to develop their own accounts must learn to be guided by his remarks without turning them into dogma, following them as long as they keep the texts fresh and alive while not being afraid to jettison them when they seem to drain the texts of their vitality.

52 *SKS* 13, 407 / *M*, 343.

53 *SKS* 13, 407–8 / *M*, 343–4. (Translation modified.)

54 *SKS* 13, 408 / *M*, 344.

> Just as irony has something deterring about it, it likewise has something extraordinarily seductive and fascinating about it. Its masquerading and mysteriousness, the telegraphic communication it prompts because an ironist always has to be understood at a distance, the infinite sympathy it presupposes, the fleeting but indescribable instant of understanding that is immediately superseded by the anxiety of misunderstanding—all this holds one prisoner in inextricable bonds.[55]

Sometimes we will feel certain we have got hold of Kierkegaard, only in the next moment to have the familiar experience of having him slip away yet again. Despite these difficulties, I remain convinced that there is much to be gained from taking Kierkegaard up on his suggestion that we view his activity as a writer and thinker as a Socratic task. Readers of "My Task" who share my conviction will be aware, however, that I have been operating at a fairly general level of description in this article. Kierkegaard's main claim is that the refusal to call himself a Christian is analogous to Socrates' stance of ignorance. He claims that so adopted, this stance gives him the ability to make his fellow citizens aware of a deeper sense in which they are not Christians, while also allowing him at the same time to pursue an authentic ethical and religious life.

With Kierkegaard's Socratic point of view now hopefully before us, the next natural step would be to turn to other texts in the *corpus* in order to consider further how Kierkegaard conceives of what he calls his Socratic method and where in the *corpus* we should look if we want to discover concrete examples of this method actually at work. But that will have to wait for another article. Let me conclude by noting that there is perhaps a touch of irony in Kierkegaard's suggestion that it is only the activity of Socrates that sheds any meaningful light on his own activity. For Socrates, of all people, is about as enigmatic and elusive a character as we can find within philosophy, and is the very person who Alcibiades claims is utterly unlike any other human being:

> [Socrates] is unique; he is like no one else in the past and no one in the present—this is by far the most amazing thing about him....[He] is so bizarre, his ways and his ideas are so unusual, that, search as you might, you'll never find anyone else, alive or dead, who's even remotely like him. The best you can do is not to compare him to anything human, but to liken him, as I do, to Silenus and the satyrs.[56]

If Kierkegaard's claim bears out, then a proper investigation of his writings will reveal that Alcibiades was mistaken in his claim about Socrates' uniqueness by one person. When investigating further Kierkegaard's claim that Socrates provides his only analogy and that his task is a Socratic task, it is worth keeping in mind that Kierkegaard devoted the bulk of his first mature work, *The Concept of Irony with*

---

55 *SKS* 1, 109 / *CI*, 48–9. And to seek such an understanding, as I do, while inviting others to accompany one is to run the further risk of having one's moments of misunderstanding very much on display. As Kierkegaard's pseudonymous author Johannes Climacus puts it, "Anyone who begins to exercise himself in this understanding no doubt will frequently enough catch himself in a misunderstanding, and if he wants to become involved with others, he had better take care" (*SKS* 4, 299 / *PF*, 102).

56 Plato, *Symposium*, 221c–d.

Continual Reference to Socrates, to developing an account of who he thinks Socrates is. Despite the prominence given in the title to the concept of irony, Kierkegaard spends nearly three-quarters of his discussion examining the very individual he will later model himself upon and toward whom he now points us.[57] In this way Kierkegaard brings us full circle from his last words in "My Task" to the first words of his dissertation. His first true act as a writer and thinker was to stake his claim as the best interpreter of Socrates; in the end of his life he maintains that if we want to become interpreters of him who avoid the superficial readings he attributes to his contemporaries, then we should take his suggestion and examine his writings in the light of Socrates. In effect Kierkegaard suggests that one riddle, the riddle of Socrates (which he once thought he had solved in his dissertation and which continued to occupy him throughout his life), is the key to our trying to solve a second riddle, the riddle of Søren Kierkegaard.

[57] Kierkegaard focuses on Socrates in all of Part One of the dissertation and in Part Two in the second half of the chapter entitled "The World-Historical Validity of Irony, the Irony of Socrates" (*SKS* 1, 69–278 / *CI*, 7–237. *SKS* 1, 302–8 / *CI*, 264–71). In the introduction to Part Two, Kierkegaard claims that he has "dealt in the first part of the dissertation solely with Socrates" (*SKS* 1, 281 / *CI*, 241). Perhaps because of Kierkegaard's focus on Socrates in the dissertation, his dissertation director, Frederik Christian Sibbern, suggested that he change the title of his dissertation to "Socrates as Ironist with a Contribution to the Development of the Concept of Irony in General, Particularly with Regard to the Most Recent Times" (quoted in Olesen, "Kierkegaard's Socratic Hermeneutic," p. 103, see also *SKS* K1, 134; Bruce Kirmmse, "Socrates in the Fast Lane: Kierkegaard's *The Concept of Irony* on the University's Velocifère (Documents, Context, Commentary, and Interpretation)," in *The Concept of Irony*, ed. by Robert L. Perkins, Macon, Georgia: Mercer University Press 2001 (*International Kierkegaard Commentary*, vol. 2), pp. 17–99, see p. 23.

Meno:
Kierkegaard and the Doctrine of Recollection

David D. Possen

In three of Plato's dialogues,[1] Socrates praises a striking myth, known as "Plato's Doctrine of Recollection," which explains all human learning as a process of *remembering*. According to this myth, our souls are as old as the hills; they have already experienced countless lives and afterlives; and they have already learned, eons ago, everything that there is for souls to know. Just before entering and animating our infant bodies, however, our souls forgot all that they once knew. Hence a newborn baby, on this account, is not an ignorant little creature. It is actually an astonishingly *forgetful* little creature: a creature with a world to remember.

We often speak of people learning new things. By "learning" we normally mean that a person encounters a truth that they have never known before, and then manages to discover its truth—to recognize it *as* a truth—for the very first time. Against this common view, Socrates' myth insists that there is no such thing as discovering new truths; there is only the remembering of truths that our souls once knew and have forgotten. Put another way, human learning is really a wholly *immanent* activity. All the knowledge that we can ever gain is already present, albeit dormant, within our souls. This, in barest outline, is Plato's Doctrine of Recollection.

Søren Kierkegaard has often been characterized as an energetic *foe* of the Doctrine of Recollection.[2] At times he is depicted, more specifically, as a

---

This article has benefited greatly from the editorial advice of Jon Stewart and K. Brian Söderquist, from comments by P. Brickey LeQuire and Aaron Tugendhaft, and from discussions of related material with Jonathan Lear, James Conant, David Tracy, Jennifer Stith, Erin Leib, and Richard Purkarthofer. I thank them all.

1 Plato, *Meno* 81b–d; *Phaedo* 72e–73a, 77d–e; *Phaedrus* 249b–c.

2 The most recent full-length Anglophone essay on the subject, by Anne Freire Ashbaugh, attributes the following view to Kierkegaard: "Recollection takes an existentially inauthentic stance regarding time and eternity which leads to the loss of historicity and to a monolithic view of the past which ultimately vitiates into an objectification of the subjective and a universalization of the individual." A. Freire Ashbaugh, "Platonism: An Essay on Repetition and Recollection," in *Kierkegaard and Great Traditions*, ed. by Niels Thulstrup and Marie Mikulová Thulstrup, Copenhagen: C.A. Reitzel 1981 (*Bibliotheca Kierkegaardiana*, vol. 6), pp. 9–26; see pp. 12–13. Ashbaugh goes on to assert, at p. 15, that Kierkegaard's purpose in engaging the Doctrine of Recollection was to demolish it and replace it with his own theory of "repetition," set forth in "sharp contrast" to recollection in the pseudonymous work *Repetition*. Ashbaugh does not address, however, the insistence

defender of "transcendent" Christianity—a religion that exposes its adherents to a paradoxical, radically new truth—against "immanent" forms of religiousness rooted in recollection.[3] These portraits are popular for a reason: they benefit from what appears to be clear textual support. Yet such portraits are nonetheless misleading. As the present article reveals, Kierkegaard's actual assessment of the Doctrine of Recollection was in fact carefully *mixed.* Kierkegaard distinguished sharply, if subtly, between two opposed approaches to recollection: one Platonic, speculative, and devoted to immanence; the other Socratic and focused on human ignorance. While Kierkegaard indeed sought to defend Christianity against an immanent form of religiousness rooted in what he called the "Platonic" approach to recollection, he took care to praise the "Socratic" approach to recollection as a form of thought and life—indeed, as a form of "faith"—that is deeply analogous to Christian faith.[4] For Kierkegaard, put briefly, the Doctrine of Recollection plays a vital role not just on one side, but on *both* sides, of the gulf between immanent religiousness and Christianity.

This article details Kierkegaard's nuanced approach to the Doctrine of Recollection. We begin (in Section I) by reviewing Kierkegaard's painstaking distinction between the Socratic and Platonic approaches to the myth. We then turn

---

in *Repetition* that "repetition and recollection are the same movement, except in opposite directions" (*SKS* 4, 10 / *R*, 131), or Climacus' remark that "repetition," like recollection, "is basically the expression for immanence" (*SKS* 7, 238 / *CUP1*, 263). Nor does Ashbaugh take account of *Repetition*'s underlying and untiring attack on Hegelian philosophy, which "does not have the category of recollection or of repetition," and for which "all life dissolves into an empty, meaningless noise" (*SKS* 4, 26 / *R*, 149). For a comprehensive account of the place of recollection in *Repetition*, see Karsten Friis Johansen, "Kierkegaard und die griechische Dialektik," in *Kierkegaard and Dialectics*, ed. by Herman Deuser et al., Aarhus: University of Aarhus 1979, pp. 51–124; see pp. 101–6.

3 See, for example, C. Stephen Evans, *Kierkegaard on Faith and the Self: Collected Essays*, Waco, Texas: Baylor University Press 2006, pp. 99–101; Patrick Gardiner, *Kierkegaard*, Oxford: Oxford University Press 1988, pp. 68–76; and Merold Westphal, *Kierkegaard's Critique of Reason and Society*, Macon, Georgia: Mercer University Press 1987, p. 106 note 3. For a perceptive discussion and critique of this way of characterizing Kierkegaard's relation to the thought of Socrates and Plato, see Arne Grøn, "Transcendence of Thought: The Project of *Philosophical Fragments*," *Kierkegaard Studies Yearbook*, 2004, pp. 80–9, especially pp. 83–4.

4 *SKS* 7, 192, 189 note 1 / *CUP1*, 210, 206 note. Three commentators who productively discuss this wrinkle in Kierkegaard's thought are Jacob Howland, Mary-Jane Rubenstein, and Merold Westphal. Cf. Jacob Howland, *Kierkegaard and Socrates: A Study in Philosophy and Faith*, Cambridge: Cambridge University Press 2006, pp. 188–208; Mary-Jane Rubenstein, "Kierkegaard's Socrates: A Venture in Evolutionary Theory," *Modern Theology*, vol. 17, no. 4, 2001, pp. 441–73, see pp. 442–3; Merold Westphal, *Becoming a Self*, West Lafayette, Indiana: Purdue University Press 1996, pp. 120–30. For further discussion of Kierkegaard's distinction between Socratic and Platonic recollection, see Wolfdietrich von Kloeden, "Sokrates," in *Kierkegaard's Classical Inspiration*, ed. by Niels Thulstrup and Marie Mikulová Thulstrup, Copenhagen: C.A. Reitzel 1985 (*Bibliotheca Kierkegaardiana*, vol. 14), pp. 104–81, see p. 153; and Henry E. Allison, "Christianity and Nonsense," in *Essays on Kierkegaard*, ed. by Jerry H. Gill, Minneapolis: Burgess 1969, pp. 127–49, see pp. 133–4.

more closely (in Section II) to *Philosophical Fragments*, a work that has sown much confusion among Kierkegaard's commentators. We observe that *Philosophical Fragments* boldly collapses Kierkegaard's usual distinction between "Platonic" and "Socratic" recollection; but we demonstrate that this conflation is conscious, indeed satirical. We conclude (in Section III) by clarifying Kierkegaard's own stance on recollection. While he bore little love for the Doctrine of Recollection as a metaphysical *doctrine*, Kierkegaard venerated Socrates' own comportment toward the *myth* of recollection as a laudable form of faith: indeed, as our best analogy to authentic Christian piety.

I. Recollection: Socratic Myth, Platonic Doctrine

In *The Concept of Irony*, Kierkegaard famously claimed that some of Plato's representations of Socrates are more accurate than others. In particular, he praised Plato's *Apology* as "an authentic portrait of the actual Socrates," while elsewhere in the dialogues, he maintained, Plato did little more than put "his own professions" into Socrates' mouth.[5] Kierkegaard characterized his own approach to Plato's dialogues as an effort to extract "the unalloyed Socratic" from the dialogues' mixed Platonic-Socratic ore.[6] To this end, he distinguished between two rival philosophical *methods* at work in the dialogues: the "ironic" method, which he classified as Socrates' own, and the "speculative" method, which he attributed wholly to Plato.[7]

Kierkegaard summarized the difference between the Socratic-ironic and the Platonic-speculative methods of philosophy as follows: "Socrates' philosophy began with the presupposition that he knew nothing [and] ended with the presupposition that human beings know nothing at all; Platonic philosophy began in the immediate unity of thought and being and stayed there."[8] On Kierkegaard's account, Socrates—the *real* Socrates—was none other than the doughty ignoramus who appears in Plato's *Apology*. This Socrates was a man who genuinely knew nothing at all, aside from the fact of his own ignorance; his philosophical activity consisted in his coming to terms with his own ignorance and in disclosing the ignorance of all other human beings. Plato, meanwhile, appears as a sharply different kind of thinker: an ambitious theorist who aimed to explore and specify the immanent wisdom—the "immediate unity of thought and being"—that he assumed we all already possess.

Much of Kierkegaard's dissertation is devoted to the project of classifying whole stretches of Plato's dialogues as either "Socratic" or "Platonic."[9] Yet Kierkegaard held that there are also passages in Plato that are simultaneously Socratic *and* Platonic. Kierkegaard interpreted the Doctrine of Recollection, in particular, as a

5 *SKS* 1, 138, 92 / *CI*, 80, 30.

6 *SKS* 1, 102 / *CI*, 40.

7 *SKS* 1, 97, 108 / *CI*, 36, 46–7.

8 *SKS* 1, 98 / *CI*, 37.

9 On Kierkegaard's adaptation of the method of classifying Plato's dialogues set forth by Friedrich D.E. Schleiermacher (1768–1834), see *SKS* 1, 114 / *CI*, 53–4 and *SKS* 1, 172–3 / *CI*, 119–21.

text of this last sort: an utterance that may have meant one thing to Plato, and still another to the authentic Socrates. Kierkegaard wrote:

> It would be Platonic to fortify existence by the upbuilding thought that man is not driven empty-handed out into the world, by calling to mind his abundant equipment through recollection. It is Socratic to disparage all actuality and to direct man to a recollection that continually retreats further and further back toward a past that itself retreats as far back in time as that noble family's origin that no one could remember.[10]

To Plato, recollection is a thought that *reassures* us about our present lives, inasmuch as it invites us to take ownership of the rich stores of knowledge that already lie within us. To Socrates, by contrast, recollection is a thought that *unsettles* us. For it confronts us with the claim that we have fallen far, indeed farther than we can remember, from our former state of knowledge.

Later in his dissertation, Kierkegaard harnesses a vivid metaphor—that of motion backward and forward in time—in order to expand upon the same distinction: "The one [Socrates] maintains recollection negatively and *retrogressively* in contrast to the current of life; the other [Plato] maintains recollection *forward* in its outflowing into actuality."[11] To Plato, recollection affirms our intuition that we are continually growing in knowledge; it directs us forward to a future bright with newly remembered truths. To Socrates, meanwhile, recollection points us both humbly downward and longingly backward. For it encourages us to see our present selves as essentially diminished, wilted creatures—as shadows of our souls' lost glory.

Kierkegaard's account of the difference between Platonic and Socratic recollection is best understood as a corollary of his general account of the difference between Platonic and Socratic philosophy. As we saw above, Kierkegaard characterizes Plato as a speculative thinker whose philosophical activity both begins and ends "in the immediate unity of thought and being."[12] Put another way, Kierkegaard's Plato assumes that (1) *the world is in some sense already known to our minds*; he then proceeds to explore the content of our minds' world-knowledge. Yet in order for the latter activity to be both meaningful and potentially successful—that is, in order for it to be possible for us to make *progress* in clarifying our minds' knowledge of the world—it must further be the case that (2) *some of our minds' knowledge of the world is not yet fully available to us*; and that (3) *it is nonetheless possible for us to gain full access to at least some of the knowledge described in (2).*

Taken together, assumptions (1), (2), and (3) also constitute the metaphysical core of a Doctrine of Recollection. To "recollect" a piece of knowledge means, after all, to *re-collect* it: to make it again one's own. And if it is true that our souls *do* in some sense already know everything there is to know; and if it is true that, though we may not at present have access to that vast knowledge, we really *can* recover elements of it piece by piece; then it is also true that what we call learning is really a form of recollection—of coming back into possession of knowledge that is in some sense already our own.

---

10 *SKS* 1, 120 / *CI*, 60.

11 *SKS* 1, 176 / *CI*, 124–5.

12 *SKS* 1, 98 / *CI*, 37.

From the point of view of Kierkegaard's Plato, therefore, the tale of recollection is an elaborate expression, coded in the language of memory and amnesia, for the operating principles—the unity of mind and world, and the possibility of our progressively unfolding and clarifying this unity—that underpin his own philosophical method. The Doctrine of Recollection thus literally functions as a *doctrine* for Kierkegaard's Plato: it is a belief held true by assumption. And it is a belief, moreover, that motivates Kierkegaard's Plato to continue what he takes to be his own main task as a thinker: to speculate on what we have to recollect, and on how we might go about doing so.

Kierkegaard's Socrates, by contrast, is a man whose thought begins and ends not with the presumption of knowledge, but with the earnest acknowledgment of ignorance. This Socrates, the Socrates of Plato's *Apology*, opens by recognizing that he has no knowledge at all; he thus has no doctrines to hold or propound, not even the very myth of recollection that he himself puts forward in conversation. Kierkegaard expresses this point by writing that Socrates "does not adhere to [the] thesis" of recollection.[13] (As we shall soon see, Kierkegaard's pseudonym Johannes Climacus will explain that Socrates "did not pursue" recollection because he "continually parts with it."[14]) From the point of view of Kierkegaard's Socrates, recollection is not truly a doctrine, but more of a *myth* that has its uses: a tale that "disparage[s] all actuality," and "negatively" prompts its hearers to become aware of their ignorance and that of their fellows.[15]

Here a brief look at Plato's *Meno* will be helpful. For the notion that recollection is a myth that is useful for Socrates to promulgate, rather than a doctrine whose truth he can demonstrate with confidence, derives directly from that text.[16] The *Meno* records a debate about virtue between Socrates and the title character, an exuberant young orator who boasts that he has "spoken about virtue hundreds of times," even "in front of large audiences."[17] Socrates, for his part, claims to "have no knowledge of virtue at all"; he interrogates Meno to see what the latter really knows.[18] Despite all of his expertise, Meno soon falters under Socrates' questioning. He eventually confesses that he cannot even say what virtue is.[19] This admission signals the classic Socratic predicament of *aporia*: Socrates and his interlocutor join in acknowledging their shared ignorance of the matter under discussion.

While Meno expresses irritation at this outcome, Socrates remains unfazed. "I don't know what virtue is," Socrates announces, "[and] you look as if you don't

13 *SKS* 1, 120–1 / *CI*, 60.

14 *SKS* 7, 188 / *CUP1*, 205. *SKS* 7, 189, note / *CUP1*, 206, note.

15 In stating that recollection functions for Kierkegaard's Socrates as a myth, rather than a Doctrine, I am paraphrasing Kierkegaard rather than quoting him. Kierkegaard himself had good reason to avoid using the word "myth" in this manner: he elsewhere commits himself to the claim that "the mythical in Plato…*does not belong* to Socrates." *SKS* 1, 158 / *CI*, 104.

16 All subsequent references to the *Meno* are indexed by Stephanus page. The translation is that of W.C. Guthrie in Plato, *Protagoras and Meno*, Harmondsworth: Penguin 1956, pp. 115–57.

17 *Meno*, 80b.

18 *Meno*, 71b.

19 *Meno*, 80a–b.

[either]. Nevertheless I am ready to carry out, with you, a joint investigation and inquiry into what it is."[20] Meno retorts: "But how will you look for something when you don't in the least know what it is?...Even if you come right up against it, how will you know that what you have found is the thing you didn't know?"[21] It is in response to this last objection, commonly called "Meno's Paradox," that Socrates propounds his myth of recollection. Socrates' aim is to show Meno how it can be that, even though he does not know the truth, he still hopes to recognize it when he sees it.

Our focus here, however, is not on the details or plausibility of the myth of recollection, but on the status that Socrates accords it and the arguments that he marshals on its behalf. Socrates introduces recollection as a tale that he has heard "from men and women who understand the truths of religion," as well as from Pindar and other poets.[22] He asserts that he believes it too.[23] And yet, apart from these arguments from authority,[24] the only real *reason* Socrates provides for believing the myth is curiously utilitarian. "We ought not...to be led astray by the contentious argument you quoted," Socrates admonishes Meno. "It would make us lazy, and is music in the ears of weaklings. The other doctrine produces energetic seekers after knowledge; and, being convinced of its truth, I am ready, with your help, to inquire into the nature of virtue."[25] Socrates' point is not that recollection is true (he merely *announces* that he believes it) but that Meno's "contentious" argument is one that would be bad for us to believe[26]—whereas recollection is a myth that is good for us to believe, whether or not it is true of our souls or of the world.

What is it, then, that makes the myth of recollection so useful? By depicting our *aporia* as a middle stage between our souls' loss of knowledge and recapture of it, recollection motivates us to remain "energetic seekers after knowledge" *despite* our ignorance. In a footnote to *Philosophical Fragments*, Kierkegaard's pseudonym Johannes Climacus explains how this works: "The contradiction of existence is explained by positing a 'pre' as needed (by virtue of a prior state, the individual has arrived at his present, otherwise unexplainable state) or by positing a 'post' as needed (on another planet the individual will be better situated, and in consideration of that, his present state is not unexplainable)."[27] By supplying both a "pre" and a "post" that prompt us to face our ignorance squarely and seek knowledge nonetheless, the

---

20 *Meno*, 80d.

21 Ibid.

22 *Meno*, 81a–b.

23 *Meno*, 81a, 81d–e.

24 Howland, noting the weakness of Socrates' strategy of "appeal to...authority," remarks that "these features of the text cast doubt on whether we should understand the principle of recollection literally." Howland, *Kierkegaard and Socrates*, p. 43.

25 *Meno*, 81d–e.

26 As Howland points out, the name Meno (Mένων) means "staying or tarrying" (*Kierkegaard and Socrates*, p. 39); Meno, "who doubts the very possibility of learning" (p. 109), is in a very real sense at a philosophical standstill.

27 *SKS* 1, 219, note 1 / *PF*, 10, note.

myth of recollection serves—if I may borrow a phrase from Jacob Howland—to "guarantee the meaningfulness" of our Socratic quest for knowledge.[28]

Climacus expands on the significance of recollection to Socrates in his *Concluding Unscientific Postscript*. He there describes recollection as a "thesis" of which Socrates has no objective knowledge. Yet Socrates nonetheless lives *by* this thesis and *up* to it, in so far as he devotes his entire existence to the *possibility* that, despite his present ignorance, he will someday recognize the truth.[29] In Climacus' terms, recollection is for Socrates an "objective uncertainty" toward which he directs his entire existence in "faith"; whereas for Plato recollection is a "thesis" in the ordinary sense of the word—a doctrine whose truth Plato assumes—and indeed "an intimation of the beginning of speculative thought."[30] Climacus explains this distinction in a pivotal footnote:

> The thesis [recollection] certainly belongs to both [Socrates and Plato], but Socrates continually parts with it because he wants to exist. By holding Socrates to the thesis that all knowing is recollecting, one turns him into a speculative philosopher instead of what he was, an existing thinker who understood existing as the essential. The thesis that all knowing is recollecting belongs to speculative thought, and recollecting is immanence, and from the point of view of speculation and the eternal there is no paradox. The difficulty, however, is that no human being is speculation, but the speculating person is an existing human being, subject to the claims of existence. To forget this is no merit, but to hold this fast is indeed a merit, and that is precisely what Socrates did. To emphasize existence, which contains within it the qualification of inwardness, is the Socratic, whereas the Platonic is to pursue recollection and immanence.[31]

At the core of this passage lies a riddle. The upshot of the Doctrine of Recollection, we have seen, is that we already contain all of the knowledge we seek; and yet Socrates' great achievement is precisely that he never lost sight of his ignorance. How can it be, then, that Socrates was a believer in recollection? Climacus answers that Socrates could not and did not adhere to the doctrine *as a thesis*. By continually confessing his ignorance, Socrates departed from the thesis of recollection "continually" as well: for he thereby acknowledged not only that he had no knowledge of the myth's

---

28 Howland, *Kierkegaard and Socrates*, p. 119. Howland's phrase is a gloss on Climacus' account of the sense in which Socrates may be said to have presupposed the existence of the divine: "[Socrates] presumably would have explained that he lacked the courage needed to dare to embark on such a voyage of discovery without having behind him the assurance that the god exists." *SKS* 4, 249 / *PF*, 44.

29 In general, Climacus explains, "Socratic ignorance [is] the expression, firmly maintained with all the passion of inwardness, of the relation of the eternal truth to an existing person, and therefore must remain for him a paradox as long as he exists." With regard to the immortality of the soul, for example, Socrates has no knowledge of its truth, but "stakes his whole life" on its possibility; "he dares to die, and with the passion of the infinite he [so orders] his life that it might be acceptable—*if* there is an immortality." *SKS* 7, 185 / *CUP1*, 201–2.

30 *SKS* 7, 186–8 / *CUP1*, 203–5.

31 *SKS* 7, 189, note 1 / *CUP1*, 206, note. The text immediately preceding this passage is cited in Section II below; the text that follows it is cited in Section III.

truth, but also—and more deeply—that he himself, as a being bereft of all truth, had no experience of recollection's workings in his soul.

All the same, however, there is a sense in which we may say that Socrates did remain committed to recollection.[32] For without ever neglecting to face up to his ignorance, Socrates dedicated his entire life to the *possibility* that he might someday know its truth firsthand, that is, the possibility that he might someday recognize the truth to which his myth of recollection refers. In Climacus' terms, Socrates directed himself toward an "objective uncertainty"—the truth of his myth—with the "infinite passion of inwardness."[33] Climacus' name for this form of life is "faith": in particular, a "Socratic faith" analogous to Christianity.[34]

For Climacus' Plato, meanwhile, recollection does indeed serve as a "thesis." Climacus' Plato prefers not to dwell on his present state of ignorance (to "focus on existence"); he is content simply to assume the doctrine's truth and to "pursue recollection and immanence," that is, to speculate abstractly on the nature of the immanent knowledge that our recollection may bring to light. And in so doing, Climacus quips, Plato displays a curious kind of *forgetfulness* about himself. Plato, who pursues recollection, fails to recollect the fact of his "existence"—who he is, how he lives, and how little he really knows—while he engages in speculation; whereas Socrates, who does not presume to recollect any knowledge at all, is not nearly so forgetful. To put the point more broadly, the Doctrine of Recollection can be as dangerous as a thesis as it is useful as a myth. For the doctrine tempts us, once we assume that it is true, to speculate about the content of our hypothesized immanent knowledge; and once we do this, we lose sight of our ignorance—we forget "that no human being is speculation."

Before proceeding further, let us note that the distinction between Platonic and Socratic recollection that we have just examined—a distinction made by Climacus in his *Postscript*—is entirely consistent with the account of Platonic and Socratic recollection with which we began (due to Kierkegaard in *The Concept of Irony*).[35] In the sections that follow, we will have much to say about *differences* between what Kierkegaard and Climacus have to say about recollection. For now, however, let us simply take stock of two basic commonalities. First, both Climacus and Kierkegaard stress Socrates' intrepidity in acknowledging his ignorance at every moment; and both contrast this intrepidity in Socrates with Plato's readiness to lose himself in speculation about our stores of immanent knowledge. Moreover, according to both Climacus and Kierkegaard, Plato and Socrates treat the tale of recollection quite

---

32 Here I disagree with Merold Westphal, who writes that Climacus "portrays Socrates as shying away from [recollection] and leaving it to Plato." Westphal, *Becoming a Self*, p. 121. To my mind, Climacus' claim that Socrates "constantly only parts ways with" [*bestandig kun tager Afsked med*] Recollection indicates that Socrates retains an intimate, continuous, and indeed unending relationship to the Doctrine.

33 *SKS* 7, 187 / *CUP1*, 204.

34 *SKS* 7, 187 / *CUP1*, 204. *SKS* 7, 190, note / *CUP1*, 206, note.

35 Here I follow Mary-Jane Rubenstein, who describes Climacus as "refining the Plato/ Socrates distinction that Magister Kierkegaard had set in *Irony*." Rubenstein, "Kierkegaard's Socrates," p. 452.

differently. Plato affirms recollection as a doctrine—an axiom of his metaphysics; while for Socrates, recollection is a myth well worth living by.

II. The Conflation of Platonic and Socratic Recollection in Philosophical Fragments

In Section I we noted that the account of Platonic and Socratic recollection set forth by Kierkegaard in *The Concept of Irony* (1841) is consistent with the account propounded by Climacus in his *Concluding Unscientific Postscript* (1846). In this section, we will consider a number of intervening statements about Socrates and recollection—found in Climacus' 1844 work *Philosophical Fragments*—which clash plainly with both of the above accounts. In the excerpts below, it certainly sounds as though *Socrates*, rather than Plato, is the speculative philosopher who took recollection to be his fundamental doctrine and metaphysical starting-point: (1) "In the Socratic view, every human being is himself the midpoint, and the whole world focuses only on him because his self-knowledge is God-knowledge."[36] (2) On "the Socratic line of thought…it appeared that basically every human being possesses the truth."[37] (3) "That the God once and for all has given man the condition [for understanding the truth] is the eternal Socratic presupposition."[38] In *Fragments* Climacus speaks gamely of "the *Socratic* theory of recollection and of every human being as universal man."[39] The word "Platonic" never appears. And as a result, it has been easy for readers to misjudge the book's critique of immanent religiosity as Climacus' (or Kierkegaard's) grand attack upon Socrates, the "Socratic theory of recollection," and the Socratic approach to truth.

Kierkegaard seems himself to have been troubled by the ease with which *Fragments* invites this reading. In *Concluding Unscientific Postscript*, published two years after *Fragments*, he has Climacus apologize for painting a distorted picture of Socrates in his earlier book:

> This may be the proper place to elucidate a dubiousness in the design of *Fragments*, a dubiousness that was due to my not wanting immediately to make the matter as dialectically difficult as it is, because in our day terminologies and the like are so muddled that it is almost impossible to safeguard oneself against confusion. In order, if possible, to elucidate properly the difference between the Socratic (which was supposed to be the philosophical, the pagan philosophical position) and the category of imaginatively constructed thought, which actually goes beyond the Socratic, I carried the Socratic back to the thesis that all knowing is a recollecting. It is commonly accepted as such, and only for the person who with a very special interest devotes himself to the Socratic, always returning to the sources, only for him will it be important to distinguish between Socrates and Plato on this point. The thesis certainly belongs to both of them, but Socrates continually parts with it because he wants to exist. By holding Socrates to the thesis that all knowing is recollecting, one turns him into a speculative philosopher

---

36 *SKS* 4, 220 / *PF*, 11.

37 *SKS* 4, 222 / *PF*, 13.

38 *SKS* 4, 264 / *PF*, 62.

39 "…*den* socratiske *Theori om Erindringen.*" *SKS* 4, 244 / *PF*, 38. (My emphasis.)

> instead of what he was, an existing thinker who understood existence as the essential.... To emphasize existence, which contains within it the qualification of inwardness, is the Socratic, whereas the Platonic is to pursue recollection and immanence.[40]

Here Climacus admits that, in the writing of *Fragments*, he knowingly attributed Platonic recollection to Socrates, and thereby conflated Socrates with the "speculative philosopher" Plato. By conceding this point, Climacus prompts us to take a fresh look at such statements as (1), (2), and (3) above. He invites us to interpret or reinterpret those lines as conscious departures from his *actual* understanding of Socratic and Platonic recollection—an understanding which is consistent (as we saw in Section I) with that of Kierkegaard in *The Concept of Irony*.

Climacus' apology is itself fairly straightforward. The question it prompts, however, is *why*: Why would Climacus write a book that collapses the very distinction between Plato and Socrates to which he is otherwise firmly committed? Why would he not simply draw this distinction properly the first time? In the passage that we have just examined, Climacus provides a superbly cagey and convoluted answer to these questions. He did not wish to trouble his reader, he explains, with complex terminological niceties. He wished to focus, instead, on the larger purpose of *Fragments*: namely, "to elucidate properly the difference between the Socratic (which was supposed to be the philosophical, the pagan philosophical position) and the category of imaginatively constructed thought, which actually goes beyond the Socratic."[41] It is for this last purpose, Climacus asserts, that he "carried the Socratic back to the thesis that all knowing is a recollecting"[42]—even though, he now admits, it is really "Platonic" rather than "Socratic" thought that adheres to this thesis.

The oddity of Climacus' answer comes into focus the moment we try to summarize it. "It was in order to show how we can *go beyond Socrates*," Climacus appears to be saying, "that I conflated Socrates with Plato." But this makes little sense. If Climacus' objective in *Fragments* was truly to sketch an advance *beyond* Socrates—and to "elucidate properly" how this advance *differs* from the Socratic position—then it should surely have been of paramount importance for him to begin with an accurate depiction of Socrates and "the Socratic." Why would Climacus instead begin by portraying Socrates as if he were Plato, and by labeling Platonic recollection "the Socratic theory?" It is as though the *Fragments* were a carefully orchestrated sham: a book that sketches an advance beyond *Plato*, only to advertise the same as an advance beyond Socrates.

As we shall soon see, Climacus elsewhere suggests explicitly that *Fragments* is a sham of just this sort.[43] And this suggestion has vast implications, when we consider that the claim to have gone beyond Socrates is both central and essential to the book's argument. Briefly, Climacus begins *Fragments* by asking what it would take for the Doctrine of Recollection to be false—that is, what must be the case if not all learning is recollection, if not all knowledge is immanent, and if it is possible for us

40 *SKS* 7, 189, note 1 / *CUP1*, 206, note. The continuation of this passage is cited in Section I above.

41 *SKS* 7, 189, note 1 / *CUP1*, 206, note.

42 Ibid.

43 *SKS* 7, 249, note 1 / *CUP1*, 275, note; and see below.

to learn things that are radically new to us.[44] In the remainder of his book, Climacus explores the conditions and ramifications of this possibility, and in so doing just "happens" to derive all the fundamentals of Christian doctrine: a theory of original sin, a tale of divine incarnation and atonement, a category of faith, a symptomatology of offense, and a call to contemporaneity with the incarnate god. Climacus concludes the *Fragments* with a rather smug declaration of success, accompanied by a dart aimed at all those who have falsely claimed to have done the same: "This project indisputably goes beyond the Socratic, as is apparent at every point....But to go beyond Socrates when one nevertheless says essentially the same as he, only not nearly so well—that, at least, is not Socratic."[45]

Yet it is far from indisputable, given what we now know about the views of Climacus and Kierkegaard on recollection, that the project of *Fragments* actually succeeds in going "beyond the Socratic." For even if we grant that the book succeeds in sketching a robust, quasi-Christian alternative to the Doctrine of Recollection; and even if we grant that the book does manage to point the reader outside the sphere of immanent thought that the doctrine allows for—all this would still only amount to an advance beyond what Climacus and Kierkegaard consider to be *Platonic* recollection, speculation, and immanence. Our question returns, therefore, with renewed vigor: what is at stake for Climacus in describing the argument of the *Fragments* as an advance beyond *Socrates*?

Our first hint of an answer emerges a little later in the *Postscript*, in a footnote devoted to castigating Andreas Frederik Beck (1816–61), one of *Fragments*' few reviewers. Beck, Climacus complains, dissects the book as though it were "didactic"; but this is in fact "the most mistaken impression one can have."[46] What Beck neglects in the *Fragments*—and what the attentive reader should take care to observe—is "the contrast of form, the teasing resistance of the imaginary construction to the content, the teasing audacity (which even invents Christianity), the only attempt made to go further (that is, further than the so-called speculative constructing), the indefatigable activity of irony, the parody of speculative thought in the entire plan, [and] the satire in making efforts as if something [new] were to come of them."[47] There is much to say about this passage.[48] For our purposes, however, it suffices to note that (1) Climacus here describes the *Fragments* as a thoroughgoing parody of speculative thought; and that (2) he describes the attempt in the *Fragments* to go beyond Socrates as a crucial component of this parody, namely, as a *farce* in which a speculative thinker merely tries and fails to think his way out of speculative thinking itself ("further than the so-called speculative constructing").

---

44 *SKS* 4, 222 / *PF*, 13.

45 *SKS* 4, 306 / *PF*, 111.

46 *SKS* 7, 250, note 1 / *CUP1*, 275, note.

47 Ibid.

48 On this see Paul Muench, "The Socratic Method of Kierkegaard's Pseudonym Johannes Climacus: Indirect Communication and the Art of 'Taking Away,' " in *Søren Kierkegaard and the Word(s): Essays on Hermeneutics and Communication*, ed. by Poul Houe and Gordon D. Marino, Copenhagen: C.A. Reitzel 2003, pp. 139–50.

To understand the workings of claim (2) above—to see *how* and *why* the pretense of an advance beyond Socrates in *Fragments* is crucial to the book's larger parody—we need to take a closer look at this parody, its purpose, and its context. In this we may rely on the results of Jon Stewart's exhaustive recent research, which identifies Climacus' chief polemical target in *Fragments* as Professor Hans Lassen Martensen (1808–84).[49] The name Martensen, we shall now see, provides the link to Socrates that we have been seeking. Martensen, a longstanding rival of Kierkegaard's, was an accomplished speculative philosopher with an unfortunate habit: he punctuated his career with intermittent announcements that he or his allies had *advanced beyond* one well-known thinker after another, superseding such luminaries as Hegel, Goethe, Dante, and even Socrates.[50] Kierkegaard found this habit of Martensen's enormously irritating. He pilloried and parodied it unceasingly—to the point where references to "going further" or "going beyond" in Kierkegaardian texts "immediately suggest," as Stewart remarks, that the polemical target is Martensen.[51] Kierkegaard was especially piqued by Martensen's 1841 claim that Protestantism makes it possible for us to advance beyond Socratic thought ("irony") to a "higher," Christian sphere ("humor") in which human beings gain immanent access to God's knowledge of the fate of our souls.[52]

These facts give us good reason to read Climacus' farcical "advance beyond Socrates" as part and parcel of his larger parody of Martensen; namely, it is a satire directed specifically at Martensen's 1841 efforts to sketch a Christian sphere of immanent knowledge that supersedes the thought of Socrates.[53] To savage Martensen on this point, Climacus first *mocks* him by purporting to have gone beyond "Socrates"

---

49 For Stewart's complete discussion of *Fragments*, see Jon Stewart, *Kierkegaard's Relations to Hegel Reconsidered*, Cambridge and New York: Cambridge University Press 2003, pp. 336–77.

50 Martensen's claim to have "gone beyond Hegel" is widely attested. For an account of what may have been his earliest such statement, see Hans Lassen Martensen, *Af mit Levned: Meddelelser*, vols. 1–3, Copenhagen: Gyldendal 1882, vol. 2, p. 45. On Martensen's prescription for how a "Protestant poet"—presumably his ally Johan Ludvig Heiberg (1791–1860)—might improve upon Goethe's *Faust*, see Hans Lassen Martensen, "Betragtninger over Idéen af Faust med Hensyn paa Lenaus *Faust*," *Perseus: Journal for den speculative Idee*, vol. 1, 1837, pp. 91–164; see also George Pattison, *Kierkegaard, Religion, and the Nineteenth Century Crisis of Culture*, Cambridge: Cambridge University Press 2002, pp. 101–3. For Martensen's praise of Johan Ludvig Heiberg as a poet who had superseded Dante, and had further pioneered a mode of aesthetic and ethical discernment (humor) that outstripped that of Socrates (irony), see Hans Lassen Martensen, "Nye Digte af J.L. Heiberg," *Fædrelandet*, January 10, 1841, columns 3210–12; see also Pattison, *Kierkegaard, Religion*, pp. 111–12.

51 Cf. Stewart, *Kierkegaard's Relations to Hegel Reconsidered*, p. 566; cf. p. 65; p. 467.

52 Martensen, "Nye Digte," column 3212. For Kierkegaard's crisp response on behalf of irony at the close of *The Concept of Irony*, see *SKS* 1, 357 / *CI*, 329.

53 On a more general note, in the *Postscript*, Climacus mocks Martensen and other Hegelians for attempting to explain the life and work of Socrates as a *stage* within the progressive unfolding of human thought: "Even in his [naked] hide, [Socrates] was not nearly as ludicrous as he later became in the system, where he shows up fantastically wrapped in the rich systematic drapery of a paragraph." *SKS* 7, 137, note / *CUP1*, 147, note.

himself—in a thought-experiment that culminates (as we shall see in Section III) in a marvelously Socratic mire of confusion and ignorance. Climacus then *berates* Martensen for having claimed to discover a sphere of immanent knowledge "higher" than that described in the Doctrine of Recollection: "But to go beyond Socrates when one nevertheless says essentially the same as he, only not nearly so well—that, at least, is not Socratic."[54] What Martensen represents as Christian and supra-Socratic thought, in other words, is merely a reprise of Platonic recollection and immanence—albeit more poorly expressed.

We are left with a plausible account of why *Fragments* so boldly conflates distinctions between Plato and Socrates, and between Platonic and Socratic recollection, that matter so deeply to both Climacus and Kierkegaard. Yet there remains still more for us to learn from Climacus' thought-experiment in *Philosophical Fragments*. In Section III, we will sketch how this experiment theatrically breaks down. In that failure, we will detect rudiments of a theological approach that may surprise us: a *celebration* of Socratic recollection as analogous to, compatible with, and perhaps even essential for the experience of Christian faith.

III. The View Behind Philosophical Fragments: *Socratic Recollection as a Guide to Christian Experience*

In Section II we made much of the fact that, in the *Postscript*, Climacus openly repudiates his quixotic description of Socrates in *Fragments*. In point of fact, however, even if Climacus had never written another word on the subject, we would still have cause to view his initial portrait of Socrates with skepticism. This is because the thought-experiment at the core of *Fragments*—Climacus' farcical attempt to "go beyond Socrates"—in fact culminates by ostentatiously falling to pieces; and the way that the argument collapses makes it clear that Climacus cannot have really viewed Socrates as a theorist of immanence and recollection.

The controlled argumentative implosion in *Fragments* is one of the most remarkable literary and philosophical feats in Kierkegaard's *corpus*. I discuss the matter in more detail elsewhere in this volume;[55] here, however, a brief review will suffice. In Chapter III of *Fragments*, Climacus attempts to describe how non-immanent learning takes place: how a human being can come into possession of a truth that is radically new to him. Climacus contends that, in the instant of transcendent learning, the learner must simultaneously become aware of the absolute untruth in which he has been living. In good Christian fashion, Climacus terms this awareness "the consciousness of sin"; he insists that it cannot be acquired or communicated except via direct divine revelation.[56]

Climacus next explains why it is that Socrates never managed to burst the bounds of immanence and recollection. This is because, Climacus tells us, despite all of Socrates' attempts to come to terms with his own ignorance, the god nonetheless

---

54 *SKS* 4, 306 / *PF*, 111.

55 David D. Possen, "*Phaedrus*: Kierkegaard on Socrates' Self-Knowledge—and Sin," in this volume.

56 *SKS* 4, 224 / *PF*, 14–15.

never allowed him to discover the secret of his absolute untruth. Citing *Phaedrus* 230a, Climacus writes that Socrates

> became almost confused about himself [*næsten raadvild over sig selv*] when he came up against the different; he no longer knew whether he was a more curious monster than Typhon or whether there was something divine in him. What did he lack, then? The consciousness of sin, which he could no more teach to any other person than any other person could teach it to him. Only the god could teach it—if he wanted to be teacher.[57]

The logic of this passage is clear. Because Socrates never acquired the consciousness of sin, he remained in a state of confusion, and never gained access to the transcendent truth ("the different"[58]).

The Christian, by contrast, is said to *succeed* in moving from untruth to truth and, simultaneously, in gaining the consciousness of sin. In his Appendix to Chapter III, Climacus summarizes what must take place in the Christian's "moment" of trans-Socratic transformation:

> Let us recapitulate. If we do not assume the moment, then we go back to Socrates, and it was precisely from him that we wanted to take leave in order to discover something. If the moment is posited, the paradox is there, for in its most abbreviated form the paradox can be called the moment. Through the moment, the learner becomes untruth; the person who knew himself becomes confused about himself [*raadvild over sig selv*] and instead of self-knowledge he acquires the consciousness of sin.[59]

In his moment of transcendent learning, the Christian becomes "confused about himself" [*raadvild over sig selv*] and so gains the consciousness of sin. In this he curiously resembles Socrates, who, we saw above, became "*almost* confused about himself" [*næsten raadvild over sig selv*] and yet *failed* to gain the consciousness of sin. Clearly there must be an important difference between these parallel states of bafflement, Christian and Socratic. What, then, might this difference be?

We may certainly point to the qualifier *næsten*, "almost," as evidence that Climacus does not believe that Socrates' confusion about himself is quite the same as the perplexity that befalls the incipient Christian. But what more can we say about this difference? Remarkably, Climacus has only one single answer to offer, and that is an answer that we have already seen: "What did [Socrates] lack, then? The consciousness of sin."[60] The difference between Socrates and the incipient Christian lies in the enormity of sin, which is and remains beyond Socrates' ken.

This answer, however, is of little use to us. For on Climacus' own account, sin cannot be discovered, recognized, or revealed to a human being except in a direct encounter with the divine. Climacus certainly cannot *himself* show us what sin is; and for this reason, he can hardly explain how the moment of confusion in which a

---

57 *SKS* 4, 251 / *PF*, 47. For the sake of consistency with a subsequent citation, I have emended the Hongs' "bewildered about himself" to "confused about himself."

58 "What, then, is the unknown [truth]? …It is the different, the absolutely different." *SKS* 4, 249 / *PF*, 44.

59 *SKS* 4, 255 / *PF*, 52.

60 *SKS* 4, 251 / *PF*, 47.

Christian moves "beyond Socrates" differs from Socrates' own bafflement in *aporia*. In order to indicate that difference—and so to mark off what is Christian from what is supposed to be merely Socratic—Climacus can in fact do little more than point at Socrates, intone the word "sin," and gesture heavenward.

With this we encounter what is, to my mind, the deepest and most biting irony in the *Fragments*: that Socrates appears as a model not just on one side, but on both sides, of the gulf the book posits between "Socratic" and Christian life. Climacus employs Socrates as both his foil *and* his analogy for Christian conversion. He thereby refutes the conceit that the royal road to Christianity lies in rejecting Socratic thought. He instead suggests that, precisely in and through the ignorance and bewilderment that accompany Socrates' *failure* to become a Christian, Socrates provides our best illustration (barring divine revelation) of what it means to *succeed* in becoming a Christian; namely, we must become earnestly "confused" about ourselves; more literally, we must become utterly "helpless" [*raadvild*] with regard to ourselves; or again, to use the Socratic term, we must reach a state of complete *aporia*, or "resourcelessness," with respect to our self-knowledge.

The last point becomes explicit in the *Postscript*, where Climacus painstakingly explains the above irony—evidently to edify readers who had missed his point the first time:

> To emphasize existence, which contains within it the qualification of inwardness, is the Socratic, whereas the Platonic is to pursue recollection and immanence. Basically Socrates is thereby beyond all speculation, because he does not have a fantastical beginning where the speculating person changes clothes and then goes on and on and speculates, forgetting the most important thing, to exist. But precisely because Socrates is in this way beyond speculative thought, he acquires, when rightly depicted, a certain analogous likeness to what the imaginary construction set forth as that which truly goes beyond the Socratic: the truth as paradox is an analog to the paradox *sensu eminentiori*; the passion of inwardness in existence is then an analog to faith *sensu eminentiori*. That the difference is infinite nevertheless, that the designations in *Fragments* of that which truly goes beyond the Socratic are unchanged, I can easily show, but I was afraid to make complications by promptly using what seem to be the same designations, at least the same words, about the different things when the imaginary construction was to be presented as different from these.[61]

Unlike speculative thinkers, who pursue immanence and Platonic recollection while ignoring the fact of their own ignorance, Socrates (the *real* Socrates) faced and contended with his ignorance at every moment, and pressed on with his search for knowledge nonetheless. He thus exhibited a lifelong commitment to a possibility that he had no reason to believe would come to fruition: the possibility that, despite his present ignorance, he would someday be granted knowledge. As we noted earlier, Climacus elsewhere defines this form of life—a life of "contradiction between the infinite passion of inwardness and the objective uncertainty"—as "faith," albeit only "the Socratic faith."[62] In the present passage, Climacus remarks that Socrates' way

61 *SKS* 7, 189, note 1 / *CUP1*, 206, note. Earlier portions of the same footnote are cited in Sections I and II above.

62 *SKS* 7, 187 / *CUP1*, 204. *SKS* 7, 190, note / *CUP1*, 206, note.

of life bears "a certain analogous likeness" to the life that the *Fragments* depicts as *beyond* Socrates: namely, the Christian's life of faith in a transcendent truth.

Let us rephrase. Properly understood, the life and faith of Socrates is itself an "advance beyond Socrates" in the sense that the thought-experiment in the *Fragments* sought to specify: it is an advance beyond Platonic recollection and immanence. In this regard, Socratic faith and Christian faith are similar. All the same, Climacus insists, "the difference is infinite nevertheless, [as] I can easily show."[63] That is to say, there really *is* a gulf between Christian and Socratic faith, and an infinite one no less. Climacus boasts that he could easily have demonstrated the existence of this gulf, but chose not to do so. For it would have been too *confusing*, he tells us, to have to explain how such words as "faith," "paradox," and "inwardness" apply to both Socratic and Christian life despite the infinite difference between them.

We have good reason to be skeptical of this last set of claims. It is difficult to imagine, first of all, that Climacus' bewildering subterfuge in the *Fragments* can really be best explained as an attempt to *avoid* "complications." In Section II, we encountered a far more plausible explanation for the charade: Climacus slyly employs the terms "Socrates" and "the Socratic" for Platonic recollection and immanence so that he can parody Martensen's talk of advance beyond Socrates with a farcical "advance beyond Socrates" of his own.

Moreover, it is not at all clear why we should believe that Climacus "can easily show" the infinite gap between Socratic ignorance and Christian experience. We may recall that it was Climacus' *inability* to provide such a demonstration that signaled the collapse of his thought-experiment in the *Fragments*. And as we shall now see, the *Postscript* too culminates—just like the *Fragments*—in a push and failure to describe Christianity's infinite difference from Socratic categories. While this last argumentative turn is too complex to summarize here, it may be sketched in four parts as follows: (1) Near the close of the *Postscript*, Climacus *appears* to offer a serious, schematic account of Christianity, under the heading "Religiousness *B*...or paradoxical-religiousness."[64] (2) In the body of that account, Climacus insists that it is "ludicrous" to attempt to understand paradoxical-religious life. The best we can do is employ *analogies* to it, while "continually bear[ing] in mind the absolute difference that there is no analogy to the sphere of the paradoxically religious."[65] (3) Climacus then supplies a number of candidate analogies for paradoxical-religious Christian life. On closer inspection, all of these candidate analogies turn out to be depictions of the thought and life of Socrates.[66] (4) In order to speak of paradoxical-religiousness, it emerges, we need to employ Socrates as our analogy to it—all the while bearing in mind the "absolute difference" that renders the Socratic analogy invalid. Yet Climacus can tell us nothing, once again, about the "absolute difference" itself. It soon emerges that in the *Postscript*, just as in the *Fragments*, Climacus can in no way demonstrate the infinite gap between the Socratic and the Christian. The

63 *SKS* 7, 189, note 1 / *CUP1*, 206, note.

64 *SKS* 7, 505 / *CUP1*, 556. *SKS* 7, 511–33 / *CUP1*, 561–86.

65 *SKS* 7, 511 / *CUP1*, 562. *SKS* 7, 515 / *CUP1*, 567.

66 *SKS* 7, 515 / *CUP1*, 566. *SKS* 7, 516–17 / *CUP1*, 568. *SKS* 7, 517, note 1 / *CUP1*, 569, note.

best he can do, once again, is to point at Socrates and attempt to gesture beyond him.

In all of these provocative attempts and failures to specify Christianity's advance beyond Socrates, what Climacus *does* manage to demonstrate—despite himself, as it were—is that simply the life of Socrates indeed bears powerful analogies to that of a faithful Christian. The main such analogy concerns the way in which both Socrates and the Christian comport themselves toward Truth and the divine. Neither Socrates nor the Christian relate to the Truth as a doctrine, that is, as a metaphysical postulate. Instead, both Socrates and the Christian devote their lives to learning the truth, even though neither has objective grounds for thinking that they could ever come to know it (in Socrates' case, because he has no knowledge of the truth; in the Christian's case, because he is a sinner and the truth is absurd). In so doing, both Socrates and the believing Christian wrestle faithfully with their ignorance, confusion, and anxiety about their relation to truth. And both rely, at every moment, upon the possibility that the truth itself can and will intervene to enlighten them.

A second analogy concerns the structure and status of the guiding tales themselves—the myth of recollection, on the one hand, and the traditional Christian account of the fall, sin, and redemption, on the other. Both of these tales—if I may generalize to the point of crudity—divide our history into three grand epochs, a "pre," a present, and a "post": a union with the truth (the unity of thought and being, or Eden); a distance from the truth (our ignorance, or our vale of tears); and a reunion with the truth (the reconciliation of thought and being, or eternal happiness). Both tales situate us within the second of the three epochs, where we long for the truth yet do not know it. Both tales imply that our path toward the truth will involve a painful confrontation with our own present inadequacy (the depth of our psychic amnesia; the enormity of our sin). Finally, both tales indicate that, because of our own present distance from the truth (our ignorance; our sin and offense), we may not yet be in a position to recognize the tales themselves as truth. Accordingly, both tales call us to stake our lives upon their truth (to seek knowledge intrepidly; to live in faith). And this is precisely what both Socrates and the Christian do.

It is thus a lamentable distortion to claim that Climacus opposed Socrates and Socratic recollection in the name of "higher" Christian thought. On the contrary, both the *Fragments* and its *Postscript* imply that Socratic faith and Christian faith are so closely analogous that *no one* can discover or communicate (save by direct divine revelation) what knowledge the latter provides but the former does not. It is most accurate to say that, for Climacus, a Christian life is a peculiar *kind* of Socratic life: a life that seeks escape from its own state of ignorance and helplessness, yet does so in a distinctively Christian way—by appealing to the paradoxical grace of the God-man.[67]

This same view may, moreover, be safely imputed to Kierkegaard himself. It is often forgotten that Kierkegaard claimed to be, simultaneously and without contradiction, both a student of Socrates and a believer in Christ.[68] "I calmly stick

---

67 Cf. *SKS* 4, 252 / *PF*, 47.

68 "Formally I can very well call Socrates my teacher—whereas I have believed and believe in only one, the Lord Jesus Christ." *SV1* XIII, 541 / *PV*, 54.

to Socrates," he wrote in *The Point of View*. "True, he was no Christian, that I know, although I also definitely remain convinced that he has become one."[69] The notion that Socrates could convert to Christianity without ceasing to be Socrates suggests that the Socratic model is entirely compatible with, even if it is insufficient for, a Christian life-commitment. Kierkegaard in fact described his own authorship as an effort to imitate or become the converted Socrates whom he invokes. As an author, Kierkegaard aimed to serve as an ignoramus who demolishes others' fantasies about Christianity, and thereby recruits them to join him in the *aporia* necessary for any genuinely Christian experience of conversion. "The only analogy I have before me is Socrates," he wrote in 1855. "My task is a Socratic task, to audit the definition of what it is to be a Christian. I do not call myself a Christian, but I can make manifest that the others are that even less."[70] By showing others how they fail to live up to Christianity's demands, even while refraining from calling himself a Christian, Kierkegaard sought to recruit his readers to join him in the Socratic *aporia* he believed necessary for *any* genuinely Christian experience of conversion.

In commending Socrates to his nominally Christian audience, Kierkegaard found himself forced to reeducate his readers in the wake of writers like Martensen, who had encouraged them to revel in having "gone beyond" the Socratic standpoint. To counter this view, Kierkegaard labored to distinguish Plato's cosmological postulates and speculative method from Socrates' earnest engagement with ignorance. He then worked to promote the latter as a viable and indeed indispensable analogy to Christian life. As this essay has shown, a strong distinction between Platonic and Socratic senses of the Doctrine of Recollection proved crucial to Kierkegaard's effort. If we wish to summarize Kierkegaard's stance on recollection, therefore, we must accord this distinction its full importance. We must say that while Kierkegaard disdained the Platonic *thesis* of recollection as a spur to speculation, immanence, and paganism, he championed the Socratic *relation* to recollection as a priceless precursor—indeed, as our best analogy—to authentic Christian faith.

---

69 *SV1* XIII, 541 / *PV*, 55.

70 *SKS* 13, 405 / *M*, 341.

Phaedo and *Parmenides*:

Eternity, Time, and the Moment, or From the Abstract Philosophical to the Concrete Christian

Janne Kylliäinen

This article will investigate Kierkegaard's interpretation of Plato's views of eternity, time, and the moment. The dualistic Platonic view of time and eternity—and its concrete realization in Socrates—form the basis upon which Kierkegaard explicates his ethical-religious and Christian views.

I will investigate the major published texts in which Kierkegaard confronts Plato's conception of eternity and time—*The Concept of Irony*, *Either/Or*, *Repetition*, *The Concept of Anxiety*, *Philosophical Fragments*, and the *Concluding Unscientific Postscript*—as well as material from Kierkegaard's journals and notebooks. I will also examine the secondary literature that Kierkegaard used—or could have used—when formulating his views. I will then argue that he uses the Platonic-Socratic position as a human standard, which allows him to clarify the Christian conception of eternity, time, and the moment.

I. Time and Eternity in Plato's Works

Plato treats time and eternity relatively rarely as explicit themes in his dialogues. Most of the important passages are from the late dialogues. The *Timaeus* (37c–38c) explains the genesis of time (χρόνος) from the eternal (αἰών). The Demiurge creates the moving cosmos as an image of the eternal, unchanging world of ideas. The perpetual movement of the heavens "takes place according to number" (κατ᾽ ἀριθμὸν ἰοῦσαν αἰώνιον εἰκόνα) and this image of the eternal is the ground for our conception of time. Time is thus a function of bodily movements. The *Parmenides* (140e–142a and 151e–157b) contains a host of interesting insights into the concept of time, including insights into the concept of the moment. These concepts give rise to just as many puzzling contradictions, however, when predicated of "the one" (τὸ ἕν).[1] Nonetheless, Plato's enormous influence on the subsequent discussion of time and eternity is not based only on these few passages but also on what has become

---

The work for the present article has been made possible by a grant from the Academy of Finland.

1 Eva T.H. Brann, "Plato," in *Encyclopedia of Time*, ed. by Samuel L. Macey, New York: Garland 1994, pp. 467–8.

known as his doctrine of ideas or forms. In most of Plato's early dialogues—in the *Phaedo*, for example—Socrates strives to comprehend the being of the unchangeable forms in themselves and their relation to the sensual world of becoming. These eternal forms or ideas may be comprehended with intellect alone; the soul, which is immortal, longs to see these ideas and to remain with them. In the myths told by Socrates, the unchangeable world is located above and beyond the changeable sphere, and the movement of the soul towards them is depicted as a journey up into heaven, which is what we see described in the *Phaedrus* and the *Symposium*. As we will see, Kierkegaard was inspired both by the dualistic view implied in the doctrine of ideas and by what Plato wrote about the moment in the *Parmenides*.

II. The Concept of Irony, with Continual Reference to Socrates *(1841)*

The Concept of Irony presents Plato as a philosopher who lost himself in abstractions and who was not interested in synthesizing the eternal and the temporal in his personal existence. Kierkegaard presents the Socratic-Platonic position as abstract in every respect. It is abstract, first of all, because eternal ideas are separated from what is concretely given. Second, the eternal soul is separated from the temporal body. Third, the abstractly intellectual individual becomes separated from his or her historical surroundings. As result, eternal ideas, the soul, and the ahistorical individual tend to vanish into nothingness. At the same time, the sensuous, the corporeal, and the historical likewise vanish into nothingness as they become separated from the eternal. From his world-historical point of view, however, Kierkegaard is able to justify and rescue the Socratic-Platonic position: at that historical time, the Socratic-Platonic position was necessary for the development of Greek spirit as well as a position that was to follow it, namely, Christianity.

Kierkegaard maintains that ancient Greek culture (*Græciteten*) was defined by a dichotomy characterized in Plato's dialogues. This dichotomy determines the train of thought in a less developed way than the trichotomy of rigorous speculative thought. As a result, in the Platonic dialogues the unity of concept and intuition remains absent. In essence, the kind of thought at work in the dialogues amounts to simplifying the complexities of life by leading them back to an ever more abstract abbreviation.[2]

This dichotomy that had come to define the Greek spirit is manifest in the dualism of the eternal and the temporal in the *Phaedo*.[3] In *The Concept of Irony*, Kierkegaard argues against Friedrich Ast's (1778–1841) interpretation of the *Phaedo*, according to which Socrates was not a genuine representative of the Greek spirit. In his *Life and Works of Plato* (1816), Ast, a professor of classical literature in Landshut and Munich, claims that Socrates is idealized in the *Phaedo* and turned into an Indian Brahmin, whose spirit "flees from sensuousness, besetting and distressing it, and pines for release from the bodily shackles imprisoning it."[4] Against this view Kierkegaard argues that the spirit of the *Phaedo* is genuinely Greek:

---

2 *SKS* 1, 93–4 / *CI*, 32.

3 *SKS* 1, 122–37 / *CI*, 62–79.

4 Friedrich Ast, *Platon's Leben und Schriften*, Leipzig: Weidmann 1816, pp. 157–8.

> [T]he Grecian sky is high and arched, not flat and burdensome [as the Oriental one]; it rises ever higher, does not anxiously sink down; its air is light and transparent, not hazy and close. Therefore the longings to be found here tend to become lighter and lighter, to be concentrated in an ever more volatile sublimate, and tend not to evaporate in a deadening lethargy. Consciousness does not want to be soaked to softness in vague qualifications but to be stretched more and more. Thus the Oriental wants to go back behind consciousness, the Greek to go over and beyond the sequence of consciousness. But this sheer abstractness that it desires becomes ultimately the most abstract, the lightest of all—namely, nothing.[5]

In the *Phaedo*, eternal existence resulting from the successive "dying to" (*Afdøen*) is understood altogether abstractly. Kierkegaard refers first to the passage in which Socrates explains the *philosophers' wish to die*. Socrates argues that one never encounters the essential nature of a thing—that by which it is what it is such as magnitude, health, strength,—via sense perception.[6] Instead, genuine knowledge depends upon an abstraction from lower sense perceptions. Therefore, philosophers, who desire to comprehend the pure essence of things, are bound to wish to have as little as possible to do with the body.[7] And if death is a separation of soul and body as is generally acknowledged, then one understands why philosophers wish to die.[8] Even if the argument itself is solid, Kierkegaard finds the resulting conception of the eternal rather precarious. According to Kierkegaard, "the soul is here understood just as abstractly as the pure essence of the things that are the object of its activity."[9] The "purely abstract" as such, in contrast to the concrete, tends to become nothing in Socratic dialogue. Consequently, the eternal soul also becomes nothing.[10]

According to Kierkegaard, the nothingness of the eternal soul also results from the *recollection argument* for the immortality of the soul.[11] Socrates argues that certain universal concepts—equality, the in-and-for-itself beauty, the good, justice, piety, for example—are presupposed in all experience, and thus we must be born with a knowledge of them. The point of the argument is that just as these ideas exist prior to palpable things, so the soul exists before the body. In a Hegelian spirit, Kierkegaard criticizes the slackness of this kind of Socratic thinking:

> Here the speculatively unexplained (indeed, anything speculative is at first glance paradoxical) synthesis of the temporal and the eternal is poetically and religiously set at ease. What we confront here is not the eternal self-presupposing of self-consciousness that allows the universal to enclose the particular, the individual, tightly and constrictively—on the contrary, the universal flutters loosely around it.[12]

5 *SKS* 1, 125 / *CI*, 65–6.

6 *Udvalgte Dialoger af Platon*, vols. 1–3, trans. by C.J. Heise, Copenhagen: Gyldendal 1830–38 [vols. 4–8, Copenhagen: C.A. Reitzel 1851–59, cf. *ASKB* 1167 and 1169. Kierkegaard owned vols. 1–7], vol. 1, p. 17 (*ASKB* 1164–1166). (See *Phaedo* 65d.)

7 *Udvalgte Dialoger af Platon*, vol. 1, p. 18. (See *Phaedo* 66a–e.)

8 *Udvalgte Dialoger af Platon*, vol. 1, p. 20. (See *Phaedo* 68b.)

9 *SKS* 1, 125–8 / *CI*, 66–9.

10 Ibid.

11 *Udvalgte Dialoger af Platon*, vol. 1, pp. 33–8. (See *Phaedo* 72e–77e.)

12 *SKS* 1, 130 / *CI*, 70–1.

There is no explanation as to how, or in what sense, ideas exist before things do. If it goes no better with the pre-existence of the soul than with these universal concepts, it vanishes into infinite abstraction, Kierkegaard argues.[13]

While the eternal becomes abstract, the temporal becomes abstract, too: just as the existence of the soul in eternity is abstract, so is its temporal existence. Because the eternal signifies an abstract pre-existence and an equally abstract post-existence for Socrates and Plato, one might think that temporal existence would become the full center of life for them, Kierkegaard suggests. But this not the case. Kierkegaard points out that life on earth is "the incomplete" for Socrates and Plato, and it is the formless existence that results from the "dying to" which their longing aspires to. While still living on earth, the best activity of the soul is to lead the particular back to the universal, that is, to lead the temporal back to the eternal.[14]

In the *Phaedo* Socrates also argues for the immortality of the soul on grounds of its *unchangeableness*. The non-compounded is that which always remains invariable, since it cannot be disintegrated, cannot perish. The soul belongs to the non-compounded, and therefore it cannot perish.[15] But, argues Kierkegaard, here an equally abstract view of the relation between the soul and body results. The soul is forever divine, immortal, rational, homogeneous, indissoluble, self-consistent, and invariable—the body is human, mortal, irrational, multiform, dissoluble, and never self-consistent. The soul and the body are not related to each other, and the soul continually tries to sneak out of the body "instead of moving freely in the body produced by it."[16]

It seems that what Kierkegaard seeks in vain in the *Phaedo* are the "concrete" speculative and Christian views, in which the soul and the body are synthesized with each other. With a clear reference to the Hegelian point of view, he points out that "the concrete relation of the particular to the universal as given in and with individuality" is unknown to Socrates and Plato.[17] On the other hand, the Greek philosophers lacked the Christian idea of the resurrection of bodies.[18] Neither Socrates nor Plato could imagine that out of "the body of sin" could arise "the full-grown God-man," that is, that the human being could be created anew in the image of God. For them the successive dying to is an intellectual movement toward abstraction. In his abstract intellectualism Socrates lacks a positive moral view: "In the intellectual dying to, that which is to be died to is something indifferent; that which is to grow during this dying to is something abstract."[19] Due to the ironic spirit of Socrates the movement in the *Phaedo* ends negatively: both the temporal and the eternal end up being nothing.[20]

---

13 *SKS* 1, 130 / *CI*, 71.

14 *SKS* 1, 130–1 / *CI*, 71–2.

15 *Udvalgte Dialoger af Platon*, vol. 1, pp. 44–7. (See *Phaedo* 78b–80d.)

16 *SKS* 1, 131–2 / *CI*, 72–3.

17 *SKS* 1, 130 / *CI*, 71.

18 *SKS* 1, 133 / *CI*, 74.

19 *SKS* 1, 134–5 / *CI*, 76.

20 *SKS* 1, 134–7 / *CI*, 75–9.

Kierkegaard uses the *Phaedo* as evidence for his view that Socrates' existence was defined or determined by irony. However, Kierkegaard does not allow Socrates' existence to be swallowed completely into the nothingness of irony in his dissertation. He maintains that, as ironist, Socrates was altogether *appropriate to his times* and that his existence signified a turning point in the historical development of world spirit.[21] Why was he world-historically appropriate? Kierkegaard explains that Socrates was needed to introduce a concept of the "eternal" that could be held up against the immediate concept of the "moment" familiar to the Sophistic Greek consciousness. The Socratic moment (*Øieblikket*) demolished definitively the old Greek culture and the relativism typical to it. Socrates thereby made room for the Christian moment in which the eternal and the temporal became concrete, that is, the moment in which they became one.

In the early Greek culture everything was true: Greek consciousness was immersed in the immediate existence and naïvely relied upon what it received from the past "like a sacred treasure," writes Kierkegaard. The Greeks still considered everything given to be true and were not yet aware that, in truth, "life is full of contradictions." But, according to Kierkegaard, "what is supposed to be absolutely certain and determinative for men (laws and customs, for example), places the individual in conflict with himself."[22] Moreover, all this is something external to him, and as such he cannot immediately accept it. While the immediate consciousness does not notice this, reflection discovers this at once. Kierkegaard agrees with Hegel's rational reconstruction of the historical process and explains that in Sophistry reflection was awakened, and through the activity of the Sophists, reflection started to shake the foundations of the substantial ethical life (*den substantielle Sædelighed*) typical to Greek culture. However, Sophistry was able to lull reflection to sleep again with reasons. The grounds and reasons that the Sophists gave were only of a provisional nature, valid only for a "moment" (*Øieblik*). But the next moment never came for Sophistry, because it lived in the moment: Sophistry lacked a comprehensive consciousness; it lacked the *eternal moment* in which it would have to give an account of the whole, Kierkegaard claims.[23]

Kierkegaard writes that the Sophists provided "the next moment," the moment in which the momentarily true dissolved into nothing. But Socrates' irony was not turned against the Sophists only; it was turned "against the whole established order." Socrates demanded ideality and this demand was the judgment that condemned all Greek culture.[24] As Kierkegaard sees it, the judgment of Socrates by the Athenian state was a justified reaction. Socrates was, in effect, a threat for the existing ethical order of the state, and he did indeed lead the youth astray. Kierkegaard describes how Socrates seduced the youth:

> He discussed some subject that was personally important to them....He became their confidant without their quite knowing how it had happened....And then, when all the bonds of their prejudices were loosened...then the relation culminated in the

21 *SKS* 1, 244–5 / *CI*, 198–200.
22 *SKS* 1, 249 / *CI*, 204.
23 *SKS* 1, 247–50 / *CI*, 201–5.
24 *SKS* 1, 258 / *CI*, 213–14.

> meaningful moment, in the brief silvery gleam that instantly illuminated the world of their consciousness, when he turned everything upside down for them at once, as quickly as a glance of the eye (*Øieblik*) and for as long as a blink of the eye, when everything is changed for them ἐν ἀτόμῳ, ἐν ῥιπῇ ὀφθαλμοῦ [in a moment, in the twinkling of an eye][25]....By means of his questions, he quietly sawed through for toppling the primeval forest of substantial consciousness, and when everything was ready—look, then all these formations vanished, and the eyes of the soul delighted in a vista such as they had never seen before.[26]

The irony of the procedure lay in the fact that Socrates had nothing more to give the seduced.[27] Quoting 1 Corinthians 15:52 in Greek, Kierkegaard brings *the Socratic moment* and *the moment of the coming of Christ* side by side. Kierkegaard seems to be pointing out that with the glance of his eye (*Øieblik*), Socrates could not envision the coming of Christ and the resurrection of bodies as the apostle Paul could, after Christ, a few centuries later.[28] Socrates could not envision *the eternal in time*. He could rescue the souls of his disciples from the snares of relativity, but that was all: as an ironist he had the absolute only in the form of nothing.[29] He had no positive new knowledge to share with his disciples since, indeed, he was ignorant: "He was ignorant of the ground of all being, the eternal, the divine—that is, he knew that it was, but he did not know what it was."[30]

Kierkegaard maintains that Socrates broke the spell in which human life lay in "the form of substantiality."[31] The merit of Socrates was that he related as an individual human being to that which is absolute, divine, eternal, and in-itself. But his deficiency was that he did not know what the absolute was. As a result of Socrates' activity, the pagan gods took flight and took the fullness with them, and what remained was man as a form, which was to receive the fullness into itself.[32] "Yet this, of course, is only a moment of transition," writes Kierkegaard. "In many ways, man was still on the right road, and therefore what Augustine says about sin may be said about this: *beata culpa* (happy fault).[33] The heavenly hosts of gods rose from the earth and vanished from mortal sight, but this disappearance was the condition for a deeper relationship."[34]

How is the new, deeper relationship to the divine built? What fills the form of the person that irony leaves empty? Kierkegaard refers to "subjective thinking"—the "speculation" that remained purely subjective—that appears in the later dialogues

---

25 1 Cor 15:52.

26 *SKS* 1, 237 / *CI*, 189–90.

27 *SKS* 1, 237–8 / *CI*, 190–1.

28 1 Cor 15:51–54.

29 *SKS* 1, 136 / *CI*, 77.

30 *SKS* 1, 217–18 / *CI*, 169.

31 *SKS* 1, 219 / *CI*, 171.

32 *SKS* 1, 219 / *CI*, 171.

33 A reference probably to Augustine, "De diligendo Deo," Chapter 6. See *Sancti Aurelii Augustini Opera*, vols. 1–18, 3rd ed., Bassani: Remondini 1797–1807, vol. 17, column 1705. Here Augustine praises the fall of man: "*O felix culpa, quae talem ac tantum meruit habere redemptorem* (O happy fault, which has deserved to have such and so mighty a Redeemer)!"

34 *SKS* 1, 221 / *CI*, 173–4.

of Plato such as the *Parmenides*, *Theaetetus*, *Sophist*, and *Statesman*. This Platonic thinking desires fullness and presupposes an immediate unity of thought and being.[35] The reconciliation with the gods, then, would seem to occur already in the *Timaeus* where the good God, without envy, wants to create a good world.[36] It is obvious, however, that in his dissertation, Kierkegaard does not consider Plato's "abstract dialectic" to be the ultimate, positive reconciliation of the temporal and the eternal; it is rather a way to lose oneself in abstraction. Plato could not understand—not to mention, master—Socratic irony; he was its enthusiastic victim.[37] Instead, Kierkegaard refers repeatedly to Christ as the fullness, πλήρωμα.[38] At the same time, he writes that irony met its master in Hegel[39]—and this might be said without irony.

Thus, Kierkegaard's interpretation of Plato that emphasizes the abstractness of Plato's thought and of Socratic existence alike appears already in *The Concept of Irony* to drive at Christianity, in which the synthesis of time and eternity was to take place in the fullness of time. With this synthesis Kierkegaard, apparently, still regarded as compatible the Hegelian speculation that unites the particular and the universal in the singular.

Addendum on the Influence of Contemporary Sources

The Hegelian influence on Kierkegaard's evaluation of Socrates and Plato and their dualistic conceptions of time and eternity is clear enough. Kierkegaard refers to the trichotomy typical of the modern, more rigorous speculative development and to "the eternal self-consciousness that allows the universal to enclose the particular, the individual, tightly and constrictively"; he looks for "the concrete relation of the particular to the universal as given in and with individuality."[40] It is in light of such Hegelian ideals that Greek dualism is considered to be a less developed manifestation of world spirit and that Socratic existence is judged to be abstract. Moreover, Kierkegaard's analysis which follows a development beginning with the substantial ethical life of the early Greek culture, via the Sophists, and then to Socrates follows closely Hegel's analyses in the *Lectures on the Philosophy of History* and the *Lectures on the History of Philosophy*.[41] It is important to note

---

35 *SKS* 1, 174–6 with 97–9 / *CI*, 122–5 with 36–7.

36 *SKS* 1, 221 / *CI*, 173.

37 *SKS* 1, 65 (thesis III) / *CI*, 5 (thesis III). *SKS* 1, 90–2 / *CI*, 28–30. *SKS* 1, 125 / *CI*, 66. *SKS* 1, 177–6 / *CI*, 124–5.

38 See for example, *SKS* 1, 74–5 / *CI*, 13–15. *SKS* 1, 243 / *CI*, 197. *SKS* 1, 265 / *CI*, 220–1. Cf. Col 2:8–10 and Gal 4:4.

39 See *SKS* 1, 282 / *CI*, 242.

40 *SKS* 1, 93 and 130 / *CI*, 32 and 70–1.

41 See *Jub.*, vol. 11, pp. 297–352 and *Jub.*, vol. 18, pp. 3–122 (*Jub.* = Georg Wilhelm Friedrich Hegel, *Sämtliche Werke. Jubiläumsausgabe*, vols. 1–20, ed. by Hermann Glockner, Stuttgart: Friedrich Frommann 1928–41). Kierkegaard quotes both Hegel's *Vorlesungen über die Philosophie der Geschichte* (ed. by Eduard Gans, Berlin: Duncker und Humblot 1837 (vol. 9 in *Georg Wilhelm Friedrich Hegel's Werke. Vollständige Ausgabe*, ed. by Philipp Marheineke et al., Berlin: Duncker und Humblot 1832–45)) and *Vorlesungen über*

how Kierkegaard's account *differs* from Hegel's, however. Both of them agree that immediate life is indeed full of contradictions and that this state of affairs comes to light with the Sophists and Socrates. But while Hegel considers the matter in terms of the contradictions between different maxims, principles and truths of spirit,[42] Kierkegaard concentrates on the discrepancy between the inner and the outer, where the inner refers to the eternal and the infinite.[43] Kierkegaard analyzes the differences between the substantial consciousness, the Sophists, and Socrates as differences in orientation in temporality: the immediate consciousness typical of early Greek culture receives the past as given, the Sophists live in the abstract present moment, and Socrates reaches for the next moment, the moment that negates all the previous ones.[44] Such an analysis is absent in Hegel's discussion, and although the analysis is not downright anti-Hegelian, it does not derive directly from Hegel. It is as if the Kierkegaardian conception of temporality forces its way here into a Hegelian discussion of the development of world spirit.

In addition to Hegelianism, Christianity also clearly bears on Kierkegaard's reading of Plato and on his interpretation of Socrates' existence in *The Concept of Irony*. A treatise in which Platonism and Christianity had been brought side by side systematically was *The Christian Element in Platonism or Socrates and Christ* (1837) by Ferdinand Christian Baur (1792–1860), Professor of Protestant Theology in Tübingen.[45] Kierkegaard refers frequently to the part of the work in which Baur discusses the personality of Socrates.[46] Generally speaking, Kierkegaard accepts Baur's views. He appreciates especially the way Baur, in contrast to Friedrich Schleiermacher (1768–1834), emphasizes the significance of the personalities of Socrates and Christ for the doctrines that originated in them, Platonism and Christianity, respectively. Kierkegaard, however, contrasts the two personalities in a more radical way than Baur does: while the fullness of the deity resided in Christ, in Socrates appearance and essence were ironically separated from each other and the eternal—the divine—was present only as absent under the form of ignorance.[47] The ironic personality of Socrates affected the enthusiastic young Plato: it is the spirit of

---

die Geschichte der Philosophie (vols. 1–3, ed. by Carl Ludwig Michelet, Berlin: Duncker und Humblot 1833–36 (vols. 13–15 in *Georg Wilhelm Friedrich Hegel's Werke. Vollständige Ausgabe*) (*ASKB* 557–559)) while discussing the Sophists and Socrates; see *SKS* 1, 247–8 / *CI*, 201–3 and *SKS* 1, 251 / *CI*, 206.—For an analysis of Kierkegaard's *The Concept of Irony* as a sort of a commentary for the part of Hegel's *Lectures on the History of Philosophy* that treats the Sophists and Socrates, see Jon Stewart, *Kierkegaard's Relations to Hegel Reconsidered*, Cambridge and New York: Cambridge University Press 2003, pp. 150–81.

42 *Jub.*, vol. 18, pp. 5–7, where Hegel discusses the case of the Sophists, and pp. 117–21, where he discusses Socrates.

43 *SKS* 1, 249 / *CI*, 204. *SKS* 1, 253 / *CI*, 208–9.

44 *SKS* 1, 249–50 / *CI*, 204–5. *SKS* 1, 258 / *CI*, 213.

45 Ferdinand Christian Baur, *Das Christliche des Platonismus oder Sokrates und Christus*, Tübingen: Ludwig Friedrich Fues 1837 (*ASKB* 422).

46 Ibid., pp. 90–154. This part of Baur's book had been published in Danish in *Tidsskrift for udenlandsk theologisk Litteratur*, vol. 5, 1837, pp. 485–533. Kierkegaard had become acquainted with the text already then. See *SKS* 17, 245–6, DD:75 / *KJN* 1, 236–7.

47 *SKS* 1, 76 / *CI*, 14–15. *SKS* 1, 217 / *CI*, 169. *SKS* 1, 169 / *CI*, 220–1.

Socrates that shows in the movement towards the abstract nothingness that is typical of the early Platonic dialogues, including the *Phaedo*.[48] Thus, there is a more radical difference between Platonism and Christianity than Baur leads us to believe, argues Kierkegaard.[49] It is true that Baur looks at the similarities rather than differences between Platonism and Christianity, but at the end of his treatise, Baur points out the difference between Socrates and Christ very much as Kierkegaard does.[50] Kierkegaard was aware of this since in the *Journal DD* from 1837 he commends precisely this passage of Baur's work.[51]

It seems that the plan for the dissertation had crystallized for Kierkegaard around the time of the journal entry on Baur, that is, in the summer and fall of 1837.[52] It is possible that Kierkegaard's teacher Poul Martin Møller (1794–1838) was the one who gave shape to, or at least confirmed, Kierkegaard's view on the decisive difference between the Socratic and the Christian relationships to the eternal. Kierkegaard had already pondered the difference between philosophy and Christianity in 1835–36.[53] Passages in his journals from 1837 indicate that a conversation with Professor Møller might have helped him identify the differences between philosophy, as the human standpoint, and Christianity with the differences between Socratic irony and redemption in Christ. In the *Journal DD*, entry 5, Kierkegaard writes about the importance of distinguishing philosophy, "the purely human view of the world—the *humanistic* standpoint," from Christianity.[54] In another entry, DD:18, he refers to a "most interesting conversation" with Poul Møller on June 30, 1837 as he considers the differences between Socratic irony and Christian redemption. The influence of Socrates was simply to awaken, but not to redeem, "except in an inauthentic sense."[55] This is essentially the view that Kierkegaard maintains in *The Concept of Irony*, so it seems that the main inspiration for the dissertation might, indeed, have come from the discussion with Møller.

Besides the private discussion(s) with Møller, his essay "Thoughts Concerning the Possibility of Proofs of Human Immortality" (1837)[56] might have helped Kierkegaard conceive the differences between the pagan and Christian relationships to the eternal. The essay is mentioned by Kierkegaard in the *Journal BB* in an entry written on February 4, 1837.[57] Møller argues there that human immortality cannot be proven *a priori* on the basis of pure concepts and abstract reasoning only. Instead, a human being may become convinced of his immortality on the basis of a concrete,

---

48 *SKS* 1, 90–150 / *CI*, 28–96.

49 *SKS* 1, 76 / *CI*, 14–5. *SKS* 1, 265 / *CI*, 220–1.

50 See Baur, *Das Christliche des Platonismus oder Sokrates und Christus*, pp. 147–54.

51 *SKS* 17, 245–6, DD:75 / *KJN* 1, 236–7.

52 *SKS* 17, 240, DD:58 and DD:75 / *KJN* 1, 232 and 236–7. See also *SKS* K1, 126–7.

53 *SKS* 17, 30–6, AA:13–18 / *KJN* 1, 25–31. On the dates Kierkegaard wrote these notes, see *SKS* K17, 15.

54 *SKS* 17, 216, DD:5 / *KJN* 1, 208.

55 *SKS* 17, 225–6, DD:18 / *KJN* 1, 216–17.

56 P.M. Møller, "Tanker over Muligheden af Beviser for Menneskets Udødelighed, med Hensyn til den nyeste derhen hørende Literatur," *Maanedsskrift for Litteratur*, vol. 17, 1837, pp. 1–72 and pp. 422–53.

57 *SKS* 17, 134, BB:41 / *KJN* 1, 127–8.

organic world-view built on Christian tradition, true emotion, and true science.[58] There might be an echo of these views in Kierkegaard's dissertation in his distinction between the abstract Greek eternity and the concrete Christian one.[59] Møller also lectured on the history of ancient philosophy at the University of Copenhagen in 1834–35. In these lectures that were published posthumously in 1842, he also points out that the immortality of a sensuous human individual by no means follows from the Platonic doctrine of recollection.[60] However, it is not known if Kierkegaard attended these lectures.

III. Either/Or *(1843) and* Repetition *(1843)*

The Concept of Irony described how the eternal and the temporal were separated from each other and understood equally abstractly by Socrates and Plato. The positive moment of unity between God and man, and between the eternal and temporal, was lacking. The abstract, empty existence of Socrates, however, cleared the way for the true incarnation of the eternal: the Socratic moment of abstraction cleared the way for the moment of fullness. In *Either/Or* and *Repetition* the abstract philosophy of the Greeks is in the background while the idea of a concrete synthesis of the temporal and the eternal that would take place in the moment of time is being developed.

In *Either/Or*, Part II, there is a kind of afterimage of the Socrates described in *The Concept of Irony*. In his dissertation, Kierkegaard criticized the ethics of Socrates for being completely abstract. With Socrates virtue became detached from its natural element, from the concrete actuality of soul and state. His virtues were not civic virtues based on an earnest sense of responsibility; they were his personal virtues based on light-hearted ironic experiments.[61] In *Either/Or* Judge William describes how in ancient Greece a single individual isolated himself from the surrounding world in order to develop into a paragon of virtue. But, complains William, the virtues the individual developed were not civic, but personal. For Judge William this serves as an example of how the *ethical choice of oneself* can go wrong by leading the subject to abstraction and permanent isolation.[62] In the ethical choice of oneself there is, indeed, an abstract moment of isolation. But, as William sees it, this moment of deliberation will not last long. Like the *Platonic moment*, it actually does not exist at all—even during the choice, the individual continues to live as the concrete person that he is.[63] In the true choice of oneself the individual rises above his temporal existence and is transformed by the eternal, but then he receives back his concrete self. "The true concrete choice is the one by which I choose myself back into the world the very same moment I choose myself out of the world."[64] At the *moment*

---

58 *Efterladte Skrifter af Poul M. Møller*, vols. 1–3, Copenhagen: C.A. Reitzel 1839–43, vol. 2, pp. 175–237 (*ASKB* 1574–1576).

59 For example, in his exposition of the *Phaedo* and in *SKS* 1, 72, note 2 / *CI*, 10, note 2.

60 *Efterladte Skrifter af Poul M. Møller*, vol. 2, p. 430.

61 *SKS* 1, 270–2 / *CI*, 228–30.

62 *SKS* 3, 229–30 / *EO2*, 240–1.

63 *SKS* 3, 160 / *EO2*, 163.

64 *SKS* 3, 237 / *EO2*, 249.

of choice a decisive change takes place: when the subject truly chooses, or rather, receives himself, the temporal and the eternal are brought together, consciousness integrates and the person becomes his concrete, historically given self.[65]

Judge William's ethical view is an alternative to the abstract, ahistorical existence of a Greek philosopher; but, for William, it is also an alternative to the distracted existence of Hegelian philosophers who one-sidedly lose themselves in the past. The judge is displeased with the young men who, lost in the "pet philosophy" of the day, play with the titanic forces of history but are unable to tell a plain man what he is to do in life, and who do not know any better what they themselves are to do. This seems to be due to a confusion between *two spheres*: the sphere of thought and the sphere of freedom. Between these spheres there is a difference: in the sphere of thought, necessity rules, but for the acting individual there is an either/or. A distracted philosopher, absorbed in philosophy, in the past, in necessity, knows not the blessed life of freedom. Contrary to this, Judge William fights for freedom, for the time to come, for either/or.[66]

A forward orientation in time and a critique of Hegelian mediation also characterize the spiritual movement that Constantin Constantius is after in *Repetition*. Trying to characterize the *movement of repetition*, Constantin, somewhat unexpectedly, pits Greek philosophy against Hegel:

> It is incredible how much flurry has been made in Hegelian philosophy over mediation and how much foolish talk has enjoyed honor and glory under this rubric. One should rather seek to think through mediation and then give a little credit to the Greeks. The Greek explanation of the theory of being and nothing, the explanation of "the moment," "non-being," etc. trumps Hegel.[67]

Again a reference is made to *the moment*. As with the ethical choice of oneself, the issue at stake is a transition in the sphere of spirit, the transition that the Greeks called κίνησις: when and how a transition from possibility to actuality takes place. One should attempt to think through Hegelian mediation, Constantin suggests, since there is no explanation for how the reconciliation of the opposites takes place in it.[68] An examination of the Platonic view of life as recollection could clarify the issue and clarify, by its contrast, the modern movement of repetition. The Greek movement of recollection goes backward; recollection is like a beautiful old woman who is never of help at the moment. Repetition makes an opposite movement, a forward movement; the person who chooses repetition does not sit like an old woman turning the spinning wheel of recollection but calmly goes his way, happy in repetition. Repetition should play a very important role in modern philosophy, Constantin

---

65 *SKS* 3, 172–3 / *EO2*, 177. *SKS* 3, 213 / *EO2*, 222–3.

66 *SKS* 3, 166–72 / *EO2*, 170–6.

67 *SKS* 4, 25 / *R*, 148–9. The phrase translated as "trumps" (*siger Spar To til*) implies that Constantin still has something better than the Greeks up his sleave. In the card game l'hombre *spar to* is the second highest trump (*manille*), which is still overcome by *spar es* (*spadille*). See *SKS* K4, 41.

68 *SKS* 4, 25–6 / *R*, 148–9. Cf. *SKS* 18, 160, JJ:65 / *KJN* 2, 148. *SKS* 19, 395, Not13:27/ *JP* 1, 258–9. *SKS* 19, 415, Not13:50–50.a / *JP* 1, 260, and *JP* 2, 1603.

thinks.[69] Currently, however, modern philosophy makes no movement at all; it only makes a commotion (*Ophævelse* [also translated "sublation"], a reference to the Hegelian *Aufhebung*); or, if it makes any movement, it is always within immanence, whereas repetition is and remains a transcendence.[70]

In drafts of a letter to Johan Ludvig Heiberg (1791–1860), Constantin Constantius explains that the repetition his book really was about is the repetition of individual freedom:[71]

> In my little book, I always spoke about the issues of freedom for the life of the individual. The Greek mentality was in one sense happy, but if this happiness ceased, recollection manifested itself as freedom's consolation; only in recollection and by moving backward into it did freedom possess its eternal life. The modern view, on the other hand, must seek freedom forward. For the Greek outlook, eternity, regarded from the point of view of the moment, appears through the past; the modern view must look at eternity, regarded from the point of view of the moment, through the future.[72]

The point of *Repetition* was that, once lost, repetition of freedom is possible only as a transcendent, religious movement by virtue of the absurd: ultimately, the concept of repetition signifies reconciliation (*Forsoningen*).[73] Constantin argues that when the repetition of individual freedom is considered, Hegelian mediation should be kept out. Hegelian mediation belongs to the *sphere of logic* where everything lies in immanence, but the movements of spirit take place in the *sphere of freedom*, and they take place not by virtue of immanence, but of transcendence. Movement belongs to the world of spirit, and it is always dialectical with respect to time. Hegel has mistakenly applied movement to logic, whereas both ancient and modern philosophy have consistently assigned it a place in the philosophy of spirit.[74]

In Socrates' existence and in Plato's philosophy the eternal and the temporal are separated from each other. In *Either/Or*, Part II, Judge William sketches a solution to the problem of dualistic existence. It is not a Hegelian insight that the concepts and the phenomena are fundamentally identical as manifestations of absolute spirit. Such insights belong to the sphere of thought, whereas Judge William is concerned with the practical sphere, the sphere of freedom, where the dualism of eternal thought and temporal individual existence remains despite such insights. In practice, Hegelian philosophers do not solve the problem of dualism, but fall prey to it: the young philosophers become immersed in the sphere of thought and forget that there is the sphere of freedom, the sphere of action, too. According to Judge William, what

---

69 *SKS* 4, 9–11 / *R*, 131–3.

70 *SKS* 4, 56–7 / *R*, 186.

71 *Pap.* IV B 111, 263–5 / *R*, Supplement, pp. 288–9.

72 *Pap.* IV B 117, 298 / *R*, Supplement, p. 317.

73 *Pap.* IV B 117, 285 / *R*, Supplement, p. 305. *Pap.* IV B 293–4 / *R*, Supplement, p. 313. *Pap.* IV B 118, 1, pp. 300–1 / *R*, Supplement, p. 320.

74 *Pap.* IV B 117, 288–9 / *R*, Supplement, pp. 308–9. See also *Pap.* IV B 118, 7, pp. 302–3 / *R*, Supplement, pp. 321–2.

solves the dualism and brings the eternal and the temporal together in the sphere of freedom is the ethical choice of oneself.[75]

The dichotomy that Hegelian mediation was supposed to have done away with is thus taken up as a problem that demands a practical solution. In the manuscript *Johannes Climacus, or De omnibus dubitandum est*, which Kierkegaard wrote during the last months of 1842 and the first months of 1843, the same movement is carried out in a more rigorous way. In the *Journal JJ*, Kierkegaard himself suggests that he might have been influenced by Plato while writing *Johannes Climacus*,[76] so we might look for some Platonic traits there.

The protagonist of the manuscript, Johannes Climacus, is puzzled by modern philosophy, which claims to be both the historical and the eternal simultaneously. For Climacus, this union appears to be a mystery: "Indeed, it is a union similar to the union of the two natures in Christ."[77] Modern philosophy wants to be in the present and above the present at the same time, in the same moment:

> Philosophy...wanted to permeate everything with the thought of eternity and necessity, wanted to do this in the present moment, which would mean slaying the present with the thought of eternity and yet preserving its fresh life. It would mean wanting to see what is happening as that which has happened and simultaneously as that which is happening; it would mean wanting to know the future as a present and yet simultaneously as a future.[78]

Unable to get inside this mysterious philosophy as his contemporaries do, that is, through doubt alone,[79] Climacus tries to begin with the beginning: he tries to first search out the ideal possibility of doubt in consciousness.[80] He reasons as follows: In immediacy there is no possibility of doubt. But when immediacy is expressed in language, contradiction is present, since language does not simply express reality, but produces something else. "Immediacy is reality, language is ideality; consciousness is contradiction. The moment I make a statement about reality, contradiction is present, for what I say is ideality."[81] Reflection is the possibility of the relation between *reality* and *ideality*, and consciousness is the relation. The categories of reflection are always *dichotomous*, the categories of consciousness are *trichotomous*. Consciousness is spirit. "If there were nothing but dichotomies, doubt would not exist, for the possibility of doubt resides precisely in the third, which places the two in relation to each other." In other words, doubt resides in consciousness, in spirit, which is *interesse* (being between), that is, a relation and thus an interest.[82] Ideality and reality collide, not in time or in eternity, but in consciousness. The collision is present as soon as the question of a *repetition* arises, claims Climacus. But as the

---

75 *SKS* 3, 166–73 / *EO2*, 170–7.

76 *SKS* 18, 231, JJ:288 / *KJN* 2, 212.

77 *Pap.* IV B 1, 122–3 / *JC*, 139–40.

78 *Pap.* IV B 1, 125–6 / *JC*, 142–3.

79 *Pap.* IV B 1, 141 / *JC*, 159.

80 *Pap.* IV B 1, 144–5 / *JC*, 165–6.

81 *Pap.* IV B 1, 146 / *JC*, 168.

82 *Pap.* IV B 1, 147–8 / *JC*, 169–70.

question of repetition arises, the manuscript ends. In the closing lines, repetition is distinguished from recollection, but the closer characterization of both is left indeterminate.[83]

The link to Platonism in *Johannes Climacus* might be Climacus' insight that the activity of spirit begins with the dichotomy. Climacus vindicates a Platonic dichotomy as a starting position for the human striving for a synthesis.[84] For doubt and error to be possible, there must be a discrepancy between immediate reality and conceived ideality, and before there can be talk of the unity of the real and the ideal, the ideal must first appear for reflection as separate from the immediate. So both the possibility of error and the actual overcoming of error lie in the dichotomy familiar to us from the works of Plato.

Kierkegaard also vindicates dichotomy in an entry in *Notebook 13*, written in 1842–43, that discusses Karl Werder's (1806–93) version of Hegelian logic:

> In the doctrine of being, everything *is*, there is no transition, (this is something that even Werder admitted, see the small books).
>
> In the doctrine of essence there is *Beziehung*.—The malpractices in Hegel's logic. Essentially this part [the doctrine of essence] is just dichotomies—cause–effect—ground–consequent—reciprocal effect is problematic, belongs maybe somewhere else.
>
> The concept is a trichotomy.
>
> Being does not belong to logic at all.
>
> It [i.e. logic] ought to begin with dichotomy.[85]

Here we find the same insight: the beginning should be made with a dichotomy. But once dichotomy is posited, it still is not clear how the transitions should take place. The note continues:

> Hegel has never justified the category of transition. It might be significant to compare it with the Aristotelian doctrine of κίνησις.
>
> Is mediation the zero point, or is it a third?—Does the third itself emerge through the immanental motion of the two, or how does it emerge?—The difficulty appears especially when one seeks to transfer it to the world of actuality.[86]

Judge William, Constantin Constantin, and Johannes Climacus want to transfer the problematic of transition from the world of thought into the world of actuality. In the actual life of an individual, one begins in immediacy, the determinate representation

---

83 *Pap.* IV B 1, 149–50 / *JC*, 171–2.

84 Maybe it seems a little forced to speak here of a Platonic dichotomy, while the term reflection refers in Hegelian language rather to Kant and Fichte than to Plato. However, since the Socratic existence is the paradigm of dualistic existence both in *The Concept of Irony* and later in the *Concluding Unscientific Postscript*, and since Kierkegaard himself refers to Plato in connection with *Johannes Climacus*, one may argue that in essence the dichotomy equals the Platonic one.

85 *SKS* 19, 415, Not13:50 / *JP* 2, 1602. (Translation slightly modified.) Cf. with *SKS* 19, 406, Not13:41 and 41.b / *JP* 2, 1602, where Kierkegaard argues that being is not a category, not a quality, that is, not a determinate being.

86 *SKS* 19, 415, Not13:50 / *JP* 1, 260. (Translation slightly modified.) *JP* 1, 1603.

of the ideal follows, but the individual is then faced with problems in bringing them together. The point of the pseudonyms is that the solution to these problems depends on the free acts of spirit.

As opposed to the tendency of philosophical thinking, Judge William situates the subject in temporal actuality and gives him a forward orientation in time: contemplation of the past is not enough; as a married man and father, the judge has to take care of the future, and the same holds with all human beings. Thus, there is not a moment to waste. The abstract moment of deliberation does not exist; the moment of ethical choice is now.[87] Against the backward orientation typical of Greek recollection, Constantin Constantius posits the modern, forward-oriented movement of repetition. In his thought experiment, in the main story of the book *Repetition*, a young man suffers from the burden of his history, but expects the eternal to show itself in time again. As Constantin explains in his letter to Heiberg, the young man looks at eternity, from the point of view of the moment, not in the past as the Greeks did, but in the future.[88]

Both pseudonyms refer to the Greek, that is, to the Platonic moment. Judge William alludes to the Platonic moment where "actually is not at all," and Constantin Constantius celebrates the Greek development of "the moment" and "non-being." In *The Concept of Anxiety* and *Philosophical Fragments*, the Platonic moment will become a central point of reference in clarifying the Christian moment.

Addendum on the Influence of Contemporary Sources

The emergence of the Platonic concept of the moment in Kierkegaard's texts demands some explanation. Where does Kierkegaard get it from? Constantin Constantius claims that "the Greek explanation (*Udvikling*) of the theory of being and nothing, the explanation of 'the moment,' 'non-being,' etc. trumps Hegel."[89] The reference is no doubt to Plato. Plato develops the concepts of being and non-being in the *Sophist* and the *Parmenides*, and he treats the concept of the moment (τὸ ἐξαίφνης) in the *Parmenides* 155e–157b. It is possible that Kierkegaard might have come across this passage already while preparing *The Concept of Irony*. As noted above, he plays with the concept of the moment in his dissertation when discussing the Sophists and Socrates; moreover, he creates a parallel between the Socratic moment with the Christian moment with his Greek quotation from the first letter of Paul to the Corinthians. In his dissertation, he also alludes to Plato's *Parmenides* as the source for the concept of "becoming" understood as a synthesis of being and non-being.[90] However, he does not mention the Platonic moment in his dissertation or the extant journals from that time, nor is the Platonic moment discussed extensively in the secondary literature on Plato and Socrates that Kierkegaard refers to in his dissertation and journals. Friedrich Ast mentions it in one single sentence.[91] In the "Introduction"

87 *SKS* 3, 160–1 / *EO2*, 163–4. *SKS* 3, 166–73 / *EO2*, 170–7.

88 *Pap.* IV B 117, p. 298 / *R*, Supplement, p. 317.

89 *SKS* 4, 25 / *R*, 148–9.

90 *SKS* 1, 305 / *CI*, 268. For the explanation of the passage, see *SKS* K1, 338.

91 Ast, *Platon's Leben und Schriften*, p. 242.

to the *Parmenides* in his translation of *Plato's Works*, Friedrich Schleiermacher notes "the concept of the momentary" (*der Begriff des Augenblicklichen*) as a remarkable achievement of Platonic speculative dialectics.[92] That is all.

It is unlikely that these short notes would have been enough to capture Kierkegaard's interest; it is more likely that Kierkegaard began serious consideration of the Platonic moment later. Judge William's letter on "The Balance Between the Esthetic and the Ethical in the Development of the Personality," where the Platonic moment is first mentioned in *Either/Or,* was in all likelihood written after Kierkegaard's return from Berlin.[93] Jon Stewart has suggested that the philosophical and theological implications of the Platonic moment could have been brought to his attention by the above-mentioned Karl Werder in Berlin in winter 1841–42.[94] In Berlin, Kierkegaard attended Werder's lectures entitled "Logics and Metaphysics with a Particular Consideration of the Most Important Older and New Systems," and presumably studied Werder's *Logic: As Commentary and Supplement to Hegel's "Science of Logic"* (1841).[95] Werder wrote his *habilitation* on Plato's *Parmenides*, and in his *Logic*, he quotes the passage 155e–157b, which treats the concept of moment.[96]

It is not easy to understand Werder's use of the Platonic moment with regard to Hegelian logic. He seems to suggest that determinate beings come into existence from pure being and disappear into it in the moment (*Augenblick*), which Plato treats in his *Parmenides*. These transitions take place in the moment; it is the eternal presence of thinking from which everything begins and into which everything disappears.[97] The strongest evidence that Werder is Kierkegaard's source for understanding the significance of the Platonic moment is entry 50 in *Notebook 8*.[98] Here Kierkegaard seems to refer precisely to that passage of Werder's work in which the Platonic moment is identified as the category of transition.[99] The passage from *Repetition*

---

92 *Platons Werke*, vols. 1–3 in 6 parts, trans. by Friedrich Schleiermacher, vols. 1.1–1.2 and vol. 2.1, Berlin: Realschulbuchhandlung 1817–18, vols. 2.2–2.3 and vol. 3.1, Berlin: Reimer 1824–28, vol. 1.2, p. 97 (*ASKB* 1158–1163).

93 *SKS* K2–3, 55–7.

94 Jon Stewart, "Werder: The Influence of Werder's Lectures and *Logik* on Kierkegaard's Thought," in *Kierkegaard and His German Contemporaries*, Tome I, *Philosophy*, ed. by Jon Stewart, Aldershot: Ashgate 2007 (*Kierkegaard Research: Sources, Reception and Resources*, vol. 6), pp. 335–72. Klaus Schäfer notes that when Vigilius Haufniensis takes up the Platonic concept of the moment in *The Concept of Anxiety*, he opposes Werder's understanding of it; see Klaus Schäfer, *Hermeneutische Ontologie in den Climacus-Schriften Sören Kierkegaards*, Munich: Kösel-Verlag 1968, pp. 295–6, note 202.

95 Karl Werder, *Logik. Als Commentar und Ergänzung zu Hegels Wissenschaft der Logik*, Erste Abtheilung, Berlin: Veit und Comp. 1841 (*ASKB* 867). (No further installments were ever published.)

96 Ibid., pp. 93–6.

97 Ibid., p. 100; p. 121; p. 151. Here I follow Schäfer's interpretation; see Schäfer, *Hermeneutische Ontologie in den Climacus-Schriften Sören Kierkegaards*, pp. 259–60, note 130, and pp. 295–6, note 202.

98 *SKS* 19, 245, lines 4–9, Not8:50, / *JP* 1, 257.

99 Werder, *Logik. Als Commentar und Ergänzung zu Hegels Wissenschaft der Logik*, p. 100.

quoted above indicates that having listened to Werder's lectures, Kierkegaard began to think that the problematic transitions implicit in Hegelian mediation could be clarified by considering the Platonic moment anew.

Kierkegaard might also have read about the Platonic moment in *The History of Philosophy* by Wilhelm Gottlieb Tennemann (1761–1819). Tennemann mentions the moment in his exposition of Plato's metaphysics.[100] An entry in *Notebook 13* shows that Kierkegaard read the chapter on Plato in Tennemann.[101] However, the entry was probably written after Kierkegaard finished *Either/Or*.[102]

IV. The Concept of Anxiety *(1844) and* Philosophical Fragments *(1844)*

The ethical choice and the religious repetition described by Judge William and Constantin Constantius are, to use the expression introduced by the latter, transitions in the sphere of freedom. As movements, they are dialectical with respect to time and take place in a moment of time. In *Repetition*, Constantin Constantius suggests that the Platonic moment could clarify what happens in the moment of transition, and the Platonic movement of recollection could clarify, by contrast, the modern movement of repetition. Constantin does not explain what separates the ancient from the modern, but the authorship that follows points toward Christ. In *The Concept of Anxiety* and *Philosophical Fragments*, the differences between the Platonic and Christian moments come into focus.

In the long, pregnant footnote at the beginning of the third chapter of *The Concept of Anxiety*, Vigilius Haufniensis paraphrases and examines *Parmenides* 156e–157a, the passage in the *Parmenides* in which Plato develops his concept of the moment. According to Vigilius, "Plato conceives of the moment as purely abstract."[103] The moment appears as "this strange thing" (ἄτοπον, that is, "something that has no τόπος, place") "that lies between motion and rest and does not occupy any time." In the moment, that which is in motion comes to rest, and that which is at rest comes into motion. The moment is the general category of "transition" (μεταβολή) since all transitions—the transition of the one to the many, the many to the one, from likeness to unlikeness, etc.—take place in the moment.[104]

According to Vigilius, Plato deserves credit for showing how difficult it is to place transition in the realm of the purely metaphysical. In Hegelian logic transitions take place from one concept to the next. Plato shows that in the realm of the purely metaphysical, that is, in the realm of Hegelian logic, the moment of transition is ἄτοπον, without place.[105] Plato deserves credit for showing this, for once it becomes clear that logic does not have the category of transition, "it will become clearer that

---

100 Wilhelm Gottlieb Tennemann, *Geschichte der Philosophie*, vols. 1–11, Leipzig: Johann Ambrosius Barth 1798–1819, vol. 2, pp. 354–6 (*ASKB* 815–826).

101 *SKS* 19, 245, lines 20–4, Not13:8.b / *JP* 3, 2339.

102 After December 1842, while Kierkegaard was done with "The Balance Between the Esthetic and the Ethical" in September 1842. See *SKS* K19, 535, and *SKS* K 2–3, 57.

103 *SKS* 4, 385 / *CA*, 82.

104 *SKS* 4, 386–7 / *CA*, 83.

105 *SKS* 4, 384–5 / *CA*, 81–2.

the historical spheres and the knowledge that rests on a historical presupposition have the moment."[106] However, as we approach the concrete moment that belongs to the historical spheres, the limitations of Plato become evident. The Platonic moment is and remains "a silent atomistic abstraction"; for Plato the moment remains "non-being under the category of time."[107] Plato remains in the world of abstraction and cannot conceive of the concrete moment that stands at the center of history.

According to Vigilius, another passage from the *Parmenides* indicates the consequences of treating the moment as an atomistic abstraction: "It shows how, if the one is assumed to have the determination of time, the contradiction appears that 'the one' (τὸ ἕν) becomes older and younger than itself and 'the many' (τὰ πολλά) and then again neither younger nor older than itself and the many (§ 151. E.)"[108] In passage 151e, "to be" is defined as "participation in an essence or a nature in the present time (τὸ δὲ εἶναι ἄλλο τί ἐστιν ἤ μέθεξις οὐσίας μετὰ χρόνου τοῦ παρόντος § 151. E.)."[109] But developed further, it appears that the concept of the present (τὸ νῦν) vacillates between an indication of the present, the eternal, and the moment: "This 'now' (τὸ νῦν) lies between 'was' and 'will become,' and naturally 'the one' cannot, in passing from the past to the future, bypass this 'now.' It comes to the halt in the now, does not become older but is older."[110]

The argumentation of Vigilius is somewhat unclear here. First of all, he assumes that "the moment" spoken of at *Parmenides* 156d is identical with "the present time" mentioned at 151e and "the now" at 152b–e. Thus, for Plato the moment means both the eternal present, in which movement stops, and the transitory moment of transition, which lies between the past and the future. Second, Vigilius argues that with such a conception of the moment, Plato ends in a contradiction: "the one" both *is* and *becomes* in the moment of time. The lesson Vigilius wants to draw from his reading of the *Parmenides* seems to be that the concept of the moment cannot belong to logic because it is a self-contradictory concept. However, Vigilius claims that regardless of whether it is contrary to thought or not, the moment belongs "to the historical spheres"; for Plato it was impossible to think the moment, but that does not mean that the moment—the combination of being and becoming, state and transition—would not exist in the historical spheres.

The passage 151e–152e might also be important for Kierkegaard because of the theological significance "the one" had in later Platonism. If we take τὸ ἕν to refer to the god understood as "the one," what Plato encounters in the *Parmenides* at the level of abstract concepts turns out to be the paradox of the eternal God coming into time and receiving predicates that belong to temporal beings. What Plato tried to think, but could not, was the presence of the absolute in the sphere of becoming, that is, in the historical spheres. For Plato, the god never makes an appearance in time, never becomes present in the moment in time, and consequently an irreconcilable dualism of eternity and time remains. If interpreted in this way, Vigilius' idiosyncratic

---

106 *SKS* 4, 387, note / *CA*, 84, note.

107 Ibid.

108 Ibid.

109 Ibid.

110 Ibid. Cf. *Parmenides* 152b–e.

reading of Plato points towards Christ, in whom the eternal God comes into time and in whom reconciliation is brought about. Given the context, this interpretation is not farfetched, for in the text that follows the footnote, Vigilius brings the Platonic and the Christian moments side by side.

According to Vigilius, it is symptomatic that what the Danes call *Øieblik* (moment, glance of an eye), Plato calls τὸ ἐξαίφνης (the sudden, or, something that takes place with one unaware). The Greek "moment" is related to the category of the invisible; it is an abstraction of thought that never becomes visible in the temporal, sensuous realm. Time and eternity "were considered equally abstractly" by Plato and his compatriots. Vigilius claims that this was because the Greeks lacked "the concept of temporality, and this again was due to the lack of the concept of spirit."[111] What are the concepts of temporality and spirit, then, that the Greeks did not have? And what is the proper concept of the moment that Vigilius contrasts with the deficient concept that Plato had, the concept of the concrete moment that belongs to the historical spheres?

Vigilius writes that spirit is the eternal that unites the eternal and temporal, the soul and body. As soon as the spirit is posited (or posits itself) in the individual life, the moment in which time and eternity touch each other is there, and with it temporality.[112] Time, taken in itself, is "an infinite succession" in which there is no foothold to be found, that is, no present. Each moment is a process, a passing by. As a concept of time, the present refers only to something infinitely contentless, to the infinite vanishing that takes place at each moment of time. In time itself there is neither present, nor past, nor future, but there is just the process of passing by.[113] On the other hand, the eternal is the present, the present that is not without content, but is full. As soon as the eternal spirit that unites the eternal and temporal is posited (or posits itself), the present moment is there and, with it, the temporality in which time constantly cuts off eternity and eternity constantly permeates time. Only with this moment does history begin. Only here is the division of time into the present, past and future endowed with its meaning.[114]

In the "Introduction" to *The Concept of Anxiety*, Vigilius Haufniensis explains that he is not practicing psychology as an immanent science, but explores the phenomena of human spirit on dogmatic presuppositions.[115] In the book itself, Vigilius indeed works out a "dogmatic" understanding of how temporality is constituted. In the development of the individual, the eternal appears first as a future possibility; the future is the incognito in which the eternal appears. In the concrete individual the possibility of the eternal—of spirit, of freedom—expresses itself as anxiety. Anxiety is the dizziness of freedom and in anxiety freedom succumbs.[116] This moment of the Fall marks the beginning of the human history. At the moment of the Fall, sin is

---

111 *SKS* 4, 391 / *CA*, 87–8.

112 *SKS* 4, 392 with 394 / *CA*, 88–9 with 90–1.

113 *SKS* 4, 388–9 / *CA*, 85–6.

114 *SKS* 4, 390 / *CA*, 86. *SKS* 392 / *CA*, 88–9.

115 *SKS* 4, 317–31 / *CA*, 9–24.

116 *SKS* 4, 365–6 and 392–4 / *CA*, 61 and 89–91.

posited and temporality emerges as sinfulness.[117] The individual who has personally experienced the Fall now has good reasons to be anxious about the future, and anxiety thereby determines the present moment in which he lives; as Vigilius puts it: "In the individual life, anxiety is the moment."[118] Together "the moment and the future in turn posit the past."[119]

After the Fall, anxiety thus determines the three temporal dimensions of individual life. In the world-historical development, such a predicament characterized Judaism after the Fall and before Christ. Judaism knew only the moment as a *discrimen* (i.e., as the moment of the Fall and separation)[120] and the eternal appeared to it as the future. In Christianity the pivotal concept is the fullness of time. The fullness of time is the moment as the eternal, the full presence of the eternal that is also future and past. This—apparently Christ as the eternal in time (Galatians 4:4)—signifies the moment of conversion, reconciliation (*Forsoning*), and redemption both in world-history and in "individual historical development."[121] For the individual, Christianity offers a possibility of faith that extricates itself from "anxiety's moment of death." Vigilius claims that only faith is able to do this, for "only in faith is the synthesis eternal and at every moment possible."[122]

So here we have the concrete moment that belongs to the historical spheres: the history of the individual and the history of the human race. It is the moment as an atom of time in which eternity appears as undivided, ἐν ἀτόμῳ.[123] However, the moment does not simply reconcile time and eternity, but also shows the opposition between them: whereas "dialectical sorcery" makes eternity and the moment signify the same thing, in Christianity "eternity and the moment become extreme opposites."[124] Vigilius writes that the moment—the appearance of Christ in time—posits the temporality in which eternity constantly permeates time, while time constantly cuts off (*afskærer*) eternity.[125] Moreover, in a footnote Vigilius also refers to the eschatological dimension of the Christian moment: the world will pass away in the moment, ἐν ἀτόμῳ καὶ ἐν ῥιπῇ ὀφθαλμοῦ.[126] Thus, the anxious expectation of the eternal in time apparently characterizes not only Judaism, but also Christianity. But, as noted above, Vigilius maintains in another passage that Christian faith extricates itself from "anxiety's moment of death" and in Christian faith the synthesis "is eternal and at every moment possible."[127]

Plato, as a representative of Greek culture, knew neither the Fall nor redemption, had neither the Jewish nor the Christian concept of the moment. The Greeks did not define the moment forwards but backwards: as Platonic recollection shows, for them

117 *SKS* 4, 392 / *CA*, 89.
118 *SKS* 4, 384 / *CA*, 81.
119 *SKS* 4, 393 / *CA*, 89.
120 Cf. *SKS* 4, 355 / *CA*, 50.
121 *SKS* 4, 393 / *CA*, 90.
122 *SKS* 4, 419 / *CA*, 117.
123 *Pap.* V B 55, 6.
124 *SKS* 4, 387–8 / *CA*, 84.
125 *SKS* 4, 392 / *CA*, 89.
126 *SKS* 4, 391 / *CA*, 88.
127 *SKS* 4, 419 / *CA*, 117.

the eternal lay "behind as the past that could only be entered backwards."[128] Thus, the Greeks had only an abstract concept of the eternal, for "the eternal thought of as the past is an altogether abstract concept....In a deeper sense they did not have the concept of eternal."[129] In other words, the Greeks neither anticipated the becoming of the eternal in a Judaic manner, nor did they have the Christian concept of an eternal spirit that at every moment permeates time. The moment for the Greeks was not an atom of time, but "an atom of eternity" and for Greek culture, "the atom of eternity was essentially eternity."[130]

In the *Philosophical Fragments*, too, the Greek moment serves as a clarifying parallel to the Christian moment. Here the question is how a human being comes to know the eternal truth, and the issue between the Socratic and the Christian is formulated as follows: can a historical point of departure be given for an eternal consciousness?[131]

Referring to the doctrine of recollection in Plato's *Meno* (80e–86b) and to the maieutic method that Socrates describes in the *Theaetetus* (148e–151d), Johannes Climacus argues that in the Socratic view the moment of time has no decisive significance for learning the eternal truth. The human being has had the condition for learning the truth for all eternity: he has had the capacity to recollect it. The point in time when he actually recollects the truth is merely an accidental occasion for using the capacity that belongs inherently to his eternal soul. Therefore, "viewed Socratically, any point of departure in time is *eo ipso* something accidental, a vanishing point, an occasion."[132] The temporal point from which the movement of recollection departs is a nothing because "in the same moment I discover that I have known the truth from eternity without knowing it, in the same instant that moment is hidden in the eternal, assimilated into it."[133] In another passage Climacus notes that, according to the Socratic and Platonic understanding, the bringing forth of "the many beautiful and glorious discourses" (*Symposium* 210d) is only an appearance of what had "already for a long time" been present within the learner (*Symposium* 210c)—therefore, "in this birth the moment is instantly swallowed by recollection."[134]

Nevertheless, Climacus suggests in several passages of his treatise that the moment must be there, even if undetectable, whenever transitions take place between the factual and the ideal, the temporal being and the eternal essence. Thus, for example, when one regards events in time as work of the eternal God, a leap from the temporal to the eternal takes place in the moment. Similarly, also a quality appears or disappears in the moment as a result of a change in quantity: for example, when one continues to add individual seeds one after another, at some moment in time a new

128 *SKS* 4, 393 / *CA*, 90.

129 *SKS* 4, 392 / *CA*, 89.

130 *SKS* 4, 392 / *CA*, 88.

131 *SKS* 4, 213 / *PF*, 1.

132 *SKS* 4, 218–20 / *PF*, 9–11.

133 *SKS* 4, 221 / *PF*, 13.

134 *SKS* 4, 237 / *PF*, 31.

quality emerges from the seeds, namely, the quality of being a pile.[135] Furthermore, in a teleological progression, which Climacus apparently understands as a temporal process that aims at a timeless ideal, there is always a moment, a pause, in which wonder stands and waits for the free coming into existence of an essence.[136]

A note from 1844 shows how Kierkegaard was trying to comprehend the similarities and differences between these momentary transitions or leaps:

> *How does a new quality emerge from an unbroken quantitative determining?*
>
> I am a poor man who does not have many ideas; if I get one, I must take care that I hold on to it.
>
> A leap.
>
> The Platonic moment.
>
> *unsre Zuthat.* (see a passage in the *Phänomenologie*). *Hinter den Rücken*
>
> Every quality emerges then with a leap
>
> *Are these leaps, then, of just the same quality.*
>
> The leap by which water turns to ice (the leap by which I understand an author.) and the leap which is the transition from good to evil. (more sudden, Lessing's Faust, the evil spirit, who is hasty as the transition from good to evil.)
>
> *The qualitative difference between leaps.*
>
> The Paradox.
>
> Christ's entry into the world.[137]

Here the Platonic moment seems to be "where" the mysterious leaps "behind the back" of consciousness—something that Hegel writes about in the "Introduction" to his *Phenomenology of Spirit* (1807).[138] There are leaps at every event, in which a new quality breaks into existence. But there is also a qualitative difference between the leaps described and the paradoxical leap that Christianity is centered on.

In Christianity the leap and the moment are decisive. In Christianity there is a historical point of departure for an eternal consciousness, and a certain historical moment is of decisive significance. This moment is the fullness of time—a unique moment, "short and temporal" as moments are, and yet decisive and "filled with the eternal."[139] Such a moment emerges when the eternal resolution of the God is fulfilled in time.[140] This moment is the paradox, the paradox of God coming into existence as a man, living among men in the humble form of a servant, and dying as a man.[141] With respect to this world-historical moment, a moment may take place also in the history of a human individual. In the life of the individual, the moment of

---

135 *SKS* 4, 246–8 / *PF*, 40–43.

136 *SKS* 4, 279–81 with 273–5 / *PF*, 80–1 with 73–5.

137 *Pap.* V C 1 / *JP* 3, 2345. (Translation slightly modified.)

138 See *Hegel's Werke*, vol. 2, pp. 71–2.

139 *SKS* 4, 226 / *PF*, 18.

140 *SKS* 4, 232 / *PF*, 24–5.

141 *SKS* 4, 255 with 300 / *PF*, 51 with 104.

Christ's life may give rise either to a moment of offense or to a moment of faith.[142] In the thought experiment developed in *Philosophical Fragments*, the Christian moment thus means, first, God as a man,[143] and secondly, the moment in which faith in the God-man takes place in the individual, that is, the moment of receiving faith from the God-man.[144] This moment, in all its aspects, is to be understood as a work of God, as a wonder;[145] and only the believer, he who receives the condition from the God and is never able to forget it, may be considered as a contemporary with such a moment.[146]

In *Philosophical Fragments*, "the moment" thus becomes the decisive point of contrast between the Socratic and the Christian points of view. From the Socratic point of the view "the moment is not to be seen or to be distinguished; it does not exist, has not been, and will never come." From the Socratic point of the view the learner is himself the truth, his self-knowledge is God-knowledge, and the moment of decision is foolishness.[147] From the Christian point of view, everything centers on one moment of history which, for the believer, comes to mean the moment of liberation, the moment of conversion, the moment of rebirth, the moment of break with the past, and which the believer will never be able to forget, neither in time nor in eternity.[148]

There is no sign that Kierkegaard used any secondary literature on Socrates and Plato that he had not already consulted while formulating his view of *the moment* in *The Concept of Anxiety* and *Philosophical Fragments*. In fact, there are no references to any secondary literature on Plato in the journals and notebooks from that time, and in the texts themselves, Kierkegaard only cites Plato. The above-mentioned works by Werder, Schleiermacher, and Tennemann might have inspired Kierkegaard to explore the *Parmenides* in detail, but Vigilius' reading of it in *The Concept of Anxiety* is quite original. The view Climacus presents as the Socratic view in *Philosophical Fragments* seems to have been reconstructed from the material collected from various Platonic dialogues. The view that Climacus explicates—any

---

142 *SKS* 4, 252 / *PF*, 48. *SKS* 4, 261 / *PF*, 59.

143 "Whether or not [the disciple] is to go any further, *the moment* must decide (although it already was active in making him perceive that he is untruth)." (*SKS* 4, 229 / *PF*, 20.) "In its most abbreviated form the paradox can be called the moment." (*SKS* 4, 255 / *PF*, 51.) "In order for the teacher to be able to give the condition, he must be the god, and in order to put the learner in possession of it, he must be man. This contradiction is in turn the object of faith and is the paradox, the moment." (*SKS* 4, 264 / *PF*, 62.)

144 "How, then, does the learner come to an understanding with this paradox…It occurs when the understanding and the paradox happily encounter each other in the moment, when the understanding steps aside and the paradox gives itself, and the third something, the something in which this occurs…is that happy passion…*faith*." (*SKS* 4, 261 / *PF*, 59.) "How, then, does the learner become a believer or a follower? When the understanding is discharged and he receives the condition. When does he receive this? In the moment." (*SKS* 4, 264 / *PF*, 64.)

145 *SKS* 4, 242 / *PF*, 36. *SKS* 4, 267 / *PF*, 65–6.

146 *SKS* 4, 222 / *PF*, 1. *SKS* 4, 267–70 / *PF*, 66–9.

147 *SKS* 4, 220 / *PF*, 11. *SKS* 4, 255 / *PF*, 51–2.

148 *SKS* 4, 222–8 / *PF*, 13–20.

point of departure in time is just "a vanishing point, an occasion" for learning the eternal truth—cannot be found, as such, in any single Platonic dialogue.

In *The Concept of Anxiety* and *Philosophical Fragments*, the difference between the static Platonic conception of *eternity* (there, in itself, wanting nothing to do with the temporal) and the dynamic Christian conception of eternity (permeating time and encompassing temporality in all its dimensions) is explicated in clear terms. Also here, it is hard to find predecessors for Kierkegaard's view in the secondary literature he used. It seems that Kierkegaard relied upon his own intuitions that were formed while studying Plato for his dissertation, *The Concept of Irony*. In a footnote at the beginning of the work, Kierkegaard writes:

> Philosophy relates in this respect to history—in its truth, as eternal life to the temporal according to the Christian view—in its untruth, as eternal life to the temporal according to the Greek and the antique view in general. According to the latter view, eternal life began when one drank of the river Lethe in order to forget the past; according to the former, eternal life is attended by the bone-and-marrow-piercing consciousness of every idle word that is spoken.[149]

The story about deceased souls drinking from the stream of oblivion is told by Socrates in Plato's *Republic* 620d–621d. As early as 1840, Kierkegaard writes in the *Journal HH* that this story shows how the pagan world posited future existence in a "negative, polemical way" with the present.[150] In *The Concept of Anxiety*, the story is taken up again as an example of a demonic metaphysical way of conceiving of the eternal. Here Vigilius writes: "[T]he teaching of Christianity cannot be more sharply illuminated by any opposite than that of the Greek conception that the immortals first drank of Lethe in order to forget."[151] In harmony with the story, and in stark contrast to the Christian view, the temporal moment vanishes in *Philosophical Fragments* into eternity as the eternal is recollected.[152] The Christian understanding, which Kierkegaard contrasts with this pagan view in 1844, is eternity as the fullness of time, that is, eternity as revealed in Christ. Kierkegaard records this view as early as 1839 in the *Journal EE*: "*Eternity is the fullness of time* (this saying also understood in the sense in which it is used when it is said that Christ has come in the fullness of time)."[153] In the same journal, another entry anticipates the idea that eternity as the fullness of time could be attained by a human being in a transitory moment of time: "Such is the relationship between time and eternity—as it is found in the Hebrew word עד ['ad], which in the first place means *transitus* and thereafter eternity, only in such a way that eternity may not be thought of simply as a denominative of *transitus*, but also as a constant position of fullness."[154]

In *The Concept of Anxiety* and *Philosophical Fragments*, the contrast between the Greek and the Christian views is brought to a head; but at the same time the Greek

149 *SKS* 1, 72 / *CI*, 13.

150 *SKS* 18, 126, HH:5 / *KJN* 2, 120.

151 *SKS* 4, 453 / *CA*, 154.

152 *SKS* 4, 220 / *PF*, 11. *SKS* 4, 221 / *PF*, 13. *SKS* 4, 237 / *PF*, 31.

153 *SKS* 18, 31, EE:78 / *KJN* 2, 27.

154 *SKS* 18, 62, EE:185 / *KJN* 2, 57.

thinkers are presented as the best that the human race has been able to reach on its own. In Christianity, the life of the God in time fills time, which for Plato signified a vanishing, and it makes concrete the eternal that Plato and Socrates could conceive only as a timeless abstraction. But without God in time, faith, and the consciousness of sin, one cannot go beyond the Socratic. In fact, modern speculation works under the paradigm of recollection. It is essentially the Socratic view, even if it purports to go beyond the Socratic by "scientifically" confusing faith with the immediate and reconciliation with mediation.[155]

In *The Concept of Irony*, the speculative trichotomy was regarded as an advance beyond the Greek dichotomy.[156] *Either/Or*, *Repetition*, and *Johannes Climacus* show that it is much more difficult to attain the trichotomic spiritual structure in practice than in thought. In *The Concept of Anxiety* and *Philosophical Fragments*, speculative mediation is declared to be confusion and the paradoxical moment of faith is presented as the only possible point of unity between the eternal and temporal. On the other hand, Socratic ethical self-knowledge and Platonic dualism are now presented as the main alternatives for Christian faith: they make up the only alternative worth considering, whereas Hegelian speculation just confuses the concepts.

V. Concluding Unscientific Postscript *(1846)*

In the *Concluding Unscientific Postscript*, human existence in general is understood in light of the Platonic dualism of eternal and temporal. Climacus writes that, like *eros* in the *Symposium* (202c–204a), existence is "begotten by the infinite and the finite, the eternal and the temporal, and is therefore continually striving."[157] He characterizes existence also with a simile that resembles the famous one in the *Phaedrus* (253c–253e), "eternity is infinitely quick like the winged steed [Pegasus], temporality is an old nag, and the existing person is the driver."[158]

For Climacus, the dualistic structure of existence is the ground for continuous ethical striving. In *The Concept of Irony*, it was the lack of a positive moral view typical of irony that explained the continuous striving typical of Socratic *eros*.[159] In the *Concluding Unscientific Postscript*, a continuous striving expresses the ethical relationship of a temporal, finite subject to the eternal and the infinite. Climacus declares that every Greek thinker was occupied with ethics and existence and, therefore, each was involved in continuous striving. In existence, the eternal is that which gives continuity to the process of becoming. While an abstract eternity is outside motion, a concrete eternity is present in the existing person in passion: the idealizing passion anticipates the eternal in existence. Because Climacus also declares that every Greek thinker was essentially a passionate thinker, one may conclude that Socrates and Plato

---

155 *SKS* 4, 318–20 / *CA*, 10–12. *SKS* 4, 219 / *PF*, 10. *SKS* 4, 220 / *PF*, 11. *SKS* 4, 306 / *PF*, 111.

156 *SKS* 1, 93 / *CI*, 32.

157 *SKS* 7, 91 / *CUP1*, 92.

158 *SKS* 7, 283–4 / *CUP1*, 311–12.

159 *SKS* 1, 106–7 / *CI*, 45–6.

are now declared "not guilty" of abstract existence.[160] The accusation of abstraction is now directed toward modern speculative thought, that "absolutely" annuls the distinction between "here and hereafter" in the pure being of the eternal.[161]

The merit of having "paid attention to the essential meaning of existing"[162] belongs especially to Socrates. He realized that the eternal truth is a paradox when it is essentially related to the person that exists in temporality. Plato, on the other hand, forgot this and lost himself in recollection, that is, in speculative thought. But Climacus considers the Socratic and the Platonic views of how one comes to conceive of the eternal to be identical: the eternal truth is recollected in time.[163] Climacus associates this view with Religiousness *A*, the immanent ethical-religious view that Climacus has apparently developed from the Socratic view presented in *Philosophical Fragments* under the symbol *A*. According to this view, every individual is essentially related to the eternal and is structured equally eternally. In the realm of time, the individual discovers that he must presuppose himself to be eternal. Thus, the moment in time is swallowed by the eternal. In this view "my existence is an element within my eternal consciousness."[164]

The *Concluding Unscientific Postscript* is the last work in which Kierkegaard discusses time and eternity with direct reference to Socrates and Plato. The *Postscript* presents the Socratic relation to the eternal as an ethical and religious relationship for the subject. It is not hard to explain how Kierkegaard ends with this view of Socrates: it is the standard view presented by Xenophon and Plato. Rather, what would demand explanation is why he did not assume this standard view right away: in *The Concept of Irony*, Socrates was depicted as an amoral ironist with only a purely intellectual relationship to the eternal. On the other hand, some aspects of the later view are consistent with this early view presented in the dissertation. In the *Postscript* Socrates is still on the road to nowhere: objectively he is in untruth since he does not have the right conception of the eternal because he does not know Christ.

In the *Postscript* Socrates serves as an example of an existing individual who never forgets that he exists. As was the case in the *Fragments*, it is hard to find precursors to Climacus' reconstruction of Socrates in the secondary literature Kierkegaard used; and it is just as hard to find any single statement in Plato's works that corresponds to Climacus' language. In these dialogues Socrates, of course, never pays attention to the essential meaning of existence,[165] although his ethical and philosophical life as described by Xenophon and Plato might be considered to express it. Nor does Socrates point out anywhere that the eternal truth is a paradox when it is essentially related to the person that exists in temporality,[166] but his philosophical ignorance and his fascination for the endless philosophical quest for the eternal truth might be considered to express it indirectly. As an imaginative observer and reconstructing

160 *SKS* 7, 90–1 / *CUP1*, 91–2. *SKS* 7, 117 / *CUP1*, 121–2. *SKS* 7, 283–5 / *CUP1*, 311–13.
161 *SKS* 7, 518 / *CUP1*, 570–1.
162 *SKS* 7, 187 / *CUP1*, 204.
163 *SKS* 7, 187–9 / *CUP1*, 204–7.
164 *SKS* 7, 520–1 / *CUP1*, 573.
165 See *SKS* 7, 187 / *CUP1*, 204.
166 See *SKS* 7, 187–8 / *CUP1*, 205–6.

thinker, Climacus diagnoses and tries to capture the essential characteristics of the spiritual life of Socrates. And for all we know, perhaps Socrates would have accepted his diagnosis.

Kierkegaard begins *The Concept of Irony* with a Hegelian criticism of the abstract dichotomy typical both of Socratic existence and Platonic thought, both of which are said to separate the temporal from the eternal. In *The Concept of Irony*, both Hegelian speculation and Christianity represent syntheses that overcome the Greek dichotomy.

In the second phase, this Hegelian criticism is turned against Hegelian philosophy itself. In *Either/Or*, Judge William criticizes the abstract and dualistic existence of the distracted Hegelian philosophers that imagine that they exist in the sphere of thought and, at the same time, turn a blind eye to the problems pertaining to personal existence in concrete historical actuality. Criticism of Hegelian philosophy is repeated by Constantin Constantius in his letter to Heiberg as well as by the young Johannes Climacus in the manuscript that bears his name as its title: Hegelian philosophy does not help the individual overcome the dualism of the eternal and the historical. Recollection of the eternal in time is not enough; what is needed is the repetition of the eternal in time.

In *The Concept of Anxiety* and *Philosophical Fragments*, then, the Christian moment is introduced. The paradoxical coming of the eternal God into time overcomes the dichotomy of time and eternity; his existence in temporality as a man makes up the world-historical moment in which the temporal and the eternal are synthesized. Corresponding to this, in the history of an individual a moment of faith may occur that makes the eternal present in the succession of time and gives significance for temporality. It is worth noticing, however, that in the Christian "concretion" that results from the acceptance of faith, the dichotomy of human existence is not only annulled but also preserved. The eternal does not become concrete only in faith, but also in the simultaneous sin-consciousness. Hence, it is correct to speak about "infinite qualitative difference between time and eternity,"[167] also with respect to Kierkegaard's *Christian* conception: as long as he is "on the earth" the sinful individual remains partly separated from God who is "in heaven."[168]

In the light of this, it is understandable that in the *Concluding Unscientific Postscript*, Climacus criticizes Hegelian speculation with the help of Socrates. In contrast to Hegelians, Socrates was at least conscious that in his personal existence, the eternal and temporal were separated. The consciousness of the problem and the ethical striving of Socrates are, thus, to be preferred to the illusory Hegelian solutions: there is more concretion in the existing Socrates than in all the abstract syntheses of Hegel.

If we consider the movement that takes place from *The Concept of Irony* to the *Concluding Unscientific Postscript*, we may regard it as a kind of double negation in which Socrates and Hegel are used to negate each other. The dialectical movement aims beyond philosophical positions towards Christian existence, in which the eternal becomes concrete for the existing individual: positively in faith and negatively in sin-consciousness.

---

167 See Karl Barth, *Der Römerbrief*, Zürich: Theologischer Verlag 1978, p. XIII.

168 Ibid.

Phaedrus:
Kierkegaard on Socrates' Self-Knowledge—and Sin

David D. Possen

We need not "appeal to statistics," Sophia Scopetea rightly notes, to show that "Kierkegaard makes his Socrates revolve around a very few recurring Platonic passages."[1] Though it is complex and revolutionary, Kierkegaard's portrait of Socrates indeed centers on a tiny group of core citations from Plato. These texts include Socrates' professions of ignorance in the *Apology*; his talk of recollection in the *Meno*, *Phaedo*, and *Phaedrus*; his praise of wonder, together with his self-description as a midwife, in the *Theaetetus*; and his confession, at *Phaedrus* 229e–230a, that he cannot tell whether he is a simple being, gentle and divinely blessed, or "a complex creature...more puffed up with pride than Typhon."[2]

The present article will focus on the last of these passages—and its extraordinary importance to Kierkegaard. Kierkegaard interpreted Socrates' remark about Typhon, we will see, not just as a sign of Socrates' intrepidity in facing his ignorance, but also as evidence that something analogous to the Christian consciousness of *sin* may already be discerned in Socrates' self-understanding. Kierkegaard used the latter suggestion, in turn, to bolster a thesis fundamental to his authorship: that the "simple wise man" Socrates, though a pagan and millennia out of date, still has much to teach the laity and clergy of Lutheran Denmark.[3]

In what follows, we will explore the significance of *Phaedrus* 229e–230a for Kierkegaard's broader authorial aims. We will begin, in Section I, with a detailed tour of Kierkegaard's interpretive approaches to the passage. Kierkegaard worked methodically, we will see, to depict Socrates' apprehension of his monstrousness as an analogy for the Christian consciousness of *sin*. In Section II, we will turn to *Philosophical Fragments*, the book in which this Socratic-Christian analogy takes center stage. We will observe how this book both tries and fails to dispense with its

---

1 Sophia Scopetea, "Becoming the Flute," *Kierkegaardiana*, vol. 18, 1996, pp. 29–43, see p. 37.

2 Plato, *Collected Dialogues*, ed. by Edith Hamilton and Huntington Cairns, Princeton, New Jersey: Princeton University Press 1963, p. 478.

3 "That [noble] simple wise man [of old]," *hiin* [*ædle*] *eenfoldige Vise* [*i Oldtiden*], is Kierkegaard's standard epithet for Socrates in this context. See, for example, *SKS* 10, 226 / *CD*, 218–19.

own Socratic portrait, rooted in *Phaedrus* 229e–230a, of the transformative process of Christian conversion.

We will close by inquiring, in Section III, *why* Kierkegaard sought to harness Socrates' line about Typhon for so controversial a purpose. We will suggest that Kierkegaard's goal was to refute the claims and assumptions about Socrates and Christianity that had been promulgated by Hans Lassen Martensen (1808–84), his bitterest rival. Whereas Martensen sought to characterize Christian thought as an advance beyond Socratic ignorance and irony, Kierkegaard appealed to the Typhon passage, we will argue, in order to stress the *similarity* between Christian faith and Socrates' self-knowledge—and thereby to insist, *contra* Martensen and following the strictures of Lutheran tradition, that human reason cannot possibly think its way around (let alone beyond) its unceasing need of grace.

I. "A Corrupt and Corruptible Man": Socratic Self-Knowledge and the Discovery of Sin

Kierkegaard's interpretation of *Phaedrus* 229e–230a is both idiosyncratic and highly imaginative. It became "philologically possible," Scopetea aptly notes, only in the wake of a "chain of successive displacements of meaning."[4] When we examine the passage in its original context, we find that it functions as the punch line of a consequential opening *retort* by Socrates to Phaedrus, his seductive interlocutor. This retort then sets the tone for much of the dialogue that follows.

The *Phaedrus* records a debate about a series of *tensions*: tensions between *eros* and trickery, between openness and concealment, and between speech and writing. Most fundamentally, the *Phaedrus* dramatizes the tension between *temptation* and *resistance*. In the dialogue's middle act, Socrates finds himself briefly seduced into donning a blindfold and praising the "non-lover," the man who holds himself aloof from erotic love.[5] Socrates immediately regrets his speech. Hot with shame, he atones for his misdeed by offering a new speech, the Palinode, in praise of the madness of erotic love.[6]

This central scene of seduction and recantation is framed by a variety of references, spread throughout the dialogue, to Socrates' alternating susceptibility and resistance to temptation. The *Phaedrus*' pastoral setting already indicates, for example, that Socrates has in a sense allowed himself to be seduced before the conversation has even begun. For Socrates normally never ventures into the countryside—because, he insists, "Trees and open country won't teach me anything, whereas men in town do. Yet you seem," he admits to Phaedrus, "to have discovered a recipe for getting me out."[7]

Phaedrus, for his part, is an avid consumer of speeches, myths, and tales.[8] In his opening banter, Phaedrus tries to charm Socrates into telling him a story—

4 Scopetea, "Becoming the Flute," p. 34.

5 *Phaedrus*, 237a–241d.

6 *Phaedrus*, 244a–257b.

7 *Phaedrus*, 230d, Plato, *Collected Dialogues*, p. 479.

8 I am indebted to Jonathan Lear for his insight on this point.

specifically, into offering a scientific interpretation of a well-known Athenian tale of seduction. "Is this not the place," he asks, where "Boreas is said to have carried off Oreithuia from the banks of the Ilissus?"[9] Once Socrates assents, Phaedrus asks him whether he *believes* the myth. Socrates replies that he doubts its literal meaning; yet he refuses to take Phaedrus' bait and delve into an extensive discussion of the myth's scientific basis. Were he to do so, Socrates remarks, he would eventually have to provide a naturalistic account of the entire Athenian mythological bestiary—of centaurs and the Chimera, of Gorgons and of Pegasuses. But Socrates has no time, he tells Phaedrus, to busy himself with such inquiries:

> I myself have certainly no time for the business, and I'll tell you why, my friend. I can't as yet "know myself," as the inscription at Delphi enjoins, and so long as that ignorance remains it seems to me ridiculous to inquire into extraneous matters. Consequently I don't bother about such things, but accept the current beliefs about them, and direct my inquiries, as I have just said, rather to myself, to discover whether I really am a more complex creature and more puffed up with pride than Typhon, or a simpler, gentler being whom heaven has blessed with a quiet, un-Typhonic nature.[10]

The opportunity to discuss and demystify the mythical beasts of Athenian lore, even if for the sake of seeking truth, is a temptation that Socrates knows he must resist. For in his present state of ignorance, Socrates cannot say whether he is not himself as furious, or as deluded by pride, as the legendary beast and arch-rebel Typhon.[11] It would be "ridiculous," Socrates argues, for him to question the existence of monsters in the heavens, or in the past, when he cannot yet rule out the possibility that a monster lurks in his own soul.

In its immediate dramatic context, Socrates' line about Typhon serves to distinguish his own philosophical project from that of a thinker interested in the nature and laws of our wider world. Unlike predecessors such as Anaxagoras or Empedocles, who concocted elaborate theories of cosmic ontology, and unlike the "Socrates" caricatured in Aristophanes' *Clouds*, who contemplates the heavens in utter indifference to his earthly surroundings, the Socrates of Plato's *Phaedrus* is wholly occupied with the puzzle of his own human nature. This is the Socrates of whom Cicero famously wrote: "Socrates was the first who brought down philosophy from the heavens, placed it in cities, introduced it into families, and obliged it to examine into life and morals, and good and evil."[12]

---

9 *Phaedrus*, 229b. Plato, *Collected Dialogues*, p. 478.

10 *Phaedrus*, 229d–230a. Plato, *Collected Dialogues*, p. 478.

11 Typhon, spawn of Gaea and Tartarus, was a fiery monster with a hundred dragons' heads and countless animal voices. He rebelled against Zeus, and nearly wrested control of the world from him, after Zeus's victory against the Titans; but Zeus defeated Typhon with a massive thunderbolt, and imprisoned him in the Underworld. Cf. Hesiod, *Theogony*, lines 820–68.

12 Marcus Tullius Cicero, *Tusculan Disputations: On the Nature of the Gods, and on the Commonwealth*, trans. by Charles Duke Yonge, New York: Cosimo 2005, p. 166. See also Friedrich Schleiermacher, "On the Worth of Socrates as a Philosopher," trans. by Connop Thirlwall, in *The Philological Museum*, vols. 1–4, ed. by Julius Hare, Cambridge: J. Smith 1832–33, vol. 2, pp. 538–55, see p. 553: "Socrates...made no excursions to points remote from

The attributes of Socrates to which Cicero's remark calls our attention—Socrates' continual focus on the question of his own nature, his intrepidity in confronting his ignorance at every moment, and his consistency in resisting (or at least regretting) distractions—are all traits that excited Kierkegaard's unceasing admiration. And occasionally, Kierkegaard does allude to *Phaedrus* 229e–230a as a passage that exemplifies these features of Socrates.[13] Yet for the most part, the references to the Typhon line in Kierkegaard's authorship address it from a rather different angle, namely, with a narrow focus on Socrates' suggestion that he might be a beast,[14] and with a view to a question that is of specialized interest to Christian scholars of Plato, namely, was Socrates' understanding of human nature rich or morbid enough to take account of the phenomenon that Christians call "sin"?

Kierkegaard's interest in the latter question was perhaps sparked by a monograph on Socrates and Christianity by Ferdinand Christian Baur (1792–1860), which is cited and parodied extensively in *The Concept of Irony*.[15] Baur's book cites *Phaedrus* 229e–230a in order to demonstrate that Socratic ignorance is compatible, even continuous, with the consciousness of sin that Christianity inspired in his followers.[16] According to Baur, Socrates' consideration of the possibility that he is a beast "more monstrous than Typhon" illustrates that "the more deeply consciousness burrows into itself, the more surely self-knowledge encounters the sin that inheres in a human being's deepest essence."[17] For Baur, when Socrates asks whether he might not be a more ferocious beast than Typhon, he is already in the act of discovering his own entanglement in sin.

Kierkegaard disagreed strongly, we will see, with Baur's understanding of the origins of the consciousness of sin. But he did detect in Socrates' Typhonic anxiety an *analogy* to the dread of sin that Christianity—particularly orthodox Lutheran

---

his centre, but devoted his whole life to the task of exciting his leading idea as extensively and as vividly as possible in others; his whole aim was [that] this foundation might be securely laid, before he proceeded further. But till then his advice was, not to accumulate fresh masses of opinions; this he for his part would permit only so far as it was demanded by the wants of active life, and for this reason he might say, that if those who investigated meteoric phenomena had any hope of producing them at their pleasure, he should be more ready to admit their researches."

13 Cf. *Pap.* X–5 B 107, p. 301: "The *summa summarum* of [Socrates'] knowledge in his seventieth year was that he did not know with certainty what a human being is. How are we to explain this? Must we not say: because he used his time first and foremost to consider what a human being is? This question goes by so quickly for the 'speedy heads.' For they leap over the question; they assume that they know the answer."

14 See Scopetea, "Becoming the Flute," p. 37.

15 On Kierkegaard's relation to Baur, see my "F.C. Baur: On the Similarity and Dissimilarity between Jesus and Socrates," in *Kierkegaard and His German Contemporaries*, Tome II, *Theology*, ed. by Jon Stewart, Aldershot: Ashgate 2007 (*Kierkegaard Research: Sources, Reception, and Resources*, vol. 6), pp. 23–38.

16 Ferdinand Christian Baur, *Das Christliche des Platonismus, oder Sokrates und Christus*, Tübingen, L.F. Fues 1837 (*ASKB* 422), pp. 23–4.

17 Ibid., pp. 23–5.

Christianity—ascribes to its followers.[18] In *Fear and Trembling*, for example, Kierkegaard's pseudonym Johannes de silentio appeals to Socrates' anxiety in order to chastise contemporary Lutheran writers who are unconcerned about sin, and who in fact preach that human beings have "already attained the highest."[19] "Oddly enough," Johannes contends, "even in the inherently more irresponsible and less reflective paganism the two authentic representatives of the Greek view of life, γνωθι σαυτον ["Know thyself!"], each in his own way hinted that, by penetratingly concentrating on oneself, one first and foremost discovers the disposition to evil. I scarcely need to say that I am thinking of Pythagoras and Socrates."[20] Here the pagan Socrates, together with Pythagoras, is lauded for having come closer to the consciousness of sin than have the nominally Christian targets of Johannes' polemic. Johannes' praise of Socrates is, in effect, a forceful reading of *Phaedrus* 229e–230a. Socrates responds to the Delphic command by devoting his life to seeking the truth about himself; and the product of his quest for self-knowledge is the discovery that he might be a monster worse than Typhon—that is, monstrously *evil*.

With this we observe a crucial link in the "chain of successive displacements of meaning"[21] to which Scopetea refers. What Socrates refers to as the possibility of being more "puffed up with pride" [μᾶλλον ἐπιτεθυμμένον] and complex than Typhon becomes, for Johannes, simply "the disposition to evil."[22] Given what Hesiod's *Theogony* tells us about Typhon's nature and conduct, the latter phrase is certainly a reasonable gloss. And yet, it can easily lead to an anachronism: for Johannes fails to consider whether what *we* mean by the "disposition to evil" could possibly have been on Socrates' mind at all.[23]

An even more daring gloss on *Phaedrus* 229e–230a appears in the *Concluding Unscientific Postscript*, whose pseudonymous author Johannes Climacus wryly reports that Socrates is said "to have discovered within himself...a disposition to all evil; it may even have been this discovery that prompted him to give up the study of astronomy, which the times now demand."[24] Here Johannes de silentio's "the disposition to evil" [*Dispositionen til Onde*] becomes Johannes Climacus' "a disposition to *all* evil" [*en Disposition til* alt *Onde*].[25] This suggests that we are no longer talking about a malicious *streak* in human nature, but are contemplating the capacity to become malicious without limit: to be as evil as can be, and perhaps even to be evil through and through.

---

18 In Luther's words: "God leaves us...in our sinful lusts in order that He may keep us in His fear and humility that we may always flee to his grace, always in fear of sinning." *Luther's Works: American Edition*, ed. by Jaroslav Pelikan and Helmut T. Lehmann, Philadelphia: Fortress Press and Minneapolis: Concordia Publishing House 1955–86, vol. 25, p. 268.

19 *SKS* 4, 190 / *FT*, 100.

20 *SKS* 4, 190, note 1 / *FT*, 100, note.

21 Scopetea, "Becoming the Flute," p. 34.

22 *Phaedrus*, 230a; *SKS* 4, 190, note 1 / *FT*, 100, note.

23 *SKS* 4, 190, note 1 / *FT*, 100, note.

24 *SKS* 7, 150 / *CUP1*, 161.

25 *SKS* 4, 190, note 1 / *FT*, 100, note; *SKS* 7, 150 / *CUP1*, 161.

Let us examine this passage more closely. It emerges in the course of a revealing aside by Climacus, in which the pseudonym explicitly compares himself to Socrates:

> Alas, it is only too well known to the few who know me and, I admit, to myself also, that I am a corrupt and a corruptible man. It is all too true. Whereas all the good people are promptly all set to attend to the future of world history, I am obliged many a time to sit at home and mourn over myself....The only one who consoles me is Socrates. He is supposed to have discovered within himself, so it is said, a disposition to all evil...I willingly admit how little I resemble Socrates otherwise. Very likely his ethical knowledge helped him to make this discovery. Such is not the case with me; in strong passions and the like, I have material enough, and therefore pain enough in forming something good out of it with the aid of reason.
>
> Let us, then, lest we be disturbed by thinking about me, stick to Socrates, to whom *Fragments* also had recourse. By means of his ethical knowledge, he discovered that he had a disposition to all evil. Now it is no longer so easy—one, two, three—to arrive at the world-historical.[26]

Climacus' polemic in this passage bears certain similarities to that of Johannes de silentio in the excerpt from *Fear and Trembling* that we examined earlier. Like Johannes de silentio, Climacus opposes contemporary thinkers who write as though they, and perhaps we, have already succeeded in becoming "good children, then good young people, then good husbands and wives."[27] Like Johannes de silentio, Climacus cites Socrates' Typhonic anxiety as a model of the self-concern that his contemporaries lack. Unlike Johannes de silentio, however,[28] Climacus goes on to exhibit *himself* as a fresh exemplar of ethical self-doubt. Climacus confesses that he is "a corrupt and corruptible man," full of strong passions, who lacks Socrates' "ethical knowledge." With this last remark, Climacus transforms his confession into a farcical attempt to out-worry Socrates. Whereas Socrates worries that he is a monster worse than Typhon, Climacus suggests that he himself is, if anything, an even more monstrous figure than Socrates.

Climacus frames his confessional soliloquy with a series of apologetic remarks—as though his words were an embarrassing imposition on the reader. Behind this apologetic tone, however, sarcasm lurks. For Climacus' words of confession—"I am a corrupt and corruptible man"—are in fact reminiscent of the words by which Lutherans acknowledge their fallenness in prayer, declaring themselves to be sinners who are prone to further sin.[29] Climacus' confession can be read as a rhetorical device

---

26 *SKS* 7, 150 / *CUP1*, 161–2.

27 *SKS* 7, 149 / *CUP1*, 161.

28 This is not entirely fair to Johannes de silentio. For he writes of how one "may in anxiety and horror discover and lure forth—if in no other way, then through anxiety—the dark emotions hiding in *every* human life"—including, presumably, in his own. *SKS* 4, 190 / *FT*, 100. (My emphasis.)

29 For an English parallel to the "General Confession" [*Almindelig Skriftemaal*] used in the Danish Church of Kierkegaard's day, see Martin Luther, *The Shorter Catechism of Dr Martin Luther*, trans. by Gustavus Anthony Wachsel, London: St George German Lutheran Chapel 1770, p. 65.

that serves the same purpose as does his invocation of the self-doubting Socrates of *Phaedrus* 229e–230a: it is to encourage his audience to think about sin in a mood of earnestness and confession (rather than in an abstract or speculative way).

In both *Fear and Trembling* and the *Concluding Unscientific Postscript*, then, Socrates' Typhonic worry is cited as an instructive analogy to the anxiety about sin that Christianity demands of its adherents. This fact prompts us to ask about the scope and limits of this analogy. What is the relationship between the Typhonic propensities that Socrates "discovered" in himself, to use Johannes de silentio's and Johannes Climacus' term, and the *sin* of which Christians are called to become aware? Baur, we saw above, suggests that the two are ultimately identical: that a Socratic search for self-knowledge is bound eventually to discover "the sin that inheres in a human being's deepest essence."[30]

Kierkegaard, unlike Baur, adhered to the traditional Lutheran claim that the consciousness of sin is a gift of grace, unavailable to non-Christians like Socrates.[31] It follows that, even if an analogy obtains between the consciousness of sin and Socrates' Typhonic anxiety, these two states of self-concern nonetheless differ at their core. What, then, is the difference between them? This last question is taken up in detail only once in Kierkegaard's authorship: in Climacus' *Philosophical Fragments*. And so it is to that compact and challenging text that we will now turn.

II. The Consciousness of Sin: An Advance Beyond Socrates' Self-Knowledge?

The conceit of Climacus' *Philosophical Fragments* is that it is a "thought-experiment" that leaves Socratic thought behind. The book ends with a boast: "This project indisputably goes beyond the Socratic, as is apparent at every point."[32] The remainder of the *Fragments* is designed to substantiate—or, rather, to *seem* to substantiate—this consequential closing claim.

In his opening pages, Climacus identifies Socratic thought with the Doctrine of Recollection: namely, with the thesis that "every human being already possesses the truth," and with the assertion that all teaching—even teaching by or about God—is merely a matter of jogging our memories.[33] Climacus then asks what would follow if these Socratic principles turned out to be false: that is, if *not* all learning were recollection, if *not* all knowledge were immanent, and if it *were* possible for us to learn things that are radically new to us.[34] The remainder of the book explores the conditions and ramifications of these anti-Socratic or, as we will call them, "trans-Socratic" assumptions.[35] Impressively, Climacus manages to derive nearly all the fundamentals of Christian doctrine from his trans-Socratic assumptions. In short

---

30 Baur, *Das Christliche des Platonismus*, pp. 23–5.

31 On Kierkegaard, Lutheran orthodoxy, and the incomprehensibility of sin, see the passage from the Smalcald Articles (Part III, Article 1, § 3) cited at *SKS* 4, 333 / *CA*, 26.

32 *SKS* 4, 306 / *PF*, 111.

33 *SKS* 4, 222 / *PF*, 13.

34 Ibid.

35 As Climacus and Kierkegaard elsewhere make clear, the failure to adopt recollection as a doctrine is by no means an "anti-Socratic" position. I use the word "trans-Socratic" in

order, he arrives at a theory of original sin, a tale of divine incarnation and atonement, a category of faith, a symptomatology of offense, and a call to contemporaneity with the incarnate god.

In his book's climactic Chapter III, Climacus undertakes to describe *how* trans-Socratic (i.e., Christian) learning takes place: that is, how a human being can come into possession of a truth that is radically new to him. Climacus contends that, in the instant of non-Socratic learning, the learner must simultaneously become aware of the absolute untruth in which he has been living. In good Lutheran fashion, Climacus calls this awareness "the consciousness of sin" and insists that this consciousness cannot be acquired or communicated except via direct divine revelation.[36] Indeed, Climacus explains, a transformative "moment" of revelation is absolutely necessary if a human being is to climb from merely Socratic learning (in this context, recollection) to the heights of trans-Socratic learning:

> If we do not assume the moment, then we go back to Socrates, and it was precisely from him that we wanted to take leave in order to discover something. If the moment is posited, the paradox is there, for in its most abbreviated form the paradox can be called the moment. Through the moment, the learner becomes untruth; the person who knew himself becomes confused about himself [*raadvild over sig selv*] and instead of self-knowledge he acquires the consciousness of sin.[37]

In the "moment" of Christian revelation, the learner is confronted with the fact of his untruth. He becomes "confused about himself" [*raadvild over sig selv*], and so gains the consciousness of sin "instead of self-knowledge." In the latter words we may detect a stark contrast between the Christian learner's consciousness of sin and Socrates' naïve self-knowledge. For as we saw in Section I, Socrates' Typhonic doubt is fêted consistently, elsewhere in Kierkegaard's writings, as a form of self-knowledge: namely, as the ignorant Socrates' earnest response to the command of Delphic Apollo: "Know thyself!"[38]

A bit earlier in the text of *Fragments*, Climacus had explained why it is that Socrates, for all his devotion to the task of self-knowledge, never managed to burst the bounds of immanence and recollection. The reason, Climacus there revealed, is that despite all of Socrates' attempts to come to terms with his own ignorance, the god simply did not allow him to discover the secret of his absolute untruth. Citing *Phaedrus* 229e–230a, Climacus writes that Socrates

> became almost confused about himself [*næsten raadvild over sig selv*] when he came up against the different; he no longer knew whether he was a more curious monster than Typhon or whether there was something divine in him. What did he lack, then? The

order to keep firmly in view the overarching conceit of *Fragments*, namely, Climacus' claim to have gone beyond Socrates.

36 *SKS* 4, 224 / *PF*, 14–15. On Lutheranism and the incomprehensibility of sin, see *SKS* 4, 333 / *CA*, 26. On Lutheranism and the necessity of Gracious revelation "to teach fallen man what sin is," see *SKS* 11, 209 / *SUD*, 96.

37 *SKS* 4, 255 / *PF*, 52.

38 *SKS* 4, 190, note 1 / *FT*, 100, note. See Section I above.

> consciousness of sin, which he could no more teach to any other person than any other person could teach it to him. Only the god could teach it—if he wanted to be teacher.[39]

Ultimately, as Climacus tells the story, God "did indeed want to be" humanity's teacher. God made himself available to each individual by coming to earth in the person of the transformative God-man, who alone reveals and heals sin.[40] Yet this event occurred too late, lamentably enough, for Socrates. Socrates never had the chance to acquire the consciousness of sin and so was never able to gain access to the transcendent truth ("the different"[41]). Rather, all of his efforts to approach the truth only left Socrates further mired in untruth. Socrates became, at best, "nearly confused about himself" [*næsten raadvild over sig selv*]: that is, confused about whether he was man or monster.

The last phrase should give us pause. In the passage cited previously, the Christian learner's *success* in gaining the consciousness of sin—an achievement that allowed the learner to progress from untruth to truth—was described as his becoming "confused about himself" [*raadvild over sig selv*]. Here Socrates' *failure* to gain the consciousness of sin—a failure that keeps him trapped in untruth—is described as his becoming "*nearly* confused about himself" [*næsten raadvild over sig selv*]. These formulations clearly imply a parallel between Christian and Socratic experience: both, it seems, are varieties of self-confusion. And yet it is equally clear that there must be an enormous *difference* between these two kinds of bafflement—a difference concealed by the tiny modifier "nearly" [*næsten*]. This difference must be nothing less than the difference between truth and untruth; the difference between Christian knowledge and Socratic ignorance; and the difference between the consciousness of sin and Typhonic doubt.

What, then, is this difference? Climacus has already indicated his answer. "What did [Socrates] lack, then? The consciousness of sin."[42] But this answer is of little use to the reader. For on Climacus' own account,[43] sin cannot be made manifest to a human being except by means of a revelation.[44] Climacus certainly cannot show us *himself* what sin is. For this reason, he certainly cannot explain how the state of self-confusion in which a Christian moves "beyond Socrates" differs from Socrates' own state of Typhonic doubt.

In his *Postscript*, Climacus acknowledges explicitly that he can do no more than gesture at the difference between Socrates' Typhonic doubt and the Christian consciousness of sin. Climacus asserts, in fact, that such gesturing is the best that

---

39 *SKS* 4, 251 / *PF*, 47. For the sake of consistency with a subsequent citation, I have emended the Hongs' "bewildered about himself" to "confused about himself."

40 *SKS* 4, 252 / *PF*, 47.

41 "What, then, is the unknown [truth]?...It is the different, the absolutely different." *SKS* 4, 249 / *PF*, 44.

42 *SKS* 4, 251 / *PF*, 47.

43 "What, then, is the difference? Indeed, what difference but sin...But how is the understanding to grasp this? ...Just to come to know that the god is the different, man needs the god and then comes to know that the god is absolutely different from him." *SKS* 4, 251 / *PF*, 46.

44 *SKS* 4, 224 / *PF*, 14–15. See also *SKS* 11, 209 / *SUD*, 96.

anyone can do. Christianity, he argues, involves "the absolute paradox, the absurd, the incomprehensible"; as a result, all "attempts at wanting to understand" it directly are "ludicrous."[45] Climacus does concede that there are various *analogies*, such as "Socrat[ic] ignorance," capable of shedding light on Christian experience.[46] He even allows that these analogies may be employed in order "to define the paradox," that is, to define Christianity as such.[47] Yet whenever we do employ analogies to Christianity for this purpose, Climacus warns, we must take care not to lose sight of the fact that our analogies are *mere* analogies. We must "continually bear in mind the absolute difference that there is no analogy...and thus the [analogy's] application, when it is understood, is a revocation."[48] If we fail to keep this fact in mind—if, for example, we attempt to comprehend Christianity in its "absolute difference" from its Socratic analogy—then we are liable simply to delude ourselves: to conflate Christianity with its analogy. In Climacus' words, we "will mistakenly revoke the paradox by means of the analogy"—instead of defining the paradox properly by first calling attention to, and then revoking, our analogy.[49]

Climacus' appeal to *Phaedrus* 229e–230a in the *Fragments* is best understood, on my reading, as a careful application of the method just described. Climacus cites Socrates' Typhonic doubt as a fruitful analogy to the trans-Socratic learner's acquisition of the consciousness of sin. He even manages to define the latter in terms of the former: both, he tells us, are forms of bewilderment (being "confused" [*raadvild*], as opposed to being "nearly confused" [*næsten raadvild*]) about our nature. Next, Climacus *revokes* the analogy: he indicates that the trans-Socratic predicament differs so starkly from its Socratic analogue that we would need a direct divine revelation in order to understand the difference between them. And finally, having said this much, Climacus demurely moves on. He leaves aside the mechanics of trans-Socratic learning—that is, Christian conversion—and proceeds (in Chapters IV and V) to a new topic: what it means to call oneself a Christian in an age when nearly everyone claims the same.

Climacus' modesty is entirely appropriate. For who is he to presume to explain the infinite difference—sin—by which Socrates' self-knowledge in ignorance differs from the Christian's consciousness of sin? What human being, indeed, is qualified to offer such an explanation at all—apart from God incarnate? In the words of a later pseudonym: "There must be a revelation from God to teach fallen man what sin is, a communication that, quite consistently, must be believed, because it is a dogma."[50] It is sheer fantasy, on this account, to imagine that we (or Climacus) can explain how the Christian consciousness of sin differs from its Socratic analogy. Put another way, we would need to be "confused" indeed—in the ordinary sense of the word—to imagine that we know the relevant difference between being "almost confused" [*næsten raadvild*] and fully "confused" [*raadvild*].

---

45 *SKS* 7, 511 / *CUP1*, 561–2.

46 *SKS* 7, 515 / *CUP1*, 566.

47 *SKS* 7, 527 / *CUP1*, 579–80.

48 *SKS* 7, 515 / *CUP1*, 567.

49 *SKS* 7, 527 / *CUP1*, 579–80.

50 *SKS* 11, 209 / *SUD*, 96.

Taken as a whole, then, Climacus' invocations of *Phaedrus* 229e–230a in *Philosophical Fragments* do not in fact help to teach us how to think our way beyond Socrates. On the contrary, they show us that we can do no better, when we try to wrap our minds around Christian conversion, than thinking through the *Socratic analogy* to such conversion, namely, Typhonic self-doubt—except in so far as revelation and grace come to our aid. In the next section, we will consider *why* Kierkegaard would have wanted us to draw this sobering conclusion; and why, more broadly, he was so eager to bring Socrates' Typhonic anxiety into conversation with the Lutheran dialectic of faith and reason.

III. Socrates as a Weapon: Kierkegaard contra *Martensen*

It is by now well-known and well-documented that Kierkegaard's pseudonymous writings are deeply polemical in character; and that Hans Lassen Martensen, a prominent Copenhagen academic and cleric, was a chief target of several of the pseudonymous books, including *Philosophical Fragments*.[51] In the pages that follow, I will suggest that it was in order to attack Martensen that Kierkegaard made such curious use of *Phaedrus* 229e–230a in his writings. Put briefly, Kierkegaard condemned Martensen for failing to pay heed to the Lutheran doctrine of *sola gratia* (the monergism of grace) in his efforts to blaze a speculative trail to Christianity's truth. In this context, Kierkegaard set forth Socrates—the self-doubting Socrates of the *Phaedrus*—as a foil for Martensen: as a better model, albeit a non-Christian one, of proper Lutheran self-regard.

Martensen had built his reputation on the claim that, by paying proper regard to the power of God's grace, a Christian thinker may *ascend*—beyond the variously ironic, ignorant, and autonomous standpoints of Socrates, Dante, Descartes, Kant, Goethe, Schleiermacher, and Hegel[52]—to a standpoint of higher, Christian

---

[51] On Kierkegaard's polemic against Martensen, see Curtis L. Thompson, "Introduction," in *Between Hegel and Kierkegaard*, ed. by Curtis L. Thompson and David J. Kangas, Atlanta: Scholars Press 1997, pp. 40–80; J.H. Schjørring, "Martensen," in *Kierkegaard's Teachers*, ed. by Niels Thulstrup and Marie Mikulová Thulstrup, Copenhagen: Reitzel 1982 (*Bibliotheca Kierkegaardiana*, vol. 10), pp. 177–207; and Jon Stewart, *Kierkegaard's Relations to Hegel Reconsidered*, Cambridge and New York: Cambridge University Press 2003. On the polemic against Martensen in *Philosophical Fragments*, see Stewart, *Kierkegaard's Relations to Hegel Reconsidered*, pp. 336–77.

[52] On Martensen's claim to have advanced beyond Hegel, see Schjørring, "Martensen," p. 185. See also Hans Lassen Martensen, *Af mit Levned*, vols. 1–2, Copenhagen: Gyldendal 1882, vol. 2, p. 45, cited and translated by Curtis Thompson in *Between Hegel and Kierkegaard*, ed. by Curtis Thompson and David Kangas, p. 8. For another source (1836) in which Martensen claimed to have "gone beyond" Hegel, see *Between Hegel and Kierkegaard*, ed. by Curtis Thompson and David Kangas, p. 9, note 11. On Martensen's prescription for how a "Protestant poet"—presumably his ally Johan Ludvig Heiberg (1791–1860)—might improve upon the poetry of Goethe, see Martensen, "Betragtninger over Ideen af Faust med Hensyn paa Lenaus *Faust*," *Perseus: Journal for den speculative Idee*, no. 1, 1837, pp. 91–164; see also George Pattison, *Kierkegaard, Religion, and the Nineteenth Century Crisis of Culture*, Cambridge: Cambridge University Press 2002, pp. 101–3. On Martensen's attempt

knowledge, indeed of "co-knowledge" with God: an immanent knowledge of the entire divine order of things, including the provenance of sin and the operations of grace.[53] In the 1840s, Martensen's view came under fierce attack in several of Kierkegaard's pseudonymous writings—most prominently in the two books attributed to Climacus. In the *Postscript*, for example, Climacus mimics Martensen's own jargon as he mocks a "speculative" thinker who "wants to enter God's council" by comprehending Christianity's truth "with the help of immanence" or "*sub specie aeterni*," that is, "from an eternal, divine, and especially theocentric point of view."[54] More broadly, the goal of Climacus' two farcical attempts to advance beyond Socrates (the first in the *Fragments*, as we saw in Section II, and the second in the *Postscript*[55]) is both to parody and to undermine Martensen's own account of such an ascent.[56] Whereas Martensen conceived of Christian life as participation in a body of knowledge that surpasses and supersedes our natural state of Socratic ignorance, Kierkegaard insisted that Socrates' intrepidity in acknowledging his own ignorance remains a potent model for all those who hope to acquire Christian faith and the consciousness of sin.

For Kierkegaard and Martensen, the burning question here concerns the place of *reason* in the Lutheran cosmos. Can living human beings make sense of the knowledge of God that Christian redemption provides? Luther, for his part, insisted that human reason "neither knows nor understands" the provenance of sin or the workings of grace. We can grasp such truth, he wrote, only by means of "the light of the gospel and the knowledge of grace."[57] On Martensen's interpretation, Luther's notion of *gratia illuminans* (enlightening grace) implies that Christianity facilitates an *ascent in knowledge* for its adherents.[58] According to Martensen, Christian redemption allows our limited natural or "autonomous" understanding of the world—epitomized by Socratic ignorance—to be replaced with a higher body of knowledge, furnished

---

to supersede Kantian and Schleiermacherian thought, see Martensen, *On the Autonomy of Human Self-Consciousness in Modern Dogmatic Theology*, trans. by Curtis L. Thompson, in *Between Hegel and Kierkegaard: Hans L. Martensen's Philosophy of Religion*, pp. 72–147. Finally, for Martensen's praise of Johan Ludvig Heiberg as a poet who had superseded Dante, and had further pioneered a mode of aesthetic and ethical discernment (humor) that outstripped that of Socrates (irony), see Martensen, "Nye Digte af J.L. Heiberg," *Fædrelandet*, January 10, 1841, columns 3210–12; see also Pattison, *Kierkegaard, Religion*, pp. 111–12.

53 Martensen, *On the Autonomy of Human Self-Consciousness in Modern Dogmatic Theology*, pp. 72–147; p. 82; p. 147.

54 *SKS* 7, 194 / *CUP1*, 212. *SKS* 7, 196 / *CUP1*, 214. *SKS* 7, 198 / *CUP1*, 216–17.

55 Climacus' second farcical advance beyond Socrates begins at *SKS* 7, 187 / *CUP1*, 204: "Just as in *Fragments*, let us from this point try a category of thought that actually does go beyond. Whether it is true or false is of no concern to me, since I am only experimenting; but this much is required, that it be clear that the Socratic is presupposed in it, so that I at least do not end up behind Socrates again."

56 This a central interpretive thesis of my dissertation, "Søren Kierkegaard and the Very Idea of Advance Beyond Socrates." See also Stewart, *Kierkegaard's Relations to Hegel Reconsidered*, p. 554; see also pp. 470–1.

57 *Luther's Writings: American Edition*, vol. 33, pp. 290–1; vol. 34, p. 166.

58 Martensen, *On the Autonomy of Human Self-Consciousness*, p. 82.

by grace. This higher knowledge is accessible to all those who incorporate *theonomy* (acknowledgment of God's gracious power) into their speculative methods.[59]

Kierkegaard deplored these claims. He countered them with an entirely different—indeed, an opposite—interpretation of Luther's account of reason and grace. As Kierkegaard saw the matter, human reason cannot make *any* headway on its own in puzzling over Christianity's truth. The best we can do, he claimed, is to acknowledge our *inability* to wrap our minds around Christianity's truth—and then to "flee" to grace.[60] To boast of theonomous speculation and Christian knowledge is, accordingly, to flout Luther's *sola gratia* doctrine. It is to attempt to turn God's grace into a mere tool of human reason.

Kierkegaard articulated this criticism of Martensen most harshly in his signed *Christian Discourses*, by way of a contrast between authentic Christian faith [*Tro*] and "superstition" [*Overtro*].[61] According to Kierkegaard,

> the Christian craves only to be *satisfied with God's grace*; he does not insist on helping himself but prays for God's grace. He does not insist that God should help him in any other way than God wills....He accepts everything by God's grace—grace also. He understands that even in order to pray for his grace he cannot do without God's grace.[62]

By contrast, the superstitious person [*den Overtroiske*]

> wants by inadmissible means to penetrate the forbidden, discover the hidden, discern the future. [He] wants to make money with the help of the Holy Spirit. He wants to force himself on God...to make himself, him the uncalled, into what only God's call can make a person. [He] wants God to serve him. What else is it, even if the superstitious person declares that it is God's help that he wants to have—when he arbitrarily wants to have it, what else is it than wanting God to serve him?[63]

In the last sentence, we meet a brutal caricature of Martensen's attempt to use grace to construct a speculative path to divine co-knowledge: namely, a man who loudly proclaims his need of grace, but in reality seeks to take advantage of grace in order to storm the heavens and "force himself on God." The root of Martensen's error—"superstition"—is that he refuses to accept that he is merely a human being, who cannot understand the "forbidden," "hidden," and "future" on his own. He is

---

59 Ibid. I thank Jon Stewart for a number of insightful comments on the relation between autonomy and theonomy in Martensen's thought.

60 The concept of fleeing to grace [*at henflye til Naade*] played a pivotal role in Kierkegaard's understanding of Christianity. See my "The Voice of Rigor," in *Practice in Christianity*, ed. by Robert L. Perkins, Macon, Georgia: Mercer University Press 2004 (*International Kierkegaard Commentary*, vol. 20), pp. 161–85.

61 For a detailed treatment of these passages, see my "On Kierkegaard's Copenhagen Pagans," in *Christian Discourses and The Crisis and a Crisis in the Life of an Actress*, ed. by Robert L. Perkins, Macon: Georgia: Mercer University Press 2007 (*International Kierkegaard Commentary*, vol. 17), pp. 35–59.

62 *SKS* 10, 73 / *CD*, 64.

63 *SKS* 10, 76–7 / *CD*, 68.

unwilling to be what he is, namely, a sinner in need of grace. But to be a Christian, to have faith, is precisely to embrace this state of affairs.

It is in this context, finally, that we may best understand Kierkegaard's invocation of Socrates' ignorance and Typhonic self-doubt as a potent analogy to Christian faith. On Kierkegaard's interpretation of *sola gratia*, the truth of Christianity is and remains incomprehensible to us except in so far as we continually appeal to grace. The true Christian indeed appeals to grace, and so receives the truth; but he nonetheless remains in need of grace so long as he lives. The true Christian, indeed, is one who acknowledges that he is *so deeply* ignorant that he does not even know how to articulate his need for grace. As Kierkegaard puts it, the Christian "understands that even in order to pray for his grace he cannot do without God's grace."[64]

It follows that the true Christian, according to Kierkegaard, lives in a state of utter ignorance analogous to that sketched by Socrates at *Phaedrus* 229e–230a. Socrates is so ignorant, he confesses to Phaedrus, that he does not even know whether or how he might extricate himself from his ignorance. He *might* be a simple being, gentle and divinely blessed, and even endowed with access to divine knowledge; but he might just as well be a more perverse and complex monster than Typhon—locked in a knot of pride and self-deception. Socrates is so ignorant, in short, that he cannot even take the measure of his own ignorance and incapacity; and so he spurns all speculation about heavenly things as a distraction, and concentrates entirely on confronting his own predicament.

Though Socrates' utter *aporia* may certainly be said to differ infinitely from the Christian's helplessness and need of grace, that difference is here beside the point. From Kierkegaard's perspective, what matters most is simply that all human beings face a *choice*, an either/or, in how we comport ourselves toward our state of ignorance and need. Either we confront our ignorance and need in anxious self-concern; or we evade our ignorance and need—say, by indulging in speculation.

As Kierkegaard sees it, our choice is clear. The former is the path trodden by the Christian and by his (infinitely inferior) analogue Socrates. The latter is the path of Martensen. Our choice, in sum, is not between Socratic and Christian life, but between true Christian self-regard—for which the Socratic self-regard modeled at *Phaedrus* 229e–230a is an instructive analogy—and Martensenian "superstition." It follows that, for the fallen individual, Martensen's portrait of Christian knowledge as a form of advance beyond Socrates is useless. It is, indeed, *worse* than useless. For not only does such talk fail to give the fallen individual any purchase on Christianity's truth; it is also liable to distract, in a blur of Chimeras ancient and modern, from the task—as Christian as it is Socratic—of coming to terms with the enormity of our ignorance.

---

64 *SKS* 10, 73 / *CD*, 64.

Protagoras and *Republic*: Kierkegaard on Socratic Irony

David D. Possen

Early on in Plato's *Republic*, the orator Thrasymachus accuses Socrates of deceptive "irony," εἰρωνεία, meaning "trickery."[1] In particular, Thrasymachus alleges that Socrates is "shamming" [εἰρωνεύεσθαι] when he claims that he cannot define justice.[2] In Plato's *Symposium*, Alcibiades similarly depicts Socrates as "dissembling" [εἰρωνεύεσθαι]—indeed, as "toying" with his hearers—when he claims to have or know nothing of value.[3] In Aristotle's *Nicomachean Ethics*, finally, Socrates is celebrated as an exemplary "self-deprecator" [εἴρων].[4] Aristotle's Socrates is a paragon of false modesty: a man who disclaims such goods as wisdom even when he actually possesses them.

These ancient portraits of Socrates as an εἴρων—as a man who falsely claims to be ignorant—have weathered well with time. In our day, it is commonplace to call Socrates an "ironist" (our cognate for εἴρων), and to assert more specifically that Socrates used "irony"—irony in the sense of εἰρωνεία, "disingenuousness" or "false modesty"—when he professed to be an ignorant man. When we speak of Socratic irony in this manner, we echo Thrasymachus, Alcibiades, and Aristotle[5] in treating Socrates' disavowal of knowledge skeptically. We also follow in the footsteps of Hegel, who characterized Socrates' professions of ignorance as a

---

I would like to thank K. Brian Söderquist for his comments and suggestions. They have improved this article substantially.

1 Plato, *Republic*, 337a.

2 Ibid.

3 Plato, *Symposium*, 216e.

4 Aristotle, *Nicomachean Ethics*, 1127b.

5 I here follow the argumentation of Gregory Vlastos in his "Socratic Irony," *Classical Quarterly*, vol. 37, no. 1, 1987, pp. 79–96, especially pp. 79–84. For a dissenting view, according to which Aristotle's use of εἰρωνεία—and with it the Latin word *ironia*, popularized by Cicero and Quintilian, which gave rise to our own term "irony"—differs in important respects from the sense of εἰρωνεία employed by Thrasymachus, Alcibiades, Callicles, and others in Plato, see Melissa Lane, "The Evolution of *Eironeia* in Classical Greek Texts: Why Socratic *Eironeia* Is Not Socratic Irony," in *Oxford Studies in Ancient Philosophy*, vol. 31, ed. by David Sedley, Oxford: Oxford University Press 2006, pp. 49–83.

"sociable pleasantry...more a conversational affectation" than "pure negation" or "negative behavior."[6]

The subject of this article is Søren Kierkegaard's view of Socratic irony: an intriguing exception to this modern pattern. Kierkegaard was as quick as any other Plato scholar in modernity to label Socrates an "ironist," and to describe Socrates' professions of ignorance as "irony." Kierkegaard departed from his contemporaries' views, however, by insisting that Socrates' "irony" does *not* amount to dissembling. As we will see below, Kierkegaard held that Socrates meant exactly what he said when claimed to be ignorant; and yet he classified Socrates' disavowals of knowledge as "irony" all the same.

This idea that Socrates could be ironic and earnest at the same time was surprising in Kierkegaard's day. As we will show below, Kierkegaard derived this idea from his unusual conception of irony as dynamic and situational, rather than static and intentional. The present article will explain and assess Kierkegaard's account. It will argue that his view, surprising in its own time, remains valuable in ours. Indeed, Kierkegaard's conception of Socratic irony, I will show, presciently forecasts an interpretive trend—the "anti-Thrasymachean" approach (as I will call it) promoted by Gregory Vlastos—that has rapidly been gaining ground among Anglophone scholars of Plato.

In what follows, I begin (in Section I) by situating Kierkegaard's account against the backdrop of the debate about Socratic irony in our day and in Kierkegaard's own. I next proceed (in Section II) to explore the interpretive steps by which Kierkegaard grounds his account in Plato's dialogues. I conclude (in Section III) by reflecting on several unscholarly features of Kierkegaard's interpretive method. I argue that these features are best understood as rhetorical tools, rather than argumentative flaws. For they allow Kierkegaard to present his account of Socratic irony as not only a thesis about history, but also—and above all—a challenging standard of human authenticity.

I. Kierkegaard on Socratic Irony: An Anti-Thrasymachean View

A. For Orientation: Kierkegaard and the Anti-Thrasymachean Approach Today

I referred above to the common view of Socratic irony as εἰρωνεία, a strategy of verbal deceit. In what follows, I will dub this view the "Thrasymachean" approach to Socratic irony, after its loudest (and perhaps oldest) exponent Thrasymachus. On the Thrasymachean view, Socrates is an ironist in the sense that he is a deceiver. More specifically, Socrates' disavowals of knowledge are disingenuous: they are ruses designed to trick his interlocutors into exposing their own ignorance.[7]

---

6 G.W.F. Hegel, *Lectures on the History of Philosophy*, vols. 1–3, trans. by E.S. Haldane and F.H. Simson, New York: Humanities Press 1974, vol. 1, p. 403. (Translation modified.) This passage is cited by Kierkegaard at *SKS* 1, 304–5 / *CI*, 267.

7 Thus Norman Gulley, for example, suggests that Socrates' disavowals of knowledge are a mere "*expedient* to encourage his interlocutor to search out the truth, to *make him think*

As I will soon explain, Kierkegaard's interpretive approach to Socratic irony diverges sharply from this Thrasymachean view. And in this respect, Kierkegaard's approach anticipates the "anti-Thrasymachean" interpretive revolution that began in Anglophone Plato scholarship during the late 1980s and early 1990s, driven by the influential work of the late Gregory Vlastos.[8] On the new anti-Thrasymachean approach, Socrates is presumed *not* to be a deceiver when he claimed to be ignorant. Rather, Socrates' disavowal of knowledge is understood as "ironic" simply in the sense that it is puzzling. It is both literally true and open to misinterpretation. This fact frustrates interlocutors like Thrasymachus: it tricks them into embarrassing self-disclosures, and so fosters a scene of *dramatic* irony.[9]

It will shortly become clear that this anti-Thrasymachean approach, championed by Vlastos, is strikingly close to the view of Socratic irony that was set forth by Kierkegaard a good century and a half earlier. Kierkegaard too, we will see below, held that Socrates' professions of ignorance were literally true, but bound to mislead. And Kierkegaard too believed that it was this *dramatic* feature of Socrates' utterances, rather than any deceitful intentions on Socrates' part, that marked his utterances as "ironic."

As interpreters of Socratic irony, in other words, Kierkegaard and Vlastos have quite a lot in common. But here there is a curious irony in the history of scholarship on irony. In his 1987 anti-Thrasymachean manifesto, Vlastos prominently but wrongly identified Kierkegaard as a typical Thrasymachean. Vlastos wrote:

> In this essay I have tried to nail down the mistake in the conception of irony that underlies [the Thrasymachean] point of view. For this purpose I have gone back to the primary, down-to-earth meaning [of irony] from which all philosophically invented ones are derived (including the one Kierkegaard fished out of Hegel: "infinite absolute negativity"), what irony means is simply expressing what we mean by saying something contrary to it.[10]

In a note to the phrase "infinite absolute negativity," Vlastos memorably added: "[Kierkegaard's] treatment of Socratic irony is hopelessly perplexed by this dazzling mystification. It seduces him into finding in the Platonic texts he purports to be glossing the vagaries of a romantic novella."[11]

I would like to dwell for a moment on these comments, for they have done great harm to Kierkegaard's reputation as an interpreter of Plato. Vlastos' remarks imply that Kierkegaard only purports to read Plato seriously. Rather, it is alleged,

---

he is joining with Socrates in a voyage of discovery." Norman Gulley, *The Philosophy of Socrates*, London: Macmillan 1968, p. 69, emphasis added.

8 Cf. Gregory Vlastos, "Socrates' Disavowal of Knowledge," *Philosophical Quarterly* 35, 1985, pp. 2–31; Vlastos, *Socrates: Ironist and Moral Philosopher*, Ithaca: Cornell University Press 1991. Vlastos was influenced strongly by Terence H. Irwin, *Plato's Moral Theory*, Oxford: Clarendon Press 1975.

9 Cf. Vlastos, "Socratic Irony," p. 86.

10 Ibid., p. 94. Cf. Vlastos, *Socrates: Ironist and Moral Philosopher*, pp. 43–4.

11 Ibid., p. 94, note 50. Cf. Vlastos, *Socrates: Ironist and Moral Philosopher*, p. 43, note 81.

Kierkegaard treats Plato's dialogues with cavalier anachronism, as though they were Romantic excrescences of his own day. The result is that Kierkegaard gets Socrates "hopelessly" wrong.

These charges deserve refutation. They are fueled by a misreading of Kierkegaard's word "negativity."[12] Vlastos seems to have assumed that, when Kierkegaard referred to Socrates as infinitely and absolutely "negative," he meant that Socrates' professions of ignorance were *deceptive* through and through. Yet in point of fact, as we will see below, Kierkegaard used the phrase "infinite absolute negativity" to make the very opposite point. Kierkegaard's point is that Socrates was precisely as ignorant—as infinitely, absolutely "negative"—as he claimed to have been; and so Socrates' professions of ignorance were *not* deceitful, but "altogether earnest."[13]

Ironically enough, Kierkegaard's actual account of Socratic irony is strikingly similar to that of Vlastos himself. The crux of Vlastos' reading lies in his insistence that Socrates' irony is "complex": it involves utterances that are literally true in one sense, but are misleading in another. Thus when Socrates "professes to have no knowledge," Vlastos writes, "he both does and does not mean what he says."[14] But this insight, as will become clear below, is quite similar to what Kierkegaard meant a century and a half earlier when he claimed that "Socrates' ignorance was simultaneously earnest and yet again not earnest."[15] In short, despite Vlastos' caricature of Kierkegaard as a shabby reader of Plato—as a Romanticizing anachronist—Kierkegaard in fact promoted a view that is as relevant to present-day research as is Vlastos' own.

B. Kierkegaard's Original Anti-Thrasymachean Dissent

Kierkegaard's own view of Socratic irony is set forth clearly in his 1841 dissertation, *The Concept of Irony with Continual Reference to Socrates*. Kierkegaard articulated his view as a strong anti-Thrasymachean dissent from the two main accounts of Socratic irony that were popular in Kierkegaard's day: those of Schleiermacher and Hegel. In explicating Kierkegaard's own approach, we will find it helpful to begin with a brief overview of these rival views. Since Schleiermacher's came first, we will begin with his.

In 1815, in a well-received lecture to the Berlin Academy of Sciences on Socrates' "Worth as a Philosopher," Schleiermacher argued that Socrates' professions of ignorance are *ironic*—that is, deceptive—in the following sense: they conceal the fact that, in so far as Socrates had the capacity to recognize his own ignorance and that of others, he must already have possessed "a more correct conception of knowledge,

---

12 This observation is due to Jonathan Lear. Cf. Lear, "The Socratic Method and Psychoanalysis," in *A Companion to Socrates*, ed. by Sara Ahbel-Rappe and Rachana Kamtekar, Oxford: Blackwell 2006, pp. 442–62; pp. 450–1 and p. 461, note 25.

13 *SKS* 1, 307 / *CI*, 270.

14 Vlastos, "Socratic Irony," p. 86.

15 *SKS* 1, 306 / *CI*, 269.

and...a more correct method founded upon that conception."[16] According to Schleiermacher, in other words, Socrates' very act of disavowing knowledge reveals that he in fact possesses a *kind* of knowledge—an epistemological expertise—that others lack. In Schleiermacher's view, it is this expertise or knowledge that marks Socrates' "worth" as a philosopher, and obviates his claim to be "wise in nothing, great or small."[17]

Schleiermacher's view soon drew opposition from Hegel. In his 1820s *Lectures on the History of Philosophy*, Hegel charged that Schleiermacher had underrated Socrates' "worth." According to Hegel, Socrates deserves credit not only as a thinker who mused about knowledge in the abstract, but also as a moral *teacher* who made the representations of moral and epistemological concepts—like "faith," "reason," or "the good"—explicit, and so "concrete."[18] While Schleiermacher may have been content to view Socrates as a master epistemologist, Hegel regarded Socrates as nothing less than the founder of morality, the first discoverer of the the good as "a principle concrete within itself."[19] It is for this reason that Hegel insists that Socrates' claim to be "ignorant" must be regarded as "social pleasantry" and mere "conversational affectation": for Socrates' self-proclaimed ignorance is belied by his robust concrete knowledge.[20]

This does not mean, however, that Hegel held a wholly Thrasymachean view of Socrates' irony. Rather, there is one sense in which Hegel *was* prepared to consider Socrates ignorant, namely, from the vantage-point of Hegel's own activity of systematic philosophizing: "It may actually be said that Socrates knew nothing, for he did not reach the point of having a philosophy or constructing a science."[21] In other words, although Socrates was in fact a moral (and epistemological) sage, his professions of ignorance may yet be considered accurate in one sense: in the sense that he did not understand ethics as Hegel did himself.

Neither Schleiermacher nor Hegel may be regarded as wholly Thrasymachean interpreters, since both took pains to identify a sincerity of some kind in Socrates' professions of ignorance. However, both Schleiermacher and Hegel were equally committed to praising Socrates as (respectively) a "worthy" philosopher or moral

---

16 F.D.E. Schleiermacher, "On the Worth of Socrates as a Philosopher," trans. by Connop Thirlwall, in *The Philological Museum*, vol. 2, 1833, pp. 538–55, see p. 541. This passage is cited by Kierkegaard at *SKS* 1, 263–4, note / *CI*, 219–20, note.

17 Plato, *Apology*, 21b.

18 Cf. Hegel, *Lectures on the History of Philosophy*, vol. 1, p. 401: "In saying that I know what reason is, or what faith is, these remain only wholly abstract representations; in order to become concrete, they must be made explicit....It is *this* explication of such representations that Socrates effected; and *this* is the truth of Socratic irony." This passage is cited by Kierkegaard at *SKS* 1, 304 / *CI*, 266–7. For the claim that Socrates' "knowledge for the first time reached [the idea of] the good," see Hegel, *Lectures on the History of Philosophy*, vol. 1, pp. 406–7.

19 Hegel, *Lectures on the History of Philosophy*, vol. 1, pp. 406–7. This passage is cited by Kierkegaard at *SKS* 1, 274 / *CI*, 232.

20 Ibid., vol. 1, p. 403. This passage is cited by Kierkegaard at *SKS* 1, 304–5 / *CI*, 267.

21 Ibid., vol. 1, p. 399. This passage is cited by Kierkegaard at *SKS* 1, 222 / *CI*, 174.

authority.[22] For this reason, when push came to shove, both Schleiermacher and Hegel *did* end up trying to attribute some sort of positive knowledge—epistemological or moral—to Socrates. To this end, they both appealed to the old Thrasymachean idea that Socrates' disavowal of knowledge is ironic in the sense of "dissimulating." It is precisely this last point that was to provoke Kierkegaard's vigorous dissent.

In *The Concept of Irony*, Kierkegaard articulated his own more staunchly anti-Thrasymachean view of Socratic irony as a critique of both Schleiermacher and Hegel. Kierkegaard sums up his own position as follows:

> It has become clear in the foregoing that Socrates, when he declared that he was ignorant, nevertheless did have knowledge, for he knew about his ignorance; that, on the other hand, Socrates' knowledge was not a knowledge of something, that is, it did not have any positive content; and that, to this extent, Socrates' ignorance was ironic. Now since Hegel has, as it seems to me, sought fruitlessly to reclaim a positive content for Socrates, I believe that the reader must agree with me. Had Socrates' knowledge been a knowledge of something, then his ignorance would merely have been a conversational technique. On the contrary, *his irony was complete in itself.* Inasmuch, therefore, as Socrates' ignorance was *simultaneously earnest* and *yet again not earnest*, it is *on this point* that Socrates must be grasped. To know that one is ignorant is the beginning of coming to know; but if one does not know more, it is a mere beginning. Such knowledge is what kept Socrates ironically afloat.[23]

Let us unpack this paragraph slowly. In the first sentence, Kierkegaard accepts Schleiermacher's core claim that Socrates' disavowal of knowledge presupposes that he knows something about knowledge. But Kierkegaard also endorses Hegel's critique of this claim, namely, that any such knowledge-about-knowledge would merely be abstract, negative, and regulative. In other words, such knowledge-about-knowledge could tell us only that we have *failed* to arrive at true knowledge. It cannot tell us what the positive *content* of true knowledge might be. As Kierkegaard explains, Socrates' epistemological expertise is merely "the beginning of coming to know." It is not knowledge of anything definite, and so cannot count as "positive" knowledge.

Kierkegaard next turns his critical gaze toward Hegel. He rejects as "fruitless" Hegel's attempts to attribute "positive" knowledge to Socrates: particularly Hegel's efforts to paint Socrates as a thinker who succeeded in "making the abstract concrete."[24] Kierkegaard protests that Hegel does not adequately defend this claim.[25] Most tellingly, Kierkegaard shows that Hegel himself elsewhere admits—in the context of his portrait of Socrates as the founder of morality—that Socrates' thought actually aimed and moved in the *opposite* direction: "it proceeded not from the

---

22 Similarly Vlastos, in our own day, insisted that Socrates was not only an "ironist" but also a "moral philosopher." Cf. the title of his last book: *Socrates: Ironist and Moral Philosopher*.

23 *SKS* 1, 306 / *CI*, 269. (Translation modified, original emphasis restored.)

24 *SKS* 1, 304 / *CI*, 267.

25 Ibid. According to Kierkegaard, Hegel's "examples" of the positivity of Socratic irony—that is, Socrates' alleged concretization of "reason" and "faith"—are "poorly chosen" and "so modern that [they] hardly remind us of Socrates."

abstract to the concrete but from the concrete to the abstract and continually arrived at this."[26]

This is not the place to analyze the details of Kierkegaard's critique of Hegel.[27] For our present purposes, what matters most is this critique's basic thrust. Namely, against Hegel, just as against Schleiermacher, Kierkegaard insists that Socrates has no "positive" knowledge to offer at all. Rather, Kierkegaard describes Socrates as a wholly *negative* figure: a man whose ignorance was "earnest," and who—as Kierkegaard puts it elsewhere—was "altogether earnest about being ignorant."[28]

Let us pause to clarify what this last point does and does not entail. Like most Plato exegetes today, Kierkegaard did not take Socrates' profession of ignorance—his claim to be "wise in nothing, great or small"[29]—to be a blanket denial of *all* knowledge whatsoever.[30] Instead, on Kierkegaard's account, Socrates' profession of ignorance pertains solely to *wisdom* about "philosophical" matters—to "the ground of all being, of the eternal, of the divine"—rather than to "empirical" or experiential knowledge, which Socrates had in spades.[31] With respect to philosophical knowledge, Kierkegaard held that Socrates truly *was* as ignorant as he claimed to be. As Kierkegaard put the matter, Socrates' stance of philosophical ignorance was "a true philosophical position," albeit a "completely negative" one.[32]

This explains what Kierkegaard means when he describes Socrates' ignorance as "earnest." But why then, in the paragraph cited previously, does Kierkegaard go on to say that Socrates' ignorance is *both* "earnest" and "yet not earnest"? Fortunately for the reader, Kierkegaard soon clarifies this point. With respect to Socrates' ignorance of the afterlife, Kierkegaard writes, "Socrates…does not take this ignorance greatly to heart; on the contrary, he genuinely feels quite liberated in this ignorance. Consequently, he is not in earnest about this ignorance, and yet he is altogether earnest about being ignorant."[33] This passage suggests strongly that,

---

26 Ibid. This line likely refers to Hegel's claim that, in his moral reasoning, Socrates was constrained by his "*abstract* attitude" toward the Good—an attitude that "has no further development." Cf. Hegel, *Lectures on the History of Philosophy*, pp. 70–1, cited at *SKS* 1, 274 / *CI*, 232.

27 For a discussion of this critique and its significance, see Jon Stewart, *Kierkegaard's Relations to Hegel Reconsidered*, Cambridge and New York: Cambridge University Press 2003, pp. 169–70.

28 *SKS* 1, 307 / *CI*, 270.

29 Plato, *Apology*, 21b.

30 On the interpretive and logical perils of attributing an "unrestrained skepticism" to Socrates, see J.H. Lesher, "Socrates' Disavowal of Knowledge," *Journal of the History of Philosophy*, vol. 25, no. 2, 1987, pp. 275–88; pp. 280–1.

31 *SKS* 1, 217 / *CI*, 169. This reading is consistent with the many particular professions of ignorance scattered throughout Plato's dialogues, which restrict themselves in scope to matters of theology, eschatology, and the definitional essence of various aesthetic and ethical concepts and standards. (The "aesthetic" concept I here have in mind is beauty, or "fineness" (τὸ καλόν); but this is arguably as much an "ethical" concept as an aesthetic one for Socrates.) For documentation, see David Wolfsdorf, "Socrates' Avowals of Knowledge," *Phronesis*, vol. 49, no. 2, 2004, pp. 75–142, pp. 80–4.

32 *SKS* 1, 217 / *CI*, 169.

33 *SKS* 1, 307 / *CI*, 270.

when Kierkegaard makes the general claim that Socrates' ignorance is "not earnest," he is referring to the light-hearted *attitude* that Socrates takes toward the matter of which he is ignorant (e.g., the afterlife). Socrates' *professions* of ignorance, however, remain "altogether earnest" in Kierkegaard's view.

We are now equipped to appreciate the distinctive sense in which Kierkegaard characterizes Socrates as *ironic*. When Kierkegaard states that Socrates' ignorance "was ironic" and kept him "ironically afloat,"[34] he does not mean to return (like Hegel or Schleiermacher) to the Thrasymachean view that Socrates merely pretends to be ignorant. Rather, Kierkegaard emphatically denies that "irony" requires "dissimulation," or presupposes some external "purpose."[35] Instead, when he speaks of Socrates' irony, Kierkegaard refers not to Socrates' subtle intentions in disavowing knowledge, but to the open and dramatic effects of his disavowal: to the "annihilating enthusiasm of negativity" with which Socrates, professing ignorance, demolishes his fellow Athenians' "vanity" (pretensions) and "free[s]" them to confront their ignorance just as he acknowledges his own.[36]

What makes Socrates' claim of ignorance *ironic* to Kierkegaard, in short, is not that the claim is inaccurate, but that it is destructive: its effect is to induce bewilderment and to dispel false illusions of knowledge. By earnestly acknowledging his ignorance, Socrates prompts his listener to face the prospect that they might be less knowledgeable than they had assumed. Early on in *The Concept of Irony*, Kierkegaard characterizes Socrates' "ironic method" as precisely such a provocation: it "began with the presupposition that [Socrates himself] knew nothing," and "ended with the presupposition that human beings know nothing at all."[37] *Contra* Thrasymachus, Kierkegaard here defines Socratic irony on terms that have nothing to do with inaccuracy or disingenuousness on Socrates' part. Socratic irony here consists, instead, in the humbling *effect* that his professions of ignorance have on their hearers.[38]

One way of putting this is that Kierkegaard's anti-Thrasymachean account locates the irony of Socrates not in a *static* account of his utterances or intentions, but in a *dynamic* account of how Socrates' utterances affect his contemporaries. Accordingly, when he refers to Socrates' irony as "infinite absolute negativity,"[39] Kierkegaard hardly means (as Vlastos would have it) that Socrates was infinitely and absolutely *deceptive*. Rather, he means that Socrates was precisely as "negative"—as ignorant—as he claimed to be; and that, by continually and earnestly articulating his own negativity, Socrates managed to expose the negativity and ignorance that was endemic to "the entire given actuality"—the Athenian polity—of his day.[40]

---

34 *SKS* 1, 306 / *CI*, 269.

35 *SKS* 1, 293–4 / *CI*, 255–6.

36 *SKS* 1, 222–3 / *CI*, 175–6.

37 *SKS* 1, 98 / *CI*, 37.

38 Cf. *SKS* 1, 101–2 / *CI*, 40: "Here, then, we see irony in all its divine infinitude, which allows nothing whatever to endure. Like Samson, Socrates grasps the pillars that support knowledge and tumbles everything down into the nothingness of ignorance."

39 *SKS* 1, 292 / *CI*, 254.

40 Ibid.

II. Kierkegaard's Interpretation of Socratic Irony in Plato's Dialogues

A. Kierkegaard's Method for Detecting Socratic Irony in Plato

It should not surprise us that Vlastos' anti-Thrasymachean revolution has taken Anglo-American Plato scholarship by storm. As an interpretive assumption, the anti-Thrasymachean approach to Socratic irony is attractive for several reasons. Most prominently, such an approach allows us to treat Socrates as a trustworthy speaker: a coherent thinker who *means what he says* when he claims to be ignorant. More broadly, this view allows us to guard Socrates' utterances against the "exegetical abuse" (as Iakovos Vasiliou calls it) that follows when scholars sense that any interpretation may be attacked or defended "merely by crying 'irony.' "[41]

These interpretive benefits are substantial. But they come at a price. For in order to make the anti-Thrasymachean view seem plausible as a reading of Plato, its advocates must explain what can appear to be a glaring contradiction in Plato's Socrates. Namely, while Socrates disavows knowledge in certain passages, there are others in which he avows knowledge, and plenty of it; not to mention whole dialogues that consist essentially of lectures by Socrates peppered with perfunctory interruptions. This means that the advocate of an anti-Thrasymachean reading has two tough questions to answer. The first question runs roughly as follows: "If Socrates *really* is the self-proclaimed ignoramus of the *Apology*, then what are we to make of the lecturing know-it-all of the *Republic*, the *Timaeus*, or the *Critias*?" The second is: "What about passages in the *Apology* itself in which Socrates seems to avow moral or epistemological knowledge?"

Today's anti-Thrasymachean exegetes typically answer the first question by conceding that we have here to deal with two different *kinds* of Socrates figures.[42] On this view, Plato's authorship contains early dialogues, late dialogues, and perhaps other kinds of dialogues (middle, transitional) as well; and the Socrates at issue here—the Socrates who earnestly disavows knowledge—is a distinctive creature of the *early* dialogues. Accordingly, the fact that the late dialogues *Timaeus* or *Critias* portray Socrates as a fountain of knowledge poses no problem for anti-Thrasymachean interpreters, who merely state that these dialogues are outside their interpretation's range.

In *The Concept of Irony*, Kierkegaard responds to the first question above with a close intellectual ancestor of the strategy just described. Rather than speak of

---

[41] Iakovos Vasiliou, "Conditional Irony in the Socratic Dialogues," *Classical Quarterly*, vol. 49, no. 2, 1988, pp. 456–72, see p. 456.

[42] On this line of argument, see David Wolfsdorf, "Interpreting Socrates' Early Dialogues," *Oxford Studies in Ancient Philosophy*, vol. 27, 2004, pp. 15–41; pp. 24–31. Wolfsdorf's list of "early" dialogues—the *Apology*, the *Charmides*, the *Crito*, the *Euthydemus*, the *Euthyphro*, the *Gorgias*, *Hippias Major*, *Hippias Minor*, the *Ion*, the *Laches*, the *Lysis*, and the *Protagoras*—reflects the broad consensus of Plato scholars today; though Book I of the *Republic*, and some or all of the *Meno*, are often included in the list, and *Hippias Major* and *Hippias Minor* are sometimes left out of it.

"early" and "late" dialogues (though he occasionally does this too[43]), Kierkegaard distinguishes between texts that he considers accurate representations of the "actual" Socrates, such as the *Apology*, and other texts in which—he alleges—Plato has put "his own professions" into "the mouth of Socrates."[44] In drawing this distinction, Kierkegaard relies on a division proposed by Schleiermacher between "constructive" dialogues, such as the *Republic*, *Critias*, and *Timaeus*, and those that are more authentically "dialogical," "ironic," or "Socratic."[45] Kierkegaard then declares: "I shall have very little to do with these constructive dialogues, inasmuch as they cannot contribute much to the view of Socrates' personality," since in them Socrates is "practically" Plato's mouthpiece, "a *nomen appellativum* that merely designates the one speaking, the one expounding."[46]

So much for the first question—at least for now. (We will return to it later.) The second question is perhaps the greater challenge, and continues to beguile anti-Thrasymachean interpreters today. For it just so happens that, even *within* the dialogues that might be labeled "early" or "Socratic," Socrates' professions of ignorance coexist uneasily with other passages in which Socrates avows, or seems to avow, knowledge of theological and ethical truths.[47] This cries out for an explanation from the anti-Thrasymachean approach. For it would certainly seem that, if Socrates both avows and disavows the same kinds of knowledge, then he must be dissembling somewhere.

In recent Plato scholarship, considerable attention has been devoted to this problem.[48] Kierkegaard, however, sidesteps the problem by judiciously expanding his account of the "Socratic" and "Platonic" strands in Plato. After classifying certain dialogues as Socratic and others as Platonic, Kierkegaard suggests further that that certain dialogues, like the *Republic*, can contain both Socratic and Platonic parts and passages;[49] that other dialogues, like the *Phaedo*, "can simultaneously be Socratic and Platonic;"[50] and that certain Socratic utterances, like the Doctrine of Recollection, can have meant one thing to Socrates, and another to Plato.[51] In

---

43 See Kierkegaard's reference to "earlier," "later," and "intermediate" dialogues at *SKS* 1, 171 / *CI*, 119.

44 *SKS* 1, 171, 92 / *CI*, 119, 30.

45 Cf. F.D.E. Schleiermacher, *Introductions to the Dialogues of Plato*, trans. by William Dobson, Cambridge: J. & J.J. Deighton 1836, pp. 355–6.

46 *SKS* 1, 115 / *CI*, 54.

47 These have been helpfully documented by David Wolfsdorf in Wolfsdorf, "Socrates' Avowals of Knowledge."

48 This effort has been spearheaded by David Wolfsdorf, particularly in Wolfsdorf, "Socrates' Avowals of Knowledge"; "Interpreting Socrates' Early Dialogues"; and *Trials of Reason: Plato and the Crafting of Philosophy*, New York: Oxford University Press 2008. Wolfsdorf has managed persuasively to narrow down the list of Socrates' *genuine* avowals of knowledge to a single pair of passages in the "early" dialogues—at Plato, *Apology*, 29ab and 37b—where Socrates claims to "know" an ethical truth about justice, namely, that disobeying one's superior is unjust. But containing the problem is not the same as solving it.

49 *SKS* 1, 169–71 / *CI*, 118–19.

50 *SKS* 1, 134 / *CI*, 85.

51 Cf. *SKS* 1, 120–1 / *CI*, 60.

effect, this expedient allows Kierkegaard to *dismiss* passages that do not conform to his model of Socrates—such as passages in which Socrates confidently avows knowledge—as "Platonic" impurities in otherwise Socratic texts.

In this context, Kierkegaard portrays himself as a kind of literary chemist, whose analysis aims to isolate the purely Socratic *element* from the Socratic-Platonic amalgam of Plato's dialogues. Kierkegaard introduces this chemical metaphor in a pivotal passage in which, after identifying Socrates' irony with his practice of (earnestly) acknowledging his own ignorance and exposing that of others, he takes note of Socrates' celebrated wish to continue this practice on into the afterlife.[52] Kierkegaard remarks:

> Here...we see irony in all its divine infinitude, which allows nothing whatever to endure. Like Samson, Socrates grasps the pillars that support knowledge and tumbles everything down into the nothingness of ignorance. That this is genuinely Socratic everyone will certainly admit, but Platonic it will never become. Here, then, I have arrived at one of the duplexities in Plato and the very clue I shall pursue in order to find the unalloyed Socratic.[53]

The lines offer a capsule view of Kierkegaard's general method for detecting Socratic irony in Plato. In so far as passages in Plato confirm Kierkegaard's starting portrait of Socrates as an ironist—as a man who earnestly acknowledges his own ignorance and exposes that of his interlocutors—Kierkegaard will admit them as "Socratic." In so far as passages contradict this portrait, Kierkegaard will classify them as "Platonic."

This method simply oozes with circular reasoning. It presupposes the very account of Socratic irony that it proposes to find; and it insulates this account against all conceivable counterevidence by the ingenious expedient of classifying all such counterevidence as "Platonic." We will say more about this circularity and its implications in Section III. For the moment, however, let us briefly turn to some examples of how Kierkegaard puts this method into practice.

B. Case Studies: Kierkegaard on Socratic Irony in Protagoras *and* Republic *I*

Nearly a hundred pages of *The Concept of Irony* are devoted to extracting and analyzing instances of Socratic irony in five Platonic dialogues: the *Symposium*, the *Protagoras*, the *Apology*, the *Phaedo*, and Book I of the *Republic*. The result is a mountain of argumentation that cannot be paraphrased easily, particularly in an article as brief as the present one. I will therefore limit myself to the briefest of summaries of Kierkegaard's analysis of three dialogues—the *Symposium*, the *Apology*, and the *Phaedo*—in order to make room for a fuller treatment of the remaining two.

We saw in Section I that, on Kierkegaard's anti-Thrasymachean account, the irony of Socrates consists in his intrepid activity of earnestly acknowledging his ignorance and exposing that of others. Kierkegaard defines Socrates' "ironic" method as his movement from "the presupposition that he knew nothing" to "the

52 See Plato, *Apology*, 41b.

53 *SKS* 1, 101–2 / *CI*, 40.

presupposition that human beings know nothing at all."[54] Kierkegaard goes on to characterize this process as the analogue, in philosophical dialogue, to Samson's suicidal revenge upon the Philistines: "grasp[ing] the pillars that support knowledge and tumbl[ing] everything down into the nothingness of ignorance,"[55] with all the "annihilating enthusiasm of negativity."[56]

With the above definition of Socratic irony in place, Kierkegaard proceeds to detect its presence in five dialogues that he deems reliably or partly Socratic. In the *Symposium*, Kierkegaard points to the drama of Alcibiades' unrequited love for Socrates as the main locus of the dialogue's Socratic irony. What fascinates Alcibiades about Socrates is precisely his epistemic and rhetorical negativity, his irony; but it is precisely this that makes it impossible for Socrates to satisfy him.[57] In offering this drama as a representation of love, Kierkegaard concludes, the *Symposium* as a whole acquires an ironic cast. For both "the love-relation that has developed between Socrates and Alcibiades and what we can learn from it about the nature of love are negative."[58]

In the *Phaedo* and *Apology*, Kierkegaard associates Socratic irony with the ignorance about the afterlife that Socrates hints at in the *Phaedo*, and avows openly in the *Apology*.[59] As we mentioned earlier, Kierkegaard characterizes the *Phaedo* as "simultaneously…Socratic and Platonic," inasmuch as it is full of putative demonstrations of the immortality of the soul to which Plato might have assented, but Socrates surely would not.[60] The *Apology*, by contrast, is judged to be Socratic and ironical "in its totality," largely because Socrates is there explicit, consistent, and unyielding in his effort to expose his accusers' ignorance and hypocrisy, as well as in his admission that he does not know what death will bring.[61]

Beyond the *Symposium*, *Phaedo*, and *Apology*, Kierkegaard also examines the role of Socratic irony in two other Platonic texts: the *Protagoras* and Book I of the *Republic*. What is distinctive about the latter texts, Kierkegaard writes, is that they are marked by irony in their *structure*, as well as in their content. This can be seen in the fact that both texts end not "without a conclusion," as Schleiermacher had claimed, but rather "with a *negative* conclusion."[62] That is, both the *Protagoras* and Book I of the *Republic* culminate not in indifference but in emphatic affirmations of human ignorance. In so doing, both texts reflect the motion and rhythm of Socratic irony—the progression from Socrates' own disavowal of knowledge to a shared *aporia*—writ large, on the scale of an entire conversation.

The *Protagoras* famously ends with an argumentative switch. Socrates comes around to the view with which Protagoras had begun, namely, that virtue can be

---

54 *SKS* 1, 97–8 / *CI*, 36–7.

55 *SKS* 1, 101–2 / *CI*, 40.

56 *SKS* 1, 222 / *CI*, 175.

57 *SKS* 1, 109–10 / *CI*, 48–9.

58 *SKS* 1, 110 / *CI*, 49.

59 *SKS* 1, 137, 142 / *CI*, 78–9, 85.

60 *SKS* 1, 142 / *CI*, 85.

61 Ibid.

62 *SKS* 1, 115 / *CI*, 54. The Schleiermacher reference is to Schleiermacher, *Introductions to the Dialogues of Plato*, pp. 354–5.

taught; while Protagoras adopts Socrates' initial stance, namely, that virtue is not teachable. While this symmetrical development might be thought simply to be the "ridiculous" duet of an "absurd pair," from which no conclusion may be inferred,[63] Kierkegaard rejects this interpretation "on Socrates' behalf."[64] In point of fact, Kierkegaard maintains, Socrates' exchange with Protagoras has a clear, if negative, philosophical destination: the shared acknowledgment of ignorance.

To demonstrate this, Kierkegaard points to the ironic character (in his sense of "ironic") of the two main *arguments* that Socrates puts forth in the *Protagoras*: (1) his argument that all virtues must be one and the same, and (2) his corollary argument that virtue, as knowledge, must be teachable. With regard to (1), Kierkegaard remarks that "the ironic consists in" the way in which, by persuading Protagoras that there is a single unitary virtue, Socrates "tricks him out of" the illusion that he knows any particular "concrete virtue."[65] That is, Socrates persuades Protagoras that he cannot really know courage (for example) unless he already knows justice, or temperance, or piety; what Protagoras ultimately needs to know is the *unitary virtue* of which every concrete virtue is a part. The "trick" in this argument, Kierkegaard explains, is that the unitary virtue of which Socrates speaks is necessarily "so abstract...that it only becomes the rock on which the individual virtues, like well-freighted sailing ships, run aground and are smashed to pieces."[66] In sum, what makes Socrates' argument "ironic" is not that he deals deceptively with Protagoras; it is, rather, the simple fact that Socrates' argument leads Protagoras from an imagined "positivity," in which he thinks he knows many virtues, to a state of "negativity," in which he acknowledges his ignorance of the "one and only one" fundamental virtue.[67]

Argument (2) is the one in which Socrates and Protagoras seem to switch places. Socrates, in particular, moves from maintaining that virtue cannot be taught to (seemingly) defending Protagoras' claim that virtue *can* be taught. Kierkegaard notes that this argumentative maneuver also involves a turn toward abstraction and negativity, since Socrates rests his defense of the claim that virtue is teachable on the basis of an utterly impractical presupposition: that the virtuous teacher has comprehensive knowledge of "the circumstances of pleasure" and pain.[68] By structuring his defense of Protagoras' claim in this manner, writes Kierkegaard, Socrates in effect eviscerates it. For if virtue can be taught in theory, provided that we have knowledge of "the limitless sum of experience," but *we do not have* such knowledge—then for all practical purposes virtue *cannot* be taught.[69]

Once again, then, the thrust of Socrates' argument is to deprive Protagoras of the illusion that he has knowledge. Kierkegaard remarks that there are in a sense two kinds or levels of irony in operation here:

---

63 *SKS* 1, 116–17 / *CI*, 56, citing Plato, *Protagoras*, 361a.

64 *SKS* 1, 117 / *CI*, 57.

65 *SKS* 1, 119 / *CI*, 59.

66 *SKS* 1, 119 / *CI*, 58.

67 *SKS* 1, 253 / *CI*, 208–9.

68 *SKS* 1, 121 / *CI*, 61.

69 Ibid.

> The ironic to the first power lies in the erection of a kind of epistemology that annihilates itself; the ironic to the second power lies in Socrates' pretending that by accident he found himself defending Protagoras' thesis, although he in fact crushes it by the defense itself.[70]

On its surface, then, argument (2) is ironic inasmuch as it prompts us, as we saw above, to recognize the *ignorance* that prevents us from knowing or teaching virtue. On another level—the level of the dialogue's drama—argument (2) is ironic in the sense that it exposes the self-confusion that underlay Protagoras' initial formulation of the thesis that virtue can be taught. Originally, Protagoras had declared that virtue can be taught in order to express his confidence in his own expertise in virtue (that is, that he knows virtue well enough that he could teach it). Yet Socrates' defense of Protagoras' thesis makes clear that this confidence is misplaced. For while virtue may be teachable in theory, *we* do not know it well enough to teach it.

This is, in brief, what Kierkegaard calls the *Protagoras*' "negative conclusion." Rather than close on a note of sheer indeterminacy (as the argumentative switch might at first seem to indicate), the dialogue ends by exposing Protagoras' ignorance, and by allowing that ignorance to take its place beside Socrates' own. Taken as a whole, the *Protagoras* thus follows precisely the rhetorical trajectory that Kierkegaard associates with Socratic irony. The dialogue moves from Socrates' initial acknowledgment of his own ignorance to a shared recognition of *aporia*.

Let us now turn briefly to Kierkegaard's analysis of Book I of the *Republic*, which presents a close parallel to his discussion of the *Protagoras*. Here again Kierkegaard seeks to show that Plato's text "does not merely end without a conclusion, as Schleiermacher thinks, but rather with a negative conclusion."[71] And once again, Kierkegaard works to demonstrate that "irony is an essential element" in the text by documenting its ironic trajectory: namely, Socrates' efforts to expose Thrasymachus' ignorance about justice, culminating in his declaration that "the present outcome of the discussion is that I know nothing."[72]

What is distinctive in Kierkegaard's discussion of the *Republic* is the fact that he here excludes nine-tenths of the dialogue in question (Books II–X) from consideration. In essence, Kierkegaard treats Book I of the *Republic* as a "Socratic" dialogue distinct from the "Platonic" subsequent Books. At one point he even refers to Book I as an independent "dialogue."[73] To justify this procedure, Kierkegaard appeals to Schleiermacher, who had noted a gap between the Socrates portrayed in *Republic* I and the Socrates of *Republic* II–X. While Socrates' method of Book I, Schleiermacher had written, resembles that in Plato's "earlier ethical pieces," in later Books

> the method is completely changed: Socrates no longer comes forward with questions in the character of a man who is ignorant, and only looking for greater ignorance in

70 *SKS* 1, 121–2 / *CI*, 61.

71 *SKS* 1, 164 / *CI*, 111.

72 Plato, *Republic*, 354b.

73 *SKS* 1, 165 / *CI*, 112: "*Dialogen*."

> the service of the god, but as one who has already found what he seeks, he advances onwards, bearing along with him in strict connection the insights he has acquired.[74]

On Kierkegaardian terms, this note boils down to the claim that the Socrates of *Republic* I is an ironic, negative, and "Socratic" figure, while the Socrates of *Republic* II–X is a positive mouthpiece for Plato. For Kierkegaard, this provides sufficient justification for him to divide the *Republic* into two distinct domains—the Socratic Book I, and the Platonic remainder—and to treat the former in isolation as a distinct ironic "dialogue."

It is interesting to note the difference in argumentative thrust between Kierkegaard and Schleiermacher on this point. When Schleiermacher investigates the differences in "method" between *Republic* I and *Republic* II–X, he does so precisely in order to disclose what he takes to be the *unity* of vision that binds the *Republic*'s "constructive" and "ethical" elements together. Schleiermacher's goal is to appreciate how the entire *Republic*, and behind it Plato's entire authorship, functions as a harmonious if differentiated whole.[75]

Kierkegaard's goal, by contrast, is to carve Plato up. Kierkegaard has little interest in the Socratic-Platonic amalgam of Plato's dialogues as such. Instead, he prefers to dissolve the amalgam or to crack it open in order to get at the "unalloyed Socratic" element that it contains.[76] To this end, Kierkegaard eagerly breaks Plato's *corpus* apart into "Socratic" and (presumably) "Platonic" pieces, split along a jagged fissure separating *Republic* I from *Republic* II–X. He then portrays these Platonic and Socratic elements as fundamentally irreconcilable.[77]

In our next and final section, we will pause to reflect on the scholarly deficiencies—the circularity and derivative character—of the argumentation just cited. We will observe that, in his zeal to extract a purely ironic, negative Socrates from Plato, Kierkegaard violates a number of scholarly norms. Yet we will also note that Kierkegaard indicates that he does so deliberately; and that, in flouting the norms of scholarship in this way, Kierkegaard resembles no one so much as the very Socrates—the trenchantly negative, destructive Socrates—who is the object of his interpretive search.

III. Kierkegaard's Method: An Unscholarly Plea for Irony?

Let us briefly return to Gregory Vlastos' attack on Kierkegaard's view of Socratic irony. Vlastos, we saw in Section I, casts Kierkegaard as "hopelessly perplexed" about Socrates, thanks to the "dazzling mystification"—the phrase "infinite

---

74 Schleiermacher, *Introductions to the Dialogues of Plato*, pp. 355–6, cited at *SKS* 1, 163 / *CI*, 110–11.

75 See Schleiermacher, *Introductions to the Dialogues of Plato*, pp. 354–6.

76 *SKS* 1, 102 / *CI*, 40.

77 Cf. *SKS* 1, 102 / *CI*, 40: "That this is genuinely Socratic everyone will certainly admit, but Platonic it will *never become*. Here, then, I have arrived at one of the duplexities in Plato and the very clue I shall pursue in order to find the unalloyed Socratic."

absolute negativity"—that he had "fished out of Hegel" and read into Plato.[78] This critique combines several distinct charges, all serious: (1) that Kierkegaard was an unscholarly reader of Plato, who did not so much read him as read things *into* him; (2) that Kierkegaard was an unoriginal interpreter, who simply rehashed (and poorly so) an idea of Hegel's; and, most significantly, (3) that Kierkegaard's account of Socratic irony as "infinite absolute negativity" is staunchly Thrasymachean, and is as such incorrect.

Our study of Kierkegaard has refuted Vlastos' most consequential charge (3). We have shown that Kierkegaard was in fact—like Vlastos himself—a staunchly *anti*-Thrasymachean interpreter of Socratic irony. What is more, we have seen that Kierkegaard's word "negativity" does not mean what Vlastos apparently assumes it does. The term does not cast aspersions on Socrates' sincerity. Rather, Kierkegaard uses "negativity" to highlight the dynamism in dispelling illusions ("the annihilating enthusiasm"[79]) with which Socrates, confessing his own ignorance, prompts his interlocutors to acknowledge their ignorance as well.

Thus Vlastos' charge (3) is unfounded. His charges (1) and (2), however, are somewhat less wide of the mark. It is certainly far-fetched to imply that Kierkegaard mistook Plato for a Romantic, or that he pilfered his conception of Socratic irony from Hegel. But there still remains a sense, I believe, in which Vlastos' instincts hold true.

Kierkegaard's argumentation *does* fall short of ordinary scholarly norms. In Section II, we observed a glaring circularity in Kierkegaard's method for isolating "the unalloyed Socratic" in Plato. We also noted the extent to which Kierkegaard relies on others (such as Schleiermacher) to legitimate his choices of "Socratic" texts. In this concluding section, I will briefly reflect on these features of Kierkegaard's argumentation. I will suggest that they are deliberate and purposeful: they highlight the Socratic, ironic character of Kierkegaard's own enterprise in *The Concept of Irony*.

Following his five-dialogue tour of Socratic irony in Plato, Kierkegaard offers a brief "Justifying Retrospection."[80] Here he undertakes to explain—indeed, to justify—why his analysis included these dialogues and not others. He begins as follows:

> As far as the choice of dialogues is concerned, I have continually had regard for only one thing—namely, to limit myself to the dialogues that according to the common opinion would disclose to me, even though fragmentarily, a view of the *actual Socrates*. Most scholars, in their grouping of the dialogues, have a first division (and to me this is the primary concern); all of them are closely connected with Socrates…because they are assumed to be most kindred to him in spirit, even though not all scholars explicitly call them the *Socratic* dialogues.[81]

Reviewing his five chosen dialogues (the *Symposium*, the *Protagoras*, the *Apology*, the *Phaedo*, and Book I of the *Republic*), Kierkegaard then offers a "retrospective

78 Vlastos, "Socratic Irony," p. 94; *Socrates: Ironist and Moral Philosopher*, pp. 43–4.

79 *SKS* 1, 222 / *CI*, 175.

80 *SKS* 1, 171–7 / *CI*, 119–26.

81 *SKS* 1, 171 / *CI*, 119–20.

justification" for their classification as Socratic by appeal to the views of Schleiermacher, Friedrich Ast (1778–1841), and an unspecified set of "most scholars."[82] When he appeals to these predecessors, Kierkegaard is pointedly deferential to them: he maintains that he has "continually" restricted himself to texts whose Socratic character is affirmed by a consensus of other scholars ("the common opinion").

It is thus somewhat jarring that Kierkegaard next asserts that he has *also* subjected these consensus selections to an independent, "unbiased" review of his own. "If in my choice of dialogues," Kierkegaard writes, "I have in one respect kept in mind the conclusions of scholarly researchers, adapted myself to them as far as possible, leaned upon them as much as they allowed me to, I have also, on the other hand, endeavored to ascertain their correctness by an unbiased examination of a large portion of Plato."[83] Here Kierkegaard does claim to have made an original contribution to Plato scholarship: namely, by verifying on his own the consensus view that these five dialogues are Socratic. It soon emerges, however, that Kierkegaard's method of "unbiased examination" is *also* derived from Schleiermacher: it involves analyzing these dialogues by disentangling their Platonic or "constructive" rhetorical strands from Socratic strands focused on the acknowlegment of ignorance.[84]

My aim here is not to join Vlastos in labeling Kierkegaard an unoriginal thinker. I wish simply to point out that Kierkegaard *himself* takes pains to depict his interpretive method as fundamentally derivative. Intriguingly, the same can be said with regard to his method's *circularity*. In Section II, we noted that Kierkegaard rejects in advance (as Platonic) every depiction of Socrates in Plato that conflicts with his anti-Thrasymachean portrait of Socrates as infinitely negative and earnestly ironic. While this pattern of circular argumentation—that is, the fact that Kierkegaard presupposes the very account of Socratic irony that he proposes to verify—is certainly convenient for Kierkegaard, it also leaves him vulnerable to the Vlastos' charge that he is not so much reading Plato as he is reading his interpretation *into* Plato's texts.

Before we issue such a charge ourselves, however, we would do well to note the following passage, which comes shortly after Kierkegaard's "Justifying Retrospection":

> But what was Socrates actually like? What was the point of departure for his activity?... The answer is: Socrates' existence is irony. Just as this answer, in my opinion, removes the problem, so the fact that it removes the problem makes it the right answer as well—thus it *simultaneously appears* as a hypothesis and as the truth.[85]

I read this passage as a sign that Kierkegaard's forays into scholarship are unscholarly by design. For Kierkegaard here admits that he does not follow the standard scholarly procedure of articulating a hypothesis and demonstrating its truth. Rather, he simply *declares* that his hypothesis (his anti-Thrasymachean account of Socrates and his irony) "simultaneously appears as the truth." But this is not scholarship; it is dogma.

---

82 *SKS* 1, 172 / *CI*, 120.

83 *SKS* 1, 172 / *CI*, 120–1.

84 *SKS* 1, 175 / *CI*, 124.

85 *SKS* 1, 178–9 / *CI*, 127.

Hence while Kierkegaard might refer to his study of Plato as an "unbiased examination," this passage makes clear that he does have biases—and they are proud and clear from the start. Hence in a sense Vlastos is right: Kierkegaard is indeed an *unscholarly* interpreter. But I do not think that Kierkegaard would have been troubled by this accusation. For he in fact invites it himself. After noting that Socratic irony concerns "the purely personal life, with which science and scholarship [*Videnskab*] admittedly are not involved," Kierkegaard issues a kind of manifesto of unscholarliness:

> Grant that science and scholarship are right in ignoring [Socrates and his irony]; nevertheless, one who wants to understand the individual life cannot do so. And since Hegel himself has said somewhere that with Socrates it is not so much a matter of speculation as of individual life, I dare to take this as sanction for my method of proceeding in my whole venture.[86]

Here Kierkegaard defines the "method of proceeding" [*Fremgangsmaade*] that structures *The Concept of Irony* as a whole. This method consists in defying the norms and interests of "science and scholarship," and in exhibiting Socratic irony as a potent challenge, or paradigm,[87] for "individual life" as such. (Thus, for example, Kierkegaard closes *The Concept of Irony* by depicting "irony as the negative" as the *sine qua non* for any authentic human life.[88])

In my view, it is this same method that informs the features of Kierkegaard's argumentation that we have here identified as unoriginal or unscholarly. When he works to detect Socratic irony in Platonic texts, Kierkegaard simply dismisses all interpretive trouble spots as *distractions* from his more urgent task of exhibiting his ironic (that is, earnestly ignorant) Socrates as a model of human authenticity. And for this same reason, Kierkegaard sees no need to strike out on his own as an interpreter. It is more efficient for him to rely on the scholarly bonafides of an Ast or a Schleiermacher.

In all of this, I submit, Kierkegaard resembles no one so much as the ironic Socrates that he works to promote. For much as Socrates, in *Phaedrus* 229de–230a, is so preoccupied by his own ignorance that he has no time to inquire into heavenly affairs, so too Kierkegaard is ultimately content to leave to others—to "scholarly researchers"[89]—the scholarly details of analyzing and clarifying Plato's texts. Kierkegaard does not aspire to contribute positive knowledge on this score. Rather, Kierkegaard's interpretive work is *negative* in character, as befits the model of Socratic irony that he defends. Much as Socrates challenges his contemporaries by insisting upon his "presupposition"—his confession of ignorance—at every turn, Kierkegaard does the same with *his* presupposition: his assumption that Socrates was "earnest" in professing his ignorance.[90]

---

86 *SKS* 1, 215 / *CI*, 166–7.

87 As I argue in Chapter 1 of my dissertation: David D. Possen, *Søren Kierkegaard and the Very Idea of Advance Beyond Socrates*, University of Chicago.

88 *SKS* 1, 355–6 / *CI*, 326–7.

89 *SKS* 1, 172 / *CI*, 121.

90 *SKS* 1, 307 / *CI*, 270.

Symposium:
Kierkegaard and Platonic Eros

Rick Anthony Furtak

I. The Theory of Eros in Plato's Dialogues: A Brief Synopsis and Commentary

To call something divine is to assert that it is a higher power, something not created by human beings and not within our control; we do not dispose of it, but it holds sway over us. For Plato, "any power, any force we see at work in the world, which is not born with us and will continue after we are gone could thus be called a god, and most of them were."[1] Clearly, one of the most prominent divinities in the Platonic universe is Eros, the god of love: this personified emotional force is mentioned repeatedly throughout Plato's collected works and is the theme to which two of his greatest dialogues are largely devoted. In the *Theages*, a short dialogue having to do with his divine sign, the character Socrates admits that love is one subject about which he does have knowledge; in the *Cratylus*, which deals with the meanings of words, Socrates says that Eros flows into us from the outside; and there are passages in the *Republic* and the *Laws* that focus on the place of erotic love in the ideal society.[2] But the primary sources for the Platonic discussion of Eros are two dialogues, the *Symposium* and the *Phaedrus*.

The *Symposium*, which is also known as the *Banquet* or the *Drinking-Party*, consists of a series of speeches made in praise of Eros, the god of love. The participants are Phaedrus, Pausanias, Eryximachus, Aristophanes, Agathon, Socrates, and Alcibiades; and one common theme shared by almost all of the speeches is that Eros plays an important role in guiding human beings toward the appropriate objects of love.[3] The highlight of the dialogue, and the place where scholars tend

---

1 G.M.A. Grube, *Plato's Thought*, Boston: Beacon Press 1958, p. 150.

2 See *Theages* 128b, *Cratylus* 420a–b, *Republic* 457a–461e, and *Laws* 836b–842a. In *Symposium* 177d–e, Socrates again says that love is "the only thing he understands," as Kierkegaard points out in *The Concept of Irony*, see *SKS* 1, 86 / *CI*, 24.

3 As is pointed out by Catherine Osborne in *Eros Unveiled: Plato and the God of Love*, Oxford: Clarendon Press 1994, p. 92: "Alcibiades needed a guide to lead him to his beloved.…Phaedrus begins by suggesting that Love is the principle that ought to guide men in all their affairs; Pausanias suggests that the proper sort of Love turns men to the correct sort of objects; Aristophanes, after describing the human quest for one's original 'other half,' assigns to Eros the role of guide, leading us to what is akin to ourselves; Agathon suggests that Eros guides his subjects to success in the arts and serves as the best pilot in all affairs and the best leader in life's choral dance." She cites *Symposium* 178c, 181a, 193b–d, and 197a–e.

to look when searching for Plato's own doctrine of love, is the speech of Socrates, much of the content of which is attributed to a mysterious priestess named Diotima, whom Socrates characterizes as "the one who taught me the art of love."[4] The speech suggests that Beauty and the Good are closely related, if not identical, and that they are the ultimate aims of all human activity.[5] So Eros is not only the power that moves human beings with sexual desire in the most explicit sense;[6] but it is also what inspires artistic creativity, moral improvement, and intellectual apprehension of eternal realities. On the Platonic view, erotic love is associated with everything from our carnal longings to the highest aspirations of the human soul, including our yearning for immortality.[7] Eros is construed in the speech of Socrates/Diotima as a sort of intermediary between mortal and divine realms of being. We cannot long for what we already have, and so if Eros is conceived as a kind of appetite or desire to possess whatever is beautiful or good, then love itself cannot be personified as a perfect being who is already in possession of such qualities as goodness and beauty.[8] Here, we see why Platonic Eros might be considered egocentric and acquisitive: *I* long for what is good *for me*, and I long to possess it for *myself*. "This violent sense of need is what Plato primarily means by love," one scholar writes, giving voice to a fairly common judgment.[9] And there is reason to be concerned about what might be left out of the picture in the erotic ascent recommended in Diotima's narrative, in which a person leaves his or her particularity behind, rising from the love of one beautiful body to the love of all, from love of bodies to love of souls, from there to a love of customs and sciences, and then on to Beauty itself.[10] Or, as Kierkegaard sums it up concisely in *The Concept of Irony*, "the object of love is: beautiful bodies—beautiful souls—beautiful observations—beautiful knowledge—the beautiful."[11] Beauty itself is said to be uncorrupted by human flesh or coloring or any of that other

---

4 *Symposium* 201d. The speech of Socrates, including the parts ascribed to Diotima, extends from 198a to 212c. See also *SKS* 20, 377, NB5:16 / *JP* 6, 6144; in this notebook entry from 1848, Kierkegaard remarks that Socrates "spoke of having learned from a woman," and adds, "I, too, can say that I owe my best to a girl. I did not learn it from her directly, but she was the occasion."

5 See *Symposium* 204e–206a.

6 Homoerotic love in particular; this, at least, is the main focus of the *Symposium*; Pausanias describes the love of boys as more "heavenly" than the love of women (see 181b–d), and in the speech of Socrates/Diotima, it is claimed that the goal of Eros is to reproduce (see 206b–e), whether in body or in soul. And the less bodily the reproduction, the better (208e–209e); what we tend to call "sublimation" is here interpreted as the expression of love that comes nearest to realizing its proper object.

7 See, for example, *Symposium*, 207d.

8 *Symposium*, 206a and 200a–e.

9 John Rist, *Eros and Psyche*, Toronto: University of Toronto Press 1964, p. 26. James Rhodes takes issue with this view, asking whether Eros can coherently be compared to an appetite which disappears when satisfied: if it is a desire for the good, then can we not have an abiding desire that whatever "gladdens our heart" be present to us, so that we love it even as we possess it? See his discussion in *Eros, Wisdom, and Silence: Plato's Erotic Dialogues*, Columbia, Missouri: University of Missouri Press 2003, pp. 310–11.

10 *Symposium*, 209e–212a.

11 *SKS* 1, 160 / *CI*, 107.

"mortal nonsense," and the person who has ascended to this level of abstraction will think less of the distinctive reality and value of contingent individuals, which are to be loved only in so far as they are instances of beauty, goodness, and other admirable qualities.[12] On this view, "beautiful individuals have only instrumental value: they are to be used, stepped on, like rungs of a ladder which leads away from any concern *for them*."[13]

It should be noted, of course, that the speech of Socrates is not the only one in the *Symposium*, nor does he get the last word: although it is questioned whether Alcibiades is too young to have developed sharp insight, he ends the dialogue with a final eulogy that points out what may be lacking in the contemplative self-sufficiency of the lover described in the previous speech.[14] After stumbling in drunk amidst a general uproar, Alcibiades learns of the theme of the conversation so far and demands to deliver a panegyric of his own, in praise of Socrates. A key moment is when he states that, although Socrates has many good qualities, these may be shared by others as well:[15] this makes us wonder if love of a person may be something more than a response to universal properties. Socrates is portrayed by Alcibiades as an exceptional, inhuman being, who is equally impervious to cold, fatigue, fear of bodily harm, or the sexual advances made by Alcibiades himself, who is madly infatuated with him. "I wonder if Socrates was that cold," Kierkegaard asks himself; "I wonder if it did not hurt him that Alcibiades could not understand him."[16] The other speech deserving of special attention is given by Aristophanes, for whom Eros is the name for our desire for wholeness, our longing to unite with our "other half."[17] Through a myth of how human beings came to exist in their present state of incompleteness and longing, Aristophanes claims that we were once whole but were cut in half by the gods, and now we search restlessly to unite with the beloved other with whom we can become whole again. Although this conception of romantic love as a merging with the other half of oneself does little to diminish the impression that Plato's account of Eros is egoistic, it does capture the feeling of lack that drives us in search of fulfillment, and it also undermines the notion of self-contained autonomy presented by Socrates. Together, the speeches of Aristophanes and Alcibiades provide strong counterpoints to the theory of Eros which is usually identified as Plato's own.

---

12 *Symposium* 211e. It would be hard to argue that what is described in 211c is anything other than a flight from the particular toward the universal: on the first step of his ascent, the lover is described as progressing ἀπὸ ἑνὸς ἐπὶ δύο καὶ ἀπὸ δυοῖν ἐπὶ πάντα τὰ καλὰ σώματα—that is, "from one to two and from two to all beautiful bodies."

13 Jonathan Lear, "Eros and Unknowing," in *Open Minded*, Cambridge, Massachusetts: Harvard University Press 1998, pp. 148–66; pp. 163–4.

14 *Symposium* 219a. Cf. Sophia Scopetea, *Kierkegaard og græciteten*, Copenhagen: C.A. Reitzel 1995, p. 325.

15 *Symposium*, 221c. For an excellent discussion of this speech and its dramatic function, see Martha Nussbaum, *The Fragility of Goodness*, Cambridge: Cambridge University Press 1986, pp. 184–99.

16 *Pap*. V B 4:3 / *JP* 4, 4262. The speech of Alcibiades occupies more of Kierkegaard's attention in *The Concept of Irony* than any other part of the *Symposium*.

17 *Symposium* 189d–193e.

The *Phaedrus* poses its own set of challenges for the interpreter. It is a metaphorically suggestive text in which the topic of Eros arises in the midst of a conversation about oratory. At first, Socrates defines Eros as an irrational desire, but later he retracts what he has said so far as it is a kind of blasphemy and promises to make up for it with another speech in honor of love.[18] This time, Eros is described as a variety of sacred frenzy, a heaven-sent blessing which provides us with insight.[19] Prophecy and poetic inspiration are among the other types of sacred frenzy, all of which demonstrate that divine madness is superior to human sanity. As in the *Symposium*, the vision of earthly beauty serves as a precipitating factor, lifting the mind to the contemplation of higher things.[20] Unlike the *Symposium*, however, the *Phaedrus* does not view the individual beloved as a dispensable step on the way to illumination. Rather, it "begins and ends with the love-relationship between individuals," presenting the erotic bond to another person as precisely what guides the lover "to an understanding of beauty and truth."[21] The madness of love has the ability to lift us to a more elevated level of happiness and wisdom than we ourselves could reach through the aid of merely human prudence or secular reason.[22] Compared with the *Symposium*, the *Phaedrus* provides the student of Plato with better resources for appreciating the significance of the most intensely particularized instances of passionate attachment. Yet the two dialogues are alike in their conviction that the experience of erotic longing which draws us toward what is beautiful has a crucial epistemic purpose: "As the most accessible of the Forms, visible in part even to the physical eye, Beauty opens up human awareness to the existence of the other Forms, drawing the philosopher toward the beatific vision and knowledge of the True and the Good. Hence Plato suggested that the highest philosophical vision is possible only to one with the temperament of a lover."[23]

II. Kierkegaard and the Theory of Eros: An Overview and Interpretation

"I have now read so much by Plato on love," Kierkegaard says in a letter to his fiancée, and this turns out to be more than just a youthful enthusiasm: even his latest religious writings contain blatant allusions to Plato's erotic dialogues, the *Symposium* and

---

18 *Phaedrus*, 238b-c and 242d–243b.

19 See *Phaedrus*, 244a–245c.

20 *Phaedrus*, 249d–250e. "That intellectual ascent has its origin in an erotic aesthetic experience is necessary due to the special nature of beauty. As a Form it belongs to the intelligible realm. But it is simultaneously the only Form that is also grasped by sensual knowledge.…The Form of Beauty abrogates the division between the visible and the intelligible." Friedo Ricken, *Philosophy of the Ancients*, trans. by Eric Watkins, Notre Dame: University of Notre Dame Press 1991, p. 103.

21 Grube, *Plato's Thought*, pp. 112–13. See also Nussbaum, *The Fragility of Goodness*, pp. 220–1.

22 *Phaedrus*, 255a–256e. Cf. Rhodes, *Eros, Wisdom, and Silence*, p. 473.

23 Richard Tarnas, *The Passion of the Western Mind*, New York: Ballantine Books 1991, p. 41. See also G.R.F. Ferrari, *Listening to the Cicadas: A Study of Plato's Phaedrus*, Cambridge: Cambridge University Press 1987, pp. 140–2.

the *Phaedrus*.[24] And it is not without justification that one commentator describes even *Works of Love* as "a courageous effort to re-introduce eros into philosophy."[25] Although Platonic Eros is not Kierkegaard's ultimate interest, it would be false to say that it is not at all what his writings are concerned about. He speaks well of the *Symposium* for its "indescribably wonderful presentation" of love's ennobling influence, and of the *Phaedrus* for its "great picture" of "the madness of love."[26] And his own works do undeniably share with these Platonic dialogues an interest in the role of love in the development of the human being. Kierkegaard's main criticism of Platonic Eros is that it is not sufficiently a love of the individual. Writing about the progress of speeches in the *Symposium*, he observes that "Love is continually disengaged more and more from the accidental concretion in which it appeared"; the abstract reflection "mounts higher and higher above the atmospheric air until breathing almost stops in the pure ether of the abstract."[27] Unfortunately, this is what happens when love is defined as a yearning for the eternal which is only mistakenly directed at a specific finite "other." Kierkegaard insists upon the unique individuality of the person who is loved, as opposed to a flight toward "that great sea of beauty" and away from the love of the particular individual in his or her distinctive singularity.[28] As he argues in *Works of Love*, in order to love the actual people we see, it is first of all necessary to "give up all imaginary and exaggerated ideas about a dream world where the object of love should be sought and found."[29] In other words, we should not use the love of an individual merely as a stimulus for taking flight from concrete reality into a contemplation of more perfect and abstract objects.

The secret of earthly love is that it bears the imprint of divine love, Kierkegaard claims, and this idea of the beloved as the stimulus for the lover's spiritual ascent is plainly reminiscent of Plato's *Symposium*.[30] Yet, for Kierkegaard, the earthly love relationship is not merely a step on the way to the eternal, just as it is not justified in merely romantic or humanistic terms: rather, it is the sacred process by which contingent existence is infused with divinity. In *Works of Love* and elsewhere, he compares Socrates' remark about loving what is ugly to the Christian doctrine of loving the neighbor, and suggests that it is a selfish person who insists on loving only

---

24 Letter to Regine Olsen, *B&A*, vol. 1, pp. 52–3 / *LD*, pp. 66–8, Letter 21. Kierkegaard alludes to *Phaedrus*, 229d–230a and *Symposium*, 220c–d, respectively, in *The Book on Adler* (*Pap.* VII–2 B 235, 226 / *BA*, 139) and *For Self-Examination* (*SKS* 13, 39 / *FSE*, 9).

25 Elsebet Jegstrup, "Text and the Performative Act," *Philosophy Today*, vol. 45, 2001, pp. 121–31; see p. 124.

26 *SKS* 19, 195, Not6:12 / *JP* 3, 2387. *Pap.* III B 26 / *JP* 3, 3323.

27 *SKS* 1, 106–7 / *CI*, 45. *SKS* 1, 102 / *CI*, 41.

28 *Symposium*, 219d. The portrait of the lover's soul in the speech of Socrates "is a totally empty abstraction," Kierkegaard writes; in the *Phaedo*, the soul is "understood just as abstractly as the pure essence of the things that are the object of its activity." *SKS* 1, 127 / *CI*, 68.

29 *SKS* 9, 162 / *WL*, 161.

30 *SKS* 5, 84 / *EUD*, 75. See also *SKS* 4, 33 / *R*, 185: "From a religious point of view, one could say it is as if God used this girl to capture him, and yet the girl herself is not an actuality but is like the lace-winged fly with which a hook is baited." Cf. Plato, *Symposium* 210a–211c.

what is "objectively" lovable.[31] In the "Young Man" of his own *Symposium*—the dialogue on love at the beginning of *Stages on Life's Way*—he presents us with a figure who believes that the category of "the lovable" is untrustworthy if it has no abstract rational essence that compels agreement from anyone and everyone.[32] This character's attitude toward Eros is that, "if I cannot understand the force to whose power I am surrendering, then I will not surrender to its power."[33] Falling in love is not a self-initiated voluntary act, of course, but "the person who from the beginning resolutely takes his stand against actuality will always have the power to drive off the inspiration of erotic love or to slay it at birth."[34] The "Young Man" in the first part of *Stages on Life's Way* should therefore be able to avoid the danger of erotic love, for better or worse, since he claims to fear it and is obviously on guard against its influence.[35]

Apart from his fairly straightforward discussion of Plato's dialogues in *The Concept of Irony*, of which the most relevant portions have already been cited, Kierkegaard treats Platonic Eros most extensively in *Stages on Life's Way*. From the moment when Constantin Constantius proposes that those assembled give a series of speeches about erotic love, the first part of *Stages* ("In Vino Veritas") is basically a revised adaptation of Plato's *Symposium*.[36] The "Young Man," at one point, justifies his aversion toward Eros by appealing to the speech of Aristophanes, who finds it ludicrous that "in the obsession of love, [the human being] is only a half running around after his other half."[37] The second part of *Stages on Life's Way* opens with an analysis of Eros in relation to marriage,[38] and the author of the third part observes in one of his diary entries that it is not with Eros that he is struggling, but with the "religious crises that are gathering over me."[39] Johannes Climacus quotes from the *Symposium* and the *Phaedrus* in *Philosophical Fragments*, but in neither case does his reference pertain directly to the theory of Eros.[40] More to the point is his mention

---

31 *SKS* 9, 364–7 / *WL*, 371–3. See also *SKS* 20, 173, NB2:77 / *JP* 1, 942. The passage he has in mind is *Symposium* 210b-c, where Socrates/Diotima says of the person starting out on the ascent of love that, upon realizing that beauty of souls is greater than bodily beauty, he must love someone who shows signs of spiritual beauty, even when this is housed in an unattractive body. As Nussbaum points out, the person who says "I'll love you only to the extent that you exemplify qualities that I otherwise cherish" leaves no room for unconditional love. See Martha Nussbaum, *Upheavals of Thought*, Cambridge: Cambridge University Press 2001, p. 499.

32 *SKS* 6, 39–44 / *SLW*, 34–40.

33 *SKS* 6, 44 / *SLW*, 40.

34 *SKS* 6, 165 / *SLW*, 176.

35 See *SKS* 6, 42–3 / *SLW*, 37–8. Cf. *SKS* 6, 37–8 / *SLW*, 32. For a good account of Eros and its relation to the aesthetic in *Stages on Life's Way* and other texts, see Chantal Anne, *L'Amour dans la pensée de Søren Kierkegaard*, Paris: L'Harmattan 1993, pp. 65–73.

36 *SKS* 6, 36 / *SLW*, 30–1.

37 *SKS* 6, 46 / *SLW*, 43. Cf. Plato, *Symposium*, 189d–193b.

38 *SKS* 6, 95–7 / *SLW*, 99–101.

39 *SKS* 6, 203 / *SLW*, 216.

40 *SKS* 4, 238–9 / *PF*, 31. *SKS* 4, 245 / *PF*, 39. The passages cited are from *Symposium*, 209c–210d and *Phaedrus* 230a, respectively.

in the *Concluding Unscientific Postscript* of "the Greek conception of Eros as found in the *Symposium*," with the accompanying suggestion that the existing thinker is in a state of want and striving.[41] After all, in Plato's *Symposium* it is revealed that Eros is midway between wisdom and ignorance, and is therefore akin to the philosopher, whose love of wisdom depends on his awareness of (and lack of satisfaction with) his present state of ignorance.[42] And in *Works of Love*, in the chapter entitled "Love Hides a Multitude of Sins," Kierkegaard appropriates the term "divine madness" to refer to the capability "to be lovingly unable to see the evil that takes place right in front of one."[43]

Because he considers it "a sad but all too common inversion to go on talking continually about how the object of love must be so that it can be loveworthy,"[44] Kierkegaard might be seen as an advocate of ἀγάπη as opposed to ἔρως. And it is true that he distinguishes a right way of loving, which is difficult to achieve, from a wrong way, which is closer to our natural tendencies. But Kierkegaard is far from the neo-Manichaean view introduced by Anders Nygren, according to which the two forms of love are incompatible and engaged in "a life-and-death struggle."[45] He is much closer to Thomas Aquinas, for whom Eros is highly valued, since it inspires a striving for perfection.[46] Like the Greek authors, Kierkegaard uses multiple words to refer to love: The Danish *Elskov* and *Kjærlighed* could be roughly aligned with ἔρως and ἀγάπη, since *Elskov* indicates a love between two human beings and *Kjærlighed* tends to have broader connotations (which do not exclude intense, personal affections).[47] The latter term is used by Kierkegaard to indicate an unselfish,

---

41 See *SKS* 7, 91 / *CUP1*, 92. *SKS* 7, 117–18 / *CUP1*, 121.

42 *Symposium*, 204a. Cf. Thomas Gould, *Platonic Love*, London: Routledge and Kegan Paul 1963, p. 44: "As philosophy is not simple ignorance, but the awareness of the desirability of knowledge, so love is not merely the absence of all good things, it is the awareness of what they are, that they are absent and that they would indeed be desirable. Really to understand one's ignorance and what that implies is thus to understand love."

43 *SKS* 9, 285 / *WL*, 287. Cf. *Phaedrus*, 244b–e. "Johannes Climacus" alludes to the same Platonic notion in the *Concluding Unscientific Postscript*, see *SKS* 7, 143 / *CUP1*, 137–8.

44 *SKS* 9, 159 / *WL*, 159.

45 Anders Nygren, *Agape and Eros*, trans. by Philip S. Watson, New York: Harper and Row 1969, p. 6. Replying to Nygren, Vlastos writes that the "Greeks, being human, were as capable of genuine, non-egoistic, affection as we are." See "The Individual as an Object of Love in Plato," p. 6.

46 See the discussion by E.C. Vacek, SJ, in *Love, Human and Divine: The Heart of Christian Ethics*, Washington: Georgetown University Press 1994, pp. 244–7. On Kierkegaard's belief that "sincere erotic love" can be "an upbringing toward goodness," see Kresten Nordentoft, "Erotic Love," in *Kierkegaard and Human Values*, ed. by Niels Thulstrup and Marie Mikulová Thulstrup, Copenhagen: C.A. Reitzel 1980 (*Bibliotheca Kierkegaardiana*, vol. 7), pp. 87–99, see p. 98.

47 In notes to *Three Discourses on Imagined Occasions* and to *Christian Discourses*, the Hongs draw this parallel between *Elskov* and *Kjærlighed* and ἔρως and ἀγάπη (*TD*, 10, 161 and *CD*, 17, 444). Unfortunately, their translations often misrepresent the distinction, impertinently rendering *Elskov* as "erotic love" (as if it always meant something lewd or profane) although in many cases the single inclusive term "love" would be a more accurate translation—for example, "If you yourself have never been in love, you do not know whether

neighborly love; the former has more of a romantic tone. But these different shades of meaning do not amount to a technical separation of the two terms: Kierkegaard uses *Kjærlighed* in reference to a Platonic speech in praise of Eros, and *Elskov* even in discussing Christian love of neighbor.[48] This suggests that Kierkegaard uses the different words for love in order to distinguish various aspects or manifestations of love, not to demarcate absolutely dissimilar categories which can only be locked in violent conflict.

Kierkegaard aligns himself with the speech of Socrates in the *Phaedrus* which praises the value of sacred madness.[49] In *The Concept of Irony*, he uses the word *Kjærlighed* repeatedly in reference to Plato's *Symposium*,[50] and in *Works of Love* he cites Socrates—that "simple wise man of old"—to the effect that "Love is a son of wealth and poverty," translating the Greek ἔρως ("erotic love," as his English translators would have it), with the Danish *Kjærlighed* that he uses to refer to Christian love.[51] One of his religious discourses from 1843 contains the statement that "all human beings in all ages have confessed that love has its home in heaven and comes down from above," which could be taken as an allusion to the *Phaedrus*.[52] Even the decisively non-pagan Judge William appears to endorse the classical reverence toward Eros, which he praises as "a wonder."[53] Again and again, Kierkegaard insists that diverse forms of love can be traced to a common origin, so that Christian love does not need to abolish drives and inclinations but only to refine these crude expressions of the one "fundamental universal love" into a more unselfish kind.[54] His reason for paying attention to the "Greek form of erotic love," as Nordentoft remarks, is to emphasize that "love may take a variety of forms."[55] As Kierkegaard argues in *Works of Love*, our aim should be to distinguish unselfish love from its deviant forms. Erotic love and friendship are not "the truest form of

---

anyone has ever been loved in the world, although you do know how many have affirmed that they have loved, have affirmed that they have sacrificed their lives for erotic love [*Elskov*]." In this passage from *Christian Discourses* (*SKS* 10, 244 / *CD*, 237), the Hongs give the misleading impression that Kierkegaard suddenly changes the subject, when in fact he has been using the verb *elske* all along. He does not mean to single out Eros as *opposed* to other kinds of love at any point in this sentence, just as he does not intend to instigate an orgy by declaring "Du *skal* elske" [you *shall* love] throughout *Works of Love*: see, for example, *SKS* 9, 25–50 / *WL*, 17–43.

48 See *Three Discourses on Imagined Occasions* (*SKS* 5, 423 / *TD*, 47), where Kierkegaard alludes to *Symposium*, 178b. In *The Concept of Irony*, Kierkegaard uses the word *Kjærlighed* continually in reference to the same Platonic dialogue (*SKS* 1, 101–4 / *CI*, 41–52). See also *SKS* 3, 40 / *EO2*, 32 and *SKS* 9, 115–17 / *WL*, 112–14.

49 See *Pap.* III B 3 / *CI*, Supplement, p. 441. Cf. *Phaedrus*, 244a.

50 *SKS* 1, 101–14 / *CI*, 41–52.

51 *SKS* 9, 175 / *WL*, 175. Here, Kierkegaard is quoting from *Symposium*, 203c.

52 *SKS* 5, 158 / *EUD*, 157. Cf. *Phaedrus*, 250b–251e.

53 See *SKS* 6, 116 / *SLW*, 121.

54 *SKS* 9, 141–5 / *WL*, 139–43. In the opening chapter of *Works of Love*, Kierkegaard declares that love "flows" from a single hidden source "along many paths"; the varieties of "love in its manifestations" are to be the theme of his treatise: *SKS* 9, 17 / *WL*, 9.

55 Nordentoft, "Erotic Love," p. 92.

love," and it is crucial to identify the ways in which they fall short of the ideal.[56] Most notably, Kierkegaard's worries about the forms of love known to pagan culture include the idea that they tend to be selfish and possessive, preferential and exclusive, or preoccupied with making the judgment of whether or not the beloved has qualities which are independently admirable. Nevertheless, it would be a mistake to speak as if there were an absolute ontological difference between the love that Kierkegaard discusses in his religious writings and the love that is the topic of Plato's erotic dialogues, as if human beings were subject to a fundamentally Manichaean duality of motives, one good and the other evil.

In her book *Eros Unveiled*, Catherine Osborne points out that the phrase "God is love," in the Greek New Testament, "does not so obviously imply that God is loving"; and she adds that early Christian thinkers such as Augustine and Origen often "take it in a different sense, namely to refer to God as the source or origin from which all other lovers derive their love."[57] It is clear that Kierkegaard is operating with a similar conception of love, which he describes as the enigmatic power at the base of the psyche, and as the deepest ground of human existence. This, he says, is the explanation that we crave in our inner being, which explains the meaning of life "in the God who holds everything together in his eternal wisdom."[58] This God of infinite wisdom is also the "source of all love" in such a way that, as emotional beings, we are what we are only by virtue of being *in* love.[59] Love is the "passion of the emotions" that connects the one who loves with the second-person beloved, thereby constituting the middle term in the relation.[60] On Kierkegaard's trinitarian view, "The love-relationship requires threeness: the lover, the beloved, the love—but the love is God."[61] As M. Jamie Ferreira explains, "God is not the 'middle term' by being the direct object of our love in such a way as to marginalize the beloved; God is the 'middle term' by being the center of the relationship because 'the love is God.' "[62] Love, in other words, is the sacred power that connects us to the external world in which our duty is to love the person we see. There may be nothing in classical Greek thought that resembles Kierkegaard's ideal of an unconditional love

56 See *SKS* 9, 15 / *WL*, 7 and *SKS* 9, 263–6 / *WL*, 264–7.

57 Osborne, *Eros Unveiled*, pp. 41–2. She is referring to 1 Jn 4:8, in which it is said that "anyone who does not love does not know God, for God is love."

58 *SKS* 5, 94 / *EUD*, 87. "God is infinite wisdom," Kierkegaard writes in another discourse, and then (one sentence later): "God is love." See *SKS* 11, 157 / *WA*, 11. Cf. *Symposium* 202e, in which Eros is described as an intermediary between the human and the divine realms, binding the whole together. Sigmund Freud, identifying "the libido of psychoanalysis" with "the 'Eros' of the philosopher Plato," says that Eros is the power that "holds together everything in the world." *Group Psychology and the Analysis of the Ego*, trans. by James Strachey, New York: Norton 1959, pp. 31–2.

59 See *SKS* 9, 12 / *WL*, 3. See also Nordentoft's remarks on the differentiation of self and world out of an oceanic unity as a "subject-constituting separation," in which certain objects are charged with significance: "Erotic Love," pp. 90–1.

60 *SKS* 9, 116 / *WL*, 112.

61 *SKS* 9, 124 / *WL*, 121.

62 Jamie Ferreira, *Love's Grateful Striving*, New York: Oxford University Press 2001, p. 72.

which asks for nothing in return; but this difference should not prevent us from appreciating the degree to which Kierkegaard was inspired in his own writings by the Platonic account of Eros, the god of love. Our need to love and be loved, for Kierkegaard no less than for Plato, is the condition of our dignity as the expression of something greater than ourselves.

Theaetetus:

Giving Birth, or Kierkegaard's Socratic Maieutics

Marius Timmann Mjaaland

An old midwife helping a young mother with her delivery—that is the image introduced by Socrates to describe the process of *giving birth* to new knowledge (ἐπιστήμη).[1] This metaphor for the relation between teacher and disciple, and between knowledge and ignorance, is so rich that it has given rise to a philosophical tradition called *maieutics*, which combines pedagogy, epistemology, and a theory of communication. In Kierkegaard's dissertation, *The Concept of Irony*, he returns several times to the image of a midwife in order to describe Socrates' relation to his interlocutors. In later texts, he continues to develop this image as an ideal for *indirect* communication (*indirekte Meddelelse*). According to Kierkegaard, all communication concerning existence ought to be indirect. All the same, the influence of Socratic maieutics on his thinking cannot be limited to a "theory" of communication; it concerns rather the heart of his thinking as a whole. It is a pattern that dominates his thoughts on epistemology (for example, in *Philosophical Fragments*) as well as his plea for a fundamental rethinking of theology and philosophy (for example, in the *Postscript*). His enthusiasm for the Socratic method even amounts to an appeal for a *new* Socrates:

> Popular opinion maintains that the world needs a republic, needs a new social order and a new religion—but no one considers that what the world, confused simply by too much knowledge, needs is a Socrates. Of course, if anyone thought of it, not to mention if many thought of it, he would be less needed. Invariably, what error needs most is

I am grateful to Jonathan Weant and the editors for language assistance. Given the topic for this article, though, my deepest gratitude goes to Angela for bearing up against the travail and thus giving birth to Jonas, Maria, Tim, and Sara.

1 Cf. *Theaetetus*, 148e–151b. All quotations from Plato's works follow the translation of Hamilton and Cairns, in *Plato: The Collected Dialogues*, ed. by Edith Hamilton and Huntington Cairns, Princeton, New Jersey: Princeton University Press 1961. All references are to the Stephanus pagination. Greek quotations refer to the critical edition of the Greek text published by Société d'Édition, Les Belles Lettres, Paris 1964–68, here quoted from *Platons Werke in acht Bänden*, vols. 1–8, ed. by Gunther Eigle, Darmstadt: Wissenschaftliche Buchgesellschaft 1978–86. Kierkegaard refers to *Platonis quæ exstant Opera. Accedunt Platonis quae Feruntur Scripta*, vols. 1–11, ed. by Friederich Ast, Leipzig: Weidmann 1819–32 (*ASKB* 1144–1154).

> always the last thing it thinks of—quite naturally, for otherwise it would not, after all, be error.[2]

This statement from *The Sickness unto Death* also illustrates *how* Kierkegaard approaches Socrates. He has scarcely any historical interest in Socrates, but he sees the Socrates figure as an ideal for communication and self-knowledge in nineteenth-century Europe. Accordingly, his maieutics is not a simple copy of the Socratic pattern, but a genuinely new application of the maieutic problem in a different historical and spiritual context. To some extent Kierkegaard (or his pseudonym) even identifies with Socrates because he sees himself as the one who must *repeat* the Socratic gesture of maieutics in modernity. Here, particular emphasis must be placed on the word *repetition*. In Kierkegaard's vocabulary, "repetition" means rethinking the old in a new way;[3] in this article, it is his understanding of the *repetition of maieutics*, with all its twists and turns, which will occupy us.[4] For it is precisely via this category that he rethinks the conditions of Western philosophy and theology.

In section I, I introduce the Greek concept of maieutics and discuss its Platonic sources more thoroughly. In section II, I define the dilemma of Kierkegaard's approach to the problem of maieutics. Then, in sections III–XI, I analyze different Kierkegaardian texts with an eye to the similarities and dissimilarities between Socrates and Kierkegaard. I make this comparison from five different angles: *elenchus*, *aporia*, ignorance, death, and giving birth. Finally, I will conclude with a discussion of the conflict between Socratic and religious maieutics throughout Kierkegaard's authorship, asking why suffering in travail appears to be even more important to him than the actual possibility of giving birth.

I. The Platonic Sources

The Socratic praxis of *maieutics*, that is, midwifery (μαίευσις), brings together a wide spectrum of issues and problems. It establishes a particular nexus between epistemology and communication by situating reflection on philosophical problems within a dialogue between two persons searching for truth. Even though they both may be ignorant concerning truth itself, at least one of them (namely Socrates) has a certain insight into the world of ideas and a certain knowledge of the *difference* between what he knows and what he does not (or even cannot) know. Thus, he might seek to pass this knowledge on to his interlocutor. The problem though, is that if he knows himself and the kind of truth he reflects upon, he cannot communicate this truth without noticing the conceptual framework and the confusion surrounding

---

2 *SKS* 11, 205 / *SUD*, 92.

3 Cf. *SKS* 4, 25 / *R*, 149.

4 Maieutics is for Kierkegaard not only a way of communicating, but also a way of *rethinking* the conditions of human existence. He continually considers the possibility that the world *in its totality* might be understood *differently* while asking: How should we then be able to discover it? How could we understand it when this *other* totality transcends the possibilities of our categories? Such deliberations lead us to the category of repetition, which has all the characteristics of a maieutic category.

his interlocutor. The truth they are both seeking is a truth that must be born from the interlocutor himself, that is, he would have to *give birth* to knowledge (ἐπιστήμη) based on something other than so-called "common sense." Neither Socrates nor his interlocutors are wise in the sense that they themselves *possess* wisdom. Nevertheless, they are mutually dependent on each other in their *search* for knowledge (ἐπιστήμη) and it is their dialogue of questioning and answering that qualifies them as philosophers, that is, as lovers of wisdom. Within the *Theaetetus*, this process of questioning and answering is made vivid with the image of a young woman giving birth to a child and an old woman helping her as a midwife.[5] From this image we have the term "maieutics," or "the art of midwifery."

The use of the term "*maieusis*" is of course a metaphorical one, though it is a metaphor heavily loaded with symbolic meaning on account of its transitory position between life and death. In the process of appropriating truth, something old dies and something new is born. The concepts of life and death are essential for a Platonic understanding of philosophy. However, these concepts are at the same time religious and even mythical, and the transitory movement from death to life can be found in religious movements from East to West, in esoteric mystery cults and myths, as well as in the sophisticated doctrines of world religions. It is now well acknowledged that when it comes to the questions of life and death, Plato's thought is deeply influenced by mythical narratives; and it is so to such a degree that it is impossible to draw a strict line between *mythos* and *logos* in his thinking. For our purposes it is not even necessary to draw such a line because Kierkegaard sees a clear religious analogy to Plato's philosophy, and applies this analogy without hesitation. The Socratic metaphor of midwifery thus connects a cluster of different issues that later become important for Kierkegaard. In order to outline the significance of the notion of maieutics in Plato's philosophy, I will single out five of them; (i) *elenchus*, (ii) *aporia*, (iii) ignorance, (iv) death, and finally, (v) giving birth. I am quite aware that I am presenting an extended concept of "maieutics," but I think it is necessary in order to show the full impact of Socratic maieutics on Kierkegaard's thinking.

(i) *Elenchus*. In the *Theaetetus*, Plato introduces the following image of a midwife to describe the relation between Socrates and his interlocutor:

> SOCRATES: Well, as I said just now, do you fancy it is a small matter to discover the nature of knowledge?
> THEAETETUS: One of the very hardest, I should say...I cannot persuade myself that I can give any satisfactory solution or that anyone has ever stated in my hearing the sort of answer you require. And yet I cannot get the question out of my mind.
> SOCRATES: My dear Theaetetus, that is because your mind is not empty or barren. You are suffering the pains of travail.
> THEAETETUS: I don't know about that, Socrates. I am only telling you how I feel.
> SOCRATES: How absurd of you not to have heard that I am the son of a midwife, a fine buxom woman called Phaenarete!
> THEAETETUS: I have heard that.
> SOCRATES: Have you also been told that I practice the same art?
> THEAETETUS: No, never.

5 Cf. *Theaetetus*, 150b.

> SOCRATES: It is true, though; only don't give away my secret. It is not known that I possess this skill; so the ignorant would describe me in other terms as an eccentric person who reduces people to hopeless perplexity.[6]

The *Theaetetus* is generally accepted to be among the so-called middle dialogues, a group of dialogues where Plato reflects critically about his own philosophical method.[7] Gregory Vlastos points out that one of the main differences between the early and the middle periods is the level of critical reflection on questions concerning method, logic, and epistemology.[8] In the early period, Plato applies a method of questioning called *elenchus* (from Greek ἐλέγχειν: to examine critically, to refute), which entails a critical search for truth in the moral sense. The starting point is normally a "What is F?" question (F representing, for example, "courage" or "virtue"), which is given a positive definition by the interlocutor, that is, "F is G." Socrates then seeks to demonstrate that the definition is inconsistent, or based on wrong premises, resulting in the conclusion that "F is not G." He thus *negates* the original proposition. The discussions end without a positive answer to the question, but the point seems to be that the apparent contradiction between G and non-G presents the moral truth as an unresolved *problem*. The conclusion would then be that the failing theoretical definition opens up a space for a continuous search for moral truth by way of *praxis*, not primarily by way of theoretical deliberation.[9] Still, the *deliberation* about praxis represents a necessary guide for a wise way of living, conforming not only to everyday rules, but to a philosophical ideal for the good, moral life. In the *Theaetetus* he continues the *elenctic* form of questioning, but adds a reflection on what purpose it serves. The main point is that the search for truth—which is the goal even of the early dialogues (the dialogues without a positive result)—establishes an understanding of truth and philosophical investigation where theory is based on praxis and vice versa: The concept of truth will never be disconnected from reason's critical censorship (*elenchus*) of one's actions.

(ii) *Aporia*. This fundamental theory/praxis connection is maintained throughout Plato's more principal deliberations on method and epistemology, including that of maieutics. Also maintained is the tendency toward critical investigation by way of negation. But the negativity is in some sense radicalized when applied to principal questions such as epistemology itself, or to questions about how it is possible to appropriate true knowledge in general. The question of epistemology is posed in the dialogue *Meno*, which marks the transition from the early to the middle dialogues.[10] The protagonist Meno has been asked the question "What is virtue?" and his original proposal has been refuted by Socrates.[11] Thus, Meno is driven to confusion by the

6 *Theaetetus*, 148e–149a

7 Cf. Gail Fine, "Introduction," in *Plato*, ed. by Gail Fine, Oxford: Oxford University Press 2000, p. 3.

8 See, for example, Gregory Vlastos, "The Socratic Elenchus," in *Plato*, ed. by Gail Fine, pp. 42–3.

9 Cf. Vlastos, "Socrates' Disavowal of Knowledge," in *Plato*, ed. by Gail Fine, pp. 90–3.

10 Cf. Fine, "Introduction," pp. 9–12.

11 *Meno*, 71d–79d.

master, until he is compelled to confess that he falls short of a clear answer. He is stuck in an *aporia*: he knows neither a way out nor in.[12] Again, the negative strategy of situating the interlocutor in an *aporia* seems to have a definite aim: lacking a sufficient definition, Meno is forced to turn into himself in order to express his virtue in renewed praxis, which conforms to the *idea* of virtue. This turn from everyday moral rules to a radicalized question concerning the ideal of goodness introduces another important distinction into the search for (moral) truth: Meno cannot simply accept a proposition about virtue given by Socrates. To be true to the *idea* of virtue, he must search for his *own* truth, that is, discover the true knowledge and virtue as it is originally given in his soul. According to Plato's theory of recollection, the truth is namely found by recollecting an innate idea of virtue and goodness that has left an *original* trace in his soul.[13] Thus, the theory–praxis relation and the negative search for truth by way of an *aporia* are incorporated into a theory of innate ideas. These ideas are in some way or another present to the individual before his birth, and are brought to mind or awakened and re-collected through Socrates' aporetic questions. Socrates is not a teacher conveying a particular teaching. He is rather someone who points out the weaknesses of a definition, insists on irresolvable problems, and thereby "takes away" (false) knowledge so as to prepare the ground for the birth of truth in the interlocutor in the form of a *metabole*, a turning towards truth or goodness itself.

(iii) *Ignorance*. This dynamic of Platonic epistemology is well known through the allegory of the cave in the *Republic*, books VI–VII, supplemented by the sun allegory and the line allegory.[14] What might be less obvious is the connection between the epistemological scheme in the allegories and the famous Socratic ignorance. In the early dialogues, Socrates applies his ignorance as an ironic strategy to provoke his opponents to propose positive answers to the "What is F?" questions. This has caused several commentators to argue that his ignorance is an ironical jest: he *pretends* to be ignorant, but in fact his knowledge far surpasses that of his opponents. But such an understanding of Socratic irony and ignorance is rather insufficient and overlooks the crucial position of ignorance in Platonic epistemology.[15]

In the *Apology*, Socrates describes his own ignorance as a methodological means to identify and demonstrate inconsistencies in the philosophical positions of his adversaries. When the oracle in Delphi declared him to be the wisest man in Greece, he was surprised because he had to admit that he did not know much compared to others.[16] Yet when he started talking to other men who were called "wise," he understood what the god (Apollo) meant with the oracle's statement. They thought that they were wise because of their extensive knowledge, but when asking them critical, elenctic questions, Socrates discovered that they did not have sufficient

---

12 *Meno*, 80a–c.

13 Cf. *Meno*, 81c–86c. See also Dominic Scott, "Platonic Recollection," in *Plato*, ed. by Gail Fine, pp. 95–126.

14 *Republic*, 507a–520d.

15 See Vlastos, "Socrates' Disavowal of Knowledge," in *Plato*, ed. by Gail Fine, pp. 84–9.

16 *Apology*, 20d–23b.

reasons for their opinions. Thus, his own wisdom was expressed by knowing what he did not know, whereas the others were less wise and even a bit ridiculous, because they thought they knew much, but had no idea concerning the extent of their own ignorance.[17]

There is therefore a difference between the knowledge necessary for action—a knowledge Socrates possesses and presupposes in his arguments—and the certainty that is connected to knowledge in the strong sense, that is, the tracing of knowledge back to its first principles.[18] Socrates' wisdom is based on an ignorance concerning the first principles, even though he presupposes their absolute validity and legitimacy. On this point, Socrates and Plato differ fundamentally from Aristotle concerning the certainty of the first principles of thought. For Socrates and Plato, there is always an uncertainty attached to moral as well as theoretical knowledge, an uncertainty that is inherent to the Socratic *method* and that infects any knowledge attained with it. By insisting on his ignorance and on the statement that his wisdom is *based on* his knowledge of what he does not know, Socrates maintains the difference between knowledge and knowledge, between understanding and understanding,[19] as an undefinable presupposition or "original difference" throughout the entire Platonic *corpus*.

(iv) *Death*. This indefinable presupposition finds its expression *par excellence* in the Socratic reflections on the relationship between death and philosophy. In the *Phaedo*, where Plato describes the last hours of the philosopher sentenced to death, Socrates defines philosophy as a μελέτη θανάτου, which means something like a meditative exercise of dying or a "practice in death."[20] Socrates gives philosophical arguments for the existence of the soul after death, which are partially based on the theory of recollection. Still, he admits not knowing whether death will be for the better or for the worse for him, since it is impossible to make this judgment while still alive. Nevertheless, he suspects it is for the better because the life of a philosopher consists in an incessant exercise of death: to let the body and the sensual impressions *die* in favor of the soul and its spiritual cognition of truth.[21] Hence, the person of the senses is gradually dying away and the spiritual person is born through the *katharsis* of philosophical *episteme* and praxis. This is, so to speak, the higher goal of any philosopher: to engage in an economy of life and death, where death is

---

17 Ibid., 21c–e.

18 Cf. Vlastos, "Socrates' Disavowal of Knowledge," in *Plato*, ed. by Gail Fine, pp. 83–4.

19 Kierkegaard refers to the opposition between understanding and understanding in the following passage in *The Sickness unto Death*: "Instead of going beyond Socrates, it is extremely important urgent that we come back to this Socratic principle—to understand and to understand are two things—not as a conclusion...but as the ethical conception of everyday life." *SKS* 11, 205 / *SUD*, 92. See also the reference to a certain difference between knowledge and knowledge by Vlastos, "Socrates' Disavowal of Knowledge," in *Plato*, ed. by Gail Fine, p. 92.

20 *Phaedo*, 81a.

21 Ibid., 80a–d.

given primacy in the philosophical praxis as a purification of and preparation for (immortal) life.[22]

(v) *Giving birth*. Finally, we may return to the description of a *maieusis* in the *Theaetetus*, which gathers all the features discussed here in the image of a midwife helping the interlocutor give birth to *episteme*: *elenchus*, ignorance, *aporia*, irony, the "katharsis" of death and the (re)birth of a wiser, more responsible self. The dialogue is not elenctic in the narrow sense,[23] but it includes the *elenchus* in the form of an initial "What is F?" question, that is, "What is *episteme*?" (145c–e). Different answers to the question are discussed: *Episteme* is *aisthesis* (151d–186e), *episteme* is true *doxa* (187a–201c), and *episteme* is true *doxa* with *logos* (201c–210a). In the end, all answers are refuted and the conclusion is negative. In short, the dialogue concludes with an *aporia* (210a–d) and thus remains inconclusive. It is in this context, though, that Socrates introduces the image of a midwife to describe his relationship to the young Theaetetus. He tells him the *secret* about his mother Phaenarete (literally "*appearing virtue*"), who worked as a midwife, and describes his own praxis as a continuance of hers. As an old, unfruitful man, he identifies young men who are pregnant with truth, and converses with them, intensifying or softening the pains of travail according to what is necessary for a healthy birth. But there are also discrepancies between his praxis and that of the ordinary midwife, not only because he helps men instead of women, but also because his praxis concerns a spiritual birth, and thus birth in a "higher" sense of the word. Socrates explains:

> Socrates: My art of midwifery is in general like theirs; the only difference is that my patients are men, not women, and my concern is not with the body but with the soul that is in travail of birth...I am so far like the midwife that I cannot myself give birth to wisdom, and the common reproach is true, that, though I question others, I can myself bring nothing to light because there is no wisdom in me. The reason is this. God [ὁ θεός] constrains me to serve as a midwife [μαιεύεσθαι], but has debarred me from giving birth [γεννᾶν]. So of myself I have no sort of wisdom, nor has any discovery ever been born to me as a child of my soul. Those who frequent my company at first appear, some of them, quite unintelligent, but, as we go further with our discussions, all who are favored by god make progress at a rate that seems surprising to others as well as to themselves, although it is clear that they have never learned anything from me. The many admirable truths they bring to birth have been discovered by themselves from within. But the delivery is god's work and mine.[24]

In this passage, the function of the god, who seems to be introduced *in passing*, is of particular interest. There is someone there, though not immediately present, who is nevertheless necessary for the appropriation of knowledge. Socrates is not able to give birth, and the young man is not able to deliver a child without assistance.

---

22 Ibid., 113d–115a.

23 The initial definitions are all refuted, hence the *elenchus* is retained, but the theses discussed are not presented by the young Theaetetus, rather the theses of Protagoras and Heraclitus are presented and discussed by Socrates. Cf. Gregory Vlastos, *Socrates, Ironist and Moral Philosopher*, Ithaca, New York: Cornell University Press 1991, p. 266.

24 *Theaetetus*, 150b–d. The translation is slightly changed, since "god" indisputably is a better translation of "θεός" than "heaven."

Hence, they are both dependent on a *third*, namely the god. He is, so to speak, the (absent) father of knowledge. In this manner, the communication between the two interlocutors becomes *indirect*. And the reason for this indirectness of communication is obvious: it opens up the discussion for a third, who is not directly connected to the topic discussed, but still presupposed in the process of giving birth.

The question of how to mediate wisdom is a topic that never ceases to occupy Socrates, and I should also mention that the problem of giving birth is also part of the broader discourse on love, dominating the *Symposium* and the *Phaedrus*. Early in the *Symposium*, Socrates exclaims that it would be wonderful if the foolish could be filled with wisdom just like water flows from one cup to another through a woolen thread.[25] But as long as that is not the case, the wise person is distinguished by his ignorance, loving and seeking the wisdom that he will never *possess* as his property, as Diotima so beautifully tells him.[26] She then comes to the crucial point of her speech, where she claims that everyone is pregnant, both in body and soul, and that we all "desire to give birth."[27] According to her, giving birth is the fulfillment of a mortal's desire for immortality.[28] But the highest gift for a lover of wisdom is to see Beauty as such; when this happens, he not only gives birth to images of virtue, but to true virtue. For that reason he would even be loved by the gods and attain immortality in a perpetual movement of giving and receiving.[29] Thus, one may expect something more than the pains of travail after all; the pains are overcome by the excessive surplus of wisdom, virtue, and love.

There is no need to follow this method of midwifery in the Socratic context further. The presentation is sufficient for a discussion of how Kierkegaard applies the metaphor when dealing with epistemological problems and a theory of communication. There is, however, one last point from the *Theaetetus* concerning the relationship between *maieusis* and *aporia* which ought to be mentioned. Socrates underscores that every person who is about to give birth, either in a physical or a spiritual sense, is suffering under travails: ὠδίνουσι γὰϱ καὶ ἀποϱίας ἐμπίμπλανται.[30] The word "*aporia*" that occurs here has multiple meanings: ignorance, impasse, and travail. Hence, the metaphor of giving birth is at work every time someone experiences travails in the form of despair, an impasse, not coming further, and fundamental uncertainty.

II. Deception and Truth: Kierkegaard's Socratic Dilemma

In order to define the central dilemma in Kierkegaard's maieutics, I will start at the end, that is, with Kierkegaard's retrospective considerations of the maieutic character of his task as an author. In the posthumously published report to his contemporaries called *The Point of View of My Work as an Author* he presents his own understanding of the *art* of helping:

---

25 See *Symposium*, 175d.

26 In *Symposium*, 202a–205d.

27 *Symposium*, 206c.

28 Cf. *Symposium*, 207a.

29 Cf. *Symposium*, 212a–b.

30 *Theaetetus*, 151a.

> This is the secret in the entire art of helping....In order truly to help someone else, I must understand more than he—but certainly first and foremost understand what he understands. If I do not do that, then my greater understanding does not help him at all. If I nevertheless want to assert my greater understanding, then it is because I am vain or proud, then basically instead of benefiting him I really want to be admired by him. But all true helping begins with a humbling. The helper must first humble himself under the person he wants to help and thereby understand that to help is not to dominate but to serve, that to help is not to be the most dominating but the most patient, that to help is a willingness for the time being to put up with being in the wrong and not understanding what the other understands.[31]

This is admittedly a beautiful passage concerning the art of spiritual midwifery that is loved and quoted by philosophers, as well as health workers, business coaches, and pedagogues. The passage portrays Kierkegaard, the maiuetician, not as complicated and frightening as many will have it, rather as a humble man, denying himself in order to help others which are searching for truth. In this sense, his application of the Socratic pattern seems even more concerned with the *other* than is the case with Socrates: "The helper must first humble himself under the person he wants to help and thereby understand that to help is not to dominate but to serve."[32]

Nevertheless, the conflict between dominating and serving is one of the crucial points in Kierkegaard's maieutics, and a point that is not yet settled by this statement. This comes to the fore when one considers the following point: in the text quoted above, Kierkegaard himself is quite sure of having a greater understanding than that of his interlocutors, readers, or listeners. When he "listens" to someone, that is, when he writes about aesthetic or ethical topics, he does so only *pretending* not to know, albeit *knowing* that he is the one who knows *better*. At least on the surface level, this attitude clearly contradicts the one of Socrates, who claimed that he had never given birth to any true *episteme*. Even though Socrates seems to exaggerate his ignorance, he admits that he is dependent on his interlocutors, because they are the only ones who are still spiritually fertile. The truth Socrates is searching for is revealed through the dialogue, whereas the truth Kierkegaard is searching for seems to be a more *subjective* one, only accessible to the single individual, singularized by the thought of death or standing alone before God.

In the following passage Kierkegaard claims that the crowd, because of its massive delusion, must be "seduced into truth" by way of Socratic maieutics:[33]

> What, then, does it mean "to deceive"? It means that one does not begin *directly* with what one wishes to communicate but begins by taking the other's delusion at face value. Thus one does not begin...in this way: It is Christianity that I proclaim and you are living in purely esthetic categories. No, one begins this way: Let us talk about the esthetic. The deception consists in one's speaking this way precisely in order to arrive at the religious. But according to the assumption the other person is in fact under the delusion that the

31 *SV1* XII, 533 / *PV*, 45.

32 Ibid.

33 Concerning the problem of deceiving into the truth, see *SV1* XIII, 540–2 / *PV*, 53–5.

> esthetic is the essentially Christian, since he thinks he is a Christian and yet he is living in esthetic categories.[34]

To deceive in order to communicate the truth is Kierkegaard's definition of *indirect communication*. This follows from his appropriation of Socratic maieutics, but it also becomes apparent that the concept of midwifery has thereby been changed. In fact, Kierkegaard presupposes that deception is a *necessary* means in order to communicate with the deceived: "One can deceive a person out of what is true, and—to recall old Socrates—one can deceive a person into what is true. Yes, in only this way can a deluded person actually be brought into what is true—by deceiving him."[35] This claim, as sophisticated as it may be, is certainly very problematic in ethical respects and as an epistemological definition of "truth." It lacks any transparent or obvious criterion to distinguish between truth and seduction. Hence, the teacher or helper will have to keep his goal *secret* until he thinks that the other person is ready to appropriate the knowledge the teacher intends to convey.

So much for the problematic side of that dilemma; but it certainly has a *constructive* side as well. Kierkegaard is neither able nor willing to *solve* the problem, because the entanglement of deception and truth is precisely a topic of critical deliberation throughout his writings. The Danish philosopher is not one to seek a clear-cut solution to this dilemma. He insists on the importance of *not* solving such problems of existence—a strategy he defines as a typically Socratic way of thinking. By leaving the problem to the reader, as a problem concerning her own existence, his aim is to intensify the travail, that is, the *aporias* of human existence. This strategy is apparent, as I will show below, in almost every book published by Søren Kierkegaard, pseudonymously or not. When talking about Kierkegaard, it is not a question of maieutics or not maieutics, but a question of *how* the maieutic communication takes place and to what extent it influences his thinking. I intend to show that there is a development, however, from his early dissertation, *The Concept of Irony*, which is occupied with the person of Socrates, to texts that become more and more occupied with a *Socratic* repetition of Christianity. This change of scope makes the dilemma of deception and truth more and more acute for Kierkegaard, but he does not leave the maieutic method behind. It gradually changes into a new mode of thinking, as expressed in *The Point of View*. In my analysis, the patterns from Socratic maieutics presented in the first section will, on the one hand, serve as a template for comparing Kierkegaard's maieutics to the one presented by Plato; on the other hand, they will serve as useful analytical tools for studying the complex development of his maieutic thinking.

III. Elenchus, Love, and Secrecy: The Concept of Irony

In his dissertation on irony, Kierkegaard pays particular attention to the *elenctic* aspect of the early dialogues. Throughout the brief analyses of the *Symposium*, the *Protagoras*, the *Phaedo,* the *Republic*, Book I, and the *Apology*, he emphasizes

34 *SV1* XIII, 541 / *PV*, 54.

35 *SV1* XIII, 541 / *PV*, 53.

the negative character of the Socratic method. He refers to Schleiermacher, who observed that the early dialogues ended *without* a conclusion, and the young Danish philosopher agrees with this observation. But he also points out that this does not yet qualify the dialogues as *ironic*. It is the "*negative* conclusion" that distinguishes Kierkegaard's understanding of the ironic.[36] The negative aspect of the Socratic method undermines Plato's idealist tendencies and exhausts itself in the dialectic "sustained by irony, springing from irony and returning to irony."[37] As Kierkegaard points out, the negative result in the Socratic *elenchus* is not a coincidence. It is defined as the very goal of the early Socratic method that keeps Socrates himself *at a distance* from his interlocutor, as well as from the knowledge he seeks.

It is a bit strange, though, that Kierkegaard insists on developing a *maieutic* method on the basis of these early dialogues. He does not offer a detailed analysis of the *Theaetetus*, the only dialogue where the concept of *maieusis* is mentioned, though he *is* passionately occupied with the notion of "giving birth" in the *Symposium*. The reason is probably that the link between *elenchus* and *maieusis* is so obvious to him, namely, that *elenchus* can serve as a basis for a theory of irony as maieutics. He claims that irony is the life-view of Socrates; his questions are elenctic; thus, a maieutic dynamic develops between Socrates and his interlocutors.

In an effort to distinguish between the Platonic and the Socratic aspect of the Platonic *corpus*, Kierkegaard underscores the maieutic distance of irony. Whereas Plato constructs the world (*Tilværelsen*) dialectically, Socrates refutes any defined position in order to keep his negative freedom. For Kierkegaard, Socrates becomes irony *in personae*, and the "distinctive features" of his method are "irony in its total endeavor, dialectics in its negatively liberating activity."[38] In the later dialogues like the *Parmenides*, Kierkegaard sees Plato becoming more conscious of himself, and the *total* endeavor of irony is subsumed under an ideal totality. Nevertheless, he finds that irony continues to undermine the totality of the system. According to Kierkegaard, this is due to the maieutic praxis inscribed in the dialogues as a genre. Maieutics makes every interlocutor and every reader of the dialogue responsible for the knowledge they appropriate. Thus, the transmission of knowledge is caught up in an infinite, total negativity in so far as knowledge is not a simple repetition, but the *birth* of *episteme*.[39]

At this point, however, we might already notice a certain difference between Socrates and Kierkegaard. In the *Theaetetus*, Socrates keeps his focus on the problem of knowledge (ἐπιστήμη) whereas in *The Concept of Irony*, Kierkegaard is almost exclusively interested in the *person*. He no longer takes maieutics to be about the birth of knowledge; it concerns the birth of a new *subject*. The "infinite, negative" work of irony is thus about initiating the birth of a person in the form of a "new beginning."[40] The peak of this analysis is reached in his description of an existential

36 *SKS* 1, 115 / *CI*, 54. (My emphasis.)

37 *SKS* 1, 116 / *CI*, 55.

38 *SKS* 1, 174 / *CI*, 122.

39 *SKS* 1, 276–7 / *CI*, 235–6.

40 "But in all these and similar incidents, the salient feature of the irony is the subjective freedom that at all times has in its power the possibility of a beginning and is not handicapped

conversion, the sudden moment when "everything is changed for them ἐν ἀτόμῳ, ἐν ῥιπῇ ὀφθαλμοῦ."[41] This total change is certainly also an element in the Socratic dialogues, but Kierkegaard's suppression of the aspect of knowledge in favor of the aspect of *personhood* shows that he is strongly influenced by the literary period he belongs to, the Romantic era.

In the second part of *The Concept of Irony*, Kierkegaard criticizes some Romantic authors for not understanding the total negativity of Socrates, and on that point Kierkegaard certainly differs from other Romantic authors.[42] But his reflection on the maieutic *relationship* between Socrates and young men is nevertheless profoundly Romantic, and he places particular emphasis on the erotic intimacy between them. In his opinion, a sudden change in world-view is only possible because of the intimacy of a love-relationship. Thomas Pepper has argued that Kierkegaard in fact describes a homoerotic love-relationship, even though Kierkegaard insists on its intellectual character as a negation of sensual love.[43]

Kierkegaard's argument for emphasizing love is that only love can change a person so fundamentally. But he also notes that there is a contradiction between the intimacy of *eros* and the distance of Socrates' irony which makes it a *maieutic* relationship. Thus, he concludes that it is this *negative* love that reminds us "of the art he himself claimed to possess—the art of midwifery. He helped the individual to an intellectual delivery; he cut the umbilical cord of substantiality. As an *accoucheur*, he was unrivaled, but more than that he was not. Nor did he assume any real responsibility for the later lives of his students."[44]

In *The Concept of Irony*, Kierkegaard does not distinguish clearly between irony and maieutics, because maieutics follows from the *praxis* of irony, giving irony both its personal and its "world-historical" form.[45] At this point he follows Hegel, but

---

by earlier situations. There is something seductive about all beginnings, because the subject is still free, and this is the enjoyment the ironist craves. In such moments, actuality loses validity for him; he is free and above it." *SKS* 1, 291 / *CI*, 253.

41 "It seemed as if he had secretly listened to the most intimate conversations of their souls, as if he constrained them to speak aloud about them in his presence. He became their confidant without their quite knowing how it happened, and while throughout all this they were completely changed, he remained unbudgingly the same. And then, when all the bonds of their prejudices were loosened...when his questions had straightened everything out and made the transformation possible, then the relation culminated in the meaningful moment... that instantly illuminated the world of their consciousness, when he turned everything upside down for them at once, as quickly as a glance of the eye [*Øieblik*] and for as long as a blink of the eye, when everything is changed for them ἐν ἀτόμῳ, ἐν ῥιπῇ ὀφθαλμοῦ." *SKS* 1, 237 / *CI*, 190.

42 Cf. *SKS* 1, 321–40 / *CI*, 286–308. See also the commentaries on Schlegel and Tieck in *SKS* K1, 350, 360–1.

43 Cf. Thomas Pepper, "Male Midwifery: Maieutics in *The Concept of Irony* and *Repetition*," in *Kierkegaard Revisited*, ed. by Niels Jørgen Cappelørn and Jon Stewart, Berlin and New York: Walter de Gruyter 1997 (*Kierkegaard Studies Monograph Series*, vol. 1), pp. 460–80.

44 *SKS* 1, 238 / *CI*, 191.

45 Cf. *SKS* 1, 302–3 / *CI*, 254–65.

criticizes him for failing to notice the significance of irony in the transition from an "old" to a "new" totality, born of the infinite negativity of Socrates, which is defined as the *infinite absolute negativity*.[46] It seems, however, as if Kierkegaard has not yet discovered the more radical consequences of such an infinite difference as opposed to the speculative *sublation* (*Aufhebung*) of differences.[47] In fact, some of the most important differences between Kierkegaard and Hegel can be traced back to this infinite negativity. Kierkegaard enjoys playing the role of a Socratic thinker with a negative-ironic distance to the idealism of Plato and Hegel, respectively. Thus, it is not surprising that he is critical of the way Hegel interprets Socratic maieutics, focusing not on the questions but on the answers and the concept of "becoming":

> Hegel's description of Socrates' art of midwifery does not fare much better. Here he develops the significance of Socrates' asking questions, and his discussion is both beautiful and true, but the distinction made earlier between asking in order to get an answer and asking in order to disgrace is overlooked here. At the end, the example of the concept "to become" that he chooses is once again totally un-Socratic....[48]

According to Kierkegaard, the great merit of Socrates is that he questions *everything* that has been, even without knowing what is to come or become. In fact, this is also the very reason that he is sacrificed, and hence Plato, in the *Apology*, establishes a *secret* connection between Socrates giving birth and Socrates facing death.[49] Maieutics is introduced as a hidden or secret economy on the border between life and death.[50] Hence, the logical connection between maieutics and death is noticed by Kierkegaard as early as *The Concept of Irony*. The secrecy appears to be necessary in order to *singularize* the interlocutor. Communicating maieutically will therefore always run the risk of total misunderstanding. Still, the bigger risk is that the communication succeeds and provokes a reaction, the scandal of truth. Such a scandal is connected to the risk of giving one's life as a sacrifice for truth.[51] When a life is given, life is at risk. And even this last risk remains ambiguous concerning the *meaning* of death, of truth, of travail. Because the meaning of Socrates' life *was* irony, even the meaning of his death remains ambiguous, since finally "the ironic nothing is the dead silence in which irony walks again and haunts [*spøger*] (the latter word taken altogether ambiguously)."[52]

---

46 "Here, then, we have irony as the *infinite absolute negativity*. It is *negativity*, because it only negates; it is *infinite*, because it does not negate this or that phenomenon; it is *absolute*, because that by virtue of which it negates is a higher something that still is not. The irony establishes nothing [*Intet*], because that which is to be established lies behind it. It is a divine madness that rages like a Tamerlane and does not leave one stone upon another. Here, then, we have irony." *SKS* 1, 299 / *CI*, 261.

47 Cf. *SKS* 1, 299 / *CI*, 261.

48 *SKS* 1, 305 / *CI*, 267–8.

49 See *SKS* 1, 298–9 / *CI*, 260–1.

50 Kierkegaard repeatedly comes back to the *secrecy* and the "love-secrets" of Socratic maieutics: for example, *SKS* 1, 237–8 / *CI*, 190–1.

51 See the *Apology*, 28b–c.

52 *SKS* 1, 296 / *CI*, 258. Kierkegaard refers to Socrates' claim that "No one knows whether death may not be the greatest of all blessings...." (*Apology*, 29a.) Cf. also the reference to the well kept secrecy of maieutics in the *Theaetetus*, 149a.

IV. That Single Individual, Those Multiple Names: The Early Pseudonymous Writings

All the pseudonyms are introduced as part of a maieutic strategy. Thus, in 1849 Kierkegaard can write that the authorship "began maieutically with aesthetic production, and all the pseudonymous writings are maieutic in nature. Therefore, this writing was also pseudonymous, whereas the directly religious—which from the beginning was present in the gleam of an indication—carried my name."[53] It is not the pseudonyms as such that make the texts maieutic, but the relationship between his true name and the false or masking names, *which brings the identity of the author as well as the identity of the reader into play.*

With the "sensation" of *Either/Or*, Kierkegaard says that he addressed the "public" as such, and intentionally as the public. He then makes an effort to show the public reader, understanding themselves as part of the public, that they are also a single individual, or even primarily a single individual: "Here the beginning is made, maieutically, with a sensation, and with what belongs to it, the public, which always joins in where something is going on; and the movement was, maieutically, to shake off 'the crowd' in order to get hold of 'the single individual,' religiously understood."[54] The goal of the maieutic movement is to let the readers discover themselves by involving them in an aesthetic discussion, in a problem they are not able to solve by way of aesthetic or public categories. In the midst of the aesthetic—the analysis of Mozart's Don Juan, "The Seducer's Diary," the discussion of the limit between the aesthetic and the ethical—there are problems that situate the public reader in a decisive position: existential choice, despair, and seduction. Aesthetic discourse is fragmentary but excellent, according to the taste of the literary elite. And with a twist of the negative, maieutic strategy, the fragmentary style illustrates exactly what is lacking: the single individual *responding* to themselves, to the other, and to God. The maieutic strategy of the early pseudonymous writings inclines toward such a movement, in the direction of what is missing, in order to make the reader *aware* of their singularity, of their possibility of becoming a person in this qualified sense.[55] Not only does Kierkegaard describe different life-views, but he presents them through aesthetical and ethical authors, through dialogues and literary situations. Hence, the author (or "editor") is able to *withdraw* from his work, leaving the stage open for a multitude of different personalities.

In what sense can this be called a *maieutic* strategy? It is maieutic exactly by way of the ironic withdrawal from the positions presented. Kierkegaard is neither present as a philosopher trying to convince his readers, nor as a poet presenting his own story—that is, he is both, but neither of them unequivocally. All the arguments, all the

---

53 *SKS* 13, 13–4 / *PV*, 7. The essay *On My Work as an Author* was written in 1849, but published in 1851. The more famous *Point of View* was published posthumously.

54 *SKS* 13, 15 / *PV*, 9.

55 "Here again the movement is: to *arrive at* the simple; the movement is: from the public to 'the single individual.' In other words, there is in a religious sense no public but only individuals, because the religious is earnestness, and earnestness is the single individual; yet every human being, unconditionally every human being, which one indeed is, can be, yes, should be—the single individual." *SKS* 13, 17, 498–9 / *PV*, 10.

attitudes and personalities, are presented under the guise of other names. The author himself does not present his own view, but only the dilemma of judging between incompatible views. Just like Johannes the seducer, he is deliberately seducing his reader. He is playing with identities and positions—his own, that is, the identity of the author, as well as the positions and identities of the reader—without offering his name in any of them. Hence, the negative strategy, the distance between reader and author and the renouncement of a solution to the problem, is given priority.

All the early pseudonymous writings, from *Either/Or* to the *Postscript* are modeled on such a notion of maieutics. The role of Socrates in this maieutic strategy is not quite clear, though. The dissolution of the subject is certainly more of a *modern* problem than a problem of antiquity. Still, Socrates becomes an ideal for developing a true self because he philosophizes with the slogan "know thyself." He questions his own identity as well as the identity of his interlocutor. His self-reflection is never disparate from his action. His ethic is not reducible to the *habitus* of his contemporaries. Thus when acting in one way or another, he is at the same time questioning the totality of the ethical system to which he belongs.[56] When reflecting upon the truth, he is ready to doubt the *totality* of the present life-view. Socrates therefore becomes the prototype for an "existential thinker," who offers the maieutic praxis a concrete ideal.

There is a big difference, though, between Plato's Socrates and Kierkegaard's repetition of the Socrates figure with regard to the question of the self. Socrates is introduced in a modern context, and thus he can pose questions that concern the secularization of Christianity and the dissolution of Western metaphysics. Could it be that this modern, though anachronistic, image of Socrates comes quite close to an image of Søren Kierkegaard, as a certain *alter ego*? It may or may not, but there is obviously a kind of circularity here. The author Søren Kierkegaard is hiding behind his pseudonyms as a Socratic gesture—in order to *repeat* Socratic doubt among his contemporaries. He is writing in order to communicate with "the others," but all the while he is communicating with "himself."[57] The question concerning the identity and the "self" of reader and author alike is: *to whom* will birth be given?

V. Maieutics in the Upbuilding Discourses

Concerning the upbuilding discourses, which were published parallel to the pseudonymous writings throughout his authorship, Kierkegaard explicitly says in retrospect that these texts are *not* maieutic because they are published in his own name as an expression of direct communication (*ligefrem Meddelelse*).[58] On this point, it seems we must question the author, for the upbuilding discourses are certainly

---

56 This fact becomes apparent when he is attacked in front of the court in the *Apology*, 21d–23b.

57 Cf. Joakim Garff, *"Den Søvnløse": Kierkegaard læst æstetisk/biografisk*, Copenhagen: C.A. Reitzel 1995, pp. 30–1; pp. 56–9; pp. 85–7; p. 103; p. 155; p. 175; p. 197 et passim.

58 *SKS* 13, 13–4, 495–6 / *PV*, 7–8.

maieutic, but admittedly in a sense different from that of the pseudonymous texts.[59] Here, the maieutic is not about various authors and pseudonyms, though it is still a question of communication. The main concern of the maieutician is to singularize the reader as "that single individual" (*hiin Enkelte*). This Kierkegaardian category was introduced in the preface to a little book, *Two Upbuilding Discourses* (1843), published three months after the extensive *Either/Or*.[60] In the first preface—and later in the prefaces to all the other upbuilding discourses—Kierkegaard addresses that single individual, "whom I with joy and gratitude call *my* reader."[61] On the one hand, this address was directed to Regine Olsen, his beloved *fiancée*, whom he left to become a writer, and even when the category is extended to any reader, the discourse still echoes some of the *intimacy* of a close relationship between author and reader.[62] Furthermore, Kierkegaard stresses that he is writing "without authority," thereby underscoring the equality of reader and author in their joint search for truth. On the other hand, he underscores the *distance* by way of an alienation of the reader, using strategies to destabilize the religious discourse.[63] Hence, the *tension* between a love-relationship and withdrawnness, between the "creative word" and "silence," are given maieutic significance.[64] The upbuilding discourses, then, appear to be maieutic in a much more straightforward sense than the deceptive, pseudonymous writings. If we study one of the footnotes in *On My Work as an Author* more carefully, our view does not overtly contradict Kierkegaard's on this point:

> The maieutic lies in the relation between the aesthetic writing as the beginning and the religious as the τέλος [goal]. It begins with the aesthetic, in which possibly most people have their lives, and now the religious is introduced so quickly that those who, moved by the aesthetic, decide to follow along are suddenly standing right in the middle of the decisive qualifications of the essentially Christian, are at least prompted to become *aware*.[65]

According to this footnote, the maieutic in Kierkegaard's writings lies in the *relation* between the aesthetic and the religious. The upbuilding discourses take up problems discussed in the pseudonymous texts, but from a different point of view. They are addressed in such a way that the reader must respond existentially, not only intellectually. The reader of the discourse, addressed as "my listener," is put in focus.

---

59 See Kresten Nordentoft, *Kierkegaards psykologi*, Copenhagen: Gad 1972, pp. 463–4; p. 488. Nordentoft's analysis of Kierkegaard's maieutics is one of the most precise and differentiated analyses in the secondary literature; cf. ibid. pp. 446–88.

60 See *SKS* K5, 35–6.

61 See *SKS* 5, 13 / *EUD*, 1. *SKS* 5, 63 / *EUD*, 49. *SKS* 5, 113 / *EUD*, 103.

62 Cf. *SKS* K5, 35–6 and *SKS* 21, 351–2, NB10:185. See also Eberhard Harbsmeier, "Das Erbauliche als Kunst des Gesprächs," *Kierkegaard Studies Yearbook*, 1996, p. 297.

63 Cf. Marius G. Mjaaland, "Death and Aporia," *Kierkegaard Studies Yearbook*, 2003, pp. 395–418.

64 Cf. the description of the "Love-Secrets" between creative word and silence in *SKS* 1, 191 / *CI*, 30.

65 *SKS* 13, 13–4, note / *PV*, 7, note.

They are the one who must do the entire *work* of appropriation.[66] The author is of course giving the *occasion* for thought, a problem to reflect upon, but he is not communicating a "doctrine," nor is he presenting a result or a conclusion. Writing without authority, his role becomes more like the one of a midwife concerned "not with the body but with the soul that is in travail of birth."[67] He intensifies the travail of *episteme* by emphasizing the fundamental connection between theory and praxis, but without resolving the problems discussed. He writes, conscious that he "cannot [himself] give birth to wisdom, and the common reproach is true, that, though [he] question others, [he] can [himself] bring nothing to light."[68] The ultimate reason for this inability (and for his *disclaiming* authority) is taken directly from the Socratic paradigm: only God can give the light that is necessary for a religious *episteme*, that is, for the transition from the aesthetic or ethical to the religious. A human being—like Søren K.—is only capable of giving the occasion for religious *episteme*, primarily by intensifying the travails (that is, the *aporias*). In fact, the "upbuilding" theory of communication appears to be closer to Socrates' description of maieutic praxis in the *Theaetetus* than does the pseudonymous "deception into truth," which is more a Kierkegaardian invention.

VI. Aporia, Ignorance, Truth: Philosophical Fragments

In the *Philosophical Fragments*, Kierkegaard's understanding of *maieutics* expresses the same insight as is apparent in the upbuilding discourses: when it comes to the basis of human existence, no one can be a teacher for others unless he is familiar with the art of midwifery. The key question posed by the pseudonymous author Climacus, "Can the truth be taught?" is thus defined in the "Propositio" with reference to Socrates and his art of midwifery:

> He was and continued to be a midwife, not because he "did not have the positive," but because he perceived that this relation is the highest relation a human being can have to another. And in that he is indeed forever right, for even if a divine point of departure is ever given, this remains the true relation between one human being and another.... Socrates...was a midwife examined by the god himself. The work he carried out was a divine commission (see Plato's *Apology*), even though he struck people as an eccentric (ατοπωτατος, *Theaetetus*, 149), and the divine intention, as Socrates understood it, was that the god forbade him to give birth (μαιευεσθαι με ὁ θεος αναγκαζει, γεννᾶν δε απεκωλυσεν, *Theaetetus*, 150c), because between one human being and another μαιευεσθαι [to deliver] is the highest; giving birth indeed belongs to the god.[69]

Here we can observe that Kierkegaard is not only giving a *general* account of Socrates as a maieutician. He refers directly to and quotes from the relevant passage

---

66 Eberhard Harbsmeier analyzes the peculiar relationship between speech and writing in the written, published speeches of Kierkegaard and its relevance for maieutics, see Harbsmeier, "Das Erbauliche," pp. 296–7.

67 *Theaetetus*, 150b.

68 Ibid., 150c.

69 *PF*, 10–1 / *SKS* 4, 219–20.

in the *Theaetetus*, a passage he had studied carefully in Greek. Acting as a midwife is thus perceived as the highest expression of a relationship between human beings. This is so because *learning* and *teaching* truth in the Socratic sense depends on a recollection of innate ideas, of the truth that is there from birth, or from pre-existent life, though long forgotten.[70] Precisely because he has understood the consequences of his own ignorance, Socrates remains the wisest of all men, but his function as a teacher is nevertheless *coincidental*. Climacus claims that, in principle, any other teacher could replace him because the truth belongs *eternally* to every single person. The truth can only be discovered because it is already there, though it has been forgotten: "The truth is not introduced into him but was in him."[71]

The next step in the *Fragments* is to move to a passage in the *Meno* on the *aporia* of acquiring truth, a passage Climacus also refers to and quotes explicitly.[72] His epistemological dilemma is in fact comparable to the problem formulated here by Socrates. The *aporia* becomes even more irresolvable, however, because there is no possible recourse to recollection. Climacus then defines the fundamental difference between Socratic epistemology and the "hypothesis" that is presented as an "imagined" version of Christianity. The point of difference is preliminarily called "the moment." If the moment is of decisive significance—that is, the eternal truth is dependent on historical events—then the truth *cannot* be found by the individual person. From this presupposition it follows that truth is not given eternally as innate ideas, but conversely, the individual person cannot *possess* the truth, not even as a kind of knowledge of their own ignorance. If they are ignorant of the truth, they are defined as being *outside* the truth, in fact, as "untruth." This is the epistemological paradox that marks the beginning of the *Philosophical Fragments*.

The full significance of the moment becomes apparent when the *other* teacher is introduced in contrast to Socrates. According to the hypothesis, this other teacher brings the truth *from outside*. Moreover, he not only brings truth as such, but he even brings the epistemological *condition* for acquiring truth. Within the hypothesis, this process is called *rebirth*:

> Inasmuch as he was in untruth and now along with the condition receives the truth, a change takes place in him like that from "not to be" to "to be." But this transition from "not to be" to "to be" is indeed the transition of birth. But the person who already *is* cannot be born, and yet he is born. Let us call this transition *rebirth*, by which he enters the world a second time just as at birth....[73]

At this point, Climacus has taken the step from the Socratic birth of knowledge to the Christian concept of a rebirth, as described in John 3:3–8. It is not a big step, at least not when done hypothetically, but the consequences are quite important. The conditions for acquiring truth are redefined, as is the object of truth and the understanding of the subject who searches for truth. Climacus' understanding of

---

70 Cf. *Meno*, 80e.

71 *SKS* 4, 218 / *PF*, 9.

72 See *SKS* 4, 218, 222 / *PF*, 9, 13–14 and *Meno*, 80b–81e. Cf. also Mjaaland, "Death and Aporia," pp. 405–8 and Section II above.

73 *SKS* 4, 227 / *PF*, 19.

"rebirth" appears to be marked by the Pietistic movement in Denmark in the early nineteenth century, which also influenced Kierkegaard's father,[74] though it is easily translated into a Socratic model of maieutics:

> Just as the person who by Socratic midwifery gave birth to himself and in so doing forgot everything else in the world and in a more profound sense owed no human being anything, so also the one who is born again owes no human being anything, but owes that divine teacher everything. And just as the other one, because of himself, forgot the whole world, so he in turn, because of his teacher, must forget himself.[75]

The quotation shows how self-evident it was to Climacus (and Kierkegaard) that Socrates not only speaks of the birth of knowledge, but also of the birth of a new person, of giving birth to oneself. Here he overlooks some Socratic points, however: (i) one *cannot* give birth to oneself but only to knowledge, and (ii) when knowledge is born through travail, it is dependent on the assistance of god and of the midwife. The metaphor and the analogy is once again taken out of its original context in Plato's dialogue. This overlooked fact fits nicely with a distinction introduced by Climacus between a philosophical and a Christian conversion. Moreover, it allows him to construct Christian rebirth as a *philosophical* analogy to Socratic maieutics, although with a decisive difference. Hence, the *repetition* of Christianity as a philosophical hypothesis raises new challenges for epistemology and communication.

The difference between Socrates and "the teacher" is introduced with "the moment," which represents the decisive break between the two epistemological models.[76] Whereas Socrates leads his interlocutors back to the "old" beginning (to the truth given as innate, eternal ideas), the moment introduces a "new" beginning, a beginning where the teacher himself is given a significant position. According to Climacus, however, it remains an open question whether this possibility is thinkable, whether it is possible to "construct" such a "thought project."[77] Further, this question is deliberately left open by the author of the *Fragments*. In the "metaphysical" Chapter III, Climacus is concerned with the ultimate paradox of thought: "to want to discover something that thought itself cannot think."[78] This unknown that *disturbs* man and his self-knowledge is then given the name "the god," hypothetically of course, and only as a name.[79] Neither the existence nor the non-existence of this unknown can be proven or demonstrated with a philosophical argument.[80] It can only be posed hypothetically, or presupposed as the unknown, the absolutely

---

74 Cf. the following statement: "for presumably we can be baptized *en masse*, but we can never be reborn *en masse*," *SKS* 4, 227 / *PF*, 19. Such a distinction between baptism and rebirth is typical for Pietism, but quite unthinkable for orthodox Lutheran faith from the sixteenth and seventeenth century.

75 *SKS* 4, 227–8 / *PF*, 19.

76 See *SKS* 4, 229 / *PF*, 20–1 where the moment is defined in its relation to rebirth, yet again with another reference to the *Theaetetus*.

77 *SKS* 4, 229–30 / *PF*, 21–2.

78 *SKS* 4, 243 / *PF*, 37.

79 See *SKS* 4, 244–5 / *PF*, 39.

80 Cf. *SKS* 4, 245–9 / *PF*, 39–44.

different.[81] Thus the *aporia* of knowledge in the *Meno* is radicalized by reference to a decisive presupposition that ought to *remain* unknown with regard to conceptual knowledge.

I will leave the paradox here, though Climacus goes one step further and defines the absolute paradox as the god in the *Gestalt* of a human, that is, the teacher, who teaches the individual about truth and untruth. This hypothesis has important consequences for a theory of communication that have already been mentioned in passing: the knowledge of the paradox cannot be communicated directly, but only by relating to the unknown, to the teacher, to the paradox. The highest communicative relationship that can be acquired between human beings is to make someone *aware* of the possibility—and this is a true task for maieutic praxis.

VII. Ignorance, Paradox, and the Art of Taking Away: Postscript

In the *Concluding Unscientific Postscript to the Philosophical Fragments*, Climacus considers problems of communication in a more general way. Commenting upon misunderstandings of the *Philosophical Fragments*, he proclaims that he never intended to *add* new knowledge, that is, "*was ganz Außerordentliches und zwar Neues*."[82] In contrast, his method may be described as an art of taking away:

> Because everyone knows the Christian truth, it has gradually become such a triviality that a primitive impression of it is acquired only with difficulty. When this is the case, the art of being able to communicate eventually becomes the art of being able to *take away* or to trick something away from someone. This seems strange and very ironic, and yet I believe I have succeeded in expressing exactly what I mean.[83]

Taking away knowledge is done by a certain *estrangement* of the addressee: that which is assumed to be well-known has been *trivialized* by being presented in an unexpected way so that the reader becomes perplexed and confused.[84] Climacus is concerned with the example of Christianity: in a Christian country like Denmark in the 1840s, where Christianity was the state religion, everyone was supposed to know the essential Christian teachings. Moreover, it was simply assumed that everyone was a Christian. Climacus then makes a problem of what is apparently self-evident, proclaiming that he is *not* a Christian. He does not even know what it means to be a Christian, nor is he able to understand the central point of Christianity because it represents a paradox. The strategy is simple, but effective: when defining himself as being *outside*, he represents a continuous threat to the trivial opinion that "everyone"

---

[81] "What then is the unknown? It is the frontier that is continually arrived at, and therefore when the category of motion is replaced by the category of rest it is the different, the absolutely different." *SKS* 4, 249 / *PF*, 44.

[82] *SKS* 7, 250, note / *CUP1*, 275, note.

[83] *SKS* 7, 250–1, note / *CUP1*, 275, note.

[84] Cf. the detailed study on this topic in Paul Muench, "The Socratic Method of Kierkegaard's Pseudonym Johannes Climacus: Indirect Communication and the Art of 'Taking Away,' " in *Søren Kierkegaard and the Word(s)*, ed. by Poul Houe and Gordon D. Marino, Copenhagen: C.A. Reitzel 2003, pp. 139–50.

is *inside*. Moreover, he defines the difficulty as a difficulty in understanding the simplest things and the task of living "primitively."[85] He claims that this sort of reflection on the most basic conditions for being human is much more demanding than attaining complicated scientific knowledge or construing a "logical system."[86] Compared to the task of understanding the simplest things, seeking scientific knowledge is like a flight into the illusory certainty of "positive" knowledge.[87]

Against such an objective certainty, Climacus follows a maieutic strategy in three stages: (i) to perplex and confuse the reader with a surprising contradiction between form and content; (ii) to remind the reader of Socratic ignorance concerning *any* knowledge in general—and the knowledge of oneself in particular; (iii) to present Christian thought in the form of a paradox, thus emphasizing the immense *intellectual* difficulty of understanding the simplest things and making his readers aware of its basically *existential* scope.

Socrates, in fact, plays a double role in this maieutic investigation of Christianity. *First*, he is presented in contrast to contemporary Christianity in so far as he always insists on a point they have forgotten, namely, that *how* one understands something is just as important as *what* one understands.[88] In dealing with existential knowledge, the emphasis lies on the *how*, that is, how knowledge is actualized in concrete, personal existence. The famous statement that *subjectivity is the truth* is thus a thoroughly Socratic understanding of truth.[89] In this respect, Socrates functions as a challenge and *corrective* to contemporary Christianity. Although he was not a Christian, he has presented the paradigm for the kind of knowledge that distinguishes the Christian truth from other kinds of truth. He knew what Christianity has forgotten, and it is in such forgetfulness that Christianity has been trivialized. Thus, the first step is to *go back to* Socrates and Socratic ignorance, to Socratic negativity, and to a Socratic knowledge of the fundamental connection between theory and praxis.

The *second* role of Socrates is more complicated. It consists in re-appropriating Christianity while presupposing the above basic Socratic insight, thus conceiving of Christian doctrine in a Socratic way. This does not entail a *leveling* of Christian doctrine, rather a sharpening of the decisive difference between a Socratic and a Christian definition of truth: "So, then, subjectivity, inwardness, is truth. Is there a *more inward* expression for it? Yes, if the discussion about 'Subjectivity, inwardness,

---

85 See *SKS* 7, 148–9 / *CUP1*, 159–61.

86 Cf. *SKS* 7, 114–20 / *CUP1*, 118–25.

87 "In the domain of thinking, the positive can be classed in the following categories: sensate certainty, historical knowledge, speculative result. But this positive is precisely the untrue. Sensate certainty is a delusion...; historical knowledge is a delusion (since it is approximation-knowledge); and the speculative result is a phantom. That is, all of this fails to express the state of the subject in existence; hence it pertains to a fictive objective subject, and to mistake oneself for such a subject is to be fooled and to remain fooled. Every subject is an existing subject, and therefore it must be essentially expressed in all his knowing and must be essentially expressed by keeping his knowing from an illusory termination in sensate certainty, in historical knowledge, in illusory results." *SKS* 7, 80–1 / *CUP1*, 81.

88 Cf. *SKS* 7, 185 / *CUP1*, 202.

89 See *SKS* 7, 182–3 / *CUP1*, 199–200.

is truth' begins in this way: 'Subjectivity is untruth.' "[90] With this statement, Climacus claims that he goes *further than* the Socratic position, but he insists on doing it in a Socratic way, without losing the Socratic perspective on ignorance and knowledge. The two statements stand in a dialectical relation to one another so that any truth of importance for the single individual ought to be achieved subjectively, but the most fundamental truth that can be attained subjectively is the insight that subjectivity is untruth. The last point is, of course, based on the Christian doctrine of (hereditary) sin, but it is translated into a Socratic dialectic in order to avoid its trivialization.[91]

The entire project and style of the *Postscript* is Socratic. In fact, Climacus begins with an analysis of Socratic thinking in Christianity, but ends up with a translation of Christian thinking into a Socratic language. He remains a skeptic and a humorist concerning the actual truth of Christianity, of the paradox, of the moment, and the like. He makes a point out of not being a Christian, but he is profoundly interested in what "being a Christian" means. Even when presented in hypothetical form, he is convinced that his inquiry shows that the majority of so-called Christians are frauds. Moreover, they have totally misunderstood the philosophical presuppositions of Christianity.

Climacus inquires into different aspects of Christian thinking in order to define the possibility of becoming a Christian. And in one footnote, he describes the existential movement from the "hypothesis God" to the existential necessity of the same name:

> In this way God is indeed a postulate, but not in the loose sense in which it is ordinarily taken. Instead, it becomes clear that this is the only way an existing person can come into relationship with God: when the dialectical contradiction brings passion to despair and assists him in grasping God with "the category of despair" (faith), so that the postulate, far from being arbitrary, is in fact a *necessary* defense [*Nødværge*], self-defense; in this way God is not a postulate, but the existing person postulating God is—a necessity [*Nødvendighed*].[92]

In this case, the category of despair expresses the necessary detour for coming into relationship with God; even this, I would argue, is a Socratic point of view. Despair *is* the travail of acquiring truth maieutically. Without despair, knowledge remains abstract; through despair, it might become existentially relevant, a necessity. The category of despair thus reflects the experience of an *aporia*, of facing death, or (even more terrifying) the "sickness unto death." So far, the Socratic maieutic is inscribed into Climacus' (and Kierkegaard's) analysis of Christianity. The point where the Socratic and Christianity differ is located in an extension of the paradox: Socrates defines a subjective paradox in relation to objective knowledge. According to Climacus, however, the Christian not only faces a subjective paradox, but relates to a reality that is paradoxically structured by Christ as the God-man, even though its

---

90 *SKS* 7, 189 / *CUP1*, 207.

91 See *SKS* 7, 191 / *CUP1*, 208.

92 *SKS* 7, 183, note / *CUP1*, 200, note.

objective ontological status remains uncertain.[93] During the last half of his activity as an author, Kierkegaard explores this *double* paradox.

VIII. The Lectures on Indirect Communication

Kierkegaard's planned lectures on indirect communication from 1847 mark an important change in his reflections on the role of maieutics. Beginning in 1846, he suffered from a bitter conflict with the editors of *The Corsair*, who ridiculed him by publishing caricatured drawings of him. He then became more occupied with the radical incommensurability of Christian thought and its call to represent a *scandalon* and provocation in society. He also began to emphasize the importance of Christian suffering, following the example of Christ. These new considerations are documented in his papers as a draft for ten lectures on "The Dialectics of the Ethical and the Ethical-Religious Communication" at the University of Copenhagen.[94] Although they were neither completed nor delivered, the lectures are interesting in our context because they show how Kierkegaard developed his own theory of maieutics.

He begins with the principal distinction between communicating theoretical knowledge (*Viden*) and practical knowledge (*Kunnen*). In the case of ethics, the emphasis lies on the latter. The communication of practical ethical knowledge is carried out in the medium of *actuality*, and thus the communicator ought to *exist* in a way consistent with his teachings. This striving for actuality represents the actual situation of indirect communication. When it comes to ethical-religious knowledge, Kierkegaard claims that there ought to be some direct communication of knowledge as well, for example, about God, Jesus Christ—but at the same time, this knowledge should be reflected indirectly. In the same lecture, he even claims explicitly that he is the one to have discovered the comprehensive *maieutic* character of Christianity.[95]

Kierkegaard points out that Socrates claimed that he was not able to *give birth* to knowledge, but that is only the first moment in Christian maieutics. The Christian ought to be "reborn"—thereby not only redefining the relationship between human beings, but between God and man (who becomes a "new Creation").[96] When communicating Christian knowledge, then, it is extremely important that the other person does not become dependent on the communicator. If the communicator works as a midwife—like Socrates did—he ought to *deny himself* in order to let the other person stand alone before God. Kierkegaard understands the command to deny oneself not only as a Socratic ironic device, but as a Christian imperative to suffer the way Christ suffered by being God *incognito*.[97] That expresses a kind of irony as well, but irony redefined in relation to power.

---

93 *SKS* 7, 518–33 / *CUP*, 570–86.

94 "Den Ethiske og den ethisk-religieuse Meddelelses Dialektik," in *Pap.* VIII B 79–89 / *JP* 1, 648–57.

95 Cf. *Pap.* VIII B 82, 13 / *JP* 1, 650.

96 *Pap.* VIII B 81, 19 / *JP* 1, 649.

97 "Every witness of the truth who has been misunderstood by his contemporaries, harshly judged, even put to death, has experienced this collision: by giving the truth a less

Power is namely an important aspect of this relationship: The communicator is the powerful one in so far as he has a superior knowledge about the almighty God. Such a powerful position implies that the violent (ab)use of spiritual power is a significant problem, a problem Kierkegaard is well aware of. Thus, in order to communicate this knowledge to others, he claims that the communicator ought to totally renounce his own power in order to "suffer" the truth. That would be a "reduplication" of Christian truth in an ethical-religious sense.

Kierkegaard formulates the difference for the addressee as follows: "To stand—alone by the help of another" vs. "to stand alone—by the help of another."[98] The former alternative is a result of a communicator who misunderstands his own task or abuses his powerful position in order to be admired. The latter alternative is the repetition of the Socratic maieutic *inside* Christianity, and thus it is also defined as irony by Kierkegaard. Even in this case, there is an inherent contradiction between standing alone—and standing by the help of the other. But the dialectic of direct and indirect communication is founded upon this contradiction, and it cannot be dissolved without dissolving the tension of Christian maieutics. Kierkegaard therefore concludes that in order to de-mask the deception of modern Christendom, the communicator himself is bound to deceive, and thus "deceive into the truth."[99] From 1846 on, this problem dominates Kierkegaard's reflections on maieutics.

IX. Maieutics in the Abyss: The Sickness unto Death

Whenever he addresses seriousness, Kierkegaard returns to the thought of death.[100] Thus, thinking death is a problem that permeates his writings from beginning to end, in the pseudonymous as well as the upbuilding texts. In *Three Discourses on Imagined Occasions*, Kierkegaard analyzes *death's decision* as decisive, indefinable, and inexplicable.[101] He insists on the reality of death, and exactly because it is not illusionary, death represents a basic uncertainty concerning the end of human life. When reflecting on death, one reflects upon existence *in toto*, and when taken seriously, death tends to suspend the truth of *any* thought. Hence, Kierkegaard writes in the *Works of Love*:

> Death is the briefest summary of life, or life traced back to its briefest form. This is also why it has always been very important to those who truly think about human life to test again and again, with the help of the brief summary, what they have understood about

true form and apparently saying the same thing, he has had it in his power to gain happiness in the world, to win men—or, by being unconditionally obedient to God, expressing that God's providence shall rule and not his providence, to become misunderstood and judged. Consequently he does no adapt; he stretches himself and as mightily as he can—of course, he wins what amounts to none at all and is accused of pride." *Pap.* VIII B 88 / *JP* 1, 656.

98 *Pap.* VIII B 82, 15 / *JP* 1, 650.

99 Cf. *Pap.* VIII B 85, 24 / *JP* 1, 650.

100 For example in the *Postscript* (*SKS* 7, 153ff. / *CUP1*, 165ff.), *Works of Love* (*SKS* 10, 339–52 / *WL*, 345–58), and in the sermon "At a Graveside" (*SKS* 5, 442–69 / *TD*, 69–102).

101 Cf. *SKS* 5, 448 / *TD*, 78. *SKS* 5, 454 / *TD*, 85. *SKS* 5, 459 / *TD*, 91.

> life. No thinker grasps life as death does, this masterful thinker who is able not only to think through every illusion but is able to think it to pieces, think it to nothing.[102]

For Kierkegaard the thought of death may represent a concentration on the most essential parts of life—as a contrast to the most meaningless.[103] Almost like Nietzsche, he may write about death as a fact permeating any construction of reality, virtually annihilating the world in its very foundation (he even deliberates on the possibility of the "death of God").[104] It is possible to detect such a nihilistic tendency in the philosophical *oeuvre* of Kierkegaard as well, but he does not allow it to get the last word.[105] It is more or less like a preparation for the most serious part of the religious authorship.

In the two texts written under the pseudonym Anti-Climacus, the thought of death enters into the heart of the considerations, representing a Socratic uncertainty and a Christian abyss—the abyssal purgatory of despair. The title of Anti-Climacus' first book, *The Sickness unto Death*, suggests that death plays a decisive role. Thus, this sickness is something other than death, it defines the experience of losing oneself, described as "perpetually to be dying, to die and yet not die, to die death."[106] Whereas death is said to affect only the mortal and sensuous being, the sickness unto death affects the human self eternally. Therefore, people cannot count on death as the liberator from the sickness unto death—it might just as well mark the transition to eternal suffering.

The notion of "eternal death" itself simply represents the classical Orthodox Lutheran view, which had a strong revival in Protestant Pietism. But Anti-Climacus' use of this concept for analyzing the European *Zeitgeist* of his time is quite innovative. His point of departure is the Hegelian dialectics of spirit, constructed as a synthesis of opposites. Thus, in chapter A.A we find the famous dialectical definition of the human being as spirit.[107] In the very same chapter, however, the anthropological scheme becomes destabilized by reference to the *other*: "The human self is such a derived, established relation, a relation that relates itself to itself and in relating itself to itself relates itself to another. This is why it can be two forms of despair."[108] This construction of the self is in fact a maieutic one, that is, it is a result of maieutic considerations and has important consequences for the art of communication in the late works.

The maieutic structure of the human self follows from its fundamental dependence upon the other. When human existence is structured in such a way that you cannot

---

102 *SKS* 10, 339 / *WL*, 345.

103 See Marius G. Mjaaland, "The Autopsy of One Still Living," in *Prefaces and Writing Sampler and Three Discources on Imagined Occasions*, ed. by Robert L. Perkins, Macon, Georgia: Mercer University Press 2006 (*International Kierkegaard Commentary*, vols. 9–10), pp. 359–86, see pp. 364–8.

104 Cf. *SKS* 4, 112 / *FT*, 15 and *SKS* 5, 465 / *TD*, 97.

105 See Niels Nymann Eriksen, *The Category of Repetition*, Berlin and New York: Walter de Gruyter 1998 (*Kierkegaard Studies Monograph Series*, vol. 5), pp. 153–4.

106 *SKS* 11, 134 / *SUD*, 18.

107 Cf. *SKS* 11, 129 / *SUD*, 13.

108 *SKS* 11, 130 / *SUD*, 13–14.

know yourself unless you know the other, or more precisely, *unless you receive the knowledge of yourself from the other*, then you are certainly dependent. When, on the other hand, the knowledge of the other is impossible to communicate directly from one person to another and God as the absolute other is a *hidden* presupposition for human self-knowledge, then the human condition is defined as a "redoubled" *aporia*—or, in Anti-Climacus' words, a double despair: "In despair not to will to be oneself; In despair to will to be oneself." [109] The point is this: when you do not will to be yourself, you flee from the possibility of becoming the responsible self you might have been.[110] That is not difficult to admit. However, even when you want to be yourself, Anti-Climacus maintains that you will fail as long as you insist on your own self-view, that is, as long as you only follow your *own* will and do not receive yourself as a gift *from* the other.[111] This is the double structure of despair, which puts the human self in a quandary.[112] There is, in fact, no possibility, no way to escape, at least as long as you follow the idealistic logic of the self. Man suffers under this situation as he suffers under the yoke of death. Anti-Climacus claims that it is even worse than death, however, because death is a destiny, whereas every man is responsible for the sickness unto death: at "every moment he *is bringing* [the sickness] upon himself."[113] Either by willing or by not willing, the human being is responsible for being sick—even though he lacks the self-knowledge and the knowledge of the other that is needed to become healthy. *The maieutic question is: how to attain this knowledge?*

What makes the situation even more problematic is that the sickness is hidden. No one can be sure if someone else is infected or not. Most people cannot even make this assessment themselves because the symptoms are ambiguous. The task of the author is therefore to identify the sickness, to analyze its symptoms, and to communicate this to the reader. Even in doing so, however, he cannot *cure* the reader. He can only hope to make the reader more conscious of the illness that most probably has infected their innermost being without them even knowing it. The chosen procedure is not indirect in the same way that *Either/Or* or the *Postscript* are. Anti-Climacus presents a taxonomy of despair based on the dialectic of opposites. The intention of the psychological analysis, however, is not only to make the reader *aware* of the problem, but to make them aware of themselves. And the ultimate goal is that through this self-awareness, they will become aware of the *other* as the *ground* of their relation to their own self. Thus, the strategy is again maieutic in two respects:[114] (i) No human being can tell the other about their self-relation; the other will have to reflect upon the problem themselves in order to become aware. (ii) Neither the author nor the reader, neither the physician nor the afflicted, will be able

---

109 *SKS* 11, 129 / *SUD*, 13.

110 Cf. *SKS* 11, 136 / *SUD*, 20.

111 Cf. *SKS* 11, 130 / *SUD*, 14.

112 Cf. Marius G. Mjaaland, "X. Alterität und Textur in Kierkegaards *Krankheit zum Tode*," *Neue Zeitschrift für systematische Theologie und Religionsphilosophie*, vol. 47, no. 1, 2005, pp. 58–80, see pp. 62–6.

113 *SKS* 11, 132 / *SUD*, 17.

114 See Nordentoft, *Kierkegaards psykologi*, p. 463.

to cure the sickness. The cure is ultimately dependent on the (hidden) other, who is the only one who could establish the self-relation *differently*.

In the second part of the book, informed by theological concepts, this other is named "God" in the Christian sense of the word. But only the one who has become conscious of the problem, of the *aporia*, and how deep it goes, will be able to see God as the saving other, the ground that gives the self its transparency, or makes possible the *repetition* of self.[115] Such a repetition presupposes the *travails* of despair in order to bring about the "rebirth" mentioned by Climacus in the *Fragments*. It would be a repetition of the same self, though differently, because it had found its origin in the infinite other. However, the doubly aporetic structure of the sickness unto death—that is, of sin, as Anti-Climacus defines it—lets this possibility appear rather difficult and rare even in Christianity—at least to the well educated among its despisers.[116]

There are two reasons why the transparency of the self seems to be difficult to arrive at: the first is the *aporia* of despair, the second is the *offensive* character of any Christian category. According to Anti-Climacus, genuine Christian categories will always entail the possibility of offense. Maieutically spoken, this is a strategy for *pushing* the reader *away*. Even Socrates was careful to keep his interlocutors at a distance. He attracted young men exactly by keeping them at a distance. For any Christian category, however, the possibility of offense becomes the *conditio sine qua non* for keeping distance in a stricter sense.[117]

X. Offensive Maieutics: Practice in Christianity

In *Practice in Christianity* (1850), Anti-Climacus continues his argument for the possibility of offense as a qualification of Christian maieutics:

> In the relation between individuals, one person must and shall be content with the other's assurance that he believes him; no one has the right to make himself into an object of faith for the other person. If one is to use dialectical redoubling [*Fordoblelse*] in relation to another, he must in exactly the opposite way use it maieutically in order to avoid becoming an object of faith or an approximation thereof for another. The dialectical duplexity [*Dobbelthed*] is provisional; the next stage unconditionally brings falseness if, instead of using the dialectical duplexity for parrying, a person allows himself the presumption of becoming an object of faith for another person. But even with respect to the maieutic I do not decide to what extent, Christianly speaking, it is to be approved.[118]

The ultimate reason for writing maieutically is that nobody should risk becoming an object of faith for another person. Christianly speaking, this would be the worst

---

115 Cf. *SKS* 11, 153–5 / *SUD*, 38–40.

116 See *SKS* 11, 228–31 / *SUD*, 117–19.

117 *SKS* 11, 196–201 / *SUD*, 83–7.

118 *SKS* 12, 145–6 / *PC*, 143.

possible blasphemy.[119] The only person who could do this without committing blasphemy is the God-man, that is, his very claim of being divine is an offense, but a necessary offense. He cannot do otherwise; he must *require* faith, even at the risk of pushing everyone away. This is the offense that for Anti-Climacus belongs to any Christian communication. When the possibility of offense is overlooked or sublated (*aufgehoben*), as in German idealism and in "official Christendom," he even claims that it has lost any relation to the Christian truth. Moreover, Christianity would become distorted into a kind of modern paganism.

Given this situation of modern paganism *in the name of Christianity*, Anti-Climacus claims that any communication of Christian truth must be careful to hold on to the *infinite* difference between delusive and true Christian categories. The situation is, however, even more complex, because anyone who tries to attack modern society in the name of truth must expect to be rejected, ridiculed and—in the worst case—expelled from the society and punished. When rejected and ridiculed, there is no room for maieutics and understanding any longer. Thus, in order to start a conversation with his contemporaries, the maieutician must begin with a delusion. The delusion is that the maieutic author says the same as all the others (he operates within their language game, so to speak), but he keeps his final intention hidden; he himself remains *incognito*. Anti-Climacus considers this possibility, but he hesitates when it comes to a general defense of delusive maieutic strategies:

> Whether a person is right to mystify in this way, whether a person is capable of doing it, whether, if he could, his defense that he was maieutically developing the other person was adequate, or, from another point of view, whether it is not specifically his duty, assuming that it is self-denial and not pride—this I do not decide. Please regard this as merely an imaginary construction in thought that nevertheless does provide illumination regarding "unrecognizability."[120]

Anti-Climacus has defined the problem concerning this kind of maieutics quite clearly: it is always in danger of becoming a product of pride, that is, a very intricate way for the superior to influence the inferior without even making his superiority apparent. If every person is affected by sin, if every form of despair entails a lack of self-knowledge, even a certain blindness concerning oneself, who, then, is able to discern clearly between self-denial and pride? Even someone who wishes to *deny himself* is in danger of doing this out of pride. To practice this art of indirect communication is therefore a very risky undertaking indeed. According to Anti-Climacus, however, it is a necessary undertaking because it is the *practice in Christianity*. The example is given by Christ himself, who—being the God-man—lived in a human *incognito*. All his utterances and all his actions occur in such an incognito so that nobody can tell for sure if he is only a man or the God-man. As the former, he would be a blasphemous charlatan, as the latter he would require unconditional faith and himself become the *object of faith*.[121] At the end of the authorship, we again find an either/or. And

---

119 Cf. also the argument against any effort to demonstrate Christian faith *directly*: *SKS* 12, 43 / *PC*, 29.

120 *SKS* 12, 135 / *PC*, 131.

121 *SKS* 12, 145 / *PC*, 143.

according to Anti-Climacus, there is no option in between. Curiously enough, Christ thus becomes the master of maieutics and the final reason for using the maieutic method. Yet, this form of maieutics seems so different from the Socratic one that, in the end, we must ask if it is still the *same* maieutics as the one originally introduced in *The Concept of Irony*—with continual reference to Socrates.

XI. Discovering the Ground: Works of Love

There is a certain tendency towards negative maieutics in Kierkegaard's authorship; thus, he emphasizes *aporias* and ignorance in order to "take away" false knowledge. In the works written under the name of Anti-Climacus, this tendency becomes even stronger for theological reasons as well as for the sake of criticism. Kierkegaard sees himself fighting against the entire establishment in Denmark. Thus, the plea for suffering and direct confrontation overrules the Socratic *epoché*, the ideal of hiding in irony in order to give birth to knowledge. Such a tendency has been harshly criticized in Denmark, for example, by K.E. Løgstrup, and even though it appears to be partly unjust, the criticism points out a very problematic aspect of Kierkegaard's thought.[122] Many others, however, have defended Kierkegaard, and most of these defenders underscore a different strand in his maieutic considerations, for example, the so-called *positive* maieutics of love.[123]

There is a correlation between the maieutics of love in *Works of Love* (1847), published in his own name, and the two texts written by Anti-Climacus.[124] While the pseudonymous texts intend only to analyze and uncover despair and offense, *Works of Love* has another explicit goal: *to uncover offense in order to discover love*. As opposed to the maieutics of suspicion, this is a maieutics of confidence. The point is: one discovers love when one believes that it is *there* already, in the ground, even though it occurs "under cover":

> *"Love believes all things"* because so to believe all things means to presuppose that love, even though it is not seen—indeed, even though the opposite is seen—is still present in the ground, even in the misguided, even in the corrupted, even in the most hateful. Mistrust takes away the very foundation by presupposing that love is not present—therefore mistrust cannot build up.[125]

The maieutics of confidence gives love as a free gift, without presupposing anything except love, that love is there, *in the ground*. Thus Kierkegaard bases his maieutics on a logic of *supplement*, where *aporias*, *elenchus* and the thought of death prepare

---

122 See K.E. Løgstrup, *Opgør med Kierkegaard*, Copenhagen: Gyldendal 1968, pp. 56–68.

123 Johannes Sløk, *Kierkegaard. Humanismens tænker*, Copenhagen: C.A. Reitzel 1978; Paul Müller, *Kristendom, etik og majeutik i Søren Kierkegaard's "Kjerlighedens Gjerninger,"* Copenhagen: C.A. Reitzel 1983; Arne Grøn, *Subjektivitet og negativitet: Kierkegaard*, Copenhagen: Gyldendal 1997.

124 Grøn has argued convincingly for such a connection between *Sickness unto Death* and *Works of Love* in *Subjektivitet og negativitet: Kierkegaard.*

125 *SKS* 9, 223 / *WL*, 221.

the ground for believing all things, that is, to act as if love was there and thus to *open space* for love.

According to Kierkegaard, such a confidence *cannot* be deceived because it is based in love and returns to love. This is what Kierkegaard calls "true superiority" because it is never anxious of being inferior or becoming deceived.[126] By its very faith in the other, it overcomes deception and sees through it, regards it as a kind of self-deception. The only one who becomes deceived by the deception is the deceiver; the victim of deception will not be deceived because their confidence lies somewhere else, in the love of their neighbor. This is the maieutical logic that lays the foundation for yet another logic, the logic of a deception into truth. Love is not a static foundation for communication; it is a ground which is always moving from oneself to the other, as a "gushing spring" flowing from the bottom of the lake.[127] Giving love by presupposing it involves the self in this movement from oneself to the other; one is thus being changed all the time even though one remains oneself. The loving person is always *in need* of love, but this need of love is what changes the giver as well as the receiver. According to this logic of "overflow," in so far as both are receptive to love, both receive this gift from a source deeper than their own consciousness, from a source that is flowing over.

If we take a careful look at this logic of surplus, it has a structure similar to *eros* in Plato's *Symposium*.[128] It is the love of wisdom and the wisdom of love that moves the philosopher; thus he is moved by a source outside him, which is the common source of love and beauty. This is even the source of giving birth in the metaphorical sense, of moving the one toward the other and all others towards the One. Kierkegaard develops his theory of love from biblical texts, particularly from Paul. But this is one of the few texts that can combine the *eros* of Greek philosophy with the *agape* of the New Testament. Thus, even the break between Socrates and Christ, which in other Kierkegaard texts is fundamental, is overcome here by a logic of surplus. The author is of course not blind to all the contrary possibilities, for example, that love may become deceived, hated, mistrusted, even put to death.[129] Such a reaction is, after all, to be expected because selfless love is a provocation and an offense to the loveless. Still, as he sees it, the only possibility of overcoming the self-centric logic of despair is presupposing the other-centric logic of love in the ground.

The last chapter in *Works of Love* is again a rather provocative text, showing how dialectically complex Kierkegaard's maieutics of love is. He insists that anyone who wants to praise love must make of himself the unloveable.[130] In other words, it is an expression of true Christian self-denial, he writes. And here again, the ethical difference between Socrates and Christ comes to the fore: Socrates was himself ugly, but his ugliness made it easier for him to love the beautiful.[131] The Christian ought to *love* the ugly, the sinner, the despised, and the like, not the beautiful. This is the

126 See *SKS* 9, 237 / *WL*, 236.

127 Thus Kierkegaard defines love in the introductory chapter: *SKS* 9, 18 / *WL*, 10.

128 Cf. section I above and the *Symposium*, 202a–212b.

129 See *SKS* 9, 244–5 / *WL*, 243–4.

130 See *SKS* 9, 367 / *WL*, 373–4.

131 Cf. *SKS* 9, 365–6 / *WL*, 371–2.

paradox of Christian love, which sees beauty in the ugly and the loveable in the lost—and thus also the paradox of Kierkegaard's "positive" maieutics.

XII. Conclusion: Maieutics and the Gift of Love

I have argued for a broad understanding of Socratic maieutics, based on the *elenchus*, the *aporia*, Socratic ignorance, the thought of death, and the metaphor of giving birth. Thus, we arrived at a theory of maieutics that includes Plato's early as well as later works, and that combines such disparate aspects of his philosophy as epistemology, a theory of knowledge, ethics, ontology, and communication. A closer look at Søren Kierkegaard's early texts shows that he is a true maieutician, who has adopted all these traits of maieutic thinking, thus giving his entire authorship a maieutic character. Still, when we write about Socrates and Kierkegaard, maieutics is also about the *love* of wisdom—or the wisdom of love. This is an elliptical figure in the thought of Plato, most clearly expressed in the *Symposium*: everyone who is searching for wisdom is searching for love in so far as philosophy *is* the love of wisdom. This gives a significant perspective for our conclusion about Kierkegaard's Socratic maieutics, a perspective that throws a different light on even the more problematic parts of Kierkegaard's maieutics.

Many differences between Socrates and Kierkegaard stem from the fact that Kierkegaard applies the Socratic method to the Christian claim to truth and the fact that Christian anthropology is clearly different from that of the ancient Greeks. The most obvious conflict is found in the doctrine of sin and human freedom, but just as important are their respective understandings of reason vs. revelation, (acquiring) truth, and ethical responsibility. The Socratic philosopher is eternally searching for truth, whereas Christianity proclaims the truth. But Kierkegaard quite consistently combines the two in an effort to apply a Socratic method as a critical means to inquire into the presuppositions and the truth claim of Christian thinking. He deliberately aims to "take away" false knowledge—about the categories of Christianity as well as the categories of the self. The two sets of categories are interdependent, as far as they are understood existentially, and only when they tear down the objective as well as subjective delusions of the single individual are they able to "break down and dissolve the despairing person's defense of his despair, to lay bare, unmask, and unveil the despair which is present at the very foundation."[132]

Hence, there is a clear analogy between the Socratic *travails* (or *aporias*) and Kierkegaardian despair: addressing a theoretical problem, they both intensify the pain of searching for truth. But this pain ought to be suffered (i) in order to let the single individual struggle with their own deceptions so that they can acquire their own insights, thus giving them the full responsibility for the truth they accept or reject; and (ii) in order to prepare for the birth of knowledge or even—as a certain repetition—for the birth of the entire person, not because one has become someone else, but because one has become oneself.

---

132 Nordentoft, *Kierkegaards psykologi*, p. 463. (My translation.)

The so-called *negative* maieutics, that is, the negativity of *elenchus*, an *aporia*, or even death, plays a decisive role in this process. It is so significant, in fact, that the entire notion of maieutics is sometimes identified with negative maieutics. Thus, Kierkegaard can write in the *The Point of View* that he has aimed at *deceiving* the reader into the truth, because this is the only way the deceived can *become aware* of a truth that transcends their language game, their possibility of understanding, their stage of existence, and so on. This is a problematic figure, however, because it makes the reader totally dependent on the author, facilitating abuse of superior knowledge and manipulation of the "deceived."

This kind of "language game," in which deception replaces deceptions in order to open up the hidden truth, represents the dark side of Kierkegaardian maieutics, prompting the reader to continually be aware of its potentially dangerous consequences. His texts are written in order to "make difficulties," in order to provoke anxiety and despair, but the author cannot guarantee any cure or therapy for such diseases. The readers must take responsibility for being diseased and seek the cure themselves. Kierkegaard understands his works as maieutic in such a radical way that he has given them away for free; they are no longer "his" works. They are gifts to the reader, or even testamentary gifts from a dead author, but the reception of such a gift is not as simple as receiving other kinds of presents. In this case, receiving is just as difficult as giving because it is by receiving such a gift that the receiver could learn to stand *alone*—by the help of the other. Only then would it be a true gift in the maieutic sense, a gift of birth.

The reception of such a gift presupposes more than negative maieutics, though, more than the intensification of anxiety of despair, something more than insight about deception. The reception presupposes something given, that is, a common ground for the one who gives and the one who receives. And that common ground is described in *Works of Love* as an expectation of *love being there*—or, stated simply, *receptivity as a condition for love of oneself, of the other, of God as the absolute other and infinite source of love*. In the case of maieutics, love requires self-denial in order to avoid the abuse of a superior power, that is, the exercise of spiritual violence. But love also creates a certain interrelationship, an economy of giving without knowing, of receiving without control. Giving and receiving in this radical sense extend the limits of Socratic maieutics, but even in this case, the analogy is obvious: I am so far like the midwife that I cannot myself give birth to [love], and the common reproach is true, that, though I [give to] others, I can myself bring no [gift of love] because there is no [such love] in me. The reason is this. God constrains me to serve as a midwife [μαιεύεσθαι], but has debarred me from giving birth.[133]

[133] Modified text based on *Theaetetus*, 150c.

Cumulative Plato Bibliography

Katalin Nun

I. Plato's Works in The Auction Catalogue *of Kierkegaard's Library*

Platonis quæ exstant Opera. Accedunt Platonis quae feruntur Scripta, vols. 1–11, ed. by Friedrich Ast, Leipzig: Weidmann 1819–32 (*ASKB* 1144–1154; parts of this edition (vols. 1–7) also as *ASKB* A I 174–180).

Lexicon Platonicum sive vocum Platonicarum index, vols. 1–3, ed. by Friedrich Ast, Leipzig: Weidmann 1835–38 (*ASKB* 1155–1157).

Platons Werke, vols. 1–3 in 6 parts, trans. by Friedrich Schleiermacher, vols. 1.1–1.2 and vol. 2.1, Berlin: Realschulbuchhandlung 1817–18, vols. 2.2–2.3 and vol. 3.1, Berlin: Reimer 1824–28 (*ASKB* 1158–1163).

Udvalgte Dialoger af Platon, vols. 1–3 [vol. 1, *Phædon*; *Kriton*; *Alkibiades II*; vol. 2, *Symposion*; *Protagoras*; vol. 3, *Gorgias*; Tillæg til Indledningen til *Alkibiades II*], trans. and ed. by C.J. Heise, Copenhagen: Gyldendal 1830–38 [vols. 4–8, Copenhagen: C.A. Reitzel 1851–59; Kierkegaard owned vols. 1–7] (*ASKB* 1164–1166; for vols. 4–7 see *ASKB* 1167 and *ASKB* 1169).

Platons Stat, vols. 1–3, Copenhagen: C.A. Reitzel 1851 [vols. 4–6 of *Udvalgte Dialoger af Platon*, trans. and ed. by C.J. Heise, Copenhagen: C.A. Reitzel 1830–59] (*ASKB* 1167; for vols. 1–3 and vol. 7 see *ASKB* 1164–1166 and *ASKB* 1169).

Platon's Timaeus und Critias, trans. by F.W. Wagner, Breslau: G.P. Aderholz 1841 (*ASKB* 1168).

Platons Timæos, trans. and ed. by C.J. Heise, Copenhagen: C.A. Reitzels Bo og Arvinger 1855 [vol. 7 of *Udvalgte Dialoger af Platon*, trans. and ed. by C.J. Heise, Copenhagen: C.A. Reitzel 1830–59, cf. *ASKB* 1164–1166 and *ASKB* 1167] (*ASKB* 1169).

Plato's Unterredungen über die Gesetze, vols. 1–2, trans. by Johann Georg Shultheß, 2nd revised ed. by Salomon Vögelin, Zürich: Meyer und Zeller 1842 (*ASKB* 1170).

Platonis Eutyphro Apologia Socratis Crito Phaedo Graece, ed. by Johann Friedrich Fischer, Leipzig: Schwickert 1783 (*ASKB* A I 181).

II. Works by Modern Sources in The Auction Catalogue *of Kierkegaard's Library that Discuss Socrates and Plato*

Ast, Friedrich, "Sokrates," in his *Grundriss einer Geschichte der Philosophie*, Landshut: Joseph Thomann 1807, pp. 100–4; pp. 115–23 (*ASKB* 385).

Baader, Franz von, *Vorlesungen, gehalten an der Königlich-Bayerischen Ludwig-Maximilians-Hochschule über religiöse Philosophie im Gegensatze der irreligiösen, älterer und neuer Zeit*, vol. 1, Munich: Giel 1827, p. 41; pp. 85–6 (*ASKB* 395).

—— *Ueber den Paulinischen Begriff des Versehenseyns des Menschen im Namen Jesu vor der Welt Schöpfung. Sendeschreiben an den Herrn Professor Molitor in Frankfurt*, vols. 1–3, Würzburg: In Commission der Stahel'schen Buchhandlung 1837, vol. 2, p. 8, note (vols. 1–2, *ASKB* 409–410) (vol. 3, *ASKB* 413).

—— *Revision der Philosopheme der Hegel'schen Schule bezüglich auf das Christenthum. Nebst zehn Thesen aus einer religiösen Philosophie*, Stuttgart: S.G. Liesching 1839, p. 49; pp. 104–5 (*ASKB* 416).

Baur, Ferdinand Christian, *Die christliche Gnosis oder die christliche Religions-Philosophie in ihrer geschichtlichen Entwicklung*, Tübingen: C.F. Osiander 1835, p. 15; p. 38; p. 144; p. 150; p. 164; p. 228; p. 420; p. 430; p. 435; p. 437; p. 453; p. 470; p. 472; p. 497; pp. 527–8; p. 693; p. 711 (*ASKB* 421).

—— *Das Christliche des Platonismus oder Sokrates und Christus. Eine religionsphilosophische Untersuchung*, Tübingen: Fues 1837 (*ASKB* 422).

[Becker, Karl Friedrich], *Karl Friedrich Beckers Verdenshistorie, omarbeidet af Johan Gottfried Woltmann*, vols. 1–12, trans. by J. Riise, Copenhagen: Fr. Brummer 1822–29, vol. 2, p. 419; pp. 425–6; p. 428 (*ASKB* 1972–1983).

Buhle, Johann Gottlieb, *Geschichte der neuern Philosophie seit der Epoche der Wiederherstellung der Wissenschaften*, vols. 1–6 (in 10 tomes), vols. 1–2, Göttingen: Johann Georg Rosenbusch's Wittwe 1800; vols. 3–6, Göttingen: Johann Friedrich Röwer 1802–05 (Abtheilung 6 in *Geschichte der Künste und Wissenschaften seit der Wiederherstellung derselben bis an das Ende des achtzehnten Jahrhunderts. Von einer Gesellschaft gelehrter Männer ausgearbeitet*, Abtheilungen 1–11, Göttingen: Röwer and Göttingen: Rosenbusch 1796–1820), vol. 1, pp. 88ff.; pp. 150ff. (*ASKB* 440–445).

Cousin, Victor, *Über französische und deutsche Philosophie. Aus dem Französischen von Dr. Hubert Beckers, Professor. Nebst einer beurtheilenden Vorrede des Herrn Geheimraths von Schelling*, Stuttgart and Tübingen: J.G. Cotta 1834, p. XVII; pp. 31–2; p. 41; p. 59 (*ASKB* 471).

Eberhard, Johann August, *Neue Apologie des Sokrates oder Untersuchung der Lehre von der Seligkeit der Heiden*, vols. 1–2, Berlin: Friedrich Nicolai 1778–88 (*ASKB* A I 185–186).

Erdmann, Johann Eduard, *Natur oder Schöpfung? Eine Frage an die Naturphilosophie und Religionsphilosophie*, Leipzig: Vogel 1840, p. 115 (*ASKB* 482).

—— *Grundriss der Logik und Metaphysik. Für Vorlesungen*, Halle: Johann Friedrich Lippert 1841, p. 10; p. 27; p. 161 (*ASKB* 483).

Fichte, Immanuel Hermann, *De principiorum contradictionis, identitatis, exclusi tertii in logicis dignitate et ordine commentatio*, Bonn: Georg 1840, p. 5; p. 17, note (*ASKB* 507).

Fischer, Carl Philipp, *Die Idee der Gottheit. Ein Versuch, den Theismus speculativ zu begründen und zu entwickeln*, Stuttgart: Liesching 1839, p. III (*ASKB* 512).

Fischer, Friedrich, *Die Metaphysik, von empirischem Standpunkte aus dargestellt. Zur Verwirklichung der Aristotelischen Metaphysik*, Basel: Schweighauser 1847 (*ASKB* 513).

Flögel, Carl Friedrich, *Geschichte der komischen Litteratur*, vols. 1–4, Liegnitz and Leipzig: Giegert 1784–87, vol. 1, pp. 14–8; p. 96; p. 101 (*ASKB* 1396–1399).

Frauenstädt, Julius, *Die Naturwissenschaft in ihrem Einfluß auf Poesie, Religion, Moral und Philosophie*, Leipzig: F.A. Brockhaus 1855, p. 144; p. 148 (*ASKB* 516).

Goethe, Johann Wolfgang, "Plato, als Mitgenosse einer christlichen Offenbarung. (Im Jahre 1796 durch eine Uebersetzung veranlaßt)," in *Goethe's Werke. Vollständige Ausgabe letzter Hand* (in 55 volumes), vols. 1–40, Stuttgart and Tübingen: J.G. Cotta 1827–30; *Goethe's nachgelassene Werke*, vols. 41–55, Stuttgart and Tübingen: J.G. Cotta 1832–33, vol. 46 (*Nachlaß*, vol. 6) pp. 22–29 (*ASKB* 1641–1668).

Hagen, Johan Frederik, *Ægteskabet. Betragtet fra et ethisk-historiskt Standpunct*, Copenhagen: Wahlske Boghandels Forlag 1845, p. 90; p. 107, note; pp. 110–18; p. 113 (*ASKB* 534).

Hahn, August (ed.), *Lehrbuch des christlichen Glaubens*, Leipzig: Vogel 1828, p. 47; p. 263; p. 277; p. 288 (*ASKB* 535).

Hase, Karl, *Kirkehistorie. Lærebog nærmest for akademiske Forelæsninger*, trans. by C. Winther and T. Schorn, Copenhagen: C.A. Reitzel 1837, p. 39; pp. 38–9 (*ASKB* 160–166).

—— *Hutterus redivivus oder Dogmatik der evangelisch-lutherischen Kirche. Ein dogmatisches Repertorium für Studirende*, 4th revised ed., Leipzig: Breitkopf und Härtel 1839, p. 2; p. 4; p. 333 (*ASKB* 581).

[Hegel, Georg Wilhelm Friedrich], *Georg Wilhelm Friedrich Hegel's philosophische Abhandlungen*, ed. by Karl Ludwig Michelet, Berlin: Duncker und Humblot 1832 (vol. 1 in *Georg Wilhelm Friedrich Hegel's Werke. Vollständige Ausgabe*, ed. by Philipp Marheineke et al., Berlin: Duncker und Humblot 1832–45, pp. 382–5 (*ASKB* 549).

—— "Sokrates," in *Georg Wilhelm Friedrich Hegel's Vorlesungen über die Geschichte der Philosophie*, vols. 1–3, ed. by Carl Ludwig Michelet, Berlin: Duncker und Humblot 1833–36 (vols. 13–15 in *Georg Wilhelm Friedrich Hegel's Werke. Vollständige Ausgabe*, ed. by Philipp Marheineke et al., Berlin: Duncker und Humblot 1832–45), vol. 2, pp. 42–122 (*ASKB* 557–559).

—— "Plato," in *Georg Wilhelm Friedrich Hegel's Vorlesungen über die Geschichte der Philosophie*, vols. 1–3, ed. by Carl Ludwig Michelet, Berlin: Duncker und Humblot 1833–36 (vols. 13–15 in *Georg Wilhelm Friedrich Hegel's Werke. Vollständige Ausgabe*, ed. by Philipp Marheineke et al., Berlin: Duncker und Humblot 1832–45), vol. 2, pp. 169–297 (*ASKB* 557–559).

—— *Georg Wilhelm Friedrich Hegel's Vorlesungen über die Philosophie der Religion*, vols. 1–2, ed. by Philipp Marheineke, 2nd revised ed., Berlin: Duncker und Humblot 1840 (vols. 11–12 in *Georg Wilhelm Friedrich Hegel's Werke. Vollständige Ausgabe*, ed. by Philipp Marheineke et al., Berlin: Duncker und Humblot 1832–45), vol. 1, p. 22; p. 30; pp. 39–40; p. 142; p. 160; p. 194; p. 220;

pp. 249–50; vol. 2, p. 73; pp. 107–8; p. 130; p. 154; p. 243; p. 287; p. 295; p. 349; p. 397; p. 518; p. 551 (*ASKB* 564–565).

—— *Georg Wilhelm Friedrich Hegel's Vorlesungen über die Aesthetik*, vols. 1–3, ed. by Heinrich Gustav Hotho, Berlin: Duncker und Humblot 1835–38 (vols. 10.1–10.3 in *Georg Wilhelm Friedrich Hegel's Werke. Vollständige Ausgabe*, vols. 1–18, ed. by Philipp Marheineke et al., Berlin: Duncker und Humblot 1832–45), vol. 1, p. 134; p. 197; vol. 2, p. 2; pp. 46–8; p. 56; p. 111; p. 377; p. 452 (*ASKB* 1384–1386).

Heiberg, Johan Ludvig, "Om den romantiske Tragedie af Hertz: *Svend Dyrings Huus*. I Forbindelse med en æsthetisk Betragtning af de danske Kæmpeviser," in *Perseus, Journal for den speculative Idee*, vols. 1–2, ed. by Johan Ludvig Heiberg, Copenhagen: C.A. Reitzel 1837–38, vol. 1, pp. 165–264, see p. 261 (*ASKB* 569).

Helfferich, Adolph, *Die christliche Mystik in ihrer Entwickelung und in ihren Denkmalen*, vols. 1–2, Gotha: Friedrich Perthes 1842, vol. 1, p. 147; p. 151; p. 166; p. 175; p. 182; p. 188; p. 205; p. 288; p. 326; p. 421 (*ASKB* 571–572).

[Herder, Johann Gottfried von], *Johann Gottfried von Herder's sämmtliche Werke. Zur Philosophie und Geschichte*, vols. 1–22, Stuttgart and Tübingen: J.G. Cotta 1827–30, vol. 16, p. 29 (*ASKB* 1695–1705).

Hermann, Karl Friedrich, *Geschichte und System der Platonischen Philosophie*, Heidelberg: C.F. Winter 1839 (*ASKB* 576).

Jäger, Josef Nikolaus, *Moral-Philosophie*, Vienna: J.G. Heubner 1839, pp. 44–5; pp. 47–8 (*ASKB* 582).

Kant, Immanuel, *Critik der Urtheilskraft*, 2nd ed., Berlin: F.T. Lagarde 1793, pp. 273–4 (*ASKB* 594).

—— *Critik der reinen Vernunft*, 4th ed., Riga: Johann Friedrich Hartknoch 1794, p. 9; pp. 370–5; p. 530; p. 596; pp. 881–2 (*ASKB* 595).

Marbach, Gotthard Oswald, "Sokrates und die Sokratiker," in his *Geschichte der Griechischen Philosophie. Mit Angabe der Literatur nach den Quellen*, Leipzig: Otto Wigand 1838 (Abtheilung 1, in Gotthard Oswald Marbach, *Lehrbuch der Geschichte der Philosophie. Mit Angabe der Literatur nach den Quellen*, Abtheilungen 1–2, Leipzig: Wigand 1838–41), pp. 170–86 (*ASKB* 642; for Abtheilung 2 see *ASKB* 643).

—— "Platon und die Akademiker," in his *Geschichte der Griechischen Philosophie. Mit Angabe der Literatur nach den Quellen*, Leipzig: Wigand 1838 (Abtheilung 1, in Gotthard Oswald Marbach, *Lehrbuch der Geschichte der Philosophie. Mit Angabe der Literatur nach den Quellen*, Abtheilungen 1–2, Leipzig: Wigand 1838–41), pp. 194–233 (*ASKB* 642; for Abtheilung 2 see *ASKB* 643).

Marheineke, Philipp, *Lehrbuch des christlichen Glaubens und Lebens für denkende Christen und zum Gebrauch in den oberen Klassen an den Gymnasien*, 2nd revised ed., Berlin: Nicolai 1836, p. 6; p. 20 (*ASKB* 257).

Martensen, Hans Lassen, *De Autonomia conscientiæ sui humanæ in theologiam dogmaticam nostri temporis introducta*, Copenhagen: I.D. Quist 1837, p. 34 (*ASKB* 648).

—— *Grundrids til Moralphilosophiens System. Udgivet til Brug ved academiske Forelæsninger*, Copenhagen: C.A. Reitzel 1841, p. 95; p. 98 (*ASKB* 650).

—— *Den menneskelige Selvbevidstheds Autonomie i vor Tids dogmatiske Theologie*, Copenhagen: C.A. Reitzel 1841, p. 29 (*ASKB* 651).

—— *Den christelige Dogmatik*, Copenhagen: C.A. Reitzel 1849, p. 86; p. 96; p. 298; p. 360 (*ASKB* 653).

Meiners, Christoph, "Geschichte des Sokrates und seiner Philosophie," in his *Geschichte des Ursprungs, Fortgangs und Verfalls der Wissenschaften in Griechenland und Rom*, vols. 1–2, Lemgo: im Verlage der Meyersichen Buchhandlung 1781–82, vol. 2, pp. 346–540; pp. 683–808 (*ASKB* 1406–1406a).

—— *Geschichte des Luxus der Athenienser von den ältesten Zeiten an bis auf den Tod Philipps von Makedonien*, Lemgo: Meyer 1782 (*ASKB* 661).

Michelet, Carl Ludwig, *Vorlesungen über die Persönlichkeit Gottes und Unsterblichkeit der Seele oder die ewige Persönlichkeit des Geistes*, Berlin: Dümmler 1841, p. 33; pp. 33–9; p. 156 (*ASKB* 680).

Møller, Poul Martin, "Sokrates," in his "Udkast til Forelæsninger over den ældre Philosophies Historie," in *Efterladte Skrifter af Poul M. Møller*, vols. 1–3, ed. by Christian Winther, F.C. Olsen, and Christen Thaarup, Copenhagen: C.A. Reitzel 1839–43, vol. 2, pp. 357–75 (*ASKB* 1574–1576).

—— "Platon," in his "Udkast til Forelæsninger over den ældre Philosophies Historie," in *Efterladte Skrifter af Poul M. Møller*, vols. 1–3, ed. by Christian Winther, F.C. Olsen, and Christen Thaarup, Copenhagen: C.A. Reitzel 1839–43, vol. 2, pp. 399–453 (*ASKB* 1574–1576).

—— "Strøtanker," in *Efterladte Skrifter af Poul M. Møller*, vols. 1–3, ed. by Christian Winther, F.C. Olsen, and Christen Thaarup, Copenhagen: C.A. Reitzel 1839–43, vol. 3, p. 270; p. 287 (*ASKB* 1574–1576).

[Montaigne, Michel de], *Michael Montaigne's Gedanken und Meinungen über allerley Gegenstände, ins Deutsche übersetzt*, vols. 1–7, Berlin: F.T. Lagarde 1793–99:

—— vol. 1, p. 18; p. 30; p. 79; p. 82; p. 84; p. 143; p. 171; p. 187; p. 207; p. 213; p. 271; p. 276; p. 289; p. 291; p. 310; p. 317; p. 322; p. 347;

—— vol. 2, p. 96; p. 128; p. 176; p. 253; p. 292; p. 302; p. 304; pp. 312–13; p. 333; p. 361; p. 367; p. 372; p. 375; p. 388; p. 393; p. 402;

—— vol. 3, p. 21; p. 33; p. 41; p. 51; p. 116; pp. 139–40; p. 149; p. 155; p. 201; p. 206; pp. 221–8; p. 237; pp. 271–2; p. 290; p. 367; p. 404; pp. 429–38 passim; p. 446; p. 454; p. 480; p. 489; pp. 497–8; pp. 500–1; p. 515; p. 520; p. 526; p. 533; p. 546; p. 551;

—— vol. 4, p. 3; p. 41; p. 50; p. 55; p. 62; p. 64; p. 77; p. 113; p. 129; p. 168; p. 180; p. 183; p. 209; p. 289; p. 348; p. 394; p. 524; p. 529; p. 561;

—— vol. 5, p. 57; p. 79; p. 142; p. 188; p. 197; p. 232; p. 253; p. 273; pp. 285–6; p. 290; p. 346; p. 356; p. 359; p. 364; p. 371; p. 426; p. 479;

—— vol. 6, p. 46; pp. 51–2; p. 84; pp. 152–5 passim; pp. 168–9; pp. 194ff.; p. 202; p. 207; p. 209; p. 229; p. 233; p. 237; p. 251; p. 254; p. 263; p. 271; p. 290; p. 302; p. 309; p. 317; p. 327; p. 342; pp. 347–8; p. 351; p. 359; p. 364 (*ASKB* 681–687).

Mynster, Jakob Peter, *Om Hukommelsen. En psychologisk Undersögelse*, Copenhagen: Jens Hostrup Schultz 1849, pp. 36–9 (*ASKB* 692).

—— *Den hedenske Verden ved Christendommens Begyndelse*, Copenhagen: Schultz 1850, p. 14; p. 20; pp. 31–3; pp. 37–8 (*ASKB* 693).

—— *Blandede Skrivter*, vols. 1–3, Copenhagen: Gyldendal 1852–53 [vols. 4–6, Copenhagen: Gyldendal 1855–57], vol. 1, 18; p. 25; pp. 117–18; pp. 243–6; vol. 2, p. 156; p. 194; p. 197; p. 255; p. 355; p. 363; vol. 3, p. 43 (*ASKB* 358–363).

Nielsen, Rasmus, *Den propædeutiske Logik*, Copenhagen: P.G. Philipsen 1845, p. 12; p. 38; p. 44; p. 90; p. 119; p. 186; p. 188; p. 258 (*ASKB* 699).

—— *Evangelietroen og Theologien. Tolv Forelæsninger holdte ved Universitetet i Kjøbenhavn i Vinteren 1849–50*, Copenhagen: C.A. Reitzel 1850, pp. 133–4 (*ASKB* 702).

Petersen, Frederik Christian, *Haandbog i den græske Litteraturhistorie*, Copenhagen: Fr. Brummer 1830, p. 80; p. 90; p. 135; p. 164; p. 182; pp. 192–3; p. 205; p. 207; p. 217; p. 360 (*ASKB* 1037).

—— *Om Epheterne og deres Dikasterier i Athen*, Copenhagen: Trykt i Bianco Lunos Bogtrykkeri 1847, p. 43; p. 48; p. 78 (*ASKB* 720).

—— *Platons Forestillinger om Staternes Oprindelse, Statsforfatninger og Statsbestyrelse. Indbydelsesskrift til Kjøbenhavns Universitets Fest i Anledning af Hans Majestæt Kongens Fødselsdag den 6te October 1854*, Copenhagen: Trykt i det Schultziske Officin 1854 (*ASKB* 1171).

Ritter, Heinrich, *Historia philosophiae graeco-romanae ex fontium locis contexta*, ed. by L. Preller, Hamburg: Perthes 1838, pp. 139–59; pp. 186–228 (*ASKB* 726).

—— *Geschichte der Philosophie alter Zeit*, vols. 1–4, 2nd revised ed., Hamburg: Perthes 1836–39, vol. 2, pp. 18–89; pp. 159–211; pp. 211–59; pp. 259–388; pp. 389–443; pp. 443–522 (*ASKB* 735–738).

Schlegel, August Wilhelm, *Ueber dramatische Kunst und Litteratur. Vorlesungen*, vols. 1–2 [vol. 2 in 2 Parts], Heidelberg: Mohr und Zimmer 1809–11, vol. 1, p. 133; vol. 2.1, p. 83 (*ASKB* 1392–1394).

[Schlegel, Friedrich], *Friedrich Schlegel's Philosophische Vorlesungen aus den Jahren 1804 bis 1806. Nebst Fragmenten vorzüglich philosophisch-theologischen Inhalts. Aus dem Nachlaß des Verewigten*, ed. by C.H.J. Windischmann, vols. 1–2, Bonn: Eduard Weber 1836–37, vol. 1, pp. 28–35; pp. 361–5 (*ASKB* 768–768a).

Schopenhauer, Arthur, *Die Welt als Wille und Vorstellung*, vols. 1–2, 2nd revised and enlarged ed., Leipzig: F.A. Brockhaus 1844 [1819], vol. 1, p. 8; p. 36; p. 54; p. 81; p. 89; p. 125; p. 146; p. 152; p. 173; pp. 191ff.; p. 215; p. 239; p. 242; p. 294; p. 305; p. 308; p. 356; p. 388; pp. 394–5; p. 402; p. 414; p. 461; pp. 547–8; p. 590; vol. 2, pp. 34–5; p. 42; pp. 130–1; p. 167; p. 220; p. 296; p. 365; p. 376; p. 442; p. 507; p. 533; p. 542; p. 606 (*ASKB* 773–773a).

—— *Parerga und Paralipomena: kleine philosophische Schriften*, vols. 1–2, Berlin: A.W. Hayn 1851, vol. 1, pp. 39–45; p. 131; pp. 311–12; p. 358; p. 411; vol. 2, pp. 10–11; p. 39; p. 192; p. 236; p. 242; p. 281; p. 343; p. 449; p. 468; p. 487 (*ASKB* 774–775).

Sibbern, Frederik Christian, *Logik som Tænkelære fra en intelligent Iagttagelses Standpunct og i analytisk-genetisk Fremstilling*, 2nd enlarged and revised ed.,

Copenhagen: Paa Forfatterens Forlag trykt hos Fabritius de Tengnagel 1835, p. 2; p. 22; p. 24; pp. 173–4; p. 246 (*ASKB* 777).

—— *Speculativ Kosmologie med Grundlag til en speculativ Theologie*, Copenhagen: Forfatterens eget Forlag 1846, p. 44 (*ASKB* 780).

—— *Nogle Betragtninger over Stat og Kirke* [*Indbydelsesskrift til Kjøbenhavn Universitets Fest i Anledning af Hans Majestæt Kongens Fødselsdag den 6te October 1849. Heri: Nogle Betragtninger over Stat og Kirke*], Copenhagen: Trykt i det Schultziske Officin 1849, pp. 2–21 (*ASKB* 782).

—— *Om Forholdet imellem Sjæl og Legeme, saavel i Almindelighed som i phrenologisk, pathognomonisk, physiognomisk og ethisk Henseende i Særdeleshed*, Copenhagen: Paa Forfatterens eget Forlag 1849, p. 74; p. 104; p. 193; p. 209; pp. 241–2; p. 247; p. 448; p. 463; pp. 474–8 (*ASKB* 781).

[Solger, K.W.F.], *Solger's nachgelassene Schriften und Briefwechsel*, vols. 1–2, ed. by Ludwig Tieck and Friedrich von Raumer, Leipzig: F.A. Brockhaus 1826, pp. 650–75 (*ASKB* 1832–1833).

—— *K.W.F. Solger's Vorlesungen über Aesthetik*, ed. by K.W.L. Heyse, Leipzig: F.A. Brockhaus 1829, pp. 12–15; p. 118 (*ASKB* 1387).

Stäudlin, Carl Friedrich, *Geschichte und Geist des Skepticismus vorzüglich in Rücksicht auf Moral und Religion*, vols. 1–2, Leipzig: Siegfried Lebrecht Crusius 1794, vol. 1, pp. 233–9; pp. 250–63 (*ASKB* 791).

Steffens, Henrich, *Was ich erlebte. Aus der Erinnerung niedergeschrieben*, vols. 1–10, Breslau: Josef Max und Comp. 1840–44, vol. 4, p. 296; vol. 5, p. 312; vol. 8, pp. 380–5 (*ASKB* 1834–1843).

[Sulzer, Johann George], *Johann George Sulzers vermischte philosophische Schriften. Aus den Jahrbüchern der Akademie der Wissenschaften zu Berlin gesammelt*, vols. 1–2, Leipzig: Weidmanns Erben und Reich 1773–81, vol. 1, p. 131; p. 147; vol. 2, p. 104; p. 120 (in "Vorbericht"); p. 76; p. 192 (*ASKB* 807–808).

—— *Allgemeine Theorie der Schönen Künste, in einzeln, nach alphabetischer Ordnung der Kunstwörter auf einander folgenden, Artikeln abgehandelt*, vols. 1–4 and a register volume, 2nd revised ed., Leipzig: Weidmann 1792–99, vol. 1, p. 43; p. 74; p. 356; p. 370; p. 375; p. 378; p. 459; p. 622; p. 629; vol. 2, p. 639; vol. 3, p. 284; vol. 4, p. 310 (*ASKB* 1365–1369).

Tennemann, Wilhelm Gottlieb, *Geschichte der Philosophie*, vols. 1–11, Leipzig: Johann Ambrosius Barth 1798–1819, vol. 2, pp. 25–87; pp. 188–528 (*ASKB* 815–826).

Thiersch, Friedrich, *Allgemeine Aesthetik in akademischen Lehrvorträgen*, Berlin: G. Reimer 1846, p. 72 (*ASKB* 1378).

Tiedemann, Dietrich, *Geist der spekulativen Philosophie von Thales bis Sokrates*, vols. 1–6, Marburg: in der Neuen Akademischen Buchhandlung 1791–97, vol. 2, pp. 8–44; pp. 63–198 (*ASKB* 836–841).

Trendelenburg, Adolf, *Platonis de ideis et numeris doctrina ex Aristotele illustrata*, Leipzig: Vogel 1826 (*ASKB* 842).

—— *Logische Untersuchungen*, vols. 1–2, Berlin: G. Bethge 1840, vol. 1, p. 43, note; p. 89; p. 97; p. 102; p. 184; p. 224; p. 267; p. 315; p. 38; p. 83; p. 324; p. 360 (*ASKB* 843).

—— "Plato," in his *Historische Beiträge zur Philosophie*, vols. 1–2, Berlin: G. Bethge 1846–55, vol. 1, *Geschichte der Kategorienlehre. Zwei Abhandlungen*, 1846, pp. 205–9 (*ASKB* 848) [vol. 2, 1855 not in *ASKB*].

Weis, Carl, "Om Statens historiske Udvikling," in *Perseus, Journal for den speculative Idee*, vols. 1–2, ed. by Johan Ludvig Heiberg, Copenhagen: C.A. Reitzel 1837–38, vol. 2, pp. 49–99, see p. 82 (*ASKB* 569).

Weiße, Christian Hermann, *System der Aesthetik als Wissenschaft von der Idee der Schönheit. In drei Büchern*, vols. 1–2, Leipzig: C.H.F. Hartmann 1830, vol. 1, p. 23; p. 52; p. 88 (*ASKB* 1379–1380).

—— *Die Idee der Gottheit. Eine philosophische Abhandlung. Als wissenschaftliche Grundlegung zur Philosophie der Religion*, Dresden: Ch.F. Grimmer 1833, p. 59; p. 62, note; pp. 87–100 passim; p. 113; p. 209 (*ASKB* 866).

Waitz, Theodor, *Lehrbuch der Psychologie als Naturwissenschaft*, Braunschweig: Friedrich Vieweg und Sohn 1849, p. 35; p. 619 (*ASKB* 852).

Werder, Karl, *Logik: Als Commentar und Ergänzung zu Hegels Wissenschaft der Logik. Erste Abtheilung*, Berlin: Veit und Comp. 1841 (*ASKB* 867).

Wirth, Johann Ulrich, "Lehre des Sokrates," in his *Die speculative Idee Gottes und die damit zusammenhängenden Probleme der Philosophie. Eine kritisch-dogmatische Untersuchung*, Stuttgart and Tübingen: J.G. Cotta 1845, pp. 183–7; pp. 187–212 (*ASKB* 876).

Zeller, Eduard, *Die Philosophie der Griechen. Eine Untersuchung über Charakter, Gang und Hauptmomente ihrer Entwicklung*, vols. 1–3, Tübingen: Ludwig Friedrich Fues 1844–52, vol. 2, pp. 12–104; pp. 134–315 (*ASKB* 913–914).

Zeuthen, Ludvig, *Om den christelige Tro i dens Betydning for Verdenshistorien. Et Forsøg*, Copenhagen: Gyldendal 1838, p. 23; p. 38; p. 47; pp. 54–7 (*ASKB* 259).

—— *Om Ydmyghed. En Afhandling*, Copenhagen: Gyldendal 1852, p. 17, note; p. 18; p. 67; pp. 85–6; p. 98 (*ASKB* 916).

III. Secondary Literature on Kierkegaard's Relation to Plato and Socrates

Accard Couchoud, Marie-Thérèse, *Kierkegaard ou l'instant paradoxal. Recherches sur l'instant psychotique*, Paris: Éditions du Cerf 1981.

Allison, Henry E., "Christianity and Nonsense," *Review of Metaphysics*, vol. 20, no. 3, 1967, pp. 432–60, see pp. 440–2.

Andersen, Jørn, *Begrebet inderlighed i Kierkegaards forfatterskab—dens etiske betydning af gudsforholdet og det mellemmenneskelige forhold hos Søren Kierkegaard*, Copenhagen: Privatforlaget 2004.

Andersen, Vilhelm, "Søren Kierkegaard," in his *Tider og Typer af dansk Aands Historie*, vols. 1–4, Kristiania: Gyldendal 1915–16, vol. 4, pp. 65–108.

Anderson, Barbara, *Kierkegaard: A Fiction*, Syracuse, New York: Syracuse University Press 1974.

Arnarsson, Kristian, "Erindring og gentagelse. Kierkegaard og Grækerne," in *Filosofi og samfunn*, ed. by Finn Jor, Kristiansand, 1998, pp. 197–203.

Anne, Chantal, *L'Amour dans la pensée de Søren Kierkegaard*, Paris: L'Harmattan 1993, pp. 31–8.

Anz, Wilhelm, *Die Wiederholung der socratischen Methode durch Sören Kierkegaard*, Ph.D. Thesis, Marburg 1940.

—— "Die platonische Idee des Guten und das sokratische Paradox bei Kierkegaard," in *Die antike Philosophie in ihrer Bedeutung für die Gegenwart. Kolloquium zu Ehren des 80. Geburtstages von Hans-Georg Gadamer*, ed. by Reiner Wiehl, Heidelberg: Winther 1981, pp. 23–36.

Arnim, H., "Sokrates und das Ideal persönlicher Vollkommenheit," *Mitteilungen des Vereins der Freunde des humanistischen Gymnasiums*, vol. 21, 1922, pp. 32–46.

Ashbaugh, A. Freire, "Platonism: An Essay on Repetition and Recollection," in *Kierkegaard and Great Traditions*, ed. by Niels Thulstrup and Marie Mikulová Thulstrup, Copenhagen: C.A. Reitzel 1981 (*Bibliotheca Kierkegaardiana*, vol. 6, 1981), pp. 9–26.

Bedell, G.C., "Kierkegaard's Conception of Time," *Journal of the American Academy of Religion*, vol. 37, 1969, pp. 266–9.

Bejerholm, Lars, "Sokratisk metod hos Søren Kierkegaard och hanns samtid," *Kierkegaardiana*, vol. 4, 1962, pp. 28–44.

Bergman, Shmuel Hugo, "The Concept of Irony in Kierkegaard's Thought," in his *Dialogical Philosophy from Kierkegaard to Buber*, Albany, New York: State University of New York Press 1991, pp. 25–45.

Bohlin, Torsten, *Sören Kierkegaards etiska åskådning*, Stockholm: Svenska kyrkans diakonistyrelsens bokförlag 1918, pp. 67–71.

Bonser, Robert Dale, *The Role of Socrates in the Thought of Soren Kierkegaard*, Ph.D. Thesis, University of California, Santa Barbara 1985.

Bottani, Livio, "Malinconia e nichilismo. I: Dalla ferita mortale alla ricomposizione dell'infranto," *Filosofia*, vol. 43, 1992, pp. 269–93.

Borgvin, Rune, "En sammenligning av bestemmelsen av sokratisk og romantisk ironi i 'Om Begrebet Ironi,' " in *Kierkegaard 1993—digtning, filosofi, teologi*, ed. by Finn Hauberg Mortensen, Odense: Institut for Litteratur, Kultur og Medier, Odense Universitet 1993, pp. 153–60.

Brøchner, Hans, *Problemet om Tro og Viden*, Copenhagen: P.G. Philipsen 1868, pp. 216–19.

Burnyeat, Myles, "The Impiety of Socrates," *Ancient Philosophy*, no. 17, 1997, pp. 1–12.

Come, Arnold, "Kierkegaard's Ontology of Love," in *Works of Love*, ed. by Robert L. Perkins, Macon, Georgia: Mercer University Press 1999 (*International Kierkegaard Commentary*, vol. 16), pp. 79–119.

Cooper, Robert M., "Plato and Kierkegaard in Dialogue," *Theology Today*, vol. 31, 1974–75, pp. 187–98.

—— "Plato on Authority, Irony, and True Riches," in *Kierkegaard's Classical Inspiration*, ed. by Niels Thulstrup and Marie Mikulová Thulstrup, Copenhagen: C.A. Reitzel 1985 (*Bibliotheca Kierkegaardiana*, vol. 14, 1981), pp. 25–62.

Croxall, T.H., "The Christian Doctrine of Hope and the Kierkegaardian Doctrine of 'the Moment,' " *Expository Times*, vol. 56, 1944–45, pp. 292–5.

Crumbine, Nancy Jay, *The Same River Twice: A Critique of the Place of Eros in the Philosophy of Kierkegaard*, Ph.D. Thesis, Pennsylvania State University, Philadelphia 1972.

Daane, James, *Kierkegaard's Concept of the Moment. An Investigation into the Time-Eternity Concept of Sören Kierkegaard*, Thesis, Princeton Theology Seminary, Princeton 1947.

D'Agostino, Francesco, "La fenomenologia dell'uomo giusto: Un parallelo tra Kierkegaard e Platones," *Rivista Internazionale di Filosofia del Diritto*, vol. 49, 1972, pp. 153–72.

Daise, Benjamin, *Kierkegaard's Socratic Art*, Macon, Georgia: Mercer University Press 1999.

Davini, Simonella, "Sapere, passione, veritá nell'interpretazione kierkegaardiana dello scetticismo antico," in *Leggere oggi Kierkegaard* (*Quaderni di studi kierkegaardiani*, vol. 1), ed. by Isabella Adinolfi, 2000, pp. 61–78.

Deuser, Hermann, "Kierkegaards Sokrates—Modell und Umkehrung antiker Philosophie," in his *Kierkegaard. Die Philosophie des religiösen Schriftstellers*, Darmstadt: Wissenschaftliche Buchgesellschaft 1985 (*Erträge der Forschung*, vol. 232), pp. 31–57.

Drachmann, Anders Bjørn, "Hedenskab og Christendom hos Søren Kierkegaard," in his *Udvalgte Afhandlinger*, Copenhagen and Kristiania: Gyldendal 1911, pp. 124–40.

Dupré, Louis, "Of Time and Eternity," in *The Concept of Anxiety*, ed. by Robert L. Perkins, Macon, Georgia: Mercer University Press 1985 (*International Kierkegaard Commentary*, vol. 8), pp. 111–31.

Eriksen, Niels Nymann, "Love and Sacrifice in *Repetition*," *Kierkegaard Studies Yearbook*, 2002, pp. 26–35.

Evans, C. Stephen, *Kierkegaard on Faith and the Self: Collected Essays*, Waco, Texas: Baylor University Press 2006, pp. 99–101.

Faber, Bettina, *La contraddizione sofferente. La teoria del tragico in Søren Kierkegaard*, Padova: Il Poligrafo 1998, p. 23; p. 73; p. 123; p. 125; p. 207.

Friis Johansen, Karsten, "Platon og Kierkegaard," *Studenterkredsen*, vol. 36, 1968, pp. 10–15.

—— "Kierkegaard und die griechische Dialektik," in *Kierkegaard and Dialectics*, ed. by Herman Deuser et al., Aarhus: University of Aarhus 1979, pp. 51–124.

Furtak, Rick Anthony, *Wisdom in Love: Kierkegaard and the Ancient Quest for Emotional Integrity*, Notre Dame: University of Notre Dame Press 2005, pp. 100–7; pp. 125–30.

Gallino, Guglielmo, "Kierkegaard e l'ironia socratica," *Filosofia*, vol. 45, 1994, pp. 143–61.

Gardiner, Patrick, *Kierkegaard*, Oxford: Oxford University Press 1988, pp. 68–76.

Garff, Joakim, "Argus' Øjne: 'Synspunktet' og synspunkterne for Kierkegaards 'Forfatter-Virksomhed,' " *Dansk Teologisk Tidsskrift* no. 52, 1989, pp. 161–89. (English trasnaltion: "The Eyes of Argus: *The Point of View* and Points of View With Respect to Kierkegaard's 'Activity as an Author,' " trans. by Bruce H. Kirmmse, in *Kierkegaardiana*, vol. 15, 1991, pp. 29–54.)

Gouwens, David J., *Kierkegaard as Religious Thinker*, Cambridge: Cambridge University Press 1996, pp. 88–97.

Gramont, Jérôme, "Kierkegaard. Acheminement vers la vie," in his *Le discours de la vie. Trois essais sur Platon, Kierkegaard et Nietzsche*, Paris, Budapest, and Torino: l'Harmattan 2001, pp. 129–240.

Greve, Wilfried, *Kierkegaards maieutische Ethik*, Frankfurt am Main: Suhrkamp 1990.

Grøn, Arne, "Sokrates og 'Smulerne,' " *Filosofiske Studier*, vol. 15, 1995, pp. 97–107.

—— "Transcendence of Thought: The Project of *Philosophical Fragments*," *Kierkegaard Studies Yearbook*, 2004, pp. 80–9.

Grunnet, Sanne Elisa, *Ironi og subjektivitet. En studie over S. Kierkegaards disputats* Om Begrebet Ironi, Copenhagen: C.A. Reitzel 1987.

Gunder-Hansen, Edwin, "Gedanken über Sören Kierkegaards Zeitkritik," *Kantstudien*, vol. 42, 1942–43, pp. 210–16.

Hadot, Pierre, "The Figure of Socrates," in *Philosophy as a Way of Life*, ed. by Arnold I. Davidson, trans. by Michael Chase, Oxford: Blackwell 1995, pp. 147–78.

Hall, Amy Laura, *Kierkegaard and the Treachery of Love*, Cambridge: Cambridge University Press 2002, pp. 139–71.

Hamilton, Wayne Bruce, *Soren Kierkegaard's Conception of Temporality*, Ph.D. Thesis, McGill University, Montreal, Quebec 1972.

Hamilton, Wayne Bruce, "Existential Time: A Reexamination," *Southern Journal of Philosophy*, 13, 1975, pp. 297–307.

van Heerden, Adriaan, "Does Love Cure the Tragic? Kierkegaardian Variations on a Platonic Theme," in *Stages on Life's Way*, ed. by Robert L. Perkins, Macon, Georgia: Mercer University Press 2000 (*International Kierkegaard Commentary*, vol. 11), pp. 69–90.

—— "Was the Death of Socrates a Tragedy? Kierkegaard versus Hegel on the Possibility of the Mediation of the Tragic in Ethics," in *The Concept of Irony*, ed. by Robert L. Perkins, Macon, Georgia: Mercer University Press 2001 (*International Kierkegaard Commentary*, vol. 2), pp. 235–64.

Hennemann, Gerhard, "Die christliche und die sokratische Definition der Sunde. Nach Sören Kierkegaards Schrift *Die Krankheit zum Tode*," *Deutsches Pfarrerblatt*, vol. 52, 1952, pp. 611–13.

Henningsen, Bernd, "Søren Kierkegaard: Sokrates i København," in his *Politik eller Kaos?* Copenhagen: Berlingske Forlag 1980, pp. 134–233.

Hess, Mary W., "Kierkegaard and Socrates," *Christian Century*, vol. 82, 1965, pp. 736–8.

Himmelstrup, Jens, *Søren Kierkegaards Opfattelse af Sokrates. En Studie i dansk Filosofis Historie*, Copenhagen: Arnold Busck 1924.

Holm, Isak Winkel, "Myte: Platon," in his *Tanken i billedet. Søren Kierkegaards poetik*, Copenhagen: Gyldendal 1998, pp. 117–56.

Holm, Søren, "Platon og Kierkegaard i svensk Belysning," *Berlingske Aftenavis*, October 18, 1943.

—— *Græciteten*, Copenhagen: Munksgaard 1964 (*Søren Kierkegaard Selskabets Populære Skrifter*, vol. 11), see p. 10; p. 12; p. 15; p. 27; pp. 65–6; p. 88; p. 94;

p. 96; p. 98; pp. 103–5; p. 108; pp. 111–12; p. 115; pp. 119–22; p. 126; p. 129; p. 135; pp. 139–40.

Howland, Jacob, *Kierkegaard and Socrates. A Study in Philosophy and Faith*, New York: Cambridge University Press 2006.

Humbert, David, "Kierkegaard's Use of Plato in his Analysis of the Moment in Time," *Dionysius*, no. 7, 1983, pp. 149–83.

Jaspers, Karl, *Psychologie der Weltanschauungen*, 3rd ed., Berlin: Springer 1925 [1919], pp. 109–12.

Jegstrup, Elsebet, "Text and the Performative Act," *Philosophy Today*, vol. 45, 2001, pp. 121–31.

Jensen, Povl Johannes, "Kierkegaard og Platon," in *Studier i antik og middelalderlig filosofi og idéhistorie*, ed. by Bo Alkjær et al., Copenhagen: Museum Tusculanum 1980, pp. 699–710.

—— "Sokrates i Kierkegaards disputats," in his *Cum grano salis. Udvalgte foredrag og artikler 1945–1980*, Odense: Odense Universitetsforlag 1981, pp. 37–51.

Jolivet, Regis, "Socrate, penseur existentiel," in his *Aux sources de l'existentialisme chrétien. Kierkegaard*, Paris: Libraire Arthéme Fayard 1958, pp. 138–43.

Jones, Ozro T., Jr., *The Meaning of the "Moment" in Existential Encounter According to Kierkegaard*, S.T.D. Temple University, Philadelphia 1962.

Kangas, David, "Conception and Concept. The Two Logics of *The Concept of Irony* and the Place of Socrates," in *Kierkegaard and the Word(s). Essays on Hermeneutics and Communication*, ed. by Poul Houe and Gordon D. Marino, Copenhagen: C.A. Reitzel 2003, pp. 180–91.

Kirmmse, Bruce, " 'I Am Not a Christian'—a 'Sublime Lie'? Or: 'Without Authority,' Playing Desdemona to Christendom's Othello," in *Anthropology and Authority: Essays on Søren Kierkegaard*, ed. by Poul Houe, Gordon D. Marino, and Sven Hakon Rossel, Amsterdam: Rodopi 2000, pp. 129–36.

—— "Socrates in the Fast Lane: Kierkegaard's *The Concept of Irony* on the University's Velocifère (Documents, Context, Commentary, and Interpretation)," in *The Concept of Irony*, ed. by Robert L. Perkins, Macon, Georgia: Mercer University Press 2001 (*International Kierkegaard Commentary*, vol. 2), pp. 17–99.

Klint-Jensen, Henrik, "Platon—Kierkegaard. Tidsånden hos Platon og Søren Kierkegaard," *Fønix*, vol. 19, no. 4, 1995, pp. 24–38.

—— "Idé og dobbeltbevægelse—frigørelse hos Platon og Søren Kierkegaard," *Philosophia*, vol. 24, nos. 1–2, 1995, pp. 155–89.

Kloeden, Wolfdietrich von, "Die Ewigkeit," in *Theological Concepts in Kierkegaard*, ed. by Niels Thulstrup and Marie Mikulová Thulstrup, Copenhagen: C.A. Reitzel 1980 (*Bibliotheca Kierkegaardiana*, vol. 5), pp. 9–39.

—— "Sokrates," in *Kierkegaard's Classical Inspiration*, ed. by Niels Thulstrup and Marie Mikulová Thulstrup, Copenhagen: C.A. Reitzel 1985 (*Bibliotheca Kierkegaardiana*, vol. 14), pp. 104–81.

—— "Sokratische Ironie bei Plato und S. Kierkegaard," in *Irony and Humor in Søren Kierkegaard*, ed. by Niels Thulstrup and Marie Mikulová Thulstrup, Copenhagen: C.A. Reitzel 1988 (*Liber Academiae Kierkegaardiensis*, vol. 7), pp. 51–60.

—— *Kierkegaard und Sokrates. Sören Kierkegaards Sokratesrezeption*, Rheinland-Westfalen-Lippe: Evangelische Fachhochschule 1991 (*Schriftenreihe der Evangelischen Fachhochschule Rheinland-Westafalen-Lippe*, vol. 16).

Koskinen, Lennart, *Tid och evighet hos Sören Kierkegaard: Kierkegaard's View of Time and Eternity*, Ph.D. Thesis, University of Uppsala, Uppsala 1980.

Krentz, Arthur A., "The Socratic-Dialectical Anthropology of Søren Kierkegaard's 'Postscript,' " in *Anthropology and Authority: Essays on Søren Kierkegaard*, ed. by Poul Houe, Gordon D. Marino, and Sven Hakon Rossel, Amsterdam and Atlanta, Georgia: Rodopi 2000, pp. 17–26.

Kuypers, E., "Kierkegaards opmerkingen over de noodzaak van een Socratisch nihilisme," *Filosofie*, vol. 3, no. 4, 1993, pp. 22–8.

Leverkühn, André, "Engagement und Passion des dänischen Sokrates," in his *Das ethische und das Ästhetische als Kategorien des Handelns. Selbstwerdung bei Søren Kierkegaard*, Frankfurt am Main: Peter Lang 2000, pp. 31–40.

Levi, Albert W., "Socrates in the Nineteenth Century," *Journal of the History of Ideas*, vol. 17, 1956, pp. 104–6.

—— "The Idea of Socrates: The Philosophic Hero in the Nineteenth Century," *Journal of the History of Ideas*, vol. 17, 1956, pp. 89–108.

Lilhav, Preben, "Plato," in his *Kierkegaards valg*, Risskov: Forlaget Sicana 2003, pp. 43–7.

Lindström, Valter, "Eros och agape i Kierkegaards åskådning, reflexioner omkring Per Lønning, 'Samtidighedens Situation,' " *Kierkegaardiana*, vol. 1, 1955, pp. 102–12.

Manheimer, Ronald J., "Educating Subjectivity: Kierkegaard's Three Socratic Postures," in his *Kierkegaard as Educator*, Berkeley: University of California Press 1977, pp. 1–58.

Marini, Sergio, "Socrate 'quel Singolo'. A proposito di alcune annotazioni del 'Diario' kierkegaardiano," in *Nuovi Studi Kierkegaardiani* (*Bollettino del Centro Italiano di Studi Kierkegaardiani. Supplemento semestrale di "Velia. Rivista di Filosofia Teoretica"*), vol. 1, 1993, pp. 75–85.

Martensen, Hans Lassen, *Om Tro og Viden*, Copenhagen: C.A. Reitzel 1867, pp. 135–9.

Martinez, Roy, "Socrates and Judge Wilhelm: A Case of Kierkegaardian Ethics," *Philosophy Today*, no. 34, 1990, pp. 39–47.

—— *Kierkegaard and the Art of Irony*, New York: Prometheus Books 2001 (*Philosophy and Literary Theory*).

Masterson, Patrick, "Kierkegaard's View of Time. A Reply to J. Heywood Thomas," *Journal of the British Society for Phenomenology*, 4, 1973, pp. 41–4.

McDonald, William, "Indirection and *Parrhesia*: The Roles of Socrates' *Daimonion* and Kierkegaard's *Styrelse* in Communication," in *Kierkegaard and the Word(s): Essays on Hermeneutics and Communication*, ed. by Poul Houe and Gordon D. Marino, Copenhagen: C.A. Reitzel 2003, pp. 127–38.

McKinnon, Alastair, "Three Conceptions of Socrates in Kierkegaard's Writings," in *Kierkegaard oggi. Atti del covegno dell' 11 Novembre 1982*, ed. by Alessandro Cortese, Milan: Vita e Pensiero 1986, pp. 21–43.

Merrill, Reed, " 'Infinite Absolute Negativity': Irony in Socrates, Kierkegaard and Kafka," *Comparative Literature Studies*, vol. 16, 1979, pp. 222–36.

Mjaaland, Marius G., "Death and Aporia," *Kierkegaard Studies Yearbook*, 2003, pp. 395–418.

—— "The Autopsy of One Still Living," in *Prefaces and Writing Sampler and Three Discourses on Imagined Occasions*, ed. by Robert L. Perkins, Macon, Georgia: Mercer University Press 2006 (*International Kierkegaard Commentary*, vols. 9–10), pp. 359–86.

—— "X. Alterität und Textur in Kierkegaards *Krankheit zum Tode*," *Neue Zeitschrift für Systematische Theologie und Religionsphilosophie*, vol. 47, no. 1, 2005, 58–80.

Morris, T.F., "Kierkegaard's Understanding of Socrates," *International Journal for Philosophy of Religion*, no. 19, 1986, pp. 105–11.

Muench, Paul, "The Socratic Method of Kierkegaard's Pseudonym Johannes Climacus: Indirect Communication and the Art of 'Taking Away,' " in *Kierkegaard and the Word(s): Essays on Hermeneutics and Communication*, ed. by Poul Houe and Gordon D. Marino, Copenhagen: C.A. Reitzel 2003, pp. 139–50.

Müller, Paul, *Kristendom, etik og majeutik i Søren Kierkegaard's "Kjerlighedens Gjerninger,"* Copenhagen: C.A. Reitzel 1983.

Nagley, Winfield E., "Kierkegaard's Early and Later View of Socratic Irony," *Thought: A Review of Culture and Idea*, no. 55, 1980, pp. 271–82.

Nehamas, Alexander, *The Art of Living: Socratic Reflections from Plato to Foucault*, Berkeley: University of California Press 1998.

Neumann, Harry, "Kierkegaard and Socrates on the Dignity of Man," *The Personalist*, vol. 48, 1967, pp. 453–60.

Nizet, Jean, "La temporalité chez Sören Kierkegaard," *Revue Philosophique de Louvain*, vol. 71, 1973, pp. 225–45.

Nordentoft, Kresten, "Erotic Love," in *Kierkegaard and Human Values*, ed. by Niels Thulstrup and Marie Mikulová Thulstrup, Copenhagen: C.A. Reitzel 1980 (*Bibliotheca Kierkegaardiana*, vol. 7), pp. 87–99.

—— *Kierkegaards psykologi*, 2nd ed., Copenhagen: Hans Reitzel 1995, pp. 446–88. (English translation: *Kierkegaard's Psychology*, Atlantic Highlands, New Jersey: Humanities Press 1978.)

Nostiz, Ows von, "Kierkegaards Dämon," *Wirtschaftszeitung*, vol. 4, 1909, p. 9.

Olesen, Tonny Aagaard, "Kierkegaard's Socratic Hermeneutic," in *The Concept of Irony*, ed. by Robert L. Perkins, Macon, Georgia: Mercer University Press 2001 (*International Kierkegaard Commentary*, vol. 2), pp. 101–22.

Ottonello, Pier Paolo, *Kierkegaard e il Problema del Tempo*, Genova: Tilgher 1972.

Pascuale, Juan Edgardo de, *Kierkegaard's Socratic Philosophy*, Ph.D. Thesis, Brown University, Providence, Rhode Island 1987.

Paula, Marcio Gimenes de, *Socratismo e cristianismo em Kierkegaard: o escândalo e a loucura*, São Paulo: Annablume editora 2001.

Pentzopoulou-Valalas, Thérèse, "Kierkegaard et Socrate ou Socrate vu par Kierkegaard," *Les Études Philosophiques*, 1979, pp. 151–62.

Pepper, Thomas, "Male Midwifery: Maieutics in *The Concept of Irony* and *Repetition*," in *Kierkegaard Revisited*, ed. by Niels Jørgen Cappelørn and Jon

Stewart, Berlin and New York: Walter de Gruyter 1997 (*Kierkegaard Studies Monograph Series*, vol. 1), pp. 460–80.

Perkins, Robert L., "Two Nineteenth Century Interpretations of Socrates: Hegel and Kierkegaard," *Kierkegaard-Studiet, International Edition*, vol. 4, 1967, pp. 9–14.

—— "Woman-Bashing in Kierkegaard's 'In Vino Veritas': A Reinscription of Plato's Symposium," in *Feminist Interpretations of Søren Kierkegaard*, ed. by Nancy Tuana, University Park: Pennsylvania State University Press 1997, pp. 83–102.

Pieper, Annemarie, *Geschichte und Ewigkeit bei Sören Kierkegaard. Das Leitproblem der pseudonymen Schriften*, Meisenheim am Glan: Verlag Anton Hain 1968, pp. 167–70.

Pivčević, Edo, "Sokrates, Climacus and Anticlimacus," in his *Ironie als Daseinform bei Sören Kierkegaard*, Gütersloh: Gütersloher Verlagshaus Gerd Mohn 1960, pp. 45–71.

Politis, Hélène, "Socrate, fondateur de la morale, ou Kierkegaard commentateur de Hegel et historien de la philosophie," in *Autour de Hegel. Hommage à Bernard Bourgeois*, ed. by F. Dagognet and Pierre Osmo, Paris: Vrin 2000, pp. 365–78.

Pop, Mihaela, "L'influence platonicienne sur le concept kierkegaardien de moment," *Revue Roumaine de Philosophie*, vol. 45, nos. 1–2, 2001, pp. 165–75.

Porsing, Ole, "Græciteten, Sokrates og ironi," in his *Sprækker til det uendelige? Søren Kierkegaard i 1990'erne—en bog om bøgerne*, Århus: Slagmark 1996, pp. 17–22.

Reece, Gregory L., *Irony and Religious Belief*, Tübingen: J.C.B. Mohr (Paul Siebeck) 2002 (*Religion in Philosophy and Theology*, vol. 5).

Regina, Umberto, "Pensare l'amore. Da Socrate a Kierkegaard," in his *La differenza amate e il Paradosso cristiano. Gli Stadi sul cammino della vita di Søren Kierkegaard*, Verona: Il Sentiero 1997, pp. 3–36.

—— *Kierkegaard, L'arte di esistere*, Brescia: Editrice Morcelliana 2005 (*Filosofia*, Nuova serie, vol. 26), pp. 29–42; pp. 62–3; p. 73; p. 90; pp. 117–18; p. 180; p. 183; p. 234; p. 248.

Richter, Liselotte, "Die Sünde: Auseinandersetzung mit Sokrates," in her *Der Begriff der Subjektivität bei Kierkegaard. Ein Beitrag zur christlichem Existenzdarstellung*, Würzburg: Verlag Konrad Triltsch 1934, pp. 13–28.

Rilliet, Jean, "Kierkegaard et Socrate," *Revue de Théologie et de Philosophie*, vol. 31, 1943, pp. 114–20.

Rizzacasa, Aurelio, "Socrate e Lessing," in his *Kierkegaard. Storia ed esistenza*, Rome: Edizioni studium 1984, pp. 57–60.

Rubenstein, Mary-Jane, "Kierkegaard's Socrates: A Venture in Evolutionary Theory," *Modern Theology*, vol. 17, 2001, pp. 442–73.

—— "Ecstatic Subjectivity: Kierkegaard's Critiques and Appropriations of the Socratic," *Literature and Theology*, vol. 16, 2002, pp. 349–62.

Rudd, Anthony, "The Moment and the Teacher: Problems in Kierkegaard's *Philosophical Fragments*," *Kierkegaardiana*, vol. 21, 2000, pp. 92–115.

Sarf, Harold, "Reflections on Kierkegaard's Socrates," *Journal of the History of Ideas*, no. 44, 1983, pp. 255–76.

Schäfer, Klaus, *Hermeneutische Ontologie in den Climacus-Schriften Sören Kierkegaards*, Munich: Kösel-Verlag 1968, see p. 15; p. 43; p. 68; p. 119; pp. 138–45; p. 149.

Schalow, Frank, "Temporality Revisited: Kierkegaard and the Transitive Character of Time," *Auslegung*, vol. 17, no. 1, 1991, pp. 15–25.

Schär, Hans Rudolf, *Christliche Sokratik: Kierkegaard über den Gebrauch der Reflexion in der Christenheit*, Frankfurt am Main: Peter Lang Verlag 1977.

Scheier, Claus-Artur, "Klassische und existentielle Ironie: Platon und Kierkegaard," *Philosophisches Jahrbuch*, no. 97, 1990, pp. 238–50.

Scholtens, W.R., "Kierkegaard en Sokrates, de plaats van de ironie in het geestelijk leven," *Tijdschrift voor geestelijk leven*, vol. 30, 1974, pp. 203–7.

Schottlaender, Rud, "Sören Kierkegaards Sokratesauffassung. Bemerkungen zu dem gleichbetitelten Buche von J. Himmelstrup," *Philosophischer Anzeiger*, vol. 4, 1929–30, pp. 27–41.

Schrag, Calvin O., "Kierkegaard's Existential Reflections on Time," *The Personalist*, vol. 42, 1961, pp. 149–64.

Scopetea, Sophia, "A Flaw in the Movement," *Kierkegaardiana*, vol. 13, 1984, pp. 97–104.

—— *Kierkegaard og græciteten. En kamp med ironi*, Copenhagen: C.A. Reitzel 1995.

—— "Becoming the Flute: Socrates and the Reversal of Values in Kierkegaard's Later Works," *Kierkegaardiana*, vol. 18, 1996, pp. 28–43.

Sidgwick, Henry, "The Sophists," in *Lectures on the Philosophy of Kant and Other Philosophical Lectures and Essays*, London: Macmillan 1905, pp. 323–71.

Sinnet, M.W., *Restoring the Conversation: Socratic Dialectic in the Authorship of Søren Kierkegaard*, Fife: Theology in Scotland for St Mary's College, University of St Andrews, St Andrews 1999.

Sløk, Johannes, *Die Anthropologie Kierkegaards*, Copenhagen: Rosenkilde and Bagger 1954, pp. 52–77.

—— "Die griechische Philosophie als Bezugsrahmen für Constantin Constantinus und Johannes de silentio," *Classica et Mediaevalia. Francisco Blatt septuagenario dedicata*, ed. by O.S. Due, H. Friis Johansen, and B. Dalsgaard Larsen, Copenhagen: Gyldendal 1973, pp. 636–58 (published also in in *Materialien zur Philosophie Søren Kierkegaards*, ed. by Michael Theunissen and Wilfried Greve, Frankfurt am Main: Suhrkamp 1979, pp. 280–301).

Söderquist, K. Brian, "Kierkegaard's Nihilistic Socrates in *The Concept of Irony*," in *Tänkarnes mångfald. Nutida perspektiv på Søren Kierkegaard*, ed. by Lone Koldtoft, Jon Stewart, and Jan Holmgaard together with Centrum för Danmarksstudier vid Lunds universitet, Stockholm: Makadam Förlag 2005, pp. 213–43.

—— *The Isolated Self: Irony as Truth and Untruth in Søren Kierkegaard's On the Concept of Irony*, Copenhagen: C.A. Reitzel 2007 (*Danish Golden Age Studies*, vol. 1).

Sponheim, Paul, *Kierkegaard on Christ and Christian Coherence*, New York and Evanston: Harper & Row 1968, see p. 12; p. 23; p. 30; p. 37; pp. 69–72; p. 76; pp. 80–4; p. 125; p. 193; p. 200; p. 230; p. 257; p. 362.

Stewart, Jon, "Werder: The Influence of Werder's Lectures and *Logik* on Kierkegaard's Thought," in *Kierkegaard and his German Contemporaries*, Tome I, *Philosophy*, ed. by Jon Stewart, Aldershot: Ashgate 2007 (*Kierkegaard Research: Sources, Reception and Resources*, vol. 6), pp. 335–72.

Strawser, Michael J., "How Did Socrates Become a Christian? Irony and a Postmodern Christian (Non)-Ethic," *Philosophy Today*, vol. 36, 1992, pp. 256–65.

Stucki, Pierre-André, "Socrate ou le modèle de l'ironie," in his *Le christianisme et l'histoire d'après Kierkegaard*, Basel: Verlag für Recht und Gesellschaft 1963, pp. 33–7.

Suances Marcos, Manuel, *Sören Kierkegaard*, vols. 1–2, Madrid: Universidad Nacional de Educación a Distanca 1997, vol. 1 (*Vida de un filósofo atormentado*), pp. 145–58.

Taylor, Mark C., "Time's Struggle with Space: Kierkegaard's Understanding of Temporality," *Harvard Theological Review*, 66, 1973, pp. 311–29.

—— "Socratic Midwifery: Method and Intention of the Authorship," in *Kierkegaard's Pseudonymous Authorship: A Study of Time and the Self*, Princeton, New Jersey: Princeton University Press 1975, pp. 51–62.

—— "Love and Forms of Spirit," *Kierkegaardiana*, vol. 10, 1977, pp. 95–116.

Theunissen, Michael, "Augenblick," in *Historisches Wörterbuch der Philosophie*, vols. 1–12, ed. by Joachim Ritter and Karlfried Gründer Basel: Schwabe 1971–2007, vol. 1, pp. 649–50.

Thomas, J. Heywood, "Kierkegaard's View of Time," *Journal of the British Society for Phenomenology*, vol. 4, 1973, pp. 33–40.

Thomte, Reidar, "Socratic Midwifery: The Communication of the Truth," in his *Kierkegaard's Philosophy of Religion*, Princeton, New Jersey: Princeton University Press 1948, pp. 190–203.

Thulstrup, Marie Mikulová, *Kierkegaard, Platons skuen og kristendommen*, Copenhagen: Munksgaard 1970.

—— "Plato's Vision and its Interpretation," in *Kierkegaard's Classical Inspiration*, ed. by Niels Thulstrup and Marie Mikulová Thulstrup, Copenhagen: C.A. Reitzel 1985 (*Bibliotheca Kierkegaardiana*, vol. 14), pp. 63–103.

Thulstrup, Niels, "Kierkegaard's Socratic Role for Twentieth Century Philosophy and Theology," *Kierkegaardiana*, vol. 11, 1980, pp. 197–211.

Thust, Martin, "Das Vorbild der Redlichkeit, die Narrheit des Enstes: der Vorläufer Sokrates," in his *Sören Kierkegaard. Der Dichter des Religiösen. Grundlagen eines Systems der Subjektivität*, Munich: C.H. Beck 1931, pp. 150–70.

Torralba Roselló, Francesc, "Kierkegaard el heredero moderno de la mayéutica socrática," *Espiritu*, vol. 47, 1998, pp. 55–69.

Troels-Lund, Troels Frederik, "Kierkegaards Opfattelse af Sokrates," in his *Om Sokrates' Lære og Personlighed*, Copenhagen: University of Copenhagen 1871, pp. 51–7.

Vardy, Peter, "Socrates and Jesus," in his *Kierkegaard*, Ligouri, Missouri: Triumph 1996 (*Great Christian Thinkers*), pp. 9–21.

Vergote, Henri-Bernard, *Sens et répétition. Essai sur l'ironie kierkegaardienne*, vols. 1–2, Paris: Cerf/Orante 1982.

Vlastos, Gregory, "Socrates' Disavowal of Knowledge," in *Socratic Studies*, ed. by Myles Burnyeat, Cambridge: Cambridge University Press 1994, pp. 39–66.

Weiss, Raymond L., "Kierkegaard's 'Return' to Socrates," *The New Scholasticism*, vol. 45, 1971, pp. 573–83.

Westphal, Merold, *Kierkegaard's Critique of Reason and Society*, Macon, Georgia: Mercer University Press 1987, p. 106, note 3.

—— *Becoming a Self: A Reading of Kierkegaard's* Concluding Unscientific Postscript, West Lafayette, Indiana: Purdue University Press 1996, p. 28; p. 30; p. 32; p. 37; p. 45; pp. 60–2; pp. 65–6; pp. 68–9; pp. 120–8; pp. 135–6; p. 150; p. 158; p. 167; p. 182; p. 184.

Widenmann, Robert J., "Plato and Kierkegaards *Moment*," in *Faith, Knowledge, and Action: Essays Presented to Niels Thulstrup on His Sixtieth Birthday*, ed. by George L. Stengren, Copenhagen: C.A. Reitzel 1984, pp. 251–6.

Wild, John, "Kierkegaard and Classical Philosophy," *Philosophical Review*, vol. 49, no 5, 1940, pp. 536–51.

Wisdo, David M., "Kierkegaard and Euthyphro," *Philosophy*, vol. 62, 1987, pp. 221–6.

Wood, Robert E., "Recollection and Two Banquets: Plato's and Kierkegaard's," in *Stages on Life's Way*, ed. by Robert L. Perkins, Macon, Georgia: Mercer University Press 2000 (*International Kierkegaard Commentary*, vol. 11), pp. 49–68.

Wyller, Egil A., "Platons øyeblikks-filosofi eller dialogen Parmenides' 3. hypothese," in *Tradisjon og fornyelse. Festskrift til A. H. Winsnes*, ed. by Asbjørn Aarnes, Oslo: Aschehoug 1959, pp. 7–26.

—— "Sokrates og Kristus hos Søren Kierkegaard. En henologisk interpretasjon av forfatterskapet," *Norsk filosofisk tidsskrift*, vol. 28, 1993, pp. 207–19.

Ziolkowski, Eric, "From *Clouds* to *Corsair*: Kierkegaard, Aristophanes, and the Problem of Socrates," in *The Concept of Irony*, ed. by Robert L. Perkins, Macon, Georgia: Mercer University Press 2001 (*International Kierkegaard Commentary*, vol. 2), pp. 193–234.

PART II

Other Greek Sources on Socrates

Aristophanes:

Kierkegaard's Understanding of the Socrates of the *Clouds*

Eric Ziolkowski

I. Introduction: Aristophanes, Socrates, and the Clouds

Aristophanes' comedy the *Clouds* (*Νεφέλαι*, in Latin *Nubes*), the earliest surviving document to mention Socrates,[1] was initially performed at the Great Dionysia in 423 BC. The play features Socrates as its main subject and is generally seen to attack him as "the arch-sophist, atheist, and corrupter of the young."[2] It presents him as a quack pedagogue who holes up in his *phrontistērion* or "thinkery" amid pale, nerdish pupils; who devotes himself to astronomy, at times while suspended aloft in a basket, and to the study of subterranean phenomena; who denies the traditional deities in favor of revering clouds and air; who, like a stereotypical Sophist, allows students to be trained to win an argument whether it is right or wrong; and who charges a fee for his instruction—or so it seems to some.[3] *The Clouds* failed upon its aforementioned first and only attested performance, despite Aristophanes' opinion

---

1 As noted by Karl Jaspers, *The Great Philosophers*, vols. 1–4, New York, New York: Harcourt, Brace, and World 1962–95, vol. 1, 1962, p. 15. Cf. John Newell, "Aristophanes on Socrates," *Ancient Philosophy*, no. 19, 1999, p. 109. Neither Jaspers nor Newell mentions the fragment left from Ameipsias' comedy *Connus* which, depicting Socrates as one of its characters, was performed at the same festival as the *Clouds*. See *Socrates: A Source Book*, trans. and ed. by John Ferguson, London: Macmillan for the Open University Press 1970, p. 173.

2 Jeffrey Henderson, "Introductory Note," *Aristophanes*, vols. 1–5, new ed., ed. and trans. by Jeffrey Henderson, Cambridge, Massachusetts: Harvard University Press 1998–2007 (*Loeb Classical Library*), vol. 2 (the *Clouds*; *Wasps*; *Peace*), p. 5.

3 See the *Clouds*, lines 245–6; line 876; line 1146. (Hereafter all citations and quotations of this play are from Hendersen's edition and translation.) *Pace* the claims of many readers, including Kierkegaard (*SKS* 1, 203, note 1, 233, note 1 / *CI*, 153, note, 186, note), the text does not actually present Socrates as charging or even mentioning fees of his own. See A.E. Taylor, "The *Phrontisterion*," in his *Varia Socratica: First Series*, Oxford: James Parker 1911, pp. 176–7; Gilbert Murray, *Aristophanes: A Study*, Oxford: Clarendon Press 1933, p. 89; p. 94; Martin Andic, "The Clouds of Irony," in *The Concept of Irony*, ed. by Robert Perkins, Macon, Georgia: Mercer University Press 2001 (*International Kierkegaard Commentary*, vol. 2), p. 165.

of it as his most sophisticated comedy.[4] Apparently "too subtle for the public," the play "treated Socrates and his school too sympathetically and with too much friendly humor instead of rough satire."[5] So Aristophanes revised the script, abandoning it unfinished between 419 and 416.[6] In that incomplete form, which later circulated and remains today the only known version of the *Clouds*, Aristophanes intensified the satire by inserting the parabasis,[7] the debate between Better Argument and Worse Argument, and the torching of Socrates' domicile at the end.

Augmenting the allusions to him in three of Aristophanes' other extant comedies, all of them later (*Wasps* [*Σφῆκες*, Latin *Vespae*], *Birds* [*Ὄρνιθες*, Latin *Aves*], and *Frogs* [*Βάτραχοι*, Latin *Ranae*], produced in 422, 414, and 405 BC., respectively), the depiction of Socrates in the *Clouds* strikes most readers as discrepant with the only other surviving portrayals of him by contemporaries, Plato and Xenophon—both of whom had known Socrates personally but wrote after his death. George Grote opined in the mid-nineteenth century that the teachings of the Aristophanic Socrates seem "utterly different" from those of the real Socrates against whom the *Clouds* levels "calumnies."[8] After Grote, classicists and historians of philosophy tended to regard Aristophanes' portrait of Socrates as a "misapprehension," "astonishingly false," "unfair," and "very unfortunate."[9] Such opinions, accompanied by a sense of the play's satire as "hostile," "malicious," or "ill-natured,"[10] are thought to have "removed" the *Clouds* from consideration as a source of information about the philosophy and intellectual biography of Socrates.[11]

4 See Aristophanes, *Wasps*, lines 1037–47; the *Clouds*, line 522.

5 Murray, *Aristophanes*, pp. 87–8. See Aristophanes, *Wasps*, lines 1043–5.

6 Henderson, "Introductory Note," p. 3. See also K.J. Dover, "Introduction" to his own edition of Aristophanes, the *Clouds*, Oxford: Clarendon Press 1968, pp. lxxx–lxxxi.

7 Aristophanes, the *Clouds*, lines 518–52.

8 George Grote, *A History of Greece, from the Earliest Period to the Close of the Generation Contemporary with Alexander the Great*, vols. 1–10, new ed., London: John Murray 1888, vol. 7, p. 89; p. 147.

9 Quotations drawn successively from Friedrich Ueberweg, *History of Philosophy from Thales to the Present Age*, vols. 1–2, trans. by George S. Morris, with additions by Noah Porter, New York: Scribner 1896, vol. 1, p. 87; Jaspers, *The Great Philosophers*, vol. 1, p. 21; W.W. Merry, "Introduction" to his new edition of Aristophanes, *The Clouds*, Oxford: Clarendon 1899, p. vii; C.C. Felton, "Preface" to his edition of Aristophanes, *The Clouds*, Boston: John Allyn 1877, p. xi.

10 Quotations drawn from successively from Grote, *History of Greece*, vol. 1, p. 359, note 2; *The Oxford Companion to Classical Literature*, ed. by M.C. Howatson, 2nd ed., Oxford: Oxford University Press 1989, p. 529, s.v., "Socrates"; Albert Levi, "The Idea of Socrates: The Philosophic Hero in the Nineteenth Century," *Journal of the History of Ideas*, vol. 17, 1956, p. 93.

11 Paul A. Vander Waerdt, *The Socratic Movement*, Ithaca, New York: Cornell University Press 1991, pp. 54–5. However, Niels Thulstrup, while acknowledging that Ulrich von Wiliamowitz-Moellendorff, W. Norvin, and others "have completely rejected" the *Clouds* as a historical source, identifies several mid-twentieth-century German scholars who found in the play many "reliable historical traits for a description of Socrates" (*Kierkegaard's Relation to Hegel*, trans. by George L. Stengren, Princeton: Princeton University Press 1980, p. 233, note 12). Cf. Newell's interpretation, considered below.

In response to the description Plato proffered of his own writings as the work of an embellished, modernized Socrates,[12] Leo Strauss proclaims it "impossible to say whether the Platonic-Xenophontic Socrates owes his being as much to poetry as does the Aristophanean Socrates."[13] Nonetheless, the Aristophanic portrait is the only one that, by virtue of its comic-dramatic form, *self-evidently* constitutes a poetic fiction, even if "In the opinion of the plain man, the 'Socrates' whom Aristophanes libeled and caricatured in the *Clouds* will continue to be the historical Socrates."[14] the *Clouds* is also the only source to ascribe to Socrates an informed interest in astronomy and geology, to deny his piety, and to suggest that he taught how to succeed by exploiting such worldly arts as rhetoric and the law. According to K.J. Dover, there are three possible explanations of this basic discrepancy between Aristophanes, on the one hand, and Plato and Xenophon, on the other:

> (i) Aristophanes portrays, through caricature, the truth; Plato and Xenophon are writing fiction, putting their own ideas into [Socrates'] mouth...(ii) Aristophanes caricatures Socrates as he was in 424/3; Plato and Xenophon portray him as he became in the last twenty years of his life...(iii) Plato and Xenophon tell the truth; Aristophanes attaches to Socrates the characteristics which belonged to the Sophists in general but did not belong to Socrates.[15]

Of these explanations, the third, to which Dover subscribes, is the most widely accepted, despite the arguments of John Burnet and A.E. Taylor favoring the second. However, the idea that Aristophanes depicted the truth through caricature has not gone without espousers.[16] Furthermore John Newell suggests that the irony for which the real Socrates was known allowed Aristophanes in the *Clouds* "to present any philosophical view he pleased (or any combination of views) *without sacrificing realism*, because Socrates' irony made him a kind of mimetic actor who could believably present a variety of intellectual views, however much he might personally disagree with them."[17] In ascribing irony to the Aristophanic Socrates, this last interpretation resembles Kierkegaard's, even though Newell, who never cites Kierkegaard, approaches the *Clouds* philologically rather than philosophically.

The perception of a causal connection between the *Clouds* and Socrates' condemnation finds its *loci classici* in Plato, Xenophon, and some later Greek sources. According to Aelian and Diogenes Laertius, Anytus, one of the three men who would eventually bring Socrates to trial on the charge of impiety and corrupting youths, incited Aristophanes to write a play lampooning Socrates.[18] In Plato's

---

12 Plato, Letter 2, 314c.

13 Leo Strauss, *Socrates and Aristophanes*, New York: Basic Books 1966, p. 314.

14 W.J.M. Starkie, *The Clouds of Aristophanes*, London: Macmillan 1911, p. 1.

15 Dover, "Introduction," p. xlvi; p. xlix. Cf. Newell's distinction between "tight" and "loose" interpretations of the *Clouds* ("Aristophanes on Socrates," pp. 109–10).

16 E.g., Mario Montuori, *Socrates: An Approach*, trans. by Marcus de la Pae Beresford, Amsterdam: J.C. Gieben 1988, p. 135. Thulstrup cites other examples; see *Kierkegaard's Relation to Hegel*, p. 233, note 11.

17 Newell, "Aristophanes on Socrates," p. 114.

18 Aelian, *Historical Miscellany* (*Variae historiae*), 2.13; Diogenes Laertius, *Socrates*, 38.

Apology, the indicted Socrates cites the *Clouds* as typifying the slander with which people have long targeted him.[19] The fodder the *Clouds* furnished to the detractors of Socrates long before his trial is exemplified by the unnamed man from Syracuse who interrupts the sage's conversation in Xenophon's *Symposium* (ca. 380 BC), set at a banquet purportedly held in Athens in 421 BC, two years after the Dionysia production of Aristophanes' play. Alluding to Socrates as "a thinker on celestial subjects" (τὰ μετέωρα φροντιστής), an expression of reproach that was exploited parodically against Socrates in the *Clouds* and later bore grave implications at his trial,[20] the Syracusan evokes another passage from the play to ridicule him: "But tell me the distance between us in flea's feet; for people say that your geometry includes such measurements as that."[21]

Despite these classical linkages of the *Clouds* with Socrates' condemnation, Aristophanes oddly is seldom censured for having pilloried "the first philosopher who was tried and put to death."[22] As he is thought to have probably been in Athens during the trial, one wonders what he was doing then, and how he may have regarded this event.[23] After Socrates' death, as Socrates had prophesied (according to Plato), and as Diogenes Laertius reports, the Athenians promptly repented, executed one of the sage's accusers, and banished the rest.[24] Yet Aristophanes evidently suffered no repercussion other than to be later branded "a vulgar and ridiculous humorist."[25] Although the rumors Aelian repeated about him may have "tarnished [Aristophanes'] name, until the learning and sagacity of modern critics should redeem it from the bitter reproach of having caused the death of the noblest man of his age,"[26] some scholars argue that Socrates took no offense when the *Clouds* was performed, and that Plato and Aristophanes later remained good friends and admirers of one another.[27] It has even been submitted that the *Clouds* does not deride Socrates.[28]

Nonetheless, Plato's *Symposium*, on which such assurance is based, might be alternatively read as expressing contempt for Aristophanes. The dialogue represents him as prone to bodily intemperance (including hiccupping, perhaps from gluttony,

---

19 *Apology*, 19c.

20 Noted by E.C. Marchant and O.J. Todd in their translation of *Symposium*, in *Xenophon: in seven volumes*, vols. 1–7, London and Cambridge, Massachusetts: Harvard University Press 1979–86 (*Loeb Classical Library*), vol. 4, p. 606, note 1.

21 *Symposium*, 6.8, in *Xenophon*, vol. 4, pp. 607–9. Cf. Aristophanes, the *Clouds*, lines 144–52; lines 830–1.

22 Diogenes Laertius, *Socrates*, 20.

23 See for example, Murray, *Aristophanes*, p. 102; Levi, "Idea," p. 94, note 20.

24 Plato, *Apology*, 39c; and Diogenes, *Socrates*, 43.

25 Aelian, *Historical Miscellany*, 2.13.

26 Felton, "Preface," p. ix.

27 See for example, John Burnet, *Greek Philosophy: Thales to Plato*, London: Macmillan 1928, p. 143; Murray, *Aristophanes*, p. 102; A.E. Taylor, *Socrates*, Boston: Beacon 1951, p. 92; Povl Johannes Jensen, "Aristophanes," in *Kierkegaard's Classical Inspiration*, ed. by Niels Thulstrup and Marie Mikulová Thulstrup, Copenhagen: C.A. Reitzel 1985 (*Bibliotheca Kierkegaardiana*, vol. 14), pp. 21–2; *The Oxford Companion to Classical Literature*, p. 529; Andic, "The Clouds of Irony," pp. 174–6. See also Strauss, *Socrates and Aristophanes*, p. 5.

28 Andic, "The Clouds of Irony," pp. 178–9.

and sneezing); as devoting his life to the wine-god Dionysus and the love-goddess Aphrodite, antitheses to the Platonic ideals; as proving no match for Socrates as a drinker; and as putting everyone present but Agathon and Socrates to sleep with a speech on love, a speech centered on a theory which Socrates subsequently paints as unoriginal and dismisses. Whether or not he makes up the character of "Diotima" on the spot, perhaps to cast doubt on Aristophanes' originality, Socrates quotes her as having cited that same theory long ago as being already old-hat. Finally, theater, the forum in which Aristophanes burlesqued Socrates, is referred to here as a place filled with "an army of blockheads," and governed by "the mob's [opinion]."[29] Rather than entertaining "friendly" sentiments toward Aristophanes, might not Plato, whose *Symposium* closes with Socrates defeating Aristophanes in a debate about poetry, have the Aristophanic type in mind when recounting Socrates' banishment of the poets in the *Republic*?[30]

II. The Romantic Background to Kierkegaard's Consideration of Aristophanes

Kierkegaard's writings were not yet sufficiently known in Germany prior to World War I to earn mention in Wilhelm Süss' *Aristophanes und die Nachwelt*, which, published in 1911, surveys the reception of the Greek comic playwright from antiquity to modern times. Nonetheless, given his early, deeply informed attraction to the German Romantics, Kierkegaard could hardly have overlooked the special interest they took in Aristophanes. As Süss puts it:

> In the Romantic period all the characteristics of Aristophanic art could be sure to be understood: the unbridled, exuberant frenzy; the explosion of illusions; the farcical, popular comicality; the delight of the Romantic concept of art in Aristophanic comedy touches upon an innermost affinity of essence [*innerster Wesenverwandtschaft*].[31]

Friedrich Schlegel (1772–1829) and Ludwig Tieck (1773–1853), two of the foremost early Romantics whose theories of irony Kierkegaard scrutinizes in the second part of his dissertation *On the Concept of Irony, with Continual Reference to Socrates* (1841), played leading roles the positive reappraisal of Aristophanes during the final decade of the eighteenth century. Schlegel, with his brother August Wilhelm Schlegel (1767–1845), defended Aristophanes against the dominant opinion of their day that the tone of Attic comedy was incompatible with noble sentiments and a unified taste.[32] Characterizing the Dionysian "lawless beauty" of Aristophanes and Euripides alike as

---

29 Plato, *Symposium*, 194b, 194c.

30 I am aware that similar interpretation proffered by Léon Robin in his introduction to Plato, *Le Banquet*, ed. and trans. by by Léon Robin, 4th revised ed., Paris: Les Belles Lettres 1949, is tactfully dismissed by Taylor, *Socrates*, p. 92, note 1.

31 Wilhelm Süss, *Aristophanes und die Nachwelt*, Leipzig: Dieterich 1911, p. 127.

32 See Hans Eichner, "Einleitung" to *Kritische Friedrich-Schlegel-Ausgabe*, Abteilungen 1–4, vols. 1–35, ed. by Ernst Behler et al., Paderborn and Munich: F. Schöningh 1958-, vol. 6, 1961, p. xv, including note 2; Gerald Gillespie, "Introduction" to his edition and translation of Ludwig Tieck, *Der gestiefelte Kater*, Austin: University of Texas Press 1974 (*Edinburgh Bilingual Library*, vol. 8), p. 20.

"transporting, seductive, glittering,"[33] and pronouncing the essence of Aristophanic comedy to be a "beautiful mirth and sublime freedom" that parts with conventional theatrical illusion,[34] Friedrich Schlegel also credited Aristophanes with having exposed the moral decline of Athens in a manner and with an intensity which no historical work and no other thinker could have equaled.[35] Meanwhile Tieck emerged as the acknowledged founder of so-called Aristophanic comedy in the German theater, a man noted for his veneration of Aristophanes (*Aristophanesverehrung*).[36] His *Puss-in-Boots*,[37] a fairytale in theatrical form which Kierkegaard apparently read by 1836,[38] was found by August Wilhelm Schlegel (whether rightly or wrongly) to draw its characters "down from the stage" in a manner reminiscent of Aristophanes.[39] Friedrich Schlegel deemed that play a modern fulfillment of Romantic irony, which he construed, through an analogy to Aristophanes' prototypical defiance of dramatic illusion, as a both creative and destructive process reflecting the universal, autonomous, divine spirit of poetry.[40] Another play by Tieck, *Anti-Faust oder Geschichte eines dummen Teufels*, undertaken in 1801 but left unfinished, not only is directly modeled after Aristophanic comedy but brings on stage among its characters the shade of the ancient Greek playwright.[41]

The perception of Tieck as "a romantic Aristophanes" and of Aristophanes as "a classical Tieck,"[42] a view lastingly popularized by the Schlegels and certainly

---

33 A.W. Schlegel, "Von den Schulen der griechischen Poesie" (1797), *Kritische Friedrich-Schlegel-Ausgabe*, vol. 1, p. 15.

34 A.W. Schlegel, "Vom Ästhetischen Werte der griechischen Komödie" (1794), *Kritische Friedrich-Schlegel-Ausgabe*, vol. 1, pp. 24–30, quote on 24.

35 See *Kritische Friedrich-Schlegel-Ausgabe*, vol. 6, p. 39 (originally as *Friedrich Schlegels Geschichte der alten und neuen Litteratur: Vorlesungen gehalten zu Wien im Jahre 1812*, Vienna: Schaumburg 1815).

36 Süss, *Aristophanes und die Nachwelt*, p. 128.

37 Ludwig Tieck, *Der gestiefelte Kater, ein Kindermärchen in drey Akten mit Zwischenspielen, einem Prologe und Epiloge*, Berlin: Nicolai 1797 (premiere, 1844).

38 See the reference to Gottlieb, a character in Tieck's story, in Kierkegaard's "*Om Flyvepostens Polemik* " (1836), in *SV1* XIII, 26 / *EPW*, 22.

39 Review in *Allgemeine Literatur-Zeitung* (1797), in *Ludwig Tieck's Schriften*, vols. 1–28, Berlin: G. Reimer 1828–54, vol. 11, p. 143; quoted by Roger Paulin, who contends that this account of the play's technique "fails absolutely to capture the way in which Tieck *lifts* his audience on to the stage, playing with them before consigning them again to their place" Roger Paulin, *Ludwig Tieck: A Literary Biography*, Oxford: Clarendon Press, 1985, p. 67.

40 Paulin, *Ludwig Tieck*, p. 67, summarizing ideas expressed by Friedrich Schlegel in *Das Athenaeum*, the biannual literary periodical which he co-edited with his brother from in the years 1798–1800.

41 As noted by Raymond M. Immerwahr, *The Esthetic Intent of Tieck's Fantastic Comedy*, St Louis: Washington University 1953, p. 73. See also Paulin, *Ludwig Tieck*, p. 130.

42 See Heinrich Heine, *Die romantische Schule*, in Heinrich Heine, *Sämtliche Schriften*, vols. 1–6, ed. by Klaus Briegleb, Munich: Carl Hanser 1968–76, vol. 3, p. 416. (English translation, *The Romantic School and Other Essays*, ed. by Jost Hermand and Robert C. Holub, New York: Continuum 1985 (*The German Library*, vol. 33), p. 54.) Kierkegaard's owned Heinrich Heine, *Die romantische Schule*, Hamburg: Hoffmann und Campe 1836

known by Kierkegaard, is hardly unproblematic. Friedrich Schlegel, in casting Tieck as a modern Romantic Aristophanes while also defending Aristophanes against the "serious charge" of having "so maliciously depicted the most virtuous and wisest of his fellow citizens, Socrates,"[43] oddly overlooked that Tieck was, as one of his modern biographers puts it, "not given to his Attic forebearer's more than occasional nastiness and misanthropy."[44] And that is not the only difference. As Heinrich Heine (1797–1856) observed in his *The Romantic School*, which Kierkegaard consulted in writing the dissertation,[45] the dramas of Tieck that were routinely compared with Aristophanes' comedies differ from them structurally and stylistically "almost as a Sophoclean tragedy differs from a Shakespearean."[46] Above all, in glaring contrast to Aristophanes, "our German Aristophaneses"—a sarcastic allusion to Tieck and his German dramaturgical imitators—"abstained from any exalted philosophy of life" and kept silent about religion and politics.[47]

Denmark during its literary "Golden Age" was naturally not immune to the influence of the neighboring German vogue for Aristophanes. The Aristophanic parody of Socrates' dialectic had already been adapted in Ludvig Holberg's (1684–1754) comic play *Erasmus Montanus* (1731), to which many allusions crop up in Kierkegaard's writings, including the dissertation, where it is noted that Aristophanes' Socrates engages in behavior comparable to the "linguistic hairsplitting" of Holberg's Peer Degn.[48] In Kierkegaard's own time, the relation between Aristophanes and

(*ASKB* U 63). For a circumspect account of Tieck's relation to Aristophanes, of the Schlegels' conception of Aristophanic comedy, and of the bearing of that conception upon Tieck, see Immerwahr, *The Esthetic Intent of Tieck's Fantastic Comedy*, passim.

43 F. Schlegel, *Geschichte der alten und neuen Literatur*, lecture 2, in *Kritische Friedrich-Schlegel-Ausgabe*, vol. 6, p. 43. His ensuing defense on the same page: "*vielleicht aber war es nicht bloß poetische Willkür, und daß er den ersten besten berühmten Namen aufgriff, um unter demselben die Sophisten, die es allerdings verdienten, zu verspotten, und dem Volke so lächerlich und verabscheuungswert darzustellen als möglich. Der Dichter verwechselte und vermengte vielleicht selbst, ohne es zu wollen, den Weisen, den sein Trieb nach Wahrheit anfangs auch in diese Schule führte, mit diesen Sophisten selbst, welche Sokrates studiert hatte, um sie zu widerlegen, und deren Schule er nur besuchte, bis er ihre Leerheit erkannte und nun den Kampf gegen sie, und den Versuch begann, die Griechen auf einem ganz neuen Wege zur Wahrheit zurück zu führen*."

44 Paulin, *Ludwig Tieck*, p. 67.

45 As evidenced by *SKS* 1, 337 / *CI*, 304, where Kierkegaard cites Heine's *Die romantische Schule*. For the pertinent passage see Heine, *Sämtliche Schriften*, vol. 3, p. 376 (*The Romantic School*, p. 18).

46 Heine, *Sämtliche Schriften*, vol. 3, p. 422 (*The Romantic School*, p. 60). Heine explains: "Ancient comedy had the uniform structure, the strict course of action, and the exquisitely polished metrical language of ancient tragedy, of which it may be considered a parody, but Mr. Tieck's dramatic satires are just as daring in structure, as full of English irregularity, as capricious in their prosody, as Shakespeare's tragedies," and find their formal prototype in the Italian dramatist Carlo Gozzi's (1720–1806) "motley, bizarre fairy-tale comedies."

47 Heine, *Sämtliche Schriften*, vol. 3, p. 423 (*The Romantic School*, p. 61). Cf. Immerwahr, *The Esthetic Intent of Tieck's Fantastic Comedy*, pp. 9–10; pp. 79–84; p. 114; Gillespie, "Introduction," p. 22; Paulin, *Ludwig Tieck*, p. 298.

48 *SKS* 1, 201, note 1 / *CI*, 151, note.

Socrates occurs as a leitmotif in Adam Oehlenschläger's (1779–1850) tragedy *Sokrates* (1836), which represents Aristophanes as regretful of having derided Socrates on stage, and this play in turn is mocked in Johan Ludvig Heiberg's (1791–1860) "apocalyptic comedy" entitled "A Soul After Death" (1841).[49]

III. Kierkegaard's References to, and Uses of, Aristophanes' Socrates

While furnishing no definitive proof that he had yet read any of Aristophanes' plays, Kierkegaard's earliest recorded allusions to Aristophanes stem from discussions of him in modern sources. In a schematic outline of "the development of comedy" derived in the entry of January 16, 1837 of Kierkegaard's journal from a piece by Heiberg in *Kjøbenhavns Flyvende Post*, Aristophanes is designated to represent the "immediate" type of "universal," "higher" comedy.[50] He is again mentioned five months later, in an entry of June 8, 1837, which summarizes a recently published essay on comparative religion by the Hegelian philosopher Karl Rosenkranz (1805–79), for whom Aristophanes represents "the tragic in the comic, which absolutizes the idiosyncratic individuality."[51]

Kierkegaard must have read the *Clouds* by then or shortly thereafter. For it was around that same time or during the next several years that he drafted "The Battle between the Old and the New Soap-Cellars,"[52] a short three-act philosophical drama he never finished, published, or saw performed. Aptly described by Lee Capel as "a satirical, quasi-Aristophanic comedy,"[53] the play lampoons Hegelians and Hegelianism in a manner comparable to the satirizing of Socrates and the Sophists in the *Clouds*. In both plays the troubled protagonist—the financially-strapped Strepsiades, and Willibald, a doubter and relativist (a possible stand-in for Kierkegaard himself)[54]—seeks solutions to his problems from philosophers: the sophistical Socrates and his pupils, who lodge in the *phrontistērion*, and the Hegelians Mr von Jumping-Jack and Mr Phrase (apparent parodies of Johan Ludvig Heiberg and Hans Lassen Martensen),[55] and their associates, who lodge in the "Prytaneum," the type of Greek public building which Plato's Socrates told his judges he deserved to be maintained in after they had pronounced him guilty.[56] In a scene upon which Kierkegaard will comment in his dissertation, Strepsiades is surprised to be told by

49 See Jensen, "Aristophanes," pp. 21–2.

50 *SKS* 17, 113, BB:23 / *KJN* 1, 107; and J.L. Heiberg, "Svar paa Prof. Oehlenschlägers Skrift: 'Om Kritiken i Kjøbenhavns flyvende Post over 'Væringerne i Miklagaard,' " *Kjøbenhavns flyvende Post*, no. 13, 1828, p. 3.

51 *SKS* 17, 219–22, DD:10 / *KJN* 1, 211–13; citing Karl Rosenkranz, "Eine Parallele zur Religionsphilosophie," *Zeitschrift für spekulative Theologie*, vols. 1–3, ed. by Bauer, Bruno, Berlin: Ferdinand Dümmler 1836–38, vol. 2, no. 1, 1837, p. 8 (*ASKB* 354–357).

52 *SKS* 17, 280–97, DD:208 / *EPW*, 105–24.

53 *CIC*, 27.

54 See *EPW*, 260, note 7.

55 Cf. *EPW*, Notes, p. 261, note 9.

56 See Plato, *Apology*, 36d–37a. Cf. *SKS* 1, 242 / *CI*, 195.

Socrates that thunder and rain are produced not by Zeus but by clouds.[57] Likewise Willibald becomes mystified by a celestial phenomenon, "namely, why it was that the sun in the prytaneum never changed its position at all, as a result of which the light was always the same."[58] And just as Phidippides, after Strepsiades fails to learn from Socrates' instruction, is delivered by Socrates to "Better Argument" and "Worse Argument" to be instructed through hearing them debate,[59] so Willibald, "who had not found himself much edified or satisfied by Jumping-Jack's philosophical lectures,"[60] is referred to the "World-Historical College," where he hears pompous and convoluted lectures by the Hegelians.

Given the notoriety of the *Clouds*, the seventh of the fifteen theses heading Kierkegaard's dissertation gives pause: "Aristophanes has come very close to the truth in his depiction of Socrates," while, according to the third thesis, neither Plato nor Xenophon "finds the truth" in their own depictions of Socrates.[61] Today's consensus that the Aristophanic Socrates lacks historicity is not all that challenges or casts doubt upon Thesis VII. Numerous commentators have regarded *The Concept of Irony* itself as an ironic work,[62] a view that raises the question of how seriously any of theses should be taken. In this connection it is noteworthy that Kierkegaard had absorbed Hegel's *Lectures on the History of Philosophy* (published posthumously, 1833–36) in the winter of 1838–39,[63] for, as Povl Johannes Jensen observes, it was in consequence of the understanding of Socrates advanced therein that Aristophanes came to be "considered a source of vital importance to an appraisal of Socrates."[64] Bearing out Jensen's point, within five years after the publication of Hegel's *Lectures*, and two years after Kierkegaard's dissertation appeared, there was published in Bayreuth a book, by a pastor and professor by the name of Johannes Zorn, entitled *Aristophanes in seinem Verhältnis zu Socrates. Ein Beitrag zur gerechten Würdigung des Dichters*,[65] which took as its starting point the Hegelian view of intellectual history. Regarding Thesis VII, Capel "wonders whether Kierkegaard, being aware

---

57 Aristophanes, the *Clouds*, lines 368–424. See *SKS* 1, 197, note 1 / *CI*, 146–7, note.

58 *SKS* 17, 293, DD:208 / *EPW*, 120. See also *SKS* 17, 290, DD:208 / *EPW*, 123.

59 Aristophanes, the *Clouds*, lines 884–1111.

60 *SKS* 17, 292, DD:208 / *EPW*, 129.

61 *SKS* 1, 65 / *CI*, 6.

62 *CIC*, 8, 14; Andic, "The Clouds of Irony," p. 190. This view found early expression in the review of the dissertation in *Corsaren* 51 (October 22, 1841) col. 7: "Thank you, beloved Kierkegaard, for your irony!" (*COR*, 92–3). On the mid-twentieth century popularizers of this view, most notably Pierre Mesnard and Wilhelm Anz, see *CIC*, Notes, pp. 354–6. Thulstrup regularly detects irony in the dissertation's allusions to Hegel (*Kierkegaard's Relation to Hegel*, pp. 213–61). In contrast, for Hannay, the dissertation is "a work on irony, and not a work of irony" (Alastair Hannay, *Kierkegaard: A Biography*, Cambridge: Cambridge University Press 2001, p. 152).

63 Noted by von Kloeden, "Sokrates," p. 121.

64 Jensen, "Aristophanes," p. 20.

65 Johannes Zorn, *Aristophanes in seinem Verhältnis zu Socrates. Ein Beitrag zur gerechten Würdigung des Dichters*, Bayreuth: F.C. Birner 1845. I do not know of any evidence suggesting that Kierkegaard or Zorn (whom neither Kloeden nor Jensen mentions) were ever aware of each other's work.

of the recent rehabilitation of the Aristophanic Socrates..., is not here writing with tongue in cheek" and "follow[ing] Hegel with a serious bent on parody."[66]

Whatever the case, another scholar's claim that Thesis VII "collides with the received opinion, going back to antiquity, that Plato's view is correct and that his and Aristophanes' portraits of Socrates are in fundamental opposition,"[67] must be qualified. Tieck, for example, had already anticipated Kierkegaard in defying the assumption that Plato's portrayal of Socrates is more correct than that of Aristophanes. In *Phantasus* (1812–16), a work included in the edition of Tieck's writings that Kierkegaard owned, one of the fictive interlocutors alludes to the "delight" we take in Aristophanes' caricature of Socrates, adding:

> [I]f we want to make for ourselves a true representation of this illustrious man, we must actually, alongside the portrayals by Xenophon and Plato, adapt that by the comic poet, in order to catch sight of more than a reverend outline of him; art has no power to transport if the truth of the picture does not gaze forth out of the caricature.[68]

A vexing problem raised by Thesis VII has to do with Kierkegaard's failure to acknowledge the play's bearing upon the philosopher's indictment, trial, condemnation, and execution in 399 B.C. Remarkably, Socrates' condemnation goes unmentioned throughout the discussion of the *Clouds* in the dissertation,[69] and the *Clouds* goes unmentioned throughout the subsequent discussion of Socrates' condemnation.[70] Despite Hegel's apparent sympathy with those who deny that the *Clouds* influenced Socrates' condemnation,[71] classicists and historians of philosophy since Grote have not been content simply to see Aristophanes as having "exactly forecast[ed] the charges...against Socrates,"[72] or to accept the play's parodying of Socrates as a passive "expression" or "reflection" of the attitudes and prejudices of

---

66 *CIC*, Notes, p. 385, note 2.

67 Andic, "the Clouds of Irony," p. 161.

68 *Ludwig Tieck's Sämmtliche Werke*, vols. 1–2, Paris: Tétot Frères 1837 (*ASKB* 1848–1849), vol. 1, pp. 489–90. *Phantasus* constitutes a large compilation by Tieck of number of his shorter prose writings, including some older works and some newer, set within "a framework of conversation and discussion reminiscent of Boccaccio." (See Paulin, *Ludwig Tieck*, p. 196). As part of that framework, the passage I have quoted, which spoken by the character Manfred, occurs in a short dialogue that immediately follows the so-labeled "*Völliger Schluß*" of *Der gestiefelte Kater*.

69 *SKS* 1, 179–204 / *CI*, 128–54.

70 *SKS* 1, 215–43 / *CI*, 167–97.

71 *Georg Wilhelm Friedrich Hegel's Vorlesungen über die Geschichte der Philosophie*, vols. 1–3, ed. by Carl Ludwig Michelet, Berlin: Duncker und Humblot 1833–36 (vols. 13–15 in *Georg Wilhelm Friedrich Hegel's Werke. Vollständige Ausgabe*, ed. by Philipp Marheineke et al., Berlin: Duncker und Humblot 1832–45), vol. 2, p. 86 (*ASKB* 557–559). (English translation: *Lectures on the History of Philosophy*, vols. 1–3, trans. by Elizabeth S. Haldane and Frances H. Simson, London: Kegan Paul, Trench, Trübner 1892–96, vol. 1, 1892, p. 427.)

72 Newell, "Aristophanes on Socrates," p. 110.

contemporary Athens.[73] The tendency instead has been to charge the *Clouds* with having fostered the public antagonism that led to the philosopher's doom.[74]

Whatever effect Socrates' death may have had upon the Athenians' attitude toward Aristophanes, the playwright's burlesquing of Socrates received little criticism after Hegel "rehabilitated" the Aristophanic Socrates. In his aforementioned *Lectures*, Hegel initially turns to the *Clouds* while arguing that the condemnation of Socrates was right and just, because Socrates had subverted the Athenian "spirit" by replacing external religion with the judgment of inward consciousness as the sole criterion of truth. Anticipating the objection that the *Clouds* treats Socrates unjustly, Hegel responds that Aristophanes "was perfectly right" in this play:

> This poet, who exposed Socrates to scorn in the most laughable and bitter way, was thus no ordinary joker and shallow wag who mocked what is highest and best, and sacrificed all to wit with a view to making the Athenians laugh. For everything has to him a much deeper basis, and in all his jokes there lies a depth of seriousness....It is a pitiful wit which has no substance, and does not rest on contradictions lying in the matter itself. But Aristophanes was no bad jester.[75]

Elsewhere, in his *Lectures on Aesthetics* (published 1835–38), Hegel elaborates upon these ideas as if to preempt any counter-suggestion that Aristophanes was not a model, conservative Athenian citizen, or that any of the butts of Aristophanes' comedy, such as Socrates, were not deserving of derision.[76] Kierkegaard proved not oblivious of this view. Regardless of whatever else Kierkegaard may have accepted or rejected from the Hegelian assessment of Aristophanes, a crucial point on which he surprisingly never disagrees, at least openly, is that it was neither morally nor aesthetically wrong for Aristophanes to ridicule Socrates.

If Hegel was "a historically quite factual point of departure for the appraisal [of Socrates] during the time of SK,"[77] the German philosopher Johann Georg Hamann (1730–88)—the so-called Magus of the North—was "a forerunner for

---

73 Henderson, "Introductory Note," p. 5.

74 For example, Grote, *History of Greece*, vol. 7, p. 147; p. 154; Felton, "Preface," p. ix; W. Windelbrand, *A History of Philosophy with Especial Reference to the Formation and Development of its Problems and Conceptions*, trans. by James H. Tufts, New York: Macmillan 1893, p. 81, note 1; Alfred Weber, *History of Philosophy*, trans. by Frank Thilly, New York: Charles Scribner's Sons 1909, pp. 64–5; John Burnet, "Socrates," in *The Encyclopaedia of Religion and Ethics*, vols. 1–13, ed. by James Hastings, New York: Charles Scribner, 1908–26, vol. 11, p. 671; Murray, *Aristophanes*, p. 88; Taylor, *Socrates*, pp. 92–3; Jaspers, *The Great Philosophers*, vol. 1, 1962, p. 21; Kidd, "Socrates," pp. 480–1.

75 *Hegel's Vorlesungen über die Geschichte der Philosophie*, vol. 2, p. 86. (*Lectures on the History of Philosophy*, vol. 1, p. 427.)

76 See *Georg Wilhelm Friedrich Hegel's Vorlesungen über die Aesthetik*, vols. 1–3, ed. by Heinrich Gustav Hotho, Berlin: Duncker und Humblot 1835–38 (vols. 10.1–10.3 in *Georg Wilhelm Friedrich Hegel's Werke. Vollständige Ausgabe*), vol. 3, pp. 536–7; pp. 559–61 (*ASKB* 1384–1386). (English translation: *Aesthetics: Lectures on Fine Art*, vols. 1–2, trans. by T.M. Knox, Oxford: Clarendon Press 1975, vol. 2, p. 1202; pp. 1220–2.)

77 Jensen, "Aristophanes," p. 19.

the Kierkegaardian conception of Socrates,"[78] especially in his assessment of the Xenophantic and Platonic portraits of him: "In the works of Xenophon there prevails a superstitious, and in Plato's an enthusiastic reverence [i.e., for Socrates]."[79] It has been inferred that Kierkegaard, by the time he wrote his dissertation, was acquainted with Hamann's *Socratic Memorabilia* (1759),[80] in which the passage just quoted occurs. Although Hamann later published this work's separate *Nachspiel* (Epilogue) under the Aristophanic title *Wolken* (the Clouds),[81] only several cryptic allusions to the *Clouds* occur in *Socratic Memorabilia*. One of these is to the attestation by the Aristophanic Socrates that he and his followers believe only in "this Void, and the Clouds, and the Tongue, and only these three."[82] Kierkegaard will discuss this line while expounding Thesis VII. But whereas Hamann cited this line to illustrate the Athenians' actual accusation that Socrates did not honor the gods, and that he desired to introduce new ones,[83] Kierkegaard quotes it in conjunction with the Aristophanic Socrates' oath, "By Respiration, by Void, by Air,"[84] to suggest how the titular image of the *Clouds* is "set forth as a creed, which like any creed contains both the subjective and the objective side"[85]—the subjective being represented by "respiration" or "tongue" (γλῶττα), and the objective, by "clouds" (νεφέλαι) and "chaos" or "void" (χάος).

These different uses that Hamann and Kierkegaard make of the same line from the *Clouds* bear upon arguably the most intriguing aspect of Thesis VII's championing of Aristophanes' caricature of Socrates: Kierkegaard's almost complete silence about the pertinence of this caricature to the allegations and legal proceedings that led to Socrates' death. In contrast to Kierkegaard's silence, Hamann weaves into the penultimate paragraph of *Socratic Memorabilia* yet another ironic allusion to the fateful slandering of Socrates in Aristophanes' play,[86] and then, associating the

---

78 von Kloeden, "Sokrates," p. 109.

79 [Hamann], *Hamann's Schriften*, vols. 1–8, ed. by Friedrich Roth, Berlin: G. Reimer 1821–43, vol. 2, p. 11 (*ASKB* 536–544). (English translation: *Hamann's "Socratic Memorabilia": A Translation and Commentary*, trans. by James C. O'Flaherty, Baltimore: The Johns Hopkins Press 1967, p. 142.)

80 See Emanuel Hirsch, "Geschichtliche Einleitung" to Søren Kierkegaard, *Gesammelte Werke*, vols. 1–36, ed. by Emanuel Hirsch et al., Düsseldorf: E. Diederich 1951–66, vol. 31, p. ix; O'Flaherty, *Hamann's "Socratic Memorabilia,"* p. 107, including note 34.

81 *Hamann's Schriften*, vol. 2, pp. 51–101.

82 Aristophanes, the *Clouds*, line 424.

83 *Hamann's Schriften*, vol. 2, p. 47. (*Hamann's "Socratic Memorabilia,"* pp. 180–1, including note 57.) The German edition owned by Kierkegaard omits most of the footnotes, including the one just cited.

84 Aristophanes, the *Clouds*, line 627.

85 *SKS* 1, 188, note 1 / *CI*, 137, note.

86 Hamann suggests that whoever "does not know how to live on crumbs and alms not on prey, or to renounce everything for a sword, is not fit for the service of truth." See *Hamann's Schriften*, vol. 2, p. 49. (*Hamann's "Socratic Memorabilia,"* pp. 184–5.) To this passage's second clause Hamann provided a footnote—that is, note 62, omitted from the text in *Hamann's Schriften*—that quotes the *Clouds*, lines 1064–6: "A knife? What a civilized reward the poor sucker got! Now Hyperbolus, the man from the lamp market, has made a vast amount of money by being a rascal, but never a knife, indeed!" These are the words by

deaths of Socrates and Christ with one another, closes by remarking: "if it is true, I say, that God himself became a man, and came into the world to bear witness to the truth, no omniscience would be necessary to foresee that he would not escape from the world as well as Socrates."[87]

By following up on his allusions to the *Clouds* with this thought, Hamann comes close to implying that if Socrates and Christ are to be juxtaposed, then Aristophanes' satiric contribution to the slander that led to Socrates' trial and death might seem analogous to the vilification of Jesus that led to his crucifixion. If Kierkegaard noted this implication, he never pursues it, possibly because he considers any comparison of the deaths of Socrates and Christ to be blasphemous,[88] and also because, contradicting the tradition that originated with the early church fathers of likening Socrates to Christ,[89] his perception of the two men's relation is such that he felt compelled to open his dissertation by positing the paradoxical thesis that "The similarity between Christ and Socrates consists essentially in their dissimilarity."[90] Therefore, even if Kierkegaard did read Hamann's *Wolken*, and there is no evidence that he did read it, he remains silent about the slyly ironic manner in which Hamann there makes a final allusion to Socrates by evoking the titular image of Aristophanes' play precisely by rehearsing a reference to Christ drawn directly from Luther's Bible: "Behold, he is coming with the clouds!"[91]

In harking back (albeit with no acknowledgment by Kierkegaard) to Tieck's advocacy of appealing to Aristophanes along with Plato and Xenophon to achieve "a true representation" of Socrates, the pronouncement that the Aristophanic depiction of Socrates approaches "very close to the truth" distinguishes Kierkegaard from both Friedrich Schleiermacher (1768–1834) and Hegel in their views on the so-called Socratic problem: the historical-philosophical quandary of ascertaining who the "historical" Socrates really was and what he actually taught. Scheiermacher, providing the initial formulation of that problem in what Kierkegaard can call his "well-known treatise"[92] on Socrates as a philosopher, suggested that Plato and

---

which Worse Argument mocks Achilles' father Peleus for having been given by the gods a knife with which to defend himself against wild beasts in the woods. Although, in the myth, the gods meant that gift as a reward for Peleus' having refused a proposition by Acastus' wife, Worse Argument offers the counter-anecdote about Hyperbolus to suggest that a rascal is likely to garner more wealth in life than is someone decent like Peleus. The irony of Hamann's allusion to this passage is that, whereas Worse Argument would have been taken by Socrates' critics as representing what they considered to be Socrates' own morally corruptive teaching, Hamann appropriates Worse Argument's own words to associate "renounc[ing] everything for a sword" with "service of truth."

87 *Hamann's Schriften*, vol. 2, p. 50. (*Hamann's "Socratic Memorabilia,"* pp. 184–5.)

88 See *From the Papers of One Still Living*, in *SKS* 1, 54 / *EPW*, 99.

89 See Eric Ziolkowski, "From the *Clouds* to *Corsair*: Kierkegaard, Aristophanes, and the Problem of Socrates," in *The Concept of Irony*, ed. by Robert Perkins, Macon, Georgia: Mercer University Press 2001 (*International Kierkegaard Commentary*, vol. 2), pp. 199–203.

90 *SKS* 1, 61 / *CI*, 6.

91 *Hamann's Schriften*, vol. 2, p. 100.

92 *SKS* 1, 263 / *CI*, 219.

Xenophon, *combined*, give the most accurate representation of Socrates.[93] In contrast, Hegel in effect subverted that suggestion by favoring Xenophon's representation over Plato's, at least with regard to Socrates' teaching.[94] Kierkegaard, for his own part, finds Schleiermacher's discussion "lacking" in "an awareness of Socrates' significance as personality," and Hegel's presentation failing to offer anything "to illuminate the relations of the three different contemporary views of Socrates."[95] Having contended through Theses II–VI that Xenophon, "like a huckster, has deflated his Socrates," whereas Plato, "like an artist, has created his Socrates in supranatural dimensions,"[96] Kierkegaard submits that Aristophanes' view "will provide just the necessary contrast to Plato's and precisely by means of this contrast will open the possibility of a new approach for our evaluation."[97] What makes the Aristophanic appraisal of Socrates so valuable is its comic nature, for "just as every process usually ends with a parodying of itself...so the comic view is an element, in many ways a perpetually corrective element, in making a personality or an enterprise completely intelligible."[98] This association with a "perpetually corrective" comic perspective helps justify Kierkegaard's anachronistic approach to the play. As he later acknowledges, he has classified these three interpretations of Socrates "more according to their relation to the idea (the purely historical [i.e., Xenophon]—the ideal [i.e., Plato]—the comic [i.e., Aristophanes]) than according to time," although he does not desire "to deprive the Aristophanic view of the weight it does have because it is closest to Socrates in time."[99]

---

93 Friedrich Schleiermacher, "Ueber den Werth des Sokrates als Philosophen," in *Abhandlungen der philosophischen Klasse der königlich-preussischen Akademie der Wissenschaften aus den Jahren 1814–1815*, Berlin: Realschulbuchhandlung 1818 (the lecture was delivered in 1815), p. 59: "What *can* Socrates have been, in addition to what Xenophon reports of him, without however contradicting the distinguishing features and principles of life which Xenophon assuredly puts forward as Socratic; and what *must* he have been to have given Plato motive and justification to present him as he does in his dialogues?" For discussion see Burnet, "Socrates," p. 672; V. de Magalhâes-Vilhena, *Le Problème de Socrate: le Socrate historique et le Socrate Platon*, Paris: Presses Universitaires de France 1952, p. 131; Jaspers, *Great Philosophers*, vol. 1, p. 29.

94 *Georg Wilh. Friedr. Hegel's Vorlesungen über die Geschichte der Philosophie*, ed. by G.J.P.J. Bolland, Leiden: A.H. Adriani 1908, p. 312 (*Lectures on the History of Philosophy*, vol. 1, p. 414): "in regard to the personality and method, the externals of his teaching, we may certainly receive from Plato a satisfactory, and perhaps a more complete representation of what Socrates was. But in regard to the content of [Socrates'] teaching and the point reached by him in the development of thought, we have in the main to look to Xenophon." This passage does not occur in the first edition of the *Vorlesungen über die Geschichte der Philosophie* (in *Hegel's Werke. Vollständige Ausgabe*, ed. by Philipp Marheineke et al.). It was among the additional materials from notes and transcripts of Hegel's lectures that were incorporated by Carl Ludwig Michelet into the second revised edition, Berlin: Duncker und Humblot 1840.

95 *SKS* 1, 265, / *CI*, 221.

96 *SKS* 1, 178 / *CI*, 127.

97 *SKS* 1, 179 / *CI*, 128.

98 *SKS* 1, 179–80 / *CI*, 128. Cf. *Pap.* I A 285 / *JP* 4, 4066. *SKS* 18, 77, FF:15 / *KJN* 2, 71. *SKS* 17, 269, DD:168 / *KJN* 1, 260.

99 *SKS* 1, 204, note 1 / *CI*, 154, note.

That Kierkegaard will continue to ignore the question of the bearing of the *Clouds* upon Socrates' trial is ensured by an interpretive maneuver he now makes, which resembles Hegel's resolution "not to consider the real nature of the comedy of Aristophanes, nor the wanton way in which he was said to have treated Socrates."[100] Having viewed Socrates near the close of Plato's *Symposium* as "a sculptural image of the abstract unity of the comic and the tragic,"[101] and having also taken into account Socrates' sense of a unity of pleasure and pain in Plato's *Phaedo*,[102] Kierkegaard nonetheless sets in opposition the "tragic ideality" of the Platonic depiction of Socrates and the "comic [ideality]" of the Aristophanic.[103] As for the question of what may have motivated Aristophanes to see Socrates this way, he dismisses it as "totally irrelevant."[104]

In choosing, unlike Hegel, to focus upon the accusation against Socrates as "a historical document," Kierkegaard will bracket the question of whether the Athenians were right to execute him.[105] Yet he does not confine his focus to the *Clouds* in arguing that Aristophanes' depiction of Socrates approaches "the truth." For support, he adapts an anecdote from another classical source. Submitting that it would have been both beneath Aristophanes' dignity to portray Socrates empirically "as he walked and stood in life," and outside the interest of Greek comedy "to idealize him on a scale whereby he became completely unrecognizable," Kierkegaard finds the latter point "attested by antiquity, which recounts that the performance of the *Clouds* was honored in this respect by the presence of its severest critic, Socrates himself, who to the public's delight stood up during the performance so that theater crowd could see for themselves the fitting likeness."[106] Citing no source, Kierkegaard is unaware that this anecdote comes from Aelian,[107] according to whom Socrates rose from his seat on that occasion not to demonstrate the verisimilitude of Aristophanes' portrayal, as Kierkegaard infers, but, oppositely, to show his contempt for comedy and the Athenians.[108]

This anecdote is cited out of context by the German Hegelian philosopher and aesthetician Heinrich Theodor Rötscher (1803–71) in his "philological-philosophical" study *Aristophanes und sein Zeitalter* (1827), which is presumably where Kierkegaard

100 *Hegel's Vorlesungen über die Geschichte der Philosophie*, vol. 2, p. 85. (*Lectures on the History of Philosophy*, vol. 1, p. 427.)

101 *SKS* 1, 113 / *CI*, 52. See Plato, *Symposium*, 223d.

102 Plato, *Phaedo*, 60b–c. See *SKS* 1, 127, note / *CI*, 67, note. *SKS* 1, 139 / *CI*, 81.

103 *SKS* 1, 180 / *CI*, 128.

104 *SKS* 1, 180 / *CI*, 128–9.

105 See *SKS* 1, 215.26–216.12 / *CI*, 167–8 (quotation at *SKS* 1, 216.13 / *CI*, 168).

106 *SKS* 1, 180 / *CI*, 129.

107 Aelian, *Variae historiae*, vol. 2, p. 13. Kierkegaard did not learn until after he wrote his dissertation that Aelian was the source of this anecdote (*SKS* 24, 298–9, NB23:197 / *JP* 4, 4251), nor had he even read Aelian prior to writing the dissertation (*SKS* 24, 483, NB25:66 / *JP* 4, 4289).

108 During a performance of a Euripidean drama, Socrates is likewise said to have got up and left the theater in protest against what he considered an absurdity in the script. See Diogenes Laertius, *Socrates*, 33.

encountered it.[109] In his next breath, "agree[ing] with the perspicacious Rötscher,"[110] Kierkegaard avers that the Greek audience would not have accepted a portrayal of Socrates discrepant with the actual Socrates' character. This is but the first of numerous appeals Kierkegaard makes to Rötscher, whose monograph, although its publication preceded that of Hegel's *Lectures on the History of Philosophy*, is deemed "the most comprehensive expression of Hegelian understanding of Aristophanes' place in history."[111] Of the several other Germans to whom Kierkegaard refers in discussing the *Clouds*, namely, Hegel, the aesthetic philosopher Johann Georg Sulzer (1720–79), and the classical philologists Johann Wilhelm Süvern (1775–1829) and Karl C. Reisig (1792–1829), he cites Sulzer and Süvern as supporting the idea of the accuracy of Aristophanes' depiction of Socrates.[112] Yet Rötscher is the scholar whom Kierkegaard favors the most, and with whom, excepting Hegel, he most deeply and fruitfully engages.[113] While summarizing the play's titular symbol, its plot, its comic and ironic elements, and its portrayal of Socrates' personality, teaching, and existential "position,"[114] he approves of Rötscher's interpretation on the following points: the notion that Socrates became comic for Aristophanes only inasmuch as Aristophanes saw him as "the representative of a new principle";[115] the perceived unity of the Aristophanic Socrates and "the actual Socrates";[116] and the representation of the play's chorus as clouds,[117] the very image that conveys "Socrates' thoughts objectively envisioned."[118] (By this latter point we may be

109 H. Theodor Rötscher, *Aristophanes und sein Zeitalter. Eine philologische-philosophische Abhandlung zur Alterthumsforschung*, Berlin: Voss 1827, p. 18. Cf. *Pap.* III B 30 / *JP* 4, 4246, where Kierkegaard reproduces other information on Socrates from Rötscher's book.

110 *SKS* 1, 180 / *CI*, 129.

111 Jensen, "Aristophanes," p. 19. Cf. von Kloeden, "Sokrates," p. 125.

112 See *SKS* 1, 181, note 1 / *CI*, 129, note and *SKS* 183 / *CI*, 130–1, citing *Charaktere der vornehmsten Dichter aller Nationen; nebst kritischen und historischen Abhandlungen über Gegenstände der schönen Künste und Wissenschaften, von einer Gesellschaft von Gelehrten* [Nachträge zu Johann Georg Sulzer, *Allgemeine Theorie der schönen Künste: in einzeln, nach alphabetischer Ordnung der Kunstwörter auf einander folgenden, Artikeln abgehandelt*, vols. 1–2, Leipzig: Weidmann & Reich 1771–74], vols. 1–8, ed. by Johann Gottfried Dyck and Georg Schatz, Leipzig: im Verlage der Dykischen Buchhandlung 1792–1808, vol. 7, p. 162 (*ASKB* 1370–1377) and Johann Wilhelm Süvern, *Ueber Aristophanes Wolken*, Berlin: Königlich Akademie der Wissenschaften 1826, pp. 3ff. The name Schaz, alternatively spelled as Schatz, is cited at *CI*, Notes, p. 511, note 309 as Schütz. Kierkegaard mentions Reisig once in passing (*SKS* 1, 193, note 1 / *CI*, 143, note).

113 Cf. Thulstrup, *Kierkegaard's Relation to Hegel*, p. 233, note 12. *SKS* 1, 182 / *CI*, 130: "I cannot help ranging myself behind the deservedly exultant Rötscher, who so triumphantly leads the idea through and out of its battle with the misunderstandings of earlier views."

114 *SKS* 1, 183–203 / *CI*, 132–53.

115 *SKS* 1, 182 / *CI*, 130. Cf. Rötscher, *Aristophanes und sein Zeitalter*, pp. 319–30.

116 *SKS* 1, 183 / *CI*, 131–2. Cf. Rötscher, *Aristophanes und sein Zeitalter*, pp. 276–88; pp. 312–19.

117 *SKS* 1, 183 / *CI*, 132. *SKS* 1, 187 / *CI*, 136. Cf. Rötscher, *Aristophanes und sein Zeitalter*, pp. 50–9; p. 325.

118 *SKS* 1, 188 / *CI*, 137.

reminded that it was to Aristophanes' play that Hegel himself is putatively alluding when, in his discussion of Greek Comedy in his *Phenomenology of Spirit* (1807), he asserts that rational thinking rendered divine beings into "clouds, an evanescent mist, like those imaginative representations."[119]) Kierkegaard bases his analysis of the *Clouds* so extensively upon Rötscher's that in one instance he reproduces Rötscher's language without acknowledgment.[120]

Aside from his quibbling elsewhere over Rötscher's interpretation of a specific passage in the *Clouds*,[121] Kierkegaard only questions "whether the earnestness [Rötscher] so definitely claims for this play does not make him somewhat at odds with the irony he otherwise attributes to Aristophanes."[122] This reservation introduces an element of confusion in Kierkegaard's discussion of the *Clouds*. If an overriding assumption in the dissertation is that "irony was constitutive in Socrates' life,"[123] Kierkegaard now also speaks of "Aristophanic irony" and "irony worthy of an Aristophanes."[124] Because he never differentiates between Aristophanic irony and Socratic irony, his conceptions of them seem indistinguishable.

Exerting an even greater influence upon Kierkegaard is Rötscher's allusion to Aristophanes' "total earnestness of attitude" in the *Clouds*.[125] Accordant as it is with Hegel's perception of "deep political earnestness"[126] underlying Aristophanes' merriment over the Athenian democracy, this characterization furnishes Kierkegaard with a foil against which to defend the play's comic dimension, and later to counter the charge that Aristophanes slandered Socrates. If Socrates' life consisted of irony,

> this affords a much more comic side than would be the case if the principle of subjectivity, the principle of inwardness, along with the whole train of ensuing ideas, were taken to be the Socratic principle, and if the authorization of Aristophanes were to be sought in the earnestness with which he as an advocate of early Greek culture had to try to destroy this modern monstrosity. This earnestness bears down too heavily, just as it restricts the comic infinity, which as such recognizes no limits. Irony, on the other hand, is simultaneously a new position and as such is absolutely polemical toward early Greek culture.[127]

---

119 *Georg Wilhelm Friedrich Hegel's Phänomenologie des Geistes*, ed. by Johann Schulze, Berlin: Duncker und Humblot 1832 (vol. 2 in *Georg Wilhelm Friedrich Hegel's Werke. Vollständige Ausgabe*), p. 560 (*ASKB* 550). (English translation: *Phenomenology of Spirit*, trans. by A.V. Miller, Oxford: Oxford University Press 1979, pp. 451–2.)

120 As Rötscher can conjecture about the Aristophanic Socrates that "*unter seiner Maske die Sophisten gemeint wären*" (*Aristophanes und sein Zeitalter*, p. 288), so Kierkegaard asks "whether Aristophanes, behind the mask of Socrates, wanted to mock the Sophists" (*SKS* 1, 189 / *CI*, 138).

121 See *SKS* 1, 194, note / *CI*, 144, note.

122 *SKS* 1, 182 / *CI*, 130. See Rötscher, *Aristophanes und sein Zeitalter*, p. 325.

123 *SKS* 1, 182 / *CI*, 131. See also *SKS* 1, 65 / *CI*, 6. *SKS* 1, 74 / *CI*, 12. *SKS* 1, 99 / *CI*, 37.

124 *SKS* 1, 185 / *CI*, 135. *SKS* 1, 189 / *CI*, 139.

125 See Rötscher, *Aristophanes und sein Zeitalter*, pp. 319–30; see p. 319.

126 *Hegel's Vorlesungen über die Geschichte der Philosophie*, vol. 2, p. 86. (*Lectures on the History of Philosophy*, vol. 1, p. 428.)

127 *SKS* 1, 182 / *CI*, 131.

Confusingly, again, the mention of irony here could refer to either Socratic irony or Aristophanic irony, because Kierkegaard wants "irony" substituted for "earnestness" as the designation of Aristophanes' attitude toward Socrates. This confusion is exacerbated by Kierkegaard's assurance that irony is "something that at rock bottom is comic."[128] Is irony "comic" in the sense that Kierkegaard has designated Socrates as comic,[129] or in the sense that he will later designate Aristophanes as such?[130] Kierkegaard offers no clarification, nor seems to suspect, as Burnet will, that Socrates' irony "comes entirely from Plato."[131] Kierkegaard is familiar with Hegel's perception of the Platonic Socrates' irony as "a controlled element, a way of associating with people."[132] Further in the dissertation, he adopts Hegel's notion of irony as "infinite absolute negativity,"[133] which Gregory Vlastos views as a "dazzling mystification" by which Kierkegaard's treatment of Socratic irony "is hopelessly perplexed."[134] Nonetheless, just as his presentation of Socrates as totally negative represents a break from Hegel, who, in keeping with his own comprehensive perspective, "necessarily had to find a positive element in Socrates, as he had to find it in every philosopher,"[135] so Kierkegaard's ascription of irony to the Aristophanic Socrates is entirely original.[136]

Later, regarding the delineation of the Socratic dialectic in the *Clouds*, Kierkegaard comments again upon Rötscher's ascription of earnestness to the poet, and alludes for the first and only time to the play's bearing upon Socrates' condemnation. The Socratic dialectic can be discussed only as a purely intellectual construct, "whereas we have nothing at all to do with the altogether immoral conduct in which such a dialectic can become an active collaborator in the service of a corrupted will."[137] An example is when the dim-witted farmer Strepsiades hoodwinks his creditors, and his own prodigal son then beats him, as a consequence of their both having been corrupted by their witnessing a dialogue between Better Argument and Worse Argument in Socrates' *phrontistērion*: "Aristophanes himself must have been aware of this; if not, I really do not see how Aristophanes can be saved from the old accusation of having slandered Socrates."[138]

---

128 Ibid.

129 *SKS* 1, 181 / *CI*, 129. See also *SKS* 1, 195 / *CI*, 145. *SKS* 1, 202 / *CI*, 152.

130 *SKS* 1, 202, note 1, 204 note 1 / *CI*, 153–4, including footnotes.

131 Burnet, *Greek Philosophy*, p. 127, note 2. Cf. Taylor, *Socrates*, pp. 21–2. The development of the meaning of the word εἰρωνεία is traced by Gregory Vlastos, *Socrates, Ironist, and Moral Philosopher*, Ithaca, New York: Cornell University Press 1991, pp. 23–4. See also Newell, "Aristophanes on Socrates," p. 112.

132 *SKS* 1, 278 / *CI*, 237.

133 *SKS* 1, 292 / *CI*, 254. *SKS* 1, 297 / *CI*, 259. *SKS* 1, 299 / *CI*, 261. Cf. *Hegel's Vorlesungen über die Aesthetik*, vol. 1, pp. 89–90; p. 205. (*Aesthetics*, vol. 1, pp. 68–9; p. 160.)

134 Vlastos, *Socrates, Ironist*, p. 43, note 81.

135 Thulstrup, *Kierkegaard's Relation to Hegel*, p. 232.

136 *Pace* Vlastos, *Socrates, Ironist*, p. 29: "The anti-hero of the *Clouds* is many things to many men, but an ironist to none."

137 *SKS* 1, 199 / *CI*, 149.

138 Ibid.

Bringing to a head his converging views of the two figures, Kierkegaard immediately proceeds to defend *both* Aristophanes against the charge of slander *and* the Aristophanic Socrates against the charges of corrupting morals. This convergence, being dependent upon the conviction that Aristophanes' portrayal was justified, presupposes Hegel's stimulus. It is in part from Hegel that Kierkegaard derived this justification of Aristophanes, together with the recognition of Socrates' dialectic as negative, a recognition Hegel credited Aristophanes with having been the first to reach.[139] Likewise it was in apparent emulation of Hegel that Kierkegaard above dismissed "the bombast about [Socrates'] virtue," and that he will later ridicule "the scholarly professional mourners and the crowd of shallow but lachrymose humanitarians whose blubbering and sighing" over Socrates' death "still echo through the centuries."[140] Only when he invokes Rötscher once again as a foil, this time to his own defense of Aristophanes, does he implicitly make Hegel a foil as well: "Let Rötscher inflate as much as he wishes the earnestness with which Aristophanes laid hold of his task in the *Clouds*—Aristophanes is not exonerated thereby."[141]

Just as he will later recall Hegel's analysis of Socrates' irony,[142] so must Kierkegaard now recall Hegel's perception of a deep "earnestness" in Aristophanes. Given Kierkegaard's acceptance of "the qualification of irony, which Hegel so frequently stresses, that for irony nothing is a matter of earnestness,"[143] it seems consistent with his own ascription of irony to Aristophanes that Kierkegaard now wants to dismiss Rötscher's Hegelian "inflation" of a perceived anti-ironic earnestness in Aristophanes. This dismissal helps prepare for Kierkegaard's summary point on Thesis VII. There, he will again invoke "Rötscher's designation of Socrates' position as that of subjectivity,"[144] a designation that accords with Hegel's construal of Socrates.[145] Beforehand, however, recalling the Aristophanic image of Socrates suspended from the ceiling in a basket, Kierkegaard betrays the prominent contrast between his own understanding of Socratic subjectivity and both Hegel's and Rötscher's.[146] He suggests that if the latter understanding were correct,

---

139 See *SKS* 1, 202, note 1 / *CI*, 152, note and *SKS* 1, 269–70 / *CI*, 226–7, citing *Hegel's Vorlesungen über die Geschichte der Philosophie*, vol. 2, p. 85; p. 89. (*Lectures on the History of Philosophy*, vol. 1, p. 426; p. 430.) See also Kierkegaard's Thesis IV in *SKS* 1, 65 / *CI*, 6; expounded in *SKS* 1, 96–9 / *CI*, 34–7.

140 *SKS* 1, 216 / *CI*, 167–8.

141 *SKS* 1, 199 / *CI*, 149.

142 *SKS* 1, 278 / *CI*, 237.

143 *SKS* 1, 276 / *CI*, 235.

144 *SKS* 1, 202 / *CI*, 152. See Rötscher, *Aristophanes und sein Zeitalter*, pp. 247–58. Thulstrup considers this point "Rötscher's main theme" (*Kierkegaard's Relation to Hegel*, p. 233, note 12).

145 See *Hegel's Vorlesungen über die Geschichte der Philosophie*, vol. 2, pp. 71–9. (*Lectures on the History of Philosophy*, vol. 1, pp. 407–4.)

146 This contrast is well emphasized by Glen A. Cosby, who relates this contrast to the equally marked contrast between Kierkegaard's later association of subjectivity "with the intensive inwardness of religious passion,....that most private of all human relations: the relation between the individual and God," and "the progressively public unfolding of 'cosmic

"in terms of the comic it would have been more appropriate to present Socrates as infinitely vanishing and to have accentuated the comic in Strepsiades' inability to catch a glimpse of him rather than to present him suspended in a basket."[147] Radically qualifying, yet not fully disagreeing with Rötscher's equation of Socrates with subjectivity,[148] Kierkegaard finds Aristophanes' view of him "to be more true in terms of the comic and consequently more just" (here he cites Hegel's claim that "it is Aristophanes who has understood Socrates' philosophy merely from its negative side"), "and likewise one will also see a way to remove some of the difficulties that otherwise would remain in this Aristophanic play if one defines this position more specifically as an ironic position—that is, allows the subjectivity to pour out in its profusion, but prior to this lets it egotistically terminate in irony."[149]

Here, by associating the Aristophanic Socrates with both subjectivity and irony, Kierkegaard confirms his own movement beyond Hegel and Rötscher, and thus fulfills his own earlier insight that "irony is beyond subjective thinking."[150] Rounding off his exposition of Thesis VII, he concludes that Aristophanes contains elements of both Xenophon's and Plato's views. For if "Plato tried to fill up the cryptic nothing that actually constitutes the point in Socrates' life by giving him the idea," and if "Xenophon tried to do it with the prolixities of the useful,"[151] then "with respect to Plato Aristophanes has subtracted, and with respect to Xenophon has added."[152]

For Kierkegaard, the Aristophanic Socrates thus represents the mean between the Platonic Socrates and the Xenophontic Socrates, and thus approximates closely "the truth." In arguing this thesis, as we have seen, Kierkegaard himself did some "subtracting" and "adding." From Aristophanes he subtracted the earnestness ascribed by Hegel and Rötscher, and to the Aristophanic Socrates he added the irony he himself perceives in him. As a result, the images of Aristophanes and Socrates, the poet and the philosopher, the satirist and the satirized, converge in the categories of irony and the comic. What is the legacy of Thesis VII in Kierkegaard's writings after *The Concept of Irony*? Rötscher's view of Socrates' position as subjectivity, a view Kierkegaard adopted in expounding Thesis VII, proves pertinent to the conception of subjectivity that runs through the pseudonymous *corpus*.[153] But how do Aristophanes and his representation of Socrates bear upon Kierkegaard's thinking and writing beyond the dissertation?

---

subjectivity' found in Hegel's system" (*The Living Word: Kierkegaard, Nietzsche, and Their Relation to Socrates*, Ph.D. Thesis, Emory University, Atlanta, Georgia 1998, p. 87).

147 *SKS* 1, 202 / *CI*, 152.

148 *Pace* Jensen, "Aristophanes," p. 20. Aside from the passage cited below, see *SKS* 1, 212 / *CI*, 163. *SKS* 1, 214 / *CI*, 165. *SKS* 1, 243 / *CI*, 197. *SKS* 1, 243 / *CI*, 197. *SKS* 1, 255 / *CI*, 211. *SKS* 1, 260 / *CI*, 215. *SKS* 1, 268 / *CI*, 224. *SKS* 1, 307–8 / *CI*, 271. Kierkegaard's Thesis VIII, that "Irony...is the lightest and weakest indication of subjectivity" (*SKS* 1, 65 / *CI*, 6), notably refrains from totally negating the relation of irony to subjectivity.

149 *SKS* 1, 202–3 / *CI*, 152–3.

150 *SKS* 1, 176 / *CI*, 124.

151 *SKS* 1, 203 / *CI*, 153.

152 *SKS* 1, 204 / *CI*, 154.

153 As noted by the Hongs, *CI*, Notes, p. 515, note 348.

Kierkegaard and his pseudonyms make relatively few allusions to the *Clouds* during the first five years after the dissertation. In 1842 or 1843, inside the cover of a copy of his dissertation, he belatedly notes that it was Aelian who purported that the historical Socrates was present at the play's performance.[154] In addition, the religious thinker Frater Taciturnus in *Stages on Life's Way* (1845) has Quidam refer without acknowledgment to the pre-Socratic principle of existence ascribed to Socrates in the *Clouds*,[155] and, from the draft and the final copy of the *Concluding Unscientific Postscript* (1846), Kierkegaard deletes two iterations of a jocular reference by Climacus to Strepsiades' notion of rain as Zeus urinating through a sieve.[156] That is all, although, as Jacob Howland notes, Climacus' representation of Socratic philosophizing in *Philosophical Fragments* (1844) bears a suggestive resemblance to two passages in Plato that "present the philosopher as a human being who aspires to be a god," and that thus, echoing the Aristophanic image of Socrates looking down upon gods as well as humans from his basket, "are clearly intended as caricatures, insofar as neither one acknowledges, or can account for, Socrates' own comprehensive engagement with the affairs of his friends and fellow citizens."[157]

Nonetheless, jottings from 1842–43 on the back end-sheet of a copy of *The Concept of Irony* reveal Kierkegaard, in those first two years after the dissertation, to be filling in gaps in his knowledge about the relationship of the *Clouds* to Socrates, and reading (or rereading) other plays by Aristophanes as well.[158] He notes that Socrates was depicted by comic poets other than Aristophanes;[159] that Aristophanes' *Frogs* ends by branding Socrates a gossip and a denigrator of the art of poetry;[160] and that Aristophanes, through the chorus leader of the *Wasps*,[161] "names the evil of which [Aristophanes] wanted to cleanse the state with the *Clouds*: idleness and legal trickery."[162] Kierkegaard surely recognizes the reference in the *Frogs* as an insult to Socrates. Yet, true to his earlier refusal to see the *Clouds* as slandering Socrates, and consistent with the fact that the *Wasps* nowhere mentions Socrates by name, he may not assume, as scholars typically do,[163] that the allusion to the *Clouds* in *Wasps* implicitly associates Socrates with the "evil" that Aristophanes "wanted" to purge. Like Hegel and Rötscher, Kierkegaard evidently still regards Aristophanes as

154 *SKS* 24, 298–9, NB23:197 / *JP* 4, 4251.

155 See *SKS* 6, 209 / *SLW*, 224.

156 *Pap*. VI B 35:34 / *CUP2*, Supplement, p. 37. See Aristophanes, the *Clouds*, line 375.

157 Jacob Howland, *Kierkegaard and Socrates: A Study in Philosophy and Faith*, Cambridge: Cambridge University Press 2006, p. 192; comparing Plato, *Theaetetus*, 173d-e and 500b-c to Aristophanes, the *Clouds*, lines 223–7 and lines 247–8.

158 See, for example, *SKS* 2, 45–6 / *EO1*, 36–7, which quotes Aristophanes, *Knights*, lines 32–5 in the Greek (see *Pap*. III B 179, p. 57 for J.G. Droysen's German rendering of the same passage); and *SKS* 2, 272–3 / *EO1*, 282–3, which quotes *Plutos*, lines 189ff. in the Greek.

159 *Pap*. IV A 211 / *JP* 4, 4258.

160 *Pap*. IV A 209 / *JP* 4, 4256.

161 See line 1036 of the Loeb edition. As the Hongs' note, the line numbers there differ from those cited by Kierkegaard from Johan Krag's Danish translation, *Aristophanes's Komedier*, trans. by J. Krag, vol. 1, Odense: S. Hempel 1825, p. 271 (*ASKB* 1055).

162 *Pap*. IV A 210 / *JP* 4, 4257.

163 For example, Ferguson, *Socrates: A Source Book*, p. 172.

a conservative reformer or "cleanser" of the state. Yet, unlike them, he still refrains from associating Socrates with what he thinks Aristophanes meant to attack.

Kierkegaard thus protects his own esteem for Aristophanes as reformer from conflicting with his ever-growing reverence for Socrates as ironist. Mirroring the convergence already observed in his association of the two men with irony and the comic, Kierkegaard's view of Aristophanes as having wanted "to cleanse the state" of "idleness and legal trickery" (for example, Sophistry) matches his view of Socrates as someone out "to destroy [the Sophists] so radically."[164] Together with these converging images of Socrates and Aristophanes, Kierkegaard's writings convey a pessimistic perception of a similarity between the ancient era of those two men and Kierkegaard's own modern era. The dissertation, in reference to Hegel and Rötscher, spoke of "the decline of the Athenian state" brought about by "the principle of decay,"[165] which boded that "the hour of disintegration was at hand."[166] Accordingly, referring to Greece "at the time when the state was in the process of disintegration," the aesthete "A" of *Either/Or* (1843) asks: "And does not our age have a striking likeness to that age, which not even Aristophanes could make more ludicrous than it actually was?"[167] Sensing that his own age is one of political and religious dissolution, one "more depressed and therefore deeper in despair" than Aristophanes' age, and one that "excels" that age in the unwillingness of anyone "to have responsibility," "A" exclaims: "Would not this inverted story of responsibility be an appropriate subject for Aristophanes!"[168]

That Aristophanes had become for Kierkegaard the prototypical satirist and comic poet, as well as a classic ironist, is further attested in *Fear and Trembling* (1843), whose pseudonym Johannes de silentio speaks of Aristophanes as an ironist who "knows that he has the power of laughter," and that only "one solitary voice will speak up to restrain him."[169] If this "solitary voice" is, as it would seem, a synechdochic allusion to the Socrates of Plato's *Symposium*, it represents a significant acknowledgment of the tension between Socrates and Aristophanes. Johannes de silentio proceeds to elaborate upon the particular use that this Aristophanic ironist makes of laughter:

> He has infallible information about the way laughter sneaks in and lives secretly in a person, and once it has taken up residence, it watches and waits. Let us imagine such an Aristophanes, such a slightly altered Voltaire, for he is also sympathetic: he loves existence, he loves men, and he knows that even if denunciation by laughter may rear up a new, redeemed generation, at the same time a great number of his contemporaries will be destroyed. So he remains silent and as far as possible forgets himself how to laugh. But dare he remain silent?...Ethics is a dangerous branch of knowledge, and it

164 *SKS* 1, 247 / *CI*, 201.

165 *SKS* 1, 245–6 / *CI*, 200.

166 *SKS* 1, 246 / *CI*, 201.

167 *SKS* 2, 141 / *EO1*, 141.

168 *SKS* 2, 142 / *EO1*, 142.

169 *SKS* 4, 196, note 1 / *FT*, 107, note.

> was surely possible that Aristophanes for purely ethical reasons decided to let laughter pass judgment on the perverse age.[170]

By the time Kierkegaard pursues his self-appointed role as a Christianized Socratic "gadfly" against the established Danish church, in the years 1854–55,[171] he will perceive Socrates as his sole "analogy" and pronounce his own "task" to be "a Socratic task, to audit the definition of what it is to be a Christian."[172] However, even while identifying with the wish of *Either/Or*'s aesthete to have the laughter always on his side, Kierkegaard will qualify that the kind of laughter that he himself wants to use—Socrates' laughter—"must first of all be divinely consecrated and devoutly dedicated."[173] In contrast, the quotation above seems almost to strain to avoid acknowledging the harm Aristophanes' employment of a different sort of laughter did to Socrates' reputation. There is no evidence that Kierkegaard read Voltaire; yet in view of Voltaire's notoriety as a mocker, the characterization of Aristophanes as "a slightly altered Voltaire" seems almost to cast Aristophanes as a mocker.

Still it would be hard to overlook here the implicit acknowledgment of the damage Aristophanes did to Socrates. If what makes Aristophanes a modified Voltaire is that he is "sympathetic" (*unlike* Voltaire), we must remember that Socrates would head the list of that "great number of [Aristophanes'] contemporaries" who were "destroyed" by Aristophanic satire. That Johannes de silentio, like Kierkegaard, views Aristophanes ambivalently is further suggested by the Catch-22-like "paradox" he proceeds to introduce: if Aristophanes "remains silent" and "forgets himself how to laugh," it is because he is magnanimous; but anyone so magnanimous will not dare remain silent, because a sense of ethics will lead such a person to employ laughter to "pass judgment on the perverse age."

Despite Johannes de silentio's denial that "aesthetic nobility" might help in catalyzing the use of Aristophanic laughter to judge a corrupt age, Aristophanes' pertinence to the aesthetic stage seems punctuated by a declaration made in "Literary Quicksilver, or a Venture in the Higher Lunacy with *Lucida Intervalla*," an unsigned satirical article that appeared in *Ny Portefeuille* two weeks before *Either/Or*'s publication, and was later ascribed, albeit disputably, to Kierkegaard: "Life parodies itself and does it with an esthetic thoroughness that puts every Aristophanes to shame."[174] Regardless of whether Kierkegaard wrote that article, or whether he seemingly suspected his secretary Peter Vilhelm Christensen had composed it from ideas stolen from him through their private conversations,[175] a similar allusion to Aristophanes as a comic touchstone occurs some years later in Kierkegaard's journal.[176] Accordingly, two different speakers at the aesthetic banquet of Kierkegaard's *Stages on Life's Way* (1845) appeal to Aristophanes

170 *SKS* 4, 196, note 1, 197 / *FT*, 108, note.

171 *Pap.* XI–3 B 53, p. 102 / *JP* 6, 6943, p. 555. Cf. *SKS* 13, 149 / *M*, 107.

172 "My Task" (draft), September 1, 1855, *SKS* 13, 405 / *M*, 341.

173 *Pap.* XI–3 B 55 / *JP* 6, 6945. See also *SKS* 2, 52 / *EO1*, 43.

174 "Litterært Qvægsølver eller Forsøg i det høiere Vanvid samt *Lucida Intervalla*," *Ny Portefeuille*, vol. 1, no. 7 (February 12, 1843) columns 198–216 (included in *SV1* XIII, 471–85 / *COR*, 73–86; quotation in *SV1* XIII, 479 / *COR*, 80).

175 See *SKS* 18, 186–7, JJ:144 / *KJN* 2, 173. See also *KJN 2*, Notes, p. 501.

176 *SKS* 21, 370–1, NB10:208 / *JP* 6, 6392.

as a similar touchstone on the subject of love. Having summarized the theory of erotic attraction ascribed to Aristophanes in Plato's *Symposium*, according to which the gods divided the primeval human being into two parts, which now seek each other,[177] the anonymous Young Man takes up this thought again. Noting that whenever two persons "in union and in love form one self," they end up subordinated to serving the species, the Young Man "find[s] this more ludicrous than what Aristophanes found so ludicrous. For the ludicrousness in that bisection lies in the contradiction, which Aristophanes did not adequately emphasize": the contradiction of a "complete" human individual betraying himself to be "only a half running around after his other half."[178]

Perhaps inspired by the Young Man, Constantin Constantius too appeals to Aristophanes, specifically as a portrayer of Socrates, but he does so for a different reason: to make the following point about the incompatibility of jealousy with intellect. In contrast to Shakespeare's Othello, who, in Constantin's racist view, as a colored man "cannot be assumed to represent intellect," a person of intellect "either does not become jealous or in becoming that becomes comic, and most of all if he comes running with a dagger."[179] One can hardly imagine Socrates surprising Xanthippe *in flagranti*, since "it would already be un-Socratic to imagine Socrates essentially concerned about or even spying on Xanthippe's faithfulness."[180] On the other hand,

> since Aristophanes at times wanted to portray Socrates as ludicrous, it is inconceivable that it never occurred to him to have Socrates come running on stage shouting: Where is she, where is she, so that I can murder her, that is, the unfaithful Xanthippe. Whether Socrates was made a cuckold or not really makes no difference....Socrates, even with horns on his forehead, remains the same intellectual hero; but that he could become jealous, that he could want to murder Xanthippe—ah, then Xanthippe would have had a power over him that the whole Greek state and the death penalty did not have: to make him ridiculous.[181]

This passage is significant for two reasons. First, reflecting the cynicism of Constantin's aesthetic disposition, it breaks from Kierkegaard's own general refusal to acknowledge Aristophanes' desire "to portray Socrates as ludicrous." Secondly, through its drawing that desire of Aristophanes vis-à-vis Socrates into a more-than-subliminal association with the failure of the state "to make him ridiculous," the passage associates the *Clouds* with Socrates' trial. This is not the last time Kierkegaard will hint at that association, but it is perhaps the closest he comes to making it explicit.

Aside from the depiction of Socrates, the one Aristophanic theme by which Kierkegaard proves most deeply captivated is that of the Athenian sausage peddlar who, as a series of oracles predicted, becomes the deliverer and reformer of the state. For Taciturnus, as for Kierkegaard, this theme in *Knights* epitomizes the principle of

---

177 *SKS* 6, 39 / *SLW*, 35. See Plato, *Symposium*, 189d–193b.

178 *SKS* 6, 44 / *SLW*, 43.

179 *SKS* 6, 52 / *SLW*, 50.

180 Ibid.

181 *SKS* 6, 53 / *SLW*, 50.

contradiction that underlies anything "comic in the Aristophanic sense."[182] In several other instances between 1845 and 1849 Kierkegaard appeals to the sausage-peddlar theme in order to parallel his contemporary age with that of Aristophanes',[183] and he speaks of the modern concern with the natural sciences, and of modern Christian scholarship, as furnishing motifs superbly suitable to an Aristophanic comedy—especially if the poet "has Socrates present and has him peer into a microscope."[184]

Given his own experience as the butt of public satire during the *Corsair* fiasco of 1846, it is not surprising that Kierkegaard should strive then to distinguish the mean, destructive, "improper" use made of satire and the comic by that Copenhagen tabloid, from the "proper," Aristophanic brand of comedy.[185] In contrast to the corrupt "present" form of satire that *The Corsair* employed against him, as he points out, the comedic attacker in antiquity had to appear personally in the square so that one got to see who it was; the attack was open, and when it was over, forgotten.[186] Moreover "the public," an abstraction created by the modern press, "simply could not have appeared in antiquity."[187] He concludes:

> The concept of *literary contemptibility* can be defined with the following predicates: it lacks the legitimacy of an idea; even if it has some talent; it is without a life-view, cowardly, slavish, impudent, covetous; and it is therefore essential to it to be anonymous. If, to see the difference, one thinks by way of comparison of the dissolution of Greece and Aristophanes' comedy, then Aristophanes stands warranted with an idea, distinguished by genius, elevated through personal courage....But just as antiquity was altogether unable to attain the abstraction of modern dissolution, so it lacked, even in the period of depravity, any real analogy to the sort of abject paltriness that anonymity wants to encourage. It is true that Socrates says in the *Apology* that his real accusers, those who had already accused him for many years, were like shadows no one could grasp hold of, but even if town gossip and man-to-man talk are like shadows, in a way it is still made by real people, but through anonymity one single person can conjure forth a legion of shadows.[188]

Here Kierkegaard manages in one breath to distinguish Aristophanic comedy favorably from modern, anonymous "literary contemptibility," and to recall the allusion by Socrates to his accusers. Yet unlike Constantin, he again avoids acknowledging that Aristophanes satirized Socrates with the *Clouds*. Why? As

---

182 *SKS* 6, 379 / *SLW*, 409. An earlier draft of this passage is found in *Pap*. V B 150, 3, p. 254. Cf. *SKS* 8, 79 / *TA*, 82. See also *SKS* 6, 380 / *SLW*, 410; cf. *SKS* 6, 381 / *SLW*, 412.

183 See *Pap*. VII–1 B 116 / *TA*, Supplement, p. 133, which was crossed out in the final draft of the discussion of *Knights* in *SKS* 8, 79–80 / *TA*, 82–3. See also *Pap*. VII–1 B 55, p. 242 / *COR*, Supplement, p. 193; and *SKS* 21, 370–1, NB10:208 / *JP* 6, 6392.

184 *SKS*, 20, 70, NB:81 / *JP* 3, 2814. See also *Pap*. VII–2 B 235, p. 86 / *BA*, 45.

185 *SKS* 8, 71–2 / *TA*, 74. See also Andrew J. Burgess, "A Word-Experiment on the Category of the Comic," and Lee C. Barrett, "The Uses and Misuses of the Comic: Reflections on the *Corsair* Affair," both in *The Corsair Affair*, ed. by Robert L. Perkins, Macon, Georgia: Mercer University Press 1990 (*International Kierkegaard Commentary*, vol. 13), pp. 85–121, 123–39.

186 See *Pap*. VII 1 B 48 / *COR*, Supplement, pp. 177–8.

187 *SKS* 8, 87 / *TA*, 91.

188 *SKS* 18, 280–1, JJ:422 / *KJN* 2, 259.

augured by *The Corsair*'s derisive reference to Taciturnus as "Socrates' successor,"[189] Kierkegaard imagines that the destruction of his own personality by the Copenhagen press is now so comparable to Socrates' predicament amid the Athenians that "It would be most interesting to talk with Socrates about the matter."[190] A journal entry labeled "The Dialectic of Contemptibleness" brings to bear upon Kierkegaard's experience as an abused innocent, what Socrates reportedly said to Xanthippe when asked how a guiltless man could be sentenced to death: "Would you rather have me guilty?"[191] With his self-image as a Socratic dialectician augmented by a sense of kinship with Socrates as a slandered victim, Kierkegaard can emphasize Aristophanes' satire of Socrates without subverting his own sense of affinity with Aristophanes as an employer of the proper form of the comic.

The senses of affinity with both men coalesce most fully in Kierkegaard's unpublished essay of 1846, "A Personal Statement in Costume." Contemplating the comic as antithetical and antidotal to *The Corsair*, Kierkegaard here aims "to deal with the comic in fear and trembling, to maintain the conception of responsibility rooted in ethical and religious earnestness together with the delight of the jest."[192] Feeling "rather alone in my thinking and perhaps the only one who herewith renounces any reputation for having a sense of the comic," he is reminded of the question Socrates asked at the trial: does everybody except one know how to ride horses, or do only a few riding masters know this art, while others know nothing about it?[193] Claiming that "in a small country like Denmark a disproportionate and immoral phenomenon such as *The Corsair* does great harm and is of no benefit whatsoever...because it counterfeits and taints the comic and thereby silences the authentic comic," Kierkegaard knows that "the proof" of this claim "is valid only on the basis of my understanding of the comic and thus only for the individuals who Socratically [*socratisk*] assume that the comic is like riding, that only a few know how but the majority do not."[194]

Although Kierkegaard makes this assumption "Socratically," it is not to Socrates but to Aristophanes that he appeals at the essay's end. With regard to the derisive cartoons by Peter Klæstrup (1820–82) that *The Corsair* had published of him that accentuate his physical peculiarities,[195] he distinguishes Aristophanic comedy from *The Corsair*'s crude satire. The poet, he concedes, must exaggerate in order to draw

---

189 "Efterlysning," *Corsaren*, no. 277 (January 9), 1846, column 6 / *COR*, 117.

190 *SKS*, 20, 30, NB:20 / *JP* 5, 5899.

191 *Pap*. VII–1 B 9, p. 172 / *COR*, Supplement, p. 161. See Diogenes Laertius, *Socrates*, 35.

192 "En personlig Yttring i Costüme," *Pap*. VII–1 B 55, p. 226 / *COR*, Supplement, pp. 178–9.

193 *Pap*. VII–1 B 55, pp. 226–7 / *COR*, Supplement, p. 179. See Plato, *Apology*, 25a–b.

194 *Pap*. VII–1 B 55, p. 227, 22 / *COR*, Supplement, pp. 179–80.

195 See especially *Corsaren*, no. 277 (January 9), 1846, column 4 / *COR*, Supplement, p. 116. *Corsaren*, no. 278 (January 16), 1846, columns 4–5 / *COR*, Supplement, pp. 119–20. *Corsaren*, no. 279 (January 23), 1846, column 1 / *COR*, Supplement, p. 126. *Corsaren*, no. 280 (January 30), 1846, column 11 / *COR*, Supplement, p. 130. *Corsaren*, no. 285 (March 6, 1846, columns 9–10 / *COR*, Supplement, pp. 132–3. *Corsaren*, no. 381 (January 7), 1848, column 8 / *COR*, Supplement, p. 137. See also *COR*, pp. xxi–xxii.

out the pathos and the comic: "For example, to depict the topsy-turvy situation in Athens, Aristophanes had a sausage dealer become the supreme power in the country. So it was in the play; in actuality it was not quite that bad. But in Copenhagen a pair of trousers has actually attained the position of highest standing and importance. I wonder what Aristophanes would think of that?"[196]

Such wonderment about Aristophanes recalls Kierkegaard's earlier expressed desire to discuss with Socrates the destructive power of the modern press. One of *The Corsair*'s most infamous caricatures of Kierkegaard shows him standing on a cloud at the center of the universe.[197] We cannot know whether this reminded him of the titular image by which Aristophanes' play ridiculed Socrates. Yet, seeing his own physique derided in print must have bolstered Kierkegaard's feeling of affinity with Socrates, whose reputation as "the ugliest of men" he had discussed in the early 1840s in his journal and dissertation.[198]

Remarkably, the identification with the victimized Socrates never leads Kierkegaard to turn openly against Socrates' most famous derider. It was left to a contemporary sympathizer, unbeknownst to Kierkegaard, to associate with Aristophanes' satiric mode the brand of derision by which Kierkegaard himself was now parodied in the role of a theologian named "Søren Kirk" (later renamed "Søren Torp") in Jens Christian Hostrup's (1818–92) musical comedy, *The Neighbors Across the Way*.[199] After attending a performance of the play, the poet Bernhard Severin Ingemann (1789–1862) complained in a letter of December 14, 1847 to Hostrup: "The Aristophanean presentation of well-known personalities (namely Søren K.) conflicts with my principle of poetic freedom, and I believe that what you gain in immediate effect is offset by a loss in the higher artistic sphere."[200]

By 1848, far from condemning Aristophanes, Kierkegaard comes to identify with him as an exemplar of the "good" comic form. He is indignant at the thought of *The Corsair*'s "attempt at being a sort of moral enterprise in which ethical satire would be beneficial to the good (à la Aristophanes)."[201] Two years later he lambasts the suggestion by Meïr Aron Goldschmidt, *The Corsair*'s editor, that *The Corsair* and the comic embody "the first stage" in the development of a life: "As a rule, the comic is at the end—comedy quite properly concludes Hegel's *Aesthetics*, and an Aristophanes certainly would feel strange if he were advised to make his life as comic poet the first part—and then become 'earnest.' "[202] Consistent with his dissertation's dismissal of the Hegelian ascription of "earnestness" to Aristophanes,

196 *Pap.* VII–1 B 55, p. 242 / *COR*, Supplement, p. 193.

197 *Corsaren*, no. 285 (March 6), 1846, column 10 / *COR*, Supplement, p. 133.

198 *Pap.* III B 8 / *JP* 4, 4244. Cf. *Pap.* III B 30 / *JP* 4, 4246. See also *SKS* 1, 198–9 / *CI*, 148. *SKS* 1, 256, note 1 / *CI*, 212, note.

199 Jens Christian Hostrup, *Gjenboerne: Vaudeville-Komedie*, Copenhagen: F.H. Eibe 1847.

200 *Breve Fra og til C. Hostrup*, ed. by Elisabeth Hostrup, Copenhagen: Gyldendal 1897, pp. 105f. See Hostrup, *Gjenboerne*.

201 *SKS* 21, 170, NB8:57 / *JP* 6, 6282.

202 *SKS* 23, 185, NB17:32 / *JP* 6, 6602.

Kierkegaard insists further: "As a writer, I have never banned the comic; it was utilized in an auxiliary way by the pseudonyms."[203]

That Kierkegaard is *both* a "modern Socrates" *and* an Aristophanes of sorts will be suggested by a contemporary shortly before Kierkegaard's death.[204] During and after the *Corsair* affair, Kierkegaard evidently preserves his balanced dual esteem for Socrates and Aristophanes by not fully acknowledging the pertinence of the *Clouds* to Socrates' fatal condemnation. Otherwise, given his acceptance from the late 1840s on of "the clinical task assigned to me: Copenhagen in moral disintegration,"[205] such an acknowledgment would require him to side *either* with the poet whose comedies sought to reform and preserve Athens in its "age of disintegration," *or* with the philosopher whose dialectic was seen, perhaps by Aristophanes himself, as contributing to that "disintegration."

Kierkegaard never makes that choice, except perhaps once, implicitly. In opening his *For Self-Examination* (1851), he once again alludes obliquely to Aristophanes' implication in Socrates' doom. Having noted the correspondence between Socrates' circumstance with the contemporary Danish situation, Kierkegaard adopts as his own the imagined voice of Socrates from Plato's *Apology*: "The thoughts, ideas, and concepts that I, known by everyone, ridiculed by your comic poets, regarded as an eccentric, daily attacked by 'the anonymous' (it is his word)…have developed in conversation with the first person to come along in the marketplace—these thoughts are my life."[206] The words, "ridiculed by your comic poets," stand out. A year later, Kierkegaard still cannot keep Aristophanes' relation to Socrates off his mind, as a passage in Eduard Zeller's (1814–1908) *Die Philosophie der Griechen* leads him to note that the general practice which Plato ascribes to the Sophists, namely, that "of debating for and against on any question...and to instruct the listeners in this art," is "the same art of which Aristophanes accuses Socrates, that he gives instruction in both just and unjust discourse."[207] By 1854, contemplating Socrates' life-and-death stakes in the *Apology*, Kierkegaard recognizes: "On a small scale something like this is apparent in my life." Without mentioning Aristophanes, but clearly with him in mind, he then declares: "How ridiculous for a poet to want to seize hold of Socrates—Socrates' whole intention was to put an end to the poetic and to apply the ethical."[208]

---

203 Ibid.

204 See Fr. Helweg, "Et Ord om Thurahs Riimbrev," *Dagbladet*, October 26, 1855; quoted by Habib C. Malik, *Receiving Søren Kierkegaard: The Early Impact and Transmission of His Thought*, Washington, D.C.: Catholic University of America Press 1997, p. 108.

205 *SKS* 23, 185, NB17:32 / *JP* 6, 6602. See also *SKS* 21, 170, NB8:57 / *JP* 6, 6282. *SV1* XIII, 605 / *PV*, 119. *Pap*. IX B 64, pp. 377–9 / *PV*, Supplement, pp. 276–9.

206 *SKS* 13, 39, 301–2 / *FSE*, 9.

207 *Pap*. X–6 C 6.1 / *JP* 3, 3331, referring to Eduard Zeller, *Die Philosophie der Griechen. Eine Untersuchung über Charakter, Gang und Hauptmomente ihrer Entwicklung*, vols. 1–3, Tübingen: L.F. Fues 1844–52, vol. 1, p. 256 (*ASKB* 913–914).

208 *SKS* 26, 71, NB31:94 / *JP* 4, 4301.

Bibliography

I. Aristophanes' Works in The Auction Catalogue *of Kierkegaard's Library*

Anthologia graeca, ed. by Paul Hagerup Tregder, Copenhagen: C.A. Reitzel 1842, pp. 74–7 (*ASKB* 1041).

Aristophanis Comoedias accedunt perditarum fabularum fragmenta, vols. 1–2, ed. by Wilhelm Dindorff, Leipzig: Weidmann 1830 (*ASKB* 1051).

Des Aristophanes Werke, vols. 1–3, trans. by Johann Gustav Droysen, Berlin: Veit 1835–38 (*ASKB* 1052–1054).

Aristophanes's Komedier (contains the Danish translations of the *Frogs*; the *Clouds*; *Plutos*; and *Acharnians*), trans. by Johan Krag, Odense: S. Hempel 1825 (*ASKB* 1055).

II. Works by Modern Sources in The Auction Catalogue *of Kierkegaard's Library that Discuss Aristophanes*

[Becker, Karl Friedrich], *Karl Friedrich Beckers Verdenshistorie, omarbeidet af Johan Gottfried Woltmann*, vols. 1–12, trans. by J. Riise, Copenhagen: Fr. Brummer 1822–29, vol. 2, p. 407 (*ASKB* 1972–1983).

Dyck, Johann Gottfried and Georg Schatz (eds.), *Charaktere der vornehmsten Dichter aller Nationen; nebst kritischen und historischen Abhandlungen über Gegenstände der schönen Künste und Wissenschaften, von einer Gesellschaft von Gelehrten* [Nachträge zu Johann Georg Sulzer, *Allgemeine Theorie der schönen Künste: in einzeln, nach alphabetischer Ordnung der Kunstwörter auf einander folgenden, Artikeln abgehandelt*, vols. 1–2, Leipzig: Weidmann & Reich 1771–74], vols. 1–8, Leipzig: Dyk 1792–1808, vol. 7, p. 162 (*ASKB* 1370–1377).

Flögel, Carl Friedrich, *Geschichte der komischen Litteratur*, vols. 1–4, Liegnitz and Leipzig: David Giegert 1784–87, vol. 1, pp. 14–20 passim; p. 77; p. 86; p. 101; pp. 34–341 (*ASKB* 1396–1399).

Hagen, Johan Frederik, *Ægteskabet. Betragtet fra et ethisk-historiskt Standpunct*, Copenhagen: Wahlske Boghandels Forlag 1845, p. 111, note; p. 114 (*ASKB* 534).

Hamann, Johann Georg, *Hamann's Schriften*, vols. 1–8, ed. by Friedrich von Roth, Berlin: Bey G. Reimer 1821–43, vol. 2, p. 82, p. 303; vol. 3, p. 23; p. 331; vol. 7, p. 224 (*ASKB* 536–544).

[Hegel, Georg Wilhelm Friedrich], *Georg Wilhelm Friedrich Hegel's Vorlesungen über die Geschichte der Philosophie*, vols. 1–3, ed. by Carl Ludwig Michelet, Berlin: Duncker und Humblot 1833–36 (vols. 13–15 in *Georg Wilhelm Friedrich Hegel's Werke. Vollständige Ausgabe*, ed. by Philipp Marheineke et al., Berlin:

Duncker und Humblot 1832–45), vol. 1, p. 388; vol. 2, p. 52; p. 56; p. 64; pp. 85–90; p. 101; pp. 112–13; p. 183; vol. 3, p. 217; p. 232; pp. 509–10; pp. 518–19; pp. 536–7; pp. 559–62; p. 579 (*ASKB* 557–559).

—— *Georg Wilhelm Friedrich Hegel's vermischte Schriften*, vols. 1–2, ed. by Friedrich Förster and Ludwig Boumann, Berlin: Duncker und Humblot 1834–35 (vols. 16–17 in *Georg Wilhelm Friedrich Hegel's Werke. Vollständige Ausgabe*, ed. by Philipp Marheineke et al., Berlin: Duncker und Humblot 1832–45), vol. 2, pp. 461–2 (*ASKB* 555–556).

—— *Georg Wilhelm Friedrich Hegel's Vorlesungen über die Aesthetik*, vols. 1–3, ed. by Heinrich Gustav Hotho, Berlin: Duncker und Humblot 1835–38 (vols. 10.1–10.3 in *Georg Wilhelm Friedrich Hegel's Werke. Vollständige Ausgabe*, vols. 1–18, ed. by Philipp Marheineke et al., Berlin: Duncker und Humblot 1832–45), vol. 1, p. 497; vol. 2, p. 59; pp. 112–13; p. 232; vol. 3, pp. 509–10; pp. 518–19; pp. 536–7; pp. 559–62; p. 576; p. 579 (*ASKB* 1384–1386).

—— *Georg Wilhelm Friedrich Hegel's Vorlesungen über die Philosophie der Religion*, vols. 1–2, ed. by Philipp Marheineke, 2nd revised ed., Berlin: Duncker und Humblot 1840 (vols. 11–12 in *Georg Wilhelm Friedrich Hegel's Werke. Vollständige Ausgabe*, ed. by Philipp Marheineke et al., Berlin: Duncker und Humblot 1832–45), vol. 2, p. 109 (*ASKB* 564–565).

Petersen, Frederik Christian, *Haandbog i den græske Litteraturhistorie*, Copenhagen: Fr. Brummer 1830, p. III; p. 253 (*ASKB* 1037).

—— *Om Epheterne og deres Dikasterier i Athen*, Copenhagen: Bianco Lunos Bogtrykkeri 1847, pp. 27–8; p. 72 (*ASKB* 720).

[Richter, Johann Paul Friedrich], Jean Paul, *Vorschule der Aesthetik nebst einigen Vorlesungen in Leipzig über die Parteien der Zeit*, vols. 1–3, 2nd revised ed., Stuttgart and Tübingen: J.G. Cotta 1813, vol. 1, p. 258 (*ASKB* 1381–1383).

Schlegel, August Wilhelm, *Ueber dramatische Kunst und Litteratur. Vorlesungen*, vols. 1–2 [vol. 2 in 2 Parts], Heidelberg: Mohr und Zimmer 1809–11, vol. 1, pp. 283–325 (*ASKB* 1392–1394).

[Schlegel, Friedrich], *Friedrich Schlegel's sämmtliche Werke*, vols. 1–10, Vienna: Jakob Mayer und Co. 1822–25, vol. 1, pp. 53–5; vol. 4, pp. 25–45 passim; vol. 5, p. 145 (*ASKB* 1816–1825).

Schopenhauer, Arthur, *Parerga und Paralipomena: kleine philosophische Schriften*, vols. 1–2, Berlin: A.W. Hayn 1851, vol. 1, p. 36 (*ASKB* 774–775).

Sibbern, Frederik Christian, *Om Forholdet imellem Sjæl og Legeme, saavel i Almindelighed som i phrenologisk, pathognomonisk, physiogonomisk og ethisk Henseende i Særdeleshed*, Copenhagen: Paa Forfatterens eget Forlag 1849, p. 387; p. 448 (*ASKB* 781).

[Solger, Karl Wilhelm Ferdinand], *Solger's nachgelassene Schriften und Briefwechsel*, ed. by Ludwig Tieck und Friedrich von Raumer, vols. 1–2, Leipzig: F.A. Brockhaus 1826, pp. 493–628 (*ASKB* 1832–1833).

—— *K.W.F. Solger's Vorlesungen über Aesthetik*, ed. by K.W.L. Heyse, Leipzig: F.A. Brockhaus 1829, p. 107; p. 165; p. 234; p. 313 (*ASKB* 1387).

Steffens, Henrich, *Christliche Religionsphilosophie*, vols. 1–2, Breslau: Josef Max 1839, vol. 1, p. 137 (*ASKB* 797–798).

Sulzer, Johann Georg, *Allgemeine Theorie der Schönen Künste, in einzeln, nach alphabetischer Ordnung der Kunstwörter auf einander folgenden, Artikeln abgehandelt*, vols. 1–4 and a register volume, 2nd revised ed., Leipzig: Weidmann 1792–99, vol. 1, p. 40; p. 80; p. 98; p. 214; p. 259; pp. 497–9; p. 505; p. 508; p. 511; p. 513; p. 707; vol. 3, p. 141; vol. 4, p. 770 (*ASKB* 1365–1369).

Thiersch, Friedrich, *Allgemeine Aesthetik in akademischen Lehrvorträgen*, Berlin: G. Reimer 1846, p. 261 (*ASKB* 1378).

Weiße, Christian Hermann, *System der Aesthetik als Wissenschaft von der Idee der Schönheit. In drei Büchern*, vols. 1–2, Leipzig: C.H.F. Hartmann 1830, vol. 1, p. 222; p. 233 (*ASKB* 1379–1380).

III. Secondary Works on Kierkegaard's Relation to Aristophanes' Socrates

Andic, Martin, "Clouds of Irony," in *The Concept of Irony*, ed. by Robert Perkins, Macon, Georgia: Mercer University Press 2001 (*International Kierkegaard Commentary*, vol. 2), pp. 161–92.

Himmelstrup, Jens, *Søren Kierkegaards Opfattelse af Sokrates. En Studie i dansk Filosofis Historie*, Copenhagen: Arnold Busck 1924, pp. 290–4.

Holm, Isak Winkel, "Herskerens stemme. Kierkegaard som erotisk læser af Aristophanes' 'Skyerne,' " in *Læserens åndedrag: en antologi om den læsende digter og den digtende læser*, ed. by Uffe Hansen et al., Copenhagen: Museum Tusculanum 1996, pp. 85–105.

Howland, Jacob, *Kierkegaard and Socrates: A Study in Philosophy and Faith*, Cambridge: Cambridge University Press 2006, p. 8; p. 58; p. 60; pp. 73–4; p. 83; p. 99; p. 114; p. 131; p. 192.

Jensen, Povl Johannes, "Aristophanes," in *Kierkegaard's Classical Inspiration*, ed. by Niels Thulstrup and Marie Mikulová Thulstrup, Copenhagen: C.A. Reitzel 1985 (*Bibliotheca Kierkegaardiana*, vol. 14), pp. 118–24.

Kleinert, Markus, *Sich verzehrender Skeptizismus. Läuterungen bei Hegel und Kierkegaard*, Berlin and New York: Walter de Gruyter 2005 (*Kierkegaard Studies Monograph Series*, vol. 12), pp. 106–18; p. 139; p. 180; p. 191; p. 194; p. 197; pp. 207–8.

Kloeden, Wolfdietrich von, "Sokrates," in *Kierkegaard's Classical Inspiration*, ed. by Niels Thulstrup and Marie Mikulová Thulstrup, Copenhagen: C.A. Reitzel 1985 (*Bibliotheca Kierkegaardiana*, vol. 14), pp. 104–81, especially pp. 124–7.

Paula, Marcio Gimenes de, *Socratismo e cristianismo em Kierkegaard: o escândalo e a loucura*, São Paulo: Annablume editora 2001, see pp. 47–50.

Scopetea, Sophia, *Kierkegaard og græciteten. En kamp med ironi*, Copenhagen: C.A. Reitzel 1995, p. 15; p. 19, note 59; p. 22; p. 24; p. 83, note 24; p. 99; pp. 108–19 passim; p. 122, note 24; p. 125, note 29; pp. 135–6; p. 155; p. 291, note 5; p. 293; p. 294, note 7; p. 309, note 42; p. 324; p. 325, note 43; p. 333; p. 346, note 39; p. 412, note 19; p. 463.

Tjønneland, Eivind, *Ironie als Symptom. Eine kritische Ausenandersetzung mit Søren Kierkegaards Über den Begriff der Ironie*, Frankfurt am Main: Peter Lang

2004 (*Texte und Untersuchungen zur Germanistik und Skandinavistik*, vol. 54), see pp. 107–91.

Ziolkowski, Eric, "From the *Clouds* to *Corsair*: Kierkegaard, Aristophanes, and the Problem of Socrates," in *The Concept of Irony*, ed. by Robert Perkins, Macon, Georgia: Mercer University Press 2001 (*International Kierkegaard Commentary*, vol. 2), pp. 193–233.

Xenophon:
Kierkegaard's Use of the Socrates of the *Memorabilia*

William McDonald

Almost all of the references to Xenophon in Kierkegaard's work occur in the first part of his dissertation, *The Concept of Irony*.[1] Kierkegaard's aim in this first part, entitled "The Position of Socrates Viewed as Irony," is to reveal the essence of the historical Socrates as irony. Part One of the dissertation is divided into three sections: "The View Made Possible," "The Actualization of the View," and "The View Made Necessary." These sections are preceded by a short introduction, in which Kierkegaard clarifies his methodology, and they are succeeded by an appendix on "Hegel's View of Socrates." It is necessary to understand Kierkegaard's methodology, and the relation of his view on Socrates to that of Hegel, before we can fully understand his use of Xenophon's accounts of Socrates.

Kierkegaard posits the view that Socrates is essentially an incarnation of irony, but does not want to apply this as a procrustean philosophical preconception to the historical phenomenon of Socrates as an individual. Rather, he wants the hypothesis to be able to explain both the actual individual Socrates, and the essential truth about irony, as well as to show why all of the accounts by Socrates' contemporaries fail to discover the truth about either the phenomenon of Socrates or the concept of irony. In the course of his investigation, Kierkegaard seeks to steer a path between history, which he takes to deal with "the particular" phenomenon, and philosophy, which he takes to give conceptual explanations in terms of eternal truth.[2] It is difficult to reconcile historical and philosophical accounts of the same phenomenon, since history focuses on particular phenomena in a fragmentary manner, and philosophy focuses on essential concepts as totalities.[3] While history has linked the word "irony" to Socrates, "it by no means follows that everyone knows what irony is."[4]

To compound the difficulties, concepts themselves have histories, and history can be conceptualized philosophically. Both these difficulties are further compounded

---

1 Of Xenophon's works, Kierkegaard refers to the *Memorabilia* most, to the *Apology* fewer times, and to the *Symposium* only once. He did not refer to any other of Xenophon's works. Cf. *SKS* K1, 166.

2 *SKS* 1, 72–3 / *CI*, 9–11.

3 *SKS* 1, 73 / *CI*, 11.

4 Ibid.

in the case of Socrates, since he was silent (in the sense that he wrote nothing for posterity)—and "this is his whole life in terms of world history."[5] Kierkegaard aims, in his dissertation, to take into account the history of the concept of irony, starting with its introduction by Socrates,[6] and to capture the essential philosophical truth about irony by showing how it manifests in the particular individual Socrates and in the misunderstandings by his contemporaries. At the same time he offers a critique of Hegel's view of Socrates, as seen through the lens of Hegel's philosophy of history.

The difficulty of giving congruent historical and philosophical accounts of Socrates as both individual phenomenon and universal concept is made even more difficult when Socrates is posited as irony. Since irony points "to something other [than] and opposite" to the literal, or "the outer," the task of portraying it is "as difficult as to picture a nisse [household sprite] with the cap that makes him invisible."[7] In order to capture the "angle of refraction" by which Socrates transforms "the inner" to what is witnessed as "the outer," Kierkegaard looks to "a new combined reckoning."[8] Instead of finding the truth about either Socrates or irony represented positively in the accounts by Socrates' contemporaries, Kierkegaard strives to find these in the empty space that the contemporary accounts define collectively—in a way analogous to the picture of Napoleon's grave, in which the only positively portrayed elements are two trees and a grave; but from the empty space between them emerges an image of Napoleon himself.[9] By close examination of the extant accounts by three eyewitnesses, namely, Xenophon, Plato, and Aristophanes, Kierkegaard argues that it is *possible* to view Socrates as irony in the space found between them.[10] Kierkegaard summarizes this first step in his hermeneutic method as follows:

> Wherever it is a matter of reconstructing a phenomenon by means of what could be a view in the stricter sense of the word, there is a double task: one must indeed

---

5 *SKS* 1,74 / *CI*, 11–12.

6 Cf. Thesis X of Kierkegaard's dissertation. *SKS* 1, 65 / *CI*, 6–7. Note, however, that by Socrates' time, the *eiron* was a well-established figure in Greek fertility rites and the theatrical forms they spawned. If Kierkegaard is correct in claiming that Socrates was the first to introduce irony, he can only be correct if he means "irony" in the special sense he gives it in his dissertation. For the figure of the *eiron* in early Greek thought, see Wylie Sypher, "The Meanings of Comedy," in *Comedy*, ed. by Wylie Sypher, Baltimore and London: Johns Hopkins University Press 1956, pp. 216–30.

7 *SKS* 1, 74 / *CI*, 12.

8 Ibid.

9 *SKS* 1, 80–1 / *CI*, 19. For a reproduction of the picture of Napoleon's grave, see *SKS* K1, 169.

10 Note that of the three eyewitnesses, only Aristophanes' *The Clouds* was written while Socrates was alive. Both Plato and Xenophon knew Socrates personally, but wrote their accounts after Socrates' death. It has been argued, by Kenneth Dover and others, that Aristophanes' caricature does not deal with the historical Socrates, and we might also question whether Xenophon's accounts are based primarily on his own acquaintance with Socrates or whether they are due to others' reports. See Tonny Aagaard Olesen, "Kierkegaard's Socratic Hermeneutic in *The Concept of Irony*," in *The Concept of Irony*," ed. by Robert L. Perkins, Macon, Georgia: Mercer University Press 2001 (*International Kierkegaard Commentary*, vol. 2), pp. 113–14.

> explain the phenomenon and in doing so explain the misunderstanding, and through the misunderstanding one must attain the phenomenon and through the phenomenon break the spell of the misunderstanding.[11]

After establishing that it is *possible* to view Socrates as irony, and thereby both explain him as an historical phenomenon and explain the misunderstandings of his contemporaries, Kierkegaard proceeds to show how this view is *actualized*, and then how it is made *necessary*. His hermeneutic approach involves in this manner a modal dialectic. The first stage proves the conception possible, by showing how it explains both the phenomenon and its misunderstandings; the second stage shows how the conception maps onto the *facts* that are agreed upon by the contemporary accounts, principally the facts about Socrates' *daimonion* and about his trial and condemnation; and the third stage shows how Socratic irony is a necessary development in the evolution of "world spirit." This understanding of the evolution of spirit as subject to "world-historical" necessity owes a lot to Hegel's philosophy of history, though Kierkegaard reserves some criticisms of Hegel's view for his appendix to Part One of the dissertation. This third stage of the hermeneutic also points towards Part Two of the dissertation, which strives to apprehend Socrates *via eminentiae* [by way of idealization], in contrast to the attempt in the first part of the dissertation to apprehend Socrates *via negationis* [by way of negation].[12]

I. Kierkegaard's View Made Possible

Most of the references to Xenophon occur in the section entitled "The View Made Possible," with a few references in "The Actualization of the View," and no references in "The View Made Necessary." A few references crop up again in the appendix on "Hegel's View of Socrates," but no mentions of Xenophon occur in Part Two of the dissertation. The examination of the eyewitness accounts purports to be historical, philological, and philosophical, but is also informed by Kierkegaard's more immediate context of cultural history and theology. Kierkegaard's attempt to find the essence of Socrates was not the first. Two major types of investigation of this question preceded his own: one type used primarily historical-philological methods, and the other type used historical-philosophical methods.[13] During most of the eighteenth century, Xenophon was taken to be the most reliable source of information about the historical Socrates. This developed over the course of the century to giving equal weight to Xenophon's and to Plato's accounts, until by the beginning of the nineteenth century, preference was given to Plato's account.[14] The problem of trying to disentangle the historical Socrates from the conflicting accounts

---

11 *SKS* 1, 205 / *CI*, 155.

12 *SKS* 1, 244 / *CI*, 198–9.

13 Cf. Olesen, "Kierkegaard's Socratic Hermeneutic in *The Concept of Irony*," p. 108.

14 Cf. Jens Himmelstrup, *Søren Kierkegaards Opfattelse af Sokrates*, Copenhagen: Arnold Busck 1924, pp. 256ff.

by contemporaries and their successors, in the absence of any writings by Socrates himself, came to be known as "the problem of Socrates."[15]

The early nineteenth century also produced several new editions of the primary sources, both in the original language and in German and Danish translations. Georg Anton Friedrich Ast (1778–1841) produced a new edition of Plato's writings,[16] as well as an influential commentary, *Platon's Leben und Schriften*,[17] which is quoted at length in Kierkegaard's dissertation. Gottfried Stallbaum (1793–1861) also produced a selection of Plato's dialogues in Greek, with his own prefaces in Latin.[18] In addition, Kierkegaard had access to the German translation of Plato's works by Friedrich Schleiermacher (1768–1834),[19] and to Danish translations of Aristophanes[20] and of selections of Plato and Xenophon.[21]

This flurry of philological activity, taken together with the emerging orthodoxy that Plato was the most reliable guide to the historical Socrates, gave rise to the problem of differentiating within Plato's existing dialogues those which most accurately reflect the historical Socrates. Friedrich Schleiermacher produced the most influential historical ordering of Plato's work, based on philological evidence and on the hermeneutic principle of philosophical development. These methods were used to establish both the authenticity of works attributed to Plato and their order of composition. Schleiermacher superimposed a conception of the systematic representation of Plato's theory of forms on the textual evidence in order to arrive at their order of composition. On the basis of this abstract approach, Schleiermacher arrived at the view that the early dialogues of Plato were those which best represent the historical Socrates, and that Socrates' great contribution to philosophy is the idea

---

15 Cf. V. de Magalhâes-Vilhena, *Le Problème de Socrate: le Socrate historique et le Socrate de Platon*, Paris: Presses Universitaires de France 1952, which is probably the most comprehensive historical survey of attempts to solve this problem. Cf. Eric Ziolkowski, "From *Clouds* to *Corsair*: Kierkegaard, Aristophanes, and the Problem of Socrates," in *The Concept of Irony*, ed. by Robert L. Perkins, Macon, Georgia: Mercer University Press 2001 (*International Kierkegaard Commentary*, vol. 2), pp. 198–206.

16 *Platonis quæ exstant Opera. Accedunt Platonis quae feruntur Scripta*, vols. 1–11, ed. by Friederich Ast, Leipzig: Weidmann 1819–32 (*ASKB* 1144–1154). Cf. *SKS* K1, 381.

17 Friedrich Ast, *Platon's Leben und Schriften. Ein Versuch, im Leben wie in den Schriften des Platon das Wahre und Aechte vom Erdichteten und Untergeschobenen zu scheiden, und die Zeitfolge der ächten Gespräche zu bestimmen. Als Einleitung in das Studium des Platon*, Leipzig: Weidmann 1816. Cf. *SKS* K1, 377.

18 *Platonis dialogos selectos*, published with commentary by G. Stallbaum, Gotha and Erfurt: Hennings 1827. Cf. *SKS* K1, 381.

19 *Platons Werke*, vols. 1–3 in 6 parts, trans. by Friedrich Schleiermacher, vols. 1.1–1.2 and vol. 2.1, Berlin: Realschulbuchhandlung 1817–18, vols. 2.2–2.3 and vol. 3.1, Berlin Reimer 1824–28, vol. 1.2, p. 97 (*ASKB* 1158–1163). Cf. *SKS* K1, 377.

20 *Udvalgte Dialoger af Platon*, vols. 1–3, trans. by C.J. Heise, Copenhagen: Gyldendal 1830–38 [vols. 4–8, Copenhagen: C.A. Reitzel 1851–59, cf. *ASKB* 1167 and 1169. Kierkegaard owned vols. 1–7] (*ASKB* 1164–1166). Cf. *SKS* K1, 382.

21 *Xenophons Sokratiske Merkværdigheder*, trans. by J. Bloch, Copenhagen: Möller & Sön 1792. Cf. *SKS* K1, 383.

of the dialectic.[22] The latter claim is central to Kierkegaard's later view of Socrates, but Schleiermacher's imposition of an abstract, systematic view of the development of a philosophical concept as a hermeneutic principle for discovering historical truths is explicitly rejected by Kierkegaard.

Schleiermacher's approach was pursued further both by Hegel, in terms of his notion of "world-historical" necessity in the evolution of "the concept," and by Friedrich Ast in his determination that Plato's *Apology* is inauthentic.[23] Ast then used this claim as a basis for preferring Xenophon's *Apology* to the *Apology* attributed to Plato. Kierkegaard agrees that if Ast is right in his claim about Plato's *Apology*, then Xenophon's *Apology* should be preferred as an account of the historical Socrates. Ast bolstered his argument about the inauthenticity of the *Apology* with philological and literary evidence, but Kierkegaard seeks to refute Ast's interpretation by showing that his own hypothesis about Socrates as an embodiment of irony is consistent with all the passages in Plato's *Apology* which develop Socrates' view of death.[24] Death, as a confrontation with nothingness, is a special test case for the hypothesis that Socrates' standpoint is irony. Kierkegaard contends that Socrates' fearlessness in the face of death, as portrayed in Plato's *Apology*, is entirely consistent with a life-time of dwelling with the nothingness of irony. This is in stark contrast to Ast's interpretation of the portrait of Socrates in this work as "listless and spiritless"—which seems quite at odds with the "inspired enthusiast" Socrates is otherwise depicted to be.[25]

Kierkegaard then proceeds to attack Ast's assertion that there is no Platonic irony in the *Apology*, or more damagingly still for his own point of view, the possibility that there is no irony at all in the *Apology*.[26] Ast's assertion looks at first glance to be a direct contradiction of Kierkegaard's thesis that Socrates' essence is irony, and that this is present (albeit negatively) in Plato's *Apology*. Kierkegaard goes on to argue that the reason Ast has failed to find irony in the *Apology* is that he was looking for it in particular places in the text, while it really applies to the text as a whole.[27]

While irony is present in Plato's *Apology* as a whole, according to Kierkegaard's argument, Plato was not consciously aware that Socrates' nature was irony. Kierkegaard quotes Ast at length, not to refute Ast's contention that Plato did not consciously portray Socrates as an ironist, but to show that implicit in Plato's portrait of Socrates in the *Apology*, despite the truth of Ast's contention, we can discern Socratic irony everywhere, *via negationis*. As Kierkegaard goes on to demonstrate in the subsection on "The Mythical in the Early Platonic Dialogues," Plato erred on the side of speculative idealism in his apprehension of Socrates.[28] By identifying the complementary mistakes of the contemporary accounts, Kierkegaard not only gets

---

22 Wolfdietrich von Kloeden, "Sokrates," in *Kierkegaard's Classical Inspiration*, ed. by Niels Thulstrup and Marie Mikulová Thulstrup, Copenhagen: C.A. Reitzel 1985 (*Bibliotheca Kierkegaardiana*, vol. 14), p. 120.

23 Cf. Himmelstrup, *Søren Kierkegaards Opfattelse af Sokrates*, p. 254; and Ast, *Platon's Leben und Schriften*, passim.

24 *SKS* 1, 138–50 / *CI*, 80–96.

25 *SKS* 1, 142–3 / *CI*, 87.

26 *SKS* 1, 143–4 / *CI*, 88.

27 *SKS* 1, 146–50 / *CI*, 90–6. See also *SKS* 1, 99 / *CI*, 37.

28 *SKS* 1, 150–62 / *CI*, 96–109.

closer to identifying the historical phenomenon of Socrates correctly, but he also shows how the original sources are to be understood in relation to one another.

Despite his hermeneutic method of looking for the actual Socrates in the space between the accounts by Socrates' contemporaries, and despite his claim that Aristophanes' account comes closest to the truth,[29] Kierkegaard lays by far the most weight on his examination of Plato's texts—in fact, he devotes over twice as much text to Aristophanes as he does to Xenophon, and about four times as much to Plato as to Aristophanes.[30] He devotes a subsection of his dissertation to a direct comparison between Xenophon's and Plato's accounts, and another to a three-way comparison of Xenophon, Plato, and Aristophanes, but does not bother with separate sections for direct comparisons between Xenophon and Aristophanes or between Aristophanes and Plato.

In placing the emphasis on Plato in this way, Kierkegaard is following the dominant trend in classical scholarship of his time, which identified the early Platonic dialogues as those which best represent the historical Socrates. He justifies his choice of the Platonic dialogues he uses by saying that he follows "most scholars," and in emphasizing the importance of the first book of the *Republic* he proceeds "under the auspices of Schleiermacher."[31] But there were other important influences too on Kierkegaard's understanding of Socrates and the contemporary accounts. Not least were those attempts to show that Socrates was a spiritual precursor of Christ.[32]

Johann Georg Hamann (1730–88), in *Socratic Memorabilia*, found in Socrates' declaration of ignorance, evidence that faith has precedence over reason. Hamann identified Socrates as a forerunner of Christ, and saw in Socrates' irony a method of indirect communication analogous with Christ's.[33] Hamann also influenced Kierkegaard's interpretations of Xenophon and Plato, whose representations of Socrates Hamann characterized respectively as superstitious, and a gushing devotion.[34] Yet Hamann wrote *Socratic Memorabilia* without having read either Xenophon or Plato. Instead he relied primarily on a German translation of François

---

29 Cf. Thesis VII: "Aristophanes has come very close to the truth in his depiction of Socrates." *SKS* 1, 65 / *CI*, 6.

30 The amount of text Kierkegaard devotes to each of the contemporaries is as follows: Xenophon (*SKS* 1, 77–89 / *CI*, 15–27); Plato (*SKS* 1, 89–178 / *CI*, 27–126); Aristophanes (*SKS* 1, 179–203 / *CI*, 128–53).

31 *SKS* 1, 171–2 / *CI*, 119–20.

32 Cf. Ferdinand Christian Baur, *Das Christliche des Platonismus oder Sokrates und Christus. Eine religionsphilosophische Untersuchung*, Tübingen: Fues 1837 (*ASKB* 422); Johann Eduard Erdmann, *Vorlesungen über Glauben und Wissen als Einleitung in die Dogmatik und Religionsphilosophie*, Berlin: Duncker und Humblot 1837 (*ASKB* 479).

33 Cf. von Kloeden, "Sokrates," pp. 108–10. See also James C. O'Flaherty, *Hamann's Socratic Memorabilia: A Translation and Commentary*, Baltimore: The Johns Hopkins Press 1967, p. 6.

34 *Johann Georg Hamanns Hauptschriften*, vols. 1–4, ed. by Fritz Blanke, Gütersloh: Mohn 1956–63, vol. 2, p. 76, cited in von Kloeden, "Sokrates," p. 109.

Charpentier's *The Likeness of a True and Non-Pedantic Philosopher, or the Life of Socrates*,[35] as well as John Gilbert Cooper's *The Life of Socrates*.[36]

Hamann's conception of Socrates was mediated for Kierkegaard by Poul Martin Møller (1794–1838). Kierkegaard took up the idea that Socrates educed a type of love in his pupils, through what Hamann referred to as "spiritual pederasty," after a conversation with Poul Martin Møller, in June 1837.[37] From this conversation, Kierkegaard formed the kernel of his ideas that Socrates' essence lies in irony, that irony is a form of indirect communication, and that it can be used to elicit love—and in this respect Socrates and Christ are analogous. The difference between them is that Socrates uses irony, which is egotistical, and Christ uses humor, which is irony to a higher power.[38] Kierkegaard's first thesis in his dissertation runs as follows: "The similarity between Christ and Socrates consists essentially in their dissimilarity."[39] This gives Kierkegaard the opportunity to discuss an issue in contemporary theology, with reference to the work of Ferdinand Christian Baur (1792–1860), with Hamann in the background.[40]

In addition to the literature on the parallels between Socrates and Christ, there was also a considerable literature on irony. This includes work by Kierkegaard's philosophy teachers at Copenhagen University, Frederik Christian Sibbern (1785–1872) and Poul Martin Møller,[41] as well as the work of the Hegelian Johann Eduard Erdmann (1805–92) on "religious irony,"[42] and of course all the work by the German Romantics, which Kierkegaard criticizes in Part Two of his dissertation, as well as the work of Hegel himself, who characterized Solger's irony as "absolute infinite negativity."[43]

By hypothesizing that the essence of Socrates is irony, understood as "absolute, infinite negativity," Kierkegaard finds an explanation of the misunderstandings by

---

35 François Charpentier, *Das Ebenbild eines wahren und ohnpedantischen Philosophi, Oder: Das Leben Socratis*, trans. by Christian Thomas, 2nd ed., Halle: Salfeld 1720 [1693].

36 John Gilbert Cooper, *The Life of Socrates, collected from the Memorabilia of Xenophon and the Dialogues of Plato, and illustrated farther by Aristotle, Diodorus Siculus, Cicero, Proclus, Apuleius, Maximus Tyrius, Boethius, Diogenes Laertius, Aulus Gellius, and others*, London: R. Dodsley 1749. Cf. also James C. O'Flaherty, *Hamann's Socratic Memorabilia: A Translation and Commentary*, p. 59.

37 von Kloeden, "Sokrates," p. 111. Cf. *SKS* 17, 225–6, DD:18 / *KJN 1*, 216–7.

38 Cf. *Pap*. II A 101–8. Note that Poul Martin Møller had already associated Socratic irony with humor, as "the cast of mind [*Sindstemning*] from which irony springs." See Poul Martin Møller, "Sokrates," in *Efterladte Skrifter af Poul Martin Møller*, vols. 1–6, 3rd ed., Copenhagen: C.A. Reitzel 1855–56, vol. 4, p. 99.

39 *SKS* 1, 65 / *CI*, 6.

40 Cf. Sophia Scopetea, *Kierkegaard og græciteten. En kamp med ironi*, Copenhagen, C.A. Reitzel 1995, p. 107.

41 In 1822 Sibbern had suggested the irony of Socrates as the topic of a prize essay for the Academy of Science; see Jens Himmelstrup, *Sibbern. En Monografi*, Copenhagen: J.H. Schultz Forlag 1934, p. 265; P.M. Møller, "Om Begrebet Ironie," in *Efterladte Skrifter*, vol. 3, pp. 152–8. Cf. Møller, "Sokrates," pp. 92–110.

42 Erdmann, *Vorlesungen über Glauben und Wissen*, cited in von Kloeden, "Sokrates," p. 119.

43 Cf. *CI*, Notes, pp. 475–6, note 64.

his contemporaries. Since for Kierkegaard, following Hegel, irony makes its first appearance in the person of Socrates, Socrates' contemporaries failed to recognize it.

II. Kierkegaard's Actual View of Xenophon

Whereas Plato idealizes Socrates and makes him the basis of his own positive philosophy, Xenophon errs by being too prosaic, empirical, and utilitarian in his view of Socrates.[44] Like Poul Martin Møller, Kierkegaard thinks that Xenophon was too caught up in the practicalities of life, to have any philosophical insight.[45] In particular, Xenophon failed to realize that Socrates concerned himself with dialectic, and that Socrates was essentially an ironist.[46] Xenophon's representations of Socrates also suffer from the fact that they are subordinated to the purpose of showing "what a scandalous injustice it was for the Athenians to condemn Socrates to death."[47]

Xenophon had no eye for the situation, and no ear for rejoinder, in recounting Socrates' conversations.[48] As a result, Xenophon was quite blind to irony. By failing to take the situation into account, Xenophon failed to show that "the true center for Socrates was not a fixed point but an *ubique et nusquam*."[49] By having no ear for rejoinder, Xenophon had no idea of the "infinitely resonating reverse echoing of the rejoinder in the personality"[50]—which is an intimation of Socrates' irony as infinite negativity. In short, Xenophon, unlike either Plato or Aristophanes, was no artist. He tried to tell it plainly, as he saw it—and in so doing gave only superficial, prosaic descriptions of external events, and missed the essential inner life of Socrates the ironist and midwife of subjectivity.

Whereas Plato added something to Socrates, because of his own artistic and philosophical nature, Xenophon took something away: "Xenophon, like a huckster, has deflated his Socrates and...Plato, like an artist, has created his Socrates in supranatural dimensions."[51] In particular, Xenophon took away Socrates' characteristic "infinite negativity," which radically cleared the ground for the positive philosophical activity of others. Xenophon did this by representing Socrates as a utilitarian:

> But if we remember the conclusion we arrived at through Xenophon, namely, that here we found Socrates busily functioning as an apostle of finitude, as an officious bagman for mediocrity, tirelessly recommending his one and only saving secular gospel, that here we found the useful rather than the good, the useful rather than the beautiful, the established rather than the true, the lucrative rather than the sympathetic, pedestrianism

---

44 Cf. Thesis II: "The Xenophontic Socrates stops with an emphasis on the useful; he never goes beyond the empirical, never arrives at the idea." *SKS* 1, 65 / *CI*, 6.

45 Cf. Møller, "Sokrates," p. 99.

46 Ibid., pp. 100–2.

47 *SKS* 1, 77 / *CI*, 15.

48 *SKS* 1, 78–81 / *CI*, 16–19.

49 *SKS* 1, 78 / *CI*, 16.

50 *SKS* 1, 80 / *CI*, 18.

51 *SKS* 1, 178 / *CI*, 127.

> rather than harmonious unity, then one will surely admit that these two conceptions cannot very well be joined.[52]

Xenophon was an empiricist, a utilitarian, and confined to the realms of finitude in existence. He was not a speculator, or a philosopher, or an artist, and failed to discern any difference between the inner world of Socrates and his outward behavior. Plato, on the other hand, was a speculative philosopher, and elevated Socrates "into the supramundane regions of the idea."[53] For Kierkegaard, Socrates actually occupied the invisible dividing line between these accounts, oscillating "between the ideal *I* and the empirical *I*; the one would make Socrates a philosopher, the other a Sophist; but what makes him more than a Sophist is that his empirical *I* has universal validity."[54] It is this universal validity, for Kierkegaard and for Hegel, which makes Socrates' irony *necessary* as a moment in the world-historical dialectic of spirit. Because Xenophon has no trace of philosophical speculation, he is not mentioned in that section of the dissertation which deals with "The View Made Necessary." Nor does he rate more than one mention in the subsection on Aristophanes, since his role in the negative portrait of Socrates is only by way of contrast with Plato.

Nevertheless, Xenophon's account is useful when it comes to Kierkegaard's attempt to map his possible view of Socrates as irony onto Socrates as actual historical phenomenon. Kierkegaard does this by focusing on what the contemporary accounts agree upon as facts about the life of Socrates. In particular, Kierkegaard examines the facts of Socrates' belief in his *daimonion*, and the facts about Socrates' trial and condemnation. For these purposes, Xenophon is quite a reliable guide, though Kierkegaard argues that Plato's account of the *daimonion* as something that only communicates negatively, in terms of warnings and deterrence, is preferable to Xenophon's account, in which the *daimonion* "orders, prompts, as well as commands doing something."[55] Plato's view is preferable because it is more consistent with an interpretation of Socrates as essentially ironic. In his interpretation of Socrates' *daimonion* as "a qualification of subjectivity,"[56] Kierkegaard concurs with Hegel, and has little to add other than to reiterate that this character of the *daimonion* is consistent with his interpretation of Socrates as irony.

III. Kierkegaard's View of Hegel Made Necessary

Kierkegaard takes Hegel to task for his slap-dash methods in arriving at his conclusions about Socrates. He accuses Hegel of using "only one single dialogue from Plato as an example of the Socratic method, without explaining why he chose this particular one. According to Kierkegaard, Hegel "uses Xenophon's *Memorabilia* and *Apology*, and also Plato's *Apology*, quite uncritically"; he does not bother to distinguish the phenomenal and conceptual presentations of Socrates; and "there is nothing at all in

---

52 *SKS* 1, 178 / *CI*, 127.
53 *SKS* 1, 179 / *CI*, 128.
54 Ibid.
55 *SKS* 1, 208–9 / *CI*, 158.
56 *SKS* 1, 214 / *CI*, 165.

his presentation of Socrates in *Geschichte der Philosophie* to illuminate the relations of the three different contemporary views of Socrates."[57] Hegel even dismisses Schleiermacher's effort to order the Platonic dialogues according to literary and philological criteria, and to examine them for authenticity, since for Hegel it is much more urgent to discern the world-historical import of the ideas, and he does not bother with philological justification of his own distinction between "the really Platonic" dialectic, and the "merely negative dialectic" of Socrates.[58]

Yet, as Jon Stewart has argued, "Kierkegaard follows almost to the letter Hegel's treatment of Socrates in his *Lectures on the History of Philosophy*."[59] This apparent Hegelianism, together with Kierkegaard's later antipathy to the Danish Hegelians, is taken as evidence by some commentators that Kierkegaard is being thoroughly ironic in his use of Hegel in the dissertation. Neither position is right, in my view. Stewart marshals compelling evidence that Kierkegaard had no particular ax to grind against Hegel or Hegelians when he wrote his dissertation. Only one Danish Hegelian, Hans Lassen Martensen (1808–84), ended up on his dissertation panel, and he was a last-minute substitute, so Kierkegaard could not have anticipated an academic audience "to dupe with meta-irony."[60] On the other hand, he could well have treated Hegel's views ironically, to enjoy an in-joke with the anti-Hegelians, such as F.C. Sibbern, whom he expected to be on his dissertation panel.

But there is no need to assume that the dissertation treats Hegel ironically, even if it were possible to demonstrate the presence of something as slippery and invisible as irony. Kierkegaard's overt task, while drawing heavily on Hegel's insights about Socrates, is to give a methodologically more rigorous means of arriving at those insights. In the process of doing this, Kierkegaard also manages to criticize Hegel on some crucial points, while maintaining the central thesis of Part One of the dissertation, that Socrates' nature is irony. From Kierkegaard's point of view, Hegel identified "the form of interrogation employed by Plato" with his own notion of the negative, which in turn he superimposed on his understanding of Socratic irony.[61] This is due to Hegel's methodological flaw of fitting the phenomenon to the concept, rather than trying to find a concept appropriate to the phenomenon. Furthermore, Hegel imposed the modern concept of irony on Socrates, rather than the ancient one, which Socrates introduced.[62] Hegel found in Socrates an individual who embodied the (modern) universal concept of irony, whereas Kierkegaard finds in Socrates an individual with universal validity. That is, whereas Hegel started with a universal and found its exemplar in Socrates, Kierkegaard starts with Socrates and finds in him the potential to generate a universal.

---

57 *SKS* 1, 265–6 / *CI*, 221–2.

58 *SKS* 1, 266–7 / *CI*, 222–3.

59 Jon Stewart, *Kierkegaard's Relations to Hegel Reconsidered*, Cambridge and New York: Cambridge University Press 2003, p. 135.

60 Ibid., pp. 137–9.

61 Cf. Thesis IV, *SKS* 1, 65 / *CI*, 6.

62 Cf. Thesis XII, *SKS* 1, 65 / *CI*, 6.

Kierkegaard sums up Hegel's diverse views on Socrates under the rubric "the founder of morality."[63] Hegel borrowed examples of Socrates' positive and negative side of the universal in Socrates' morality from Xenophon's accounts.[64] But ultimately, for Kierkegaard, Hegel strove to understand Socrates' morality too positively, both by trying to interpret the content of the good for Socrates, and by trying to show where Socrates' arrived at the good:

> The real difficulty with Hegel's view of Socrates is centered in the continual attempt to show how Socrates interpreted the good, and what is even more wrong in the view, as I see it, is that it does not accurately adhere to the direction of the trend in Socrates' life. The movement in Socrates is toward arriving at the good. His significance in the world development is to arrive there (not to have arrived there at some time). His significance for his contemporaries is that they arrived there. Now, this does not mean that he arrived there almost toward the end of his life, but that his life was a continual arriving at the good and having others arrive at this....The same with the true.[65]

Kierkegaard also criticizes Hegel for ignoring the weight Socrates put on his divine mission.[66] This faith enabled Socrates to erase his ego, and in humbling himself to his divine mission, to become a "world-historical" individual.[67] Finally, the irony Hegel attributed to Socrates was "a controlled element,"[68] whereas Kierkegaard thinks this is characteristic of modern irony.[69] For Kierkegaard, Socratic irony is "absolute, infinite negativity," which in the person of Socrates "was entirely negative" in relation to the established order, and rather than appear as "a mastered element in discourse...finally sweeps Socrates away with it."[70]

Despite the criticisms and corrections of Hegel's view of Socrates, Kierkegaard was caught up in the Hegelian project of rendering Socratic irony a necessary moment in the world-historical evolution of spirit. Had Kierkegaard not been such an Hegelian fool, heir to Plato's speculative idealism, he might have abandoned this part of his thesis and heeded a little more closely the empirical stolidity of Xenophon's reporting.

---

63 *SKS* 1, 268 / *CI*, 225.
64 *SKS* 1, 274–5 / *CI*, 232–3.
65 *SKS* 1, 276–7 / *CI*, 235–6.
66 *SKS* 1, 277 / *CI*, 236.
67 *SKS* 1, 277 / *CI*, 236–7.
68 *SKS* 1, 278 / *CI*, 237.
69 *SKS* 1, 353–7 / *CI*, 325–9.
70 *SKS* 1, 262 / *CI*, 217–18.

Bibliography

I. Xenophon's Works in The Auction Catalogue *of Kierkegaard's Library*

Xenophontis Opera graece et latine ex recensione Edvardi Wells accedunt dissertationes et notae virorum doctorum cura Caroli Aug. Thieme cum praefatione Io. Aug. Ernesti, vols. 1–4, Leipzig: Gleditsch 1801–04 (*ASKB* 1207–1210).

Xenophontis Memorabilium Socratis dictorum Libri IV. Editio minor, ed. by F.A. Bornemann, Leipzig: Hahn 1829 (*ASKB* 1211).

Xenophons sämmtliche Schriften, vols. 1–6, trans. by August Christian Borheck, Lemgo: Meyer 1778–1808 (*ASKB* 1212–1213).

Ξενοφῶντος Ἀπομνημονευμάτων βιβλία τέσσαρα = *Commentarii Dictorvm Factorvmqve Socratis Ad Defendvm Evm Scripti A Xenophonte Libris IV. Cvm Apologia Socratis Eidem Avctori Vvlgo Adscripta. Ex Fide Librorvm Editorvm Sriptorvmqve Et Virorvm Doctorvm Coniectvris Annotationibvsqve Tertivm Recensvit Et Interpretatvs Est Io. Gottlob Schneider*, ed. by Johannes Gottlob Schneider, Leipzig: Hahn 1816 (*ASKB* A I 196).

II. Works by Modern Sources in The Auction Catalogue *of Kierkegaard's Library that Discuss Xenophon*

[Hegel, Georg Wilhelm Friedrich], *Georg Wilhelm Friedrich Hegel's Vorlesungen über die Aesthetik*, vols. 1–3, ed. by von Heinrich Gustav Hotho, Berlin: Verlag von Duncker und Humblot 1835–38 (vols. 10.1–10.3 in *Georg Wilhelm Friedrich Hegel's Werke. Vollständige Ausgabe*, vols. 1–18, ed. by Philipp Marheineke et al., Berlin: Duncker und Humblot 1832–45), vol. 1, p. 355; vol. 2, p. 377; vol. 3, p. 257 (*ASKB* 1384–1386).

Meiners, Christoph, "Xenophon," in his *Geschichte des Ursprungs, Fortgangs und Verfalls der Wissenschaften in Griechenland und Rom*, vols. 1–2, Lemgo: Meyer 1781–82, vol. 2, pp. 622–36 (*ASKB* 1406–1406a).

— *Geschichte des Luxus der Athenienser von den ältesten Zeiten an bis auf den Tod Philipps von Makedonien*, Lemgo: Meyer 1782 (*ASKB* 661).

Petersen, Frederik Christian, *Haandbog i den græske Litteraturhistorie*, Copenhagen: Fr. Brummer 1830, p. 135; p. 164; p. 184; p. 209; p. 217 (*ASKB* 1037).

Sibbern, Frederik Christian, *Om Forholdet imellem Sjæl og Legeme, saavel i Almindelighed som i phrenologisk, pathognomonisk, physiogonomisk og ethisk Henseende i Særdeleshed*, Copenhagen: Paa Forfatterens eget Forlag 1849, p. 470; pp. 476–7 (*ASKB* 781).

[Sulzer, Johann Georg], *Johann Georg Sulzers vermischte philosophische Schriften. Aus den Jahrbüchern der Akademie der Wissenschaften zu Berlin gesammelt*, vols. 1–2, Leipzig: Weidmann 1773–81, vol. 1, p. 131 (*ASKB* 807–808).

Sulzer, Johann Georg, *Allgemeine Theorie der Schönen Künste, in einzeln, nach alphabetischer Ordnung der Kunstwörter auf einander folgenden, Artikeln abgehandelt*, vols. 1–4 and a register volume, 2nd revised ed., Leipzig: Weidmann 1792–99, vol. 1, p. 370; p. 391; p. 459; p. 507; p. 517; vol. 2, p. 305; p. 407; vol. 3, p. 285 (*ASKB* 1365–1369).

III. Secondary Literature on Kierkegaard's Relation to Xenophon

Hadot, Pierre, "The Figure of Socrates," in *Philosophy as a Way of Life*, ed. by Arnold I. Davidson, trans. by Michael Chase, Oxford: Blackwell 1995, pp. 147–78.

Himmelstrup, Jens, *Søren Kierkegaards Opfattelse af Sokrates. En Studie i dansk Filosofis Historie*, Copenhagen: Arnold Busck 1924, pp. 271–4.

Holm, Søren, *Græciteten*, Copenhagen: Munksgaard 1964 (*Søren Kierkegaard Selskabets Populære Skrifter*, vol. 11), p. 100.

Kloeden, Wolfdietrich von, "Sokrates," in *Kierkegaard's Classical Inspiration*, ed. by Niels Thulstrup and Marie Mikulová Thulstrup, Copenhagen: C.A. Reitzel 1985 (*Bibliotheca Kierkegaardiana*, vol. 14), pp. 104–81.

Mesnard, Pierre, *Le Vrai Visage de Kierkegaard*, Paris: Beauchesne et ses fils 1948, p. 8; pp. 120–2; p. 136; p. 138; p. 140; p. 143, note 1; p. 144, note 1; p. 148.

Nagley, Winifred, "Kierkegaard's Early and Later View of Socratic Irony," *Thought*, vol. 55, 1980, pp. 271–82.

Olesen, Tonny Aagaard, "Kierkegaard's Socratic Hermeneutic," in *The Concept of Irony*, ed. by Robert L. Perkins, Macon, Georgia: Mercer University Press 2001 (*International Kierkegaard Commentary*, vol. 2), pp. 101–22.

Rubenstein, Mary-Jane, "Kierkegaard's Socrates. A Venture in Evolutionary Theory," *Modern Theology*, vol. 17, 2001, pp. 442–73.

Sarf, Harold, "Reflections on Kierkegaard's Socrates," *Journal of the History of Ideas*, vol. 4, no. 2, 1983, pp. 255–76.

Scopetea, Sophia, *Kierkegaard og Græciteten: en kamp med ironi*, Copenhagen: C.A. Reitzel 1995, p. 17, note 48; p. 41, note 11; pp. 108–9; p. 117; pp. 119–20; p. 133, note 84; p. 347, note 48; p. 464.

Ziolkowski, Eric, "From *Clouds* to *Corsair*: Kierkegaard, Aristophanes, and the Problem of Socrates," in *The Concept of Irony*, ed. by Robert L. Perkins, Macon, Georgia: Mercer University Press 2001 (*International Kierkegaard Commentary*, vol. 2), pp. 193–233.

PART III

Later Interpretations of Socrates

Kierkegaard's Socrates Sources

Eighteenth- and Nineteenth-Century Danish Scholarship

Tonny Aagaard Olesen

> "A human being, who, in his 25th year, understood Socrates as well as I did."[1]
>
> "As a man is, so is his Christ-image."[2]

The old saying that the history of philosophy "consists of a series of footnotes to Plato,"[3] could perhaps be corrected somewhat since Plato himself was a devoted disciple of the well-known *scurra Atticus*,[4] or as Kierkegaard liked to call him *that great ironist*. Therefore, one should probably rather regard the philosophical tradition as a series of footnotes to Socrates—who never wrote anything. Kierkegaard would certainly regard the matter in this way since if he was a passionate reader of Plato, it was nonetheless Socrates whom he sought in Plato's dialogues.

Many scholars have noted Kierkegaard's profound affinity—to use another title—with *that simple wise man*. Kierkegaard constantly reminds us of him. As early as the first newspaper article from 1834 we find the ironic remark that Socrates' wife, Xanthippe, still stands "as a pattern of feminine eloquence and as founder of a school that has lasted to this very day, whereas Socrates' school has long since disappeared."[5] And in the final—posthumously published—issue of *The Moment* from 1855 Kierkegaard confesses that Socrates is his sole human measuring rod and that his task "is a Socratic task," namely, "to audit the definition of what it is to be a Christian."[6] It is easy to understand why Kierkegaard is often called "the

---

1 *SKS* 23, 455, NB20:118.

2 *SKS* 23, 482, NB20:165 / *JP* 1, 355.

3 Cf. Alfred North Whitehead, *Process and Reality: An Essay in Cosmology*, New York: The Free Press 1979, p. 39.

4 Cicero, *De Natura Deorum*, I, 93.

5 Cf. Kierkegaard, "Another Defense of Woman's Great Abilities" (December 17, 1834), printed in Teddy Petersen's *Kierkegaard's polemiske debut. Artikler 1834–36 i historisk sammenhæng*, Odense: Odense Universitetsforlag 1977, p. 17 / *EPW*, 3.

6 *SKS* 13, 405 / *M*, 341. Cf. Paul Muench, "Kierkegaard's Socratic Point of View," in *Kierkegaardiana*, vol. 24, 2007, pp. 132–62.

Danish Socrates," "the Socrates of the North," "the modern Socrates," or even "the Christian Socrates."[7]

The ever growing literature on Kierkegaard's Socrates testifies to the fact that this is a central theme. Although Kierkegaard was so good at Greek that he could directly read the surviving sources, his conception of Socrates did not come to him directly from heaven. It is to a large degree stamped by the historical-hermeneutical situation that he found himself in, that is, by the German research. Almost in a class of its own with respect to importance stands Hegel's philosophical Socrates, followed then by an important influence or inspiration from the historical-critical Plato research with central figures such as Friedrich Schleiermacher, Friedrich Ast and Johann Gottfried Stallbaum, along with partial inspiration from Ferdinand Christian Baur and Heinrich Theodor Rötscher, and quite possibly with a broader, more indeterminate undercurrent from Johann Georg Hamann.[8] Finally, one finds in this a group a number of important sparring partners, who are continually introduced into the discussions in Kierkegaard's dissertation, *The Concept of Irony*.[9] Kierkegaard's Socrates is simply unthinkable without this German literature.

The task that I have here undertaken consists in presenting an overview of the *Danish* sources of Kierkegaard's picture of Socrates, or at least, the Danish context for Kierkegaard's Socrates. From a general perspective, this is a somewhat strange task since the sources, as noted—and according to time-honored tradition—are for the most part German. For this reason no one has previously wasted their precious time by making a systematic investigation of the possible Danish influences on Kierkegaard. But is this not a sin of omission? It is certainly now well known that there are not many authors who are so interwoven with their local contemporary age as Kierkegaard. This is precisely the situation that is noted now and again when scholars quote the ceremonial words Danish professor of literature, Paul V. Rubow (1896–1976): "One cannot hold Kierkegaard and Copenhagen cultural life from 1830–50 close enough to each other. The great poets and thinkers cannot be separated from their city, their contemporary age and their language."[10] Let us begin by making a series of necessary demarcations in the material. The first restriction: a complete investigation of the Danish Socrates reception would begin in the eighteenth century, when Socrates was treated as the moral ideal of humanity, a human hero in line

---

7 See, for example, Lars O. Lundgren, *Socratesbilden. Från Aristofanes till Nietzsche*, Stockholm: Almqvist & Wiksell International 1978 (*Stockholm Studies in History of Literature*, vol. 20), p. 146; Vilhelm Andersen, "Søren Kierkegaard," in *Tider og Typer af dansk Aands Historie*, vols. 1–4, Copenhagen: Gyldendal 1907–16, vol. 2, pp. see 65–108, see pp. 67–8; Ferdinand Wagener, *Die romantische und die dialektische Ironie*, Arnsberg, Westphalen: J. Stahl 1931, p. 61; Hermann Diem, "Sokrates in Dänemark," in *Schweizer Monatshefter*, 1955–56, pp. 422–31; Thorsten Bohlin, *Sören Kierkegaards etiska Åskådning med särskild hänsyn till begreppet 'den enskilde'*, Stockholm: Svenska Kyrkans Diakonistyrelses Bokförlag 1918, pp. 52–71, see p. 71; Raymond L. Weiss, "Kierkegaard's 'Return' to Socrates," in *The New Scholasticism*, vol. 45, 1972, pp. 573–83. There are many other examples.

8 See Harald Steffes' article in this tome.

9 See the bibliography in *SKS* K1, 377–83.

10 Paul V. Rubow, *Kierkegaard og hans Samtidige*, Copenhagen: Gyldendal 1950, p. 10.

with the naturalized Jesus. Although the different images of the German Socrates of this period have long since been the object of several weighty monographs,[11] this theme in the Danish literature has still not been treated. The Danish conception of Socrates in this period built two great monuments, namely, Ludvig Holberg's (1684–1754) popular Socrates (1739),[12] which Kierkegaard unfortunately probably did not know,[13] and Jens Bloch's scholarly Socrates (1792),[14] which Kierkegaard criticizes in his dissertation more than a half century later.[15] Everything that is found between Holberg and Bloch—no one named, no one forgotten—is in the context of Kierkegaard merely a historical curiosity.[16] One can now say that if Kierkegaard's polemic against Xenophon's Socrates is legendary for its idealist sarcasm, then he is not more mildly disposed toward the Socrates literature of the eighteenth century. Kierkegaard is supposed to have been occupied with his Greek hero in the robes in which he appears in Xenophon's account: "Surely everyone perceives the unreasonableness of going so far back."[17] The Socrates of ideality (and the idea), which Kierkegaard cultivates, arises first with Romanticism, indeed, originally with the conflict with Romanticism. For this reason it does not make sense to look for positive sources of Kierkegaard's conception of Socrates in the eighteenth century. We will therefore pass over this material.

The second restriction: Since we are interested in the genesis of Kierkegaard's Socrates and not in its reception, we will omit bringing up to date and correcting the presentation of Kierkegaard's influence on the Danish Socrates tradition (1855–2009), which Himmelstrup began.[18] It is clear that it is in this tradition—of course

---

11 See, for example, Benno Böhn, *Socrates im achtzehnten Jahrhundert. Studien zum Werdegange des modernen Persönlichkeitsbewußtseins*, Neumünster: Karl Wachholtz Verlag, 2nd ed. 1966 [1928].

12 Holberg's portrayal of Socrates from *Adskillige Store Heltes og berømmelige Mænds, sær Orientalske og Indianske sammenlignede Historier og Bedrifter efter Plutarchi Maade*, Copenhagen: Høpffner 1739, is included in the scholarly standard edition, *Ludvig Holbergs Samlede Skrifter*, vols. 1–18, ed. by Carl S. Petersen, Copenhagen: Gyldendal 1913–63, vol. 11, pp. 451–500.

13 Although Holberg's Socrates is unique in its treatment of irony (see also Holberg, epistle no. 58 about Socrates' irony (1748), in *Epistler*, edited with commentaries by F.J. Billeskov Jansen, Copenhagen: H. Hagerup, vols. 1–8, 1944–54, vol. 1, p. 247–51), there is no evidence that Kierkegaard knew it. *For this reason* we can omit a treatment of Holberg, but *not* due to the anachronistic reason which Himmelstrup mentions, namely, that Holberg's Socrates is unscholarly! See Jens Himmelstrup, *Søren Kierkegaards Opfattelse af Sokrates. En Studie i dansk Filosofis Historie*, Copenhagen: Arnold Busck 1924, p. 316.

14 See *Xenophon's Sokratiske Merkværdigheder*, trans. by J. Bloch, Copenhagen: Hofbogtrykker R. Møller & Søn 1792 (2nd ed., 1802); Preface, pp. 5–12; Socrates biography, pp. 12–72; *Memorabilia*, pp. 73–381). We will later return to Bloch and his Socrates.

15 See, for example, *SKS* 1, 208 / *CI*, 157–8.

16 I can say this with certainty in the investigation that is in progress and is waiting to be published.

17 Kierkegaard, *Om Begrebet Ironi*, *SKS* 1, 263 / *CI*, 219.

18 Jens Himmelstrup, *Søren Kierkegaards Opfattelse af Sokrates* (Copenhagen: Arnold Busck 1924), pp. 314–30. This tradition stems from Hans Brøchner's *Bidrag til Opfattelse af Filosofiens historiske Udvikling* (Copenhagen: P.G. Philipsen 1869, pp. 201–15), Harald

also in the constantly growing international tradition[19]—that one finds the detailed discussion of Kierkegaard's presuppositions and results, which, so to speak, with retroactive power cast light on Kierkegaard's Socrates. This reception would be an investigation on its own.

The third restriction: Kierkegaard's conception of Socrates came about for the most part in the period leading up to the dissertation, that is, in the 1830s. This means that in the present investigation we will not explore whether in the period after the dissertation there were new Danish influences on Kierkegaard's later, apparently somewhat modified Socrates. We will likewise not unfold the entire contemporary reception of *The Concept of Irony*, or Kierkegaard's possible influence on it. With this last restriction, the period from 1841 to 1855 is placed in parentheses.

Once we lighten the load by omitting the aforementioned kinds of studies, it remains to investigate the Danish Socrates literature in the period from 1825 to 1840. One can say that there are three main paths through this reception, which, taken strictly, make a demand for closer investigation. The first of these perspectives could be called *the Socrates of philology*. What is interesting here is the appropriation of the Greek world, which is, so to speak, a presupposition for the more detailed investigation of the historical Socrates. It is the beginning of—one could almost say—— the *research on Socrates' life*, which places the focus on the sources of Socrates. Then there is the *Socrates of philosophy*, which is occupied with the content of Socrates' doctrine without any concern for the historical-philological problems. Finally, there is what one could call *the literary Socrates*, which is the entirety of antiquity translated into fictional literature, for example, in drama.

The Danish Socrates reception can be regarded as exhausted by these three perspectives. The main weight in what follows will, however, be placed on the *Socrates of philology* since it is directly connected to Kierkegaard's first appropriation of Socrates; because it is precisely this appropriation that gives Kierkegaard the dialectical tools to free himself from Hegel's influential Socrates; and finally, since this work has not been done before. The main task is thus to investigate all of the material which is connected to the historical-philological Socrates, in so far as he

---

Høffding's Habilitationschrift (*Den antike Opfattelse af Menneskets Villie*, Copenhagen: C.W. Stinck 1870, pp. 16–48), along with the very significant Habilitationschrift, Troels (Frederik) Troels-Lund, *Om Socrates's Lære og Personlighed* (Copenhagen: trykt i Bianco Lunos Bogtrykkeri 1871) to the two Kierkegaard editors, J.L. Heiberg, *Socrates' Udvikling* (Copenhagen: Tillge's Boghandel 1913), and A.B. Drachmann, *Atheisme i det antike Hedenskab* (Copenhagen: Gads Forlag 1919). Himmelstrup remarks: "From Brøchner to Heiberg and Drachmann Kierkegaard's influence is unmistakeable in the Danish Socrates literature," p. 329.

19 Jens Himmelstrup notes correctly in 1924 (*Søren Kierkegaards Opfattelse af Sokrates*, p. 314), that Kierkegaard's influence on the conception of Socrates did not extend beyond the country's borders; only in 1929 did the two German translations appear in Munich, with which the international reception began. When Albert William Levi wrote "The Idea of Socrates: The Philosophic Hero in the Nineteenth Century" (*Journal of the History of Ideas*, vol. 17, 1956, pp. 89–108), he knew only Kierkegaard's Socrates from the *Postscript*. Only with Lee M. Capel's English translation from 1966 did the now quite extensive Anglophone reception begin.

appears in Danish dress. In the conclusion, I will, however, attempt to cast a glance at the philosophical and the literary Socrates, along with the debates which were connected to them in the Danish context.

I. The Socrates of Philology

When Kierkegaard, in the first part of *The Concept of Irony*, undertakes his "combined reckoning"[20] in order to discover the historical Socrates, then, as is well known, this happens by him examining the accounts presented by Xenophon, Plato, and Aristophanes and taking into account their respective personalities. It is in this hermeneutical dialectic that Kierkegaard becomes more of a philologist than a philosopher. It is here that he with his finely tuned ears listens, so that the texts open up in a way that undermines Hegel's and philosophy's—from a historical perspective—aetherial perspective. Today no one would try to approach the historical Socrates without such a "combined reckoning," although it would typically happen on another foundation and with other conclusions than in Kierkegaard. However, prior to Kierkegaard no one had, through a close-reading and empathetic psychology, so consistently traced the sources back to the concrete individual of the author. It is in general Kierkegaard's great merit in the first chapter of his treatise—but not in the others—to have demonstrated how philology can never be reduced to being a maidservant of philosophy. It must be added here that the view for the dialectical detail and the poetic demand of the contemporary age, which led Kierkegaard to take up these philological disputes, was not so much directed against the ancient texts in themselves but rather against the ideas and the existing thinkers he found in and behind the texts.[21]

It is worth noticing that Kierkegaard for the most part keeps to the trilogy of Socrates sources: Xenophon, Plato, and Aristophanes. Kierkegaard only operates with contemporary witnesses, who each in their own way had to misunderstand Socrates in his historical appearance. Thus already due to methodological reasons—the situation of contemporaneity—he cannot make use of Aristotle,[22] who would otherwise play a certain role in Socrates research. He is likewise not tempted to use the later ancient literature (for example, Plutarch or Cicero), not even the colorful

---

[20] *SKS* 1, 74 / *CI*, 12.

[21] For this reason the philological professor of philosophy, Karsten Friis Johansen, in the article "Platon og Kierkegaard," also made this confession: "It is possible with philology's ballast and expertise to attack the interpreter Kierkegaard on many fronts, but the deepest layers in his interpretation contain a glimmer of a congeniality that very few philologists possess," *Studenterkredsen*, May 1968, nos. 1–2, p. 11.

[22] See also Himmelstrup's organization of chapter VI, 2 in *Søren Kierkegaards Opfattelse af Sokrates*, pp. 266–94, where first Aristotle is discussed, after which follow the three sections Xenophon (pp. 271–4), Plato (pp. 274–90) and Aristophanes (pp. 290–4). Kierkegaard himself stated that he had not even read Aristotle at the time that he wrote his dissertation. Cf. *SKS* 18, 231, JJ:288 / *KJN* 2, 212.

material in Diogenes Laertius receives much space. Kierkegaard has enough in his three witnesses: they constitute a kind of an analogy with the first three gospels.[23]

In addition, there comes the special order of the three sources, which is more conceptual or ideal than chronological. Xenophon, whose bourgeois limitation prevents him from capturing Socrates, is the immediate moment most lacking in spirit. Xenophon is the age of Enlightenment, and Kierkegaard's hymnic irritation with Xenophon constitutes a parallel with Friedrich Schlegel's (1772–1829) criticism of the low-ceilinged bougeoisie, the constricted morality: "In God's name, let it break to pieces."[24] Xenophon is enlightenment, but Plato is the absolute, passion, the storming of heaven, the ideas, in short: Romanticism. But where Xenophon's weapon aims too low, Plato shoots over the target. If Xenophon is finitude, and if Plato is infinity, then Aristophanes becomes the unity of these conflicting moments. Thus, conceptually, it was Plato's merit to bring Socrates up to the firmament of heaven, while it was the task of the comic writer again to bring Socrates from heaven down to the ground. If Plato represents the great tragic feeling of life, if he expresses Romanticism, then Aristophanes represents the subsequent dissolution. After the tragic there follows the comic, after Romanticism there follows what some people in the age called *the modern*, whose main representative is Hegel. One can perhaps say coarsely that where Friedrich Schlegel and especially Schleiermacher designate the transition from Xenophon to Plato, there Hegel and perhaps especially Rötscher designate the transition from Plato to Aristophanes.

Let now these interwoven trilogies designate the method's ideal horizon, whose historical implementation in Danish literature will be the subject of the present article. Before we look more closely at the Danish account of Socrates through the main sources Xenophon, Plato, and Aristophanes, we must first mention the new humanism, which Kierkegaard met in his years at the school and at the university in the form of his various instructors. This milieu certainly played its role in the fact that "Kierkegaard was, if anyone in Danish literature, the apprentice of the Greeks."[25]

A. The Greek World and Philology: From Borgerdyd School to the University

Kierkegaard grew up in a unique period in Danish culture, where the classical fields were cultivated as never before—and never since. As early as his time at the Borgerdyd School (1821–30) Kierkegaard was nurtured with an impressive amount of reading of Latin and Greek literature. In the highest class he had Greek and Latin daily for six days a week.[26] There was a significant amount of reading,

23 See *Om Begrebet Ironi*, in *SKS* 1, 76–7 / *CI*, 14–15.

24 *SKS* 1, 322 / *CI*, 288.

25 Povl Johs. Jensen, "Madvig som filolog," in *Johan Nicolai Madvig. Et Mindeskrift*, vols. 1–2, Copenhagen: Munksgaard 1955–63, vol. 2, p. 186.

26 See the scheme of the school curriculum in Per Krarup, *Søren Kierkegaard og Borgerdydskolen*, Copenhagen: Gyldendal 1977, p. 25. After a preparatory course, one continued with the eighth class level, which then counted downward as follows: VI., V., IV., III., II.B, II.A, I.B and finally I.A. One began to receive instruction in Greek in the IVth class, that is, at the age of 12, when one began with Lange's grammar; in the final two Ist classes, the students read Xenophon and then Plato.

which represented rote learning in Greek, where not only Homer and Herodotus were to be learned but also Plato's dialogues and Xenophon's *Memorabilia.*[27] The students translated Plato's Greek into Latin, but to prevent Socrates from entirely disappearing in the grammatical rigors, they also translated into Danish. It is in the period of Kierkegaard's youth, from age 8 to 17, that Socrates was introduced into his life.

As is clear from the reading that he submitted to be tested on,[28] Kierkegaard had read Xenophon's Socratic main work in Greek, that is, *all* four books of the *Memorabilia.*[29] This study gave the young student a good knowledge of Socrates. Also listed are two shorter dialogues by Plato. The first is the popular dialogue *Euthyphro*, which undeniably contains Kierkegaardian themes, not least of all the so-called "dilemma of Euthyphro,"[30] but which Kierkegaard does not really make use of in the authorship later on. The second is the even more popular *Crito*, which Kierkegaard later—according to the Kierkegaard scholar Jens Himmelstrup—consciously avoided in his dissertation since it contains an example of Socratic positivity, which does not support the absolute, infinite irony that Kierkegaard argues for.[31]

The list of readings that Kierkegaard submitted to be tested on does not exclude the possibility that he had read other texts by Plato in the school. On the contrary, the two chosen dialogues seem precisely to cry out for an explanation since the *Euthyphro* is certainly a kind of introduction to, while the *Crito* is a kind of conclusion to the *Apology.* Kierkegaard, like every other schoolboy would have had to have read this central dialogue, which later became the focal point in his conception of

---

27 See Krarup, *Søren Kierkegaard og Borgerdydskolen*, p. 27: "In Greek the number of pages the students had to submit for the examination was quite significant....The amount of Homer is quite impressive, in all 8 books of the *Odyssey*, 7 of the *Iliad*, altogether almost 10,000 lines of verse of around 300 pages. In prose they had 2 books of Herodotus, two shorter Platonic dialogues and Xenophon's *Memorabilia*, altogether around 330 pages. To this amount the Gospel of John must also be added."

28 This is printed in *B&A*, vol. 1, p. 4, / *LD*, Document V, p. 5.

29 At the school Kierkegaard presumably used F.A. Bornemann's outstanding edition *Xenophontis Memorabilium Socratis dictorum Libri IV. Editio minor*, Leipzig: Hahn 1829, Leipzig: sumtibus librariae Hahnianae 1829 (*ASKB* 1211), the text of which seems to be in agreement with the quotations from the dissertation. However, if it is true that Kierkegaard's copy survives, it is, however, without any markings. Cf. *Fund og Forskning*, 1966, p. 167.

30 See David Wisdo, "Kierkegaard and Euthyphro," *Philosophy*, vol. 62, 1987, pp. 221–6, and David Bloch, "Kierkegaard og Euthyphrons Dilemma," *Aigis*, vol. 7, no. 1, 2001, pp. 1–8.

31 See Himmelstrup, *Søren Kierkegaards Opfattelse af Sokrates*, p. 276: "What is most odd with Kierkegaard's choice is the negative, that the *Crito* is not included. It is now a time-honored custom with respect to the historical Socrates to mention the *Crito* in the same breath as the *Apology* or in any case to claim that dialogue's close connection with the *Apology*. But it is characteristic of Kierkegaard's conception of Socrates, that the *Crito* did not express the most negligible contribution to this. It would, however, also illuminate Kierkegaard's conception of Socrates' relation to the existing order in a way that was embarrassing for Kierkegaard." See note 187.

Socrates.[32] In *The Concept of Irony*, he also confesses his profound agreement with Friedrich Ast, who had reached the conclusion that the *Apology* was not written by Plato himself. Kierkegaard writes in a note:

> I recall from my early youth, when the soul demands the lofty, the paradigmatical, how when reading the *Apology* I felt disappointed, deceived, and depressed because it seemed to me that all the poetical, the courage that triumphs over death, was here wretchedly replaced by a rather prosaic reckoning executed in such a way that one could believe that Socrates wanted to say: When all is said and done, this whole affair doesn't concern me much at all. Later I learned to understand it otherwise.[33]

Kierkegaard, with reference to his "first youth" must have been thinking back to his encounter with Socrates at Borgerdyd School. It is clear that it was not Socrates *the ironist* whom he found.

We do not know with certainty who gave Kierkegaard instruction in Greek during his six years at the school.[34] In his last year at the school Kierkegaard had as his instructor the unforgettable professor Michael Nielsen (1776–1846), who in posterity has had a dubious reputation.[35] From 1811 to 1844 he was the school's authoritarian rector. He doubtlessly went through Plato with the students with great care. One of Kierkegaard's classmates later explained that if the school still had its textbooks, then one would very probably find Kierkegaard's written notes in them from Nielsen's lectures.[36] One can probably call Nielsen a kind of midwife in the Greek spirit, which in those years was born in Kierkegaard, but it was undeniably a maieutic that was based on fear and trembling.[37]

---

32 Per Krarup guesses in *Søren Kierkegaard og Borgerdydskolen*, p. 75, that Kierkegaard's school edition is the one that appears in the Auction Catalogue, see *Platonis Eutyphro Apologia. Socratis Crito Phaedo Graece*, ed. by Johann Friderich Fischer, Leipzig: Sumtu Engelh. Beni. Suicquerta Librarii 1783 (*ASKB* A I 181).

33 *SKS* 1, 139, note / *CI*, 81, note.

34 See Holger Lund's presentation of the school and its instructors in *Borgerdydsskolen i Kjøbenhavn 1787–1887. Et Mindeskrift i Anledning af Skolens Hundredaarsfest*, Copenhagen: Otto B. Wroblewskys Forlag 1887. See also Per Krarup, *Søren Kierkegaard og Borgerdydskolen*, Copenhagen: Gyldendal 1977, as well as Peter Tudvad, "Borgerdydskolen i København," in *Kierkegaards København*, 2nd ed., Copenhagen: Politikens forlag 2005, pp. 168–74.

35 See Lund, pp. 152–3, where Kierkegaard's dedications in the books he gave as gifts to Michael Nielsen are printed with the fixed predicate "unforgettable." Further, Lund sought throughout in his work to address the prejudice that Nielsen was a cramped tyrant.

36 See Frederik Welding's recollection in Bruce H. Kirmmse, *Søren Kierkegaard truffet*, Copenhagen: C.A. Reitzel 1996, p. 25. (English translation: *Encounters with Kierkegaard*, 3rd printing, Princeton, New Jersey: Princeton University Press 1998, p. 9.) Glimpses of Nielsen's Greek instruction (as recalled by Martin Attrup) are found in Kirmmse, *Søren Kierkegaard truffet*, pp. 28–9 (*Encounters with Kierkegaard*, pp. 11–12).

37 Cf. Steen Johansen's question in "Michael Nielsen," in *Kierkegaard's Teachers*, ed. by Niels Thulstrup and Marie Mikulová Thulstrup, Copenhagen: C.A. Reitzel 1982 (*Bibliotheca Kierkegaardiana*, vol. 10), p. 13: "Was the older Nielsen a kind of Socrates to the younger Kierkegaard?" Jørgen Henrik Lorck (1810–95) gave a portrayal of the situation of the Borgerdyd School at the time in the article "Fra mit Skoleliv for 50 Aar siden," in

We know that Kierkegaard's elder brother, Peter Christian Kierkegaard (1805–88), was responsible for the Greek instruction for the fourth class level, that is, in the school year 1826–27. Further, we know that Kierkegaard presumably also had been under the influence of the philologist Frederik Olaus Lange (1798–1862), called "the Greek,"[38] who in 1826 published a very popular Greek grammar.[39] When Lange in the year 1828–29 traveled abroad in order (in vain) to be cured of an eye ailment which almost made him blind, Kierkegaard tried to keep him informed about things.[40] It is also possible that for a short period Kierkegaard received instruction in Greek from the equally significant philologist, Christian Frederik Ingerslev (1803–68), who later became known for his many dictionaries.[41]

The most important instructor, with respect to Kierkegaard's study of Greek, was, however, Ernst Bojesen (1803–64), who worked as a highly valued teacher of Greek and Latin in the period from 1821 to 1840.[42] Bojesen wrote several books and treatises on different themes of antiquity, where his favorite Greek author was Aristotle.[43] In the fall of 1841 Kierkegaard sent a copy of his dissertation to Bojesen,[44]

Illustreret Tidende, no. 953, 1877, pp. 144–8. He he writes about Nielsen: "His entire external appearance was frightening for the boys; his large, wide head with the serious features, the big staring eyes, his powerful and stocky body, which was always dressed in a brown suit, the polished boots with dangling tassel, the tight beige trousers, his entire firm and determined appearance, his coarse address—all this was intended to make a strong impact on the boys, who shook and trembled, when he looked at them," p. 144, column 3.

38 See Edvard J. Anger's recollections in Kirmmse, *Søren Kierkegaard truffet*, p. 26. (*Encounters with Kierkegaard*, pp. 9–10.)

39 Frederik Lange, *Det Græske Sprogs Grammatik til Skolens Brug*, 3rd ed., Copenhagen: Gyldendal 1835 (*ASKB* 992).

40 See Kierkegaard's letter to P.C. Kierkegaard from March 25, 1829, in *B&A*, vol. 1, p. 31 / *LD*, Letter 2, p. 40. Krarup thinks that Lange had a great significance for Kierkegaard, Cf. *Søren Kierkegaard og Borgerdydskole*, pp. 66–7.

41 See *Af Søren Kierkegaard's efterladte Papirer*, vols. 1–8, Copenhagen: C.A. Reitzel 1869–81, vol. 1, p. XLI, where H.P. Barfod lists Ingerslev as an instructor.

42 Lorck, who was two years ahead of Kierkegaard, wrote in his memoirs about the instructors: "The most capable of them all was without doubt Ernst Bojesen....He read Greek with us in such a way that we not only learned what we were supposed to learn, but that we learned it such that we could not forget it again," Lorck, "Fra mit Skoleliv for 50 Aar siden," p. 145, column 2. Lorck continues by noting with regret that rector Nielsen had the unfortunate idea of wanting to give instruction in Greek to the final class since he could not match up to Bojesen.

43 See Ernst Bojesen's autobiography in *Nogle Ord til Afsked ved min Afgang fra Sorø Akademis Rektorat* (= *Indbydelsesskrift til den aarlige Hovedexamen i Sorø Akademis Skole i Juli 1863*), Sorø: [Sorø Akademi] 1863, pp. 6–7, where he lists a dozen treatises on Aristotle, among others his Habilitation, *De Problematis Aristotelis*, Copenhagen: Bianco Luno & Schneider 1836 (*ASKB* 1078) and *Aristoteles's Statslære*, Parts 1–2, Copenhagen: J.C. Scharling 1851–52 (*ASKB* 1090).

44 See Kierkegaard's accompanying letter in *B&A*, vol. 1, pp. 70–1 / *LD*, Letter 48, p. 89. It sounds like the book is a gift of gratitude to a former Greek teacher. One would think that Bojesen would have sent Kierkegaard his recently published popular schoolbook, *Haandbog i de græske Antiquiteter*, Copenhagen: C.A. Reitzel 1841 [3rd printing 1861], which won out over L. Schaaf, *Haandbog i de græske og romerske Antiqviteter*, trans. by F.E. Hundrup,

who was delighted to see his former student's more profound concentration,[45] and who many years later in return published an account of Kierkegaard's observations on irony.[46] It is certainly clear that Bojesen, who was perhaps even the person who had led Kierkegaard through Xenophon's *Memorabilia*, could not accept Kierkegaard's radical Socrates or his massacre of Xenophon's judgments of Socrates.[47] Without doubt at the school Kierkegaard had teachers who showed him the way to Socrates.

Copenhagen: Fr. Brummers Forlag 1833 (*ASKB* 1038). Bojesen's Greek handbook was translated into several languages, but, strangely enough, it was not found in Kierkegaard's book collection at his death. Bojesen likewise does not mention Socrates a single time in his presentation of the Greek institutions and customs.

45 See Bojesen's letter to Madvig in Carl Weltzer, "Endnu lidt om Søren Kierkegaard's Disputats," *Kirkehistoriske Samlinger*, 6th series, VI, 1948–50, pp. 512–13. Bojesen asks Madvig to thank Kierkegaard for sending his dissertation, which he has read "with great interest," and he was glad that Kierkegaard "had made a quite serious study of the material for the work." Bojesen, who—as Weltzer remarks—also himself "contributed to giving Kierkegaard his view of the Greeks" (ibid.), however, also adds this criticism: "But when one is reading, it certainly seems rousing, but seldom convincing; it leaves many doubts and objections unanswered or answered in an unsatisfying manner; in general it lacks calm, clarity, self-control and all artistic rounding off" (ibid.).

46 See Ernst Bojesen, *Forstudier til en Afhandling om den æsthetiske Idees Udvikling hos Grækerne i videnskabelig Retning (Indbydelsesskrift til den aarlige Hovedexamen i Sorø Akademis Skole i Juli 1862)*, Sorø: [Sorø Akademi] 1862, pp. 115–20, where the concept of irony is presented. In an introductory note one reads: "Concerning irony S. Kjerkegaard, in the second part of his master's thesis *The Concept of Irony*, has said very fittingly and sharply much that is used in the following," p. 115. After this there follows what seems to be a free paraphrase of Kierkegaard's definitions of concepts in the second part of the thesis. One can wonder why "the Greek" that Bojesen does not mention is Kierkegaard's Socrates, which would have been obvious. In his obituary for Bojesen, Madvig writes that he had "a certain irony which could be offensive if one was not used to it, but which on the whole was good-natured," *Illustreret Tidende*, no. 275, January 1, 1865, p. 113, column 1.

47 In the treatise *Bidrag til Fortolkningen af Aristoteles's Bøger om Staten. Anden Deel (= Indbydelsesskrift til Examen artium og den aarlige Hovedexamen i Sorøe Academies Skole i Juli 1845*), Copenhagen: Trykt hos J.C. Scharling 1845, pp. 41–2, Bojesen attacks a misuse of Xenophon, with which he certainly must have Kierkegaard in mind. He notes that, according to Aristotle, but also Plato, every area of proficiency must be cultivated with moderation, since everything, including knowledge, is determined precisely by its limitation. When one, he continues, "in general properly puts oneself into the ancient perspective and its consequences, one will perhaps be less inclined to make fun of Xenophon and ascribe to him an absolute and individual narrow-mindedness, when he in his *Mem. Socr.* IV, 7, has Socrates set narrow and merely practical limits for the degree to which the different sciences such as geometry, astronomy, etc., should be taught since he notes that a profession and detailed study of these sciences could take an entire human life and stand in the way of an appropriation of many other useful abilities. Morever, Xenophon already with the remark which he makes here in two places, namely, that Socrates himself was, however, not without a more profound study of these sciences or that he in his life had come beyond the limitation of his theory, seems to have protected himself against a charge of absolute narrow-mindedness being grounded in this kind of passage," p. 42. See *Om Begrebet Ironi*, *SKS* 1, 85 / *CI*, 23, where Kierkegaard by bringing in Plato, mocks this passage in Xenophon.

At the university in fall semester 1830 Kierkegaard met the first of the three professors who throughout his years as a university student constituted the country's greatest competence in the classical languages. He was Frederik Christian Petersen, 44 years old, then the best authority in the most recent German Socrates literature, although today as good as forgotten. And there was Petersen's student, the independent Johan Nicolai Madvig, only 26 years of age, but already well on his way to being one of the age's greatest classical philologists, especially with respect to textual criticism. Finally—in Kierkegaard's fourth semester—the famous 50 year-old P.O. Brøndsted came home to Copenhagen in order to take part in the Greek instruction. These three very different kinds of researchers were responsible for classicial studies during the entire decade that Kierkegaard was enrolled at the university: Petersen and Brøndsted took care of Greek, while Madvig was responsible for Latin.[48] As a result, it was also these three overburdened professors who in 1841 were on Kierkegaard's dissertation committee.[49]

Let us begin with Frederik Christian Petersen (1786–1859), who, according to Madvig in his memoirs, "was not a particularly sharp or independent philologist."[50] Posterity has also had the same opinion,[51] if indeed it had any opinion at all about Petersen. Madvig, by contrast, ascribes to him a great familiarity with the more recent German philology.[52] Petersen was perhaps not a pioneering individual, as his two colleagues were, but as a translator, scholar, editor, instructor, and critic he was *essentially* someone who conveyed ideas of others. This activity alone as a "literary observer" has, as Ivan Boserup remarked, "assured F.C. Petersen a place in Danish literary history."[53] With this quality, it was him and not his two ingenious colleagues who were the natural communicator and debater of the emergent Plato philology.

---

48 Petersen first occupied a temporary professorship (1818–27), after which he took over—and maintained (1827–59)—the *Lehrstuhl* for Greek after Niels Schow (1813–27), who again took this over from Georg Sverdrup (1803–13), while Madvig from 1826 occupied the *Lehrstuhl* in Latin, which in 1849 was expanded also to include Greek language and literature. Brøndsted occupied a professorship (1813–42), which followed him. See Ejvind Slottved, *Lærestole og lærer ved Københavns Universitet 1537–1977*, Copenhagen: Samfundet for dansk Genealogi og Personalhistorie 1978, p. 142; p. 154 and p. 164.

49 Therefore they have also been introduced in an Anglophone context. Cf. Bruce H. Kirmmse, "Socrates in the Fast Lane: Kierkegaard's *The Concept of Irony* on the University's *Velocifère*. Documents, Context, Commentary, and Interpretation," in *The Concept of Irony*, ed. by Robert L. Perkins, Macon, Georgia: Mercer University Press 2001 (*International Kierkegaard Commentary*, vol. 2), pp. 17–99.

50 Johan Nikolaj Madvig, *Livserindringer*, Copenhagen: Gyldendal 1887, p. 82.

51 See, for example, the description in Kirmmse, "Socrates in the Fast Lane," p. 49.

52 This was the same thing that Madvig said in his obituary for Petersen, when he wrote: "Petersen was not an ingenious scholar but an especially industrious and careful scholar, and he did not neglect familiarizing himself with any work which appeared in the field that he had especially chosen, Greek literature, antiquities and mythology," *Tidsskrift for Philologie og Pædagogik*, vol. 1, Copenhagen: Otto Schwartz 1860, pp. 281–2, see p. 281.

53 Ivan Boserup, "Klassisk Filologi efter 1800," in Svend Ellehøj, Leif Grane, Kai Hørby, Ditlef Tamm, and Eivind Slottved, *Københavns Universitet 1479–1979*, vols. 1–14, Copenhagen: G.E.C. Gads Forlag 1979–2006, vol. 8, *Det filosofiske Fakultet 1. Del*, by Povl Johannes Jensen and Leif Grane (1992), pp. 301–8, see p. 302.

It has been claimed that Petersen was not competent to evaluate Kierkegaard's dissertation.[54] My thesis in the following is just the opposite, namely, that he was probably the most competent.

Already at the age of 25 Petersen had in 1811 published a section of his translation of Plato's *Republic*,[55] but it was, however, not him—as we will see later—who came to translate this work in its entirety. The *Republic* was Petersen's favourite work; later, in 1854, he published a treatise on this great work by Plato.[56] However, none of Petersen's many Latin or Danish[57] treatises gives a treatment of Socrates, or even Plato, for what he expressed in this respect appeared—as we shall see—in his important reviews of the literature on Socrates.

Through the 1820s the professors at the Danish university had to do something about the miserable situation with regard to the lack of updated textbooks. Thus, it was Petersen's lot to work out two such textbooks, which were later much used and even translated into German. The one was an overview of the study of archeology, which Petersen especially gave instruction in during the time that Brøndsted was away on his journey.[58] The other textbook, *Haandbog i den græske Litteraturhistorie* or *Handbook in Greek Literary History*, is a work that Petersen had already laid the foundation for as soon as he had been made professor.[59] The first version of the handbook, which contains about the first half of the final version of the work, appeared in 1826,[60] but it soon had competition from a translation of Johann Joachim

---

54 See Carl Weltzer, "Omkring Søren Kierkegaard's Disputats," in *Kirkehistoriske Samlinger*, 6th series, vol. 6, Copenhagen: Gad 1948–50, pp. 284–311, see p. 295.

55 See "Fragment af Plato's Bøger over Statsforfatningen (Libr. VII, cap. 1–2). Socrates og Adeimantos," published in K.L. Rahbek's journal *Sandsigeren eller den danske Huusven*, nos. 29–30, August 28, 1811, pp. 457–63. The translation is without any introduction or apparatus.

56 F.C. Petersen, "Platons Forestillinger om Staternes Oprindelse, Statsforfatninger og Statsbestyrelse," *Indbydelsesskrift til Kjøbenhavns Universitets Fest i Anledning af Hans Majestæt Kongens Fødselsdag den 6te October 1854*, Copenhagen: trykt i det Schultziske Officin [1854], pp. 1–85 (*ASKB* 1171). Petersen includes everywhere the most recent philological literature, especially K.F. Hermann, but neither Socrates nor Kierkegaard is mentioned.

57 Of the shorter Danish treatises, one can mention the work *Om den aristoteliske Poetik*, Copenhagen: [Det skandinaviske Litteraturselskab], trykt hos Andreas Seidelin 1819, as well as, from a later time, *Om Epheterne og deres Dikasterier i Athen*, Copenhagen: [Det kgl. Videnskabernes Selskab] 1847 (*ASKB* 720), which Petersen bought back from Kierkegaard's book collection after the latter's death.

58 F.C. Petersen, *Almindelig Indledning til Archæologiens Studium*, Copenhagen: Gyldendal 1825; here one finds, among other things, an extensive biography of "Kunsthistoriens Heros," Johannes Winckelmann (pp. 204–274). The book was translated into German as *Allgemeine Einleitung in das Studium der Archäologie*, trans. by Pet. Friedrichsen, Leipzig: Hahn 1829.

59 He had printed in *Athene, et Maanedsskrift*, ed. by Christian Molbech, vol. 3, 1814, December, pp. 541–58, a preliminary work under the title, "Indledning til Forelæsninger over den græske og romerske Oldtids Litteratur."

60 F.C. Petersen, *Haandbog i den græske Litteraturhistorie. Første Afdeling*, Copenhagen: [Fr. Brummer] 1826.

Eschenburg's (1743–1820) somewhat outdated classic.[61] From the preface of both works it is clear that, on the one hand, there was simply lacking a work of this kind in the Danish literature and, on the other hand, the two simultaneously had worked to rectify this situation. Petersen's complete edition was, in 1830, ready to receive the new brood of students, and one of them was Kierkegaard.[62] Finally, in 1834, Petersen's work received an upgrading in the form of a German translation,[63] which of course was also known in Copenhagen. If one places the three editions beside each other, one notices how, for example, the literature on Socrates—which we will return to—constantly grows.

Petersen's Greek handbook functioned as a reference resource to the lectures, so that the professor did not need to be bothered with giving the exact references, discussing secondary literature, etc. In 471 numbered sections or paragraphs, the book ran through the Greek literature from Solon's laws to the Turk's conquest of Constantinople (1453) in all its various forms and genres. It is a kind of literary encyclopedia, or more correctly, a skeleten of one, which is constituted by brief desciptions of the authorships or notes about diverse cases followed by often extensive bibliographical information.[64] With regard to Socrates, the three versions are more or less in agreement that the central description is as follows:

> Without constructing any system, he sought by means of his own method, which is called by his name, the Socratic method, to guide others to the qualities that he himself possessed: self-knowledge, self-control, and in general a way of thinking and acting grounded in clear insight, which is designated by the term καλοκἀγαθία.[65]

The ideal of character that Socrates expresses here, this unity of the beautiful and the good, often somewhat incompletely translated as "gentleman" or "knight," seems more to represent Xenophon's Socrates than the Socrates whom we meet in Plato and Aristophanes. To be sure, one can well call the Socrates who gives an account of his divine mission in Plato's *Apology*, a highly righteous citizen, but the integrity, which is his deepest driving force, seems, however, in its consistency to come into conflict with his virtue as a citizen.

---

61 See [Johann Joachim Eschenburg, 1743–1820]: *Joh. Joach. Eschenburgs Haandbog i den klassiske Litteratur*, trans. by H.E. Wolf based on the 7th German edition [1st ed. 1783], vols. 1–2, Copenhagen: J.H. Schubothe 1828–29.

62 F.C. Petersen, *Haandbog i den græske Litteraturhistorie*, Copenhagen: Fr. Brummer 1830 (*ASKB* 1037).

63 F.C. Petersen, *Handbuch der griechischen Litteraturgeschichte. Mit einem Vorworte von August Matthiä*, Hamburg: Hoffmann und Campe 1834.

64 Most people who have read Petersen's handbook have been struck by how in one place an absolutely insignificant work can be included, while in another place an absolutely important work can be omitted. This was noted by contemporary reviews, as it was by Ivan Boserup in "Klassisk Filologi efter 1800," p. 304, note 145, which contains the most recent presentation of Petersen's accomplishments.

65 See Petersen, *Haandbog i den græske Litteraturhistorie* (1830), § 146, p. 182. Cf. also his *Haandbog i den græske Litteraturhistorie. Første Afdeling* (1826), § 143 and *Handbuch der griechischen Litteraturgeschichte* (1834), § 146.

In his first semester at the university, that is, winter semester 1830, Kierkegaard attended Petersen's lectures on Greek literature three times a week. With Petersen's handbook and all its literature, thus the year 1830 marks the point of departure for Kierkegaard's later studies of Socrates. Kierkegaard also participated three times a week in Petersen's lectures on Aeschylus' tragedy *The Eumenides*.[66] It is not known to what extent Kierkegaard continued to attend Petersen's lecture through the 1830s, since the few people who have investigated the lists of auditors seem primarily to focus on Kierkegaard's participation in theological and philosophical lectures. Petersen taught primarily Homer and Hesiod, often with reference to Greek mythology, then the Greek tragic writers, especially his favorite Aeschylus; further during a few semesters he taught the comedy of Aristophanes (always *The Wasps*) along with the lyric authors, with Pindar as his favorite.[67] Although Petersen is the one whose teaching repertoire comes the closest to the Socratic literature, it can nevertheless seem striking that one never meets Xenophon or Plato here. It is possible that Petersen used these texts in the courses where the students practiced free translation, although these, especially when Madvig was present, quickly turned into lessons on problems of grammar and syntax.[68] There are thus some indications that when we speak of the university's instructional repertoire, classical philology, represented by Petersen left Socrates to the philosophers, who had enough to attend to as it was.[69]

From Petersen's official evaluation in connection with Kierkegaard's treatise, *On the Concept of Irony*, it is clear that he was well familiar with Kierkegaard's polemical personality.[70] It would indeed be obvious that he knew Kierkegaard from the lectures, but they could also have met, for example, at Regensen College, where Kierkegaard often came and where Petersen was provost.[71] We do not know whether it was a familiarity with the master sophist Kierkegaard, which brought Petersen

---

66 See Tudvad, *Kierkegaards København*, p. 175.

67 A study of the university lectures through the 1830s shows that Petersen never lectured on Socrates. What is most interesting from the perspective of Kierkegaard's dissertation are his private lectures in 1834–35 on Aristophanes' *The Wasps*, "with an introduction to the history of Greek comedy," given for 11 auditors. Cf. *Akademiske Tidender*, ed. by Hannibal Peter Selmer, Copenhagen: Gyldendal 1835, p. 150. The course continued in the next semester with only 4 auditors, ibid., p. 465. Then it was repeated in the semester 1837–38 for "149, and later 118, auditors." Cf. *Kjøbenhavns Universitets Aarbog for 1838*, ed. by Hannibal Peter Selmer, Copenhagen: Gyldendal 1838, p. 86. In the semester 1836–37 he repeated his lectures on Greek literary history for 19 and 14 auditors respectively. Cf. *Kjøbenhavns Universitets Aarbog for 1837*, ed. by Hannibal Peter Selmer, Copenhagen: Gyldendal 1837, p. 80.

68 See Madvig, *Livserindringer*, p. 82.

69 Socrates likewise does not appear among the prize essays written through the 1830s—either in the philological or in the philosophical sections.

70 *SKS* K1, 136.

71 See Svend Aage Nielsen, *Kierkegaard og Regensen*, Copenhagen: Graabrødre Torv's Forlag 1965, where the relation between Petersen and Kierkegaard is treated, pp. 22–5. Since Kierkegaard's name is not found either in Petersen's diaries or in the Regensen provost's archive (see p. 25), Nielsen cannot add anything to the little that that we already know about Kierkegaard's relation to Petersen.

only to be an *ex auditorio* opponent at Kierkegaard's oral defense. One might well assume that the scant yield that he received from his first quick reading[72] was deepened by a more thorough reading before the defense took place. Unfortunately we do not know Petersen's evaluation of the content of the treatise; in his report he says almost nothing about this. On the whole, it is noteworthy that Petersen, who, if anyone, had the possibility of giving a review of Kierkegaard's Socrates, failed to do so. We know that the two met in subsequent years and that Kierkegaard sent Petersen at least two of his books, for which Petersen thanked him in writing, since he did not find Kierkegaard when he called on him at home.[73]

The next professor of philology whom Kierkegaard met was Johan Nicolai Madvig (1804–86), since Kierkegaard in his first semester attended Madvig's lectures on Cicero's *De finibus bonorum et malorum*, along with his lectures on Roman literary history.[74] Madvig, who was not uninterested in Greek, had to keep to Latin until Petersen died in 1859, after which Madvig took over the *Lehrstuhl* in Greek and began to do work on the Greek terrain, including Plato.[75] There are two points which make Madvig interesting in relation to Kierkegaard's occupation with Socrates. The one is that Kierkegaard himself had declared that he regarded Madvig as one of the age's three greatest men—he represented the university in its scholarly ideality.[76] When in the *Concluding Unscientific Postscript* reference is made to "the teacher of classical learning,"[77] then it is presumably Madvig, and not Petersen, to whom he refers. The other is that Madvig in his evaluation remarks that he has already read large parts of Kierkegaard's treatise.[78] This thus implies that

72 See *SKS* K136 and 142.

73 See *B&A*, vol. 1, p. 181 / *LD*, Letter 162, p. 228 and *B&A*, vol. 1, p. 253 / *LD*, Letter 234, p. 322.

74 According to Tudvad, who in *Kierkegaards København*, pp. 175–6, calculates the actual and possible lectures that Kierkegaard could have attended through the 1830s, he went only to Madvig's—and also to Petersen's—lectures in the first semester, which seems almost unthinkable!

75 The result of Madvig's treatment of Plato was not philosophical theories but textual emendations, for example, to the *Protagoras* or the *Philebus*, Cf. *Tidskrift for Philologi og Pædagogik*, Copenhagen: Otto Schwartz 1860, pp. 31ff.; pp. 40–1.

76 See the article, not used by Kierkegaard, from 1849–50 with the title: "Adskilligt foranlediget ved Prof. Nielsens 'undersøgende Anmeldelse' af Joh. Climacus." (*Pap.* X–6 B 116, p. 151 (cf. *Pap.* X–6 B 114, p. 147 / *CUP2*, 158–9): "The course of my authorship was described before in that article 'Public Confession,' which came out when I was through with the manuscript for *Either/Or*. I wanted to have no earthly reward as author, and therefore it was my desire that when the few years in which I could be an author were over, everything in literature should stand unchanged: Heiberg—Mynster—Madvig." Heiberg drops out, but the other two remain: "Madvig stands unchanged" (ibid.).

77 *SKS* 7, 564 / *CUP1*, 622.

78 Madvig writes in connection with the evaluation of *The Concept of Irony*: "With respect to the dissertation itself (a large portion of which I am already familiar with)..." See *SKS* K1, 134. (English translation: Kirmmse, "Socrates in the Fast Lane," p. 24.) Further Madvig reveals that he knows Kierkegaard's personality and preference for a lower level of style, and that Kierkegaard would not be open to negotiate this point! See *SKS* K1 135. (Kirmmse, "Socrates in the Fast Lane," p. 24.) Sibbern wanted to have Madvig be one of the

Kierkegaard stood in a closer relation to Madvig, since why would he otherwise have let the *Latin* professor read through a treatise which was only the third one in Denmark not to be written in Latin since it was deemed that the material was not suitable for the Latin language?

Kierkegaard knew Madvig from the circle surrounding Johan Ludvig Heiberg.[79] Just as Heiberg conceived of himself in the sphere of literary criticism, so also Madvig conceived of himself as a scholar. He was not a humanist who found ideals and models in ancient literature. In him the humanist piety was replaced by a critical distance and sober overview.[80] He was Denmark's first genuine professional philologist.[81] On this score, Madvig stood in direct opposition to Kierkegaard, who always had a relation to the ancient authors of someone learning and appropriating.[82] Also with what concerns disciplinary interests, Madvig seems to stand at a distance from Kierkegaard.[83] To be sure, Madvig had previously had interests in Plato, but it was the side of Plato which lay furthest away from Kierkegaard, namely, Plato's *The Laws*.

In Madvig's lifelong interest in ancient constitutions and legal systems, one can find a ground for comparison, a *tertium comparationis*, between the two, namely, in the treatise *A Glance at Constitutions of Antiquity with Respect to the Development of the Monarchy and a Comprehensive State Organism.*[84] This work is strongly

official opponents, since he is the one "who is most familiar with the dissertation." See *SKS* K1, 141. (Kirmmse, "Socrates in the Fast Lane," p. 31.) But Madvig succeeded in excusing himself: "Because the dissertation...in respect to its philological aspects is focused so much on Plato, Aristophanes, and Xenophon, my gentlemen colleagues are certainly those most suited to be official opponents." See *SKS* K1, 142. (Kirmmse, "Socrates in the Fast Lane," p. 33.) One can wonder why Madvig did not make any contribution at all—during the oral defense as was the case with H.L. Martensen who also knew the treatise ahead of time.

79 Cf. Boserup, "Klassisk Filologi efter 1800," p. 325: "For many years Madvig was a guest in the Heiberg home, just as the Heibergs often came to Professor Petersen's home. People have wanted to make Madvig into a Heibergian and even to a Hegelian, but the material that points in a Hegelian *rapsus* is hardly entirely unambiguous. Madvig was a theoretical mind, and he loved and excelled in abstract and complicated definitions."

80 See Madvig's specialist manifestos, for example, in the review of the Danish translation of Eschenburg's handbook in classical literature, where the scholarly progress from Heyne to Wolff to Boeckh is summarized (*Maanedsskrift for Litteratur*, vol. 3, 1830, pp. 99–112) along with the friendly, but overbearing criticism of Petersen's handbook on Greek literature (*Maanedsskrift for Litteratur*, vol. 6, 1831, pp. 171–86).

81 See Povl Johs. Jensen, *Cum grano salis. Udvalgte foredrag og artikler 1945–1980*, Copenhagen: Odense Universitetsforlag 1981, pp. 25–6.

82 Ibid., p. 28.

83 A presentation of Madvig's philological views is found in Brigitte Seidensticker Hauger, *Johan Nicolai Madvig (1810–1886): The Language Theory of a Classical Philologist, Investigated within the Framework of 19th-Century Linguistics*, Ann Arbor Michigan: UMI 1992.

84 *Blik paa Oldtidens Statsforfatninger med Hensyn til Udviklingen af Monarchiet og en omfattende Statsorganisme*, printed as *Indbydelsesskrift til Universitetsfesten den 6te Juli 1840 i Anledning af Deres Majestæters Kong Christian den Ottendes og Dronning Caroline Amalias Salving og Kroning*, Copenhagen: [University of Copenhagen] 1840. This program

influenced by Hegel, but on a number of points it also criticizes Hegel, discussing, among other things, Hegel's conception of the Greek world:

> With this observation of how the Greek democracy was formed and with its own one-sidedness was led to its own destruction, we would, even if *Hegel* had not reminded us of it with strong claims, hardly have been able to overlook how the development of Greek thought as drive to and capability for reasoning interfered in the course of the life of the state. Without doubt the liberated and developed reasoning and the incipient philosophizing partly with direct testing shook the circle of representations to which the earlier Greeks with conviction surrendered themselves and which corresponded to the existing arrangements: even more was the given particular interest a tool in a shrewd dialectic, whereby it could indirectly use and misrepresent those representations and make itself strong. But history allows neither in the appearance of thought and reasons to see an opposition to the previous genuine Greek life, which can be designated as its downfall, nor to agree with Hegel's determination and judgment of the point, on which it will show itself from this side. The political movement hastened ahead of the skeptical negative reasoning which cleared the way for Attic philosophy in which the Greek striving to liberate the subject from its most inward side came to break through, after the one-sidedness of the political development had virtually run its course.[85]

It is entirely correct, as has been noted,[86] that Kierkegaard's presentation, indeed, his entire conception of Socrates operates on the terrain which Madvig here sketches. But who is to say that Madvig is not under the influence of Kierkegaard? Even if Madvig's treatise appeared a year before Kierkegaard submitted his dissertation, we know nothing of when Kierkegaard wrote his dissertation, let alone when Madvig read a large part of it. If Kierkegaard had written the first part of his treatise *after* the publication of Madvig's treatise, then it seems extremely odd that his scholarly hero in classical studies is not so much as mentioned! And not least of all, when Madvig criticizes precisely the decisive point in Hegel which also Kierkegaard's world-historical Socrates rests on! By the same token, if Madvig had read Kierkegaard's presentation of Socrates, then it would be clearly understandable that he would have reservations with respect to the philosophical conception of the Greek world. Further, it would be understandable why Madvig would feel the desire to add a long, interesting note to the passage quoted above.[87]

---

was, moreover, the first university program written in Danish! It was, however, translated into German by F.H.W. Sarauw in *Archiv für Geschichte, Statistik, Kunde der Verwaltung und Landesrechte der Herzogthümer Schleswig, Holstein und Lauenburg*, vols. 1–5, ed. by N. Falck, Kiel: Schwers'sche Buchhandlung 1842–47, vol. 1, pp. 12–51.

85 Madvig, *Blik paa Oldtidens Statsforfatninger*, p. 10.

86 See Jensen, "Madvig som filolog," pp. 156–7. This outstanding treatise is translated as *J.N. Madvig. Avec une esquisse de l'histoire de la philologie classique au Danemark, trad. du danois par André Nicolet*, Odense: Odense University Press 1981, pp. 223ff.

87 Since Jon Stewart has translated most of the note in his section "Madvig's *A Glance at Constitutions of Antiquity*," in *A History of Hegelianism in Golden Age Denmark*, Tome II: *The Martensen Period: 1837–1842*, Copenhagen: C.A. Reitzel 2007 (*Danish Golden Age Studies*, vol. 3), pp. 454–67, we will keep to what is most important with regard to the relation to Kierkegaard.

Madvig wants to dwell on "Hegel's observation of the age of Socrates."[88] Hegel sees the downfall of the Greek world "arising as 'the inwardness becoming free for itself'..., where 'inwardness and subjectivity' are presented in thinking, represented by Socrates."[89] Against this, Madvig objects that the Greek world, "the Greek principle of life," does not fall into ruin due to reflection, *because* reflection itself—already ahead of time—is "a so integrated and characteristic side in the Greek life that when it is removed, this life loses its content."[90] Madvig likewise does not believe in Hegel's claim about the Greek substantiality or the moral determination of the Greeks' "*unbefangene Sittlichkeit*."[91] He does not think that what is "characteristically Greek" should be sought in an unreflective immediacy, since reflection is something characteristic of the Greeks. Further, "it was not first with Socrates that thought in its free inwardness collided with the state."[92]

Where Madvig as historian wants to go around the back of Hegel in order to elucidate the world-historical turning point which Hegel designates with Socrates, in a series of less evolutionary movements, Kierkegaard, by contrast, seems to sharpen the fracture between the ancient Greek spirit and Socrates in his own radical manner. Of course, the Sophists preceded Socrates, but with Socrates, according to Hegel and Kierkegaard, something new and decisive happened, which Madvig seems to deny. The question is whether Madvig and Kierkegaard were familiar with the breach that opened up here between their respective views of Socrates. Did Kierkegaard read Madvig's treatise, after which he went to him with his dissertation, in order to get him to read it? Or did Madvig, while he was writing his treatise, read Kierkegaard, which then occasioned the long, dismissive note? There was no one else in Denmark besides Madvig who at the time discussed Socrates' world-historical transition. Madvig seems to stand miles away from both Hegel and Kierkegaard.[93]

The last professor of philosophy whom Kierkegaard met at the university was, so to speak, a kind of archeological Odysseus who had returned home. Peter Oluf Brøndsted (1780–1842) was educated in the Greek spirit by the well-regarded philologist Oluf Worm (1757–1830)[94] and was later known for his unusal knowledge of Greek and his completely Greek disposition.[95] He appropriated all the new

88 Madvig, *Blik paa Oldtidens Statsforfatninger*, p. 24.

89 Ibid.

90 Ibid.

91 Ibid. Cf. *SKS* 1, 212 / *CI*, 162–3, where Kierkegaard virtually tries to outdo Hegel.

92 Ibid.

93 Madvig did not accept "Hegel's entire manner of placing the active moments in the life of a people, separated in sharp oppositions, in individual points of history and the choice of certain categories to designate the character of a people or an age" (ibid.), in part because they lacked the determinateness and content, and in part because they were not historically correct.

94 See, for example, the young Brøndsted's article—dedicated to Worm—about the influential annotations to Plato that were made by David Ruhnken (1723–98), in G.G. Bredow (ed.) *Epistolae Parisienses*, Leipzig: Libraria Weidmannia 1812, pp. 125–52.

95 See Vilhelm Andersen's inspired portrait of Brøndsted in *Tider og Typer af dansk Aands Historie*, vol. 2, pp. 134–64, which seems to build further on J.P. Mynster's biography, Cf. below.

philological movements which came from Germany, and not least of all Friedrich August Wolf (1759–1824), who virtually annexed Plato into modern philology, had great significance for Brøndsted. In 1818 he translated F.A. Wolf's stimulating encyclopedia from 1807.[96] He became professor in philology with a specialization in Greek in 1813—the same year as Sibbern assumed the *Lehrstuhl* in philosophy. Brøndsted's special interests, which in his youth also included Plato,[97] changed with time since he became one of the founders of archeological fieldwork.[98] Famous throughout Europe, Brøndsted found himself more and more on journeys and in the field, rather than at a desk or behind the lecturn in Copenhagen.[99] Only in November 1832—in Kierkegaard's fourth semester—did Brøndsted return home to take up the life of a professor, although in the following years he continued to take shorter journeys. Brøndsted does not seem, however, to have given lectures on the Socratic writings,[100] but he was the incarnation of the well-traveled neohumanist, in such stark contrast to his two colleagues.

Brøndsted is the one who seemed most enthusiastic about Kierkgaard's treatise, although he—almost against his own will—only had it in hand for a day: "I feel a great inclination to read the whole of it with studied attention."[101] He presumably had the time for further study of it since he drew the short straw—and thus had to appear as one of the two regularly appointed opponents at Kierkegaard's oral defense. He died nine months later at the age of 61, when he fell from his horse during a daily ride. Unfortunately he left behind no testimony about Kierkegaard.

This concludes the account about the philological side of the Greek world at school and at university, which surrounded the young Kierkegaard. About Kierkegaard's Socrates it has been said: "Never since antiquity has Socrates been brought forth with all the life and all the livliness that belongs to him."[102] This is

---

96 See *F.A. Wolfs Encyclopædiske Oversigt af Oldtids-Videnskabens samtlige Lærefag. Til Brug ved akademiske Forelæsninger*, Copenhagen: Andreas Seidelin 1818. (In German as "Darstellung der Alterthums-Wissenschaft," in *Museum der Alterthums-Wissenschaft*, ed. by F.A. Wolf and Ph. Buttmann, vol. 1, 1807 (Berlin), pp. 1–145.)

97 He wrote Platonic dialogues in his youth, gave courses on Plato at the university, and in the libraries in Paris he hunted for Plato scholia.

98 See *Peter Oluf Brøndsted. A Danish Classicist in his European Context*, ed. by Bodil Bundgaard Rasmussen, Jørgen Steen Jensen, Jørn Lund, and Michael Märcher, Copenhagen: The Royal Danish Academy of Sciences and Letters 2008.

99 Brøndsted's main work was his travel diaries, which Kierkegaard immediately bought when it appeared posthumously, *P.O. Brøndsted's Reise i Grækenland i Aarene 1810–1813*, vols. 1–2, ed. by N.V. Dorph, Copenhagen: Samfundet til den danske Literaturs Fremme 1844 (*ASKB* 2034–2035). (This book contains an outstanding biography of Brøndsted, written by J.P. Mynster, see pp. 1–86.)

100 Since Brøndsted's favorite Greek authors were the same as F.C. Petersen's, namely, Pindar and Aeschylus, and sometimes the other tragedians, he had to give up his domain to the older Brøndsted, who even translated *The Orestia*. Cf. P.O. Brøndsted, *Orestias.Trilogie af Æschylos, metrisk oversat*, ed. by N.V. Dorph, Copenhagen: Samfundet til den danske Litteraturs Fremme 1844 (*ASKB* 1049).

101 See *SKS* K1, 136. (Kirmmse, "Socrates in the Fast Lane," p. 25.)

102 Povl Johs. Jensen, *Cum grano salis. Udvalgte foredrag og artikler 1945–1980*, Odense: Odense universitetsforlag 1981, p. 29.

probably true, but this does not seem to be something that he took over from his teachers of philology. Kierkegaard's inward relation to Greek literature is unique. As he said with his thoughts turned toward modern philosophy: "the Greeks remain my consolation."[103]

B. Xenophon

Kierkegaard's Romantic attack on Xenophon is legendary. He dismisses him "with an extraordinary contempt."[104] The Socrates whom Kierkegaard finds in Xenophon is not the world-historical hero who lives and dies for an idea, but just the opposite: a spiritless *Spießburger*, a limited model of virtue, a completely innocuous utilitarist. It is customary to ascribe to Schleiermacher the honor of being the one who begins to doubt the value of Xenophon as a source, since he could not find in Xenophon's Socrates the reason for why the citizens of Athens condemned him to death.[105] This incipient subversion of Xenophon's dominance and authority is a milestone in Socrates reception: to be sure many people still held on firmly to Xenophon, but more and more began to take up a critical relation,[106] but only with Kierkegaard is Xenophon directly mocked as a second-rate author. It is with a demonic roguishness that Kierkegaard thus answers Schleiermacher's question in this way: "[I]f Xenophon's understanding of Socrates is correct, I believe that in sophisticated, inquisitive Athens people would rather have wanted Socrates done away with because he bored them than because they feared him."[107]

If one looks up § 117 in Petersen's *Handbook of Greek Literary History*, as Kierkegaard presumably did in 1830, then one already finds here the age's new insight: that Xenophon's conception of Socrates should be taken with caution:

> Not only in the philosophical (ethical) writings but also in the historical ones, Xenophon seeks everywhere to emphasize the practical-ethical, as he imaged it following the Socratic doctrine, and strives everywhere to show that the practical life ought to be led in harmony with the author of the doctrine of ethics. With this goal he recounts the events, portrays the characters and communicates the sum of his philosophy of life in descriptions of Socrates' personality and in reports about his ethical doctrine and manner of instruction. Certainly it is appreciated from his writings that he is lacking the

---

103 *SKS* 18, 231, JJ:288 / *KJN* 2, 212.

104 See Himmelstrup, "Xenophon," in his *Søren Kierkegaards Opfattelse af Sokrates*, pp. 271–4, see p. 271.

105 See the article "Ueber den Werth des Socrates als Philosophen," in *Abhandlungen der philosophischen Klasse der Königlich-Preußischen Akademie der Wissenschaften aus den Jahren 1814–1815*, Berlin: In der Realschulbuchhandlung 1818, pp. 50–68.

106 See, for example, Barthold Georg Niebuhr's (1776–1831) violent attack on Xenophon as historian in the article "Ueber Xenophons Hellenika. 1826. Mit einer Nachschrift (1828)," in *Kleine historische und philologische Schriften. Erste Sammlung*, Bonn: Weber 1828, pp. 464–82, see especially pp. 470–1 and the dismayed Ferdinand Delbrück (1772–1848), who immediately made a reply in *Xenophon. Zur Rettung seiner durch B.G. Niebuhr gefährdeten Ehre*, Bonn: Adolph Marcus 1829. In Delbrück's *Socrates. Betrachtungen und Untersuchungen*, Cologne: Bachem 1819, Xenophon's presentation plays a central role.

107 See *SKS* 1, 80, note / *CI*, 18, note.

> determinate dominant individuality, which is the special characteristic of outstandingly remarkable spirits; but those among his writings whose authenticity is certain, testify to his understanding, experience, fairness and sense of justice.[108]

The remark that Xenophon lacks personality leads further to § 147, where it is explained that there is a conflict about to what extent Xenophon with respect to Socrates—in opposition to greater personalities such as Plato and Aristotle—"is in agreement with the truth or not."[109] Petersen gives examples of this literature,[110] but refrains from entering into the discussion.

Among Xenophon's writings there is, as is well known, a group of four which are designated as "the Socratic writings," in which a portrayal perhaps of the historical Socrates is given. These were presumably intended to be a single collected composition, but they are of course separate works. In *The Concept of Irony* Kierkegaard draws especially on the main work, the *Memorabilia*, and less so on the *Apology* and only a single time does he refer to the *Symposium*, but he also certainly knew the *Oikonomikos*. Kierkegaard owned Xenophon's writings both in Greek[111] and in German,[112] but all of the Socratic writings were available in Danish during Kierkegaard's lifetime.

The most important work, the *Memorabilia*, was translated in 1792 by the young scholar and later bishop Jens Bloch (ca. 1760–1830),[113] who was schooled by one of the pioneers of modern philology, Christian Gottlob. Heyne (1729–1812). This was a very careful translation, since Bloch, who had plans to establish a new *Grundtext*,[114] introduced variants from a number of medieval *codices* which he had collected from libraries from all over Europe. Although it was only the fourth time Xenophon had

108 See Petersen, *Haandbog i den græske Litteraturhistorie* (1830), p. 135.

109 Ibid., p. 184.

110 Most important are Schleiermacher's and Delbrück's contribution, which, have already been mentioned, along with an important article by Christian August Brandis (1790–1867), "Grundlinien der Lehre des Socrates," in *Rheinisches Museum für Jurisprudenz, Philologie, Geschichte und griechische Philosophie*, vol. 1, nos. 1–2, Bonn: Eduard Weber 1827, pp. 119–50, see especially pp. 122ff., which Kierkegaard also makes use of in his discussion.

111 *Xenophontis Opera graece et latine ex recensione Edvardi Wells accedunt dissertationes et notae virorum doctorum cura Caroli Aug. Thieme cum praefatione Io. Aug. Ernesti*, vols. 1–4, Leipzig: Gleditsch 1801–04 (*ASKB* 1207–1210).

112 *Xenophons sämmtliche Schriften*, vols. 1–6, trans. from Greek by August Christian Borheck, Lemgo: Meyer 1778–1808 (*ASKB* 1212–1213).

113 *Xenophons Sokratiske Merkværdigheder.*

114 The plan was never carried out, perhaps because Bloch's teacher, Professor Laurids Sahl (1734–1805), immediately thereafter published the fourth book anew. Cf. *Xenophontis memorabilium Socratis dictorum libri IV. Ex optimis recensionibus cum selectis variorum notis paucisque suis in usum prælectionum edidit Laurentius Sahl*, Hauniæ [Copenhagen]: n.p. 1792.

been translated into Danish,[115] Bloch's was nevertheless designated as "the best Danish translation of an ancient author that we have from the 18th century."[116]

Bloch's introductory biography is well written, careful and detailed, but while he industriously draws on the many ancient sources, he only introduces the more recent research literature to a limited degree. His Socrates is the Enlightenment's common Xenophonian image of the Greek hero.[117] He is the paradigmatic model citizen who sacrifices everything, including his life, in order to benefit his fellow citizens. The Sophists do not represent—as they did for the late Romantics—the age of Enlightenment, which Socrates was responding to. On the contrary, the Sophists "hindered the true Enlightenment and ethics"[118]—the true Enlightenment man is of course Socrates, although Socrates must have been lacking "the clearer light which was the more beautiful lot of the Christian person."[119]

Bloch's biography follows the classical scheme. First the portrayal of Socrates is as the great, unambiguous moral personality. Then some irregularities, some ambiguities in Socrates' character and behavior are cast out, which are the dark clouds on the horizon that warn of forthcoming events. Then follows Aristophanes, the accusations, the trial, the judgment, the stay in prison, the sublime death, and finally all of the accusors' misfortunes and thus Socrates' world-historical resurrection.

Concerning the irregularities, the three most important must be mentioned. The one is *irony*, which Bloch mentions several times, but without actually giving an account of it. It is mentioned in connection with the discussion of Socrates' method,[120] where it is designated as a dissimulation, a piece of acting: "with his characteristic irony and repeated questions he drew out the concepts and opinions

---

115 Professor Jakob Baden in his laudatory review draws attention to the fact that this is only the third translation of Xenophon into Danish: he himself was responsible for the first in 1766 [*Xenophons Cyropædie*], the second was done by Georg Sam. Hanefeldt in 1767 [*Xenophons Lov-Tale over Kong Agesilaus*]. Baden, however, overlooked the fact that Hans Gottschalch in fact translated *The Apology* in 1781, for which reason a start had already been made on the Socratic writings. See *Kiøbenhavns Universitets-Journal*, vol. 1, 1793, pp. 39–40. To this literature one can also count the portrayal of Socrates based on Xenophon, which was printed in Claus Fasting's *Provinzialblade*, vol. 3, nos. 19–20, 1780 (Bergen).

116 Svend Ellehøj et al., *Københavns Universitet 1479–1979*, vol. 8, *Det filosofiske Fakultet 1. Del*, p. 237. See also Jakob Baden, who in his review says that the translation comes from "a man, who from very beginning of his academic life as a youth has familiarized himself with skill in the Greek language and who had the advantage over his predecessors of a mother tongue cultivated to near perfection," Baden, *Kiøbenhavns Universitets-Journal*, p. 39, column 1.

117 Cf. Jensen in *Københavns Universitets Historie*, vol. 8, p. 237: "The image of Socrates that one finds here is almost that which is known from the German Enlightenment: Socrates as the great teacher of morals, a kind of Nathan der Weise, but the presentation is precisely documented from the ancient sources."

118 See *Xenophon's Sokratiske Merkværdigheder*, trans. by J. Bloch, p. 26.

119 Ibid., p. 41.

120 Here one reads, among other things, ibid., pp. 33–4: "Socrates was very industrious in learning his auditors' nature and manner of thinking; he always organized his speech according to each one's special constitution; he humiliated, for example, the conceited and prideful, by showing them their shortcomings and their contemptibleness—by contrast, he

of those with whom he spoke."[121] In another place an explanation is given of how on earth the Athenians could condemn a man such as Socrates to death. Bloch lists a number of causes, among others, that some people were envious, others, whose ignorance had been revealed were angry, while yet others were tired of Socrates' manner of speaking: "people regarded his irony as mockery and as a trap, in which he would capture his auditors and twist the truth."[122] In addition to this is the fact that Socrates' entire way of living "was just the opposite of the dominant rich taste,"[123] indeed people even regarded Socrates "as an odd, indifferent and inactive man, who did not participate in public life."[124] Bloch is here close to discovering irony as Socrates' standpoint, but this never really dawns on him. Irony remains mostly a Socratic manner of speaking, which appears several times in the textual notes, where a passage or an expression is explained with the standard formulation: "the Socratic language of irony."[125] He never gives any account of what precisely this "language of irony" consists of.

Another ticklish question concerns Socrates as a pederast. This is the accusation, says Kierkegaard, "that has not been allowed to die over the years, because in every generation there has been some research scholar who felt constrained to defend Socrates' honor on this matter."[126] Although Kierkegaard himself does not want to discuss the matter, it is clear enough that he understands talk of pederasty as "metaphorical," since there is only talk of intellectual love. If one cannot understand that there is talk of a "spiritual pederasty," says Kierkegaard with an allusion to Hamann,[127] then he can only refer the reader to the treatise from 1752 about Socrates as an unstained pederast by Johann Matthias Gesner (1691–1761).[128] As we have already seen, he could thus also have referred to Holberg, but he could also have referred to Bloch.[129] Whereas Kierkegaard thinks that precisely the spiritual understanding of pederasty supports the conception of Socrates as an ironist, Bloch,

---

stooped down to the weak and encouraged the shy and frightful to use the abilities, he himself failed to appreciate...."

121 See ibid., p. 34.

122 Ibid., p. 46.

123 Ibid., p. 47.

124 Ibid.

125 See, for example, ibid., p. 148; p. 182; pp. 280–1 and p. 296.

126 *SKS* 1, 238 / *CI*, 191.

127 That this is an allusion to Hamann, which unfortunately is not noted in the commentaries to *On the Concept of Irony* (*SKS* 1), is clear from journal entry FF:92 (1837), in *SKS* 18, 94 / *KJN* 2, 86.

128 Johann Matthias Gesner, "Socrates sanctus Pæderasta," in *Commentarii societatis regiæ scientiarum Gottingensis*, vol. 1–5, Göttingen: Vandenhoeck ca. 1751–ca. 1755 [also ca. 1771–ca. 1778], vol. 2, pp. 1–31.

129 See *Xenophon's Sokratiske Merkværdigheder*, trans. by J. Bloch, pp. 44–5, where the section on pederastry is introduced with the strange words: "Some more recent scholars have ascribed to Socrates a certain unnatural love, which at the time defiled the Greeks' customs; but no trace is found among the ancients that he ever was once accused for this vice, neither his accussors mention it, nor Aristophanes in his biting farce, *The Clouds*."

who incidentally brings Heyne's authority into the discussion,[130] thinks that what has given occasion to such charges was Socrates himself, namely, his "ironic language," which was often misunderstood.

A third aspect of the figure of Socrates, which we have already touched on, is the interpretation of his *daimon*. Socrates often speaks of this voice, says Bloch, and then he adds:

> it seems reasonable that he himself believed this and that this feeling was a premonition or a kind of *Schwämeri*, which had its ground in part in his lively imagination and delicate nervous system, and in part in the opinion that he was the favorite of the divinity and a tool to spread enlightenment and morality.

Kierkegaard introduces this attempt to explain or explain away Socrates' *genius* in his presentation of the problem, this *crux philologorum*, where he immediately—and certainly with justice[131]—brushes aside Bloch's Xenophonian rationalism.[132] Out with Bloch, and in with Ast, who with Plato explains the context of the situation.[133] Socrates' *daimonion* does not prescribe action (Xenophon), but only warns (Plato). Then out with Ast and in with Hegel, since the situation cannot be explained but conceived conceptually,[134] and thus also in with Rötscher and Aristophanes. The daimonic in Socrates is of course—according to the Hegel-inspired Kierkegaard—nothing but negativity.

One can say that where the three aspects, *irony*, *pederastry*, and the *daimon* always give occasion for the research to be obliged to take a position, then the long tradition also follows a certain fundamental scheme. From Aristophanes' satire one is, as a rule, sent to the accusation and the trial, and thus also in Bloch, who himself declares that he follows Xenophon here. After the judgment we are led further to the prison, and here Bloch follows the common practice of using Plato's wonderful tableau in the *Crito*. Bloch many times comes to discuss the relation between Xenophon and Plato, and he believes of course that Xenophon "deserves in the true sense to be called Socrates' disciple,"[135] while "the immortal Plato deviates in many

---

130 Bloch refers both in the biography (*Xenophon's Sokratiske Merkværdigheder*, p. 45) and in the textual notes (p. 296) to his teacher, Heyne's "outstanding" treatise "de sancto Socrate Pæderasta" in *Commentarii societatis regiæ scientiarum Gottingensis*—with no further reference. Since I could not track down any such treatise by Heyne, one might conclude that Bloch, who was known for being distracted, might have meant Heyne's predecessor, the abovementioned Gesner.

131 Povl Johs. Jensen, *Københavns Universitets Historie*, vol. 8, p. 237: "In his dissertation Kierkegaard criticizes Bloch with justice for conceiving of Socrates' daimon as 'a kind of *Schwämerie*.' J.L. Heiberg's explanation of 'the daimonic' as an 'instinct' is by contrast related to what Bloch says."

132 See *SKS* 1, 207–15 / *CI*, 157–67. Bloch is quoted on p. 208 / *CI*, 158.

133 Thus Friedrich Ast in the central work *Platon's Leben und Schriften. Ein Versuch, im Leben wie in den Schriften des Platon das Wahre und Aechte vom Erdichteten und Untergeschobenen zu scheiden, und die Zeitfolge der ächten Gespräche zu bestimmen. Als Einleitung in das Studium des Platon*, Leipzig: Weidmann 1816.

134 *SKS* 1, 211 / *CI*, 161–2.

135 *Xenophon's Sokratiske Merkværdigheder*, trans. by J. Bloch, p. 68.

statements from Socrates, and often ascribed to his teacher such opinions which his splendid imagination had itself created."[136] In Bloch's time people had not yet distinguished the "Socratic" dialogues, and for this reason with Plato as a whole one seems to stand at quite a distance from the historical Socrates.[137] Xenophon, by contrast, Bloch assures his readers, "portrays for us Socrates as he really was—a boarding school teacher and moralist, whose philosophy is practical wisdom and common sense itself."[138]

With Bloch the eighteenth century is rounded out. Xenophon's star still stands high, modern Plato philology is still waiting to be founded, and Aristophanes has still not been wrested free of the Roman yoke. Nevertheless, what has been said of Bloch's presentation is true: "It is the best description of Socrates that we have before Kierkegaard."[139]

In the *Memorabilia* the goal is to show how unjust the condemnation of Socrates was, which is done by refuting the accusers and by recalling episodes from the master's life. It has often been thought also in Kierkegaard's time that the imagined defense speech which Socrates purportedly gave before his condemnation was not even written by Xenophon. Kierkegaard never discusses this. In Kierkegaard's time Xenophon's *Apology* was available in two Danish translations, but it is possible that Kierkegaard did not know them. He could, however, have had in hand Christen Thaarup's (1795–1849) *Catalogue of Danish Translations of Greek and Latin Authors* from 1836,[140] and in this case he would have known the translations from Greek literature. Concerning the translations of the *Apology*, he could nevertheless probably not use them since these translations were for the most part outdated.[141] It is clear that where Plato's *Apology* comes in and becomes one of the focal points in Kierkegaard's dissertation, since the work is read as the most perfect example of irony, there Xenophon's *Apology* cannot win in significance.[142] Where Xenophon's

136 Ibid.

137 See, for example, *Xenophon's Sokratiske Merkværdigheder*, p. 72: "Plato often puts his own opinions in Socrates' mouth, and thus ideas, which he himself had taken from the wisemen of the orient, and from that mystical and transcendental philosophy: often he captivates the reader outside the limits of the material into the worlds and states, which his wonderful imagination has created."

138 Ibid.

139 Jensen in *Københavns Universitets Historie*, vol. 8, p. 237.

140 Christen Thaarup, *Fortegnelse paa danske Oversættelser af græske og latinske Skribenter*, Copenhagen: Jens Hostrup Schultz 1836.

141 *Om Socratis Forsvars Tale*, trans. from Greek by Hans Gottschalck, Aalborg: Holzberg 1781 and *Xenofons sokratiske Forsvar*, trans. by N.L. Nissen, in *For Sandhed. Et Fierdingaarsskrift*, vol. 2, 1798, pp. 127–50. Nissen rejects the scholars who have regarded the work "as inauthentic and Xenophon as unworthy," see ibid., p. 127, since he instead conceives it as the final chapter in the *Memorabilia*.

142 Since an important argument for the ironic conception of Plato's *Apology* is Socrates' all too prosaic conception of death, one would otherwise believe that Xenophon's *Apology*, which is traditionally understood such that the old Socrates wanted to die, can at least to the same extent be interpreted ironically!

conception of death in the dissertation is "deficient" and "narrow-hearted,"[143] then he can nonetheless find in the *Apology* "some more poetic features,"[144] which in the mature Kierkegaard develop to the claim: "We read Xenophon's *Apology* and sense Socrates throughout."[145]

Just as in Kierkegaard's juxtaposition of Xenophon and Plato one does not find a close reading comparision of the two authors' respective *Apology*, so also Kierkegaard does not analyze the related versions of the *Symposium* in one shot. Kierkegaard, of course, knew Xenophon's *Symposium*,[146] and this presumably not in Odin Wollf's antiquated Danish translation from 1796,[147] which was only replaced by W.T. Kall's translation from 1854.[148] From Kall's translation it is clear incidentally that Kierkegaard did not live in vain.[149] Finally, concerning the popular work *Oikonomikos*, where Socrates gives instruction on how to keep a household, Kierkegaard presumably did not read Odin Wolf's [or Wollf's] old translation from 1801,[150] but when the pastor Johannes Søren Bloch Suhr (1807–76) published a new

---

143 *SKS* 1, 86 / *CI*, 25.

144 Ibid.

145 *SKS* 25, 464, NB25:43 (1852) / *JP* 4, 4288.

146 See the short centerpiece "Caricature" from 1841, where it is written about Socrates: "He had a little property...; no doubt he ate into his capital later, and therefore it was no wonder that he always was at hand when a banquet took place (for this reason both Xenophon and Plato have a symposium, however different their interpretations otherwise are)," *Pap*. III B 30, p. 121 / *JP* 4, 4246.

147 See Odin Wollf, "Xenophons Giestebud. Af det Græske," *Iris og Hebe*, no. 3, 1796, pp. 305–54. In a brief foreword Wolff explains that the translation is 12 years old, and he speaks of "the profound and experienced Xenophon's dialogues" (p. 305), and about "the wise and virtuous Socrates" (ibid).

148 See *Philosophen som Selskabsmand. Scene af Oldtidslivet*, trans. from Greek by W.T. Kall, Copenhagen: Jacob Lund 1854.

149 In the "Translator's Foreword" Kall was without doubt thinking of Kierkegaard, when he wrote: "However much lack of appreciation Xenophon, in later times from several sides, has been the victim to as the biographer of Socrates, because he has not conceived this great character with the profound, speculative view as his other disciple, Plato, nonetheless an unprejudiced analysis must lead to the result that great historical fidelity is precisely to be found in him, whether that be in his *Memorabilia* or his *Apology*. This is the case since although certain Athenians' injustice with the judgment of Socrates can have induced him to present Scorates as a wholly innocent and innocuous teacher of ethics and, by contrast, to avoid going into what made his conflict with a large part of his contemporary age's, both the state's and the private citizens' manner of thinking and acting inevitable and irresolvable, nonetheless in a work like the present one, in which Xenophon only intends to give his spirit free run in the circle of intimate friends, there cannot arise any founded suspicion of a mistaken conception or intentional distortion. After having read through this portrayal of Socrates, no one will be able to claim that Xenophon only presents him as a inoffensive *Spißbürger* and a boring moralist," p. [4].

150 Xenophon, *Om Huusholdningskonsten. En Veiledning-Bog for hver Mand, især for Landboen, i Socratiske Samtaler. Fra den græske Original, med oplysende Anmerkninger for Ulærde, af Odin Wollf*, Copenhagen: [trykt hos P. Poulsen] 1801. Wolff's fine introduction to the work is reprinted in Signe Isager's translation in *Klassikerforeningens kildehæfter*, 1986 (Hjørring), pp. 75–9.

translation in 1838—right at the time that Kierkegaard was working with Socrates—then this must have prodded Kierkegaard.[151] Is it from here that Kierkegaard had the inscrutable idea of having Johannes the seducer discuss farming with Cordelia's aunt? We do not know!

Xenophon's Socrates was a Greek hero conceived as the highest representative of the given morality, but it is precisely all this immediacy that Kierkegaard wants to replace with reflection. In this way Xenophon's hero becomes the absolute opposite of Kierkegaard's relentless ironist. That Kierkegaard's presentation of Xenophon awakened great amusement—but presumably also offense—is clear from *The Corsair's* laughing discussion of the dissertation,[152] and indeed also from Beck's serious review.[153]

C. Plato

Kierkegaard's rejection of Xenophon is hard. On the other extreme we find the dissertation's famous transition to Plato, where enthusiasm pours out of the author, who refers to his "own perhaps somewhat youthful infatuation with Plato."[154] No other author has, like Plato, stamped Kierkegaard right from his first intellectual awakening to the end of his life. For the same reason, Plato also belongs to the most frequently quoted authors in Kierkegaard's *oeuvre:* there one finds references to more than twenty works in the *Corpus Platonicum;* in the dissertation alone ten dialogues are mentioned, many of which are the object of Kierkegaard's characteristic close reading. To be sure, Socrates is Kierkegaard's companion throughout his life, his philosophical mascot, but without Plato the great ironic hero is simply unthinkable.

At school Kierkegaard read Plato in Greek. At university he was immediately introduced to the most recent Plato philology. F.C. Petersen in his *Handbook on Greek Literary History* had four detailed sections on Plato. In the first of these (§ 155) Plato's biography is sketched, and the works' content that ends without resolution is left to the historian of philosophy, while Petersen dwells on the masterful form of the dialogues.[155] There is no other author before Kierkegaard who had expressed in such a virtuoso manner this philosophy's *how?* Without the dramatist Plato with his "dramatic-mimic portrayal,"[156] the world before Kierkegaard would probably have never *heard* a true ironist. In the next two sections (§§ 156–7) Petersen introduced the most recent philological debate with central figures such as Dieterich Tiedemann

---

[151] See *Om Huusholdningskunsten*, trans. by J.S.B. Suhr, Copenhagen: A.F. Høst 1838. The work was reviewed as a schoolboy's poor work, Cf. *Fædrelandet*, 1841, no. 645 (September 19), columns 5173–6.

[152] See Tonny Aagaard Olesen, " 'Tak, elskede Kierkegaard, for Din Ironi!' Kierkegaard's entré in *Corsaren* 1841," in *Kierkegaardiana*, vol. 24, 2007, pp. 293–4.

[153] See *Deutsche Jahrbücher für Wissenschaft und Kunst*, no. 222 (September 17), 1842, pp. 886–7.

[154] *SKS* 1, 89 / *CI*, 27.

[155] Petersen, *Haandbog i den græske Litteratur* (1830), pp. 192–5.

[156] Ibid., p. 195.

(1748–1803),[157] Wilhelm Gottlieb Tennemann (1761–1819),[158] Friedrich Daniel Ernst Schleiermacher (1768–1834),[159] Friedrich Ast (1778–1841),[160] Joseph Socher (1755–1834),[161] and Johann Gottfried Stallbaum (1793–1861).[162] On the question of the authenticity of the dialogues, Petersen emphasizes that there are only internal criteria, and that these in the final account concern the conception that one has of Plato and his philosophy. When the *Apology* does not appear in Petersen's concluding list of the fourteen most important dialogues, this is presumably due to the fact that he concurred with the view of Friedrich Ast that the *Apology* was inauthentic. From *The Concept of Irony* it is clear that Kierkegaard was in agreement with this view—until he found a new explanation: that the whole thing was absolute irony. Concerning the question of the chronology of the dialogues, Petersen does not think that the matter can ever be definitely resolved. However, he thinks, like most of his contemporaries, including Kierkegaard, that the dialogues can be divided into three phases in Plato's life, although there is far from being any general consensus about the placement of the individual dialogues.[163] Finally—in the final section (§ 158)—he gives an extensive bibliography of the Plato literature[164]: here Kierkegaard could get the literature that he would need, and here posterity can gain an insight into what literature Kierkegaard *did not* make use of in his investigation. This was the situation in *anno* 1830.

The recent Plato philology opens in the Danish literature on two fronts, namely, first when it concerns the Greek school editions of Plato's works, and second the Danish translations of the same. Concerning the first: the edition which the Norwegian professor of Greek language and literature, Georg Sverdrup (1770–1850), published in 1811[165] was a typical school edition, but it did not contain the dialogues that the

---

157 Cf. Dieterich Tiedemann, *Dialogorum Platonis argumenta*, Biponti: Ex typographia societtis 1786. Cf. his *Geist der spekulativen Philosophie von Thales bis Socrates*, vols. 1–6, Marburg: Neue Akademische Buchhandlung 1791–97 (*ASKB* 836–841).

158 Cf. Wilhelm Gottlieb Tennemann, *Geschichte der Philosophie*, vols. 1–11, Leipzig: Johann Ambrosius Barth 1798–1819 (*ASKB* 815–826).

159 Cf. *Platons Werke*, vols. 1–6, trans. by Friedrich Schleiermacher, Berlin: Realschulbuchhandlung 1804–28 (*ASKB* 1158–1163).

160 Cf. *Platonis quæ exstant Opera. Accedunt Platonis quae Feruntur Scripta*, ed. by Friedrich Ast, vols. 1–11, Leipzig: Weidmann 1819–32 (*ASKB* 1144–1154).

161 Cf. Joseph Socher, *Ueber Platons Schriften*, Munich: Lentner 1820.

162 Cf. *Platonis dialogos selectos*, vols. 1–10, ed. by G. Stallbaum, Gotha and Erfurt: Wilhelm Hennings 1827–60.

163 See Jens Himmelstrup's chapter on Kierkegaard's use of Plato in *Søren Kierkegaards Opfattelse af Sokrates*, pp. 274–90. It is true when he here (pp. 254–5) draws attention to Kierkegaard's somewhat casual use of K.F. Hermann, *Geschichte und System der platonischen Philosophie*, Heidelberg: C.F. Winter 1839 (*ASKB* 576), but it is hardly defensible when Himmelstrup claims that "the historical view" was not found before Hermann. The developmental-psychological presentation, which Kierkegaard also relies on, *is* historical. It is another matter that one of course only naively can conclude that the closer the dialogue's composition lies to the historical Socrates, the better the portrait.

164 Petersen, *Haandbog i den græske Litteratur* (1830), pp. 198–204.

165 *Platonis libri VIII: Apologia Socratis, Crito, Alcibiades uterque, Meno, Hippias major, Symposium, Phædrus. Scholarum in usum ad optimas recensiones diligenter expressi. Partic. I*, Copenhagen: Brummer 1811.

young Kierkegaard read. More interesting, therefore, is the outstanding philologist Carl Wilhelm Elberling (1800–70) and his edition of Plato's *Apology* from 1837,[166] that is, the point in time when Kierkegaard was in the course of pulling himself together for his approaching task, which indeed had the *Apology* as one of its central points. Kierkegaard, however, made use of Ast's edition in his dissertation. Christian Frederik Ingerslev (1803–68) criticized Elberling that in his otherwise so thorough preface he should have treated Socrates more extensively, especially Socrates in his conflict with the state.[167] This theme was current at the time. Later—in 1848–51—there appeared the philologist Frederik Wilhelm Wiehe's (1817–64) exemplary *Udvalgte Dialoger af Platon*,[168] but since Kierkegaard never mentions it, and it never mentions Kierkegaard, there is no reason to dwell on it here.

Concerning the translation of Plato into Danish, we find ourselves in a pioneering time. The work that was translated earliest and most often subsequently was the popular *Crito*. It was translated in 1762 by professor Jens Schielderup Sneedorff (1724–64) in the journal *Den patriotiske Tilskuer*,[169] and in 1774 there also appeared an anonymous translation,[170] just as in 1799 there followed a new translation from the Greek philologist and later bishop Stephan Tetens (1773–1855).[171] All of these editions were forgotten in 1814 when the man of the future, C.J. Heise, published

166 See Carl Wilhelm Elberling, *Platonis Apologia Socratis et Crito. Edidit et in scholarum maxime usum interpretatus est*, Copenhagen: Gyldendal 1837.

167 This work was reviewed positively by C.F. Ingerslev in "Elberling: *Platonis Apologia Socratis*," *Maanedsskrift for Litteratur*, vol. 20, 1838, pp. 449–68. Here it is written on p. 467: "The reviewer would even wish that the editor in the part in which Socrates is treated, would have been more extensive, and namely, had spoken more about Socrates' relation to the state and especially to his accusers in general, about the justice of the accusation against him and about his conviction, about which in later times several people [note: among others, P.W. Forchhammer (*Die Athener und Socrates*, Berlin: Nicolai 1837), in whom one finds more strong words than arguments] have uttered opinions which differ significantly from the manner in which one until now has been accustomed to judge Socrates also in this respect."

168 Frederik Wilhelm Wiehe, *Udvalgte Dialoger af Platon, udgivne til Skolebrug*, vols. 1–3, Copenhagen: C.A. Reitzel 1848–51, vol. 1, *Apologien, Kriton*, 1848; vol. 2, *Eutyphron, Menon*, 1849; vol. 3, *Protagoras*, 1851. To this is attached *Plan for de bebudede Udgaver af græske og latinske Forfatteres Skrifter ved en Forening af Skolemænd samt Bemærkninger til de to udkomne Hefter af Platons Dialoger ved Udgiveren*, Copenhagen: C.A. Reitzel 1849, and F.W. Wiehe, *Bemærkninger om Udgaven af "Udvalgte Dialoger af Platon". Tredie Hefte: Protagoras, tilligemed et par Ord i Anledning af Herr cand. Fibigers Belysning osv."*, Copenhagen: C.A. Reitzel 1851, as well as "En omtvistet Læsemaade i Platons Apolog. Socr. p. 27 E," *Tidsskrift for Philologi og Pædagogik*, vol. 4, 1863, pp. 323–5. The same is true of Frederik Moltke Bugge's edition of *Platons Kritik*, Bergen: F.D. Beyer 1852.

169 See *Den patriotiske Tilskuer*, no. 164, August 13, 1762, pp. 545–52.

170 *Den døende Socrates, Hvis Endeligt skede ved at indtage Forgift*, Copenhagen: Agent Holcks Contoir 1774.

171 See Stephan Tetens, "Plato's Dialog: Kriton eller om Borgerpligt. Oversat af det Græske," *For Sandhed. Et Fjerdingaarsskrift*, vol. 3, 1799, pp. 325–62.

his *Crito*, which was later taken up in the landmark series *Udvalgte Dialoger af Platon.*[172]

Before we return to Heise, we must briefly mention the period's most successful translation, namely, *Apologi for Socrates*, translated by the adjunct and later pastor Laurits Christian Ditlev Westengaard (1795–1853). This translation appeared in two parts in the prospectus for Vordingborg grammar school: the first part in 1822,[173] and the second part in 1827,[174] but the two parts were, quite practically, circulated in a single collected volume. This short work was presumably Kierkegaard's introduction to Plato in his "early youth."[175] To be sure, Kierkegaard does not mention this translation, but we are here also in a period long before he began to write in his journals. In addition, there is the fact that Westengaard's translation is entirely unpretentious: it contains no apparatus, not even for the preface, and for this reason it would have been impossible for Kierkegaard to have made use of it in his dissertation. After having been in circulation for years, a collected—but unchanged—edition finally appeared in 1850, and this was subsequently reprinted three times.[176]

Finally, one must also mention a youthful work of the later Bible translator Christian Andreas Hermann Kalkar (1802–86), namely, *Platos Eutyphron*, which appeared in 1829,[177] that is, precisely in time for Kierkegaard to be able to secretly read for his Greek examination exercise in Danish. Of course, we do not know whether he actually did so. Kalkar's edition, which builds on Wolf's edition (Berlin 1820), is one of the first in Danish—only Heise was earlier—in which the more recent scholarly literature (primarily Schleiermacher, Ast, Stallbaum, and Tiedemann) was discussed, and in which the Greek readings were zealously discussed in the notes. However, when a dozen years later Kalker competed with Ernest Bojesen for the lectureship in Greek at Sorø, and one of his students in this context had pointed out that the Plato translation was one of Kalkar's efforts, then an *anonymous* opponent entered the field. He called Kalkar's translation "a purely dilettante work" with no philological

---

172 C.J. Heise, "Platons Kriton," *Athene, et Maanedsskrift* (ed. by Chr. Molbech), vol. 3, 1814, pp. 289–313. Later—when Plato or Socrates had become national property—one could again read a translation with the title "Socrates i Fængslet" as a feuilleton in the newspaper *Den Frisindede*, no. 30, March 12, 1846, pp. 117–19; no. 31, March 14, 1846, p. 123; no. 34, March 21, 1846, pp. 133–5; no. 35, March 24, 1846, pp. 138–40; no. 37, March 28, 1846, pp. 146–8; and no. 38, March 31, 1846, pp. 150–1.

173 Laurits Christian Westengaard, *Platos Apologie for Socrates. 1. Halvdeel*, in *Indbydelsesskrift til den offentlige Examen i Vordingborg lærde Skole i September 1822*, Copenhagen: Andreas Seidelin [1822].

174 Laurits Christian Westengaard, *Platos Apologie for Socrates. 2. Halvdeel*, in *Indbydelsesskrift til den offentlige Examen i Vordingborg lærde Skole i September 1827*, Copenhagen: Andreas Seidelin [1827].

175 *SKS* 1, 139, note / *CI*, 81, note.

176 Laurits Christian Westengaard, *Platos Apologie for Socrates*, 2nd ed. 1850; 3rd ed. 1860; 4th ed. 1872; 5th ed. 1888.

177 Christian Andreas Hermann Kalkar, *Platos Eutyphron*, trans. with an introduction in *Indbydelsesskrift til den offentlige Examen i Odense Kathedralskole den 11. September 1829*, Odense: S. Hempel 1829.

significance.[178] It was claimed that there is nothing in Kalkar's introduction which was not copied from the German masters. The notes "are for the most part only excerpts or free translations of Stallbaum's"[179] or "only a badly presented parroting of Ast."[180] After this hard judgment it could hardly come as a surprise that the Greek lectureship went to Bojesen. But who was the person who helped him? Was it the specialist in Plato translation C.J. Heise? Or was it—perhaps the most plausible possibility—the authority F.C. Petersen? Or could it have been another of Bojesen's good friends, Søren Kierkegaard? Or someone entirely different? We do not know, but it is possible that Kierkegaard *could* have done it.

The most significant event in Danish Plato research was the series of translations that Carl Johan Heise (1787–1857) began in the revolutionary year 1830—the same year that Kierkegaard began at the university and Petersen gave lectures on Greek literature. Heise's *Udvalgte Dialoger af Platon* were published in the period 1830–59 in eight volumes: the first volumes contained dialogues that Heise had already published previously, namely, the *Crito* from 1814, with which he was the first to introduce the debate from Schleiermacher's introductions to *Platon's Werke* into Danish Romanticism,[181] and the *Symposium* from 1827, which contains an extended introduction, where Schleiermacher is still the central figure, but where also Friedrich Ast with his *Platon's Leben und Schriften* (1816) is introduced.[182] The last volume was published posthumously by the professor of philosophy Frederik Christian Sibbern, who in a preface describes in detail the tortured life of his friend Heise.[183]

Already as a 14-year-old Heise was enrolled at the university, and at the age of 17 he was a candidate in theology. He became a private tutor, adjunct at the grammar school in Helsingør; he was a partly financed Plato researcher for a few years, received the title of professor, and in 1831 became a pastor, later changing to other positions. Throughout his life Heise was Plato's faithful disciple, but there were two things that plagued him and rendered him unable to do work such that not even Plato could be the consolation of philosophy: the one was that he was overburdened in his position such that he did not find the time and the energy to do that things that lay closest to his heart. The other thing—and this was the worst—was that Heise

---

178 See the anonymous article in *Fædrelandet*, nos. 75–6, February 21, 1840, p. 474, columns 474–5.

179 Ibid., p. 475.

180 Ibid.

181 C.J. Heise, "Platons Kriton," *Athene, et Maanedsskrift*, vol. 3, 1814, pp. 289–313, see pp. 289–90.

182 C.J. Heise, "Platons Symposion," *Det skandinaviske Litteraturselskabs Skrifter*, vol. 22, 1827, pp. 1–134. With Friedrich Ast reference is made to *Platon's Leben und Schriften. Ein Versuch, im Leben wie in den Schriften des Platon das Wahre und Aechte vom Erdichteten und Untergeschobenen zu scheiden, und die Zeitfolge der ächten Gespräche zu bestimmen. Als Einleitung in das Studium des Platon*, Leipzig: Weidmann 1816.

183 F.C. Sibbern says it diplomatically in the preface to the eighth volume of *Udvalgte Dialoger af Platon*, vols. 1–8, trans. and ed. by C.J. Heise, vols. 1–3, Copenhagen: Gyldendal 1830–38, vols. 4–8, Copenhagen: C.A. Reitzel 1851–59, see vol. 8, pp. V–XXXV. Kierkegaard owned vols. 1–7: vols. 1–3 (*ASKB* 1164–1166); vols. 4–6 (*ASKB* 1167); and vol. 7 (*ASKB* 1169).

suffered from an eye ailment, which rendered him almost blind over long periods of time, even to the extent that he could not read. If Heise had had money and healthy eyes, Kierkegaard might possibly never had quoted Plato in Greek.

Heise managed to translate nine of Plato's dialogues: in the first volume from 1830 one finds the *Phaedo*, *Crito*, and *Alcibiades II*,[184] while the next volume from 1831 contains the *Symposium* and *Protagoras*.[185] A few years passed before volume 3 appeared in 1838 with the *Gorgias*.[186] These are the dialogues that are constitutive for the young Kierkegaard. They all play an important role in the dissertation—perhaps with the exception of the *Crito*,[187] which had indeed been ground into his head in Greek in the school. As has been indicated in the commentaries to *Om Begrebet Ironi* in *Søren Kierkegaards Skrifter*, one often hears Heise's Plato in the dissertation: Kierkegaard has simply internalized the formulations.[188] In 1851, when Kierkegaard concluded his authorship, the next three volumes of *Udvalgte Dialoger af Platon* appeared. There was the long work *The Republic*, which Heise had worked on after he had finished the *Gorgias*.[189] From the translator's thorough introduction one sees that Heise's scholarly ambitions have almost grown in the course of the years; for example, the work's content is presented with the most recent research,

---

184 *Udvalgte Dialoger af Platon*, vol. 1 (1830): "Forerindring"; *Phædon*, pp. 1–125 (notes, pp. 193–229); *Kriton*, pp. 129–56 (introduction, p. 230, and notes, pp. 231–8); *Den anden Alkibiades*, pp. 159–89 (introduction, pp. 239–49, and notes, pp. 249–55).

185 *Udvalgte Dialoger af Platon*, vol. 2 (1831): *Symposion*, pp. 1–104 (introduction, pp. 221–30, and notes, pp. 231–51); *Protagoras*, pp.107–218 (introduction, pp. 252–7, and notes, pp. 257–79).

186 *Udvalgte Dialoger af Platon*, vol. 3 (1838): "Forord"; *Gorgias*, pp. 1–200 (notes, pp. 203–47, and introduction, pp. 247–53; "Tillæg til Indledningen til Alkibiades II," pp. 254–62).

187 See the Himmelstrup passage in note 31. Kierkegaard indeed uses the *Crito* sporadically, Cf. *SKS* 1, 114, note / *CI*, 53, note. This passage is reused in *SKS* 25, 94, NB26:93 / *JP* 6, 6819; cf. *SKS* 20, 301, NB4:29 (1847–48) / *JP* 3, 3352 and *SKS* 24, 513, NB25:99 / *JP* 4, 4291. In a copy of the dissertation he adds with explicit reference to Heise's *Crito*, that Socrates was a loafer, Cf. *Pap*. III B 29, p. 121. Concerning Himmelstrup's claim that Kierkegaard wanted to avoid the *Crito*, because it contains something positive, one might well protest. If one has understood Kierkegaard's radical reading of the *Apology*, or the *Phaido*, then one certainly cannot be surprised that Kierkegaard also found absolute irony in the *Crito*.

188 For example, the expression "*en kjælen Citharspiller*" ["an amorous zither player"] from the *Symposium*, where it is used to describe Orpheus; Kierkegaard uses it in *The Concept of Irony*, see *SKS* 1, 87, note 2 and 318 / *CI*, 26 note 1 and 282. It is later used in *Fear and Trembling*, see *SKS* 4, 123 / *FT*, 27; in *Concluding Unscientific Postscript*, see *SKS* 7, 226 / *CUP1*, 248 ["a sentimental zither player"], and *SKS* 20, 383, NB5:31 / *JP* 6, 6149. Or the expression from the *Symposium* about what is "*blødere end Alt*," ["the softest thing of all"] Cf. *SKS* 1, 105 / *CI*, 44; later used in *Works of Love*, see *SKS* 9, 311 / *WL*, 314 ["softer than the softest"]. According to F.C. Petersen, this passage does not follow Plato's Greek but is a free rendering from Heise's Danish translation (*Maanedsskrift for Litteratur*, vol. 7, 1832, p. 481).

189 See *Breve til og fra F.C. Sibbern*, ed. by C.L.N. Mynster, Copenhagen: Gyldendal 1866, p. 195.

among others, Hegel and Zeller.[190] Kierkegaard bought and read *The Republic*,[191] but he would certainly have liked to have had it 15 years earlier when he studied the first book of this work. Volume 7 with the *Timaeus* appeared during the attack on the Church in 1855, and Kierkegaard, who certainly could not resist this last pleasure, bought it immediately.[192] Neither Kierkegaard nor Heise manged to see the last volume with the *Philebus*. It was published posthumously by Sibbern, who, however, neither completed the notes nor added an introduction to the work,[193] but presumably read the proofs as he was accustomed to doing.[194] Thus ended an epoch in Danish Plato studies.

The first volume of Heise's Plato hit the Danish reading public like a kind of revelation. The Danish language still did not seem agile enough to speak Greek, but with Heise Plato became Danish. One reviewer praises the translator's thoroughness and linguistic flair,[195] and another is thankful and impressed that Heise had been successful in transferring the foreign Plato to Danish, whose linguistic borders have thus been explanded.[196] A third reviewer also notes the expansion of the language,[197] indeed, he calls the translation "beyond improvement,"[198] and adds: "How spiritual and true, and fluid is the translation of these classical passages! Everyone must admit that Plato speaks Danish like a native by upbringing."[199] Heises' translation was a major event around 1830. Never before had Plato spoken Danish so well that one could almost not miss the ironic play. Heise himself never speaks of this irony.

The best Plato experts came into a festive mood due to Heise's translations. This is true not least of all of professor F.C. Petersen, who wrote two extensive reviews, which together—almost 40 pages—give a good picture of the more recent Plato philology.[200] Reading these is almost like having an introductory lecture to

---

190 See *Udvalgte Dialoger af Platon*, vol. 4, pp. IX–LIII.

191 See, for example, *SKS* 24, 328, NB24:15 / *JP* 4, 3713.

192 *Udvalgte Dialoger af Platon*, vol. 7 (= *Timaeus*) (1855).

193 *Udvalgte Dialoger af Platon*, vol. 8 (= *Philebos. Efter Oversætterens Død udgivet af Fred. Chr. Sibbern, med en Fortale indeholdende en Skildring af den Afdøde*) (1859).

194 It is Sibbern himself who says: "Very often I together with Heise went through the second set of proofs of the translation of Plato, both for the sake of precision on the whole and for the sake of the odd dubious passage," ibid., p. XXXIV. This help that Sibbern gave to Heise—we know nothing of its extent—was later noted. Cf. Vilhelm Andersen, *Tider og Typer*, vol. 2, pp. 127–8.

195 See the anonymous discussion in *Dansk Litteratur-Tidende for 1830*, no. 27, p. 425: "The reviewer has read this translation with pleasure and without any stumbling, which could move him to take out the original. The introduction shows that Hr. H. has done his work with mature reflection."

196 See C.H. Lorenzen's review in *Kjøbenhavns flyvende Post*, 1830, no. 111, September 15, columns 1–4. Cf. Stewart, *A History of Hegelianism in Golden Age Denmark*, pp. 345–8.

197 See the art historian and philologist, Professor Torkel Baden (1765–1849), who reviewed the first two volumes in *Prøvestenen*, no. 3, 1831, pp. 106–12, see p. 106: "The limits of national language are getting expanded with translations such as this."

198 Ibid., p. 107.

199 Ibid., p. 112.

200 The first review appeared in the *Maanedsskrift for Litteratur*, vol. 5, 1831, pp. 36–54. It is signed 10/a, which points to F.C. Petersen. The date "November 1830" shows that it was

Plato studies in Danish, that is, like sitting in Petersen's lecture hall. The professor is partly original in some points, and partly he simply reacts to problems that he finds in Heise's translation, introduction, or in the scholarly notes which introduce the relevant research literature.[201] And if there was one person who read Petersen's contribution carefully, it was Heise, who was glad to take up the criticisms and suggestions in the following volumes. The exchange between Petersen and Heise was the age's first public debate about the Platonic question. There can be no doubt that Kierkegaard followed this debate.

It is translations like Heise's of Plato, Petersen explains in his first review, which make it possible for people to do philosophy in the Danish language.[202] To be sure, the dialogue form is not the modern—monological-systematic—form of scholarship, but Plato's dialogues—but also only these—can still be read because no one has surpassed Plato as a philosophical dramatist.[203] Petersen gives an overview of the collected Plato literature in Danish, in that he declares that everything before Heise "is only insignificant."[204] Then follows the central discussion of Heise's choice of dialogues, the question of their authenticity and their placement in the series of Plato's works.[205] Petersen follows Stallbaum and thus wants to ascribe the *Protagoras* and *Crito* to Plato's early period, while the *Symposium* and the *Phaedo* belong to the second phase, and *Alcibiades II*, to the extent that it is authentic, is attached to the *Crito*. It was beyond doubt that the *Protagoras*, *Symposium*, and the *Phaedo* were authentic, but when Friedrich Ast rejected the *Crito* as genuine, Petersen argued—just as Heise did—for its authenticity; here there are also many authorities to rely on.[206] Concerning *Alcibiades II*, it seems that most scholars were in agreement that it was inauthentic. Only Heise held on to it since he at least wanted to refute one of the arguments for this that he found in Schleiermacher, Ast, and others, namely, that the dialogue was supposed to be un-Platonic.[207] Heise's defense of the dialogue was then refuted by Petersen with the German authorities,[208] which later led Heise to give a new response.[209] What is interesting in this context is that Kierkegaard seems to maintain the dialogue's authenticity,[210] that is, he follows Heise.

---

written at the same time as Petersen was giving the young Kierkegaard instruction in Greek literature. The second review, which is also signed 10/a, is found in the *Maanedsskrift for Litteratur*, vol. 7, 1832, pp. 467–84, with the date "feb. 1832."

201 See *Maanedsskrift for Litteratur*, vol. 5, 1831, p. 54: "The notes testify to the translator's thorough study of Plato's writings, to his intimate familiarity with his philosophy, and are written with a judicious choice of what both in respect to criticism, antiquity and philosophy must be regarded as being the most needed and desired."

202 See ibid., p. 40.

203 See Petersen's discussion of the genre of the dialogue, ibid., pp. 40–5.

204 Ibid., p. 46.

205 Ibid., pp. 47–9.

206 Ibid., pp. 49–50.

207 See *Udvalgte Dialoger af Platon*, vol. 1, pp. 239–49.

208 *Maanedsskrift for Litteratur*, vol. 5, 1831, pp. 50–4.

209 See *Udvalgte Dialoger af Platon*, vol. 3, "Tillæg til Indledningen til Alkibiades II," pp. 254–62.

210 See *SKS* 1, 223–4 / *CI*, 176–7, and *SKS* 7, 89 / *CUP1*, 90.

Petersen continued the debate in the second review, where he, after a long general introduction, challenges Heise to examine in more detail the question of the authenticity and order of the dialogues.[211] Then follows a more extensive discussion of the *Symposium*,[212] which Heise had also treated in a more thorough manner.[213] The key issue was Schleiermacher's theory of the unity of the *Symposium* and the *Phaedo*, that is, that the two dialogues supplement one another since the first portrays Socrates in life and the second in death. This view is quite central for Heise,[214] while Petersen more or less cements this conception since he thinks that the main intention of the two dialogues, namely, of portraying Socrates, does not need to presuppose that they were written during the same earlier period: "Plato must have been occupied with tasks of this kind constantly, and he worked on them when the desire, the opportunity and the chance to do presented itself."[215] Kierkegaard explicitly follows Heise, from whom he also refers to Ast,[216] who did not believe in the unity since he thought that the two dialogues came from two different periods. But while Petersen solved the problem by doubting the premise of the relevance of their contemporaneity,[217] Kierkegaard goes in the other direction: he believes in the unity but *not* in a positive unity: what makes it possible that the two dialogues speak about the same Socrates is only that their standpoint is irony![218]

Heise does not think—as Schleiermacher does—that the main intention of the *Protagoras* is to praise Socrates' dialogical method in opposition to the Sophistic rhetoric, but by contrast—as with Ast—that the dialogue in general wants to portray the odious practice of the Sophists.[219] Since Protagoras calls himself a teacher of virtue, Heise adds, the essence of virtue must necessarily be "the philosophical substance of the dialogue."[220] Petersen's response is subtle. He invokes Ast with the conclusion: "The main thing in the *Protagoras* is to show the spirit of true research and in connection with this the genuine method."[221] Here Schleiermacher, Ast, Heise, and Petersen at bottom hold the same view: the dialogue, with the negative (the Sophistic) wants to point to the positive (Socrates' method). Here Kierkegaard's

---

211 See *Maanedsskrift for Litteratur*, vol. 7, 1832, pp. 472–3. Whereas Heise mostly keeps to Schleiermacher's organization, Petersen always sticks to Stallbaum, while Kierkegaard—as Himmelstrup says: "prefers to emphasize Ast," *Kierkegaards Opfattelse af Sokrates*, p. 276. Kierkegaard, however, also uses both Diogenes Laertius (*SKS* 1, 92 / *CI*, 30–1), Schleiermacher (*SKS* 1, 113ff. / *CI*, 52f.), Ast (*SKS* 1, 171–2 / *CI*, 120–1) and Stallbaum (*SKS* 1, 122, note / *CI*, 62–3, note; see the commentary to this).

212 *Maanedsskrift for Litteratur*, vol. 7, 1832, pp. 473–7.

213 See *Udvalgte Dialoger af Platon*, vol. 3, pp. 247–53.

214 See the introduction to the *Symposium* in ibid., vol. 2, pp. 221–30.

215 See *Maanedsskrift for Litteratur*, vol. 7, 1832, p. 475.

216 *SKS* 1, 122–4 / *CI*, 62–5.

217 Petersen also here mentions his preferred authority, Stallbaum, who claims that the two dialogues belong to the same group. Cf. *Maanedsskrift for Litteratur*, vol. 7, 1832, p. 476.

218 See *SKS* 1, 124 / *CI*, 64–5.

219 See *Udvalgte Dialoger af Platon*, vol. 2, p. 256.

220 Ibid., p. 257.

221 See *Maanedsskrift for Litteratur*, vol. 7, 1832, pp. 478–9.

move is more radical: he is glad to sign on to this unity, but with this one should implictly understand that Socrates' dialectical method is purely negative. It ends not only without a result, as Schleiermacher says, but with a negative, that is, ironic, result.[222] To this extent Kierkegaard could certainly agree with Torkel Baden's amusing remark: "The *Protagoras* has also cost the translator more difficulty than the dialogue is worth. Neither educated nor uneducated people can accept its hairsplitting. No one would therefore have any objection if it were not translated into Danish."[223] For Kierkegaard the dialogue is precisely hairsplitting, indeed, infinite hairsplitting but this, however, such that here the most refined Socratic irony is expressed. Kierkegaard would—with respect to Baden's last remark—certainly not be in agreement: for it was Heise's translation that helped Kierkegaard to see "the old grandmaster of irony."[224]

Heise's translation of Plato into Danish, his introductions and notes, where one finds a constant dialogue with the most recent Plato research, the entire enthusiastic reception of Heise's work—all this stamped the young Kierkegaard.[225] It led him far into the Socrates literature before the encounter with Hegel's Socrates in *Geschichte der Philosophie* (1836). One could claim that Heise's importance for Kierkegaard's Socrates was just as great as Hegel's, although Heise's more designates the possibility than directly causes the actualization. With Heise's Danish Socrates in his veins, one also understands from where Kierkegaard had the courage to write in Danish.

D. Aristophanes

There is nothing strange in Kierkegaard's enthusiasm for the philosophical and artistic master Plato. The rise of the new Plato philology is likewise not a surprising presupposition for Kierkegaard's Socrates. More idiosyncratic is perhaps the ritual assassination of Xenophon, but also the counterpart to this: the high evaluation of Aristophanes. It was indeed only with Romanticism—not least of all due to the Schlegel brothers—that Aristophanes again came to honor and dignity, but it was nevertheless only in the next generation's critical examination of the same Romanticism's arbitrary subjectivism that the old comic poet as a conservative—or merely someone judging from ideality—a castigator of society, became the noble representative of the Restoration. It is important that Hegel placed the Greek comic writer so high, but the landmark work was without doubt H.T. Rötscher's philological-philosophical treatise *Aristophanes und sein Zeitalter* from 1827. In the years before and after this publication there arose a new and fresh Aristophanes

---

222 See *SKS* 1, 113–22, see 115–16 / *CI*, 52–62, see 55–6.

223 See *Prøvestenen*, 1831, p. 107.

224 See *SKS* 6, 436 / *SLW*, 473.

225 Perhaps Kierkegaard in 1838 had already finished this part of the dissertation which is the reason that the otherwise so Kierkegaardian dialogue, the *Gorgias*, which was published in the same year, appears primarily in the footnotes. For explicit references to Heise's translation see, for example, *SKS* 1, 95 / *CI*, 33–4. *SKS* 1, 98 / *CI*, 36. *SKS* 1, 100–1 / *CI*, 39. *SKS* 1, 114 / *CI*, 53.

reception, which took on great significance, but which, however, could not compete with Rötscher's monograph.[226]

At the end of the 1820s Rötscher's grandiose, positive presentation of Aristophanes and Greek comedy also reached Denmark, namely, through Johan Ludvig Heiberg (1791–1860), who could use the new signals in his critical breakthrough. No one before had, like Heiberg, established the claim that the idea of aesthetics not merely culminated in drama, but—since the comic follows the tragic—in comedy. The age of tragedy is passed, said Heiberg, comedy shows reality as it is.[227] Heiberg's aesthetics led directly to Kierkegaard's prioritizing of his sources; indeed, one could go so far as to claim that certainly Rötscher is a decisive precondition for Kierkegaard, but without Heiberg, Aristophanes' poetics in the dissertation would presumably have looked entirely different. Heiberg was an Aristophanian, and Kierkegaard to a large extent was a Heibergian.

When Kierkegaard in 1830 looked up in Petersen's *Handbook of Greek Literary History*, he could read under § 105 an article about Aristophanes, to which was attached a long bibliography of Greek editions and individual overviews of the research, including Süvern's and Rötscher's.[228] Petersen raises the fundamental question without naming Socrates. Eleven comedies are preserved, of which four were rewritten by either the old Aristophanes or his sons, Petersen remarks. One of the pieces he refers to is certainly the comedy, *The Clouds*, which was performed without any great success in 423 BC and the year after, but which certainly was revised 5–10 years later to become the version that we know today, and this revised version was never performed. It is obvious that there is hidden here an abyss of obscurity which virtually makes Aristophanes' testimony hypothetical.[229] However, Kierkegaard never had such philological concerns. Then Petersen raises the big question of how Aristophanes should be conceived. It is clear enough that "the unlimited freedom with which everything is surrended for mockery and laughter

---

226 Here he is thinking of J.W. Süvern's important short work, *Ueber Aristophanes Wolken*, Berlin: Ferdinand Dümmler 1826, which Kierkegaard read, along with the interesting article by Christian August Brandis, "Ueber die vorgebliche Subjectivität der Sokratischen Lehre," *Rheinisches Museum*, vol. 2, no. 1, 1828, pp. 85–112, which is directed against Süvern and Rötscher, and finally Karl Reisig, "Ueber die Wolken des Aristophanes," *Rheinisches Museum*, vol. 2, no. 1, 1828, pp. 191–207, and "Nachtrag zu der Abhandlung über die Wolken des Aristophanes," pp. 454–6.

227 See my articles "Heiberg's Initial Approach: The Prelude to his Critical Breakthrough" and "Heiberg's Critical Breakthrough in 1828: A Historical Presentation," in *Johan Ludvig Heiberg: Philosopher, Littérateur, Dramaturge, and Political Thinker*, ed. by Jon Stewart, Copenhagen: Museum Tusculanum Press 2008, pp. 211–45 and pp. 247–307 respectively. Prior to Heiberg, Christian Molbech (1783–1857), presumably under the influence of A.W. Schlegel, had given Aristophanes and his treatment of Socrates in *The Clouds* a rehabilitation with the help of the demand for poetic truth. Cf. the article "Nogle Yttringer om den komiske Poesie, i Anledning af Hr. J.L. Heibergs Komedie: Julespøg og Nytaarsløier," in Molbech's journal *Athene*, vol. 8, 1817, pp. 366–9.

228 See Petersen, *Haandbog i den græske Litteraturhistorie* (1830), pp. 111–16.

229 Bloch had already raised this problem in his presentation of Socrates, see *Xenophon's Sokratiske Merkværdigheder*, trans. by J. Bloch, p. 48.

is foreign to our age's manner of thinking and customs."[230] The issue is, however, whether Aristophancs in his comedies lets the historical persons be representative of the larger movements of the age such that the historical figure is in a sense subordinated, or whether his satire is aimed directly at the empirical individuals. Everything depends on Aristophanes' poetics. If the former is the case, then the value of comedy as a source is minimal.[231] Kierkegaard, who claimed a both/and, under the influence of Heiberg, solved the problem by ascribing to Aristophanes an ideality of poetry; moreover, the idea that the caricature must have some truth, indeed, meant straightforwardly that the Socrates of the comedy was the one who best reflected the historical Socrates. Petersen would not go this far: "Concerning Aristophanes, whom many people think transgressed the limits of art, even when he is judged by the standard of his own time, it is impossible to determine with certainty."[232]

Petersen mentions in his bibliography that some of Aristophanes was available in Danish. Here he refers to the edition from 1825 of *Aristophanes's Komedier*,[233] which contained four comedies, namely, *The Frogs*, *The Clouds*, *Plutos*, and *The Acharnians*. The edition states that it is "volume 1," since the translator had planned to translate all of Aristophanes, but unfortunately he died shortly thereafter. His name was Johan Krag (1786–1827), and he was educated as a philologist but was active as an officer in the army until 1825, when he became adjunct at Odense Cathedralskole. There is no doubt that Krag, who was the first person in Denmark to translate one of Aristophanes' works in its entirety,[234] was really read by those people who were interested in this exclusive literature. As early as 1820 he had published a translation of *The Frogs*[235] which was positively received by the authority F.C. Petersen, who even suggested that Krag in his introduction and notes try to minimize the gap between Aristophanes' universe, which demands an enormous knowledge of the age's historical situation, and our time.[236]

It is unfortunate that Krag's translation did not manage to make use of Rötscher. It would undeniably have provided some good material for the introduction of the edition, "Concerning Ancient Comedy and Aristophanes,"[237] which Kierkegaard without doubt read very closely.[238] Kierkegaard sought everywhere in Krag what

230 Petersen, *Haandbog i den græske Litteraturhistorie* (1830), pp. 112f.

231 See Himmelstrup's account of Kierkegaard's use of Aristophanes, where the mentioned problem is precisely the key point, *Søren Kierkegaards Opfattelse af Sokrates*, pp. 290–4.

232 Petersen, *Haandbog i den græske Litteraturhistorie* (1830), p. 113.

233 *Aristophanes's Komedier, oversatte fra det Græske ved J. Krag*, Odense: S. Hempel 1825 (*ASKB* 1055).

234 The longer or shorter excerpts from Aristophanes' comedies, which are translated into Danish are registered in the *Fortegnelse paa danske Oversættelser*, pp. 6–7.

235 *Frøerne. Et Lystspil af Aristophanes*, Copenhagen: Schultz 1820.

236 See the review in *Dansk Litteratur-Tidende for 1822*, no. 46, pp. 729–36.

237 *Aristophanes's Komedier*, pp. VIII–XVIII.

238 It is Kierkegaard himself in the dissertation who refers to the edition; another indication of this, the humorous exchange from *Plutos*, which Kierkegaard uses in *Either/Or* (*SKS* 2, 272–3 / *EO1*, 282–3), is found here mentioned as one of Holberg's reminiscenses of Aristophanes. Cf. *Aristophanes's Komedier*, p. XVIII.

he could find that would be of relevance for Socrates,[239] but he especially studied the introduction to *The Clouds*, "Concerning Comedy: The Clouds."[240] Here one finds—as in Petersen—a presentation of the conflicting view of *The Clouds:* did personal hatred bring Aristophanes to undertake his coarse ridicule, or is the satire—as Lessing was the first to claim—directed not against Socrates but against the age's new movement, the Sophists? Krag places himself—just as Kierkegaard did later—right in the middle, in a both/and. Socrates was dangerous, Krag thought, since with his manner of teaching he undermined virtue and religion. Socrates sowed doubt about what was given. "Moreover, Socrates challenged others to make use of irony against him, since his entire method of teaching was irony, for which reason Cicero (*de natura Deor.* 1, 54) calls him *Scurra Atticus*."[241]

It is possible that Kierkegaard attended Petersen's instruction on Aristophanes, and thus had learned how to read the Greek comic writer in the original language. In the dissertation he indeed quotes him in Greek.[242] It is also possible that he read the comedies in German translation, from which he also later quotes.[243] It is, however, a fact that Kierkegaard, where he could—just as in the case with Plato—preferred to read the classics in Danish. Several lingistic indications in the dissertation testify to the fact that *The Clouds* was also appropriated in a Danish linguistic dress.[244] This does not mean that Kierkegaard's reading of *The Clouds* does not shine in philological details,[245] but it does mean that Kierkegaard also has a Danish support behind his Aristophanic Socrates.

---

239 See, for example, Kierkegaard's handwritten notes in his dissertation, *Pap.* IV A 209 / *CI*, Supplement, p. 450.

240 See *Aristophanes's Komedier*, pp. 265–75. See, for example, Kierkegaard's handwritten notes in his dissertation, *Pap.* IV A 210–1 / *CI*, Supplement, pp. 450–1.

241 *Aristophanes's Komedier*, p. 272.

242 No one has yet investigated which Greek edition Kierkegaard used. Such an investigation has unfortunately been unnecessarily rendered difficult by the fact that all the editions and translations of the dissertation make use of their own accents. At his death Kierkegaard owned *Aristophanis Comoediae*, vols. 1–2, ed. by G. Dindorf, Leipzig: Weidmann 1830 (*ASKB* 1051).

243 Kierkegaard used *Des Aristophanes Werke*, vols. 1–3, trans. by J.G. Droysen, Berlin: Veit 1835–38 (*ASKB* 1052–1054).

244 Kierkegaard refers directly to Krag's translation, see *SKS* 1, 192, note / *CI*, 142, note. Linguistic evidence shows that he knew the Danish translation well. See, for example, *SKS* 1, 187.13; 191.16; 194.20; 200.3; 201.3ff.; 201.9ff.; and 233.31.

245 See the outstanding articles on Kierkegaard's reception of Aristophanes, for example, Knut Klerve, "Anti-Dover or Socrates in the Clouds," *Symbolæ Osloensis*, vol. 58, 1983, pp. 23–37; Povl Johs. Jensen, "Aristophanes," in *Kierkegaard's Classical Inspiration*, ed. by Niels Thulstrup and Marie Mikulová Thulstrup, Copenhagen: C.A. Reitzel 1985 (*Bibliotheca Kierkegaardiana*, vol. 14), pp. 18–24; and not least of all Eric Ziolkowski, "From *Clouds* to *Corsair:* Kierkegaard, Aristophanes, and the Problem of Socrates," in *The Concept of Irony*, ed. by Robert L. Perkins, pp. 193–233.

II. Concluding Perspectives

Kierkegaard's Socrates is stamped by the Danish environment that he found himself in. This Danish Greekness, which imported its most essential ideas from the German Socrates literature, led Kierkegaard back to the German research. Although the *Socrates of philology*, seen ideally, is the hermeneutical precondition for the understanding of both the *Socrates of philosophy* and the *Socrates of literature*, this perspective nevertheless does not exhaust the entire Socrates reception, as it locally stamped Kierkegaard. Therefore, it is necessary to cast a glance at the remaining material.

A. The Socrates of Philosophy

When Kierkegaard in his dissertation compares his results with the research tradition, he finds only a single scholar with whom it is worth taking up a discussion. Hegel's Socrates designates not only a great turning point in the reception, but he, so to speak, sublates all previous efforts. Hegel's method is, however, not stainless. Speculative philosophy mocked Schleiermacher and the historical-philological "*Hyper-Kritik*" as completely "*überflüssig*"![246] Or as Kierkegaard expresses it regarding the possibility of giving philological support to Hegel: "Anything like this is effort wasted on Hegel."[247] But precisely the philological dialectic with its psychological hermeneutics is Kierkegaard's real weapon against the German master thinker. One can say that the existence-philosophical Socrates accurately designates the *Socrates of philosophy* in so far as this is nothing but the *Socrates of philology*. It is in this changing movement that Kierkegaard teaches the Hegelian to think concretely. It is in this "combined reckoning," that one finds the originality of the dissertation in general.[248] Now, is there a *Socrates of philosophy* in a Danish context?

In 1813, the year of Kierkegaard's birth, F.C. Sibbern was named professor of philosophy. He replaced Niels Treschow (1751–1833), who returned to Norway in order, after its independence, to work at the newly opened university in Oslo. Treschow had in 1803 taken over the professorship after Børge Riisbrigh (1731–1809), "the Danish Socrates," as he was called.[249] It is, however, not easy to find in Riisbrigh's philosophical writings any special affinity with the Greek hero.[250] What binds Riisbrigh to Socrates is Diogenes Laertius' classic history of philosophy,

---

246 See *SKS* 1, 266 / *CI*, 222.

247 Ibid.

248 Cf. my claim in the article "Kierkegaard's Socratic Hermeneutic in *The Concept of Irony*," in *The Concept of Irony*, ed. by Robert L. Perkins, pp. 101–22.

249 See B.P. Kofod, *Mindetale over afdøde Professor, Etatsraad og Ridder Børge Riisbrigh ved Hans Jordefærd den 27de April 1809*, Copenhagen [1809], p. 15.

250 See, for example, the central treatise, "Undersøgelse af den Mening, at sand Filosofi og et fuldstændigt Begreb om sand Filosofi først i vore Tider ere blevne til," *Det kongelige danske Videnskabernes Selskabs Skrivter for Aarene 1801 og 1802*, vol. 2, no. 1, 1803, pp. 1–96 (in German: "Ueber das Alter der Philosophie und des Begriffs von derselben," 1803), which is a philosophical-historical overview with emphasis on the epistemological problems, in which Socrates shines in his absence.

which the professor translated and wrote commentaries for *con amore*. With this work, which appeared in 1812, Danish literature received one of the main works of the Socrates literature.[251] Kierkegaard spent many hours in the company with this anecdotal Danish Socrates and all the Socratic schools.

There were two professorships in philosophy at the University of Copenhagen: the one was—throughout Kierkegaard's entire lifetime—that of Frederik Christian Sibbern, and the other belonged to Poul Martin Møller during the period from 1830 to 1838. After Møller's death Hans Lassen Martensen gave lectures on philosophy, but only on modern philosophy;[252] the same thing is true for the lectures which Møller's successor Rasmus Nielsen offered from 1840.[253] Thus there are only two professors of philosophy who are of interest. They were both Kierkegaard's instructors: the one primarily took care of modern philosophy, or better, his own (Sibbern), while it was the task of the other (Møller) to cover the Greek history of philosophy. One interest, which in a way bound them together, was the occupation with the essence of irony, that is, the same occupation that constitutes the basis for Kierkegaard's conception of Socrates.[254]

In fact, it was Sibbern—famous for his completely unironic naiveté[255]—who first tried to open the debate about the nature of irony in Danish literature. He did this in a

---

251 Cf. *Diogen Laërtses filosofiske Historie, eller: navnkundige Filosofers Levnet, Meninger og sindrige Udsagn, i ti Bøger*, vols. 1–2, trans. by B. Riisbrigh, ed. by B. Thorlacius, Copenhagen: J.H. Schubothe 1812 (*ASKB* 1110–1111).

252 When Martensen in his lectures on speculative dogmatics from 1838–39 can say: "Christ does not want, like Socrates to awaken dialectic but faith; Christ leads to truth, Socrates wants to seek it" (*Pap*. II C 28 in *Pap*. XIII, p. 52), such a pregnant statement does not rely on studies of Socrates. It is highly probable that it is taken from the more recent German literature, for example, F.C. Baur. If Martensen had the edge by having a little more German erudition than Kierkegaard, then the latter had more education in the ancient Greeks (Cf. *SKS* 23, 179, NB:17:23). It is perhaps also for this reason that it was a section from the second part of the dissertation that Kierkegaard read aloud for Martensen. Cf. Martensen's memoirs, which are quoted in Kirmmse, "Socrates in the Fast Lane," p. 62. It is odd that the two who had read in Kierkegaard's dissertation ahead of time, did not even turn up at the defense.

253 Rasmus Nielsen, the capable Hegelian, who almost became a Kierkegaardian, hardly contributed to Kierkegaard's Socrates. But Nielsen became Kierkegaard's fate. If Kierkegaard had finished his dissertation a few years earlier, *he* would presumably have taken over Møller's empty *Lehrstuhl*. Now it was Nielsen, who could say "no" to being on Kierkegaard's dissertation committee, and Kierkegaard had to be satisfied with always having "to pick on Nielsen"; See Kirmmse, "Socrates in the Fast Lane," p. 96.

254 See Himmelstrup, *Søren Kierkegaards Opfattelse af Sokrates*, p. 33: "When the entire question of the essence and value of romantic irony has significance in the present connection, then it is due to the fact that Kierkegaard's conception of Socrates all the way through is so closely tied to his conception and judgment of irony in its various forms. Thus, it remains for a quite large part against the background of irony that Kierkegaard in his occupation with Socrates must be seen."

255 Sibbern himself tells of an attempt to write a newspaper article from the perspective of rhetorical irony, but even this was unsuccessful, the professor of philosophy had to declare. Cf. Sibbern, *Om Poesie og Konst i Almindelighed med Hensyn til alle Arter deraf, dog især*

fragment, not previously discussed, from 1819, which for this reason will be quoted here *extenso*:

> Socratic irony, as we know it from Plato, and irony in general, which in such manifold forms comes again in the most outstanding men, for example, in Goethe—what is it really? The first thing in it is the free view of life, an unprejudiced mind's clear, calm, circumspect eye, with a completely certain and unshakable conviction that something which is raised above all change and all partical forms has infinite reality. But in addition to this there comes an eye for the many ways in which this incontestable being collides, or is met with the manifold special and momentary expressions of life's constantly changing game. The clear eye that has an overview of the whole sees, and the fresh mind amuses itself by noticing soon the insipid disharmonaries, soon the odd contrasts, in which the individual expressions of life, even the most insignificant, often come to stand with the deepest truth and being. Irony is an epic calm and clarity of mind disposed to merry jest; and the inner moving principle in its wittiness is the ever present, ever prepared to express a sense of a higher existence's infinite essence.[256]

Did Kierkegaard know this passage in Sibbern?[257] We do not know. But since Kierkegaard's favorite poem by P.M. Møller was published in the same volume,[258] and since Møller—as we will see—was interested in the nature of irony, Kierkegaard could either himself have sought out this volume or been referred to it by Møller.[259] Sibbern's question is repeated in 1822 in a proposal for a prize essay in the Academy of Sciences:

> After an initial collecting of the most important examples of Socratic irony, as they are found in Plato, one is invited to give a genuine and complete conception of this, so that one can see whether it consisted solely in a wistful concealment and dissimulation, used to mock especially the Sophists' lack of insight, or whether it was of a more profound origin and larger scope.[260]

Digte-, Maler-, Billedhugger- og Skuespillerkonst; eller Foredrag over almindelig Æsthetik og Poetik, vols. 1–3, Copenhagen: Paa Forfatterens Forlag, trykt hos J.H. Schultz 1834–53, vol. 3, pp. 279–80. See also Sibbern's letter to Poul Martin Møller from March 29, 1829, where Sibbern reports that even if he tried to be ironic in Møller's sense, it nevertheless went wrong. See also *Breve til og fra F.C. Sibbern*, vol. 2, p. 172 and *Dansk Litteratur-Tidende for 1830*, no. 40, p. 632. Cf. also Jens Himmelstrup, *Sibbern. En Monografi*, Copenhagen: J.H. Schultz Forlag 1934, pp. 263–4.

256 F.C. Sibbern, "Strøtanker," in *Iris. En Samling af Poesie og Prosa*, ed. by J.C. Hauch, Copenhagen: B. Brünnich 1819, pp. 188–98, see p. 192.

257 In another "*strøtanke*" Møller praises "Socrates' wonderful individuality" (ibid., p. 191), and Plato's dialogue the *Phaido* is lauded as the most outstanding unification of profound philosophy and immediate poetry (ibid.).

258 See the romance "Den gamle Elsker," ibid., pp. 112–15; cf. Kierkegaard's use of the poem in *Repetition.*

259 In Sibbern, Møller could also have found the inspiration for the idea of writing "*strøtanker*," which became Møller's masterpiece.

260 See Himmelstrup, *Sibbern. En Monografi*, pp. 265–6.

Since the proposal was not official, it was of course not answered—that is, before Kierkegaard some years later set about answering the question. Concerning Sibbern's response in the "*strøtanke*," which is certainly not without the influence of Jean Paul, one sees here the "Goetheian" irony introduced, which later comes to play a large role in the Danish irony debate.[261] In the first volume of *On Poetry and Art* from 1834 Sibbern—presumably under the influence of Solger—analyzes irony as a kind of sober-mindedness in reciprocal effect with enthusiasm or mood.[262] Sibbern had already printed the section on contemplative irony in 1826,[263] that is, before Heiberg—to which we will turn—in order to place irony on the agenda in earnest. We have here the form of irony that Kierkegaard later dubbed "controlled irony."[264]

One would think that Sibbern had the qualifications to judge Kierkegaard's dissertation on irony, which he in fact also read—judging by his official report.[265] However, if one casts a glance at Sibbern's careful presentation of irony in the third volume of *On Poetry and Art* from 1869,[266] one is amazed, or more correctly, it is difficult to avoid feeling disappointed. To be sure, Sibbern distinguishes truly between (1) world irony, (2) cheerful life irony (Goethe), (3) Schlegel–Tieck–Solgerian irony, (4) irony in Aristotle and Theophrastus, (5) Socratic irony, (6) rhetorical irony, and (7) the ironic-parodic, but if all of this was really written *after* Sibbern had read *The Concept of Irony*, it is striking that he has not found a single useable point in it! Let us therefore assume that when he only refers to Kierkegaard in a few footnotes,[267] the reason for this is simply that Sibbern did not update his analyses from the 1820s and 1830s but merely had them printed. However, Sibbern's

---

[261] Some of this material is presented in K. Brian Söderquist, "Kierkegaard's Contribution to the Danish Discussion of Irony," in *Kierkegaard and His Contemporaries. The Culture of Golden Age Denmark*, ed. by Jon Stewart, Berlin and New York: Walter de Gruyter 2003 (*Kierkegaard Studies Monograph Series*, vol. 10), pp. 78–105.

[262] See the lecture "Poesie og Konst betragtet in subjectiv Henseende, eller med Hensyn til Betingelserne derfor i Digters og Konstners Indre," especially the section "Ironie og Gemyt" in Sibbern's *Om Poesie og Konst*, vol. 1, pp. 367–93, see pp. 388–93. This lecture on irony, which Kierkegaard presumably heard in Sibbern's lecture hall in summer semester 1833, was called attention to by the reviewer Eggert Christopher Tryde (1781–1860) in *Maanedsskrift for Litteratur*, vol. 13, 1835, pp. 177–202.

[263] See *Gefion. Nytaarsgave for 1826*, ed. by Elisa Beyer, Copenhagen: Forlagt af Forfatterinden, trykt hos J.C. Elmquist 1826, pp. 54–70.

[264] See the concluding chapter, "Ironi som behersket Moment," in *SKS* 1, 352–7 / *CI*, 324–9, where there is also a reference to Solger's posthumous *Vorlesungen über Aesthetik*, Leipzig: F.A. Brochhaus 1829 (*ASKB* 1387), which contains the central chapter, "Von dem Organismus des künstlerischen Geistes," pp. 183–256.

[265] See, for example, Kirmmse, "Socrates in the Fast Lane," passim.

[266] See Sibbern, *Om Poesie og Konst*, vol. 3, pp. 243–81.

[267] Ibid., p. 257, where Hegel and Kierkegaard are corrected for claiming that romantic irony arises from Fichte's philosophy and not from Schelling's philosophy of nature, and on p. 276, where both Hegel and Kierkegaard are said to be right, even though the latter precisely contradicts the former. Concerning the first objection, Sibbern should have read his friend, Poul Martin Møller's remark about the nature of Romantic irony, that although "this practical resignation is infinitely different from the energetic morality which is taught in Fichte's works (which is certainly superfluous to note), it is nevertheless certain that it derives from Fichtean

presentation of Socrates and Socratic irony reveals that there is a deep intellectual gap between him and Kierkegaard.[268] It is not only striking—as Himmelstrup has already noted[269]—that Sibbern with no further ado finds that the best source for the real Socrates is Xenophon, and that Socrates is in fact not an ironist but a kind of immediate humorist, who really does not dissimulate. There is in Sibbern's Socrates—which reminds one strikingly of Sibbern himself—such an enormous lack of reflection that he almost at every point in the presentation stands in opposition to Kierkegaard's Socrates. Although Sibbern thus first posed the question, Kierkegaard with his response apparently learned nothing *positive* from Sibbern.[270]

Concerning the second professor of philosophy, Poul Martin Møller (1794–1838), there seems to be a general consensus in Kierkegaard research that Kierkegaard stands in Møller's debt, whether it is a question of Møller's wonderful personality,[271] or of the content of Møller's thoughts.[272] The proof, which is generally offered, but which proves nothing, is the dedication to *The Concept of Anxiety*, where Møller is dubbed: "The happy lover of Greek culture, the admirer of Homer, the confidant of Socrates, the interpreter of Aristotle."[273] Presumably Kierkegaard, this unhappy lover of Greek culture, with these predicates wanted to ally himself with the deceased Møller against modern speculative philosophy. It was Møller—and only Møller—who was responsible for instruction in the history of Greek philosophy, but after his death this discipline, which was not taken up by his successor, had only fallen into a slumber. Well, Møller and Kierkegaard can be juxtaposed on the question of irony and in the characterization of Socrates.

In 1834 Møller reviewed Sibbern's book on aesthetics, but he did not take up the seventh lecture's section on irony.[274] As mentioned, Tryde did, which again led Møller to begin a larger contribution on the nature of irony. This was, however, only published in 1848 as a fragment under the Kierkegaadian title: "On the Concept of

idealism, since it is also well known that Fr. Schlegel was one the most enthusiastic admirers of Fichte's *Wissenschaftslehre*." *Efterladte Skrifter*, 2nd ed., 1848, pp. 155–6.

268 Sibbern, *Om Poesie og Konst*, vol. 3, pp. 265–77.

269 Himmelstrup, *Søren Kierkegaards Opfattelse af Sokrates*, pp. 317–18.

270 This is also Jens Himmelstrup's conclusion about the relation between Kierkegaard and Sibbern taken as a whole. Cf. *Sibbern. En Monografi*, pp. 258–75.

271 Vilhelm Andersen thought straightforwardly that Møller in his own person was Kierkegaard's Socrates; cf. his *Tider og Typer*, vol. 2, p. 102.

272 See, for example, Lars Bejerholm, "Sokratisk metod hos Søren Kierkegaard och hans samtida," in *Kierkegaardiana*, vol. 4, 1962, pp. 28–44, or Wolfdietrich von Kloeden's thorough account "Socrates" in *Kierkegaard's Classical Inspiration*, pp. 104–82, especially pp. 110ff.; cf. also his *Kierkegaard und Socrates. Sören Kierkegaard's Socratesrezeption*, Bochum: Evangelische Fachhochschule Rheinland-Westfalen-Lippe 1991, pp. 9ff., and Himmelstrup, *Søren Kierkegaards Opfattelse af Sokrates*, p. 176, who believes more in "the undoubtable influence of Poul Møller on Kierkegaard in the direction of the general sense of the significance of the personality," than he actually thinks that, for example, Møller's *Efterladte Skrifter* could move anything in Kierkegaard.

273 See *SKS* 4, 311 / *CA*, 5.

274 See *Dansk Litteratur-Tidende*, no. 12, 1835, pp. 181–92 and no. 13, 1835, pp. 205–9 (also printed in Poul Martin Møller, *Efterladte Skrifter*, vols. 1–6, 2nd ed., vol. 2, Copenhagen: C.A. Reitzel 1848–50, vol. 2, pp. 105–26.

Irony."[275] If the young Kierkegaard had known these observations, it would have had to have happened by means of oral communication from Møller himself.[276] The fragment discusses Romantic irony (especially Fr. Schlegel's *Lucinde*) along with Hegel's criticism of it,[277] and thus constitutes a parallel to the second part of Kierkegaard's dissertation. These few pages could hardly have impressed the later magister in irony.[278]

Møller lectured a few times on the history of ancient philosophy.[279] We know that Kierkegaard went to Møller's lectures,[280] but we have no evidence that he attended the lectures specifically on the history of philosophy.[281] If he did not sit in Møller's lecture hall and did not read one of the circulated notebooks, then he would have had to have waited until 1841, when the lectures appeared in the second volume of Møller's *Posthumous Writings*.[282] The fact that Kierkegaard studied the lectures during the period when he was writing *The Concept of Anxiety* and *Philosophical Fragments* is demonstrated in the commentaries in *Søren Kierkegaards Skrifter*.[283]

Where the German literature can boast many histories of philosophy each with their own Socrates, Møller, by contrast, delivers the first history of philosophy in

---

275 See *Efterladte Skrifter*, 2nd ed., vol. 3, pp. 152–8.

276 The fact that the two had interesting conversations with each other is clear from the journal entry *SKS* 17, 225, DD:18 / *KJN* 1, 216–17.

277 One senses that Møller's Hegel concerns primarily § 140 in *Grundlinien der Philosophie des Rechts* (then newly published in Berlin 1833), but, by contrast, not the criticism in the introduction to the *Vorlesungen über die Aesthetik* (1835) or the Socrates portrait in *Vorlesungen über die Geschichte der Philosophie* (1836). Møller is also interested in irony in his "*strøtanker*." Cf. *Efterladte Skrifter*, 2nd ed., vol. 3, where "the degree of objectivity, which one sometimes has called irony" is defined such that "its author must have raised himself to a standpoint where egoism and sympathy are not destroyed but present as subordinate elements in a higher mental disposition," p. 85.

278 According to Himmelstrup and Vilhelm Andersen, Kierkegaard attempts in the second part of the dissertation straightforwardly to imitate Møller's criticism of Romanticism; indeed, it is claimed that Kierkegaard's portrayal of irony is a direct continuation of Møller's fragment. Cf. *Søren Kierkegaards Opfattelse af Sokrates*, p. 73.

279 Namely, in winter semester 1833–34 and in winter semester 1834–35 (for 21 auditors). The last series of lectures treated the period from Aristotle to the early Christian period. Cf. *Akademiske Tidender*, vols. 1–4, ed. by Hannibal Peter Selmer, Copenhagen: Gyldendal 1833–41, vol. 2, 1834, p. 390. Perhaps one can then conclude that the first series of lectures—1 hour three times a week—treated the period before Aristotle, that is, among other things, Socrates.

280 His name appears on the list of auditors to Møller's lectures on metaphysics in winter semester 1836–37. Cf. Tudvad, *Kierkegaards København*, p. 181.

281 Tudvad thinks that it is possible that he attended the lectures on the history of ancient philosophy in winter semester 1834–35; compare ibid., p. 179.

282 P.M. Møller, "Udkast til Forelæsninger over den ældre Philosophies Historie," *Efterladte Skrifter*, vols. 1–3, ed. by F.C. Olsen, 1st ed., Copenhagen: C.A. Reitzel 1839–43, vol. 2, pp. 275–527; an offprint had, however, appeared already in 1841.

283 See, for example, the demonstration that Kierkegaard quotes Aristotle from Møller's lectures. Cf. *SKS* K4, 217.

Danish. The portrayal of Socrates fills not quite 18 pages.[284] Himmelstrup thinks that the presentation is "schematic and quite unoriginal—building on Ritter and Hegel,"[285] although he nonetheless admits the presence of "Poul Møller's naturalness and psychological sense."[286] H.P. Rohde finds some similiarites between Møller's and Kierkegaard's Socrates, but he does not undertake a more detailed examination.[287] It is as if the more one dwells on Møller's presentation, the more bridges one finds to Kierkegaard. For example, by way of conclusion he has Socrates be the one who destroys the Greek "condition of innocence,"[288] so that humanity can no longer return to "its reflection-free conditon."[289] When this transition is thought radically, that is, when reflection in and for Socrates is thought absolutely, then we have Kierkegaard. Møller's portrayals of Socrates' irony as an ability to completely assimilate himself in the point of view of the person he is conversing with[290] are entirely Kierkegaardian. It is, however, different when Møller has humor be "the dominant mental disposition (the temperament), from which irony springs."[291] Kierkegaard would never go this far: for him humor is always baptized![292] Møller's evaluation of the sources has more affinity with Kierkegaard: Xenophon with "his lack of philosophical natural disposition" had to "misunderstand Socrates";[293] the main source Plato, with his rich speculative thinking, had aggrandized Socrates;[294] and Aristophanes had his dignity reinstated by Hegel and the Hegelians.[295] Kierkegaard could have received much inspiration from Møller. So much for the Socrates of philosophy![296]

---

284 Møller, *Efterladte Skrifter*, 1st ed., vol. 2, pp. 357–75.

285 Himmelstrup, *Søren Kierkegaards Opfattelse af Sokrates*, p. 318. Here one must, however, note that Hegel's *Lectures on the History of Philosophy* only appeared in 1836.

286 Ibid.

287 See H.P. Rohde, "Poul Møller," in *Kierkegaard's Teachers*, ed. by Niels Thulstrup and Marie Mikulová Thulstrup, Copenhagen: C.A. Reitzel 1982 (*Bibliotheca Kierkegaardiana*, vol. 10), pp. 89–109, see pp. 94–5.

288 Møller, *Efterladte Skrifter*, 1st ed., vol. 2, p. 375.

289 Ibid.

290 Ibid., pp. 363–4.

291 Ibid., p. 364.

292 Himmelstrup notes that Møller's Socrates on the strength of his humor comes to have a family resemblance with Sibbern's Socrates, *Søren Kierkegaards Opfattelse af Sokrates*, p. 318. Against this, one can object that Sibbern's humor is almost without reflection, while Møller's humor contains reflection, however, not infinite reflection. When Himmelstrup therefore sees Kierkegaard's Socrates from the dissertation as "a step backward" in relation to Møller's Socrates (ibid.), then this is presumably due to the fact that Himmelstrup to a large degree lacks a sense for the decisive significance of reflection.

293 Møller, *Efterladte Skrifter*, 1st ed., vol. 2, p. 365.

294 Ibid.

295 Ibid., pp. 368–9.

296 An important event was also the translation of a large part of Ferdinand Christian Baur's (1792–1860), *Das Christliche des Platonismus oder Socrates und Christus. Eine religionsphilosophische Untersuchung*, Tübingen: Ludw. Friedr. Fues 1837 (*ASKB* 422) (a reprint from *Tübinger Zeitschrift für Theologie*, no. 3, 1837). Cf. also "Det Christelige i Platonismen eller Socrates og Christus. En religionsphilosophisk Undersøgelse," *Tidsskrift for udenlandsk theologisk Litteratur*, 1837, pp. 485–533 (*ASKB* U 29). This treatise had great

B. The Literary Socrates

There is also a more poetic use of the Socrates figure,[297] although the Danish literature only has a single significant example, namely, Adam Oehlenschläger's tragedy *Socrates* from 1835.[298] The great debate about Oehlenschläger's Socrates has an important prelude. What is decisive here is not the distinction between the Socrates of philology and the Socrates of philosophy; Oehlenschläger's Socrates was attacked from both camps. At the time there was a rift between, on the one hand, the king of poetry, Oehlenschläger and his followers, who cultivated the immediate poetic genius, and, on the other hand, the king of criticism, Johan Ludvig Heiberg and his followers, who cultivated form, reflection, the comic, etc. Heiberg had, in an impressive critical treatise, tried to demonstrate that Oehlenschläger's genius was immediate, for which reason lyric-epic poetry, the romance, was his limitation. The tragic poet Oehlenschläger was not able to write drama. He lacked reflection, and without reflection there is no irony, and "*Without irony there can be no dramatic poet for the more recent age.*"[299] Oehlenschläger's followers were furious that their hero had been dethroned.[300] Heiberg should not believe that he was any Aristophanes, they clamed.[301] To this Heiberg responded that Oehlenschläger was even further from being a Socrates.[302] It must remain uncertain whether it was out of spite or whether it was in order to disprove every claim by Heiberg in practice that Oehlenschläger decided to write not just another tragedy but straightforwardly to make the grand master of irony to his main character. When one asked the king of the poets, he merely answered: "I loved Socrates; my fantasy, my thought, my

---

significance for Kierkegaard. Cf. Himmelstrup, *Søren Kierkegaards Opfattelse af Sokrates*, pp. 221ff.

297 See, for example, Erik Alba, *Socrates in der deutschen Literatur*, Nymwegen: Wächter-Verlag 1949.

298 In 1835–36 Christian Bredahl also wrote a few acts of a Socrates drama. Cf. Oskar Thyregod, *Christian Bredahl. Harmens og Retsindets Digter i vor Litteratur*, Copenhagen: H. Hagerup 1918, pp. 182–6. This piece was, however, only printed as "Fragmenter af fjerde og femte Act af Socrates, Tragedie af C. Bredahl," in P.L. Møller's *Gæa*, 1846, pp. 51–82.

299 This battle in Danish literature is portrayed in Olesen, "Heiberg's Initial Approach: The Prelude to his Critical Breakthrough," and his "Heiberg's Critical Breakthrough in 1828: A Historical Presentation."

300 Oehlenschläger's friend, the philosopher Henrik Steffens, agreed, however, with Heiberg, in that he wrote of the great poet: "His humor is childishly playful, without that wounded tragic sting of irony; and if one misses in him that profound view of our age's higher art, then his clarity makes us happy, the reconciling mildness, which satisfies us in its own way," *Dansk Litteratur-Tidende for 1830*, no. 31, 1830, p. 494.

301 One of the most offended of Oehlenschläger's followers, the author (Johannes) Carsten Hauch (1790–1872), wrote in 1837 a dialogue about irony, in which he discusses Heiberg's definitions. Cf. Hauch, "Bidrag til Belysningen af nogle æsthetiske Stridspuncter," in his *Afhandlinger og æsthetiske Betragtninger*, Copenhagen: C.A. Reitzel 1855, pp. 269–333.

302 See J.L. Heiberg, "Den flyvende Posts Epistel til Lanterna-magica-Doublanten i Sorø," *Kjøbenhavns flyvende Post*, no. 8, January 18, 1830, column 7.

feeling desired to occupy itself with him."[303] Indeed, Oehlenschläger felt the desire to "study the age,"[304] including Xenophon, Plato, and Aristophanes, and why not, he asked, "combine this study with my own art."[305]

Oehlenschläger's tragedy *Socrates* was no great success.[306] In spite of great acting, where Dr. Ryge played Socrates "with noble calm, profound truth and expressive force,"[307] and Madame Heiberg shined as Socrates' daimon, the piece was only performed three times in December 1835.[308] A further performance came a year later,[309] but it was a kind of gift from the theater management.[310] Oehlenschläger himself, however, regarded his *Socrates* as a masterpiece. On his deathbed he had his sons read the tragedy aloud to him, and at the obsequies after Oehlenschlägers death some scenes from *Socrates* were performed.[311] Oehlenschläger thought that the piece's fiasco was due to the negative criticism,[312] which, however, hardly explains the whole situation.

Oehlenschläger had succeeded in making Socrates into a kind of Judge William.[313] One meets on the stage "Danish Romanticism's good and upright, piously believing best citizen,"[314] who makes himself comfortable with his wife and children, although there are of course conflicts that need to be resolved. Even though there are lines that Socrates speaks that come straight out of Plato,[315] it is striking to what degree

---

303 See *Oehlenschlägers Erindringer*, vol. 1–4, ed. by J.W. Oehlenschläger, Copenhagen: Andreas Frederik Høst 1850–51, vol. 4, p. 139.

304 Ibid.

305 Ibid.

306 Adam Oehlenschläger, *Sokrates, Tragødie af Oehlenschläger*, Copenhagen: Paa Forfatterens Forlag 1836 (printed also in *Oehlenschlägers Tragødier*, vols. 1–9, Copenhagen: Forfatterens Forlag 1841–44, vol. 8, pp. 147–276 (*ASKB* 1601–1605)).

307 See Thomas Overskou, *Den danske Skueplads, i dens Historie, fra de første Spor af danske Skuespil indtil vor Tid*, vols. 1–7, Copenhagen: Samfundet til den danske Literaturs Fremme 1854–76, vol. 5, pp. 256–7 [vols. 6–7 were entitled *Den kongelig danske Skuepladses Historie, fra dens Overdragelse til Staten i 1849 indtil 1874. Efter Forfatterens Død fuldført af Edgar Collin*, 1874–76] (for vol. 1 see *ASKB* 1395).

308 It was performed at The Royal Theater on Wednesday the 16th, Saturday the 19th and Tuesday the 22nd of December 1835.

309 Namely, on October 6, 1836.

310 See Overskou, *Den danske Skuesplads*, vol. 5, p. 257.

311 Namely, on February 6, 1850. See, for example, *Bidrag til den oehlenschlägerske Literaturs Historie*, vols. 1–2, Copenhagen: Forlagt af Samfundet til den danske Literaturs Fremme 1868, vol. 1, pp. 347–8.

312 See *Oehlenschlägers Erindringer*, vol. 4, p. 139: "The entire dominant tone at that time rejected it, and I had at the time not a single aesthetician, who supported me publicly except for the good Wilster in Sorøe."

313 Later Oehlenschläger himself says—perhaps under the influence of Kierkegaard: "I wanted to present a hostility and a reconciliation between the ethical and the aesthetic principle in Socrates and Aristophanes," *Oehlenschlägers Erindringer*, vol. 4, p. 145.

314 William Norvin, *Socrates*, Copenhagen 1933 (Festskrift udgivet af Københavns Universitet i Anledning af Hans Majestæt Kongens Fødselsdag 26. september 1933), p. 9.

315 See Povl Johs. Jensen, who goes so far as to say "The Danish Golden Age could not produce a Greek tragedy, but Oehlenschläger has in his *Socrates* given the most beautiful

the character in the situation lacks reflection, not to mention double reflection; most often Socrates' wisdom positively consists of *confirming* diverse dogmas instead of *showing* that he himself is also something of a dialectician. In the very plot, which, according to one expert, was partly taken from Oehlenschläger's private life,[316] Socrates' daughter becomes the girlfriend of Aristophanes, but the two, of course, cannot have each other due to the fact that Aristophanes deprives himself of his bride from youth in *The Clouds*. He does this, of course, but whether this is out of respect for the good Socrates or because he is supposed to be in love, is merely one of the dialectical difficulties which Oehlenschläger does not have an eye for.

Kierkegaard was presumably among the select audience who saw the tragedy *Socrates*. Whether it had been out of "veneration for the Greek thinker,"[317] or out of piety towards Oehlenschläger,[318] it must in any case have been a great event for the young Kierkegaard, who, as a Heibergian, must have had low expectations about the performance itself. The criticism that Oehlenschläger refers to is the extensive article in the *Maanedsskrift for Litteratur* which appeared in November 1836[319] when the tragedy had already been removed from the billboard. The anonymous author is without doubt F.C. Petersen, whose 37 pages are probably the most extensive thing that was written about the piece,[320] as well as being a significant contribution to the contemporary Socrates literature. Kierkegaard immediately made excerpts from this review,[321] which evidences that he was following the events. Another broadside against Oehlenschläger came from the Danish-German philologist Peter Wilhelm Forchhammer (1803–94), who some months later in his brief Hegelian work *Die Athener und Socrates* complained about Aristophanes' defense; for Socrates *was* guilty.[322] Forchhammer's argumentation—along with the Hegelian reception of Aristophanes—is an important ingredient in *The Concept of Irony*.

Oehlenschläger indicated in his memoirs that there were also important men who had praised him—albeit in private—namely, P.O. Brøndsted, who sent

---

translation into Danish of Plato's *Apology*, *Crito* and *Phaido*." Cf. Povl Johs. Jensen, *Socrates*, Copenhagen: Gad 1969, p. 94.

316 See Vilhelm Andersen, *Adam Oehlenschläger. Et Livs Poesi. Manddom og Alderdom*, Copenhagen: Det Nordiske Forlag 1899, pp. 245ff.

317 See Tudvad, *Kierkegaards København*, p. 242.

318 See F.J. Billeskov Jansen, "Oehlenschläger," in *Kierkegaard: Literary Miscellany*, ed. by Niels Thulstrup and Marie Mikulová Thulstrup, Copenhagen: C.A. Reitzel 1981 (*Bibliotheca Kierkegaardiana*, vol. 9), pp. 91–111.

319 See *Maanedsskrift for Litteratur*, vol. 16, 1836, pp. 383–419.

320 See otherwise Lars O. Lundgren, *Socratesbilden. Från Aristofanes till Nietzsche*, Stockholm: Almqvist & Wiksell International 1978, pp. 143–6 and Erik Alba, *Socrates in der Deutschen Literatur*, pp. 22–8. Himmelstrup "obviously passes over" Oehlenschläger's literary treatment of Socrates; cf. his *Søren Kierkegaards Opfattelse af Sokrates*, p. 317, note.

321 See the journal entry *SKS* 18, 78–9, FF:20 / *KJN* 2, 72.

322 See P.W. Forchhammer, *Die Athener und Socrates. Die Gesetzlichen und der Revolutionär*, Berlin: Der Nicolaischen Buchhandlung 1837, pp. 50–2.

Oehlenschläger a poem,[323] and Christian Wilster's consoling letter.[324] However, Sibbern was forgotten,[325] although in fact he had delivered an extensive defense of Oehlenschläger's *Socrates*.[326] His contribution to the debate also contained a criticism of Hegel's Socrates, which had just appeared in 1836. Kierkegaard could have obtained great inspiration in the Socrates debate during these months.[327] Heiberg wrote a year later that Oehlenschläger's *Socrates* was not a tragedy at all,[328] but the culimination became a crass satire on Oehlenschläger's *Socrates* and the naive armsbearer Sibbern, who were both blind to the insight of irony; all the citizens of Copenhagen came to be familiar with this from "A Soul after Death.[329] Kierkegaard was entirely in agreement! He later noted how laughable it was that a poet wanted to add ideality to a historical figure such as Socrates, whose ideality the poet cannot even understand: "yet I have enough of the Socratic in me to understand that I did not get Oehlenschläger to understand this."[330]

The goal here has been to investigate a possible Danish context behind Kierkegaard's Socrates reception. That there is such a reception should now be obvious. Of course, many roads lead again to the German reception and perhaps also to the original Greek literature. In the end, it is, however, worth remembering that Kierkegaard's Socrates was to a large extent an original creation. This can also be found in the true words:

> Had Kierkegaard done nothing other than discover Socrates and make him comprehensible—it would have been an accomplishment that would have made him unforgettable, which would have constantly designated him as a landmark in the development of humanity.[331]

Translated by Jon Stewart

---

323 See *Oehlenschlägers Erindringer*, vol. 4, pp. 146–7. From this it is clear that Brøndsted's Socrates is so far from Kierkegaard's that it is impossible to conclude about Brøndsted's role as opponent at Kierkegaard's defense: "it is reasonable to assume that he was generally positive," Kirmmse, "Socrates in the Fast Lane," p. 73.

324 See *Oehlenschlägers Erindringer*, vol. 4, p. 263.

325 See Sibbern, *Om Poesie og Konst*, vol. 3, Tillæg, p. XXXII, where Sibbern mentions this oversight.

326 See *Kjøbenhavnsposten*, no. 323, November 16, 1836, pp. 1303–6; see also the anonymous response, "Et Par Ord i Anledning af Professor Sibberns Yttringer over Hegel i Kjøbenhavnsposten Nr. 323," *Kjøbenhavnsposten*, no. 338, December 1, 1836, pp. 1365–7.

327 One can perhaps include in this debate the reply to the professor of theology Henrik Nicolai Clausen, who had placed the speculative Plato above the didactical Socrates, which is found in *Materialier til et dansk, biographisk-literarisk Lexicon*, no. 54, December 25, 1835, column 1.

328 See Heiberg's review of Hertz's *Svend Dyrings Huus* (1837), in J.L. Heiberg, *Prosaiske Skrifter*, vols. 1–11, Copenhagen: C.A. Reitzel 1861–62, vol. 4, p. 284. Cf. also *Breve og Aktstykker vedrørende Johan Ludvig Heiberg*, vols. 1–5, ed. by Morten Borup, Copenhagen: Gyldendal 1946–50, vol. 3, p. 300.

329 J.L. Heiberg, *Nye Digte*, Copenhagen: C.A. Reitzel 1841.

330 See the journal *SKS* 26, NB31:94 / *JP* 4, 4301, p. 222.

331 A.B. Drachmann, *Udvalgte Afhandlinger*, Copenhagen: Gyldendal 1911, p. 140.

Bibliography

Eighteenth- and Nineteenth-Century Danish Scholarship in The Auction Catalogue *of Kierkegaard's Library that Discuss Plato and Socrates*

Hagen, Johan Frederik, *Ægteskabet. Betragtet fra et ethisk-historiskt Standpunct*, Copenhagen: Wahlske Boghandels Forlag 1845, p. 90; p. 107, note; pp. 110–18; p. 113 (*ASKB* 534).

Heiberg, Johan Ludvig, "Om den romantiske Tragedie af Hertz: *Svend Dyrings Huus*. I Forbindelse med en æsthetisk Betragtning af de danske Kæmpeviser," in *Perseus, Journal for den speculative Idee*, vols. 1–2, ed. by Johan Ludvig Heiberg, Copenhagen: C.A. Reitzel 1837–38, vol. 1, pp. 165–264, see p. 261 (*ASKB* 569).

Martensen, Hans Lassen, *De Autonomia conscientiæ sui humanæ in theologiam dogmaticam nostri temporis introducta*, Copenhagen: I.D. Quist 1837, p. 34 (*ASKB* 648).

—— *Grundrids til Moralphilosophiens System. Udgivet til Brug ved academiske Forelæsninger*, Copenhagen: C.A. Reitzel 1841, p. 95; p. 98 (*ASKB* 650).

—— *Den menneskelige Selvbevidstheds Autonomie i vor Tids dogmatiske Theologie*, Copenhagen: C.A. Reitzel 1841, p. 29 (*ASKB* 651).

—— *Den christelige Dogmatik*, Copenhagen: C.A. Reitzel 1849, p. 86; p. 96; p. 298; p. 360 (*ASKB* 653).

Møller, Poul Martin, "Sokrates," in his "Udkast til Forelæsninger over den ældre Philosophies Historie," in *Efterladte Skrifter af Poul M. Møller*, vols. 1–3, ed. by Christian Winther, F.C. Olsen, and Christen Thaarup, Copenhagen: C.A. Reitzel 1839–43, vol. 2, pp. 357–75 (*ASKB* 1574–1576).

—— "Platon," in his "Udkast til Forelæsninger over den ældre Philosophies Historie," in *Efterladte Skrifter af Poul M. Møller*, vol. 2, pp. 399–453

—— "Strøtanker," in *Efterladte Skrifter af Poul M. Møller*, vol. 3, p. 270; p. 287

Mynster, Jakob Peter, *Om Hukommelsen. En psychologisk Undersögelse*, Copenhagen: Jens Hostrup Schultz 1849, pp. 36–9 (*ASKB* 692).

—— *Den hedenske Verden ved Christendommens Begyndelse*, Copenhagen: Schultz 1850, p. 14; p. 20; pp. 31–3; pp. 37–8 (*ASKB* 693).

—— *Blandede Skrivter*, vols. 1–3, Copenhagen: Gyldendal 1852–53 [vols. 4–6, Copenhagen: Gyldendal 1855–57], vol. 1, p. 18; p. 25; pp. 117–18; pp. 243–6; vol. 2, p. 156; p. 194; p. 197; p. 255; p. 355; p. 363; vol. 3, p. 43 (*ASKB* 358–363).

Nielsen, Rasmus, *Den propædeutiske Logik*, Copenhagen: P.G. Philipsen 1845, p. 12; p. 38; p. 44; p. 90; p. 119; p. 186; p. 188; p. 258 (*ASKB* 699).

—— *Evangelietroen og Theologien. Tolv Forelæsninger holdte ved Universitetet i Kjøbenhavn i Vinteren 1849–50*, Copenhagen: C.A. Reitzel 1850, pp. 133–4 (*ASKB* 702).

Oehlenschläger, Adam, *Sokrates, Tragødie af Oehlenschläger*, in *Oehlenschlägers Tragødier*, vols. 1–9, Copenhagen: Forfatterens Forlag 1841–44, vol. 8, pp. 147–276 (*ASKB* 1601–1605).

Petersen, Frederik Christian, *Haandbog i den græske Litteraturhistorie*, Copenhagen: Fr. Brummer 1830, p. 80; p. 90; p. 135; p. 164; p. 182; pp. 192–3; p. 205; p. 207; p. 217; p. 360 (*ASKB* 1037).

—— *Om Epheterne og deres Dikasterier i Athen*, Copenhagen: Trykt i Bianco Lunos Bogtrykkeri 1847, p. 43; p. 48; p. 78 (*ASKB* 720).

—— *Platons Forestillinger om Staternes Oprindelse, Statsforfatninger og Statsbestyrelse. Indbydelsesskrift til Kjøbenhavns Universitets Fest i Anledning af Hans Majestæt Kongens Fødselsdag den 6te October 1854*, Copenhagen: Trykt i det Schultziske Officin 1854 (*ASKB* 1171).

Sibbern, Frederik Christian, *Logik som Tænkelære fra en intelligent Iagttagelses Standpunct og i analytisk-genetisk Fremstilling*, 2nd enlarged and revised ed., Copenhagen: Paa Forfatterens Forlag trykt hos Fabritius de Tengnagel 1835, p. 2; p. 22; p. 24; pp. 173–4; p. 246 (*ASKB* 777).

—— *Speculativ Kosmologie med Grundlag til en speculativ Theologie*, Copenhagen: Forfatterens eget Forlag 1846, p. 44 (*ASKB* 780).

—— *Nogle Betragtninger over Stat og Kirke* [*Indbydelsesskrift til Kjøbenhavn Universitets Fest i Anledning af Hans Majestæt Kongens Fødselsdag den 6te October 1849. Heri: Nogle Betragtninger over Stat og Kirke*], Copenhagen: Trykt i det Schultziske Officin 1849, pp. 2–21 (*ASKB* 782).

—— *Om Forholdet imellem Sjæl og Legeme, saavel i Almindelighed som i phrenologisk, pathognomonisk, physiognomisk og ethisk Henseende i Særdeleshed*, Copenhagen: Paa Forfatterens eget Forlag 1849, p. 74; p. 104; p. 193; p. 209; pp. 241–2; p. 247; p. 448; p. 463; pp. 474–8 (*ASKB* 781).

Zeuthen, Ludvig, *Om den christelige Tro i dens Betydning for Verdenshistorien. Et Forsøg*, Copenhagen: Gyldendal 1838, p. 23; p. 38; p. 47; pp. 54–7 (*ASKB* 259).

—— *Om Ydmyghed. En Afhandling*, Copenhagen: Gyldendal 1852, p. 17, note; p. 18; p. 67; pp. 85–6; p. 98 (*ASKB* 916).

Kierkegaard's Socrates Sources

Eighteenth- and Nineteenth-Century Germanophone Scholarship

Harald Steffes

For almost two and a half millennia, the figure of Socrates has fascinated practically every thinker who has investigated the relations between philosophy and religious conviction, between truth and subjectivity, and between philosophical teaching and the living pursuit of truth. In this Kierkegaard is no exception. As we will shortly see, Kierkegaard has his place amid a flood of eighteenth- and nineteenth-century reconstructions and approaches to Socrates. What makes Kierkegaard distinctive among the Socrates scholars of his period, however, is that he, more than most, took detailed account of the interpretations of Socrates that had preceded his own—and went on to influence modernity's view of Socrates more than perhaps any other author since the Renaissance.[1]

This article will leave aside the ramifications of Kierkegaard's portrait of Socrates for modern thought.[2] Instead, we will concentrate on the scholarly *sources in German* on which Kierkegaard relied in developing his portrait. For this reason, we will focus our attention on Kierkegaard's dissertation, *The Concept of Irony with Continual Reference to Socrates*. This text is not only the sole work by Kierkegaard that has Socrates in its title, but it is also Kierkegaard's one and only attempt to set forth an explicit and academically comprehensive engagement with the scholarly sources at issue, primarily those in German.

In what follows, we will enumerate these Germanophone sources, and will assess how Kierkegaard engaged with them. In Section I, we will summarize the main currents of Socrates reception in the eighteenth and nineteenth centuries. Section II will then offer an overview of the relevant sources in German that were present in Kierkegaard's library. In Section III, we will explore Kierkegaard's scholarly activity in his journals prior to 1841; while in Section IV, we will examine the distinctive

---

1 In the German-speaking world, however, Kierkegaard's influence took root only after a half-century's delay. The first German translations of *The Concept of Irony* did not appear until 1929! We will return to this point at the end. Cf. Kierkegaard, *Über den Begriff der Ironie. Mit ständiger Rucksicht auf Sokrates*, trans. by Hans Heinrich Schaeder, Munich and Berlin: R. Oldenbourg 1929; Kierkegaard, *Der Begriff der Ironie mit ständiger Rucksicht auf Sokrates*, trans. by Wilhelm Kütemeyer, Munich: Christian Kaiser 1929.

2 Cf. Jens Himmelstrup, *Søren Kierkegaards Opfattelse af Sokrates. En Studie i dansk Filosofis Historie*, Copenhagen: Arnold Busck 1924, pp. 314–30.

character of *The Concept of Irony* itself. Next, Sections V and VI will consider, respectively, the historical-philological approach to Socrates in Part One of *The Concept of Irony*, and the philosophical approach to Socrates in Part Two. In Section VII, finally, we will look beyond Kierkegaard's dissertation, and will consider his use of Germanophone Socrates sources in the remainder of his authorship.

I. The Main Currents of Eighteenth- and Nineteenth-Century Socrates Reception

Debate about how best to interpret Socrates' life and work began no earlier than Socrates' death, and it has never ceased. Nevertheless, the level of interest in Socrates has fluctuated noticeably over the course of history. The eighteenth century, along with the first half of the nineteenth, can be identified as the heyday of Socrates reception—particularly in the German-speaking world.

Because of the sheer volume of material from this period, the following overview of the relevant publications will necessarily be cursory.[3] Three groups of texts will be omitted from consideration at the outset. First, we will set aside for now the sources to which Kierkegaard explicitly appealed, since these will be covered in our subsequent sections. Second, we will omit discussion of the passages about Socrates in the well-known histories of philosophy of the time. Third and finally, no mention will here be made of the substantial literature on the *Socratic method* that flourished between 1780 and 1820, and which presented Socrates as a paradigm for (if not the inventor of) a distinctive pedagogical model or educational method.[4]

---

[3] For more thorough accounts, see Erik Abma, *Sokrates in der deutschen Literatur*, Nijmegen: Wächter 1949; Benno Böhm, *Sokrates im 18. Jahrhundert. Studien zum Werdegange des modernen Persönlichkeitsbewußtseins*, Neumünster: Karl Wachholtz Verlag 1966; Emil Brenning, "Die Gestalt des Sokrates in der Litteratur des vorigen Jahrhunderts," in *Festschrift der 45. Versammlung deutscher Philologen und Schulmänner*, Bremen: G. Winter 1899, pp. 421–81; Karlfried Gründer, "Sokrates im 19. Jahrhundert," in his *Reflexion der Kontinuitäten. Zum Geschichtsdenken der letzten Jahrzehnte*, Göttingen: Vandenhoeck & Ruprecht 1982, pp. 104–17; Luis E. Navia and Ellen L. Katz, *Socrates: An Annotated Bibliography*, New York: Garland 1988; Andreas Patzer, *Bibliographia Socratica. Die Wissenschaftliche Literatur über Sokrates von den Anfängen bis auf die neueste Zeit in systematisch-chronologischer Anordnung*, Freiburg: Karl Alber 1985; Wilhelm Süss, *Aristophanes und die Nachwelt*, Leipzig: Dieterich 1911.

[4] The two most prominent authors of such studies were Franz Michael Vierthaler (1758–1827) and Johann Friedrich Christoph Gräffe (1754–1816). Cf. Franz Michael Vierthaler, *Geist der Sokratik. Ein Versuch, den Freunden des Sokrates und der Sokratik gewidmet*, Salzburg: Mayr 1793; Johann Friedrich Christoph Gräffe, *Die Sokratik nach ihrer ursprünglichen Beschaffenheit in katechetischer Rücksicht betrachtet. Band II: Neuestes Katechetisches Magazin zur Beförderung des katechetischen Studiums*. Göttingen: Vandenhoeck & Ruprecht 1791. Kierkegaard, however, had little interest in these works. Even in his brief essay "The Art of Telling Stories to Children" (*SKS* 17, 122–33, BB:37 / *KJN* 1, 116–25)—Kierkegaard's first coherent text in which Socrates plays a prominent role—they are not mentioned. The same holds of the belletristic literature of the period in German, which influenced Oehlenschläger but apparently not Kierkegaard. For an example of such literature that is closely contemporaneous

The accounts of Socrates cited in *The Concept of Irony* derive almost without exception from the nineteenth century, and mainly from the 1820s and 1830s—that is, from the dissertation's immediate historical context. For this reason, studies of Kierkegaard's Socrates sources have at times confined themselves to this period.[5] A glance at *The Auction Catalogue* of Kierkegaard's library and at Kierkegaard's pseudonymous authorship indicates, however, that it is advisable to bring the eighteenth-century Socrates literature into consideration as well.

This is so because the eighteenth century was the *Socratic century*: the century that idealized Socrates. In their correspondence, for example, Princess Amalie Gallitzin (1748–1806) called the Dutch philosopher Frans Hemsterhuis (1721–90) "my Socrates," and he called her his "Diotima."[6] Similarly, Voltaire (1694–1778) and Frederick the Great (1712–86) expressed their mutual esteem by each declaring that the other was a new incarnation of Socrates.[7] The root of these invocations of Socrates lies in the Enlightenment's interest in a philosopher who, by means of his personal integrity, was able to personify the ideal human being independent of Christian faith. By the time of Pierre Bayle (1647–1706) and the Deists, the notion that morality was possible apart from Christianity had begun to gain ground; no one could seriously deny that Socrates embodied certain virtues, such as his abstemiousness, his moral integrity, and his loyalty to the ideal of justice even in the face of his impending death. These virtues all came to be viewed as possible for human beings even prior to, or without the benefit of, Christian revelation.

In other words, in the debate between secular philosophy and Christian faith about the autonomy of reason and the possibility of individual self-grounding, philosophy cited Socrates as its star witness. In this spirit, Socrates was at times represented as a prototypical freethinker persecuted by the priestly caste—as, for example, in Anthony Collins' *A Discourse of Free Thinking* (1713). Similarly, John Gilbert Cooper (1723–69) characterized Socrates as a just warrior for a pure religion of nature in his 1749 anticlerical polemic *The Life of Socrates*.[8]

---

with *The Concept of Irony*, see Carl Anton von Gruber, *Sokrates' Gespräche und Scenen aus Helena*, Pesth: J. Beimel 1836.

5 Cf. Himmelstrup, *Søren Kierkegaards Opfattelse af Sokrates*, pp. 184–226.

6 For excerpts from Princess Gallitzin's letters to Hemsterhuis, see Theodor Katerkamp, *Denkwürdigkeiten aus dem Leben der Fürstinn Amalia von Gallitzin gebornen Gräfinn von Schmettau mit besonderer Rücksicht auf ihre nächsten Verbindungen: Hemsterhuis, Fürstenberg, Overberg und Stolberg*, Münster: Theissing 1828 (photomechanical reprint, Bern: Herbert Lang 1971, pp. 117ff.).

7 For a particularly apt example, see Frederick the Great's letter of May 24, 1770 to Voltaire, in which he alludes to Erasmus' famous plea "*Sancte Socrates, ora pro nobis*": "I open with the greeting: *Sancte Voltere, ora pro nobis*." Cf. *Aus dem Briefwechsel Voltaire – Friedrich der Grosse*, ed. by Hans Pleschinski, Zürich: Haffmanns 1992, p. 446.

8 The complete title is telling: John Gilbert Cooper, *The Life of Socrates, Collected from the Memorabilia of Xenophon and the Dialogs of Plato, and Illustrated Farther by Aristotle, Diodorus Siculus, Cicero, Proclus, Apuleius, Maximus Tyrius, Boethius, Diogenes Laertius, Aulus Gellius, and Others, In Which The Doctrine of that Philosopher and the Academic Sect are Vindicated from the Misrepresentation of Aristophanes, Aristoxenus, Lucian; Plutarch, Athenaeus; Suidas and Lactantius; the Origin, Progress and Design of Pagan*

The more measured "Enlightenment" thinkers also regarded Socrates as the embodiment of their ideals and sense of life. In his *Life of Socrates*,[9] for example, François Charpentier (1620–1702) portrayed Socrates as a man of the world without explicitly depicting him as in competition with Christianity. Charpentier is also relevant for the eighteenth-century Socratic debates because he included a translation of Xenophon's *Memorabilia* in his book, and so helped to popularize that text.

Despite the stark differences between Cooper's and Charpentier's points of view, both books served as main sources for Johann Georg Hamann (1730–88) and Moses Mendelssohn (1729–86), authors of the two most famous and consequential books on Socrates in the eighteenth century.[10] This fact is significant for two reasons: first, because it reveals the remarkable impartiality with which positions as divergent as that of Cooper and Charpentier were simultaneously received; and second, because it reveals how fresh the primary sources on Socrates remained as late as the mid-eighteenth century. The wide circulation of Charpentier's book can be credited not least for its inclusion of a translation of Xenophon; while the wide variety of ancient texts cited in Cooper's book is evident from its full title, cited previously.

In 1759, Hamann published his *Socratic Memorabilia*,[11] a text that would strongly influence the *Sturm und Drang* movement, including such writers as Johann Gottfried Herder (1744–1803) and Friedrich Heinrich Jacobi (1743–1819), and through them Johann Wolfgang von Goethe (1749–1832).[12] This short text originated in Hamann's debate with his all-too-enlightened Königsberg friends, including Immanuel Kant (1724–1804), who sought to re-convert Hamann to the Enlightenment fold after the

Theology, Mythology, and Mysteries, explain'd; Natural Religion defended from Atheism on one hand, and Superstition on the other, and the destructive Tendency of both to Society demonstrated; Moral and Natural Beauty analogously compar'd; and the present Happiness of Mankind shewn to consist in, and the future to be acquir'd by, Virtue only derived from the true Knowledge of God. Herein the different Sentiments of La Mothe Le Vayer, Cudworth, Stanley, Dacier, Charpentier, Voltaire, Rollin, Warburton, and others on these Subjects, are occasionally consider'd, London: R. Dodsley 1749.

9 François Charpentier, *Les Choses mémorables de Socrate, Ouvrage de Xénophon traduit du Grec en Français. Avec La Vie de Socrates, Nouvellement composée et recueillie des plus célèbres Auteurs de l'Antiquité*, Paris, Augustin Courbé 1650. In the eighteenth century, this text gained special prominence thanks to its German translation by Christian Thomasius (1655–1728), *Das Ebenbild Eines wahren und ohnpedantischen Philosophi, Oder: Das Leben Socratis, Aus dem Französischen des Herrn Charpentier. Ins Teutsche übersetzt Von Christian Thomas*, Halle: Salfeld 1693–1720.

10 Cf. *Hamann's Schriften*, vols. 1–8, ed. by Friedrich Roth, Berlin: Georg Reimer 1821–43, vol. 7, p. 214 (*ASKB* 536–544).

11 Johann Georg Hamann, *Sokratische Denkwürdigkeiten*, Königsberg: Hartung 1759.

12 Cf. Goethe's letter to Herder in late 1771, in Johann Wolfgang von Goethe, *Briefe*, vols. 94–142, Weimar: Hermann-Böhlau 1887, vol. 95, pp. 10–13. It is noteworthy that Goethe long ruminated on the idea of composing a drama about Socrates. Ultimately he abandoned the idea, and turned his attention to a different figure: Faust. Cf. Böhm, *Sokrates im 18. Jahrhundert*, pp. 301ff. Thus when Kierkegaard writes that Socrates and Faust must be regarded as parallels, he thereby evinces a marked and surprising intellectual kinship with Goethe. (Because the editions of Goethe that Kierkegaard used include no letters, it is unlikely that Kierkegaard actually knew of Goethe's plan.)

latter's 1758 religious awakening in London.[13] Faced with the court of enlightened reason, which granted no validity to such conversion experiences, Hamann protested by sketching a Socrates who bears the features of a prophet, and who resembles a prototype of John the Baptist. In the key passages of his *Memorabilia*, Hamann links the Pauline critique of wisdom to Socrates' insistence on his own ignorance in such a way as to portray self-knowledge and the consciousness of sin as complementary acts. Against the Enlightenment, Hamann thus insists—with Socrates as his authority!—that the individual cannot ground himself autonomously with recourse to his own reason; rather, he is and remains reliant on an external force to constitute him as he is. Just as Socrates is first empowered to actualize the γνῶθι σαυτόν["Know thyself!"] by the Delphic oracle and his *daimon*, so too the Christian requires God's gracious and judging gaze in order to reach proper self-relation and self-acceptance.

The best-known book of the eighteenth century with a Socratic background is Mendelssohn's *Phaedo, or On the Immortality of the Soul*.[14] This book includes, as its introduction, a reprint of Mendelssohn's essay "The Life and Character of Socrates."[15] This popular-philosophical essay exemplifies how Socrates was treated by Enlightenment thinkers. In his Preface, Mendelssohn makes clear that he has no interest in Socrates as a historical figure, but will depict him instead as a contemporary. Mendelssohn's concern is, instead, to prove the immortality of the soul here and now. To the extent that theses from Plato's *Phaedo* are useful for this purpose, Mendelssohn will use them; but it is plainly evident that he is more interested in the *authority* of Socrates than in his actual utterances or teachings.[16]

It is typical of the late-eighteenth-century literature on Socrates that the authors involved were connected in manifold ways. Mendelssohn, for example, not only maintained a friendly correspondence with Hamann, but he also furnished the sole sympathetic contemporary review of his *Socratic Memorabilia*. Conversely, Hamann's writings contain several references to Mendelssohn's *Phaedo*, including a review.[17]

---

13 In many ways, Hamann's London transformation is comparable to Kierkegaard's experiences in the year 1838. Both describe their "conversions" in terms of Pietist theology. This is no accident, since both had fathers who were heavily influenced by the Moravian Brethren.

14 Moses Mendelssohn, *Phädon oder über die Unsterblichkeit der Seele in drey Gesprächen*, Berlin: Friedrich Nicolai 1767.

15 Moses Mendelssohn, "Leben und Character des Socrates," in ibid., pp. 1–48.

16 For example: "In the third dialogue, I needed to have full recourse to the moderns, and to allow my Socrates to speak almost like an eighteenth-century philosopher. I preferred to risk committing an anachronism than to leave out reasons that could contribute to [the reader's] conviction." Moses Mendelssohn, "Vorrede zum *Phädon*," in *Gesammelte Schriften: Jubiläumsausgabe*, vols. 1–25, ed. by Ismar Ellbogen (later volumes by Alexander Altmann) Berlin: Akademie Verlag 1932, vol. 3.1, p. 9. What is more, Mendelssohn's *Phaedo* is dedicated to a certain Thomas Abbt, who raised the Enlightenment's praise of Socrates to a polemical peak when, citing Erasmus, he cried: "*Sancte Socrate ora pro nobis*." Cf. Thomas Abbt, *Vom Verdienste*, Goslar: Hechtel 1765, p. 267.

17 *Hamann's Schriften*, vol. 3, pp. 134ff.; p. 373; p. 387; pp. 408ff.

Also worth mentioning is the most comprehensive—and bulkiest—eighteenth-century book in this field. Taken together, the two volumes of the *New Apology of Socrates, or a Study of the Doctrine of the Blessedness of the Pagans* by Johann August Eberhard (1739–1809) contain more than a thousand pages.[18] This study, a product of the Berlin Enlightenment, offers a classic plea for the case that blessedness is attainable outside of Christianity; and Socrates, once again, serves as both the paradigmatic exemplar and star witness for this thesis. Eberhard deserves mention not only because he was friendly with Mendelssohn, but also because his *magnum opus* provided Hamann with an occasion to compose an "Addendum" to his *Socratic Memorabilia*. Moreover, Kierkegaard's library contained a copy of the comparatively rare first edition of Eberhard's *New Apology*. While Eberhard's book is nowhere mentioned in *The Concept of Irony*, Kierkegaard did cite a different, shorter essay of Eberhard; but he is not known to have had that essay in his library.

While Kierkegaard's familiarity with Hamann can be attested no later than 1836,[19] he does not seem to have owned the *Phaedo* or any other writings of Mendelssohn.[20] Generally speaking, it is difficult to determine just how conversant Kierkegaard was with the eighteenth-century writings so far mentioned. But indirectly, at least—through references in Hamann's correspondence—Kierkegaard does appear to have acquired significantly more familiarity with this literature than is evident in *The Concept of Irony*.

Beyond the authors and works just mentioned, two nearly unknown eighteenth-century books on Socrates should also be mentioned here—for these shed significant light on the range of literature at issue. Both of these works seem to have gone unnoticed by Kierkegaard; for if he had been aware of them, it seems certain that he would have mentioned them in his journals. The two works in question are anonymous books, one penned by the founder of Herrnhut and the Moravian Brethren, and the other from a little-known student of Hermann Samuel Reimarus (1694–1768).

In 1725–26, Count Nikolaus Ludwig von Zinzendorf (1700–60) published an illegal and anonymous broadsheet under the title *The Socrates of Dresden*. The broadsheet's 32 pamphlets, distributed on a fortnightly basis, were aggressively suppressed by the authorities. In the 1732 edition (under the title *The German Socrates*), the total text of this broadsheet reached more than 300 pages.[21] What,

---

18 Johann August Eberhard, *Neue Apologie des Sokrates oder Untersuchung der Lehre von der Seligkeit der Heiden*, vols. 1–2, Berlin: Nicolai 1778–88 [vol. 1, 1788; vol. 2, 1778] (*ASKB* A I 185–186)

19 Kierkegaard owned the first edition of Hamann's collected works, see [Hamann], *Hamann's Schriften*, vols. 1–8, ed. by Friedrich Roth. As is well known, the motto to *The Concept of Anxiety* is derived from a comment in Hamann's *Socratic Memorabilia*.

20 In Kierkegaard's journals, Mendelssohn is mentioned only twice, in marginalia to notes to Martensen's "Lectures on the History of Modern Philosophy from Kant to Hegel"; Cf. *SKS* 22, 63–4, NB11:113. In the *Concluding Unscientific Postscript* Mendelssohn is mentioned as a friend and confidant of Lessing: *SKS* 7, 74–5 / *CUP1*, 104–5.

21 The complete title reads: Nikolaus Ludwig von Zinzendorf, *Der Teutsche Socrates, Das ist: Aufrichtige Anzeige verschiedener nicht so wohl unbekannter als vielmehr in Abfall gerathener Haupt-Wahrheiten in den Jahren 1725 und 1726: Anfänglich in der Königl. Residentz-Stadt Dreßden, Hernach aber dem gesamten lieben Vaterland teutscher Nation zu*

then, could have led a royal count in the employ of the state, who was then readying himself to become a leader of the Pietist movement, to engage in illegal activity on this scale? The answer is, evidently, that he sought to explain himself to his contemporaries. And when Count Zinzendorf addressed himself to his contemporaries who are believers in Socrates, he did so, quite naturally, in the guise of the universally beloved Socrates, and in the Enlightenment's classic medium, namely, in a weekly magazine.[22] With subtle acuity, Zinzendorf's "Socrates" uses Pauline theology to ask his Enlightened contemporaries whether their high esteem for reason has taken adequate account of reason's corruptibility.

The commonalities between Zinzendorf's Socrates and Kierkegaard's are impressive. Both authors harness Socrates to inquire into whether and how Christianity and philosophy can be united, and into the meaning of passion for the understanding. These parallel themes invite a comparison that would doubtless be fascinating. Such a comparison would also reveal that Zinzendorf served as a precursor to the theologian Friedrich Daniel Ernst Schleiermacher (1768–1834), anticipating his account of the relation between philosophy and theology (which Kierkegaard would later contest). But such a comparison will be omitted here.[23]

One particular former guest of Count Zinzendorf at Herrnhut proved to be a glowing votary of Socrates. This is Johann Christian Edelmann (1698–1767), one of the most hated and persecuted men of his day: a radical Enlightenment figure who, in 1734, sought to find his way back to established Christianity. It is precisely in Socrates that Edelmann believed he had found a comrade-in-arms in his battle to liberate "true" Christianity from the distortions of his age. Edelmann understood Socrates as a Christian, on the grounds that it is not biblical revelation, but reason, that grants human beings access to Christianity.[24]

---

einer guten Nachricht nach und nach ausgefertiget, und von dem Autore selbst mit einem kurtzen Inhalt jedes Stücks, nunmehro auch mit verschiedenen Erläuterungen, die sich in der ersten Auflage nicht befinden, und einem Anhange versehen, Leipzig: Bey Samuel Benjamin Walthern 1732. This text is available in a reprint, which appeared as Nikolaus Ludwig von Zinzendorf, *Hauptschriften in sechs Bänden*, vols. 1–6, ed. by Erich Beyreuther and Gerhard Meyer, Hildesheim: Georg Olms Verlag 1962, vol. 1.

22 Zinzendorf formulated his conception of his own Socratic role by citing 1 Cor 9:20 as follows: "Just as Paul [addressed] the Jews as a Jew would, why should not Socrates [address] the wise as a philosopher would, in order to win the wise over?" See Zinzendorf, *Der Teutsche Socrates*, p. 168.

23 In my view, it is highly unlikely that Kierkegaard could have known of Zinzendorf's "Socrates" pamphlets, since they were so effectively suppressed.

24 Cf. Johann Christian Edelmann, *Gesprächs-weise abgehandelt zwischen Doxophilo und Philaletho, Worinnen Von allerhand, theils verfallenen, theils gegenwärtig unterdruckten, theils noch unbekanten Wahrheiten, Nach Anleitung der Bibel, Auf eine freymüthige und aufrichtige Art geredet wird*, Unterredungen 1–15, [Bückeburg]: n.p. 1735–43 (photomechanical reprint, vols. 1–6, ed. by Walter Grossmann, Stuttgart-Bad Cannstatt: Frommann 1970 (vols. 1–6 in *Sämtliche Schriften in Einzelausgaben*, vols. 1–12, ed. by Walter Grossman, Stuttgart-Bad Canstatt: Frommann 1969–87)); Edelmann, *Die Göttlichkeit der Vernunft: in einer kurtzen Anweisung zu weiterer Untersuchung*, n.p. 1742 (photomechanical reprint, ed. by Walter Grossmann, Stuttgart-Bad Cannstatt: Frommann 1977 (vol. 8 in Johann Christian Edelmann, *Sämtliche Schriften in Einzelausgaben*)). On Edelmann's relation to Count Zinzendorf, and

In the case of Edelmann as well, we can rule out the possibility that Kierkegaard was familiar with his book. Kierkegaard nowhere mentions Edelmann; and in any case, thanks to their public suppression and burning, copies of Edelmann's texts had become extremely rare. Moreover, if he had been familiar with Edelmann, one would expect him to show a strong interest in Edelmann's campaign to liberate true Christianity from its contemporary counterfeits—and, equally, to have disagreed strongly with Edelmann's Neoplatonic rationalism, which sought to identify God with reason by means of the concept of *logos*.

At the same time, it should be mentioned that Gotthold Ephraim Lessing (1729–81)—who plays a prominent role in Kierkegaard's discussion of Socrates in *Philosophical Fragments* and the *Concluding Unscientific Postscript*—may have had Zinzendorf's *German Socrates* at hand. In his 1750 "Thoughts about the Herrnhut Pietists," Lessing compares Count Zinzendorf's significance to theology with Socrates' significance to philosophy.[25]

In 1785, there appeared an anonymous 142-page book, written by a student of Reimarus, bearing clear echoes of the Reimarus fragments edited by Lessing.[26] This book's allusion to the Reimarus fragments is already evident in the title, which modifies a citation from them by replacing the name "Jesus" with that of Socrates: *On the Purpose of Socrates and His Students—For Friends of the Wolfenbüttel Fragments and Similar Writings*.[27]

The author of this rationalist book was Christian Kruse (1753–1827). Much as Reimarus attempted to prove that Christ was nothing other than a political revolutionary, whose students idealized his teachings after his dishonorable defeat, so too Kruse sought to "expose" the person of Socrates as an unscrupulous politician of just this sort. And much as, for Reimarus, the Gospels were nothing other than attempts to distort history by idealizing Jesus in hindsight, so too the philosophical writings of Socrates' students are nothing other than attempts to obscure his master's political activities. As hair-raising as these theses might seem to a historian today, it should by now have become clear that, during the Enlightenment period, a purely *historical* interest in Socrates as such did not exist.

As we have so far seen, Socrates' significance is in the eye of the beholder. Depending on the author's own perspective, Socrates could be the epitome of rationalism—or of its exact opposite. He could be a forerunner of Christianity—or the exact opposite. In every case, however, Socrates served as a favorite mask or

---

on the possible influence of Zinzendorf's *Teutschen Socrates* on Edelmann's *Unschuldige Wahrheiten*, see Walter Grossmann, *Johann Christian Edelmann. From Orthodoxy to Enlightenment*, The Hague: Mouton & Co. 1976, especially pp. 50–62.

25 This text can be found in the edition of Lessing that Kierkegaard owned: *Gotthold Ephraim Lessing's sämmtliche Schriften*, vols. 1–32, vols. 1–28, Berlin: Vossische Buchhandlung 1825–27; vols. 29–32, Berlin and Stettin: Nicolai 1828 (*ASKB* 1747–1762); vol. 7, pp. 188–203.

26 In his early journals, Kierkegaard does seem to have referred to these fragments; but they do not appear in his edition of Lessing's writings.

27 [Christian Kruse], *Vom Zweck des Sokrates und seiner Schüler. Für Freunde der Wolfenbüttelschen Fragmente und ählicher Schriften*, Leipzig: Buchhandlung der Gelehrten 1785.

guise, whom an author could use to argue for his own position as convincingly as possible.

For such authors, the diversity of ancient perspectives and sources on Socrates was a convenient fact. A classic example of this convenient diversity is Socrates' *daimonion*, which Xenophon and Plato describe in markedly different terms. Accordingly, an author who wished to stress the significance of human beings' immanent powers of reason could interpret the *daimonion* as Socrates' "conscience," and could justify this by appeal to Xenophon. On the other hand, an author who wished to conceive of the *daimonion* as an external force, which demarcates the limits of a supposedly autonomous reason, could rely mainly on Plato's description of the *daimonion* as a force of warning and dissuasion.

Generally speaking, an author's assessment of the *daimonion* provides a crucial clue to his interpretation of Socrates. And so we should not be surprised to find that Kierkegaard devotes an entire section of his dissertation to this phenomenon. When he describes the *daimonion* as a "*crux philologorum*,"[28] we should not imagine that Kierkegaard's own interpretation is any less ideologically bound than are those of others. Rather, Kierkegaard is committed to his thesis that Socrates' standpoint is wholly negative; and in order to support this thesis, he can and must rely on Plato's account. That is to say, Kierkegaard's treatment of the *daimonion* allows us to pinpoint his location along the plane of Socrates interpretations. Even though *The Concept of Irony* relies on those interpretations that attempt to address Socrates historically and philologically, Kierkegaard's interest in Socrates remains philosophical through and through. In this regard, *The Concept of Irony* richly reflects a split in the Socrates debates starting around 1800.

The search for the "historical" Socrates began only a few decades before Kierkegaard's dissertation and motivated the studies of Socrates by Schleiermacher and Georg Anton Friedrich Ast (1778–1841). At the same time, there were also numerous publications, such as those of Georg Wilhelm Friedrich Hegel (1770–1831), whose main interest in Socrates was largely unhistorical, and was in any case lacking in source criticism. (Hegel's portrait of Socrates, while not the product of a historical interest in the narrow sense of that word, fits perfectly into his larger conceptions of the philosophy of history and the philosophy of religion.)

Before we proceed to examine these and other sources that were available to Kierkegaard, we should mention two last comprehensive texts that seem to have escaped Kierkegaard's notice. Both emerged in the 1820s, that is, in a period that was quite relevant to Kierkegaard; and both share a markedly philosophical interest in Socrates, for which it is Socrates' character as a philosophical paradigm, rather than his concrete person, that is of central interest. What is more, both texts were written by authors whose *teachers* were of the utmost significance for Kierkegaard.

In 1820, Jacob Salat (1766–1851) published his *Socrates or On the Most Recent Contradiction Between Christianity and Philosophy*.[29] Through his teacher Jacobi, and his friend Johann Michael Sailer (1751–1832), Salat came to be an active

---

[28] *SKS* 1, 165 / *CI*, 157.

[29] Jakob Salat, *Sokrates oder über den neuesten Gegensatz zwischen Christentum und Philosophie*, Sulzbach: Seidel 1820.

participant in the Hamannian tradition of Socrates interpretation. Three years later, the Hegelian Christian Kapp (1790–1874), later a friend of Feuerbach, published *Christ and World History, or Socrates and Science: Fragments of a Theodicy of Actuality, or the Voice of the Preacher in the Wilderness*.[30] Both books make it clear in their titles that they are comparatively uninterested in historical or philosophical issues, and are more interested in contemporary philosophical debates. They thus partake visibly of the tradition—in Salat's case deriving from Hamann and Jacobi, while in Kapp's case deriving from Hegel—in which the figure of Socrates serves as paradigmatic for the relation between theology and philosophy.[31]

As is well known, Kierkegaard himself adopted precisely this approach to Socrates starting in 1844. While in 1841, in *The Concept of Irony*, Kierkegaard seems to be primarily concerned with the other main branch of Socrates reception—namely, the "philological" branch represented by Ast, Schleiermacher, Heinrich Theodor Rötscher (1803–71), and others—this is an impression that will prove unwarranted on closer examination.

II. Survey of the Relevant Sources in German that were Present in Kierkegaard's Library but are not Cited in The Concept of Irony

It is instructive to compare the list of works cited in *The Concept of Irony* with the *Auctioneer's Sales Record of the Library of Søren Kierkegaard*. This comparison reveals that, on the one hand, Kierkegaard ultimately owned many works on Socrates that are not cited in *The Concept of Irony*; while on the other hand, well over half of the scholarly works cited in that work are not found in the auction catalogue of his library.[32] In our account of Kierkegaard's Socrates, we will begin (in the present section) by surveying some of the most important texts in the *first* of these categories: that is, texts that Kierkegaard owned, but which he made little or no explicit use of in his own study of Socrates in *The Concept of Irony*.

---

30 Christian Kapp, *Christus und die Weltgeschichte oder Sokrates und die Wissenschaft. Bruchstücke einer Theodicee der Wirklichkeit oder Stimme eines Predigers in der Wüste*, Heidelberg: Mohr 1823.

31 A similar interest is evinced in the considerably more speculative and idiosyncratic book of one philosopher and physician, Ernst Joseph Gustav Valenti (1794–1871): E.J.G. Valenti, *Sokrates und Christophorus, oder Gespräche über das Heidenthum, im Verhältnis zum Christenthum. Mit besonderer Rücksicht auf Plato's Phädon und die Unsterblichkeit*, Leipzig: J.F. Leich 1830.

32 As we will see in Section V below, while the Socrates scholarship of Hegel, Baur, and Karl Friedrich Hermann (1804–55) are attested in Kierkegaard's library, a number of other pivotal works cited in *The Concept of Irony* are missing—particularly the monographs of Ast, Rötscher, and Constantin Ackermann (1799–1877), as well as Schleiermacher's famous essay "On the Worth of Socrates as a Philosopher."

We may begin with the *History of Philosophy* of Wilhelm Gottlieb Tennemann (1761–1819),[33] which Kierkegaard regularly used as a kind of handbook.[34] In its second volume, this *History* devotes nearly a hundred pages to Socrates.[35] Why, then, did Kierkegaard omit all reference to Tennemann in *The Concept of Irony*? Several answers present themselves. First—surprising as it may sound—Tennemann nowhere discusses, or even mentions, Socratic irony. Second, Tennemann uses Xenophon as his main source,[36] in contrast to Kierkegaard, who prefers Plato and Aristophanes. Third, Tennemann follows the tradition of Kant and Mendelssohn in depicting Socrates, with his proofs of the immortality of the soul, as a guarantor of virtue.[37] This leads Tennemann to disparage Socrates' activity as a teacher and to emphasize instead the positive content of his "system." In other words, Kierkegaard's main thesis—that Socrates' standpoint lies in irony and negativity—is diametrically opposed to Tennemann's interpretation. What is most surprising, therefore, is not so much Kierkegaard's failure to refer to Tennemann in *The Concept of Irony*, as is the extent to which he does refer to him subsequently.

A similar conclusion can be drawn in the case of Christoph Meiners (1747–1810). Meiners is not mentioned in any of Kierkegaard's works; in the journals, he appears in only a small group of entries from 1852.[38] Yet in those entries, Kierkegaard engages with a book that contains significant and extensive discussions of Socrates—as we will see below. Moreover, Meiners' extensive presence in Kierkegaard's library should not be overlooked: Kierkegaard owned no fewer than 15 of Meiners' titles, amounting to 25 volumes in all.[39]

Known as "the teacher of philosophy at Göttingen," Meiners has earned notoriety for his *Outline of the History of Humanity*,[40] which exhibits ethnocentric prejudices that became—despite their refutation by Herder—forerunners of nineteenth-century racist ideas. Of relevance here are two works of history in which Socrates plays a

---

33 Wilhelm Gottlieb Tennemann, *Geschichte der Philosophie*, vols. 1–11, Leipzig: Barth 1798–1819 (*ASKB* 815–826).

34 Tennemann is mentioned roughly 70 times in the journals, as well as at the end of *Fear and Trembling* and in *The Concept of Anxiety*. His reading of Tennemann seems to have been most intense in 1842 and 1843; cf. the numerous references in *Journal JJ* and the extended excerpt found in *Pap*. IV C 3.

35 Tennemann, *Geschichte der Philosophie*, vol. 2, pp. 1–87. Socrates also plays a prominent role, naturally, in Tennemann's extensive discussion of Plato, pp. 188–528. Also of interest is the fact that, in an appendix to the volume (pp. 537–40), Tennemann provides a brief bibliography that includes the works of Charpentier and Cooper cited previously, as well as a monograph by Johann Matthias Gesner (1691–1761) that Kierkegaard cites at *SKS* 1, 238 / *CI*, 191.

36 Cf. Tennemann, *Geschichte der Philosophie*, vol. 2, p. 63.

37 Ibid., pp. 75ff.

38 *SKS* 24, 462–6, NB25:39–NB25:45.

39 See *ASKB* 657–676. *ASKB* 1406–1406a. *ASKB* 1951–1951b.

40 Christoph Meiners, *Grundriß der Geschichte der Menschheit*, Lemgo: Meyer 1787 (*ASKB* 662).

prominent role. One is the oft-cited essay "On the Genius of Socrates,"[41] in which Meiners, like Reimarus, interprets Socrates' *daimonion* rationally as a sign of nervous "hypertension." Another is Meiners' *History of the Origin, Progress, and Decay of the Sciences in Greece and Rome*, which contains a far more comprehensive treatment of Socrates.[42] As in Tennemann's case, Meiners stresses Socrates' "doctrine" rather than his method. For this reason, Meiners refers to Socrates' irony only twice and tangentially, as a rhetorical disguise used against the Sophists, in his 200 pages on Socrates.[43] Similarly, the motif of "ignorance," so important for Kierkegaard, is mentioned only superficially in a single note.[44] Another contrast to *The Concept of Irony* comes in assigning relative merit to the ancient authors on Socrates. When in doubt, Meiners follows Xenophon rather than Plato.[45] Aristophanes, meanwhile, is not even treated as a serious source. Instead, his *Clouds* is cited merely as one of the reasons why Socrates was later convicted.[46]

The *History of Philosophy* of Johann Jacob Brucker (1696–1770) need not be discussed here in detail, inasmuch as it was written not in German but in Latin.[47] Brucker was a philosopher and Lutheran theologian, a student of Johann Franz Buddeus (1667–1729) who was also influenced by the rationalism of Christian Wolff (1679–1754). As a result, Brucker found Socrates of interest primarily as a paradigm of virtue. In the single passage of *The Concept of Irony* where Brucker is mentioned,

---

41 Christoph Meiners, "Ueber den Genius des Sokrates," in his *Vermischte philosophische Schriften*, vols. 1–3, Leipzig: Weygand 1775–76, vol. 3, pp. 5–54. While this book was not included in Kierkegaard's own Meiners collection, it is cited frequently in much of the literature that he did own and use.

42 Christoph Meiners, *Geschichte des Ursprungs, Fortgangs und Verfalls der Wissenschaften in Griechenland und Rom*, vols. 1–2, Lemgo: im Verlage der Meyersichen Buchhandlung 1781–82 (*ASKB* 1406–1406a). The section on "Geschichte des Sokrates und seiner Philosophie" is found in vol. 2, pp. 346–540. See *SKS* 24, 463–4, NB25:42. *SKS* 24, 466, NB25:45. Also worth mentioning is the section on "Geschichte des Sokrates," in Meiners, *Grundriss der Geschichte der Weltweisheit*, Lemgo: Meyer 1786, pp. 67–82, of which Kierkegaard owned the second (1789) edition (*ASKB* 668).

43 Meiners, *Geschichte des Ursprungs, Fortgangs und Verfalls der Wissenschaften*, pp. 373ff. and pp. 533–4.

44 Ibid., p. 459.

45 Ibid., pp. 420–1: "When Plato attributes to Socrates thoughts that Xenophon also describes as Socratic....and especially when [Plato] communicates them in the language and style that is characteristic of his teacher, without admixture of obscurities, far-fetched arguments, or pet ideas, then I think it is justified to consider such thoughts authentically Socratic. But when Plato puts claims and investigations into Socrates' mouth that contradict Xenophon's account, or which are overly labored, artificial, or poetic, then one may confidently say that Plato has put Socrates in his own place, instead of setting himself in the place of his teacher's disposition." In other words: while Plato uses Socrates as a mouthpiece for his own ideas, Xenophon is the more historically correct.

46 Meiners, *Geschichte des Ursprungs, Fortgangs und Verfalls der Wissenschaften*, pp. 476ff.

47 Johann Jakob Brucker, *Historia critica philosophiae a mundi incunabilis ad nostram usque aetatem deducta*, vols. 1–4, Leipzig: Breitkopf 1776–77 [1742–44] (*ASKB* 446–450). In the first edition, Brucker's main discussion of Socrates begins at vol. 1, p. 522.

Kierkegaard notes that "surely everyone perceives the unreasonableness of going so far back that Brucker," or other older Socrates scholars, "would have to be included" in his study.[48] This figure of speech—whereby many classic texts in the history of philosophy, including Brucker, are set aside as irrelevant—can already be found in Hamann's *Socratic Memorabilia*.[49]

After eliminating Brucker from consideration, Kierkegaard adds that he need not be "so conscientious as to include Krug's reminiscences" either.[50] The reference here is to the *General Dictionary of the Philosophical Sciences* of Wilhelm Traugott Krug (1770–1842).[51] Krug was a Kantian, and indeed became Kant's successor in Königsberg in 1804. A dry and rational writer concerned to avoid controversy, Krug drew heavily on Xenophon, Diogenes Laertius, and the *Apology* of Plato in composing his biography of Socrates. Krug refuted the charge of pederasty as ungrounded, "exposed" Socrates' *daimonion* as a self-deception, and identified Socrates' main virtue as his piety or *eusebia*. In Krug's case, as in Tennemann's and Meiners', none of the aspects of Socrates that were most important to Kierkegaard—neither Socrates' irony, nor his negativity, nor his subjectivity—is emphasized. What would have been of interest in Krug, instead, is most likely his unusually thorough bibliography, which contained a number of titles that Kierkegaard too would mention.

The writings of Gotthard Oswald Marbach (1810–90) exhibit a marked Hegelian influence.[52] According to Marbach, Socrates was not a philosopher, but brought ethics into life.[53] Socrates "did not distinguish wisdom and ethics from one another," Marbach writes; indeed, Socrates' self-assessment in the wake of his conviction was shaped by his consciousness of his ethicality.[54] Finally, Marbach's account of the *daimonion* reads like an uncredited Hegel citation. Marbach's Socrates does not trust the Spirit that is simultaneously manifest in state and religion, but rather the general

---

48 *SKS* 1, 263 / *CI*, 219.

49 Cf. Hamann, *Sokratische Denkwürdigkeiten*, p. 14. This deserves mention because it signals—as we will see below—to what extent Hamann, though he is not mentioned even once in *The Concept of Irony*, nonetheless deserves to be reckoned among its main sources.

50 *SKS* 1, 263 / *CI*, 219.

51 Wilhelm Traugott Krug, *Allgemeines Handwörterbuch der philosophischen Wissenschaften nebst ihrer Literatur und Geschichte*, vols. 1–5 [vol. 5, Part 1, *Supplemente von A bis Z und das Generalregister*; vol. 5, Part 2, *Verbesserung und Zusätze zur zweiten Auflage*], Leipzig: F.A. Brockhaus 1827–34 (*ASKB* 604–608). Citations follow the second edition of 1832–34, along with the supplement published in 1838.

52 Gotthard Oswald Marbach, *Geschichte der Griechischen Philosophie. Mit Angabe der Literatur nach den Quellen*, Leipzig: Otto Wigand 1838 (Abtheilung 1, in Marbach, *Lehrbuch der Geschichte der Philosophie. Mit Angabe der Literatur nach den Quellen*, Abtheilung 1–2, Leipzig: Wigand 1838–41, to Abtheilung 2, see *ASKB* 643) (*ASKB* 642). Marbach's description of Socrates can be found on pp. 170–86.

53 Ibid., p. 181.

54 Ibid., p. 174. See also p. 178: "Socrates himself recognized....that he had made himself hateful to the Athenians as a bothersome preacher of ethics."

Spirit that dwells in the individual subject. Socrates' subjective experience of his *daimonion* "came in place of the Greek (objective) oracle."[55]

Alongside these histories of philosophy, Kierkegaard also owned an impressive collection of editions of the ancient sources. In themselves, these texts lie beyond the scope of the present study. But we *will* mention the editions and commentaries that are included in some of them; for these too bear the imprint of eighteenth- and nineteenth-century Socrates studies, and would have attracted Kierkegaard's notice. Thus, for example, Ast's Greek/Latin Plato edition includes two volumes of extensive annotations and indices.[56] Of special importance, meanwhile, are the introductions to individual dialogues that Schleiermacher included in his Plato translation.[57]

Kierkegaard's more strictly philosophical literature also contained stimulating material about Socrates. This is especially the case among authors influenced by Hamann, such as Hamann's student Herder, and his friend Jacobi. The preface to the fourth volume of Jacobi's *Works* provides a clear example.[58] These lines have a special, almost testamentary quality, inasmuch as they were printed immediately after Jacobi's death. In them, Jacobi emphasizes—like Kierkegaard, or more accurately like Johannes Climacus—the relationality of truth, and in particular the relation between truth and subjectivity.[59] Then—much as Kierkegaard, in *The Concept of Irony*, insists that the meaning of irony lies in its liberating negativity—Jacobi stresses: "As we are deceived [*täuschen*] by the manifold truths, so true science seeks disappointment [*Enttäuschung*]."[60] Jacobi cites Socrates as the star witness for his conception of philosophy, which accentuates the modesty of existence over and against the idealistic ideal of total knowledge:

> According to Aristotle, philosophy is science for the sake of wisdom, a knowledge based on reasons, a totality of knowledge. It seems to me that one could, with Aristotle, prize science simply for the sake of knowledge, and all the same follow Paul in wholeheartedly expressing the conviction that having Christ is better than knowing all. Socrates was unarguably more Pauline than Aristotelian.[61]

---

55 Ibid., p. 182: "*Trat an die Stelle der griechischen (objektiven) Orakel.*"

56 *Platonis quæ exstant Opera. Accedunt Platonis quae Feruntur Scripta*, vols. 1–11, ed. by Friederich Ast, Leipzig: Weidmann 1819–32 (*ASKB* 1144–1154).

57 *Platons Werke*, vols. 1–3 in 6 parts, trans. by Friedrich Schleiermacher, vols. 1.1–1.2 and vol. 2.1, Berlin: Realschulbuchhandlung 1817–18, vols. 2.2–2.3 and vol. 3.1, Berlin Reimer 1824–28 (*ASKB* 1158–1163). The first edition had appeared in 1804–10. Schleiermacher's Introductions have been conveniently made available in Friedrich Daniel Ernst Schleiermacher, *Über die Philosophie Platons*, ed. by Peter M. Steiner, Hamburg: Felix Meiner 1996.

58 *Friedrich Heinrich Jacobi's Werke*, vols. 1–6, Leipzig: Fleischer 1812–25 (*ASKB* 1722–1728); Cf. vol. 4, especially pp. XIII–XLVIII.

59 Ibid., p. XIII: "I needed a truth that was not my creation, but whose creation I was."

60 Ibid., p. XXVII.

61 Ibid., pp. XXXI–XXXII.

With allusions to Paul and Nicholas of Cusa, Jacobi interprets Socrates' insistence on his own ignorance as the ideal of "true science," and calls Socrates "a true hero of faith."[62] On these last points, however, Kierkegaard could not follow suit.

Further references to Socrates are found even in books that do not fit any of the genres that we have so far surveyed: philology, history, or philosophy. This is particularly true of a variety of books whose titles and genres would hardly lead us to expect to encounter Socrates in them.

Thus, for example, in the most famous publication of Matthias Claudius (1740–1815), that is, his newspaper *The Wandsbeck Messenger*, there appears a complete translation of Plato's *Apology*, flanked by reviews of Hamann's and Eberhard's books about Socrates.[63] Claudius' outward goal seems simply to have been to make the *Apology* available to the German reader.[64] An ulterior, anti-rationalistic motive, however, appears to have been at play as well—not only in this translation, but also in Claudius' broader and frequent adversions to Socrates; namely, Claudius wished to force the advocates of rationalism to consider whether their unreserved esteem for reason might not be one-sided and, from a Christian point of view, limiting. This position, which is quite close to that of Hamann (with whom Claudius corresponded), seems to have impressed Kierkegaard enough to prompt him to allude to Claudius unmistakably in the midst of his own treatment of the *Apology*.[65]

The poet Christoph Martin Wieland (1733–1813) presents another example where translations of Socratic texts—here of a selection of Xenophon's writings—turn out to be more than mere translations. In Wieland's case, his interest in Xenophon's Socrates was closely connected to his antirationalism. In Xenophon, Wieland saw the *negative* side of Socrates' activity: Socrates' way of destroying others' half-knowledge and rousing them out of their supposed certainties. This aspect of Socrates, Wieland held, was undervalued by Plato, who depicted Socrates' shock to common sense as immediately outweighed by his search for new, transcendental grounds for wisdom.

In this same spirit, Wieland devoted two subsequent novels to other figures from Socrates' milieu. Wieland's emphasis on Socrates' negativity would doubtless have been inspiring to Kierkegaard; and so it is no surprise that one of Wieland's Socratic novels, the *Dialogues of Diogenes of Sinope*, found its way into Kierkegaard's library.[66] In an 1847 journal entry, Kierkegaard declares that he ought to read Wieland's other Socratic novel, *Aristippus and a Few of His Contemporaries*; and

---

62 Ibid., p. XLVII: "The science of ignorance therefore consists in the knowledge that all human wisdom is merely piecemeal and must necessarily remain so: it is a knowing ignorance. Only faith can lead us above and beyond this patchwork, to the revelation that with reason is bestowed upon us."

63 See Matthias Claudius, *Asmus omnia sua secum portans oder Sämmtliche Werke des Wandsbecker Bothen*, Parts 1–8 in vols. 1–4, Hamburg: Bode 1775–1812 (some volumes had a different publisher), see vol. 3 (Part 5), pp. 60–107 (*ASKB* 1631–1632).

64 While a first German translation had appeared immediately prior to his, Claudius appears to have had no knowledge of its existence.

65 *SKS* 1, 148, note / *CI*, 94, note.

66 Christoph Martin Wieland, *Socrates Mainomenos (graece) oder die Dialogen des Diogenes von Sinope*, Leipzig: Weidmann 1770 (*ASKB* 474).

an 1850 entry reveals that he did in fact do so.[67] Meanwhile, it should be noted that Kierkegaard had already praised the originality of Wieland's irony some ten years earlier, in 1837.[68]

The writer Jean Paul (Johann Paul Friedrich Richter, 1763–1825), who is mentioned frequently in Kierkegaard's pseudonymous writings from *Prefaces* to the *Postscript*, is in fact discussed in the journals repeatedly as early as 1836 and 1837, in connection with such themes as Romanticism, irony and humor, and Socrates. As a result, Jean Paul also appears in the introduction to Part Two of *The Concept of Irony*.[69] While Kierkegaard's explicit reference is to Jean Paul's remarks on irony in his *Introduction to Aesthetics*,[70] Jean Paul's frequent reminiscences of Socrates should not be ignored. If one opens Kierkegaard's own edition of Jean Paul's writings, one finds that on the first page of the first volume, at the start of the novel "The Invisible Lodge,"[71] there stands a variation on Plato's Allegory of the Cave.

Finally, in the writings of Johann Georg Jacobi (1740–1814), that is, the elder brother of the Jacobi mentioned in Section I, that is, Friedrich Heinrich Jacobi, we find a short poem that portrays Socrates in a way that Kierkegaard would have appreciated, particularly during the *Corsair* affair. The thrust of this poem is that public ridicule is bearable—provided that one faces up to the laughter, and so gains a moral victory:

> *To the Germans*
> A clever folk, familiar with all the fair,
> permitted the sage Socrates
> to be mocked on the public stage—
> though only by Aristophanes,
> the favorite of the jesting Muse.
> But once the sage himself arrived onstage,
> the people bowed—and all fell mute.[72]

---

67 Christoph Martin Wieland, *Aristipp und einige seiner Zeitgenossen*, vols. 1–4, Leipzig: Göschen 1800–02, is not attested in *ASKB*, but is referred to in *SKS* 20, 186, NB2:114.

68 *Pap.* II A 627 / *JP* 2, 1688; cf. also *CI*, Supplement, p. 430. For an excellent illustration of Wieland's multifaceted engagement with Socrates, see Xenophon, *Sokratische Denkwürdigkeiten. Xenophons "Denkwürdigkeiten" und "Gastmahl." In Christoph Martin Wielands Übersetzungen mit seinen Erläuterungen und seinem "Versuch über das xenofontische Gastmahl,"* Frankfurt: Eichborn 1998.

69 *SKS* 1, 284 / *CI*, 244–5.

70 Jean Paul [Johann Paul Friedrich Richter], *Vorschule der Aesthetik nebst einigen Vorlesungen in Leipzig über die Parteien der Zeit*, vols. 1–3, 2nd revised ed., Stuttgart: Cotta 1813 (*ASKB* 1381–1383). Kierkegaard's reference to Jean Paul is at *SKS* 1, 284 / *CI*, 244–5; see discussion in VI.C below.

71 *Jean Paul's sämmtliche Werke*, vols. 1–60, Berlin: G. Reimer 1826–28 (vols. 61–65, *Jean Paul's sämmtliche Werke. Jean Paul's literarischer Nachlaß*, Berlin: G. Reimer 1836–38 and *Jean Paul Friedrich Richter. Ein biographischer Commentar zu dessen Werken* by Richard Otto Spazier, Neffen des Dichters, Leipzig: Wigand 1833), vol. 1, pp. 28ff. (*ASKB* 1777–1799).

72 *J.G. Jacobi's sämmtliche Werke*, vols. 1–4, Zürich: Orell, Geßner, Füßli und Compagnie 1825, vol. 2, p. 204 (*ASKB* 1729–1730): *An die Deutschen / Ein kluges Volk, bekannt mit allen*

The foregoing brief survey of titles that Kierkegaard possessed in his library, but did not use in *The Concept of Irony*, does not presume to be complete. Our goal so far has simply been to adumbrate the range of texts and sources from which Kierkegaard selected his dissertation's preferred "conversation partners." It is to the latter texts that we will now turn.

III. German Sources Cited in Kierkegaard's Journals Prior to 1841

Starting in 1835, Kierkegaard's journals began to fill with entries that anticipate the main argument of his 1841 dissertation. The first of these is the famous "Gilleleie" entry of August 1835, where Kierkegaard connects Socrates to irony and to the idea that knowledge begins *negatively* in ignorance.[73] In the summer of 1837, we find a cluster of entries—BB:37 from June, and DD:6, DD:18, and DD:36–8 from between June and August—that associate Socrates with the concepts of reflection, irony, and humor. The latter journal entries clearly anticipate Kierkegaard's portrait of Socrates in *The Concept of Irony* as a model of the ironic way of life.

Here, however, we encounter a surprising fact. For in these same journal entries, Kierkegaard also makes prominent and repeated reference to a particular modern author who does not appear at all in *The Concept of Irony*. This author is Hamann, whom we have already encountered in Section I. It is a noteworthy fact that, throughout the summer in which Kierkegaard first developed and concretized his view of Socrates, Hamann served as his most important source both qualitatively and quantitatively.[74] What is more, these pivotal early entries make clear that Kierkegaard viewed Socrates and Hamann as parallel figures: allied exponents of what in literary terms we might call *polemic*, or in philosophical terms *negativity*.

If we set *The Concept of Irony* itself aside, we find an impressive inner coherence between Kierkegaard's 1837 journal entries and his 1844 books *Philosophical Fragments* and *The Concept of Anxiety*, for which Hamann is a crucial interlocutor.[75] What, then, should we make of Hamann's absence from *The Concept of Irony*? The answer can only be a double one. For one thing, we should bear in mind that Hamann *is* present, subtly, at many points in *The Concept of Irony*, as a hidden source of

Schönen / Ließ, in Athen, den weisen Sokrates / Auf öffentlicher Bühne höhnen—— / Doch nur von Aristophanes, / Dem Liebling scherzender Camönen; / Und als der weise Mann die Bühne selbst bestieg, / Da—neigte sich das Volk, und schwieg.

[73] *SKS* 17, 28, AA:12 / *KJN* 1, 13–25. Here, however, Socrates' name is merely mentioned in parentheses, to designate a stage that must be passed through. It is hard to tell precisely what Kierkegaard thought of Socrates when he wrote this entry.

[74] On this see Harald Steffes, "Erziehung zur Unwissenheit? Kierkegaards 'Über die Kunst, Kindern Geschichten zu erzählen' und Johann Georg Hamanns 'Fünf Hirtenbriefe das Schuldrama betreffend,' " *Kierkegaard Studies Yearbook*, 2006, pp. 165–206.

[75] Just below the surface, a dialogue with Hamann pervades *Philosophical Fragments*. This is evident in the book's title and main themes, which refer to Hamannian motifs that are already present in journal entries from 1837 and 1838. Similar connections can be drawn to *The Concept of Anxiety*, which celebrates Hamann's and Socrates' shared insistence on their own ignorance. Cf. *SKS* 4, 310, 398 / *CA*, 3, 95. For more on this, see Steffes, "Erziehung zur Unwissenheit?"

Kierkegaard's ideas—as we will demonstrate below. But for another, let us recall that *The Concept of Irony* is an academic dissertation, designed to prove Kierkegaard qualified for a university post. In that context, any mention of Hamann would have been counterproductive for Kierkegaard: not only because Hamann was regarded as an "eccentric," but also because, as an enemy of "the system," Hamann's thought contrasted sharply with the idealistic theories that were prevalent in the 1830s and 1840s.

In November 1837, a name first appears that would have a presence in *The Concept of Irony*: Ferdinand Christian Baur (1792–1860). In Denmark's *Journal of Foreign Theological Literature*, Kierkegaard came across a partial translation of Baur's *The Christian Element in Platonism, or Socrates and Christ*.[76] This monograph is mentioned about ten times in *The Concept of Irony*; but Kierkegaard does not there make explicit use of the passage that he had copied into his journal.

On November 9, 1837, Kierkegaard made reference to the *Lectures on Faith and Knowledge* of Johann Eduard Erdmann (1805–1892), which he would go on to cite once in *The Concept of Irony*.[77] Erdmann's tenth lecture, on "Nihilism and Religious Irony," connects Friedrich Schlegel (1772–1829) and Karl Wilhelm Ferdinand Solger (1780–1819) to Johann Gottlieb Fichte (1762–1814) in a manner similar to *The Concept of Irony*. Socrates, however, is not mentioned.

A glance at other publications that Kierkegaard mentions in his 1837 and 1838 journals makes clear that, in developing his conception of Socrates, he made thorough use of a variety of sources that are mentioned only briefly or indirectly in *The Concept of Irony*. One example of this is the *Lectures on Anthropology* of Carl Daub (1765–1836), which Kierkegaard read in April 1838.[78] In the passage that Kierkegaard cites, Daub dryly remarks that there are no humorists to be found in Greek or Roman literature.[79] Daub identifies humorists aplenty, however, in eighteenth- and early nineteenth-century literature; and his list of German humorists—by no coincidence—consists exclusively of authors whose works Kierkegaard owned: Hamann, Jean Paul, Georg Christoph Lichtenberg (1742–99), and Theodor Gottlieb von Hippel (1741–96). Kierkegaard's interest in Daub seems to have focused primarily on the latter's account of the significance of the passions for the origin and

---

76 Ferdinand Christian Baur, *Das Christliche des Platonismus, oder Sokrates und Christus*, Tübingen: Fues 1837 (*ASKB* 422); partially translated as "Det Christelige i Platonismen, eller Sokrates og Christus: En religionsphilosophisk Undersøgelse," in *Tidsskrift for udenlandsk theologisk Litteratur*, vols. 1–20, Copenhagen: C.A. Reitzel 1833–52, vol. 5, 1837, pp. 485–534 (*ASKB* U 29).

77 *SKS* 17, 248, DD:81 / *KJN* 1, 238–9. Cf. *ASKB* 479 and *SKS* 1, 324 / *CI*, 289.

78 In the margin of *SKS* 17, 216, DD:6.a / *KJN* 1, 208; Kierkegaard noted on April 17, 1838: "I see that Daub in his lectures on anthropology, recently published, makes a very brief similar observation about why the ancients did not have humor." Kierkegaard then cites Carl Daub, *Vorlesungen über die philosophische Anthropologie*, ed. by Marheineke und Dittenberger, Berlin: Duncker und Humblot 1838, pp. 482–3, note.

79 Ibid. Daub does grant the existence of *satirists*. But these do not count as humor, since they simply set "the finite over and against the relative."

development of self-consciousness, above all "in its transition to religious feeling."[80] Surprisingly, while Daub does comment on irony and humor, these comments do not mention Socrates at all—though Socrates does appear elsewhere in his *Lectures*, in other contexts.[81]

IV. The Distinctive Character of The Concept of Irony

We will not here attempt to provide a detailed interpretation of *The Concept of Irony*. Nor will we try to answer the question, so often posed by scholars, about the relation and relative importance of book's two parts. For our purposes, it will be enough to take note of the existence of these two parts, so that we may avoid making a common but mistaken assumption about the book, namely, it is in fact *not* the case that Kierkegaard took any special interest in the philological literature on Socrates that he cited in Part One.

For the purposes of obtaining his degree, Kierkegaard was required to engage with this philological literature in order to provide a serious scholarly foundation for his account of irony. This led him to discuss this literature thoroughly—albeit passionlessly. As is well known, it was Kierkegaard's aim to highlight Socrates' negativity, as it is expressed above all in his irony; and so, to validate this portrait, it was necessary for him to eliminate from consideration ancient sources such as Xenophon, which also spoke of Socrates' positivity.

---

80 The subtitle to the entire second Part of Daub's *Vorlesungen über die philosophische Anthropologie* (pp. 121–502) reads: "Of Self-Consciousness in its Genesis, Development, and Transition to Religious Feeling." [*Vom Selbstbewußtsein in seiner Entstehung, Entwickelung und in seinem Übergang zum Religionsgefühl.*]

81 Daub, *Vorlesungen über die philosophische Anthropologie*, p. 37; p. 74; p. 134; p. 496. On p. 133, we find the well-known phrase *loquere, ut videam te*, which was a favorite of Hamann's, and which also appears in *The Concept of Irony*. Cf. *SKS* 1, 76, note / *CI*, 14, note. *SKS* 1, 284 / *CI*, 244. For further information about the genesis of *The Concept of Irony* and the relevant scholarly sources, the reader is referred to volume K1 in *Søren Kierkegaards Skrifter*, as well as to the selected journal entries included in the Supplement to the Hongs' translation. *CI*, 425–55. It should be noted that, in DD:50, Socrates is dubbed the "greatest catechist" in relation to certain problems in the philosophy of language. In an undated marginal note to this comment, Kierkegaard inserted the name "Hegel." However, a comparison with DD:10 makes clear that this has no bearing on Kierkegaard's source research on Socrates. Instead, attention should be paid to a revealing parallel in Hamann. In his "Beylage zun Denkwürdigkeiten des seligen Sokrates," Hamann discusses the suggestion that "all prospective authors be made into voices in the wilderness—and at the same time into catechumens." *Hamann's Schriften*, vols. 1–8, ed. by Friedrich Roth, Berlin: Georg Reimer 1821–43, vol. 4, pp. 106–7 (*ASKB* 536–544). The irony of this suggestion consists in the fact that the baptizer is simultaneously the baptized one, much as, in Socratic dialogue, the teacher is also the student. Generally speaking, a typological association of Socrates with John the Baptist, the Voice in the Wilderness, is fundamental to Hamann's account of Socratic negativity. This same identification also appears in *The Concept of Irony*; cf., for example, *SKS* 1, 301 / *CI*, 263 and *SKS* 1, 220 / *CI*, 173.

In attacking Xenophon, Kierkegaard took his place in the tradition of Schleiermacher, whose famous 1815 lecture "On the Worth of Socrates as a Philosopher" put a stop to the eighteenth-century veneration of Xenophon. What is less obvious, however, is that Kierkegaard could also have found plenty of passages in *Plato* that would have challenged his insistence on Socrates' negativity. It is doubtless to avoid dealing with these passages that Kierkegaard left Plato's *Euthyphro* and *Crito* out of consideration; for these two dialogues were commonly used by authors who wished to portray Socrates as a more positive figure. In my view, Kierkegaard's omission of the *Euthyphro* and *Crito* sheds important light on the character of his interest in Socrates. At root, Kierkegaard is not so much interested in uncovering the historical Socrates as he is in providing a philological basis for his position paper against Romantic irony.

Conversely, we may pose the following question about Kierkegaard's debate with the Romantics: did Kierkegaard have access to the texts in which Schlegel, for example, addresses Socrates? More to the point: even if it is self-evident today to think of irony and Socrates as inextricably linked topics, we should bear in mind the Romantics had their own distinctive conception of irony, which they did not always identify with Socrates. Finally, we should recall that there is a difference between texts that develop a theory of irony and texts that exhibit irony. As is well known, it is characteristic of Socratic irony that it does not engage explicitly with itself. (In Plato's dialogues, the word "irony" appears almost exclusively in unironic contexts, such as Socrates' trial.) That is to say that Kierkegaard's famous comment about the difficulty of depicting Socrates' irony holds equally true of the difficulty *we* face in isolating the sources on which Kierkegaard relied: "If we now say that irony constituted the substance of [Socrates'] existence...and if we further postulate that irony is a negative concept, it is easy to see how difficult it becomes to fix the picture of him—indeed, it seems impossible or at least as difficult as to picture a nisse [household sprite] with the cap that makes him invisible."[82]

The result of all of this is that, in assessing Kierkegaard's Socrates sources, we need to take account of three distinct strands in the relevant literature: (1) There are sources that inspired Kierkegaard to engage with Socratic irony; but he left those unnamed in *The Concept of Irony*. (2) There are sources that Kierkegaard could not avoid dealing with, thanks to his academic responsibilities; but these cannot have been of serious interest to him in his effort to defend the idea that *negativity* is essential for subjective life. (3) Finally, there are certain sources from which Kierkegaard did distance himself explicitly; but these were not necessarily the decisive sources for the relevant authors' accounts of Socrates.

What is most important is that we be aware of the fractured and manifold character of this material, rather than the specific details of each source. For this reason, we will not attempt, in what follows, to provide a thorough discussion of every source. Rather, topics that can be easily understood from the text of *The Concept of Irony* itself will be deemphasized in favor of examples that shed light on more hidden strands of Kierkegaard's Socrates reception.

82 *SKS* 1, 74 / *CI*, 12.

V. Part One of The Concept of Irony: *Sources for Kierkegaard's Historical-Philosophical Approaches to Socrates*

We will now survey the main sources that Kierkegaard used in the first part of *The Concept of Irony*. Our study will deepen the fundamental suspicion that we have voiced above: the suspicion that Kierkegaard is not seriously interested in these sources as such, but simply mines them for passages that make his conception of Socrates as a thoroughly *negative* figure seem more plausible.[83]

A. Friedrich Ast

Let us start by considering Friedrich Ast's *Plato's Life and Works*.[84] As its subtitle reveals ("An Attempt To Distinguish What Is True and Authentic From What Is Fabricated and Imputed, Both In Plato's Life and In His Works, and To Establish The Chronology Of the Authentic Dialogues"), Ast's book is a compilation of historical-critical analyses of the texts attributed to Plato. Of special importance to Kierkegaard was Ast's claim that the *Apology* (and the *Crito* too!) could not have been written by Plato. It is surprising how definitively Kierkegaard concludes that Ast (and others with him) is wrong on this point. It is even more surprising how little interest Kierkegaard takes—not even for the sake of argument—in Ast's detailed defense of this position, which takes up nearly twenty pages of his book.[85] It is true that Kierkegaard does mention Schleiermacher's plea for the *Apology*'s authenticity; but he then suppresses Schleiermacher's assessment that the *Apology* is an occasional piece devoid of philosophical content. Nor is he impressed by Ast's chronology of the "authentic" dialogues.[86] In sum, Kierkegaard, who must rely on the *Apology* to bolster his own reading of Socrates, sidesteps the views of the two best-known editors of Plato, in more or less elegant fashion.

In general, Ast serves Kierkegaard—as do Baur and others—primarily as a source of evidence. Where Ast is useful, Kierkegaard judges him positively; but otherwise Kierkegaard discards him. In his analysis of the *Apology*, for example, Kierkegaard makes

---

83 On this see Wolfdietrich von Kloeden, "Sokrates," in *Kierkegaard's Classical Inspiration*, ed. by Niels Thulstrup and Marie Mikulová Thulstrup, Copenhagen: C.A. Reitzel 1985 (*Bibliotheca Kierkegaardiana*, vol. 14), pp. 104–81, including his comprehensive bibliography at pp. 174–81.

84 Friedrich Ast, *Platon's Leben und Schriften. Ein Versuch, im Leben wie in den Schriften des Platon das Wahre und Aechte vom Erdichteten und Untergeschobenen zu scheiden, und die Zeitfolge der ächten Gespräche zu bestimmen*, Leipzig: Weidmann 1816. This book does not appear in *ASKB*.

85 Cf. *SKS* 1, 139 / *CI*, 81: "Ast's objections are really too important to be dispatched in this way." But this is more a polite expression of disinterestedness than an admission of methodological weakness. Of the 530 pages of Ast's monograph, Kierkegaard confines his attention to a small number of passages, pp. 53–4, pp. 157–65, and says little indeed about Ast's defense of his reading of the *Apology* (pp. 474–91).

86 Ast calls the *Phaedo* an early dialogue, and the *Symposium* a late work. Cf. Kierkegaard's lively joint treatment of these texts at *SKS* 1, 102 / *CI*, 41.

clear that he does not take Ast seriously as an interpreter of irony.[87] Here Kierkegaard identifies himself with Socrates, and indeed "reduplicates" Socrates by mocking Ast in much the same way as Socrates mocked those in his day who claimed to be wise.

B. Ferdinand Christian Baur

The case of Baur provides an excellent of example of Kierkegaard's lack of interest in the *philosophical* intentions of his "interlocutors" in Part One of *The Concept of Irony*. Throughout his dissertation, Kierkegaard expresses agreement with Baur wherever Baur's *philological* observations support his position; but he is quick to criticize Baur (along with Ast) for underestimating the importance of mythology in Plato. Baur was a prominent student of Hegel, and criticizing him was a convenient way for Kierkegaard to raise his own public profile; but it is worth noting that Kierkegaard almost always avoided engaging in direct debate with Baur—except in one single footnote.[88]

Kierkegaard's references to Baur are confined to 30 of the 150 pages of Baur's monograph *Christian Elements in Platonism*.[89] It is a remarkable fact that these pages are by no means the most significant ones for Baur's understanding of Socrates. Baur's book contains two parts, which bear the following titles: Part One: "The Kinship Between Platonism and Christianity, Considered According To The Character of Platonic Philosophy's Main Doctrines and According To Its General Standpoint"; and Part Two: "The Kinship Between Platonism and Christianity, Considered According To The Meaning That Plato Assigns To Socrates." In *The Concept of Irony*, Kierkegaard cites only from Part Two of Baur's book.[90] It is in Baur's Part One, however, that we find an important thought that will later be thematized in the Climacus writings: "Socratic philosophy and Christianity relate... to one another as do self-consciousness and sin-consciousness."[91]

Part One of Baur's book makes clear that his interest is much less in Socrates than in Plato. Indeed, Baur there considers the meaning of myth in Plato—precisely the topic that Kierkegaard accuses him of neglecting![92] Elsewhere in Baur's Part One, we encounter several claims worth attending to closely. Let us start with the following line: "[Platonic] love is...like faith, the subjective organ through which the human being receives the divine."[93] Before such "reception" is possible, Baur explains, a human being must first be purged of illusory knowledge. This purgation is accomplished by means of a negativity—namely, Socratic irony! Let us cite a bit further:

---

87 See especially *SKS* 1, 146–50 / *CI*, 90–6.

88 Here Kierkegaard agrees with Baur "that the similarity between Socrates and Christ, if anything, must be sought in the validity they both had as personalities"; but he insists "on the infinite dissimilarity that still remains within this similarity." *SKS* 1, 265, note / *CI*, 220, note; and cf. Thesis I, *SKS* 1, 65 / *CI*, 5–6.

89 Baur, *Das Christliche des Platonismus*.

90 The likely reason is that, as DD:75 indicates, Kierkegaard first encountered Baur's contribution in the form of a translation of Part Two alone.

91 Baur, *Das Christliche des Platonismus*, p. 24.

92 Ibid., pp. 44–5; p. 71, note 95.

93 Ibid., p. 51.

> The true, good, and right is, as the universal, the power that stands over the individual human being, on which he must recognize himself as dependent...The highest task of Socratic ethics...consists in prompting a human being to act in such a way that, in every walk of his life, he is guided by the good-in-itself as his ultimate end, as it expresses itself in his conscience.[94]

After this Hegelian line, which asserts the supremacy of universal principles over particular tendencies and passions, Baur adds a remark that one would like to have seen discussed in *The Concept of Irony*: "The Socratic art of midwifery and Socratic irony participate in the same way in the realization of this task."[95] To Baur Socratic irony is a disguise, and is thus a *method*. This characterization might appear weaker than Kierkegaard's account of irony as a *point of view*. Nevertheless, Baur succeeds in stressing the negativity of irony—a fact that one might expect to have been reflected in Kierkegaard's dissertation:

> The authentic essence of Socratic irony consists in this contradiction—which the questioner has anticipated at the outset, and provoked fairly deliberately, but which the respondent has not suspected—through which the purported knowledge destroys itself completely on its own, and changes, against the knower's will, into its exact opposite. This ironic method...is the negative, which has the positive element of the maieutic method as its precondition. But both [of these methods] aim, according to the Socratic soteriology, to peel natural man away from the subjectivity of his representations and tendencies, so that he is forced to sense their contradictoriness and nullity above all; and so they tear him free, by means of the knowledge of ignorance, of the vain illusion in which the outer man is content to let himself be captured.[96]

This, then, is the similarity between the Socratic and Christian "methods." Accordingly, Baur reasons:

> Truly it is not doctrine that raises Christianity above all else. Non-Christian sages have taught and declaimed nobility and divinity with almost the same purity and grandeur as did Christianity's founder. But what is more than [mere] Idea, the incarnation of the divine word—that no philosophy or speculation can reach.[97]

On the whole, Baur may be accused of waffling a bit in his assessments of the relation between Christianity and philosophy. On the one hand (following Ackermann, whose book we will discuss below), Baur claims in Part One of his book that "human salvation and beatitude is Christianity's august goal; and this salvation is also, unmistakably, the inspiring vision and final goal of Platonic philosophy."[98] On the other hand (again following Ackermann), Baur asserts in Part Two that the similarity between Christianity and Platonism is, on the whole, merely to be found in outward

---

94 Ibid., p. 26.

95 Ibid.

96 Ibid., p. 27.

97 Ibid., p. 10.

98 Ibid., p. 3. As we will note below, this is a close paraphrase of a claim made by Ackermann in his *Das Christliche im Plato und in der platonischen Philosophie*, Hamburg: Perthes 1835, p. 291.

analogies. What is more, Baur accuses Ackermann of failing to investigate the difference between Christ's significance to Christianity and Socrates' significance to Platonism; but he then fails to treat this question comprehensively himself.[99]

Generally speaking, Baur's movements are confined to the realm of Hegel's interpretation of Socrates. While Baur's emphasis on the negativity of irony might have afforded him a point of agreement with Kierkegaard, there are two aspects of his thought that separate Baur from Kierkegaard and Hamann. For one thing, Baur (in Hegelian style) emphasizes the superiority of the universal over the particular;[100] Kierkegaard, of course, took a different view from *The Concept of Irony* onward. For another, the significance of Socrates is compared *ontologically* with that of Christ, and not—as in Zinzendorf, Hamann, and Jacobi—*epistemologically* with the role of Paul or John the Baptist.

In general, Kierkegaard makes far less use of Baur than one might expect. Although Baur's book may be described as a clearing-house of references to other thinkers—including Ast, Hegel, Hermann, Schleiermacher, David Friedrich Strauss (1808–74), and Johann Wilhelm Süvern (1775–1829)—Kierkegaard seems to have relied on Baur as a secondary source for only one further author, namely, Ackermann (discussed below). Why, then, did Kierkegaard avoid engaging more directly with Baur and his sources? The answer has doubtless to do with Baur's penchant for drawing speculative parallels between Christianity and Platonism (for example, between Christian μετάνοια and Platonic recollection, or between the idea of the Incarnation and the actualization of the Idea),[101] as well as with Baur's embrace of the Hegelian view of Socrates—which, as we will see, Kierkegaard opposed—according to which Socrates' irony was a mere method, and Socrates' negativity was directed toward a positivity.[102]

We will close our discussion of Baur by mentioning four further passages in his book that are of relevance to *The Concept of Irony*: (1) At one point, Baur describes Socrates as Platonism's incarnation figure, whose role in Platonic philosophy is analogous to that of Christ in Christianity.[103] This description might have served as the foil for Kierkegaard's Thesis I.[104] (2) Like Kierkegaard, Baur regards the *Phaedo* and *Symposium* as the most valid representations of (respectively) Socrates' death and life.[105] (3) Baur claims that it is through Socrates that the standpoint of

---

99 Baur, *Das Christliche des Platonismus*, p. 90; p. 98.

100 Ibid., pp. 143–4.

101 Ibid., p. 40.

102 Ibid., pp. 145–7; p. 27; p. 102.

103 Ibid., p. 103: "If there is an inner tie of kinship between Platonism and Christianity, we find it also in the fact that, in both systems, everything proceeds from the center of a human life that is beheld as a revelation of the divine."

104 *Similitudo Christum inter et Socratem in dissimilitudine praecipue est posita*: "The similarity between Jesus and Socrates consists essentially in their dissimilarity." *SKS* 1, 65 / *CI*, 6–7.

105 Baur, *Das Christliche des Platonismus*, pp. 109–10.

subjectivity gains significance.[106] (4) Finally, Baur insists, with Ast, that the *Apology* is inauthentic.[107]

C. Constantin Ackermann

From Baur we will turn to the theologian Constantin Ackerman, archdeacon of Jena, whose monograph on *The Christian Element in Plato and in Platonic Philosophy* Kierkegaard seems to have known only from the manifold references to it in Baur.[108] If Kierkegaard *had* been directly acquainted with Ackermann's book, he would no doubt have been interested both in Ackermann's main claim[109] and in the richness of his argument. With regard to the significance of Socrates, Ackermann follows the trail that Schleiermacher blazed: he inquires into the effect that Socrates had on Plato. Ackermann considered Socratism to be a mere precursor to Platonism—even though he held that the importance to Plato of Socrates' personal, "dynamic" character cannot be overstated.[110]

Of greater interest is Ackermann's analysis of irony. For one thing, Ackermann stresses throughout his book, and not uncritically, the enduring importance of the "Schlegelian school" for the reappraisal of irony—with references to Solger and to Adam Heinrich Müller (1779–1829). For another, Ackermann defines the essence of Platonic irony with the aid of exceedingly vivid metaphors. For example: irony is the "muffler that is put to use at just the right time, when the strings of the soul are vibrating most fully and powerfully."[111] Ackermann then distinguishes between an "ordinary Socratic" irony and a "poetic-religious" or a "philosophically sharp" irony in Plato; and he emphasizes, with a glance at Proverbs 8:31, that irony in Plato can

---

106 Ibid., pp. 139–40.

107 Ibid., pp. 147–8. Baur here cites Ast in opposition to Schleiermacher. For further information on Kierkegaard's relation to Baur, see David D. Possen, "F.C. Baur: On the Similarity and Dissimilarity between Jesus and Socrates," in *Kierkegaard and His German Contemporaries*, Tome II, *Theology*, ed. by Jon Stewart, Aldershot: Ashgate 2007 (*Kierkegaard Research: Sources, Reception, and Resources*, vol. 6) pp. 23–38.

108 Ackermann, *Das Christliche im Plato*, Kierkegaard's single mention of Ackermann, at *SKS* 1, 153 / *CI*, 99, is as part of a reference to Baur; and Ackermann's book is absent from *ASKB*.

109 Ackermann, *Das Christliche im Plato*, p. XIV: "It has been my wish to illuminate and distinguish the Christian element in Plato and in his philosophy, not his theology's relation and kinship to Christianity! The Christian element of Platonic philosophy as such is no less than identical to the Christian spirit [!] of Plato's speculative doctrine of God. Plato's theology relates to his Christianness only as the particular does to the universal; it is only one of various manifestations by and in which the Christian element that rests in him reveals itself. Just as I believe that I have shown that the essence of Christianity does not rest in its salvific *doctrine*, but in its salvific *efficacy*, so too I have understandably sought to find the Christian element in Plato not in his doctrine of God's being, but exclusively in his pious consciousness of what salvific ends the power and goodness of God aims at and achieves in the world."

110 Ibid., pp. 163ff.

111 Ibid., pp. 140–1: "*zur rechten Zeit angewendete Dämpfer, wenn die Saiten der Seele am vollsten und stärksten schwingen.*"

be even more than this: "She [irony] is the sister of the true heavenly Wisdom, which plays on earth, and delights in the children of man."[112]

D. Heinrich Theodor Rötscher

One of the most distinctive characteristics of *The Concept of Irony* is the high esteem it accords to Aristophanes. In this respect Kierkegaard may be regarded as building on the philological contributions of Rötscher. In particular, Rötscher's monograph, *Aristophanes and His Age*,[113] appears to have provided Kierkegaard with the main philological and historical material for his Aristophanes portrait—particularly Rötscher's nineteenth chapter, which offers a "History of the Interpretation of the *Clouds*."[114] Surprisingly, Kierkegaard does not mention Rötscher's sixteenth chapter,[115] which would also have been worth citing. To see why this is so, consider the following excerpt from the chapter's opening:

> Inasmuch, however, as he accentuated and adhered to the principle of subjectivity in the first place, Socrates set himself against the simple ethics that excludes the decision that is derived from thought and reflection. He thus placed himself in an adversarial stance vis-à-vis the state and the consciousness of the entire Greek world. This standpoint of interiority...was granted to him by the entire ancient world. From the deepest Aristotelian dictum about Socrates' teaching to the shallow popularity of Cicero, one and the same thought resounds again and again. This thought can be expressed simply: it is that Socrates placed the inner and free decision of the spirit onto the throne of the world; and in view of this decision, nothing else can compel the subject absolutely except what it itself recognizes internally as true and obligatory.[116]

Hegel's influence is clear in this passage, particularly in Rötscher's depiction of Socrates as an exponent of subjectivity in the form of interiority. When Kierkegaard (in both *The Concept of Irony* and the *Concluding Unscientific Postscript*) describes Socrates' *daimonion* as the mark of his interiority, he is siding *with* Hegel and Rötscher—and against Ast.

It should be mentioned, finally, that Rötscher served Kierkegaard as a vehicle for acquainting him with other authors. An example is Christian August Brandis (1790–

---

112 Ibid., p. 141.

113 Heinrich Theodor Rötscher, *Aristophanes und sein Zeitalter, eine philosophisch-philologische Abhandlung zur Altherthumsforschung*, Berlin: Voss 1827 (not in *ASKB*). Rötscher wrote this book while working as a *Privatdozent* [adjunct or assistant professor] in Berlin, as is reflected in its double dedication: "To August Boeckh, perspicacious classicist and deep researcher, and to Georg Wilhelm Friedrich Hegel, grand master of authentic scholarliness."

114 Ibid., pp. 272–88. The full title of this chapter is: "*Geschichte des Verständnisses der Wolken. Widerlegung der Ansicht, daß die Sophisten in der Maske des Socrates der Gegenstand der Komödie gewesen. Erklärung der scheinbar dahin deutenden Stellen.*"

115 Ibid., pp. 247–68. The full title of this chapter is: "*Princip des Sokrates. Bewußtsein der Alten über dasselbe.*"

116 Ibid., pp. 247–8.

1867), whose *Fundamentals of the Philosophy of Socrates* Rötscher reviews at the close of his book—and which Kierkegaard then cites in *The Concept of Irony*.[117]

E. Karl Friedrich Hermann

Karl Friedrich Hermann (1805–55), professor of classical philology and editor of a six-volume revised edition of Plato, is mentioned once in *The Concept of Irony*,[118] though—interestingly—not in connection with Kierkegaard's selection of dialogues to be discussed. Hermann's book on Plato[119] contributes little to the interpretation of Socrates; it treats Socrates simply as Plato's starting "impetus." Socrates' death is thus portrayed as the "turning point" in Plato's biography, inasmuch as it gave Plato the opportunity to leave Athens for a time and visit Euclid of Megara. In Hermann's view, it was Euclid who transformed Plato into a speculative philosopher—unlike Socrates, who adopted a dismissive stance toward speculation.[120]

F. Friedrich Daniel Ernst Schleiermacher

To make matters short, *The Concept of Irony* does not engage with Schleiermacher thoroughly or genuinely. At several points, Kierkegaard refers, more or less approvingly, to Schleiermacher's philological "Introductions" to his translations of Plato's dialogues. But he does this only where their views overlap, for example, in assessing the *Symposium*, the *Phaedo*, and Book I of the *Republic*. Kierkegaard follows Schleiermacher in emphasizing the peculiar character of the *Republic*'s first book. And in evaluating the *Apology*, as we have mentioned earlier, Kierkegaard cites Schleiermacher very selectively. Kierkegaard gratefully accepts Schleiermacher's validation of the *Apology* as authentic; but he says nothing about Schleiermacher's disdain for the dialogue's philosophical content.

Schleiermacher's "philosophical" view of Socrates appears in its most concentrated form in his famous 1815 lecture "On the Worth of Socrates as a

117 At *SKS* 1, 259, note; *CI*, 214, note, Kierkegaard cites a passage from Christian August Brandis, *Grundlinien der Philosophie des Socrates*, Bonn: Rheinisches Museum 1827. Rötscher's review of this book can be found at Rötscher, *Aristophanes und sein Zeitalter*, pp. 388–400.

118 *SKS* 1, 158 / *CI*, 104. The "Hermann" cited at *SKS* 1, 194 / *CI*, 144 refers to Johann Jakob Gottfried Hermann (1772–1848), rather than to Karl Friedrich.

119 Karl Friedrich Hermann, *Geschichte und System der Platonischen Philosophie. Erster Theil, die historisch-kritische Grundlegung enthaltend*, Heidelberg: C.F. Winter 1839 (*ASKB* 576).

120 Ibid., p. 46: "As is well known, Euclid of Megara was the first who sought to unite the content of the Socratic philosophy of life with the forms of speculative philosophy as they had taken shape in the Eleatic dialectic, which Socrates did not so much abolish as avoid; and so it is an extremely likely conjecture....that it was precisely this stay in Megara that acquainted Plato more closely with the actual state of Greek speculation, and to that extent with the true needs of the philosophizing spirit of his time."

Philosopher."[121] Kierkegaard refers to this lecture five times; he thereby signals his agreement with Schleiermacher's thesis that there must lie concealed, behind Socrates' ignorance, a positive conception of knowledge. However, when Schleiermacher describes Socrates as the inventor and founder of dialectics, Kierkegaard and he part ways.[122] On Kierkegaard's reading, Schleiermacher's conception of "dialectic" must be understood as embodying a system of knowledge. Against such a conception, Kierkegaard stresses the subjective dimension of knowledge, which can be protected only by irony: "irony leads [dialectic] back into personality."[123]

This "debate" with Schleiermacher is carried out more or less clandestinely: in footnotes, in unconnected passages, and (above all) at the wrong place. It is, instead, in Schlegel's early work—composed during the period of Schlegel's intensive collaboration with Schleiermacher—that one finds texts that articulate the kind of close connection between irony and dialectic that Kierkegaard thinks is missing in Schleiermacher.[124] However, Kierkegaard does not mention Schleiermacher at all in his discussion of Schlegel.

G. Georg Wilhelm Friedrich Hegel

Hegel is, without a doubt, the interlocutor addressed most frequently and extensively in *The Concept of Irony*. Moreover, he is the only interlocutor who is given a comparable level of attention in both of the book's two parts; and he is also the sole scholarly source to whom Kierkegaard devotes a special appendix. Hegel's significance for *The Concept of Irony* is thus beyond dispute. It is Hegel's categories and points of reference that are decisive for Kierkegaard's book. However, it remains to be asked how faithfully Kierkegaard followed in Hegel's tracks—and to what extent he attempted to outdo or relativize his achievements. This question is well beyond the scope of this article, since any answer would need to rely on a comprehensive assessment of Kierkegaard's relation(s) to Hegel.

Jens Himmelstrup's classic monograph on the subject illustrates the degree to which this question remains an open one. On the one hand, Himmelstrup identifies two critical points on which Kierkegaard's conception of Socrates departs consciously

---

121 This lecture was published in a variety of settings. Kierkegaard cites a version published in the *Abhandlungen der Königlichen Academie der Wissenschaften, aus den Jahren 1814–1815*; cf. *SKS* 1, 218, note / *CI*, 170, note. Kierkegaard does not appear to have been aware of Schleiermacher's portrait of Socrates in his "Lectures on the History of Philosophy," collected in *Friedrich Schleiermacher's sämmtliche Werke*, 3. Abtheilung: *Zur Philosophie*, vols. 1–10, Berlin: G. Reimer 1835–62, vol. 2, Tome 1 (1839), particularly on pp. 80–5. This text contains several references to Schleiermacher's theory of the "indirect dialogical method." This text, together with Schleiermacher's "Introductions" to Plato's dialogues and a comprehensive bibliography, has been made accessible in Schleiermacher, *Über die Philosophie Platons*, Hamburg: Felix Meiner 1996.

122 *SKS* 1, 217–18 / *CI*, 169–70.

123 *SKS* 1, 174, note / *CI*, 122, note.

124 I refer especially to the famous Lyceum Fragment 108: *Kritische Friedrich-Schlegel-Ausgabe*, Abteilungen 1–4, vols. 1–35, ed. by Ernst Behler et al., Paderborn, Munich et al.: Schöningh 1958–2002, Abtheilung 1, vol. 2, p. 160.

from Hegel's: (1) Whereas Hegel attempts to attribute some sort of positivity to Socrates,[125] Kierkegaard regards it as an illusion to think that Socrates held positive knowledge. (2) Whereas Hegel held that Socrates' irony was merely a "method,"[126] Kierkegaard insists that Socrates' entire standpoint was that of irony. These two points combine to form Kierkegaard's central thesis that Socrates' standpoint was that of "infinite absolute negativity": itself, ironically enough, a Hegelian formulation! Himmelstrup then states explicitly that, in his view, the goal of *The Concept of Irony* is to press these two points in opposition to Hegel.[127] At the same time, however, Himmelstrup *also* remarks that it is "therefore Hegel's conception that provides the backdrop for Kierkegaard's portrait of Socrates; and Kierkegaard himself says that his conception is 'a modification' of the Hegelian one."[128]

Beyond the two contrasts that Himmelstrup draws, a third also deserves to be mentioned. Unlike Kierkegaard, who privileges Plato's portrait of Socrates over that of Xenophon, Hegel allows Xenophon to dominate his account of Socrates,[129] and cites Aristotle's testimony just as often as he cites Plato's.[130] On the other hand, Hegel and Kierkegaard do both praise Aristophanes, though for different reasons.[131]

When we ask simply about Kierkegaard's use of specific Hegelian texts, the matter becomes easier to address. Apart from a single marginal reference to *The Philosophy of Right*, there are four main texts to enumerate here. Of these four sources, it is unclear which is the most significant for Kierkegaard. Each can, in its own way, lay claim to that title: (1) The relevant section of the *Lectures on the History of Philosophy* is the text that is cited most frequently and thoroughly.[132] (2) Kierkegaard himself ascribes great importance to the *Lectures on the Philosophy of History*.[133] (3) The first volume of the *Lectures on Aesthetics* is the source for Kierkegaard's formula "infinite absolute negativity." In general, these *Lectures* provide Kierkegaard with his richest source material for evaluating Hegel's view of

---

125 G.W.F. Hegel, *Vorlesungen über die Geschichte der Philosophie*, vols. 1–3, ed. by Carl Ludwig Michelet, Berlin: Duncker und Humblot 1833–36 (vols. 13–15 in *Georg Wilhelm Friedrich Hegel's Werke. Vollständige Ausgabe*, ed. by Philipp Marheineke et al., Berlin: Duncker und Humblot 1832–45), vol. 2, p. 46; p. 59; p. 64; p. 69 (*ASKB* 557–559); *Jub.*, vol. 18, p. 46; p. 59; p. 64; p. 69 (*Jub. = Sämtliche Werke. Jubiläumsausgabe in 20 Bänden*, ed. by Hermann Glockner, Stuttgart: Friedrich Frommann Verlag 1928–41).

126 *Jub.*, vol. 18, p. 60–2.

127 Cf. Jens Himmelstrup, *Søren Kierkegaards Opfattelse af Sokrates. En Studie i dansk Filosofis Historie*, Copenhagen: Arnold Busck 1924, pp. 299–30.

128 Ibid., p. 296.

129 *Jub.*, vol. 18, pp. 80–1; and cf. p. 96.

130 *Jub.*, vol. 18, p. 59; p. 62; p. 77; p. 78.

131 For Hegel, Aristophanes is a quasi-dialectician who regarded Socrates' negativity as a "necessary" transition-stage in need of "sublation." Cf. *Jub.*, vol. 18, p. 89.

132 *Jub.*, vol. 18, pp. 42–122.

133 *Georg Wilhelm Friedrich Hegel's Vorlesungen über die Philosophie der Religion*, vols. 1–2, ed. by Philipp Marheineke, Berlin: Duncker und Humblot 1832 (vols. 11–12 in *Georg Wilhelm Friedrich Hegel's Werke. Vollständige Ausgabe*,) (*Jub.*, vol. 11, especially pp. 348–52). Cf. the extended footnote at *SKS* 1, 247–8, note / *CI*, 201–3, note.

irony.[134] (4) If we rely on Kierkegaard's Thesis XII, we could judge Hegel's extended "Review of Solger"[135] to be Kierkegaard's most decisive source, since Kierkegaard's general approach to the Romantics is grounded directly in Hegel's view of Solger.

However we choose to rank them, all four of these texts are reviewed thoroughly and carefully, and indeed not inelegantly, by Kierkegaard.[136] When Kierkegaard describes Hegel, for example, as "a turning point in the view of Socrates," this is an obvious allusion to Hegel's judgment of Socrates at the beginning and end of the section on Socrates in his *Lectures on the History of Philosophy*.[137]

While we cannot here undertake a more detailed treatment of Kierkegaard's use of Hegel, let us conclude by acknowledging that such a treatment is a necessary precondition for any thorough engagement with Kierkegaard's conception of Socrates.[138]

VI. Part Two of The Concept of Irony: *Sources for Kierkegaard's Philosophical Approach to the Irony of Socrates*[139]

This section will treat two groups of sources. We will begin with the Romantic authors Schlegel, Solger, and Johann Ludwig Tieck (1773–1853), to whom

134 *Georg Wilhelm Friedrich Hegel's Vorlesungen über die Aesthetik*, vols. 1–3, ed. by Heinrich Gustav Hotho, Berlin: Duncker und Humblot 1835–38 (vols. 10.1–10.3 in *Georg Wilhelm Friedrich Hegel's Werke. Vollständige Ausgabe*) (*ASKB* 1384–1386) (*Jub.*, vol. 12, especially pp. 105–6 and p. 221).

135 G.W.F. Hegel, "Ueber: '*Solger's nachgelassene Schriften und Briefwechsel.* Herausgegeben von Ludwig Tieck und Friedrich v. Raumer. Erster Band 780 S. mit Vorrede XVI S. Zweiter Band 784 S. Leipzig, 1826,' " in *Georg Wilhelm Friedrich Hegel's vermischte Schriften*, vols. 1–2, ed. by Friedrich Förster and Ludwig Boumann, Berlin: Duncker und Humblot 1834–35 (vols. 16–17 in *Georg Wilhelm Friedrich Hegel's Werke. Vollständige Ausgabe*), vol. 1, pp. 436–506 (*ASKB* 555–556) (*Jub.*, vol. 20, pp. 132–202).

136 The most important passages in which Kierkegaard engages directly with Hegel's texts are found at *SKS* 1, 211–15 / *CI*, 161–7. *SKS* 1, 238–48 / *CI*, 191–203. *SKS* 1, 263–9 / *CI*, 219–37. *SKS* 1, 292 / *CI*, 254. *SKS* 1, 302–8 / *CI*, 264–71.

137 *Jub.*, vol. 18, p. 42 and pp. 121–2. We find this same formulation, by the way, in Schleiermacher's 1815 lecture.

138 Beyond Himmelstrup's book and von Kloeden's article, the following secondary literature is of use: Gernot Böhme, "Große Sokrates-Interpretationen," in Gernot Böhme, *Der Typ Sokrates*, Frankfurt: Suhrkamp 1998, pp. 185–97 (on Hegel, Kierkegaard, and Nietzsche); Gerhart Schmidt, "Hegels Urteil über Sokrates," in *Sokrates. Geschichte–Legende–Spiegelungen*, ed. by Herbert Kessler, Kusterdingen: Die graue Edition 1995 (*Sokrates-Studien*, vol. 2), pp. 275–94; Eduard Spranger, *Hegel über Sokrates*, Berlin: de Gruyter 1938 (*Sitzungsberichte der Preußischen Akademie der Wissenschaften. Philosophisch-Historische Klasse*), pp. 284–96.

139 The following works are of aid in evaluating the various accounts of irony treated here. On Schlegel's position, see Ernst Behler, *Ironie und literarische Moderne*, Paderborn: Ferdinand Schöningh 1997; and Ernst Behler, *Klassische Ironie. Romantische Ironie. Tragische Ironie. Zum Ursprung dieser Begriffe*, Darmstadt: Wissenschaftliche Buchgesellschaft 1972. On Kierkegaard's conception of irony, see Edo Pivcevic, *Ironie als Daseinsform bei Kierkegaard*, Gütersloh: Mohn 1960; K. Brian Soderquist, *The Isolated Self: Truth and*

Kierkegaard devotes a chapter each. Our treatment of these figures will be brief, since there is little to add to what Kierkegaard wrote himself. Moreover, Tieck will not be considered at all, because Kierkegaard's presentation of Tieck's account of irony is based exclusively on Tieck's works of satirical drama and lyric. After this, we will turn to a number of other authors whom Kierkegaard may be have said to have treated—in a sense—ungratefully.

A. Friedrich Schlegel

For good reason, Kierkegaard addresses Schlegel's conception of irony by investigating his novel *Lucinde*. Yet mysteriously enough, neither that book nor Solger's novel *Erwin* are to be found in *The Auction Catalogue* of Kierkegaard's library.

Socrates is mentioned only once in *Lucinde*, in a single marginal passage. Elsewhere in Schlegel's writings, however, there are a number of more significant references to Socrates; but these do not seem to have provoked Kierkegaard's interest. As early as 1795–96, for example, Schlegel declares that modern history began with Socrates, inasmuch as it is with him that the conscious structuring of actuality out of thought began.[140] Next, we find an important passage on Socrates in Schlegel's 1804–05 Cologne lecture series, *The Development of Philosophy in Twelve Books*,[141] which in certain ways anticipates the critique of Xenophon in Schleiermacher's lecture "On the Worth of Socrates as a Philosopher." It should be noted that, in these lectures, Schlegel takes practically no interest in irony, and indeed ascribes some positivity to Socrates:

> All of Socrates' students agree that his philosophy was primarily directed at morality; everything else interested him only on its account. Socrates proceeded from the old saying "Know thyself," and made the inner, harmonic education and ennobling of man into the first and most necessary condition of all philosophizing.
>
> Confined solely to this end, philosophy became a merely practical individual knowledge, but to the same extent a complete *moral* wisdom; it became wisdom and science....Hence one may rightly regard [Socrates] as the ideal of worldly wisdom.[142]

Socrates also appears repeatedly in Schlegel's *Lyceum* and *Athenaeum Fragments*.[143] Here Schlegel offers the following reason for writing a novel: "Novels are the

---

Untruth in Søren Kierkegaard's On the Concept of Irony, Copenhagen: C.A. Reitzel 2007 (*Danish Golden Age Studies*, vol. 1); and especially Uwe Japp, *Theorie der Ironie*, Frankfurt: Vittorio Klostermann 1983.

140 *Kritische Friedrich-Schlegel-Ausgabe*, Abteilungen 1–4, vols. 1–35, ed. by Ernst Behler et al., Paderborn, Munich et al.: Schöningh 1958–2002, Abteilung 1, vol. 1, p. 636.

141 Ibid., Abtheilung 2, vol. 12, pp. 197–206.

142 Ibid., p. 200.

143 Cf. Lyceum Fragments no. 26, no. 42, no. 108, and no. 125; Athenaeum Fragments no. 104, no. 160, and no. 295, in *Kritische Friedrich-Schlegel-Ausgabe*, Abteilung 1, vol. 2, p. 149; p. 152; p. 160; p. 163; p. 180; p. 190; pp. 214–15.

Socratic dialogues of our day."[144] In Lyceum Fragment no. 108, Schlegel describes a "unification of the sense of *savoir vivre* with the scientific spirit," a union of Socratic irony and dialectic, which might have bridged the gap between Kierkegaard's stress on irony and Schleiermacher's accentuation of dialectic.[145]

B. Karl Wilhelm Ferdinand Solger

Both of Solger's books that are treated in *The Concept of Irony* are also attested in Kierkegaard's library, namely, his *Posthumous Writings* and *Lectures on Aesthetics*.[146] Kierkegaard's explicit references to these works allow us to trace with some precision precisely which passages he read—and the extent to which his reading was influenced by Hegel's "Review."

Surprisingly, Kierkegaard seems not to have noticed the Socratic or Platonic legacy in Solger's work. Solger, after all, wrote philosophical dialogues! Yet it should be noted that Schleiermacher—who knew Solger personally from the soirées of the Berlin publisher Georg Reimer, and who later gave the eulogy after Solger's early death—regarded Solger's switch from classical philology toward philosophical literature with great skepticism. Schleiermacher's assessment may be regarded as justified, given Solger's wholly unironic use of irony in his *Philosophical Dialogues*.[147] Moreover, the conclusion to Solger's novel *Erwin*, in which irony is explicitly addressed, seems similarly artificial and contrived; though

---

144 Lyceum Fragment no. 26, in *Kritische Friedrich-Schlegel-Ausgabe*, Abtheilung 1, vol. 2, p. 149.

145 Cf. Lyceum Fragment no. 108, in *Kritische Friedrich-Schlegel-Ausgabe*, Abtheilung 1, p. 160: "Socratic irony is the only dissimulation that is entirely automatic—and is at the same time entirely sober. It is impossible to fabricate—and is equally impossible to betray. To the one who does not have it, it will remain a riddle even after the most open act of confession. It is meant to deceive only those who consider it deceit—either those who find joy in the glorious roguishness of pulling the world's leg, or those who are angered when they discover that the joke includes them too. In [Socratic irony], everything should be jest, and everything earnestness; everything trustingly open, and everything deeply veiled. It derives from the unification of the sense of *savoir vivre* with the spirit of science, from the meeting of complete natural philosophy with the complete philosophy of art. It contains and evokes a sense of the irresolvable conflict between the absolute and the relative, between the impossibility and the necessity of total communication. It is the freest license of all, since through it one distances oneself from oneself; and yet it is also the most lawful, since it is absolutely necessary. It is a very good sign when the harmonious dullards have no idea how they should take this continual self-parody, when they oscillate unceasingly between new belief and disbelief until they become dizzy, and mistake jest precisely for earnestness, and earnestness for jest. Lessing's irony is instinct; in Hemsterhuis it is classical education; Hülsen's irony derives from the philosophy of philosophy, and can still outstrip the others by far."

146 Karl Wilhelm Ferdinand Solger, *Nachgelassene Schriften und Briefwechsel*, vols. 1–2, ed. by Ludwig Tieck and Friedrich von Raumer, Leipzig: F.A. Brockhaus 1826 (*ASKB* 1832–1833); Solger, *Vorlesungen über Aesthetik*, ed. by K.W.L. Heyse, Leipzig: F.A. Brockhaus 1829 (*ASKB* 1387).

147 Karl Wilhelm Ferdinand Solger, *Philosophische Gespräche. Erste Sammlung*, Berlin: Maurer 1817, pp. 245–6.

we do here find the artful expression that irony is a destructive glance that hovers above everything.[148]

On the other hand, Solger's emphasis on the *dialogical* principle in irony has echoes in Kierkegaard's thought. Following *The Concept of Irony*, Kierkegaard produced a pseudonymous, dialogical novel—*Either/Or*—whose focus is on concealment and dissimulation. In *Either/Or*, Socrates and irony are hardly mentioned; and yet the book is Socratic and ironic all the same. As Schlegel declared, irony is closely related to concealment—and it is best articulated in novelistic form.[149]

C. Jean Paul (Johann Paul Friedrich Richter)

As his early journals reveal, Kierkegaard took an early interest in Jean Paul's *Introduction to Aesthetics*.[150] In a revealing passage in *The Concept of Irony*, however, Kierkegaard explains why he wishes to exclude Jean Paul's thoughts on irony from consideration:

> Jean Paul also mentions irony frequently, and some things are found in his *Aesthetics*, but without any philosophic or genuinely aesthetic authority. He speaks mainly as an aesthetician, from a rich aesthetic experience, instead of actually giving grounds for his aesthetic position. Irony, humor, moods seem for him to be different languages, and his characterization is limited to expressing the same thought ironically, humorously, in the language of moods.[151]

D. Franz Xaver von Baader

In the sentence that follows the one just cited, Kierkegaard offers a similar dismissal of Franz Xaver von Baader (1765–1841). This is remarkable, because Baader does in fact treat the necessity of negativity—and so could have been a critical interlocutor for Kierkegaard's 15th and final Thesis.[152] Like Kierkegaard, Baader starts with the significance of ignorance; but unlike Kierkegaard, Baader correlates ignorance not with the ironic way of life, but with ethics. Accordingly, Baader cannot stop with negativity:

---

148 Karl Wilhelm Ferdinand Solger, *Erwin. Vier Gespräche über das Schöne und die Kunst*, Berlin: Realschulbuchhandlung 1815, pp. 277ff.

149 According to Schlegel's concept of irony, irony is intertwined with concealment, and is best expressed in the form of a novel. Cf. Lyceum Fragment 26 in *Kritische Friedrich-Schlegel-Ausgabe*, Abteilung 2, vol. 2, p. 149.

150 Jean Paul, *Vorschule der Aesthetik*. Kierkegaard's interest in Jean Paul was perhaps provoked by Sibbern. On this see Markus Kleinert, "Jean Paul: Apparent and Hidden Relations between Kierkegaard and Jean Paul," in *Kierkegaard and His German Contemporaries*, Tome III, *Literature and Aesthetics*, ed. by Jon Stewart, Aldershot: Ashgate 2007 (*Kierkegaard Research: Sources, Reception and Resources*, vol. 6), pp. 155–70; p. 160 and note 18.

151 *SKS* 1, 284 / *CI*, 244–5.

152 Cf. *SKS* 1, 65 / *CI*, 5–6: "*Ut a dubitatione philosophia sic ab ironia vita digna, quae humana vocetur, incipit*" ["Just as philosophy begins with doubt, so also a life that may be called human begins with irony"]

> As the *Wandsbeck Messenger* [i.e., Matthias Claudius] remarks, our (good) will begins precisely with not-willing (abandoning, refusing, or suppressing the not-good will), just as our true knowledge begins with ignorance (abandoning false knowledge). It too begins only by negating; but it in no way ends or rests in this negation, but rather in positive true knowledge and good will.[153]

E. Johann Georg Hamann

Precisely at the moment where Kierkegaard moves, in Part Two of *The Concept of Irony*, from treating certain authors explicitly (Schlegel, Tieck, Solger) to excluding others from consideration (Jean Paul, Baader), we find an example of Kierkegaardian irony. For if there is an author whom Kierkegaard *should* have mentioned at this point, it is surely Johann Georg Hamann. In fact, Kierkegaard does shine an indirect spotlight on Hamann at this point; for he cites a motto, "*Loquere, ut videam te*," which is already attested in Erasmus, and which is repeatedly and significantly used by Hamann, who explicitly attributes it to Socrates.[154]

All in all, there are over twenty passages in *The Concept of Irony* that may be read as allusions to Hamann, or at least as inspired by him. The influence of Hamann's richly metaphorical style is evident throughout. For example, at times Kierkegaard employs analogies and metaphors that Hamann pioneered, such as the subtle correlation of the biblical pericope of the pool of Bethesda with Socrates' polemic,[155] or the association of Mark 5 with philosophy.[156] Moreover, the notion that Socrates was the greatest Sophist of all, in so far as he outgunned the Sophists' illusory wisdom with his own ignorance, is already to be found in Hamann, namely, in the latter's "Five Pastoral Letters On the School Drama," which Kierkegaard studied thoroughly in 1837.[157] It is especially appropriate that Kierkegaard takes up the latter notion (that Socrates was "the greatest practicing Sophist"[158]) when discussing Aristophanes' Socrates. For as it happens, Hamann's own most detailed image of

---

153 Cf. Franz von Baader, *Revision der Philosopheme der Hegel'schen Schule bezüglich auf das Christenthum. Nebst zehn Thesen aus einer religiösen Philosophie*, Stuttgart: Liesching 1839, p. 72 (*ASKB* 416).

154 *SKS* 1, 284 / *CI*, 244; and see *Hamann's Schriften*, vol. 2, p. 261; vol. 6, p. 35.

155 *SKS* 1, 79 / *CI*, 17. The two notes on this page may be indirect references to Hamann's "Fünf Hirtenbriefen das Schuldrama betreffend," to which Kierkegaard refers in *SKS* 17, 128–9, BB:37 / *KJN* 1, 122–3. Cf. *Hamann's Schriften*, vol. 2, p. 430.

156 *SKS* 1, 246 / *CI*, 201. Cf. *Hamann's Schriften*, vol. 4, pp. 310–11. More controversial are a number of further passages, in which Kierkegaard cites off-handedly certain Platonic images that are of pivotal importance to Hamann, for example, the analogy to a doctor who is to be prosecuted before a jury of children (*Gorgias* 521e, cited at *SKS* 1, 144 / *CI*, 88, and at *Hamann's Schriften*, vol. 2, p. 47). Whether or not one speaks of a direct influence in such cases, it is clear that a spiritual kinship of sorts is reflected in the two authors' preference for the same images.

157 Hamann, "Fünf Hirtenbriefen das Schuldrama betreffend," in *Hamann's Schriften*, vol. 2, pp. 413–50. At *SKS* 17, 128–9, BB:37 / *KJN* 1, 122–3, Kierkegaard cites precisely the passage in which Hamann states that ignorance is the "great Sophist." *Hamann's Schriften*, vol. 2, p. 425.

158 Letter dated October 12, 1759, in *Hamann's Schriften*, vol. 1, p. 494.

Socrates is found in his short 1761 piece "Clouds," which culminates by identifying reason with "law" in the Pauline sense. Hamann repeated this identification in one of his letters; and Kierkegaard copied down the latter passage both approvingly and in full in his journals.[159]

Kierkegaard's notion that an ironic understanding of nature is only possible "through the contemplation of sin"[160] is also a product of Hamann's influence, as the 1837 journal entry DD:18 reveals.[161] In another 1837 entry, DD:36, Kierkegaard identifies Hamann as "the greatest and most authentic humorist."[162] This thought is repeated in *The Concept of Anxiety*, where a parallel is drawn between Hamann, as humorist, and the ironist Socrates.

Apropos of *The Concept of Anxiety*: the motto to that book not only draws the parallel just described, but also includes a citation from Hamann's *Socratic Memorabilia*.[163] It is worth noting that in the original passage in Hamann, immediately after the sentence that Kierkegaard cites, we find the remark that Socrates spoke, at every opportunity, of readers who could swim.[164] Remarkably, this same motif of a swimming reader is what we find in the Greek motto appended to the bookseller's edition of *The Concept of Irony*: "Whether one tumbles into a little diving pool or plump into the great sea, he swims all the same."[165]

The continual, underlying presence of such Hamannian images in Kierkegaard's development of his own conception of Socrates—or, more precisely, the fact that Kierkegaard made use of images that had previously been used by Hamann—leads him at times to identify Socrates and Hamann indirectly. When Kierkegaard, in *The Concept of Irony*, depicts Socrates as "enigmatically attracting and repelling" simultaneously,[166] this is strongly reminiscent of a May 1839 journal entry about Hamann: "*Allicit atque terret.*"[167]

All of these allusions and cross-connections (and others as well) are carefully veiled by Kierkegaard. Viewed in isolation, each could appear to be simply a coincidental similarity. Yet the impressive number of such "coincidences" ought to awaken our suspicions. Indeed, after one has taken note of the continual juxtaposition of Socrates and Hamann in the 1837 and 1838 journals, one will scarcely be able to believe in such "coincidences" anymore.

---

159 Cf. *Pap.* I A 237; cf. *Hamann's Schriften*, vol. 1, p. 405; vol. 2, p. 100.

160 *SKS* 1, 293, note / *CI*, 255, note.

161 Cf. *SKS* 17, 225–6, DD:18 / *KJN* 1, 216–17.

162 *SKS* 17, 234, DD:36 / *KJN* 1, 225.

163 *SKS* 4, 310 / *CA*, 3. The reference is to *Hamann's Schriften*, vol. 2, p. 12.

164 *Hamann's Schriften*, vol. 2, p. 12.

165 Plato, *Republic* 459d, cited at *CI*, 418–19.

166 *SKS* 1, 196 / *CI*, 146.

167 *SKS* 18, 32, EE:82 / *KJN* 2, 27.

VII. Prospects

As is well known, *The Concept of Irony* was not Kierkegaard's last word on Socrates. This is not the place to take account of Kierkegaard's later refinements and modifications of his portrait of Socrates. Our focus is simply on Kierkegaard's use of Germanophone Socrates sources. But even on this narrow topic, one clear tendency can be discerned: namely, that with few exceptions, Kierkegaard did not consider any new sources on Socrates after completing his dissertation. Two reasons may be given for this: (1) Kierkegaard had by then already accumulated an immense library of sources; and (2) his perception and representation of Socrates was by then growing more and more self-sufficient.

If we set aside Kierkegaard's renewal of interest after 1841 in histories of philosophy like Tennemann's and in the novels of Wieland—as we discussed in Section II—it is his engagement with Lessing that is his most significant use of a German Socrates source after 1841.

The opening question of *Philosophical Fragments* indicates that Kierkegaard was familiar with Lessing by the time of its writing. However, evidence from the journals indicates that Kierkegaard did not study Lessing intensively until he had begun to compose the *Concluding Unscientific Postscript*.

As the *Postscript* reveals, Kierkegaard shared Lessing's insight that the subjectivity of truth requires that one reflect upon the mode in which it is to be appropriated. That is to say: the subjectively existing thinker must be aware of the dialectic of communication. Kierkegaard credits Socrates with discovering the indirect method, and cites the *daimonion* as the sign of an interiority that knows the necessity of appropriation. Like Lessing, Kierkegaard insists that both direct and indirect discipleship is impossible. Above all, Part Two of the *Concluding Unscientific Postscript* insists—with reference to the problem of contemporaneity, which had already been discussed in *Philosophical Fragments*—that Lessing's classic formulation is correct: "contingent truths of history can never become the demonstration of necessary truths of reason."[168]

Kierkegaard also cites Lessing's famous insistence, in "A Rejoinder,"[169] on the anti-systematic, process-oriented quality of truth. According to Lessing, truth is not an objective result, but is best encountered in subjective striving: "If God held all truth enclosed in his right hand, and in his left hand the one and only ever-striving drive for truth, even with the corollary of erring forever and ever, and if he were to say to me: Choose!—I would humbly fall down to him at his left hand and say: Father, give! Pure truth is indeed only for you alone."[170] Lessing himself, let us note, makes no reference to Socrates in either "A Rejoinder" or in "On the Proof of the Spirit and of Power."[171] Nevertheless, Kierkegaard here apprehends a clear Socratic

---

168 *SKS* 7, 96 / *CUP1*, 97. Kierkegaard here cites *Lessing's sämmtliche Schriften*, vol. 5, p. 80.

169 G.E. Lessing, "Eine Duplik," in *Lessing's sämmtliche Schriften*, vol. 5, pp. 95–212.

170 *SKS* 7, 103 / *CUP1*, 106. Kierkegaard here cites *Lessing's sämmtliche Schriften*, vol. 5, p. 100.

171 G.E. Lessing, "Ueber den Beweis des Geistes und der Kraft," in *Lessing's sämmtliche Schriften*, vol. 5, pp. 75–85.

legacy. That Kierkegaard is correct in doing so can be confirmed by a glance at (among other texts) Lessing's "Thoughts About the Herrnhut Pietists."[172]

As we have noted, Kierkegaard's later works do not introduce any new secondary literature on Socrates. Rather, Kierkegaard there emphasizes new aspects of his portrait of Socrates, and so comes to reevaluate the sources that he had used previously. More specifically, Kierkegaard assigns greater significance, in his later works, to Schleiermacher's distinction between the speculative Plato and the existentially interested Socrates. As a result, Kierkegaard now treats all speculative philosophy as un-Socratic and improper. (This is a change that would affect his relation to Hegel significantly.)

On another front, one pivotal source now appears explicitly—particularly in *The Concept of Anxiety* and *Philosophical Fragments*—whose influence had been pointedly disguised in *The Concept of Irony*. This is Johann Georg Hamann, author of the *Socratic Memorabilia*: a man who continually emphasized, with Socrates, the subjective and existential character of truth.

Like Lessing, Hamann was a writer who sought to live up to the question of truth by devoting himself to indirect communication. For this reason, Hamann's characteristic style is one of continual ironic concealment. And for the same reason, Hamann's main influence on Kierkegaard can be difficult to detect: it derives not so much from individual statements (though these too have their significance) as from Hamann's overall mode of thinking and writing.

In what follows, we will focus our attention on a single and—to my knowledge—unnoticed "citation" that discloses Kierkegaard's subtle but persistent reliance on Hamann.[173] This "citation" is embedded in Climacus' Appendix, entitled "Offense at the Paradox (An Acoustical Illusion)," to Chapter III of *Philosophical Fragments*.[174]

Let us begin by noting that Hamann and Kierkegaard share an interest in the phenomenon of *offense* as a product of the incommensurability of faith and reason. They similarly share the insight that the difficulty of apprehending faith is an "acoustical" matter. Hamann's "Fragments" draws its epigraph from John 6:12, a verse that Climacus similarly uses to describe how one might gather the letters of faith ("catch every syllable so that nothing would be lost"[175]). Following this epigraph, Hamann offers an interpretation of John 6:13 that had attracted

---

172 This text can be found in the edition of Lessing that Kierkegaard owned, see *Lessing's sämmtliche Schriften*, vol 7, pp. 188–203.

173 For this reliance, see Steffes, "Erziehung zur Unwissenheit." In terms of form, Hamann's presence is evident in the books' title pages and closing passages. In terms of content, the key connection arises in Hamann's notion that Socratic philosophy and Christianity relate to one another as self-consciousness does to the consciousness of sin. The existential dimension *shared* by self-consciousness and the consciousness of sin brings both Christianity and Socratic philosophy into a common opposition to rational and speculative attempts to describe the constitution of the self. An identical account may be easily recognized as constitutive for the books attributed to Johannes Climacus and Anti-Climacus.

174 *SKS* 4, 253–7 / *PF*, 49–54.

175 *SKS* 4, 262 / *PF*, 60.

Kierkegaard's attention as early as 1837,[176] and which culminates in a reference to Luther's translation of Romans 10:17: faith comes through the sense of *hearing*. That this sense of hearing can be deceived is due to the character of the paradox.

At the beginning of Chapter III of *Fragments*—the chapter whose "Appendix" we are about to consider—Climacus expresses this thought as follows: "The paradox is the passion of thought, and the thinker without the paradox is like the lover without passion: a mediocre fellow."[177] Compare to this the following passage from one of Hamann's letters: "A heart without passions, without affects, is a head without concepts, without marrow. And I doubt very much whether Christianity desires such heads or hearts."[178] For both thinkers, this general insight is brought to a head in the case of a man who loved the paradox, but was no Christian, namely, Socrates. Elsewhere in the same letter, Hamann writes: "An unsalted salt and a Christian Socrates belong in the same category. The Socrates whose Memorabilia I have written was...the greatest practicing Sophist...My Socrates remains great as a pagan."[179] Many of this passage's themes are echoed elsewhere in Kierkegaard's writings.

At the center of his *Socratic Memorabilia*, Hamann addresses the question of Socrates' *daimonion*. He reviews several classical accounts of this mysterious being, and intermixes a number of "plausible" inventions of his own; but his true goal is to establish that Socrates *himself* could not undertake any inquiry into the essence of his *daimonion*, because it consistently refused all speculative explanation, and remained an external voice. Like Kierkegaard's paradox, the *daimonion* can only be perceived through indirect (that is, cited) utterances. Hamann chooses to translate *daimonion* as *Genie* ["genius"], the foundation of Socratic negativity: for it was Socrates' trust in the external sovereignty of his genius that allowed him to cling to his own negativity.

Remarkably, Climacus ascribes the same place to the paradox in his account of Christianity as Hamann assigns to the *daimonion* in his account of Socratic philosophy! Kierkegaard's paradox refuses all speculation, just as the *daimonion* does for Hamann's Socrates; although of course there are certain classic paradoxical utterances that may be cited—as Climacus' Appendix to Chapter III of *Fragments* shows.

In this Appendix, Climacus makes a total of seven attempts to allow the paradox to speak. These attempts—all citations or paraphrases of statements by other authors—are influenced through and through by Hamann's attempt to describe Socrates' *daimonion*. Hamann's influence can be seen, first of all, in the *form* of Climacus' attempts: his extended list only serves to underline the fact that a universal account of the paradox can no more be given than can an explanation on the *daimonion*. (The fact that an *existential* answer, rather than a universal one, is needed here links the problem of sin-consciousness to that of self-consciousness.) Second, Hamannian

[176] *SKS* 17, 128–9, BB:37 / *KJN* 1, 122–3, with reference to Hamann's "Pastoral Letters."

[177] *SKS* 4, 242–3 / *PF*, 37.

[178] *Hamann's Schriften*, vol. 1, p. 494.

[179] Ibid.

language can be detected in the particulars of Climacus' seven attempts to "hear" the paradox. Two of his seven formulations are directly derived from Hamann. Significantly, one of these is drawn from the same letter that contains the notion, cited elsewhere by Climacus that it is passion that makes the thinker.[180] The other Hamannian citation is remarkable because of the formula with which Climacus introduces it: "the paradox itself says: comedies and lies must be probable, but how could I be probable?"[181] It would seem that, when "the paradox itself" speaks, it does so with Hamann's voice. And it then expresses, in all clarity, that it will have nothing to do with the sphere of approximation knowledge, since it will not allow itself to be reduced to the level of probability. This remark is, simultaneously, a metacommentary on Climacus' ironic attempt to approach the truth of the paradox by listing any number of relevant declarations.

All that remains, for our purposes, is to show how these cross-connections relate back to Kierkegaard's inquiry into Socrates and his negativity. To see this, we need only turn to the sixth of Climacus' seven citations. Here the paradox calls the understanding "a clod and a dunce."[182] While Climacus identifies this statement as a citation from Luther, it is in fact a paraphrase derived from Hamann's *Socratic Memorabilia*. In his "Commentary to the Seven Psalms of Confession," Luther compares natural man to a rough "clod and rock."[183] Hamann then lifted this expression and put it to a new use: namely, to describe how both self-consciousness and sin-consciousness must take something away from the rough "clod and rock" (that is, natural man) in order to shed light on his predicament. This is what every sculptor knows—particularly Socrates, who was not only the son of a sculptor, Sophroniscus, but had himself worked as a sculptor in his youth: "Socrates thus imitated his father, a sculptor"—and here Hamann cites Luther—"the one who 'develops the sculpture's form precisely by carving away and removing what should not be in the wood.' "[184] Hence when Climacus appeals to Hamann's admixture of Socrates' insight (about self-consciousness) and Luther's insight (about sin-consciousness), he thereby proclaims that both kinds of consciousness are *negative* in nature. Like the *daimonion* and the paradox, self-consciousness and sin-consciousness defy the speculative, constructive understanding; they refuse all attempts at positive definition; and instead become visible in their liberating efficacy only in so far as they seek to free the rough "clod and rock" to become his own true shape.

This detailed example should make clear that, by the mid–1840s, Kierkegaard had abandoned his earlier philological inquiry into the nature and history of Socrates. Instead, his interest in Socrates had become a nearly self-sufficient attempt to harness

---

180 This is one example among many of Hamann's efforts to radicalize the question of truth: "The truth in the mouth of a hypocrite is dearer to me than to hear it from an angel or an apostle." *SKS* 4, 256 / *PF*, 52. Cf. *Hamann's Schriften*, vol. 1, p. 497.

181 *SKS* 4, 256 / *PF*, 52. Cf. *Hamann's Schriften*, vol. 1, p. 425.

182 *SKS* 4, 256 / *PF*, 53.

183 Cf. *Martini Lutheri Geistreiche Erklärung der Sieben Buß-Psalmen*, ed. by Johann Jacob Rambach, Jena: Johann Friederich Ritter 1741, p. 103. Luther's commentary dates to 1525.

184 *Hamann's Schriften*, vol. 2, p. 22.

the insights of Socratic philosophy for use in a Christian anthropology or theory of subjectivity.

One result of this is that, during his final attack on the Church, Kierkegaard referred to Socrates almost entirely without appealing to other sources. In the last two years of his life, we find Kierkegaard granting Socrates the title "Reformer," which he was by then no longer willing to attribute to Luther. Kierkegaard's reason for this lay not in a repudiation of Luther's theology, but in his conviction that Lutheranism had been corrupted by its history.[185] The disciples had usurped the place of their master: Luther's pupils had turned Lutheranism into a (political) system. In protest against this development, Kierkegaard maintained his lifelong, dedicated friendship with the Athenian sage who did not presume to be able to teach others, because he always remained convinced that he knew nothing.

It is therefore appropriate that Kierkegaard himself remained without disciples. This has been his fate particularly in the German-speaking world of Plato scholarship. For though Kierkegaard's view of Socrates did leave some traces in late-nineteenth-century Plato scholarship in Denmark—specifically, in the work of Hans Brøchner (1820–75) and Harald Høffding (1843–1931)—in Germany the debate about Socrates proceeded, at least for the time being, as though Kierkegaard and *The Concept of Irony* had never existed.

It was not until several decades after his death that Kierkegaard's significance for the understanding of Socrates and his irony was finally uncovered. During the long period of unbroken oblivion that preceded his rediscovery, Kierkegaard shared—"with fitting irony," one is tempted to say—the fate of Aristophanes, his own star witness. Perhaps this, then, is the question that most truly haunts the study of Kierkegaard's use of scholarly sources: from whom did Kierkegaard get the idea of disclosing Aristophanes as the one who knew Socrates best? As we have seen, such an idea can be found neither in the philosophical writings of Baur and Hegel, nor in the philological studies of Ast and Rötscher.

We might look next to the Romantics, who ascribed more significance to Aristophanes than did their predecessors. And indeed, Kierkegaard does allude to a passage in Heine's *The Romantic School*—a book in which Tieck is identified with Aristophanes.[186] However, Tieck's standpoint differs considerably from that of Kierkegaard's Aristophanes.

Instead, among all the eighteenth- and nineteenth-century authors with whom Kierkegaard can be shown to have intensively engaged, one single author stands out as having attributed the same Aristophanic distinguishing marks to Socrates as did the Dane. Socrates' *negativity* had already been recognized by Hegel and his students. That *irony* is the fundamental form of subjectivity was proclaimed by the Romantics as well. But the idea that Socrates' negativity was no mere transitional phase, but was a complete and enduring articulation of subjectivity with irony as its main feature—there is only one single author who shared this idea with Kierkegaard: Johann Georg Hamann. And when we turn to the book in which Hamann, in a

---

185 Cf., for example, *SKS* 25, 303-4, NB29:12.

186 *SKS* 1, 337 / *CI*, 304, with reference to Heinrich Heine, *Die romantische Schule*, Hamburg: Hoffmann und Campe 1836, pp. 43–4 (*ASKB* U 63).

decisive second step, defends and deepens the Socratic standpoint that he had set forth in his *Memorabilia*, we find that he gives this sequel a deeply resonant title: *The Clouds*.[187]

Translated by David D. Possen and Merle Denker Possen

[187] Johann Georg Hamann, *Wolken: Ein Nachspiel sokratischer Denkwürdigkeiten*, in *Hamann's Schriften*, vol. 2, pp. 51–102.

Bibliography

Eighteenth- and Nineteenth-Century Germanophone Scholarship in The Auction Catalogue *of Kierkegaard's Library that Discuss Plato and Socrates*

Ast, Friedrich, "Sokrates," in his *Grundriss einer Geschichte der Philosophie*, Landshut: Joseph Thomann 1807, pp. 100–4 (*ASKB* 385).

—— "Platon," in his *Grundriss einer Geschichte der Philosophie*, Landshut: Joseph Thomann 1807, pp. 115–23 (*ASKB* 385).

Baader, Franz von, *Vorlesungen, gehalten an der Königlich-Bayerischen Ludwig-Maximilians-Hochschule über religiöse Philosophie im Gegensatze der irreligiösen,*

—— *Ueber den Paulinischen Begriff des Versehenseyns des Menschen im Namen Jesu vor der Welt Schöpfung. Sendeschreiben an den Herrn Professor Molitor in Frankfurt*, vols. 1–3, Würzburg: Stahel 1837, vol. 2, p. 8, note (vols. 1–2, *ASKB* 409–410) (vol. 3, *ASKB* 413).

—— *Revision der Philosopheme der Hegel'schen Schule bezüglich auf das Christenthum. Nebst zehn Thesen aus einer religiösen Philosophie*, Stuttgart: S.G. Liesching 1839, p. 49; pp. 104–5 (*ASKB* 416).

Baur, Ferdinand Christian, *Die christliche Gnosis oder die christliche Religions-Philosophie in ihrer geschichtlichen Entwicklung*, Tübingen: C.F. Osiander 1835, p. 15; p. 38; p. 144; p. 150; p. 164; p. 228; p. 420; p. 430; p. 435; p. 437; p. 453; p. 470; p. 472; p. 497; pp. 527–8; p. 693; p. 711 (*ASKB* 421).

—— *Das Christliche des Platonismus oder Sokrates und Christus. Eine religionsphilosophische Untersuchung*, Tübingen: Fues 1837 (*ASKB* 422).

Buhle, Johann Gottlieb, *Geschichte der neuern Philosophie seit der Epoche der Wiederherstellung der Wissenschaften*, vols. 1–6 (in 10 tomes), vols. 1–2, Göttingen: Rosenbusch 1800; vols. 3–6, Göttingen: Röwer 1802–05 (Abtheilung 6 in *Geschichte der Künste und Wissenschaften seit der Wiederherstellung derselben bis an das Ende des achtzehnten Jahrhunderts. Von einer Gesellschaft gelehrter Männer ausgearbeitet*, Abtheilungen 1–11, Göttingen: Röwer and Göttingen: Rosenbusch 1796–1820), vol. 1, pp. 88ff.; pp. 150ff. (*ASKB* 440–445).

[Becker, Karl Friedrich], *Karl Friedrich Beckers Verdenshistorie, omarbeidet af Johan Gottfried Woltmann*, vols. 1–12, trans. by J. Riise, Copenhagen: Fr. Brummers Forlag 1822–29, vol. 2, p. 419; pp. 425–6; p. 428 (*ASKB* 1972–1983).

Cousin, Victor, *Über französische und deutsche Philosophie. Aus dem Französischen von Dr. Hubert Beckers, Professor. Nebst einer beurtheilenden Vorrede des Herrn*

Geheimraths von Schelling, Stuttgart and Tübingen: J.G. Cotta 1834, p. XVII; pp. 31–2; p. 41; p. 59 (*ASKB* 471).

Eberhard, Johann August, *Neue Apologie des Sokrates oder Untersuchung der Lehre von der Seligkeit der Heiden*, vols. 1–2, Berlin: Nicolai 1778–88 [vol. 1, 1788; vol. 1, 1778] (*ASKB* A I 185–186).

Erdmann, Johann Eduard, *Natur oder Schöpfung? Eine Frage an die Naturphilosophie und Religionsphilosophie*, Leipzig: Vogel 1840, p. 115 (*ASKB* 482).

—— *Grundriss der Logik und Metaphysik. Für Vorlesungen*, Halle: Lippert 1841, p. 10; p. 27; p. 161 (*ASKB* 483).

Fichte, Immanuel Hermann, *De principiorum contradictionis, identitatis, exclusi tertii in logicis dignitate et ordine commentatio*, Bonn: Georgi 1840, p. 5; p. 17, note (*ASKB* 507).

Fischer, Carl Philipp, *Die Idee der Gottheit. Ein Versuch, den Theismus speculativ zu begründen und zu entwickeln*, Stuttgart: S.G. Liesching 1839, p. III (*ASKB* 512).

Fischer, Friedrich, *Die Metaphysik, von empirischem Standpunkte aus dargestellt. Zur Verwirklichung der Aristotelischen Metaphysik*, Basel: Schweighauser 1847 (*ASKB* 513).

Flögel, Carl Friedrich, *Geschichte der komischen Litteratur*, vols. 1–4, Liegnitz and Leipzig: Giegert 1784–87, vol. 1, pp. 14–18; p. 96; p. 101 (*ASKB* 1396–1399).

Frauenstädt, Julius, *Die Naturwissenschaft in ihrem Einfluß auf Poesie, Religion, Moral und Philosophie*, Leipzig: F.A. Brockhaus 1855, p. 144; p. 148 (*ASKB* 516).

Hahn, August (ed.), *Lehrbuch des christlichen Glaubens*, Leipzig: Vogel 1828, p. 47; p. 263; p. 277; p. 288 (*ASKB* 535).

[Hamann, Johann Georg], *Hamann's Schriften*, vols. 1–8, ed. by Friedrich Roth, Berlin: G. Reimer 1821–43, vol. 1, pp. 114–15; p. 138; p. 296; p. 311; p. 321; p. 342; p. 435; pp. 437–8; vol. 2, p. 11; p. 12; pp. 20–6; pp. 29-35; pp. 38–50 passim; p. 77; pp. 51–102; p. 90; p. 94; p. 156; pp. 252–3; p. 257; p. 263; p. 340; p. 367; p. 370; p. 375; p. 426; p. 515; vol. 3, p. 62; pp. 150–1; vol. 4, p. 20; pp. 82–3; pp. 99–102; p. 111; pp. 113–14; p. 173; p. 188; p. 209; p. 243; p. 246; p. 272; p. 301; p. 305–8; p. 311; pp. 315-7; p. 422; vol. 5, p. 48; p. 60; p. 271; vol. 6, p. 231; vol. 7, p. 68; p. 75; p. 94; p. 126; p. 187 (*ASKB* 536-544).

[Hase, Karl], *Hutterus redivivus oder Dogmatik der evangelisch-lutherischen Kirche. Ein dogmatisches Repertorium für Studirende*, 4th revised ed., Leipzig: Breitkopf und Härtel 1839, p. 2; p. 4; p. 333 (*ASKB* 581).

Hegel, Georg Wilhelm Friedrich, *Georg Wilhelm Friedrich Hegel's philosophische Abhandlungen*, ed. by Karl Ludwig Michelet, Berlin: Duncker und Humblot 1832 (vol. 1 in *Georg Wilhelm Friedrich Hegel's Werke. Vollständige Ausgabe*, ed. by Philipp Marheineke et al., Berlin: Duncker und Humblot 1832–45, pp. 382–5 (*ASKB* 549).

—— "Philosophie des Sokrates," in *Georg Wilhelm Friedrich Hegel's Vorlesungen über die Geschichte der Philosophie*, vols. 1–3, ed. by Carl Ludwig Michelet, Berlin: Duncker und Humblot 1833–36 (vols. 13–15 in *Georg Wilhelm Friedrich Hegel's Werke. Vollständige Ausgabe*, ed. by Philipp Marheineke et al., Berlin: Duncker und Humblot 1832–45, vol. 2, 42–122 (*ASKB* 557–559).

—— "Philosophie des Plato," in *Georg Wilhelm Friedrich Hegel's Vorlesungen über die Geschichte der Philosophie*, vols. 1–3, ed. by Carl Ludwig Michelet, Berlin: Duncker und Humblot 1833–36 (vols. 13–15 in *Georg Wilhelm Friedrich Hegel's Werke. Vollständige Ausgabe*, ed. by Philipp Marheineke et al., Berlin: Duncker und Humblot 1832–45), vol. 2, pp. 169–297 (*ASKB* 557–559).

—— *Georg Wilhelm Friedrich Hegel's Vorlesungen über die Philosophie der Religion*, vols. 1–2, ed. by Philipp Marheineke, 2nd revised ed., Berlin: Duncker und Humblot 1840 (vols. 11–12 in *Georg Wilhelm Friedrich Hegel's Werke. Vollständige Ausgabe*, ed. by Philipp Marheineke et al., Berlin: Duncker und Humblot 1832–45), vol. 1, p. 22; p. 30; pp. 39–40; p. 142; p. 160; p. 194; p. 220; pp. 249–50; vol. 2, p. 73; pp. 107–8; p. 130; p. 154; p. 243; p. 287; p. 295; p. 349; p. 397; p. 518; p. 551 (*ASKB* 564–565).

—— *Georg Wilhelm Friedrich Hegel's Vorlesungen über die Aesthetik*, vols. 1–3, ed. by von Heinrich Gustav Hotho, Berlin: Duncker und Humblot 1835–38 (vols. 10.1–10.3 in *Georg Wilhelm Friedrich Hegel's Werke. Vollständige Ausgabe*, vols. 1–18, ed. by Philipp Marheineke et al., Berlin: Duncker und Humblot 1832–45), vol. 1, p. 134; p. 197; vol. 2, p. 2; pp. 46–8; p. 56; p. 111; p. 377; p. 452 (*ASKB* 1384–1386).

Helfferich, Adolph, *Die christliche Mystik in ihrer Entwickelung und in ihren Denkmalen*, vols. 1–2, Gotha: Friedrich Perthes 1842, vol. 1, p. 147; p. 151; p. 166; p. 175; p. 182; p. 188; p. 205; p. 288; p. 326; p. 421 (*ASKB* 571–572).

Hermann, Karl Friedrich, *Geschichte und System der Platonischen Philosophie*, Heidelberg: C.F. Winter 1839 (*ASKB* 576).

Kant, Immanuel, *Critik der Urtheilskraft*, 2nd ed., Berlin: F.T. Lagarde 1793, p. 9; pp. 273–4; pp. 370–5; p. 530; p. 596; pp. 881–2 (*ASKB* 594).

Marbach, Gotthard Oswald, "Sokrates und die Sokratiker," in his *Geschichte der Griechischen Philosophie. Mit Angabe der Literatur nach den Quellen*, Leipzig: Otto Wigand 1838 (1. Abtheilung, in Gotthard Oswald Marbach, *Lehrbuch der Geschichte der Philosophie. Mit Angabe der Literatur nach den Quellen*, Abtheilung 1–2, Leipzig: Wigand 1838–1841), pp. 170–186 (*ASKB* 642; for Abtheilung 2 see *ASKB* 643).

—— "Platon und die Akademiker," in his *Geschichte der Griechischen Philosophie. Mit Angabe der Literatur nach den Quellen*, Leipzig: Wigand 1838 (1. Abtheilung, in Gotthard Oswald Marbach, *Lehrbuch der Geschichte der Philosophie. Mit Angabe der Literatur nach den Quellen*, Abtheilung 1–2, Leipzig: Wigand 1838–41), pp. 194–233 (*ASKB* 642; for Abtheilung 2 see *ASKB* 643).

Marheineke, Philipp, *Lehrbuch des christlichen Glaubens und Lebens für denkende Christen und zum Gebrauch in den oberen Klassen an den Gymnasien*, 2nd revised ed., Berlin: in der Nicolai'schen Buchhandlung 1836, p. 6; p. 20 (*ASKB* 257).

Meiners, Christoph, "Geschichte des Sokrates und seiner Philosophie," in his *Geschichte des Ursprungs, Fortgangs und Verfalls der Wissenschaften in Griechenland und Rom*, vols. 1–2, Lemgo: Meyer 1781–82, vol. 2, pp. 346–540 (*ASKB* 1406–1406a).

—— "Geschichte des Plato und seiner Philosophie," in his *Geschichte des Ursprungs, Fortgangs und Verfalls der Wissenschaften in Griechenland und Rom*, vols. 1–2, Lemgo: Meyer 1781–82, vol. 2, pp. 683–808 (*ASKB* 1406–1406a).

—— *Geschichte des Luxus der Athenienser von den ältesten Zeiten an bis auf den Tod Philipps von Makedonien*, Lemgo: Meyer 1782 (*ASKB* 661).

Michelet, Carl Ludwig, *Vorlesungen über die Persönlichkeit Gottes und Unsterblichkeit der Seele oder die ewige Persönlichkeit des Geistes*, Berlin: Verlag von Ferdinand Dümmler 1841, p. 33; pp. 33–39; p. 156 (*ASKB* 680).

Ritter, Heinrich and L. Preller, *Historia philosophiae graeco-romanae ex fontium locis contexta*, Hamburg: Perthes 1838, pp. 139–59; pp. 186–228 (*ASKB* 726).

Solger, K.W.F., *Solger's nachgelassene Schriften und Briefwechsel*, ed. by Ludwig Tieck und Friedrich von Raumer, vols. 1–2, Leipzig: F.A. Brockhaus 1826, pp. 650–675 (*ASKB* 1832–1833).

Tennemann, Wilhelm Gottlieb, "Sokrates," in his *Geschichte der Philosophie*, vols. 1–11, Leipzig: Barth 1798–1819, vol. 2, pp. 25–87 (*ASKB* 815–826).

—— "Plato," in his *Geschichte der Philosophie*, vols. 1–11, Leipzig: Barth 1798–1819, vol. 2, pp. 188–528 (*ASKB* 815–826).

Trendelenburg, Adolf, *Logische Untersuchungen*, vols. 1–2, Berlin: G. Bethge 1840, vol. 1, p. 43n; p. 89; p. 97; p. 102; p. 184; p. 224; p. 267; p. 315; p. 38; p. 83; p. 324; p. 360 (*ASKB* 843).

—— "Plato," in his *Historische Beiträge zur Philosophie*, vols. 1–2, Berlin: G. Bethge 1846–55, vol. 1, *Geschichte der Kategorienlehre. Zwei Abhandlungen*, 1846, pp. 205–9 (*ASKB* 848) [vol. 2, 1855 not in *ASKB*].

Weiße, Christian Hermann, *Die Idee der Gottheit. Eine philosophische Abhandlung. Als wissenschaftliche Grundlegung zur Philosophie der Religion*, Dresden: Ch.F. Grimmer'sche Buchhandlung 1833, p. 59; p. 62, note; pp. 87–100 passim; p. 113; p. 209 (*ASKB* 866).

Wirth, Johann Ulrich, "Lehre des Sokrates," in his *Die speculative Idee Gottes und die damit zusammenhängenden Probleme der Philosophie. Eine kritisch-dogmatische Untersuchung*, Stuttgart and Tübingen: J.G. Cotta 1845, pp. 183–7 (*ASKB* 876).

—— "Lehre des Plato," in his *Die speculative Idee Gottes und die damit zusammenhängenden Probleme der Philosophie. Eine kritisch-dogmatische Untersuchung*, Stuttgart and Tübingen: J.G. Cotta 1845, pp. 187–212 (*ASKB* 876).

Zeller, Eduard, "Sokrates," in his *Die Philosophie der Griechen. Eine Untersuchung über Charakter, Gang und Hauptmomente ihrer Entwicklung*, vols. 1–3, Tübingen: Fues 1844–52, vol. 2, pp. 12–104 (*ASKB* 913–914).

—— "Plato und die ältere Akademie," in his *Die Philosophie der Griechen. Eine Untersuchung über Charakter, Gang und Hauptmomente ihrer Entwicklung*, vols. 1–3, Tübingen: Fues 1844–52, vol. 2, pp. 134–315 (*ASKB* 913–914).

Index of Persons

Dante Alighieri (1265–1321), Italian poet, 83.
Daub, Karl (1765–1836), German Protestant theologian, 284, 285.
Descartes, René (1596–1650), French philosopher, 83.
Diogenes Laertius, 169, 170, 220, 254, 279.
Diotima, 106, 122, 171, 271.
Dover, Kenneth J., 169.

Eberhard, Johann August (1739–1809), German philosopher, 272, 281.
Edelmann, Johann Christian (1698–1767), German pietist, 273, 274.
Elberling, Carl Wilhelm (1800–70), Danish philologist, 243.
Empedocles, 75.
Erasmus of Rotterdam, i.e., Desiderius Erasmus Roterodamus (1466/69–1536), Dutch humanist, 300.
Erdmann, Johann Eduard (1805–92), German philosopher, 205, 284.
Eryximachus, 105.
Eschenburg, Johann Joachim (1743–1820), German literary historian, 227,
Euclid of Megara, 293.
Euripides, 171.
Euthyphro, 221.

Faust, 66.
Ferreira, M. Jamie, 113.
Feuerbach, Ludwig (1804–72), German philosopher, 276.
Fichte, Johann Gottlieb (1762–1814), German philosopher, 284.
Forchhammer, Peter Wilhelm (1803–94), Danish-German philologist, 263.
Frederick the Great (1712–86), King of Prussia, 269.

Gallitzin, Amalie, Princess (1748–1806), 269.
Gesner, Johann Matthias (1691–1761), German classical scholar, 237.
Goethe, Johann Wolfgang von (1749–1832), German poet, author, scientist and diplomat, 38, 83, 256, 257, 270.
Goldschmidt, Meïr Aaron (1819–87), Danish author, 193.
Grote, George (1794–1871), English classical historian, 168, 176.

Hamann, Johann Georg (1730–88), German philosopher, xi, 177, 178, 205, 237, 270–2, 276, 279, 280–4, 290, 300–6 passim.
Hegel, Georg Wilhelm Friedrich (1770–1831), German philosopher, xi, 38, 49, 52, 55, 58, 59, 66, 71, 83, 87–94 passim, 102, 104, 126, 127, 175–87 passim, 193, 199–209 passim, 216, 218, 220, 231–2, 238, 247, 250, 254, 259–60, 264, 277, 279, 288–98 passim, 308, 306.
Heiberg, Johan Ludvig (1791–1860), Danish poet, playwright and philosopher, 56, 59, 71, 174, 175, 230, 251, 252, 257, 261, 262, 264.
Heiberg, Johanne Luise (1812–90), Danish actress, 262.
Heine, Heinrich (1797–1856), German poet and author, 173, 308.
Heise, Carl Johan (1787–1857), Danish pastor and translator, 243–50 passim.
Hemsterhuis, Frans (1721–90), Dutch philosopher, 269.
Herder, Johann Gottfried (1744–1803), German philosopher, 270, 277, 280.
Hermann, Karl Friedrich (1805–55), German classical philologist, 293.
Herodotus, 221.
Hesiod, 77, 228.
Heyne, Christian Gottlob (1729–1812), German philologist, 235, 238.
Himmelstrup, Jens, 217, 221, 258, 260, 294, 295.
Hippel, Theodor Gottlieb von (1741–96), German author, 284.

Høffding, Harald (1843–1931), Danish philosopher, 306.
Holberg, Ludvig (1684–1754), Danish-Norwegian dramatist and historian, 173, 217, 237.
Homer, 221, 228, 258.
Hostrup, Jens Christian (1818–92), Danish poet, 193.
Howland, Jacob, 33, 187.

Ingemann, Bernhard Severin (1789–1862), Danish poet, 193.
Ingerslev, Christian Frederik (1803–68), Danish philologist, 223, 243.

Jacobi, Friedrich Heinrich (1743–1819), German philosopher, 270, 275, 276, 280–2, 290.
Jacobi, Johann Georg (1740–1814), German poet, 282.
Jean Paul, i.e. Johann Paul Friedrich Richter (1763–1825), German author, 257, 282, 284, 299, 300.
Jensen, Povl Johannes, 175.
John the Baptist, 271, 290.

Kall, W.T., 240.
Kalkar, Christian Andreas Hermann (1802–86), Danish Bible translator, 244, 245.
Kant, Immanuel (1724–1804), German philosopher, 83, 270, 277, 279.
Kapp, Christian (1790–1874), 276.
Kierkegaard, Peter Christian (1805–88), Danish theologian, elder brother of Søren Kierkegaard, 223.
Kierkegaard, Søren Aabye (1813–1855),
- *The Battle between the Old and the New Soap-Cellars* (1837), 174.
- *The Concept of Irony* (1841), ix, 18, 24, 29, 34–6, 45, 46–54 passim, 59, 68–71 passim, 76, 90, 92, 94, 95, 97, 102, 104, 106, 110, 112, 115, 124–7 passim, 143, 171, 175, 186, 187, 199–211, 216, 218, 219, 222, 228, 235, 257, 263, 267–9, 272, 275, 276, 277–306 passim.
- *Johannes Climacus, or De omnibus dubitandum est* (ca. 1842–43), 57, 58, 69.
- *Either/Or* (1843), 45, 54–6, 60, 69, 71, 128, 129, 130, 140, 188, 189, 299.
- *Fear and Trembling* (1843), 78, 79, 188.
- *Two Upbuilding Discourses* (1843), 130.
- *Repetition* (1843), 45, 54–6, 59, 61, 71.
- *Philosophical Fragments* (1844), ix, 29, 32, 35–45 passim, 59, 61–72 passim, 73, 78–84 passim, 110, 115, 131–7 passim, 141, 187, 259, 274, 283, 302–4.
- *The Concept of Anxiety* (1844), 45, 59, 61–8 passim, 71, 259, 260, 285, 303, 305.
- *Prefaces* (1844), 282.
- *Three Discourses on Imagined Occasions* (1845), 138.
- *Stages on Life's Way* (1845), 110, 187, 189, 191.
- *Concluding Unscientific Postscript* (1846), ix, 33–45 passim, 69, 70, 71, 77, 79, 81, 84, 111, 115, 129, 134, 136, 140, 187, 229, 274, 282, 302.
- *Works of Love* (1847), 109, 111, 112, 138, 143–6 passim.
- *Christian Discourses* (1848), 85.
- *The Point of View for My Work as an Author* (ca. 1848), 44, 122, 124, 146.
- *The Sickness unto Death* (1849), 116, 138–41.
- *Practice in Christianity* (1850), 141, 142.
- *On My Work as an Author* (1851), 130.
- *For Self-Examination* (1851), 194.
- *The Moment* (1855), x, 3–6, 215.
- Journals, Notebooks, *Nachlaß*, 45, 53, 57, 58, 60, 67, 68, 283–5, 301.

Klæstrup, Peter (1820–82), Danish cartoonist, 192.

Stallbaum, Johann Gottfried (1793–1861), German classical scholar, 202, 216, 242, 244, 245, 248.
Stewart, Jon, 38, 52, 60, 83, 93, 208, 232.
Strauss, David Friedrich (1808–74), German theologian, historian and philosopher, 290.
Strauss, Leo (1899–1973), American political philosopher, 169.
Suhr, Johannes Søren Bloch (1807–76), Danish pastor, 240.
Sulzer, Johann Georg (1720–79), German philosopher, 182.
Süss, Wilhelm (1882–1969), German classical philologist, 171.
Süvern, Johann Wilhelm (1775–1829), German classical philologist, 182, 251, 290.
Sverdrup, Georg (1770–1850), Norwegian classical scholar, 242.

Taylor, A.E., 169.
Tennemann, Wilhelm Gottlieb (1761–1819), German historian of philosophy, xi, 61, 67, 242, 277–79, 302.
Tetens, Stephan (1773–1855), Danish classical philologist and bishop, 243.
Thaarup, Christen, 239.
Theaetetus, 121.
Thrasymachus, 87, 88, 94, 100.
Tieck, Ludwig (1773–1853), German poet, 171–3, 176, 179, 257, 296, 297, 300, 306.
Tiedemann, Dieterich (1748–1803), German philosopher, 241, 244.
Treschow, Niels (1751–1833), Norwegian philosopher, 254.
Tryde, Eggert Christopher (1781–1860), Danish theologian and pastor, 258.
Typhon, 40, 73–83 passim, 86.

Vasiliou, Iakovos, 95.
Vlastos, Gregory (1907–91), American classical scholar, 88–90, 94, 95, 101–4 passim, 118, 184.
Voltaire, i.e., François-Marie Arouet (1694 - 1778), French Enlightenment writer, 188, 189, 269.

Werder, Karl Friedrich (1806–93), German philosopher and literary critic, 58, 60, 61, 67.
Westengaard, Laurits Christian Ditlev (1795–1853), Danish pastor and translator, 244.
Wiehe, Frederik Wilhelm (1817–64), Danish philologist, 243.
Wieland, Christoph Martin (1733–1813), German poet, 281, 282, 302.
Wolff, Christian (1679–1754), German philosopher, 278.
Wolf, Friedrich August (1759–1824), German classical scholar, 233.
Wolff, Odin (1760–1830), Danish author, 240.
Worm, Oluf (1757–1830), Danish philologist, 232.

Xanthippe, 190, 192, 215.
Xenophon, ix, x, 70, 169, 170, 175–80 passim, 186, 199–211, 217–21 passim, 224, 227, 228, 234–41, 250, 258, 260, 262, 270, 275–81 passim, 285, 286, 295, 297.
  Apology, 203, 207, 235, 239, 240.
  Symposium, 170, 240, 235.

Zeller, Eduard (1814–1908), German polyhistor, 194, 247.
Zinzendorf, Nikolaus Ludwig von, Count (1700–60), German religious reformer, 272–4, 290.
Zorn, Johannes, 175.

Index of Subjects